Undelivered Letters

Edited by Judith Hudson Beattie
and Helen M. Buss

Undelivered Letters to Hudson's Bay Company Men on the Northwest Coast of America, 1830-57

With introductions and narratives by
Judith Hudson Beattie and Helen M. Buss
and notes by Judith Hudson Beattie

UBC PRESS • VANCOUVER • TORONTO

09 08 07 06 05 04 03   5 4 3

Printed in Canada on acid-free paper. ∞

National Library of Canada Cataloguing in Publication Data

Main entry under title:

Undelivered letters to Hudson's Bay Company men on the Northwest Coast of America, 1830-57 / edited by Judith Hudson Beattie and Helen M. Buss.

   Includes bibliographical references and index.
   ISBN 0-7748-0973-6 (bound); ISBN 0-7748-0974-4 (pbk)

1. Hudson's Bay Company – Employees – Correspondence. 2. Hudson's Bay Company – Employees – Biography. 3. Fur traders – Northwest Coast of North America – Biography. I. Buss, Helen M. (Helen Margaret) II. Beattie, Judith Hudson.

FC3213.1.A1U52 2003   971.1′102′0922   C2002-911143-9
F1060.3.U52 2003

Canadä

UBC Press gratefully acknowledges the financial support for our publishing program of the Government of Canada through the Book Publishing Industry Development Program (BPIDP), and of the Canada Council for the Arts, and the British Columbia Arts Council.

This book has been published with the help of a grant from the Humanities and Social Sciences Federation of Canada, using funds provided by the Social Sciences and Humanities Research Council of Canada.

UBC Press is also grateful for the financial assistance of the Hudson's Bay History Foundation in support of this work.

Printed and bound in Canada by Friesens
Set in Adobe Garamond by Brenda and Neil West, BN Typographics West
Copy editor: Susan Quirk
Text designer: Neil West
Proofreader: Gail Copeland
Cartographers: Eric Leinberger (pp. 9, 10, 16); Dawn Huck (p. 4)

UBC Press
The University of British Columbia
2029 West Mall
Vancouver, BC V6T 1Z2
604-822-5959 / Fax: 604-822-6083
www.ubcpress.ca

This book is affectionately dedicated to loved ones absent through distance or death, and to those who have accompanied us on our long journey. We each wish to pay a special tribute: Judy to her mother, Beatrice M. Hudson, and Helen to her father, Harold James Clarke, who both care about ordinary people and their extraordinary stories.

Contents

Maps and Illustrations

The "Sundry letters" wrapper that once enclosed the undelivered letters.

James Blackie's 1832 letter from Fort Vancouver to his sister in London, proposing marriage to his friend Kitty (entry 5).

Tailor order listing the outfit supplied to Henry Harmsworth for his work with the Company, 1832 (entry 13).

John Spence's 1835 letter from the *Prince Rupert,* inquiring about Margaret, his "old lady," at Fort Vancouver (entry 16).

Cross-written letter to George Prattent, 1837, illustrating how a single sheet of paper could be used to hold the maximum amount of news (entry 20).

Mrs. Hooten's 1839 letter to the Company enclosing her dead son's baptismal certificate (entry 26).

Thomas Heath's 1838 letter mentioning the good fishing and local gossip to his brother William (entry 29).

Several of the letters from Margaret Simpson to her husband, James, written in 1842 and 1849 from Kincardine, Scotland (entry 37).

Edward Wallis's 1847 letter to his brother describing his plans to follow him to sea (entry 54).

Edward Wallis's 1847 picture of himself enclosed by the ribs of a whale, and of his brother Charles in the crow's nest of his ship, the *Columbia* (entry 54).

A few of the seventeen letters written in 1844 and 1848 by the very literate Buck family of Cork, Ireland, to young Jonathan Buck (entry 47).

Following page 306

Mary Ann Harrier's 1845 letter to her husband, John, enclosing one of her many ringlets after receiving a lock of his "beautiful hair" (entry 48).

J.E. Holman's 1852 letter to Thomas on letterhead intended to remind him of their home in Harbledown (entry 71).

Two of the three letters written in 1831 by Joseph Grenier's father to his *voyageur* son, as well as the yellow feather enclosed (entry 75).

John Mongle's 1830 letter from Fort Colvile to his wife in Maskinongé, describing how much he missed her (entry 76).

Mary Macdonald's 1851 letter to her sweetheart, Allan McIsaac, enclosing a lock of her hair (entry 87).

Jane Lloyd's 1857 letter to John Tod with the sad news of Eliza Tod's death and the bill for her funeral expenses (entry 92).

Portrait of Chief Trader John Tod, shown with his books and a distinguished bearing, date unknown (entry 92).

Acknowledgments

This work would not have been possible without the enthusiasm, generous support, and cooperation of many people. Families indulged our obsession with these letters and provided help and encouragement throughout the long process. Vacations were often planned around the requirements for research opportunities and familiarity with conditions in such places as Fort Vancouver, Victoria, California, and Hawai'i. We are grateful to our husbands: to Richard Buss, for helping us in our pursuit of accuracy by comparing the original letters with the typed transcriptions; and to Francisco Valenzuela, for taking on research assistant duties in the Public Archives of Nova Scotia.

One group of letters to *voyageurs* – those in French – required special help to transcribe, translate, and understand another culture. We are deeply indebted to the many people who have helped provide details on the lives of the *voyageurs* and their families, and interpret and correct the transcriptions and the translations. Foremost among them are Carolyn Podruchny, who shared the results of her research in the Archives nationales du Québec in Montréal; Alfred Fortier, who guided our research in the wonderful reference resources of the Société historique de Saint-Boniface at the Centre du Patrimoine in Winnipeg; Robert Vézina, who applied his knowledge of old French to the interpretation of the language of the letters; and Roger Baron, who read the translations and offered suggestions and interpretations. Many of the staff at the Provincial Archives of Manitoba read the results and provided helpful suggestions, including Monique Clément, Martin Comeau, Gilbert Comeault, Janelle Reynolds, and Diane Schipper. Our thanks to all.

Among the most helpful in tracking down personal details and publicizing the names of the letter writers are a number of genealogists. Bruce Watson generously shared his findings on individuals who served on the west coast, compiled after many years of diligent research. His vast compilation of thousands of names, which has restored their personalities and histories, will be a boon to researchers when it is published. The tireless efforts of Sharon Osborn-Ryan have created indispensable indices to the baptisms, marriages, and burials in the early years of Washington and Oregon territories, published by Harriet Munnick in an earlier monumental task. Through their dedication, the family history on the coast is quickly accessible and easy to find. Janice Sinclair, an enthusiastic genealogist in Harray, Orkney, connected us with many descendants of letter writers and provided details on the families of the Orkney employees. Others from Orkney – such as Jim Troup, James R. Harvey, Alison Fraser, and Phil Astley – offered the results of their research and knowledge. Bill Lawson, a genealogist from the Isle of Harris, searched his extensive files; and he and William Macleod provided useful information about some of the families from the Isle of Lewis and the Hebrides. John Steele made it his task to publicize the names of Scots and interested a freelance journalist, Campbell Thomas, in the project. Through their efforts, our project was mentioned in BBC broadcasts in English and Gaelic, in articles in at least twelve different newspapers in Scotland and Ireland, and in genealogical publications and websites. Gordon Innes posted the English names on a website that generated considerable interest; Mrs. P.J. Sisam, Laura Arksey, William Torrens, and Jonathan Catton went out of their way to track down helpful details and share their information on specific Englishmen. Others who offered the results of their genealogical research included Barbara A. Macleod, Robin McLay, Professor Donald Smith, and Roxanne Woodruff.

The result of all this publicity has been interest and helpful suggestions, with the occasional gold mine of information. One such lucky strike was Dr. Alicia St. Leger, a descendant of the Oldens who wrote so many letters to Jonathan Buck. She is a professional historical researcher and was invaluable in hunting down details on the fascinating family of the man who never received seventeen delightful letters. She has helped deliver these letters to a wide audience with enough background to make them meaningful and significant.

We have also benefited from the specialized knowledge of many in various fields. Dick Wilson was generous in his sharing of information on the ships and seamen on the west coast as well as the results of his research in countless archives for images of the posts, people, and ships. The readers of the manuscript for UBC Press and the Aid to Scholarly Publications Programme provided valuable suggestions for further reading in British and Quebec social history, and Marion McKay and Dr. Ian Carr gave helpful hints on medical diagnoses.

Early in the project Grace Ewart used her typing skills to take on the very difficult task of transcribing the letters. All our colleagues have been supportive; special thanks go to Debra S. Moore, whose suggestions on the photography improved the end product, and to Steve Halek of The LabWorks, who took such care with capturing the letters on film. Ann Hindley, Brad Froggatt, Katherine Pettipas, and Sharon Reilly at the Manitoba Museum provided their expert advice about the artifacts, which added so much to the images of the letters. At the end of the project, Richard Buss collaborated with us to create the index. With such a large body of letters and such a long time during which the work took place, there are inevitably some whose names will be missed. Every contribution was valuable and we appreciate the help that has been given freely at every turn.

The enthusiasm of Jean Wilson and all those at UBC Press who have prepared catalogues, planned book launches, and given suggestions on production have helped to create this book. We are especially grateful for the sensitive and meticulous assistance of our editor, Camilla Jenkins. Of course, no matter how much help we received, any errors are ours and we welcome corrections or new interpretations.

Special thanks are due to our employers, the Provincial Archives of Manitoba and the University of Calgary, both of which were enthusiastic about the project, and to the Hudson's Bay History Foundation and the Aid to Scholarly Publications Programme, which provided funds to help publish this book.

Undelivered Letters

Introduction

The Hudson's Bay Company, founded in 1670, had its headquarters in London, England, but most of its operations in North America. The London governor, deputy governor, and Committee members made decisions about the pursuit of the trade, but they rarely visited the North American continent where the trade occurred. Most of the officers and men at the posts and the ships were recruited in Britain, and for the first 150 years of the Company's history went out in ships to Hudson Bay and from there inland to various fur-trading activities operating under its own hierarchical system. The vast territory west of the present Ontario-Manitoba border formed the Northern Department, with communications radiating from its headquarters at York Factory out to the various district headquarters and from there to the posts and outposts. The Company secretary provided the communication link between these two distinct and distant parts of the Company. The HBC built a successful trade, initially based on the popularity of a hat made from felt using the soft underfur of the beaver. The union with the North West Company in 1821 changed not only the extent of its trade but also the traditional routes and the focus on fur because the Company inherited posts on the Pacific Ocean. The western coast of North America – the Columbia Department – required a new approach around Cape Horn that changed the length of the return voyage from months to years. It offered new products, such as salmon and wood, and eventually new markets along the route from Chile and California in the south to the posts of the Russian American Company in the north (Alaska) and into the Pacific Ocean in the Sandwich Islands (Hawaiʻi).

From the late 1820s to the 1850s, Hudson's Bay Company vessels sailed yearly from London, England, to the Company's Pacific headquarters at Fort

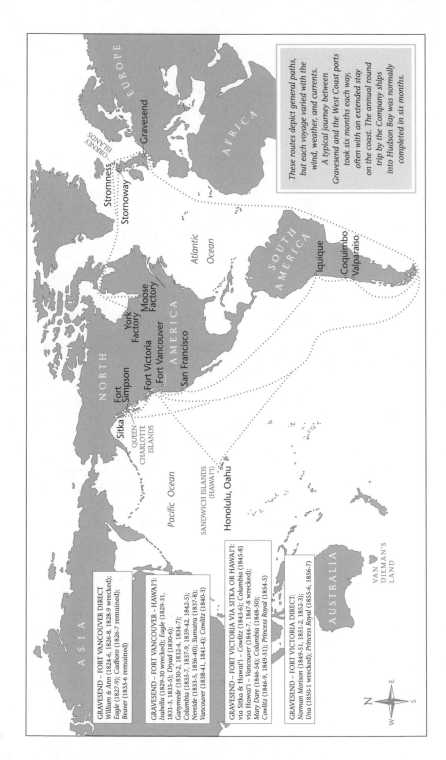

GRAVESEND – FORT VANCOUVER DIRECT
William & Ann (1824-6, 1826-8, 1828-9 wrecked); *Eagle* (1827-9); *Cadboro* (1826-7 remained); *Beaver* (1835-6 remained);

GRAVESEND – FORT VANCOUVER – HAWAI'I:
Isabella (1829-30 wrecked); *Eagle* (1829-31, 1831-3, 1833-5); *Dryad* (1830-6); *Ganymede* (1830-2, 1832-4, 1834-7); *Columbia* (1835-7, 1837-9, 1839-42, 1842-5); *Nereide* (1833-5, 1836-40); *Sumatra* (1837-8); *Vancouver* (1838-41, 1841-4); *Cowlitz* (1840-3)

GRAVESEND – FORT VICTORIA VIA SITKA OR HAWAI'I:
via Sitka & Hawai'i – *Cowlitz* (1843-6); *Columbia* (1845-8)
via Hawai'i – *Vancouver* (1844-7, 1847-8 wrecked); *Mary Dare* (1846-54); *Columbia* (1848-50); *Cowlitz* (1846-9, 1849-51); *Princess Royal* (1854-5)

GRAVESEND – FORT VICTORIA DIRECT:
Norman Morison (1849-51, 1851-2, 1852-3); *Una* (1850-1 wrecked); *Princess Royal* (1855-6, 1856-7)

Hudson's Bay Company routes around Cape Horn.

Vancouver, which today is the city of Vancouver, Washington, on the north shore of the Columbia just opposite Portland, Oregon, on the south shore. After the establishment of Fort Victoria – the present-day Victoria, capital of British Columbia – on Vancouver Island in 1849, the new colony became their destination. The Company ships made this long journey around the southern tip of South America in order to supply their business interests from California to Alaska with men and goods and to bring back the results of their trade. Usually, the round trip took almost two years and men who went out on these ships were often away for longer, staying to transport agricultural products and conduct trade along the coast and as far away as Oahu (Hawai'i) and Valparaiso, Chile. Others stayed for longer periods as workers in the posts, on the Company farms, and, after the international border was agreed upon in 1846, in the mines and farms of the new British colony on Vancouver Island. While they were away, their relatives – wives, parents, sisters, and brothers – as well as sweethearts and friends wrote letters to them. Most of the letters took the same long journey around the Horn and sometimes arrived after the men had left for home or, as occasionally happened, after they had met with tragic accidents. As west coast trade and settlement grew, men also left the Company's employment for better prospects. As a result, a large number of letters remained undelivered.

Postal arrangements developed and expanded during the period under consideration. Ships' letters were the main method, where the next ship – usually the Company's own – carried the mail. However, by the end of the period, mail was sometimes shipped to Panama and crossed the isthmus to be picked up by ships on the Pacific coast. Occasionally the express brigade, following the fur trade routes across the continent, carried mail between the regular sailings. Initially, separate envelopes were not used; the paper on which the letter was written was left blank on one side and folded to form a cover where the address could be written. Then the folded sheet was carefully sealed with sealing wax, round wafers of various colours, or colourfully decorated gummed seals. Occasionally additional sheets or small items, such as a lock of hair, were inserted in the enclosure. Mail was costly and families used various methods to cut costs, including limiting the number of sheets and filling them completely with writing, even cross-writing messages on the page. The page was filled with writing, then turned at right angles and filled in the other direction. This can increase the challenge of reading the letters, but with practice most are remarkably easy to decipher.

The Hudson's Bay Company kept very detailed and informative records of all its activities. Since the Company had scruples about private property – an extension of its very careful handling of its own property – it was most respectful of its employees' letters. Since the Company was not in the habit of throwing away any written material, when a letter failed to reach a man in the Columbia district, it was preserved – often unopened – and returned to the Company's London secretary. Although we have evidence that some letters were returned to the families, many were not, perhaps because return addresses were insufficient. Therefore, the secretary of the Company – William Smith during much of the period when the ships went regularly to the west coast – marked each letter and filed it meticulously. About 250 letters collected during several decades were never claimed. Of those located – and there may be others not yet traced – only about forty, sent to men in regions other than the west coast, were excluded from this volume.

These undelivered personal letters became part of the archival collection of the Company in London, England. In 1974 the large and varied collection of documents of the fur trade was moved to the Provincial Archives of Manitoba in Winnipeg. For more than a decade, Judith Hudson Beattie and Helen M. Buss have been reading the undelivered letters, transcribing them, organizing them, discussing them, as well as studying related materials. Judith Hudson Beattie, Keeper of the Hudson's Bay Company Archives, has a broad knowledge of the Company, its history, and its men, and has researched the biographical backgrounds of the men to whom the letters were addressed. This information appears in the notes of this book alongside information about the ships and posts where many of the men served. Helen M. Buss, whose research has been in memoirs, letters, and diaries, has collaborated with Judith Hudson Beattie to write narratives that introduce the letters and their writers as well as the men for whom they were intended. Together, we have grouped the letters in terms of the different positions of the men who were to receive these letters – the sailors whose lives were lived primarily on ships and in seaports, the French-speaking *voyageurs* hired in villages along the St. Lawrence River, the largely English and Scottish Company men who served at the posts and occasionally retired there, and the emigrant workers who hoped to be part of a new colony. Although the men and their correspondents share many concerns, we have divided their letters into these categories in order to provide introductions that take into account their historical, linguistic, and social differences, as well as their varied relationships to the Company and its activities.

Because the men generally remain silent within this correspondence, we include contexts for their lives in these introductions. The biographical background that introduces each man's entry is largely from Company records and is supplemented by the biographical information in the notes. Since the letter writers speak for themselves, we offer only contextual information in most cases and additional biographical information only when it is available. Our narratives are aimed at helping a wide variety of readers to enter the letters with the essential information they need to read them as representations of individuals. Although we expect a wide variety of researchers – from genealogists through social historians and cultural theorists – to find these letters useful, we do not expect our narratives to provide all of the contexts that such scholars may require. Rather, we hope they will serve as a basis for understanding the human subjects who wrote and received the letters as well as provide some directions for the further research of the reader. Our first aim is to put ordinary people, who have not been central to either the history or the literature of the period, in the primary position of attention.

Even though we wish to highlight the lives of working people, there are a number of prominent Company officials whose decisions profoundly affected the lives of ordinary folk. Three names in particular recur in these pages. George Simpson, governor in North America, had enormous powers in terms of both the careers of men and the operation of posts. Chief Factor John McLoughlin of Fort Vancouver, where west coast trade centred, had most of the day-to-day power over men's lives – except for men on ships, who were under captains' orders – and was the local court of last resort in all disputes. Later in the period, James Douglas became an important authority in the lives of seamen, immigrant workers, and men at various posts. In his roles first as McLoughlin's second-in-command, then as chief factor and governor of Fort Victoria and the new colony of Vancouver Island, his decisions enter the stories of these workers, sailors, and emigrants.

These voices from a past world are vividly present through the vehicle of their personal letters, which we reproduce with only very minimal additions, such as essential punctuation and a few helpful translations of phonetic spellings and words no longer in current use. The letters from the families of *voyageurs* appear both in their original French and in full English translations. Within each of the book's divisions, we have ordered the entries and letters chronologically, with only a few exceptions where a strict chronology would separate related stories, in order to give readers a sense of the changing world of the early nineteenth century.

This collection of letters offers us an unusual look into a broad spectrum of lives in this period and is unique in terms of the variety of human subjects that speak directly to us out of the past. The letters are from multiple correspondents to multiple addressees and thus represent a variety of perspectives in terms of age, place of residence, class, and gender. Yet because the common situation of all of the letters is that they are being sent to men who are far away from home – working to make a living for themselves and their loved ones – common themes prevail: concerns about safety (both physical and spiritual), worries about money, and about the ability of love and loyalty to survive over time and distance. The letter writers range from clever young women of the country gentry class – who write in prose reminiscent of a Jane Austen novel full of romance, parties, and money – to barely literate, poor parents too old to work their farms, who are desperate for a son's return. There is, as well, the wife who gets a portion of her husband's pay quarterly from the Company but only sees her husband for three months in three years – just long enough to conceive a child that he will not see for years. In contrast, there is the brother who makes sly jokes about the quality of women in faraway places. There are the deserted women who have been left behind, with memories and little else. While the bulk of the letters are from people in Lower Canada (Quebec), England, Ireland, Wales, and Scotland – including a substantial number from the western islands and Orkney and a few from the Shetlands, a few letters are from men themselves at posts in the Company's service.

Readers in Britain may find that their towns, their districts, or their family names are mentioned in some letters, while readers in Canada and the United States will discover that some of the men settled in North America or left "country wives" – that is, Aboriginal (First Nation and Métis) women – they may have married according to the "custom of the country," in which marriages were blessed by Aboriginal ceremonies or by declared cohabitation. These wives and their children became founders of their communities, ancestors of extended families. The history of the Company and its men has always been closely related to Canada's history as a colony and as a nation. In the United States there is a growing awareness of the many interconnections between the Company's activities and western expansion. One of those historical moments, the settlement of the Oregon Territory, coincides with these letters. But beyond these appeals, there is the power of the letters themselves. When we first began to read them we found ourselves intensely and personally involved in their vivid re-creation of peoples' lives, peoples' selves. Over the years of our research and writing, the ability of these letters to bring their writers to life for us, to make us feel and imagine their situations and those of the men they wrote to, has never faded. They are powerful evocations of the lives of actual people in a period now distant but made close to us by these personal letters that reach out across time.

One of the strongest reminders of past lives are the letters of women. Women's lives have not always been part of traditional historical narratives because of our society's reliance on what Robert B. Shoemaker calls "written discourse" as the "dominant discourse" (1998, 4). This has meant that women's activities have been behind the scenes of these traditional narratives and therefore not generally the subject of commentary. In contrast, in these letters we see women engaged in multiple activities of work and influence. Company records reveal just how hard the men in their service worked; these

S = Men on the ships
P = Men at the posts
E = Emigrant labourers

0   50 miles

0   50 kilometres

N

Shetland (S, P)

OUTER HEBRIDES

Stromness

Orkney (S, P, E)

Stornoway

Lewis (P)

Uist (P)

Nairn
(P, E)

Aberdeen
(S)

SCOTLAND

Kincardine (S)

Forfar (S)

Stirling (S)

Edinburgh (S)

Renfrew (S)

Atlantic
Ocean

North
Sea

Wigtown (S)

Cumberland
(S)

Louth (S)

Yorkshire (S)

Irish Sea

Lancashire
(S)

IRELAND

ENGLAND

Cork (S)

Waterford (S)

WALES

Suffolk (S)

Pembroke
(S)

Buckingham
(S)

Essex (S, E)

Middlesex (S)

London (S, P)

Kent (S, E)

Somerset (S)

Hampshire
(S)

Devon (S)

Dorset (S)

Cornwall (S)

Atlantic
Ocean

English Channel

Origins of men on the ships, men at the posts, and emigrant labourers.

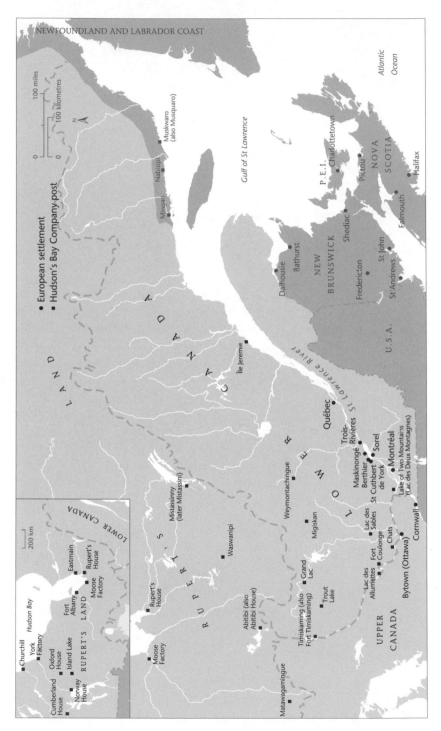

Origins of the *voyageurs* and some Hudson's Bay Company posts.

letters confirm that the families left behind often had equally hard, if different, forms of service. In fact, being in domestic service was the common way for a woman to earn a living in this period. Historian Bridgit Hill finds that it is "from the letters, journals, diaries and memoirs of their employers" (1996, 4) that we learn of the lives of servants. In this text we hear some of these servants speak for themselves in their own written discourse: their letters.

Both the men and the women who write these letters also help us address the absence of the lives of working-class and lower-middle-class people in historical and literary accounts of the period. They reveal just how difficult were the conditions of many working families, how quickly financial situations could change, how poor health speedily became tragic death in the days before modern medicine, employee benefits, and social welfare plans. The place of servants, like the place of women in the social structure, was part of the growing great change in English society in the first half of the nineteenth century. When we read their accounts of work-related difficulties, we can more easily understand why, especially in the later part of the period covered, a number of our correspondents mention emigration as a possible cure for their situation.

A Note on the Text

Our main aim has been to let the general reader enjoy the flow of the letters, uninterrupted by such academic apparatus as footnotes, while supplying full references for those who wish to pursue further research. Each entry is numbered, and each letter within each entry includes the date on which it was written at or near the beginning. As transcripts, the letters are reproductions as faithful as possible to the originals; as noted above, we have added only necessary closing punctuation to separate sentences and, occasionally, an explanatory or missing word. A word may be missing, for instance, where the seals that held the letter closed, on being opened, have torn the paper. All our insertions are shown in square brackets. Where handwritten originals include one or more lines underscoring words for emphasis, we follow the modern typesetting convention of showing such words in italics. Indentation in the originals is erratic. We have regularized the placement of the date, inside address, and salutation and placed return addresses, where they are given, on a single line, rather than as a series of increasingly indented parts. All letters that begin with the symbol ᔪ are among the undelivered correspondence. A few letters reproduced in the book are not in this collection and are therefore not marked with the symbol. These appear on pages 46, 68, 83, 144, 247, 292, 295, and 297.

All source citations for the letters, as well as for some related subjects, are in the notes at the end of the book. Source citations for letters are at the end of the notes for each entry listed in their order of appearance; wherever possible, letters, extracts, and quotations are identified by the date on which they were written. Hudson's Bay Company Archives material at the Provincial Archives of Manitoba is signified by the acronyms HBCA, PAM; all other citations are indicated with the author's last name and the date of publication in parentheses. Full bibliographical information is available in the references. When "the Company" is cited, it always refers to the Hudson's Bay Company. On a number of occasions, since events in one man's life often connect with another, we refer readers to other men's stories with a cross-reference to his entry number. The reader will also find the stories indexed by the men's names at the end of the text.

On the first mention of a post or fort we give the present-day name of that location (e.g., Fort Vancouver is Vancouver, Washington), and this information is also available in Appendix B.

As money is often a central topic in the letters, we offer this rough guide to purchasing power, gleaned from the letters themselves. A loaf of bread could be purchased for fivepence and a gallon of flour for ninepence. A young apprentice boy was given sixpence for a week's pocket money, while his family paid £10 per annum for the rent of a modest home in London and £15 for the funeral expenses of the boy's mother. A seaman earned between £24 and £30 a year, and a second mate's salary rose to £50. While £8 would buy you a small boat "to go on the river to sell beer," you would need £800 to buy "a pleasantly situated cottage" with some land in the country. During the period when American ships began to recruit British seamen with higher wages, the English pound was worth approximately five American dollars. The letter writers transcribed sums of British currency in various ways in their texts, but it is safe to say that the standard order of pounds (£), shillings (s), and pence (d) is always intended.

Finally, we found when confronted with the phonetic spelling of some letters that by reading them aloud and thus pronouncing the words as they were written, we not only understood more of the meaning but could also hear something of the accent of the time and place.

Letters to Men on the Ships

Until the 1820s, the Company had mainly operated annual ships into Hudson Bay, a trip completed in one shipping season. But, with the acquisition of the North West Company – including its operations on the west coast – the shipping increased in complexity and in financial commitment, and so did the possibilities that personal letters might not be delivered, given the time and distance involved. Whereas trips into Hudson Bay occupied a season, from May to October, the voyage to the west coast required almost two years from the time a ship left Gravesend, England, until its return, providing there were no mishaps or delays. Often a ship would be ordered to stay on the west coast for a year or more to conduct the coastal trade and the voyage became a three-year venture. In later years the lengthy time of the voyages was less, the ship *Norman Morison* accomplishing voyages to the Columbia Department in 1849 and 1851 in only five months. Most of the crew – apprentices, seamen, officers, and masters – had close ties to the sea and they generally signed their contracts in London. Two-thirds were of British origin – English (71 percent), Scottish (14 percent), Orkneymen (11 percent), Welsh (2 percent), and Irish (1 percent) – and the rest were made up of Europeans (1 percent), North Americans (17 percent), and Sandwich Islanders (i.e., Hawaiians) (15 percent). However, even though their contracts and the accounting records often give the "parish of origin" as London, where the men were hired, family letters in the undelivered files indicate where the men originally resided. Half of our sample came from the London and Thames estuary, but the rest came from seaports in Ireland, Wales, Scotland, and the coast of England. They were not like the usual Hudson's Bay Company employees, who were predominantly Scottish (including Orkneymen), long-serving, and invested with great loyalty to the Company. While a number of the ships' officers remained in the Company's service for many years, many of the seamen signed on for only one trip and, on returning to England, took the first ship available with another mercantile company in order to remain steadily employed. Often our accounts of them break off suddenly as a voyage ends or, as in the later years of the coastal service, when they desert their ships for the temptation of the gold fields, free land, or just better-paying ships in a labour-short and competitive mercantile market.

Among the letters to sailors we find a number to youths. These boys were the apprentices from the Royal Greenwich Hospital School hired at as young an age as fourteen after completing three years of schooling in marine craft. The school provided education for the sons of seamen serving in the Royal Navy, the merchant marine, Trinity House, and the Royal Marines. In 1830 the Company hired eight "lads intended to go out by the Brig *Dryad* to Columbia River [who] were bound apprentices to the Company for a period of 7 years each." Instructions to Chief Factor John McLoughlin, officer in charge at Fort Vancouver, regarding the apprentices were very detailed and included the request that "they be treated with kindness" and that attention be "paid to their instruction and the care of their morals." The chief officer was obliged to make sure that "accurate priced statements ... be sent home yearly of the articles with which they are supplied." In exchange for the Company's close supervision of the apprentices, the school was to supply spaces for the sons of Company employees, which might include some sons born to the employees' North American wives. But, soon after, the school was fiercely defending its students in a long list of complaints against the Company – some of which are the subject of the letters and narratives that follow – so that large-scale hiring of apprentices was curtailed.

For all the sailors, be they apprentices, seamen, or officers, the voyages to the west coast of North America would require two years at a minimum. A ship headed for the Columbia River that left England in the fall would round Cape Horn at the tip of South America in February or March, during the southern hemisphere's late summer. On arrival in the Columbia Department in the northern hemisphere's spring or summer, a ship would unload its supplies, destined to provision the posts and fur brigades that headed inland. The summer months might be passed waiting in Fort Vancouver for the return of the brigades and furs in the fall. Or, after a few months supplying the coastal forts of the Hudson's Bay Company and the Russian American Company, the ship would return to the Columbia River, load up with timber, salmon, and agricultural products as well as furs, and head out, bound for home, with trading calls at such places as Yerba Buena (San Francisco) and Monterey in California, as well as Honolulu in Hawai'i and Valparaiso in Chile. As a result, sailors had many opportunities to get into trouble or, seeking better pay and new adventures, to slip away from the Company ships. Those who did work out their contracts would arrive back in London by spring the next year. Although seamen signed on for the length of the voyage or signed a three-year contract, apprentices were obligated for the duration of their seven-year apprenticeships, engineers signed five-year contracts, and ships' officers were more or less continually employed by the company. Of all the seamen and landsmen hired for the Columbia trade, only one-third remained for more than three years.

Life on board ship was hard work for the average seaman. They took their turn in various duties: each qualified seaman doing a trick at the helm each day, trimming sail, acting as foretopman, doing four-hour watches, and assisting the carpenter in recaulking the seams, as well as working with the boatswain rerigging the yards and spars. Work days were often sixteen hours a day, except for Sundays when, in good weather and after morning divine services led by the mate or master, a sailor could wash or mend his clothes and chat with other men on deck. But even on Sundays, he would have to serve one four-hour watch. Yet, above-deck work was often preferred to time off below decks, as the conditions in the fo'c'sle (forecastle), near the bow of the ship, were not such as to make a man want to spend too much time in what was "home" for the almost two years on the average voyage. The area of the fo'c'sle, on the largest Company ship, was 7.6 by 5.0 by 1.7 metres (25 by 16 by 5.5 feet). It housed the bunks – which the Company supplied rather than the usual hammocks – the eating table slung up to the ceiling when not in use, the privy, and the personal possessions of the sailors. Because the bow was under pressure from the weight of the ship's fixtures above it, the deck seams were constantly opening up, allowing water that swept over the boat from the waves or during rainy days, to drip into the men's quarters. The tallow candles used for light in the windowless fo'c'sle allowed soot to penetrate the wood, making the area dark as well as damp. Smell was also a problem: bilge water from the adjoining cargo holds and the covered bucket the men used as a privy on days when they could not hang over the side of the boat blended with the men's sweat, wet clothing, and carbon-penetrated damp wood to yield a stink that would send men above decks whenever they were permitted to be there. Once on deck they could see the more adequate quarters of the mate and captain, housed above deck, where the officers ate their more elaborate meals, served by the ship's steward. Officers slept and ate in a drier, less malodorous environment. However, advancement to a higher rank was a real, if long-term, possibility. Apprentices who had a schooling in mathematics so that they could take the navigation exams leading to mate's papers would eventually become officers. An ordinary seaman without education could, after a number of years, become a boatswain or, if he showed

Hudson's Bay Company operations on the west coast, 1830-57. In 1853 the portion south of the boundary line was named Oregon Department and the northern portion, Western Department.

special abilities, he might become cook or steward. A number of the men represented in our sample did receive promotion with the Company.

In fact conditions on Company ships were usually better than for seamen on other vessels. Not only did they have bunks in place of hammocks but they were well, if plainly, fed on stores of dried beans, salted pork and beef, as well as ship's biscuit, and on fresh vegetables and fruits whenever the ships stopped at one of the several ports on their journeys. On coastal service, ships traded with Aboriginal peoples not only for furs but also for fresh fish and game. The Company preferred no corporal punishment and men were generally not punished with anything worse than being kept in irons in the cargo hold long enough for tempers to cool. In 1853 Governor George Simpson commented to Chief Factor Donald Manson, "We duly appreciate the necessity of maintaining discipline and enforcing obedience; that end is not to be attained by the display of violent passion and the infliction of severe and arbitrary punishment in hot blood. When a servant is refractory or disobeys orders he should be allowed a full hearing, his case examined fairly and deliberately, and if guilty, either taken out to the depot, put on short rations, or under arrest – in fact almost any punishment rather than knocking about or flogging" (Loo 1994, 32). However, tempers sometimes flared, and floggings and cruelty were not unknown. In theory, Chief Factor John McLoughlin, the highest-ranking Company officer on the west coast, was the court of last appeal in regard to discipline. His judgments were generally humane but, as our research on the letters reveals, sometimes he had to support his captains against his own desire to be fair to the men or risk losing these highly qualified masters in an increasingly competitive market.

Given the tensions of close quarters aboard ship, it is surprising that mutinous outbreaks recorded in the company records and some of these letters were rare. Drunkenness was generally not a problem when the ship was under way, since men were served only a quarter pint of grog (half rum and half water) a day with their daily medicine of lime juice to fight scurvy but, once men arrived at attractive ports such as Honolulu, misbehaviour driven by drink was a real danger, as our narratives and the letters reveal. In the late 1840s and into the 1850s desertions become more frequent because of the presence of American vessels paying much higher wages – US$120 and $160 per month compared to the £4 monthly paid by the Company (equivalent to £24 to £32 per month, approximately a year's salary aboard Company ships). As well, opportunities for work opened up by the California gold rush and the new settlements springing up in the Oregon Territory offered competition to the Company's employment.

Despite the demanding life of seafaring in the early nineteenth century, the sailors proved to be a hardy lot, with only 1 percent off sick at any given time and only 1 percent dying of injury or disease over the three decades of the Columbia service. There were shipwrecks that took lives, as in the loss of the crew of the *William & Ann* on the bar of the Columbia in 1829 but, when the *Isabella* was wrecked on the bar the next year, her whole crew was saved. When in port at one of the Company forts, especially Fort Vancouver, sick and injured men were well cared for by the Company, often by a trained doctor.

The Company was scrupulous in its records of money transactions with its employees. A seaman's pay was kept on account for him. He could draw from this account or arrange for regular disbursements to be made to family back home, either through prior arrangement in London or by sending a signed draft for cash that his family could use to obtain funds from the Company. We see evidence of many grateful families as well as those less well provided for in these letters. The Company secretary sometimes had to make difficult judgment calls about the distribution of a sailor's pay in response to appeals by needy relatives of far-away sailors or when a sailor died without naming his beneficiary.

The letters to sailors are from family members who represent a broad range of education, class, and place. They contain news of home, of births, marriages, and deaths along with concern for the well-being of a son, husband, or brother away at sea. Some letters give financial advice and spiritual counsel; others offer gossip and reports about girls on the marriage market. Families often have more than one son at sea and collectively offer a sense of how widespread were Britain's mercantile interests. Many, in the earlier years, speak of the dull economic times in Britain and, toward the end of the period, there is more talk of family members emigrating to places as far away as Australia and New Zealand. A number of correspondents show a good knowledge of not only civic affairs in their local districts but also of national and international news. For example, Robert Nicholls's brother, writing in 1832, mentions the Reform Bill, the resignation of Prime Minister Earl Grey, as well as news from Portugal, Poland, and Egypt.

Some of the most compelling letters come from mothers, especially those who are economically dependent on their sons and those who have not heard from their sons in a long time. Anger, fear, and love combine in these letters, sometimes in the same sentence. The letters of lonely wives and yearning sweethearts gain intensity for us as readers, since we know that these heartfelt emotions never reached the intended recipients. Ann Duncan wrote several undelivered letters to her husband, in which she becomes increasingly more frustrated – especially so when she receives a letter from him in which he scolds her for not writing! There are humorous letters as well, ones in which sisters tease their brothers and satirize the locals, and letters in which brothers manage to work in an off-colour joke while reporting on the home scene. Because the sailors range from apprentices through regular seaman to those who have risen to mate or master, the families and friends writing to sailors represent a broad range of early nineteenth-century British working- and middle-class citizens of all ages and both sexes. Their letters paint us a wide and very human portrait of that society.

1 WILLIAM WILSON: *I niver was in more nide*

William Wilson, an Orkneyman, left London as a seaman on the *Cadboro* on 25 September 1826. The *Cadboro* arrived on 24 April 1827, taking close to seven months to make the voyage. William worked on the coastal service until 1830 and arranged to have his parents receive £15 at a rate of £5 per year by way of another person, Mrs. Cromarty. However, his father wrote that they had not received all they had expected through the woman, who by then was deceased.

∾ William Wilson, Seaman on Board the Cadboro, Fort Vancouver, Columbia River

Kirkwall 17 June 1830

Deare and Loving Son
I recived your Letter of the 20 March 1828 and was hapey to hear of your good health and well appointed which mentions to me that I will recive five pounds yearly from Mrs Cromarty[.] the first that I recived from her was one Soverin by A Letter Deted the 1 June 1827 the next was Two Pounds 17 Aprill 1828 the next was Two pounds by letter of 8 November 1828 and Three pounds in May 1829 and Three pound in November 1829 in all eliven pounds that I have recived from Mrs Cromarty and by information from her Sister in Kirkwall that recived her dead Letter she departed this life the 12 day of May 1830[.] as I have seated [stated] to you what I have recived you Will best Judge of what may be in her handes belongin you[.] I have at present to send to you by the first oppertunety for London Two frokes and Eight pairs of Stockiens and some metons [mittens] which I hope you will recive in seaftey[.] Deare Son I have to inform you that your Sisters and Brothers is in good health only times in Orkey [Orkney] is verey dull for A suport to them and thee can hardly meake A life for them- selves only Janey in A Coures day [the course of a day] drives the Cart to and from to Stromness for me when I am not fite to go or thene we would be much worse of[f] as I am fite to do nothing in Kirkwall with the Cart[.] The Littel that I have recived from you is bine A verey great help to me[.] I hope the Lord will prosper you in all your undertakiens on account of it

but had I recived what you desiered me to gete it would still bine the
greater bennifite as I am needfull but it was not for want of your good will
that I did not recive it[.] ✝ [crossed out] as my former house is nue bine
sold and puled doune I have bine obldged to remove to A house that that
[repetition] cost me more thine double rent A thing which at present I am
verrey unfite to pay but I hope the Lord will bliss you on account of your
former Kindness and hopes you will continue it as I niver was in more
nide[.] Dear Son your Mother is bine so pourlie this last Twelve monthes
that she could not beake A Bineck [bake a bannock] for herself and you
may consider what my treyels is[.] Dear Son if the Lord Speares you I
should be hapey to see your feace ounces more in time or at at [repetition]
aney reat to hear of you being again in Briton [Britain] as nothing can give
me greater pleasuer thene to heare of you being being well[.] I should wish
to know when you think to be home[.] dear Son if you intend remainen
where you are I will [do all] in my power to send you aney litell thing that
may be in my power that you may stand in nide of only mention it[.] Dear
Son how soune I recive word from you nothing can give me greater pleasuer
in this side of time and I remain your Dear and Lovin Father till Death
    Donald Willson

    Less than a week later, William's parents sent out a second letter, on receiv-
ing one from him telling of his new appointment to a different ship.
William's letter had taken ten months to reach them.

~ William Willson, on Bord the Scouner Vancover, at Fort Vancover in
Columbia River

Kirkwall 22 June 1830

    Dear and Loving Son We have this day recived your letter of 20 Agust
1829[.] how earnestly we embresed it we cannot tell you[.] we was sorey to
hear of you being pourly in health for some time but hapey that you are
again recoveded and gote well[.] we are sorry that you are engeaged for
Another year in such A deangers Countrey as nothing would give us greater
pleasuer then to see you[.] I am affreyed that your Mother will niver see
you as she is so pourely[.] Dear Son we have recived with your letter four
poundes which we cannot tell you our necesiety when we gote it[.] Shuerlie
it is the Lordes doeins that has provided such a wey of help for us and he
will reward you but your letter was above the whole to hear that you was
still in time[.] Dear Son your Cousien William Miller has left the Soldiers
and Came home and died A Twelve month ago died and his Sister Ceatren
touke her bede on his Buriel day and died also[.] nue the Old people has

not one of there Children in time at tall and thee hive no laberers[.] your
Sister Ann and har husbant is well at present and thee hive A Boy and
Girell[.] your Sister Marey is in Ceathness [Caithness] at Serviss[.] your
Brother is not home at present but his wife is well and has four Children[.]
all your Sisters sendes there kind love to you[.] your Sister Betcy sendes her
kind Complimentes to you and she hopes to see you home soune[.] we are
verey sorrey that we could not gete your artickels sent out to you before
nue[.] Blind Bobe sendes his Compliments to you[.] we have no more
partickler nues to inform you but that we remain your dear and Lovin
father and Mother Till death

    Donald & Jean Willson

    The first Company ship to go out to the Columbia Department after these
letters were written was the *Ganymede,* which left in November, so they
were probably sent by another conveyance. By the time they arrived, however,
William was sailing home on the *Eagle,* which had left the west coast on 29
October 1830 and arrived in London 18 April 1831. Men sometimes went briefly
to their homes before shipping out again. William's father had appealed to
his son's sense of responsibility, claiming "I am fit to do nothing in Kirkwall,"
"I am needful," and "I niver was in more nide." William did not continue in
the HBC's service. However, in light of his father's demands and the dull economic times, William likely remained as a seaman in another company's service. Unless his new ship stopped in the Orkney Islands for water and crew, he
may not have been able to make the expensive trip home to see his family.

2 JAMES CURTIS, WILLIAM CURTIS, AND HENRY BEE: *You shall be sold*
    to the Doctors for your Beauty

James Curtis left London, with his eighteen-year-old son William, aboard
the *Dryad* in January 1830 and they were at the west coast by August. Neighbours James and William Curtis and Henry Bee had all signed contracts at
the same time, James with an "x" and the two younger men with full signa-
tures. Henry's mother inserted a message to him in the letter written to James
Curtis by his wife, Mary Litchfield, with a postscript by her mother, named
Ward – or could it have been Mary from Lichfield, now within London?

James Curtis, on board the Dryade, Colombia

[1 February 1832 with insert dated 28 January 1832]

    My Dear Husband & Son

    I have this Oppotunity of wrighting these few lines to you and William
hoping you are both in good health[.] I am sorry to say I am very indifirent

in my heelth at this present time[.] Mary sends her Love to you both
wishes you was come home[.] my Mother sends her Love to you and her
grandson and Sarah Collet send her Love to you both and all your Cousons
and will be happy to see you safe in England once more[.] Mrs Towers send
her Love to you she as got one Child[.] phillip is still in Ameraca still but
they cannot speak well of the Country[.] I sent you word they had lost one
Child and they have lost one since and when Abby got to Ameraca she was
Confined with twins one she as lost[.] my Sister Ann send her love to you
both[.] Robert Warner he send his love to you[.] he comes and see me once
a fortnight[.] I have seen Mrs Simpson once but I have never been up in her
place[.] Mrs Allen sends her respects[.] Caroline Allen as garne a voyage to
sea[.] Mrs Boxall I do see some times but seldom[.] her Husband is at sea[.]
Peter the Swept send his love to you[.] They kep[t] the first of May up
respecting Mary Leaving[.] I can not say much about it[.] I keep her at
school but she cannot git on[.] we have had shocking bad going on in
London Burking people a line and selling their Bodies to Docter and some
as got Hang for it
PS your Old Litchfield Mother Ward send her respects to you and if she
can git you Burke you shall be sold to the Doctors for your Beauty
[upside down in what appears to be another hand] Henry Bee[']s Mother is
much Obliged to Wm Litchfield for sending her word about Henry and
should wish him to be kind Enough to Inquire further for her as she wishes
to know where he his to be found & Please to send word in the next letter
to your Mother & shall be very glad on your coming to England to call on
me[.] I hope your all in good Health & will soon be Home
Jany 28th
1832
[original hand]   I remain your affect[ionate]
                                   Wife and Mother
                                   M. Litchfield

Feby 1 1832
[sideways on cover] Mary wishes to know if her Cat is alive and liffing
[living]

   In the postscript James, or possibly William, is teased about his good looks
as a potential victim for William Burke. Burke perpetrated an 1827 scandal
in which he and his accomplice and landlord, William Hare, enticed people
into their Edinburgh house with drink, then suffocated them. Seventeen people were either killed or disinterred and sold for a lucrative fee to Dr. Robert
Knox for anatomy classes. Burke was hanged in 1829 after Hare turned king's

evidence; as a result of the scandal the law was changed to allow dissection. Their manner of suffocation in a way that left no sign of violence on the bodies became known as "burking." During this period body snatchers, or "resurrectionists," operated widely, and Mother Ward either refers to recent events in London, or she has mistaken the city where Burke and Hare operated.

Once on the coast James, the father, worked as a boatswain aboard the *Vancouver* and his son worked as a seaman aboard the *Ganymede.* James returned to London aboard the *Ganymede* on 7 November 1831 and would have missed his wife's first letter sent in January 1832, when he was on his way home. William – known as both Curtis (his father's name) and Litchfield (his mother's name) – stayed on the west coast to work as a seaman aboard the *Cadboro.* Since the letter was not addressed to the son, however, it would not be delivered to him but returned. Mrs. Bee's enclosure, asking for news of her son, would have brought bad news had the inquiries gone further. After serving as a cook on the *Dryad* from December 1829 to 1831, Henry deserted his ship, probably at Monterey, California. In her next letter, William's mother indicated that she had received news of his whereabouts directly from her husband.

For William Curtis, belongs to Dride [*Dryad*], laying for Columby

August 27 1832

My Dear Son William

I have the pleasure of saying [seeing] your Farther Come home safe but was much hurt to hear you had left the Ship your Father was in[.] Ally and prise [Price] Just come home before your Farther did and Sail with them in Bord of the Winsor [*Windsor*][.] your Farth[er] not getting the money he expected he as took a voyage with Aly and price to new South Wales and by that time your time is up your Farth[er] will be at home[.] what you takes up in the Ship I mean Mony be shure you take an examine of it[.] Mary sends her kind Love to you and your Grandmother Sarah Collet and all your Cousens send their Love to you[.] Your Aunt Warner and Couson send their Love to you[.] John Allin [Allan or Allen] as sail in the ship with your Farther[.] Mothr Ward send her Love to you and Harriet Ayres

I shall be happy to see you

I remain your ever effectant

Mother M. Litchfield

William's mother warned him about his father "not getting the money he expected" and to be careful to check what he is paid, given her husband's disappointment with his pay. She could not have predicted the more serious fate that awaited her son. As her August 1832 letter was on its way to the west

coast, William and two other seamen, Peter Calder and Robert Nicholls (see
Nicholls story, entry 3), went ashore without supervision, bought liquor, got
drunk, and became involved in a riot aboard the *Cadboro* on 5 October. They
were "sent in irons for getting drunk and using insolent language to their
officers." Arriving back in England aboard the *Eagle* on 30 May 1833, William
may have had to wait some time to face his father on the latter's return from
the New South Wales colony in present-day Australia. One possible solution
for a sailor who did not want to face his family was to seek work on another
vessel before a bad reputation could catch up with him. Perhaps he was looking for a new ship with other seafaring friends on 1 June 1833 at The George
and Vulture tavern, near the Hudson's Bay Company headquarters, when he
and several other crewmates signed a letter to Charles Fraser (entry 9).

3   ROBERT NICHOLLS: *A large sheet of paper to write to you all the news (which
    by the bye I do not know how to fill up)*

Arriving in the Columbia Department in July 1831 aboard the *Ganymede*,
after being at sea since November of the previous year, seaman Robert
Nicholls wrote to his family on 13 August and again on 17 August. Perhaps
because he worked for a newspaper, brother William's letter included news
of the larger world, from riots in Bristol in the unsettled times of the Reform
Bill (see further discussion in Joseph Binnington's story, entry 4) to wars in
the Middle East, as well as the details of local romances, births, and deaths.
Like many who wrote in the early 1830s, he complained of the dull economic
times. Despite his protestations that he would not know how to fill the pages,
there is little blank space in the surviving letter.

〜   Hudson Bay House, Fenchurch Street, London,
     To Mʳ Robᵗ Nicholls, Fort Vancouver, New Caledonia

     Penryn [Cornwall] 13ᵗʰ May, 1832

         Dear Brother
         We have receivd your letters of the 13ᵗʰ August and 17ᵗʰ ditto, within two
     days of each other and are all most highly gratified to hear of your being in
     good health and comfortable; and agreeably to your request I have pro-
     cured a large sheet of paper to write to you all the news (which by the bye I
     do not know how to fill up) – To begin with our own – we are all in good
     health, thank God, but are still as you may imagine but poorly off in the
     world, but better than thousands of others, Mother enjoys very good
     health; Betsy and Mary Ann are at Mr Lavin's; and Harriet enjoys her
     health much better than when you left; – Dennis's time has been out nearly

twelve months but such is the depression of trade in this country at present that he has been unable to procure but very little work, in fact, he has done nothing since Christmas. I have had the good fortune to continue in work till this time, but know not how much longer it may continue, as our trade is exceedingly dull, I am now employed on the *Cornubian* weekly newspaper at Falmouth. John James and Catherine are still at school. Pearce and Aunt are very well but as yet have no children they were at Penryn a fortnight since[.] Ann Sophia and the child are well (as yet but one but worse luck another on the road). Captain Spershott is well and has the command of a Schooner called the Helston, which was built for the Union Company, at Fowey last year, Capt. H. Hosken is put out of the Enterprize and has been at home 15 or 16 months doing nothing and Jack Roberts has got the command of her, and got a wife into the bargain, – Haldgate is Mate of HM Packet Calypso and was very well the last time I saw him and kindly enquired after you. – Cuttings is now steward of HM Packet *Emulous* but is in very bad health and I fear is not long for the land of the living. the last voyage when I saw him he was looking shocking ill[.] Maunder was very well in health about five weeks since when he sailed for the Brazils on board of HM Packet *Opossum* but in spirits shocking bad. (alas this way-wardness of fate, Cupid has planted his dart in his heart and God knows what will be the result) but in despite of all obstacles has continued to fall in love with that *beautiful* Brunette Miss Araminta Earle. Mother, Grandfather, Sister, and Brothers all against him but to make the old adgae [adage] good the more opposition the greater the constancy so with poor Ned in despite of wind and weather, Mother and fire-irons (for by-the-bye the old dame called the shovel to her aid with the very laudable intention of knocking out the brains that could imagine her accomplished daughter as the partner of a common man-of-wars-man, without chance of promotion, on the half-pay of 4s. 10d. a week!) has been a constant nightly visitor at the Elephant and Castle. – Miss Elizabeth Earle is still in a state of single blessedness, but Bob its no go with you unless you continue to make yourself a Captain or chief-mate, at least, of a West Indiaman. – John Truran is master of old Trenery's schooner the Commerce, but will never make his fortune in that employ. Tom has got two children, and as far as appearances go may be supposed to be doing well. – Andrew has also two children but not doing so well as Tom. – Richard, Cousin Mary, and Susan are well and desires particularly to be remembered. – Within this month we have lost your old friend, and my dearest acquaintance poor Robert Blenkinsop, he was stationed at Chester in the Excise and being in a declining state of health petitioned to be removed into Cornwall, which being granted he left Chester for home and arrived here on a Thursday and the Sunday week following I had the melancholy satisfaction of following him to the receptacle appointed for all living. John Blenkinsop has obtained a situation as clerk under Lord Falmouth, at Tregothnan; James is an apprentice to a Tinman at Penzance and the rest remain at home. Old Jack Bunster has made a fool of himself – to use his own words – he has got a dear little wife and a dear little girl[.] he married Jane Bennett who he was courting when you was home[.] Barnicoat is working in the same office with me at Falmouth, and is most desperately in love with Ann Fenency who he has been going with this long time and I [have] no doubt that he will marry her as soon as he is able. Joseph Boswarthick, our old Sunday School companion has been dead this several months having received a kick from a horse and lived but two or three days after[.] Henry Dyson was at home last year but is now out with Capt Sowell; Moyle fell in love with Hannah Powson and made her an offer of marriage which she refused and Harry came home to see her and prevent Moyle from cutting him out. I know not what more to write to you to fill up the sheet as you do not feel much interest in politics but in the absence of other things you must take that – We have had an election these two years following and shall most likely have another this year as the Reform Bill is not settled[.] Earl Grey has resigned the office of Prime Minister and it is expected that the Duke of Wellington will have the place – there have been great disturbances in different parts of the country, at Bristol the mob resisted the military broke open the prisons and burnt them together with the Proton[otary's] House, Bishop's Palace, Mansion House and a number of other houses and a great many lives were sacrificed before the disturbances could be quelled and it is the general opinion that there will be the second part of the same tune but to a greater extent without there is an alteration in the times – Don Pedro has come home from the Brazils and is now at the Western Islands preparing an expedition to invade Portugal to recover the throne from Don Miguel for his daughter Donna Maria – Poland has been subdued by the Russians and is now in a more degrading state of vassalge than ever. The Turks are at war with the Egyptians and I am brought up as I know not what more to say and must conclude in the usual way by sending Mother's Sisters', Brothers' kindest love your friends and acquaintances remembrances and believe me your

   Affectionate Brother
    Will A.Nicholls

[cover] I forgot to mention Mr Lavin and family to you. Mr Lavin has been very unwell with a swelling in the neck but is now I hope much better. Henry is gone to sea in the Camden packet to Halifax to see

whether he will like the sea or not. Sarah and all the rest are very well – .
I've seen Cuttings today and he is much better and desires to be
remembered to you. I must again conclude and hope that on your arrival
you will at once pay us a visit as we are all very anxious to see you –
    W.A.N.

Robert Nicholls would probably have not had much to offer if he pursued
Elizabeth Earle to relieve her of her state of single blessedness, as he was certainly not a captain or chief mate. Nor perhaps would he have been in any
shape to contribute to the family income, as brother William might have
hoped. Company records show that as a result of being part of a riot aboard
the *Cadboro,* he was put aboard the *Eagle* and "sent home in irons for getting
drunk," along with two other seamen, William Curtis (entry 2) and Peter
Calder.

4 JOSEPH BINNINGTON: *Trade in every branch is very dull and brighter
    prospects are at present visionary*

The two letters written to Joseph Binnington in late 1832 and early 1833 reveal
the importance to ordinary Englishmen of the great parliamentary reform
movement toward more equal representation of the populace. It was just
then reaching a peak of interest because of the 1832 Reform Bill. The letters,
from a more well-educated hand than many in this collection, show enough
trust in the new reformed parliament and its potential to do away with the
undemocratic representation formerly characteristic of English parliaments
to hope for a more prosperous state for Joseph to return to, despite the dull
prospects for contemporary tradespeople. This writer was able to see the very
close connections between national politics and the economic well-being of
ordinary citizens, and to convey to his brother a sense of the state of things
at home while encouraging him to assess carefully his own decision about
coming home or staying in North America, both in regard to his economic
as well as his physical health.

～ Joseph Binnington on board the Cadborough

[12 September 1832, London]

    Dear Brother
    I embrace the oppertunity of sending these few lines to inform you that
I am spared to return to my family and that Mrs B and myself and children
are well. I have had an increase of another little boy named Alfred and that
Francis and his family are well and I am sorry to inform you that Mr Croft

his [is] dead and your Sister left with the Children[.] she has bore her loss
with a christian fortitude and shows her respect to her deceased husband in
her affection to the children[.] she continues to reside at the same house she
occupied when you was at home[.] she has been very ill but at Present is
better and employd at the upolstering buisness, – which I am sorry to state is
not very brisk – indeed trade in every branch is very dull and brighter prospects
are at present visionary[.] the bill of Reform is passed after great resistance
from the tory part and great determination by the reformers and the election
for the reform candidates will shortly take place, and I hope should you be
spared to return home things will then be in a more prosperous state

   I am sorry to state that we have not had any letter from you since leaving
the downs and was much surprized that you did not inform us of your
motives for stoping in the country and If any promises has been held out
to induce you to stop that you will realize your expectations and I shall be
happy to congratulate you on your success and trust you will write to
inform us on the first oppertunity and direct either to your sister, or to
me- at the old residence N° 9 Queen St. Ratcliff[.] we all unite in our kind
love to you
      and remain yours affect[io]n[atel]y
         Brothers & Sister
         T [or F] Binnington
12 Sept 1832

   By the time he wrote his second letter, Joseph's brother had heard from
him. He told his brother the latest political news: the election in 1832 of
William Cobbett (1762-1835) in Oldham.

∼ Joseph Binnington

[20 February 1833]

   Dear Brother
   I now write to inform you that I & my family are well and that Sister Mary
is very unwell at present – and I hope you find yourself better than you was
when we last heard from you. francis and his family are well.
   I hope the climate you are in you will not be subjectt to any more
diseases[.] if it do not agree with you I recommend you to come home
altho things are at present in a precarious state[.] I hope things will turn
out better as the new reformed parliment have met[.] I hope something
will be done to benefitt the country as some seem determined to effect a
reformation of abuses[.] Cobbett is a member for Oldam [Oldham] and is
staunch to the cause of reformation – I remain in Queen St. at present and

I do not know how long I may remain here as I wish to get into a better situation for buissnes and where to go too for the best is dificult to ascertain but must trust to providence for the benifitt. The Eagle is shortly expected and I hope we shall hear from you and shall be glad to give us some account of the country you are in and what prospects you may have in the employ you are in and I shall be glad to hear from you every oppertunity and Conludere with our kind love to you and remain yours Affectionatly
    Your Affectionate Brother
      T [or F] Binnington
20 Feby 1833

    The mention of Joseph having been ill when he last wrote may be related to the disease that frequently struck Fort Vancouver between 1830 and 1836, when the fort was subject to a "dreadful visitation" of what was called "intermittent" or "trembling" illness. What was certainly malaria emerged semi-annually; many whites were incapacitated by it and the disease killed 75 percent of the Aboriginal peoples who caught it. Joseph Binnington may well have had malaria, since he arrived at Fort Vancouver aboard the *Ganymede* on 17 July 1831, a year when malaria was so virulent that it brought Company business to a standstill for a while.

    Binnington's record shows that he served aboard the *Cadboro* from 13 August 1831 to 25 October 1832 but, if suffering from malarial fever, Joseph may have languished below decks in the dark and dampness. Perhaps his experience turned him against the country, as he left on 6 November 1832. At the end of May of the following year, his brother received – not the letter that he expected to arrive on the *Eagle* – but Joseph himself, who would have missed the two letters that contained his brother's analysis and advice.

5 JAMES BLACKIE: *Give my kind lov to Kity for i meny time mentchon her name out hear*

After sailing on the May to November round trip to Hudson Bay in 1828 as a seaman aboard the *Prince of Wales,* James Blackie enlisted for the longer voyage to the Columbia Department, leaving in January 1830 aboard the *Dryad* and arriving on 10 August 1830. He worked aboard that ship until 1833, during which time he was promoted to boatswain, a senior seaman in charge of the rigging, anchors, cables, and so forth. This letter, written by James on 2 October 1832, is one of the rare undelivered letters from a man serving in the Columbia Department.

〜 Mrs Mitchison, N° 17 Angles Gardins, Back Road, St. George's In the East, London

Fort Vancouver 2 October 1832

   Dear Sister i rite thes few Lines to you to you [repetition] hoping to find you in ~~good~~ [crossed out] and the Children in good health as it leves me at present thanks be to god for it for i ave ben very Luckey since i ave ben in this Country not one day sik[.] i am very sory to hear of the death of your husband tho it a deat [debt] that we must pay and i am very sory to hear that Walter ban so onWell [unwell][.] give my best respect to Mrs Nouland and like wise to Mrs Burns and her daughter and husband and i am very much blitch [obliged] to him for riting the last Leter that you sent to me[.] you may se me home in 12 month time[.] give my best respext to Mrs Robinson and Betsey and i very much blitch to hear [her] for taking care of the bed and i send money to pay the intrest and leve it in hear charge till i return[.] sister i hope you do as i say hear in this Leter for the Bed will be a service to me wen i retuorn home and i hope you take care of my chest if your not parted with it and as for any other smal artickle i nead not to mentchon. give my kind lov to Kity for i meny time mentchon her name out hear[.] if you ~~ave~~ [crossed out] she [if she have?] aney regard of maken a Pardner i will not forgit what i am riting of[.] if you fix you mind aney other way i hope you will not wate for me tho if you do not my mind will not alter for i maney a time was a going ~~but~~ [crossed out] Put the queston to you so i hope you will not forgit thes few lines that ave rot to you in this Leter[.] Dear sister i hope you not pas this Leter a bout to no one but betwen you and Kity[.] we are lying all Loaded redy for sailing for Fort Simpson[.] give my Kind Love to Mrs Rainer and her husband[.] i am very sory that the most of your Friend is forgot you since your husband is dead tho i am not forget you yeat my self and mind be shure and pay for the bed and do not forgit to drink my health so nead not to mind riting to me aney more leters till you se me[.] give my best respext to all inquiring Friend[.] Oct 27 sister we ave a new Captin Joined our ship to day one Captin Keppling [Kipling] and Mr Duncan [entry 14] is Left us and to Join another Ship i bleve[.] i do not now how i may agre to gether[.] we are all strang[ers] hear together but me and the Carpenter[.] so no more at present from your loving and fathful Brother James Blackie and i hope Shely mend on it

Dear Sister i ave rote to Mr Smith to let you ave 5 pound and lay it out to the best advantage a pon your self and your Famly and do not forigit what i rite to you

It is interesting that the concerns of the men working in North America with the Company seem to be similar to those writing from Britain: money and possessions, family news, and romance. James's mention of the new captain and crew members was not a casual concern. In the close inter-dependency of shipboard life, it would be a worrisome situation to be "all strang[ers] hear together but me and the Carpenter." In fact, as boatswain, he would be in charge of general maintenance of the ship and its small boats, and thus a direct supervisor of the work of the seamen and apprentices. It would be a good thing to be able to count on the carpenter's friendship if he were to carry out his new captain's orders.

It would have been a relief for James's sister to hear that he was going to stand by her when most of her friends had forgotten her since she had become a widow. His loyalty as well as his financial contribution (one-sixth of his year's pay) would be essential in a time when few working men could make any provision for their families in case of their death. If her male rela-tives would not support her, a woman would probably have to be parted from her children to work in domestic service. James's marriage proposal to Kitty may well have been accepted in person, since James Blackie never went on the long trip to the west coast again. He returned home aboard the *Ganymede,* arriving in late February 1834. After that he chose to travel as boatswain on the Company's ships to Moose Factory in James Bay, a six- or seven-month voyage that would allow a man to winter at home. He made this voyage many times, the last being in 1858. We have no record of whether or not he found both his Kitty and the "Bed [that] will be a service" waiting when he arrived home.

6 ARCHIBALD CAMPBELL: *Ef we Should Never meet in thes woorld mey We meet in that place wher We Shall never part*

Archibald Campbell had been away from home for almost four years – since autumn 1829 – when his sister Margaret sent this letter full of the many changes, both happy and tragic, that had occurred in their Scottish family since he left. Foremost in her mind was the loss of their brother John, a cap-tain, and its impact on his young family. Her disappointment and worry at only receiving one letter from Archibald, in November 1831, indicates that one brother's death increased her concern for another. But it also reveals how little some families understood – especially in the early history of the Columbia Department trade – of the vast distance and slow communication involved in such an enterprise. It is quite possible that Archibald wrote his letter, referred to by his sister, shortly after his arrival in Columbia aboard the *Isabella* in 1830. From what she writes, the contents of Archibald's letter seemed to have given Margaret hope that he would quickly follow it home, but she had waited through 1832 and early in the new year she took up her pen to write to her beloved brother.

∿ To M[r] Arch[ibal][d] Campbell, Stewart of the Dierd [*Dryad*] Brig, C[o]lumbia River, Capt. Sim[p]son, To the Hon[ble] Hudsons Bay house, London

Alexandrea [Alexandria] Jenry [January] 27 1833

My Dearst Brother
    Should thes letter Com To your hand it Will let you now that We Are All wall At present and i hope it will find You in the Sam[.] Dear Brother Whe[n] we Recved your letter in Novm 1831 we looked forwerd too May 1832 with gret plisure but how was we disapinted[.] we then thoght You would be hom in Nov 1832 And then I wrot to london to the Compney And Mr Smeth [h]is Answer was that AS ther wis no particular mark to your Neam he thought that you Was Well[.] My dear brother ef you Could Not Com hom you Might At least hav Sent A letter AS you Most be Awear that your old father would be hapy to hear from you[.] ~~That we that~~ [crossed out] you was wishing to No [know] What Collen And John Was doing[.] At that time your letter Came hom John was Capten of the Belfast and Colen was Stewart with But on the 21 of disember When he Was Alleyeng on bord part of hes Cargou Out of A lighter layeng Along Side he Slept his foot And Was Drownd ~~drand~~ [crossed out][.] he his [has] left A Soreful Wif and 2 prety babys[.] Archd was not 2 years And margret 9 Weeks At ther father is death[.] My Dear Brother I may Say AS jacob did that My father will go to the greav With Sorow for hes Soon [son][.] oh archd if you [k]new What your father is Sofiring for the want of his Sons[.] John is [John's] corps was not got for 3 weeks and it was At the bathes in Elensborugh [Helensburgh][.] oh my dear Brother What A day brings about And what [al]most 5 years[.] how meney has been taken Awe this last year by a pestlenc that the lord Sent Among us[.] Our frende hes All escept AS yet thank god[.] M[rs] hamalton [Hamilton] And Willin And rosenne All ded with it[.] dear brother AS for news About gourock I [k]now lettel of them ther is Shich Alteration On it that you would not [k]no[w] it[.] ther is A church bilt in the middel of the town And A hous on the top of Campock And the form of A battere Along the rok[.] Margret hastock And devd Storm was Mared About the time that John And Jenet was mared And margret is ded And deved is mared Agen[.] Jennet li[v]es Chrestena mills is Choul[.] She has 12 p A year And A fre hous And At John is death the owenars geav her 50 p for hes Seak And he

had A letel hem Self[.] She is young And will Soon forget hem but oh et was A heavily Strock to us All[.] he rot 4 or 5 letters to you but you never Answert them[.] I hop my dear Brother Should thes Com to your hand that you will Answert thes[.] may God grant that you will be the bearer your Self[.] My Dear Brother i hop that you well Make out thes Scrol As it is with A Sorefull hart And trembleng hand I wret to you At thes tim[.] Jennet is Stopeng in edenbrough [Edinburgh][.] She hes lost one of her famelay And his 2 She Cam hear to Se hes last Sumer[.] Collen is Stewart [steward] of the aren castle Stembot And pad 50 p year[.] they Go from glasgow to rothsay [Rothesay] And Is doing well[.] Christin And ellen Are boath well[.] Catren and donald Are Well And much AS you Saw them[.] Jemes And i is doing vere Well[.] we has had A Cloth Shop thes 2 years and im verey Comfble[.] Oh My Dear Brother if you hav forgot All your frends they hav Not forgot you[.] dear Brother by thes time yu most hav experenced Much of the goodness of the Almight[y] towards you[.] may you remember that Altho your in the midst of heathens dod will be with you ef you Ask hcs ead[.] oh ef we Should Never meet in thes woorld mey We meet in that place wher We Shall never part[.] ef Colen is Sparet he will writ you with the Shep that Sals in may[.] Non of our frends Nos of me writting At thes tim but i no that thay will Send ther kind love to you
Jems hes hes [repetition] kind lov to you[.] I hav Only one Son And he often Speks About hes Oncle Archd[.] my Adres is Jemes glen Marhtonet [Merchant] Alexendrea [Alexandria] by dombarton [Dumbarton] Scotland
I remen your afecnet Sister til deat
　　Margret Glen

If Margaret knew about the shipwreck of her brother's ship, the *Isabella*, on its arrival, her concerns and worry would have been even more understandable. In a letter dated 11 October 1830, Chief Factor John McLoughlin described the loss:

The Isabella entered the Columbia River on the 2nd of May, but Capt. Ryan mistook Chinook Point for Cape Disappointment and came in through the south Breakers; south of the Channel the Vessel struck and carried away her Rudder, the wind and Tide drifting her on very heavy Breakers though she was still Stricking Capt. Ryan was obliged to cast anchor and to lighten her by throwing as much of her cargo (as he could) overboard but getting afraid she would go to pieces in the night, and conceiving he had no other means of saving the lives of the crew, abandoned her and proceeded in the Boats to this place [Fort Vancouver] which he reached on the night of the 4th May. Immediately I sent a party of our people down, but on their arriving there on the morning of the 6th May, they found the Vessel had parted from her anchor and drifted on shore at the place I already mentioned, and though I arrived there on the morning of the 7th with all the remaining people we could spare from this place includiung Capt. Simpson with the Cadboro and crew, we were unable to get the vessel off, but succeeded in saving the greater part of her cargo.

Crossing the bar of the Columbia River was a risky venture. The year before the *William & Ann* had wrecked there, losing the entire crew and most of the cargo.

Archibald's letter to Margaret, even if it had been sent on the return ship, the *Eagle,* would not have reached London until spring 1831. As well, Margaret had since married and was living with her merchant husband in Alexandria, Scotland. Perhaps this interfered with mail delivery. The family's worries about Archibald had led Margaret to inquire with William Smith at Company headquarters in London. Basically, all he could usually tell families was that, if there was "no particular mark" beside a man's name, they must assume that no news is good news. This state of uncertainty was part of having a man in the service of such an intercontinental venture of the British colonial world. In such a vast and growing empire, with men at danger on land and at sea, the comfort that religion gave was essential to women in Margaret's situation.

Despite a shipwrecked start, Archibald Campbell did well in the Columbia service. After arriving in the district in 1830, in recognition of his valiant efforts to save the ship and salvage the cargo, he was promoted to steward, superintending culinary affairs and serving food on the ship. He stayed to serve aboard the *Cadboro* and the *Dryad* in their duties along the west coast, leaving for home aboard the *Eagle* in November 1832. When he left the ship in London in early June 1833, he may have gone to Scotland and received firsthand the news contained in this letter from his sister. Margaret had prayed that "ef we Should Never meet in thes woorld mey We meet in that place wher We Shall never part." She may or may not have been able to meet her brother in this world. Since many men went quickly from one trading company's service to another, Archibald may have shipped out without having learned anything about the family at home.

7 JOHN FLINN: *Took away rich and poor without distinction*

Henry Ridgway of Waterford, Ireland, wrote to his friend John Flinn serving as a seaman on the ill-fated *Isabella,* to tell him that four years after his departure from England his family and Ireland in general have been struck by cholera deaths.

⌖ Waterford January 29ᵗʰ 1833

Dear John

A short time ago I wrote to Mr Smith the agent to the Hudson's bay Company at his office at Threadneedle Street London to know whether you were living or not or where you were when they last heard and he informed me that you were well and on board one of their ships at Columbia river – I now write a few lines to tell you of your family

Your mother sends a letter with this which will also inform you – Your father died last September and your brother Nick also a few days after him of the Cholera Morbus which complaint raged here in Ireland and England this last Summer and Autumn very severely and took away rich and poor without distinction – My father though a healthy man always, also died of it the beginning of last month – Your uncle William Flinn came home from Newfoundland about a year ago and also died last Summer but I believe he did not leave any money to signify after him as he said there was a great deal due to him in Newfoundland which he could not collect or get paid – Therefore in consequence of these deaths your Mother and family are left very desolate and of course unprovided for, and for this reason I wished to write you thinking that perhaps you would soon come home to see us and if so I would do all in my power to get you whatever situation I could here so that you might live here or go in some vessel from this Port – At all events when you receive this letter if you dont come home I would be glad you would write me or your Mother – I will do what I can for her but I have a great many looking to me since my father died for support and it is hard for me to make out living for all of them – Should you come home We should be glad to see you – In the mean time

I remain
Your friend
Henry Ridgway

You can direct any letters for your mother to my care

John was lucky in that the crew of the *Isabella* was saved (see the Archibald Campbell story, entry 6), but it must have been a frightening start to his service in the Columbia Department. He had obviously written home about it since the incident is mentioned in the following letter from a friend in London.

~ Mr John Flinn, Seaman in the Hudsons bay C^o, Columbia River

May [1833] London

    Mr John Flinn

    Mrs Hunter rec[eive]^d your kinde Letter and sorry to here of your Missfortune of you loosing your ship but glad to finde you are well as this leaves us at present and hoping to see you by the returne of the next Ships[.] all your old commorades is well but things is Veary dead in London[.] coal traid ha[s] bee[n] at a stop as the Pitt Me[n] has all be off in consequinc[e] of Wagges and Veary little Commerce or yet Baltic traid as the Rushings [Russians] and Pools [Poles] is at ware and Lickley to be a ware in Ingland [England] as thare is great disturbens on acc[oun]^t of the reforme Bill[.] Things in England lookes bad[.] old Charley is yett alive but can not work[.] old rodney is alive[.] John Kairnes is well[.] McGee Doron and all the rest Just the same[.] Mrs Hunter and Miss Hunter and Mr Hunters' all well[.] Mrs Jones and all thare fambly is well[.] my young man Henry and Brown is at Peter'sberge [St. Petersburgh][.] Old Larry and Old Jimmy Beardy and fambly is well[.] Andrew and Anderson is at home and several of your aquentences[.] thare was a number of David [Davis] Straits and Greenland Men Less a the year and Very few has proceeded this[.] I think by your Letter you have seen some service and will see more before you leave that Quarter[.] I think you will not finde this Enterprizing Voyage so Comfortable a Voyage as you Expected[.] All the rests of your commorades I think has a Choice for it as I send this letter out by Morrise[.] he has ship'd in one of the Nore West men and by him you Obtain this Letter[.] I understand Mrs Hunter has remmembred you to all friend as you wish'd in your Letter[.] I suppose you would know of Walter being Loss'd before you Left London[.] Whe have got the Docks nearley all compleat[.] ware the ruins was is all a Compleat Wet London Dock[,] Wapping Wall is a Little Island surrounderd with water Penetrable only by the Dean Bridges[.] Little Field [Littlefield] has command of a small shoone[schooner.] his Son is Mate with him[.] I have remmemberd you to all your Old acquaintances M^r and Mrs Kenny McGee M^r and Mrs Finnigan Roudy Ryan[.] Old Charly Beady he is past work[.] Old rodney is yet a Live[,] Grace and Billy Little Billy[.] My son John is a Shooe Make[r] and a good hand[.] he would astonish you how well he has got forward[.] Henry is Mate of the Hand of Providence belonging to Maldon[.] all the old aquainences sends all thare Best respects to you[.] Robt Newholom has turned out Very Bad[.] he could not Get [h]is Coal undertaker Licenses renew'd[.] John Kairnes is Undertaker and Vearynear Licenced[.] Johonathan Thomson he is in the W Indias his landlad[y] old M^{rs}

Anderson is dead[.] Mr Ofield is dead[.] Thomas Caines the Wheat Chaff opposed to my House is dead[.] Wapping Wall is much olterd[.] thare has been Seaveral deaths amongst the coal shippers[.] old Mrs Hunters Mother is dead[.] the Parliment has be desolved on ac/ [account] the reform Bill[.] Great o/c [outcry?] in Members[.] Every man renting a house of ten pounds p^r year can give a Voat[.] all the Irish 40/ feeholder will again give a Voat[.] we have had a grand Elumination inconsequence of the good King William acting so well with the People of England[.] He is well Lik'd[.] not such a King England Eaver produced [be]fore[.] Seaveral Men of Ware is fitting out a War Expected but not sertain nowne yet the Pooles [Poles] and the Rushings [Russians] has hard fighting for Liberty[.] We have had a strong reverlution in Franc[e] Last June the abdicated the Throne and is now at Holirood house in Scotland[.] thare has been a Strong reverlution all over but in England[.] I would have sent you a News paper but I understand it would not be admmitted[.] If you fall in with any thing Curuis [curious] I wish you would not for get me[.] I have Loss'd my fine Gray Parrot[.] it got Poison'd[.] I must conclude with My best wishes for your safe returne[.] yours Truly C. Crawford

    for Mr Hunter

[on the cover] Betty is Marrid to a Carpenter of a Ship is all the Weddings sinc[e] you went away
Reeds of the three Marinors was burt Down in less than One hour to the Ground[.] Garland

    The news that the Russians and Poles were "hard fighting for Liberty," that there was revolution all over, and that politics and the economy were both suffering from the many disturbances of the time show the kind of detailed knowledge of events that people in London possessed. Hunter's letter, written with the help of Miss Crawford and often straying into her words, is a good indication of the changing times in terms of the dockyards and other London economic ventures as well as the nation's precarious condition and the effects of foreign disturbances on England's economy. For Hunter, however, the poisoning of his parrot seems to be at least as important as such large issues as the Reform Bill and King William's popularity. The line at the end of the letter from Garland on the subject of a fire appears to be from a drinking buddy, if the Three Mariners is a pub.

    Records show that John Flinn arrived in London on 30 May 1833 aboard the *Eagle*. We do not know if he returned to Ireland to help his family; however, from the sounds of Hunter's letter, Flinn had a considerable friendship network in London where opportunities for sailors would be greater than in

Waterford. In fact, he was still in London a month after his arrival when he joined his friends in a tavern near the Company's headquarters, The George and Vulture, to sign his name to a letter addressed to Charles Fraser (entry 9), a crewmate in the Columbia Department. Back in Ireland, Henry Ridgway, left with the responsibility of so many, may have been indulging in wishful thinking when he hoped Flinn would "live here or go in some vessel from this Port."

8　Samuel Parsons: *You Shall be Welcome to my place providing you had not a shirt to your Back*

Letters from families – often serious, practical, and full of yearning for the absent member – predominate among the undelivered letters. The following letter from a blunt-speaking woman friend, reveals another side of life – a side about which, perhaps, a man might not tell his family.

☙　To Samual Parsons, On Board the Brigg Dryad, Captain Kickling [Kipling] – Hutson's Bay, N.W.C[oast]

London No 22 Robinhood Lane[,] Popler 31ˢᵗ May 1833

　　Dear Friend
　　I received your much esteemed Letter of 27ᵗʰ of October 1832[.] nothing gives us greater pleasure and Satisfaction than to here you are well, and this Leaves us all will ~~God~~ [crossed out] thank God for and hopes we will have the pleasure of seeing you once more here[.] as for your friend Mʳˢ Dubery she is Dead twelve months ago and also William Casady and for your old friend Needham he has been in prison, he is not in the ship and sheers ["Ships and Shears" tavern?], and I expect he is Gone to hell or some other better place of Worship, Give my best respects to Robert Stewart[.] Dick, your old favourite is Still alive Carring on the old game I mean Biddy Leary[.] as for the Child it lived only a fiew Weeks, Give my best respects to young Barton, I shall be happy to here from you every oppertunity[.] you Shall be Welcome to my place providing you had not a shirt to your Back, I have Got nothing more perticular to say at preasant, Connor Joins me in Kind Respects to you and all others & believe
　　Us your Cincere Friend –
　　　Catherine Connor

　　The "young Barton" referred to in this letter is probably George Barton (entry 31). The words of the generous Catherine, that she would make Samuel welcome, even if he "had not a shirt to [his] Back," may make us imagine a special relationship but the fact that she also sent the "Kind Respects" of Connor may indicate a husband in the picture. One of the tantalizing aspects of these letters is that we are left to imagine the before and after of these men's stories of which we have but small glimpses, and in what we imagine we reveal our own predisposition. For example, we can never know what Dick's "old game" with Biddy Leary was. We cannot even be sure who had the child that is mentioned. Even though this letter might suggest a number of scenarios, it may simply be the words of a landlady who kept a boarding house for sailors, where they could count on her generous hospitality even when their board money was not readily available.

As for Samuel Parsons, after serving as a seaman on the *Ganymede* on its outward voyage in 1830-1, he continued in that capacity on the *Vancouver* and the *Dryad* in the Columbia Department and returned once more on the *Ganymede,* leaving on 1 July 1833 and arriving in London in late February 1834. We might want to assume that Samuel heard all the gossip firsthand from his sincere friend when he returned to London and perhaps received her hospitality once again, before shipping out with another mercantile company.

9 CHARLES FRASER: *The Ship is going to sail to day by which you will receive this letter*

Charles Fraser began his service as a ship's boy or apprentice aboard the *Eagle,* leaving London on 1 November 1829 and arriving in the Columbia Department in early June 1830. Charles served on the coast as a seaman aboard the *Eagle,* the *Dryad,* and the *Cadboro* from 1830 to 1833, travelling up and down the coast from Fort Simpson, Nass (present-day Port Simpson, British Columbia), in the north to Monterey in the south. Trading trips to Hawai'i were also part of the schedule of the coastal service. His cousin, also named Charles Fraser, and other pals sent their greetings from a pub.

Charles Fraser, Columbian river, North West Coast of America
George & Vulture Tavern, 39 ratcliff Highway [London]

June 1st 1833

D[ea]ʳ Cousin
I take this opportunity of writing to let you know I have left whitechapel road, your mother who is quite well wish'd me to write to you[.] I saw a Shipmate of yours name'd Sterling [Starling] who call'd at my house[.] he told me you was quite well which I was happy to hear – your mother is gone in the Country and I do not think she has received your letter which Sterling put in the post

I write now thinking you would like to hear from us, as the Ship is going to sail to day by which you will receive this letter, I was glad to hear from your Shipmate that you are so comfortable, things are very bad in London, my brother Peter is doing well[,] in fact all the Fraser's I am happy to say are doing very well, if you have any opportunity of sending a letter I shall be glad to hear from you[.] wishing you health prosperity and happiness I am

	yours Truly
	Charles Fraser
To Charles Fraser	Tho⁵ Wood
Columbian river	John Flinn
north west Coast of	Wᵐ Curtis
America	send their best respects
	and *hope you are well*

Charles Fraser left the Columbia Department on the *Ganymede* on 19 September 1833, a few months after his cousin hurried to the ship that could take his letter; if this was a Company ship, it must have been the *Nereide*, which had been delayed in Spithead, Plymouth, because of a leak after a May departure from Greenwich. The other friends adding their names to the letter included John Flinn and William Curtis, who were also the intended recipients of undelivered letters (see entries 7 and 2, respectively). Fraser arrived back in London on 23 February 1834.

10 ROBERT ALLAN: *I remain your Affect[ionate] and Afflicted Mother*

Robert Allan's entire service, from 1829 to 1844, was as a seaman. He left London at the age of twenty-nine aboard the *Isabella,* which wrecked on the bar at the Columbia River (see Archibald Campbell story, entry 6). After having been rescued with the rest of his mates, he worked as a seaman on the vessels *Cadboro* and *Dryad* between 1830 and 1832. In 1833 Robert Allan was serving on his third ship in the Columbia region and records show he was actually aboard the *Ganymede* when his mother wrote this pained letter to him, care of the *Cadboro,* in the spring of that year. While many letters reveal the happier ties of love and devotion that bind nineteenth-century families despite great distances and lengthy absences, Mary Allan's letter gives us a glimpse of an unhappier side of this strong family interdependence.

∽ Robert Allan on Board Cadboro, Columbia

Greenwich June 4 1833

My Dear Son
I am Greatly suprised in not hearing from you when the Ship arrived &
Son I am avery bad and have been so a long time and I am in Great ~~deserd~~
[crossed out] destress[.] I have nothing Comeing in as I am not able to
work[.] your Sister Gives her Kind Love to you and is avery Sorrow that
you did not Send a letter home an I also James as it so long since I see
you[.] Ann gives her kind Love to you an her Brother also & son I hope
you will answere this Letter by return poast
I have not received aney of your mony this two years an half[.] your own
heart must know what state I am in[.] Mr Starling delived [h]is message to
me & son I think avery hard that you did not Come nor send to me
I have now to say but God bless you and send you a pleasant Voyage and
speedy return[.] I remain
your Affect[ionate] and Afflicted Mother
Mary Allan

A working-class mother could be in desperate straits if unemployed and
without the support of her children. Despite her disappointment with her
son, Mary signed herself hopefully as Allan's affectionate as well as afflicted
mother. Mary may have remained afflicted, as the Company obviously had
no instructions from Robert to disburse a portion of his pay; however, he did
return to England on the *Ganymede* arriving in London 23 February 1834 and
served with that ship on its trip to Hudson Bay between 2 June and 10
November. Since the *Ganymede* did not leave for its next Columbia voyage
until 10 December, he may well have gone to see his mother at Greenwich
and helped her out financially. However, there is reason to believe that he
formed another attachment in North America as the years went by, one that
would have first call on his pay packet.
After returning to the Columbia Department, Robert Allan served another ten years on the coastal service as a seaman and settled at Chinook,
Oregon, in 1844, dying there on 7 March 1845. But the record does not end
with his death. His wife was probably the daughter of a white man and an
Aboriginal mother. Their daughter, Mary Anne, was baptized on 10 August
1846, at Fort Dunvegan (in present-day Alberta), where she had been taken
after her father's death. Mary Anne was well past infancy by that time. Since
she was ninety years old when she died in 1930, she was probably about six,
making her seventeen when she married William Lucas Hardisty, an officer
of the Hudson's Bay Company, in 1857. She told her husband that she

recalled brothers and sisters who were then living in Oregon, and that both her parents died when she was very young. Robert Allan's daughter married twice, gave birth to seven Canadian children, and now lies in All Saints Victoria Cemetery near Stonewall, Manitoba, having lived until January 1930.

Mary Anne's history illustrates an important part of Canada's settlement. The line of succession from Aboriginal and European grandparents to Canadian prairie dweller is not an unusual one. Governor Simpson attempted to stop the intermarriage of Europeans with Aboriginal peoples in 1830, when he brought his young wife Frances to Lower Fort Garry in present-day Manitoba. Perhaps one of his motivations was that he himself had a number of former "country wives" and children to keep hidden from his new bride. While Simpson discarded his Aboriginal wives, many country marriages were of lifetime duration.

Simpson's policy, while causing personal pain for many families, did not stop the long custom of unions between Company men and Aboriginal women – as evident from William Hardisty's marriage to Robert Allan's daughter. But Simpson's policy did have the effect of making men like Hardisty need to explain their choices, as indicated by this letter that Hardisty wrote about Mary Anne to George Simpson in 1857, a letter obviously gauged to appease the boss:

> I got married last fall, with Mr Anderson's permission – The girl is of respectable parentage, altho' without education – We – the officers of M^{c}K[enzie]R[ive]^r have been greatly scandalized by [crossed out] of late, by one of our Colleagues Keeping a Mistress –, and not being certain when I might be allowed to leave this district, I considered it better to marry *even* an ignorant girl, than pine away in solitary misery at the Youcon – or disgrace myself, and the service to which I belong, by imitating the example set us by M^r C[hief] T[rader] [Bernard Rogan] Ross . . . I have been more comfortable and happier since I [crossed out] my marriage than I have been at any time during the last 10 or 12 years – Even the absence of my wife would be less unpleasant & more bareable than the consciousness of being single, unthought of, and uncared for, by any one – It is my intention therefore to request Mr Anderson to take M^{rs} H[ardisty] down with him to Canada next summer in order to have her placed at school there for three or four years, by which time I trust she will have improved sufficiently both in mind and person – to enable her to mix in decent society, and to do credit to my rank in the service.

The irony of Hardisty's letter is that he himself was the product of a country marriage, born in 1824 and baptized at St. John's Church in the Red River settlement in present-day Manitoba on 13 April 1838. Although the sons of country marriages often served only in the lower ranks of the Company, Hardisty obtained promotions, becoming a chief trader, and his letter to Simpson indicates that he intends to do the right things that will do credit to his rank in the service. His wife, Mary Anne Allan, the daughter of a seaman, granddaughter to a humble Greenwich working woman and a North American Aboriginal woman, became an educated member of the elite of fur trade society. In her first marriage, she was the mother of Isabella, the future wife of Sir James Alexander Lougheed (1854-1925) and grandmother of an Alberta premier, Peter Lougheed.

11 JAMES WILSON: *Never neglict your parents let them be ever so poor or ever so mean*

After serving from the fall of 1828 at York Factory, James Wilson went overland to Columbia in 1829. He served on the *Dryad* from 1829 to 1833 and would have been away from home for four or five years by the time these family pleas were sent. The parents addressed the letter to "Columbae, York Factory, Hudsonsbay," indicating their uncertainty about where James was serving and about the geography of this distant land.

~ James Wilson, Sailor at Columbae, York Factory, Hudsonsbay

Stromness 21 st June. – 1833

Loving son we come to enquire after your health and we hoop it is very good but I am sorry to tell you that my health is along with my strength gone to leave me my sight and hearing far faild[.] I am not abl to build and I cannot see to sew[.] but why were you so mindfull of us as not to write us last year nor yet by the Eagle[.] shurely you Could hade an Oppertunity[.] neather dide your Brother make any mention of you in his letter[.] your time is out[.] shall we expect you home[?] your brother John was at the straits last year and got a full ship[.] he is in the same ship again[.] he married soon after he came home and beheaved middling well[:] we shall have a young Cobler soon[.] we have Ordered your Brother should you come his way to give you a small suply of stockings and mittons and hade you wrote us we would sent you some[.] now for news[:] Our minister is dead and and we have got a fine young man in his place[.] the parishes is Devided and Mr Charles Clouston is placed in Sandwick[.] Blessed be God the pleague is done away[.] it came as near us as week [Wick] in Caithness[.] we are getting herrings here Just now at a Uncomon time of the year[.] plenty of bread and a grand Appearance but my farm is lying laye because I was not able to doo anthing to it[.] this is been the poorest

year I ever saw not being able to earn any thing and your mother is much
the same[.] different people has been asking after you such as Baikie Goudie
and Mr Spence and Wm Brown and Wm Corigill [Corrigal][.] Peter Garson
is married to Margaret Heddle[.] Betty Spence was married yesterday to a
walls lade named M^cpherson[.] many people old and young dying and a
general complaint such as I suffer is in many families[.] now Dear James
you Ordered W^m corrigill to give your mother and brother John such things
and they got some of it but he seems Uneasy about it[.] John is much
Obledged to you for the compliement you sent him and hopes to Reward
you if ye be spared to meet[.] old Madie a Bushel of Compliements to you

now James see that you slip no oppertunity of writting to us and make
Our Old Age as comfortable as you can[.] this may be the last time I write
you[.] should it be so mind your poor mother and God will Reward you[.]
I comitt you to his care and with earnest prayers for your well fare we
Remain in Affection your Parents while we are Robert & Jannet Wilson

The great disruption in the Presbyterian Church was a major topic of concern and commentary for the people of Orkney, as the changes affected the
lives of rich and poor alike. For more on the effects of this major social reor-
ganization, please see the letters to James Dickson (entry 83).

The second letter is especially interesting, as it is one of the few undelivered letters from a man working for the Company. His brother Robert wrote
the letter at York Factory, on Hudson Bay, but his post was as a boatbuilder
at Norway House, just north of Lake Winnipeg. Robert Wilson wrote to give
James some brotherly advice.

To James Wilson, Sailor, Columbia

York Factory July 7 1833

Dear Brother
As Opportunity offers itself I sit down to Write you this few lines hooping they may arrive safe to your hand and find you in good health, as this
leaves me at present,

Dear James since I wrote you last summer I have not experienced good
health I have been troubled with a sore Breast But I cant say that I feel
much of that at present, James I wrote you last year that I was determined
for home But as you was inclined to leave the service I made a nother
agreement to remain at this place with an expectation of seeing you this
summer but my expectations was frustrated which I am not sorry for if you
can find yourself comfortable although after an absence of 13 years I should
been glad to seen you at this place[.] [I rec]eived a letter from our Parents

last year[.] they ar Both [the] same Way as when you left them only fast failing[.] [Fat]her writes me that he had no letter from you last fawl which is a wrong thing of you, Dear Brother take this as a Brothers advice never neglict your parents let them be ever so poor or ever so mean. I hoop that you have more of a natural feeling then to neglict those that never will in my oppinion neglict you providing you was reduced to the meanest and lowest extream,

Dear Brother I had a letter from George Spence Merch[t] last and he desired me to acquent you of some old debt that you contracted with him[.] he seems to be surprised that you have forgot him when in your power[.] he tells me that he used you as a Brother when at home and that he thinks you doo not use him well in return[.] Now James you should always remember on people that assisted you when you could not asist yoursilf[.] you are not certain But you may com to bee at the necesity of him again[.] Dear Brother as I doo not keep my health at this place I am fully determined to go home with the Ship this fawl but whether I go or not I hoop that you will write me next year either for hear or elsewhere

James I have no particular news to inform you of at present only I hoop that you will take care of your old hulk as you are sailing on a dangerous coast where you may get your Vessel so much injured that you may never bee able to put to sea again so that you require to keep yourself free from these dangerous ports in a storm that you find numerous on the shores of the Pacifict Ocean or Columbia[.] I suppose that you may understand what I mean[.] James there is nothing that could give me more pleasure than to hear of your prosperity[.] our Brother John was a David [Davis] Straits again last year by Father letter but the ungreatfull Brother never writes me one scripe of a pen our [father] gives me a poor account of him which I am so[rry for] But I hoop that you Will not bee so neglectfull as to [forget] Father Mother and Brothers as he has don

So Dear Brother I Conclude hooping that you may injoy good health and tranquility while I remain

Your Affect[te] Brother &c

Robt Wilson

James was on his way home as a passenger on the *Ganymede* when these letters were sent. His brother Robert echoed the family duty sentiments of the parents, exhorting James not to neglect their parents but added what may well be a special warning about sexual behaviour, disguised in the imagery of sailing. Indeed, there were some literally dangerous ports on the Columbia coast but, when the brother added the comment, "I suppose that you may understand what I mean," his words may take on a different meaning.

The politics of family are made more complex by the presence of letters from two points of view. Robert does not know that his brother John, after his ungrateful behaviour at Davis Strait, is home, married, and – in his parent's estimation – has behaved "middling well," since he is expecting a child. Robert might well be resentful of John's situation, given that he himself had served thirteen years away from home and his latest hope of family connection, James, had failed to stay in touch. In 1840 he wrote a letter to Thomas Halcrow, a merchant in Stromness, Orkney, which was filed with the Hudson's Bay Company's inward London correspondence and is therefore not among the undelivered letters. It reveals that John had fallen back into disgrace and Robert continued to be a loyal support to his distant relatives.

Thomas Halcrow, Merchant, Stromness, Orkney

Y Factory 5ᵗʰ Sepʳ 1840

Dear Sir

I duly read your favour by the safe arrival of the Prince Rupert as well as the articles sent me which gave due satisfaction.

You will as usual supply my Dear Parents with 8£ sterᵍ or to that amount for the ensuing Year & be shure send my by return of Company Ship a statement of ther supply in full.

You will also please supply to my accᵗ my name son Robert with a full suit of desent Clothᵍ & pay his schooling for the Year.

his mother also my Sister-in-Law you will please supply with £3 sterling that is to say if she is in misery & her thoughtless reprobate of a husband (my Brother John, I am ashamed of the Compliment) not made his appearance or sending her any thing for her & family support but if he is at home Cancel this order unless sickness or any unforseen misfortune may happen at all event, whither suppᵈ or Not Keep this a secret and let them know nothing of my wish

[He continues with instructions to send a gown and "two tippets for little Girls of Net Work Laced round the eges" and a watch, ending with further expressions of his filial devotion:]

I hoop you will be kind to my Father & Mother & act in a measure in my stead & if in my Power your Kindness shown them Shall not be unrewarded by their Son ... please write me by Canady next Spring & Give me all the news you can[.] My Eys at present for want of sleep & Rest are g[lued] together & I hav wrote this Letter I may say Blind.

With every good wish for your health & success

I add no more at present but remain

Your Humble & Ob^d Ser^t
R. Wilson

While James left the Company service on his return in 1834, Robert stayed on in the Hudson Bay area, first as a boatbuilder at Norway House, then as postmaster at Severn (1834-9) and at York Factory (1839-49), then as clerk at York Factory (1849-54). From 1840 until her departure in 1851, he shared the mess table with Letitia Hargrave, the wife of Chief Factor James Hargrave, in charge at York Factory. Her inquisitive eyes missed very little, and she recorded a rather uncharitable description of him when he was her messmate: "Last is Mr Wilson who trades with the Indians & has charge of all the workmen. He is the Butt of the party being an Orkney man who came here as a boat carpenter but was promoted no one knows why for he is an ass. All energy, never saying or doing right & yet very willing. He lives in the gent^s house & altho' each has a different nickname for him he is constantly working for one or other. He never opens his mouth at table that there is not a burst of laughing on all sides, he looks bewildered sometimes but generally joins at last" (Macleod 1947, 86-7). Later she noted, "He is the very image of Miss Harriet Loudoun, both face figure & manner only his eyes are rather whitish. His pose & affectation atone for the difference & the conceit he has of himself" (Macleod 1947, 91). Letitia delighted in recounting Robert's attempts to find a wife, noting in 1848,

> Miss Mary Taylor, or Mrs Stewart ... intimated that the Govr made her remain at York that Mr Wilson might marry her. Mr W. either had too much pluck or too little sense but Mrs Stewart intimated to Mrs N. Finlayson that Mr Lane had popped [the question]. She refused him ... Mr Wilson had met with a disappointment from a Miss Fanson. He & another man asked her from the master of the Fort where she lived. He told Wilson that if he finished a boat by Spring he c^d have her. The other man was a house carpenter & he promised her to him if a house was finished by a certain time. In the meantime he went off on a voyage & was so delighted by the canoe navigation of a M^r McShay that when he got home he made her marry *him*. (Macleod 1947, 87-8)

Just three days before Letitia Hargrave left York Factory in 1851, Robert Wilson – or, as she refers to him, "Old Panum" (which could mean that he had a pasty complexion, or that he looked as ragged as a scarecrow) – married "a widow from Orkney her name Mrs Flett who came out by the ship & set up in Red River as a dress maker, with her relative Mr Cumming of Baring's [Beren's] River's patronage. She is a 'native' but has been in Orkney for 30 years. Wilson ... made up his mind while he was escorting her up from the ship to the house. The woman had an excellent character & is very industrious, her age 37. All the beauty & fashion at York assisted" (Macleod 1947, 263). Letitia was scathing in her ridicule of Wilson, making fun of his pretensions and physique – calling him "an ass" and a "scarecrow" – but she concluded, "He is the derision of all & sundry but every one likes the poor man & he does not care in the least for being laughed at every time he opens his mouth" (Macleod 1947, 135).

Robert Wilson's last ten years with the Company were as clerk at Oxford House, where he died on 29 March 1864 at age sixty-five. He, like his brother John, behaved "middling well" and had a son, Robert Cummings Wilson, who followed his father into a career in the Hudson's Bay Company service.

12 WALTER PREDITH: *Mary Ann thinks she shall never see you any more*

Walter Predith from Stepney was just beginning his service as a steward aboard the *Nereide* when these letters were sent to him in 1833. As steward, he had charge of the ship's provisions, cutlery, and table service.

∽   Walter Predith, Captain's Steward to the Ship Nearit, Belonging to the Honble Hudsons Bay C°

London October 2nd 1833

Dear Walter
I have to inform you that Monrose [Munro] is expected home every day by the Cumbrian. I have called on Miss Boxall[.] she sends her love to you and wishes you well, and hopes you will meet with a quick and safe return, be so kind as to write to us by the first conveyance.
Your friend Walter stoped with me about 8 weeks and is now gone out to the Mediteranean in the ship Tuscan and is expected home about Christmas. My Brothers and Sisters their love to you, also Mary Ann who thinks it is a long while to be from home and hopes you will return long before the time mentioned[.] I must now conclude with love to you,
I remain Dear Walter
Your affectionate Sister
S[arah] Kidman

P.S Please address N° 14 Bethnal Green East

Henry Kidman's letter dated two months later, added further details on friends and relations.

For Walter Predith on Board the Ship Nereide Belonging to the Honble Hudsons Bay Company

Dec^m 4th 1833

Dear Walter

I write these few Lines to inform you we are all well hoping you are the same[.] we shall be glad to hear from you as soon as you Can send – Walter has Left the tuscan at Leghorn & Come to London by another ship. Sarah says Miss Boxall has left where she was and Don't Know where she is gone to – Since Sarah wrote the last Letter she has recieved a Letter from Munro, wrote at Bombay on July 29th and was then under sail for China, expects not to Come to England for 2 or 3 years[.] he sent home his 2 Suits of Clothes from Gravesend by Andrews of Limehouse which he understood By your Letter that I had not Received them and a half Sovereign[.] Sarah has seen him and he has acknowledged having them[.] I expect having an increase in my family Early next year[.] Sarah & mary Ann Desire to be remembered to you[.] mary Ann thinks she shall never see you any more

We all Join with our
respects to you
Henry Kidman

P.S. Sarah Lives at N° 14 Bethnal Green and has taken the house and is full of Lodgers –

Sarah's letter bears the Company's notation that Walter returned "Home per *Nereide* 1834," and Henry Kidman's letter the notation "Paid by Mr. Budge at Valpa^{so}." Walter Predith had deserted at Valparaiso, Chile. The Hudson's Bay Company's agent there at the time, Robert Forbes Budge (known as Roberto Budge in his adopted country), was responsible for finding cargo for the ships returning to England and for trying to sell consignments of salmon and shingles from the Pacific northwest – neither with much success. He paid the postage for the letters from the wages due Predith. Valparaiso was a major port, and no doubt Walter found another ship to join, although some – such as Budge himself – found the Chilean climate, prospects, and women so much to their liking that they married and settled permanently. It is quite possible that Mary Ann was right and she never did see Walter again.

13 HENRY WILLIAM HARMSWORTH: *We have no outher Earthly Protecter*

We know a great deal about Henry Harmsworth because of a detailed family history privately published in 1984, *A Harmsworth Saga of the Nineteenth*

Century, by a descendant of the family, Evelyn Glegg. Henry came from a sea-faring family, his father Henry senior having been in the East India Company and the Royal Navy. According to Glegg, Henry senior had "appalling bad luck" with both his mental and physical health (1984, 18). He was accused of desertion when he came back to try his mariner's exam, which, to rub salt in the wound, he failed for lack of knowledge about the English Channel. He also had a propensity for disobedience and "peculiar behaviour" which led to a court martial for inappropriate use of supplies in 1825, at which time he was dismissed from the service (Glegg 1984, 19). Between 1825 and 1827 he desperately and unsuccessfully petitioned the Admiralty to reverse the decision. He was successful in placing Henry junior in the Royal Hospital School in Greenwich where the sons of Royal Navy men were accepted as apprentices, not only on the basis of "the comparative merits, services and suffering of the father in the Royal Navy [but, luckily for Henry] regard being also had to the number and destitution of the family" (Glegg 1984, 41, citing *Illustrated London News,* 19 February 1848). The Harmsworth family's descent into poverty would accelerate in the future, as their undelivered letters indicate.

After completing three years of schooling at Greenwich, Henry was bound for seven years as an apprentice with the Hudson's Bay Company in 1830 when he was fourteen. He was sent out on the *Ganymede,* arriving at Columbia River 11 August 1831, where he served aboard the *Nereide* and the *Cadboro,* as well as the *Columbia,* until he left for home on the *Nereide* in June 1834. Some of the apprentices sent out on the *Dryad* complained bitterly about their lot, claiming to have been served black biscuit and dried salmon. In his defence, Chief Factor John McLoughlin wrote that the sailors "when in Harbour ... have as much fresh fish, Venison or Game with potatoes or other vegetables according to the season as they can eat, and when they have nothing fresh they have the usual allowance of salted Beef, Pork Biscuits &c. and in no instance have they been Kept alone on Salmon or Grain with fat." The boys also complained of having been ill treated by a mate, but McLoughlin defended the late Captain Aemilius Simpson, claiming "I am certain he would not have allowed them to be ill treated by anyone, as he was so anxious about their comforts, and to promote their Interest that he had a place built up in the Vessel to keep them a part from the men and to enable them to go on with their studies."

Henry finally arrived home on 27 May 1835 after his captain, J.M. Langtry, took a long time to find suitable cargo in Valparaiso and Copiapo. His father had written in June 1832 inquiring after his son and was told that he would only expect to receive letters if the ship had put in to port before Cape Horn or if it fell in with ships bound to England. In October he wrote again and was told that he should write by 20 February 1833 to make the next overland packet. By the time Henry arrived home, however, his father had died (in 1833). The support of the family now fell squarely on his shoulders. He was granted a brief leave of absence from 29 May to 10 June 1835 to visit his family, then quickly set out on the *Esquimaux,* fitting at Bristol, for a voyage to Ungava Bay with Captain Duncan (entry 14). The voyage was an adventurous one, as the ship became blocked in ice passing Cape Resolution and once again on sailing into Ungava Bay. Escaping the ice, the *Esquimaux* went aground on a reef. Freed by a rising tide, it delivered its cargo and made a fast twenty-two-day trip home to London, arriving on 18 October, giving Henry less than a month in England before boarding the *Nereide.* He was granted another leave from 21 December 1835 to 2 January 1836, and in February he purchased an outfit consisting of a pea coat, trousers, leather shoes, mitts, four blue shirts, two Guernsey frocks, two cotton shirts, four cotton handkerchiefs, a sou'wester, soap, knives, scissors, thread, worsted, needles, and a comforter, before he sailed for the Columbia. For those men who made a summer voyage into Hudson Bay during the summer layover between the arrival and departure of the Columbia ships, it must have been an exhausting service. But it was made necessary by needy families and the fact that a man was unemployed and unpaid the minute his ship arrived in port. An apprentice like Henry would have had no choice in his assignments.

Elizabeth Ann Burney had married Henry Harmsworth senior in 1811 as a twenty-five-year-old widow with three small children, only two years after her husband, Francis Burney, had died. Then a widow for the second time, her letters reveal the typical concerns of a mother for a son, particularly for his spiritual health. She gave him news of both his little sister, Elizabeth (age eleven), who "will be provided for by her Aunt," and Mary Ann (age eight), who so ardently wishes Henry home. The letter was sent in the parcel of letters put together by Mrs. Langtry, the wife of the captain of the *Nereide.*

Henry W. Harmsworth, H.H.B. Company, ~~Columbia River~~ [crossed out and redirected in the Company secretary's hand to] Brig Esqx YF

Havant Jenry [January] 12 1835

My Dear Henery
you are now 19 years Old and I hope a stead[y] good lad[.] Oh how happy should I bee to see you once more[.] I trust that the Lord will in his murcy grant me that plesher but should that not be the case I hope my dear Boy you will be kind to your Dear sisters as Elizebeth will be provieded for by her Aunt, I am quit[e] well at present but this is a dying world and I wish to impress this on your mind and never treet them as John Armstrong as don[.] we never here from him[.] Elizer and Margratt

was quit well as Mr Davis your Teacher ad been to Welas [Wales] and saw
them[.] Maryann is still with me[.] your littil sister often tolks of you and
wishes the time wos com for you to come home to ous[.] Mr Watson at
Castel is here[.] the[y] are bouth well and disers to be remberd to you[.]
Deborah and Mrs Watson send there Love to you[.] your Aunt Saley is quit
well and sends her Love to you and so do all your Frends[.] as Mrs Langtree
[Langtry] is goin to send this in her parsell I shall not troubel Mr Smith
this time but if eney thing should happen I will send to you a gin befor the
ships sails that will bring this to you[.] I hope my dear H. you reads your
bibel as that will make you wise unto selvation[.] your Dear father often
rejoiced that he was broke out of the Navy as it was the sevaing of his Soul
and wot a plasher it well be for you and me and your Dear Sister to meat
him in Havan[.] Oh My Dear you are a Child of many preyers and I trust
you prey for ous –
poor Thomas Burney as Blown A part of his Hand and is quit Blind with
one eye[.] he was in the London Hospitel 13 weeks and was not expected to
live[.] I am shore you will be sorry for them[.] all the rest of the Famaly is
quit well when I herd from them[.] Maryann Armstrong sends her Love to
you and your sister sends hundreds of kiss[e]s and except my best Love

My Dear Boy may the blessing of god be with you is the constant pray
of your d[ea]r Mother EA Harmsworth

Besides his little sister there seems to be another Mary Ann (Armstrong),
who sends her love in this and the next letter. It is interesting to see how
Henry senior had come to terms with his dismissal from the navy before his
death, as Ann recounts that he "rejoiced that he was broke out of the Navy
as it was the sevaing of his Soul."

His mother's next letter, written less than a month later, was sent by the
family's adviser, the Dowager Lady Grey of Belgrave Square, to Company Secretary William Smith in a vain effort to make sure the family's news reached
Henry and to receive the latest word on his welfare. William Smith assured
Lady Grey that Henry's conduct was satisfactory as of the previous April. In this
letter his mother continued to urge Henry to look to his prayers and his soul.

Henry William Harmsworth, ~~Col~~ [crossed out and redirected in the
Company secretary's hand to] Brig Esqx YF

Havant Feby 4 1835

My Dear Henry
As I sent you a Letter in Mrs Langtrees [Langtry's] packett I have but
littil to say only as I am writing to our kind frend Lady Grey I shall get her

to send this Letter to Mr Smith[.] I hope you will not let eney opertunety pase with out sending home to me[.] I should much like to know how late you are and do send me word whot time I might expect you to come home[.] I recved a letter from your Dear Elizebath yesterday and she sends her love to you, and hopes we shall come and see her when you coms home[.] you would be suprised to see how very nicly she writes[.] Maryann disers me to say that you shall not go with out you take her[.] there is not a day but she is wishing to see you and eney littil thing she gets it is all put by for you[.] I trust you often thinck of ous and My Dear boy I hope you read and pray to God for ous[.] I should like to know if there is eney Mishonry where you are and what is neme is[.] I beleve your Dear Father rote this once to you but you did not say eney thing a bout it, Mrs Watson recved a letter from Philip[.] he was quit well and disers to be remberd to you[.] Oh Henry you can not thinck what a good lad he is[.] I trust that your Dear Fathers preyers will be answard on your behalf and that we might all meat him in Hevan is the constant preyers of yur Dear Mother[.] Mrs Watson and Deborah sends there love to you and Watson of Rolands Castel is here and hopes he shall see you again to eat some of his Appels[.] Aunt sally is quit well and so is her famly and the Wellers disers me to give ther Love to you and so do Maryann Armstrong

I have nothing more to say but I trust the Lord will bless you
and bring you home to me and beleve me My Dear Boy your affectatn
Mother EA Harmsworth

In her next letter Elizabeth Ann tells her son that she has had to move to Portsea from Havant to take up a position at an orphan's school because she "cannot live on the Mony." Positions such as teacher or governess would be typical for educated women without means in a time when few other career paths were open. Less educated women would be eligible for positions as matron, laundress, cook, or cleaner.

~ Henry W. Harmsworth, an Apprentice to the Hudson Bay Com^y, N° 3 Fenchurch Street, London

[1836] Orphan school, Sent georges squar [St. George's Square], Portsea

My Dear Henry
I shall right to you by this ship and I hope you got the boxes on your arival at Clombia[.] I ashore you your Dear sister wos dreadfully disopinted at not seeing you[.] she as ad a Fevour and wos home for 8 Weeks and your Aunt says I must take her home next year[.] I trust Henry when you are out of your time you will help keep your Old Mother and sisters as we have

no outher Earthly Protecter[.] I trust the Lord well spear you to ous[.] Maryann [Armstrong] is gon to Wales to her sisters[.] I hope the will do well[.] Philip and Deborough Watson came to see me yesterday[.] the bouth disers there best wishes for your sefe return and Watson and his Wife came here for a few days[.] I do thinck if it should please god to speare my Life untel you return I shall come to London[.] Mrs Haydon as lost her Eldest Son and Tom as been here for some time[.] he is second Mate of a timber ship[.] the girls with there F[ather] and M[other] sends there Love to you, Maryann is now my only compainen[.] I viry of ten feel my lonly condishion and wish I wos back to Havant but I cannot live on the Mony[.] I have not heard from the burneys for some time[.] your Aunt Saly as been dredfuly ill but is a littil better[.] we cannot here eney thing of poor John[.] I do thinck he must be dead[.] I hope you will bring ous all the shalls you can get and with my preyers and blesing My Dear Henery

    I remain your affectnat

      Mother

        E A Harmsworth

Henry, a mere apprentice, far away on the Columbia coast, is unaware that his sister will soon be home, that his cousin John has died, that his mother has had to take a job, that he will have to "keep [his] Old Mother and sisters as we have no outher Earthly Protecter," and that Mary Ann Armstrong has gone to join her family in Wales. The next two letters, from Henry's Aunt Sarah and his mother, Elizabeth Ann, show that the family is counting on his finishing his apprenticeship by late 1838.

Henry W. Armsworth, Apprentice Hudson Bay Company, N° 3 Fenchurch St

N° 12 Hawke Street, November 26 [1836] Portsea

My Dear Henry

    as Mr Burney is going to London I shall send you this Letter[.] I am still at the school and in better health then when you left me[.] I reved a letter from Elizebath and she is quit well and wishes much to know if you will be soon home[.] I have to inform you that your Unckel Edwerd is dead[.] he died quit[e] sudent and his Wife sent me 10 pounds at her Death[.] the fortun will go to young Collett with a trifull for you and your sisters but how much I can not tel[l][.] Lady Grey is very sorry that you did not Make a will and Leave me your porshen of Money if it should please god that I should be the Longest Liver but I hope My Dear Boy you will Live to ease me if I should Live to be hold but this is whot she wishes you to do to

right your self that if it should please god to take you that I am to have
your shear of whot ever Money might be Left to you by your Aunts or
Unckle and get the Captn ~~to~~ [erased] or Mate to sine it and send it to
me[.] Maryann Armstrong is gon to Weles [Wales][.] I rec[ei]ved a Letter
from them this day[.] ther are all well but not Hapy to gether[.] Tomas
Haydon is Cheafe Mate and such a dandy you cannot thinck[.] Aldina
Burney is soon to be Married to Franck Banks[.] poor Severs is in prison
for Debt and Mrs Burney as got them all to cope[.] I can not thinck how
she Manages with them all[.] all the Haydons send there Love to you and
wishes you wos heare this Christmas and so do I for i am shore it is a long
time since I spent so happy a forghtnight but I trust we shall soon meat a
gain[.] Lady Grey rote to know when you would to out of your time and I
sent to sey in sepetember next[.] I am looking for that time with much
plsher[.] all your Havant Frends disers to be remberd to you when I saw
them

I hope I shall soon get a Littre from you by the next ship[.] I recved a
Letter you sent on the pasage out[.] oh you can not tel how happy I wos to
recve it
adue My Dear Henery I r[e]ma[i]n yor
affetnat Mother E A Harmsworth

Perhaps the next letter did not reach him because it was addressed to his
former ship, the *Esquimaux.*

∾ Henry Harmsworth, on board the Esquimaux, Columbia

15 Victory St Newtown, Deptford Septr 1837

My Dear Nephew
I have heard from your Mother and she was quite well and Mary Ann
and wished me to write to you and to inform you that she has only
received five pounds from Lady Grey since January last and she does not
expect any more untill you come home which she hopes will be as soon as
possible[.] she is still living at – Portsea 12 Hawke Street[.] we cannot tell
you how the School gets on for we have not heard for your Mother has not
said any thing about it some time[.] we saw Elizabeth the beginning of
June when she was going to spend her Mid summer Holidays at her Aunt
Collets[.] she has grown a fine Girl but is uncommon proud[.] Aldeana
Burney is Married to Mr Banks[.] John Burney has lost one of His
Children[.] he was living a board the steamer in the docks and poor John
the eldest Boy was drowned for he fell over while he was drawing a pail of
water for his father to wet the decks[.] his death was a great shock to all the

family[.] old Mrs Burney felt it viry much[.] it was only about five or six
weeks before Aldeana was maried[.] Mr Charles Burney is captain of a
Gentlemans yatch which was laid off at Greenwich so that M^rs C Burney
has been up this summer[.] our King Willian is dead and we have got a
new queen Victoria[.] it is reported that she will be crowned next May
when she will be Nineteen years of Age at which time we hope that you
will be home[.] we have had a very backward season in almost every thing
this year and as for Grapes we do not expect to have hardly any at all[.]
Captain Napier again put up for the brough of Greenwich to be Elected for
a mimber of parliment but did not get in which makes the third time that
He has put up twice at portsmouth[.] the first time he had 20 votes and the
next 173 but here at Greenwich He had very Good prospects and most likely
he would have Got in had not bribery been carried on by the Tory party[.]
trade has been very dull this season and particular about a week after the
King died for the people all going in mourning put a very great stop to trade
and particular as it was in Middle of the summer for he died the 22nd of
June[.] I hope that your health is well[.] We join in sending our Kind love
to you[.] poor Tom has been home and has gone out again in the Sattlelite.
    I remain your
    Affectionate Aunt
    Sarah Feyer

His aunt's comment on Elizabeth becoming "uncommon proud" may
indicate why she is being sent home. The death of one of the Burney boys –
Elizabeth Ann's late husband's relatives – in a fall from a ship in harbour
reminds us that sailors were always in danger and often could not swim. Aunt
Sarah's hope that Henry would be home by the time Victoria was crowned
was realized, as the Company records show that he received "clothes supplied
at the expiry of apprenticeship," and a letter of recommendation written by
the Company secretary on 16 April 1838 when Henry was twenty-two years
old. He had arrived in London on 10 April aboard the *Sumatra* and Victoria
was crowned on 28 June. Henry's safe return must have given his mother
Elizabeth Ann a great deal more pleasure and peace of mind than the queen's
coronation – pleasure because she could finally "clasp to my bosom my dear
child" and peace of mind because the young man on whom Uncle Edward's
trifle had been settled – and who failed to make a will leaving it to her in case
he met a similar fate to that of the Burney boy – is by then safely home where
he could do his duty as his widowed mother's son.
    Elizabeth Ann's final letter is written in a more sophisticated but also more
formulaic language than is typical of her. It also has more religious overtones.
The different handwriting observed in the originals indicates that someone

else wrote the letter for her, and no doubt reflects Elizabeth Ann's deteriorated health.

Henry Harmsworth, Apprentice to Hudson Bay Com, Fenchurch Street, London
Obliged to Mr Smith to forward it

Portsea November 12/37 [1837]

My dear Son,
I have just been informed that I can send you a few lines if they are written quickly and however discordant it may be with my feelings to send and with yours to receive a short epistle I do not like to let pass an opportunity of enquiring into your welfare as it is at all times pleasant to hear of those we love particularly when separated from them. I long to see you my dear Harry and do hope the time is not far distant when I shall again clasp to my bosom my dear child[.] I assure I am very solicitous to hear of you and none but a mother can imagine the anxiety I suffer on your account far far from home, destitute of the means of grace, surrounded by profligate companions, with no one to care for your never dying soul to what tempta[tion] are you not exposed. But you have my prayers imperfect as they [are], you have a Bible wherein you may look for counsel and direction and read of him who died to redeem you from misery and raise you to everlasting life. and what is more than all beside you have a throne of grace to which you may resort[.] there Jesus waits to answer prayer "Guilt holds us back and fear alarms but still he bids us come" O my dear boy hasten to the Friend of sinners ere it be for ever too late. Remember life is uncertain Death is sure[.] this world with all its fashions is passing away and we are passing away with it[.] soon we may be prostrated in death[.] Let us seek then to answer with sincerity the important enquiry Am I prepared to die? and let your prayers ascend with mine to the throne of mercy on behalf of your immortal soul.
You will be pleased to hear that I received a letter a few days since from Elizabeth[.] she is very well and sends her love to you[.] I expect to see her at Christmas[.] she is to spend her vacation at Portsmouth[.] little Mary anne is very much grown since you saw her[.] Mrs Arter Watson and all Friends are I am happy to inform quite well and unite with me in love to you[.] I must now conclude and believe me to remain
Your affectionate mother E A Harmsworth

Henry went on to do his mother proud. He passed his officer's examinations and gained regular employment aboard ships trading between London and Hobart (Tasmania), a route increasingly profitable as Australia became less a prison colony and more a settlement. Henry rose to second officer of the *Mayflower* and chief mate on the *Waverley* and received his mariner's certificate in 1845, which describes him as "5′9 and ¾ inches, brown hair, fresh complexion, hazel eyes, scar on chin." In the same year he became chief mate on the *Calcutta,* a position he held until 1848 when he became a master. Henry, in spite of his many travels, settled in England. The family record shows that he married Ann Brooke in 1856, at the age of forty. They had seven children born between 1857 and 1872. By 1859 he was prosperous enough to be one of the shareholders of the cargo of the ship *Ethel,* which he commanded. In the 1861 Census, the entire family was living in Camberwell, Surrey, including his widowed mother, listed as head of the household, her two unmarried daughters, Elizabeth and Mary Ann, and her son Henry, his wife and child. He continued his seafaring life as a master of ships until 1878 when he retired. He and his wife settled in retirement in the town of Deal where he lived until he was ninety-two, dying in 1908. His mother had died in 1870, his sister Elizabeth in 1903. His wife Ann lived until 1917.

14   ALEXANDER DUNCAN: *I dont no wat pleasure a Man has at all stoping away from his wife and Family so long*

Alexander Duncan had a twenty-four-year career with the Hudson's Bay Company, beginning as a seaman and boatswain aboard the *William & Ann,* which went to the Columbia Department in 1824, and finishing as the master of the *Columbia* in 1848. His voyages included two to Moose Factory in Hudson Bay, but mostly consisted of the long journeys to and from the west coast of North America. After marrying Ann Simpson at Larbert, Stirling, in Scotland in 1829, he undertook his longest stay on the west coast from 1830 to 1835, when he was promoted from mate to master. In those years he commanded the *Dryad, Ganymede,* and *Vancouver.* The *Vancouver* was driven ashore and wrecked on Point Rose, Queen Charlotte Islands, on 3 March 1834 but Duncan was exonerated of all blame in this incident and appointed as master of the *Cadboro.* His wife Ann wrote to him in 1835, by now weary of his long absence and more than willing to join him if she could.

∾   Capt Alexander Duncan, Columbia, [in another hand] c/o J. Tod Esqʳ

Kincardine 3ᵈ Feb 1835

Dear Husband

I am once more afforded the opportunity of letting you know that I am well hoping this will [find] you the same[.] I wrote you on the 13ᵗʰ of November and sent it to the office in London to go out with the vessel that

Peter [Duncan] is with[.] there was a M^r [Archibald] McDonald from
Columbia river – called on your brother John[.] he says he left you about 8
months ago and he said you was in good health[.] he says there is a strong
bropability of your being on your road home[.] also he told them there was
not a married man out there save you and the Governer[.] also he says
there is not a white woman out there but the Governers wife and two
daughters – he says the true secrets of your not coming home last year that
you would need to have descended to a mates station in the home coming
vessel but I am sorry you did not come home for it was a great
disappointment to me[.] it is now 5 years past since you left home[.] you
may well think how uneasy I have been all that time but I am still living in
the strong hopes of seeing you in the month of March[.] I hope you shall
never receive this letter for I think you will be on your road home before it
reaches Columbia[.] I have much to say to you that I cannot put in write[.]
I send this with Mr Todd that called at your brother Johns and said he
would take out any little word we had to send to you[.] he says he never
knew you for he had never been at Columbia he had been at Hudsons Bay
and on his way home he fell in with an English Lady on her road home
from America to Glasgow and married her and he brings her out with him
and he says he wuld liked much to have taken me out with him but M^r
McDonald holding out that you were on your road home[.] I would liked
very well to have gone with him and M^r McDonald but it would have been
a sore disappointment to us both if you had left the place and me gone
out[.] Mr Todd and wife leaves Liverpool next week[.] M^r McDonald joins
him there to sail for New York then to travel to Columbia both in company[.] perhaps you may receive this letter before the ones sent with Peters
vessel[.] I go off to Glasgow tomorrow with this letter to Mr Todd[.] M^rs
John Duncan wrote me all these news[.] I ~~might like~~ [crossed out] would
liked much to have seen M^r McDonald but he was off to London before
Mrs Duncan had time to write for me[.] I will get more news from them
when I go up for they got more news from him than from your own
brother[.] the news I got was like a letter from yourself[.] your brother
John and his wife has been two good friends to me and appears to continue
so but your brother Peter used me very bad[.] I mentioned some of his
behaviour to you in my last letter I sent you and I trust If you are not away
before you receive this letter you will come away with the first oportunity
and If not I would be willing to go out to you[.] the friends are all well as
far as I know[.] If Mr Langlan is not on his way let him know Miss Ro[?]
still staying in Glasgow and is well and If he is ~~not~~ [crossed out] on his way
and not you I will get more news when I see him, my brother John is
married about two months ago also my brother Roberts wife is married

again about 2 weeks ago[.] your brother John is to write you with M^r
Todd[.] hoping we will see you home soon I remain your loving
  and affectionate wife
    Ann Duncan

Ann's information that there is "not a married man out there save you and
the Governer . . . [and] not a white woman . . . but the Governer's wife and
two daughters" was not strictly accurate. Many men in Fort Vancouver at this
time maintained relationships with Aboriginal women, their unions – while
not Christian marriages – being sanctioned by Chief Factor McLoughlin.
The men were permitted to build dwellings for their Aboriginal wives, and
the Company allowed rations to be allotted to these women, whose unpaid
labour contributed so mightily to the fur trade's success. Aboriginal women's
abilities in every skill necessary to the conduct of the fur trade – fishing, gath-
ering edible roots and berries, snaring small animals, dressing skins, handling
canoes, carrying heavy packs – were depended on by their trader husbands.
There were no European women in the sense Ann might understand, since
Chief Factor McLoughlin's wife, Marguerite, was an Aboriginal woman.
Archibald McDonald, who travelled out to North America with John Tod
after visiting Captain Duncan's family, was also married to an Aboriginal
woman after his first wife, the daughter of Chief Concomely, died. As for
John Tod, who carried her letter and even offered to bring out Ann herself,
the story of his own marriage and the fate of his wife can be found in the
story of his undelivered letter (entry 92). If Ann had gone out to Fort Vancouver she might well have been very unhappy, since the next year the
Reverend Herbert Beaver, an English missionary, arrived with his wife and
upset everyone by condemning all the men's Aboriginal wives as concubines
(Hussey 1991), enraging McLoughlin and dividing the community.
  Ann's wish to travel to join her husband was prevented by his arrival back
in England. But her other wish – that he was on his way home and would
miss her letter – was fulfilled. He shipped home aboard the *Dryad* in October
1835, arriving in April 1836. On 1 June 1836 he wrote to the Company committee protesting that his pay had been docked for three months after the wreck
of the *Vancouver* and expressing his disappointment at returning as a passenger "in consequence of Captn Eales refusing to give up the command of the
Ganymede." He asked for permission to visit his relations in Kincardine,
Scotland, which was granted, with an extension for a month in response to a
further request in early July. Although Ann and Alexander Duncan had been
married for several years, there were no children, owing to his long absence.
A child was conceived on his 1836 visit but in early February 1837 he was away
again on the *Sumatra*. Before he left, he authorized the Company to pay £20

to Ann on 1 July and 1 February each year. The regular stipend would have
been a comfort to Ann, living in Midpark, Kincardine, when she birthed her
daughter Ann on 15 May 1837 while her husband was once again on the high
seas. She wrote to Alexander to tell him the news and her state of health.

〜 Mr Alex^r Duncan, Columbia River
To the care of William Smith Esqr, 4 Fenchurch Street, London

Kincardine May 21st 1837

My Dear Husband
    I recived your kind letter on the 20th of may Dated 30th of march, and
was happy to hear of your Wellfare, I was ~~deleve~~ [crossed out] delivered of a
daughter 15th may, I am now to inform you that I am not so well as might
have been expected owing to my nipples being sor, but I am happy to let
you know that this young Duncan that you spoke of in your letter is in
good health and Christian was over from Carronshore and she says that it
has the Duncans feet and tocs[.] Mary is to be over this week[.] I had a
leter from Mrs Duncan afortnight ago and Alex^r is still subegeck [subject] to
fites as it was when you received there letter[.] I sent a letter to glasgow
letting them know that I got a daughter and one to your Father to let him
know I was up at glasgow and was happy to find them both in good
health[.] your Brother John is removing from his present house owing to
some other person taking his house and shop[.] he is removing to union
street opposit Mrs Bells shop[.] If you wright him you must Derect to union
Street[.] I intend wright to London to Mr John Anderson next Monday[.]
M^r and Mrs Anderson was very kind to me in Convaing me to the ship and
stoped till she started[.] I had avery pleasent pasage ~~home I hope that~~
[crossed out] till friday morning about 3 oClock when we arived at
Carronmouth and did not get ashore till satrday for the pilate Could not
come off[.] the house was all safe when I arived[.] I went to Mr Rintoul
about my money and he told me that it would Cost 4/6 each time I recived
it[.] he is gone since that time and I went to one Mr Stephen another Banker
in Kincardine[.] I am to recive it from him –
    This has been three and ahalf long months to me but I expekt you home
the next year[.] I will give you more particulars in the next letter when if
god spare me I will be able to wright[.] I intend to have her Crisned as
soon as I am able to be out of my Bed[.] the pain that I am suffering with
my Breasts I wish to have no more[.] her name is to be Ann[.] she is more
like you than me[.] I expect that you are going round Cap[e] horn this
month[.] as you said your old aquintince James Black is no more he died
that week that I came home

My Brother John sailed from London 18ᵗʰ for Culcuta [Calcutta][.] We
are all in god health and they have all there Compliments to you
I shall add no more at present but remins
    Your most affect wiff
        Ann Duncan

By August Alexander Duncan had progressed only as far as Hawai'i after
almost six months in which all the crew was affected with scurvy. In a second
letter, illness and loneliness are beginning to show, as Ann worried about
Alexander being away for five years. He had signed a five-year contract in
January 1837.

Mʳ Alexʳ Duncan, Columbia River
To the care of Willᵐ Smith Esqʳ, 4 Fenchurch Street, London

Kincardine Novr 5ᵗʰ 1837

My Dear Husband
    I take this opportunity of writting to you to let you know that Ann and
I are quite well at present hopes this will find you in good health and safe
arrived at Columbia and I hope you will have recived the letter that was
sent you deited [dated] in the month of may and it would let you kow of
My recovery[.] My niples was sore for 8 weeks[.] I am weared to hear from
you it will be a long time before next april if you have got no chance since
the Month of March but I trust that you will return with the Sumatra[.] it
is a long Nine Month and two dayis since you and I parted[.] this will be a
dull winter to Me be the last[.] I am very Dull[.] if you be away for 5 years
again ithink it will be weared time for me to stop away from our house all
that time[.] little Ann will Not know that she has a Father if you stop away
all that time but God was kind to Me that gave me a daughter[.] she is a
healthy Child she takes no food, I have plenty of milk for her[.] she is good
Company to Me[.] I am sure that you would love to see her[.] she is much
like your self she has dark Eys like your self she has long hair down her
brow it is aburin [auburn] Colour she is a swet bosomful [or bosompal?] all
night to Me[.] she will be good company to Me if she be spared to Me[.] I
have got a Clock and a ship on the top of it[.] I draw my money there it
costs me 2 and a penny Every time[.] I have been over at Carronshore 3
times with Ann and once at Glasgow[.] Mʳˢ Duncan was going to the salt
water at Elnsburgh [Helensburgh] for Alex health[.] the fits has left him[.] I
went with her it is oppossite Greenock and we stopped there three week
there and Alex was much beetr and John thought we was all much the
Better of being there[.] Mʳˢ D is very fond of Ann and she says she would
like to see you meet with her[.] I had a letter from Mʳˢ D to weeks ago and

thy were all well and they hav left there old house and shop and they are removed to the corner of union street[.] if you write them direct it to there and Elisbeth is to be Married the first of the Month in papleshier [Peebleshire][.] I had a luiter from M^rs anderson and hir and John is both well and they say that you will be proud of your Daughter when you hear about her[.] Cristina was over here four week ago and they were all well she stopt all night here[.] Mrs Simpson has got son three weeks ago[.] She looks for John home the first of april from Calcutta[.] Ann is as fond of her uncle James as Margret Simpson was of you for ahoble and a song she will not get one from you In Her young days[.] friends are all well at present here and they have their Compliments to you

    no more at present
      but remains your
        Most affect Wife
        Ann Duncan

Excuse all mistakes here for I have not much time for Ann dont sleep much through the day

Although Ann Duncan used the fondness of her brother, James, and his wife, Margaret Simpson, for their niece Ann as a way to try to bring her husband home, relations were not always cordial between the former Ann Simpson and her family (see James Simpson's story, entry 37). Ann was truly weary of the long separations when she wrote this letter that she hoped would find him on his way home. Once again her wish came true, as Alexander came home on the *Sumatra,* arriving in London on 10 April 1838 after a pleasant voyage of four months and twenty days. By 25 April 1838 Captain Duncan was ready to visit his "relations in Scotland."

Once again his stay at home was a short one, and by November 1838 he had left on the long voyage to the Columbia Department as master of the *Vancouver.* By the time Ann wrote her next letter in 1840, she was of the opinion that her husband should be home. She had good reason to feel that way as by then there was a second daughter, conceived during his leave home but born in March 1839 when Alexander was two oceans away.

Captn Alex^r Duncan, Barque Vancouver, Columbia River, To the care of William Smith Esqr, 4 Fenchurch Street, London – prepaid

Kincardine 11th May 1840

My Dear Husband
    I received your letter and was happy to hear that you was quite well but sorrey sorrey [repetition] to think that you was kept out their and I am

happy to inform you that both the Children and I are quite well at present[.] little Ann says that she is quite weaired to see her Father[.] now
Margret is beginning to walk now she is not weaned yet[.] I received your
parcel and I received a leeter from Mrs Anderson this Morning that I would
receive the Money this week[.] your Brother peter and his wife paid Me a
Viset and gave me all the news about you being kept[.] he says that he is
not going out till two years and he takes his Wife and Family with thim[.] I
dont no wat pleasure a Man has at all stoping away from his wife and
Family so long[.] Peter says that you May be kept longer than next year yet
But I will live in good hopes of seeing you next year if God spares us all to
meet again[.] I have taken the house all to My self now[.] I do fell Very dull
for the want of My Company[.] I do intend going to glasgow the and of
this Month[.] I will take docter Watt pipe with me and one to John[.] I
received 4 pipes and three Cups[.] give my Compliments to My Brother
James [Simpson] and his Wife is Very sorry that he will hav to stop out for
his five years[.] thir is no word from your brother Andrew since he sailed[.]
friends are all well at present Friends here sends ther Compliments to you
   no more at present
     but Remains
       your Affect[ionate]
        Wife Ann Duncan

Ann's concern that Alexander may be kept longer than the next year
proved not to be the case, as he arrived in London on 3 June 1841. In the
meantime, however, as indicated in the following letter from Ann written on
28 January 1841, he had written an angry letter, which left his wife wounded
and upset.

~ Captn Alex^r Duncan, Barque Vancouver, Columbia River,
To the care of William Smyth Esqr, 4 Fenchurch Street, London

Kincardine Jan[u]ary 28th 1841

   My Dear Husband
   I take this opportunity of writting to you to let you know that I received
your letter in the Month of Octber dated the 2 of April informing Me that
you have received no letter from Me[.] I was happy to hear that you was
quite well and I trust this will find you well[.] your letter afflicted Me
much when I received it[.] now when I think of your long absence from
Me Makes my life like a dreary Wildrness[.] it is now twelve years since we
was Married now and we have been only seventeen months to gether all
that time[.] do you think that you dont punish me sore enough without

sending me a letter of the kiend frome such a distance you had more ned to send altter of more comfort to me[.] I have wrote you 4 letters to now and this is the 5[.] i know not wether you will receive it or not[.] I Wrote to the Company to see what was the reason that our letters did not go foret and they wrote me saying that the had sent them all of[.] I sincerely hope you hav received all them before this time[.] the first I wrote to you was about the bierth of your daughter in the month of May 1839 and the Eext in the Month of Octber and my letter came back to me and I was sorrey for the ship was sailed tow Monthes sooner than I Expected and the next I wrote you after your Brother J[ohn] arrived here and I sent up to London in the month of September 1840 and the shipe was sailed in Agust and that was another opportunity I lost[.] so if you dont receive this letter I can do no more than I have done

I inform you that the two Children are quite well at present Ann is astout gerl now if you was at home now she would amuse you know[.] Margret is now 22 Months old now she is a anticeng [enticing] Child for she Chated whan she ws fiftwen Monthes old as well as Ann Could do[.] you Mentioned in your letter if you was to remain in the Country ten years that you would not write me another letter until you received one from me but Many Fatherless Children is ben left here since you want away[.] thay want away after you[.] Mr Martin son is one amongst the number and left his Weif and two Children but I trust that God that h[as] procteced you through the Mighty ocean will bring you in safty here to your Dear Children[.] my brothe James [Simpson's] wife wreetes him at the same time[.] your brother peter is with Cap nickel [Captain Nichol] at the present tim[.] friends are all well at present[.] loving[?] [insertion] friends sends ther kind love to you

I add no Mor at present but remains your loving and affectionate Wife Ann Duncan

As readers, imagining this past time in the present moment, we share Ann's frustration. We know that three of her four missing letters are undelivered, and the letter she has just written will have the same fate. Her letter to William Smith dated 11 December 1840, seeking the speediest means of getting word to her husband, is also preserved. A passenger described Duncan in 1840: "The Captain was an old British tar, with a heart full of generosity for his friends, and a fist full of bones for his enemies. A glass of cheer with a messmate, and a rope's end for a disobedient sailor, were with him impromptu productions, for which he had capacity and judgment; a hearty five foot nine inch, burly, stout-chested Englishman, whom it was always pleasant to see and hear" (Farnham 1844, 8). Ann had encountered his harsh written words during a time when he was contending throughout the voyage with a disobedient and drunken boatswain, James McLoughlin, and was feeling neglected by his wife. One wonders how the two would greet each other – both so angry and hurt – on his arrival home in the summer of 1841. While Ann's accusing letter never reached Alexander, she had received his threat that if he "was to remain in the Country ten years" he would not write her another letter until she wrote him. On 9 May 1841, she wrote once more to the Company governor and committee in a desperate attempt to get word to her husband. Ann's letters give us a rare glimpse into the frustrations, worries, and sorrows that undelivered letters caused both men and families.

Whatever his reception by his wife in 1841, Alexander's visit was brief and far from peaceful. During this time he had to defend himself against accusations by his boatswain, James McLoughlin, of assault and mistreatment. For his part, Duncan defended his actions in dealing with McLoughlin in the Sandwich Islands, where he went ashore without leave and returned to the ship "intoxicated, singing songs and disturbing the peace of the Ship." The British consul in the Islands got involved in the matter when McLoughlin was put in double irons in a dungeon in Honolulu, and McLoughlin engaged J. Pelham to represent him in a legal action for assault. While Duncan defended himself successfully, he was further bothered during his stay in Kincardine by a return of the fever and ague (possibly malaria) he first contracted on the coast. When he was able to return to his ship in August – still employed as master of the *Vancouver* – he asked to be permitted to return home in 1842 and be given the command of a ship heading into Hudson Bay. His wish was not granted. A letter to Duncan from a friend in Moose Factory puts another light on the long absences of men in the Company employ.

◠ Capt Alex^r Duncan, H. H. B. Co. London or Columbia River

Moosefactory 10 March 1841

My Dear Sir

I duly receive your kind favor of 2 April last and am concerned to find that the present state of things at the Columbia is not to your liking & trust you may soon get reconciled to the changes in affairs should you remain in the country. for myself I never have been more comfortable than at this place & altho' it has not the varieties of [Fort] Vancouver it is in many respects very snug quarters & the long steady winters suit my constitution better than a warm climate[.] As for news I could give you none that could be interesting to you. Mag with all her faults was a most convenient commodity & has one great quality of never troubling her Cust[o]mers with any Squallers. As Missionaries are all the thing we have at last got one here to correct the Morals of the South. I shall be satisfied with the sale of the Trunk of Clothes you were good enough to take charge of & trust that French may be made to pay it. I understand the French have forced their Missionaries on the Islands again of course much against the grain of the Binghamites. Any news you can give me about Oahu or the Columbia will be very acceptable. & I am with best wishes

    Yours very truly

      R. Cowie

    Robert Cowie's reference to the French forcing their missionaries on the islands points to the ambiguous relationship between missionaries and the Company. Missionaries often interfered with the unions between European men and Aboriginal women that so well served the fur-trading interests; they also condemned the easy prostitution that plagued some forts. There was, as well, the problem of some local traders welcoming Protestant missionaries and others being more tolerant of Catholic missionaries. Chief Factor John McLoughlin of Fort Vancouver tolerated and was kind to missionaries of both faiths, welcoming the democratizing influence of the American Protestants and helping the Catholic missionaries to settle in the Oregon Territory. He was eventually married to his Aboriginal wife, Marguerite, by a priest. With the exception of the disruptive Reverend Beaver, who was English, Fort Vancouver was generally welcoming to this new element in its midst. Cowie's casual and harsh remark about "Mag . . . a convenient commodity . . . never troubling her Cust[o]mers with any Squallers," speaks to a side of the fur trade that is often not written about in any detail. Although the marriages of Company men to Aboriginal women are analyzed by Van Kirk (1980), Brown (1980), and others, the easy acceptance of prostitution is not as carefully documented. Cowie certainly makes his joke in a manner that would seem to expect no censure from Duncan. We have no record of Alexander Duncan's possible relationships with women on his many travels.

    Duncan remained in the employ of the Company, first as master of the *Vancouver*, briefly commanding the *Beaver* and then the *Columbia*. Records show that Ann had to do without her husband from September 1841 to May 1845, occasioning another anxious letter from Ann to the Company on 21 March 1844. When Duncan was leaving on yet another tour of duty on the distant Pacific coast, he petitioned for recognition for his devotion to duty.

To The Govr, Deputy Govr and Committee of the Honourable Hudsons
Bay Comp^y

Barque Columbia
Septr 9th 1845

Honb^leSirs

I beg leave with great respect, to submit the following facts to your
favourable consideration.

I entered the service of the Honb^le Comp^y in the year 1824; and since
1832 I have been a commander,

It does not become me to speak of the manner in which I have
endeavoured to discharge my duties. The kind way in which my services
have been appreciated by Messrs McLoughlin and Douglas has always been
a great satisfaction to my mind; and I hope that in my next voyage, for
which I am now actively preparing, I will be able to manifest the same zeal,
assiduity and care, which in former voyages have I trust, met with the
approbation of your Honb^le Comp^y.

Though still in the prime of life, and able to encounter any labour or
fatigue, I am not unconscious that I am advancing in years; and from time
to time indulge the wish that I could make some provision for my growing
family, The hope of promotion, either to a Chief Tradership, or to the
command of one of the Hudsons Bay ships, has encouraged me; and I trust
that my ambition will not be considered presumptuous, when it is
recollected that out of the twenty-one years during which I have been in
the service of the company, at least twelve have been spent on the N.W
Coast of America.

My respectful request to your Honours is, that, taking into consideration
the length of my services, and the manner in which I have discharged my
duties, you will be pleased to place me on the same rating as to Pay with
the commander of a Bay Ship.

It would be wrong in me to say that this favour would increas my
diligence and zeal, because I have always endeavoured conscientiously to do
my utmost, but it would at least stimulate me, and render me content to
spend the best energies of my life in your Honourable Company's Service.

I have the Honour to be
    Honourable Sirs
Your most Obed^t & very Humble Servt
    Alex^r Duncan

Duncan's next long absence, which stretched from the autumn of 1845
to the spring of 1848, saw the birth of a son, John Alexander, born on 28

April 1846. Perhaps discouraged by lack of advancement, Duncan left the Company's service on his return to England in 1848. On 7 June 1848 he submitted his resignation "being now desirous of returning from such lonely voyages" in an "endeavour to spend the remainder of my life with my family." On 13 June 1848, he asked for a certificate of character and a payment for the five cabin passengers he carried from the Columbia Department to the Sandwich Islands and for the four passengers that he carried to England. He was duly reimbursed £94 6s. 6d. on 15 July 1848. After having spent only twenty-three months of nineteen years of marriage (by her estimate and ours) in the company of her husband, Ann emigrated with him to the United States (see entry 37). They settled to farming, first in New York and later in Oakland County, Michigan.

15   JAMES JOHNSTON: *Your mother & I have been very poorly all the winter*

Peter Johnston wrote to thank his dutiful son James, who had sent £5 – the equivalent of a little more than two months' pay for a seaman or one month for an officer – to help his family. James Johnston had been in the Company's service for six years by the time this letter was sent. He left in 1829 from London aboard the ill-fated *Isabella,* which was wrecked on 2 May 1830. He served as a seaman on the *Vancouver, Dryad,* and *Cadboro* on the west coast service until 1833, when he was promoted to boatswain aboard the *Ganymede,* where he rose to second mate in 1834.

∽   Mr James Johnston, Seaman at Fort Vancover, Columbia

Stromness 27th June 1835

My Dear James
   I received your most welcom letter of the 19th march 1834 inclosing a bill of £5 for which we are exceedingly oblidged to you. It came in a most seasonable time for your mother & I have been very poorly all the winter, and haveing your Brother to cloath & maintain while learning the shoemakeing has rendered us exceding mean but we hope he will now do for himself as he has gone to David [Davis] Straits where we expect he will please for his last master to whom he served his appenticeship was very well satisfyed with him – Your Mother wishes to be most affectionately remembered to you & hopes to have the pleasure of haveing you yet in Stromness to ~~settle~~ [crossed out] be a comfort to her in her old age[.] Mr Spence's family wish to be particularly remembered to you[.] Mr Spence is not yet married – If you have any money in the Companys hands I think that you cannot do better with it than give an order to Mr Spence to draw

it in his own name so that it may be kept for your old or sickly years –
We were very glad to see John Moar who told us particularly about you –
he wishes to offer you his best compliments[.] May the Lord direct you in
all that you need both for time and eternity is the wish of your

    most affectionate

      Father

        Peter Johnston

To Mr James Johnston at Fort Vancover

Perhaps this letter did not reach the right James Johnston, since there were four men by that name serving at that time. Confusion owing to the common names of the day occurred often. A John Johnston of Orphir wrote on 17 April 1847 to the Hudson's Bay Company inquiring about his brother James, stating that a man who recently left the Company "gives me to understand that he was personally acquainted with one to name James Johnston, that came from the Orkneys, as I have a brother that left it of that name many years ago and has not hard any word of him since . . . I was informed that he was a Master on one of the Packets on Columbia River." While some aspects of the described man seem to fit James, the son of Peter Johnston, this James Johnston left the district as second mate on the *Ganymede* on 19 October 1836, arriving in London on 30 March 1837 and finishing his service with the Company on 8 April 1837. The Company secretary wrote that "only one person of the name" was in the service in 1847 and he was a native of Shetland who came out in 1839. It was all too easy for families to lose touch completely, in spite of attempts to locate missing members.

16 JOSEPH AND JOHN SPENCE: *I Sometimes think of old times yet we had*
    Pleasure and Sorrow togeher

John Spence, an Orkneyman, began his forty-year career with the Company in 1820 when he went to York Factory as a young boatbuilder in his early twenties. Within a year he moved to Cumberland House in present-day Saskatchewan, and by 1825 he had gone overland to the Pacific to build boats at Fort Simpson, Nass, and at Fort Vancouver. After eight years on the coast, he left to return home to Britain by going cross-country, wintering at Churchill and York Factory on the way. In his letter to Joseph Spence (a friend, not a relative), serving as a seaman on the west coast, we find an insight into not only the hard life of men in the Company's service but also the life of a man who entered and left a union with an Aboriginal woman.

To Joseph Spence, Seaman Fort Vancouver, Columbia River

On Board the Ship P[rince] Rupert laying in 5 fathom hole Y[ork] Factory, Sept{superscript}r{/superscript} 17{superscript}th{/superscript} 1835

Joseph Spence

In Remembrance of our old acquantance I write you this to let you know that I am in good health at present hoping this will find you and all old acquaintance well also. the year I left you I did not get home[.] it was the 27{superscript}th{/superscript} Sept{superscript}r{/superscript} before the Ship was ready to leave York[.] we proceeded as far as the mouth of the Straits where It was all Blocked with Ice[.] we than bore up for Churchill and the Prince of Wales for Charlton[.] we got in Churchill River the 17{superscript}th{/superscript} Oct{superscript}r{/superscript} when we had it very Cold[.] we passed a hard winter both with hunger and Cold and to Crown all got 5 Plank and 4 timbers in the flat of our ships Bottom stove in and all the Cargo Damaged[.] we had a very hard Job to get it repaired[.] the rock was in through the bottom and we Could not get it out only by Blasting in with Powder[.] I Bored 6 different holes in the rock Sitting in water to the Breast but we got it repaired and got the ship home and I am now on Board of her at York Factory as Carpenter in Place of Belter (Captn J. C. Grave Commands us)[.] I am well appointed for the time but the Voyage will be short if we get home this year which I hope we will

Joseph Give My Compliments to My Old lady Although I Suppose she has altogether forgot Me[.] I Sometimes think on old times yet we had Pleasure and Sorrow together but I think now I paid too much head to Stories not Saying but they were true but when it was only for a time that I thought of remaining with her we might been quieter had I been More Careless

I would be happy to See you all and I Still think I will but I am not Sure how Circumstances may go[.] I am not Married as yet nor yet thinking of it[.] they are plenty of girls in Orkney but by their appearance to me they want Money to keep them up they are remarkable dressy now at home an old fellow like me wanted a Clean Pocket handkerchief every day they dazeled my eyes so[.] My Compliments to all old acquantance French and English[.] I hear Lackie is there yet[.] I am afraid he is not been so real as I took him to be by what you Said in your letter but little ods it will be a lesson to you and me never to trust any one too much[.] your letter Came first to my Sisters hands and she read the Contents before I Came home but she never said a Single word of displeasure but asked me very pleasantly if I had any Children to which I replied no she then said she hoped if I had any I was surely not so hard hearted as leave them there to Starve as she understood white people's Children left there was poorly appointed. Joseph

take my advice and be Carefull of your money[.] a Fool on time will give a good advice[.] I Could not take this to myself but I assure you if you are Spared to Come home or go to any other Civilised Country you will find the Benefit of it[.] I do not mean you to be a miserd for that I abhor nor yet to deny youself needfull necessaries of whatever Sort as nature will have its way but do not give it its full way or alas it will perhaps go too far. I passed a very Comfortable winter at home but I spent all my mony[.] I remained three weeks in London from that took a Cabin Passage in a Smack down to Leith from thare took Co[a]ch for 50 Miles in the Country from there to Glasgow, from Glasgow to Port Glasgow, from Port Gasgow to Greenock and back the same way to Leith again than took a Cabin Passage to Stromness in one off the packets[.] so you See I have been as bad at home as I was with you but never mind I have good health and I am now at my hands with a good Chest of towels [tools] of my Own[.] My Compliments to Margaret again and tell her I never knew a woman since I left her as sure as I write this, Joseph hoping this will Come Safe to your hand Some time or other. I am done and may God bless you and may you meet with all the Comforts that Can be expected where you are is the earnest wish of you real
   Well Wisher
   John Spence

NB Henry Wards goes home with us this time.

   This intriguing look at the psychology of someone who left his Aboriginal partner behind – as was often the case – reveals the conflicts that a man might have in this situation. Although some men who left women made careful provision – the Company in its later history insisted they make provision for long-term partners and under-age children – others seemed to have no qualms about abandoning such women. John seems unsure how to feel. At first he merely sends "Compliments to my Old Lady [who he is sure] has altogether forgot me." With his observation about the dressy girls at home who "want money to keep them up," there is an implicit comparison with the woman left behind, who in terms of her economic value as a worker in the fur trade would have been an asset to a man rather than an expense. The letter, which began as a description of John's working life, is increasingly a kind of unwilling meditation on his past love, as he recounts the opinion of his sister on European men who leave their children "poorly appointed" back in North America. Being found out at home by a sister whose judgment, no matter how pleasantly put, might have prodded the writing of this letter, seems to bring on a kind of regret and a confession on John's part, as he ends by giving "My Compliments to Margaret again" – then, not merely an "old lady," but a person with a name – "and tell her I never knew a woman since I left her as sure as I write this." John Spence's confession of the "pleasure and sorrow" he felt thinking of his Margaret never reached her. The letter's intended recipient, Joseph Spence, who had begun his career with the Company in the Northern Department in 1828 and moved on, as did John, to Fort Vancouver in 1833, was headed back to Britain on the *Columbia* in August 1836 and deserted at Hawai'i. The actual notation was: "Gone to Woahoo [Oahu]."

After John Spence left Margaret and the coast, he returned to the Company's service working as a carpenter on the *Prince Rupert,* plying its summer route between Stromness and York Factory, thus allowing him to visit and be a support to his sister Betsey, whom we assume is the sister referred to in the letter to Joseph. By 1838, three years after his letter to Joseph, he was on his way back to the Columbia Department aboard the *Vancouver.* He then stayed, serving at Fort Vancouver and on the *Cadboro.* His sister Betsey wrote in September 1843, worried that the only support of herself and her children might not come home.

～ John Spence C Carpenter, Fort Vancouvur, Columbia,
Care of William Smith Esqur, Secratre to the Honourable Hudson Bay Company, London

Stromness 18th June 1843

My Dear
Brother I recived your welcome Letters which gave me great pleasure to hear that you were than well and had arrived of your Voyage but it is So long from the time that the letters are wrote and before they reach Me that I can scarce be glad[.] they are So many changes that I dont know what may be happnd to you ere your letter reaches me. –
I am sorry to find that you have not made up your mind to come Home and you say dont be disapointed if you dont Come[.] My Dear Brother I will be Very Much disapointed if you dont Come but I fondly hope you will ere this reaches you [crossed out] Columbia be on your passage Home and on that account I will not Say much fore I do hope you will have left but I am affraid to put of writing altogether that you may take it in your Head to Stop and than you would think Me careless and neglectful
My Dear Brother you wish me to give you all the News but I am affraid from the State my Health is in I will not recolect much[.] I mentioned in my last that I had been along time ill[.] I were extremely ill for Six Months and yet I am not in My usual way[.] I never had Such a winter and Spring

in My life[.] I never thought to have wrote you again in my life[.] I Saw
nothing but Death before me and the thoughts of My poor delicate
destitute Children rent my very heart but I may I never foreget the goodnes
of him who has promised to be the Orphans stay and the Widows Shield
that has again restored me a little to watch over them for they are
uncommonly delicate[.] Cristina has been declining fore this last twelve
Months[.] Some days She is able to go to School and then for weeks She
will be that ill that you would think she wouldn't live any time[.] the
Doctor Says She must be alowed to Move about any way she finds herself
able fore She is fit for no Medcine but you would be astonished at her
patience when she is Scarce able to Speak[.] She will Scarce confess She is
ill[.] if asked if She is worse She will say rather worse but I am meddling[.]
Janet keeped remarkably well all winter but Could not attend School on
account of My illness as there are no person in the House but them and
Me but about 6 weeks ago She was Seized with a Severe illnes which has
turned out to be dropsy[.] how it is to end is only known to him who is
the wise disposer of all things & that I may be resigned to his will in all
things[.] I had bought New Books and Sent her to School as Soon as ever I
could be left alone and it is to no purpose but if her Heavenly Father Sees
fit to take her to himself She will not need any of this Worlds learning[.]
but in the Midst of all My troubles I have Many Mercies first that he I
trust has given them Grace fore they are realy amiable in their dispotions
and has the good will of all who knows them and next that he has Stirred
you up to be More like a Father to them than any thing else and I trust
that he will bles and reward you fore it[.] My Dear Brother I have taken up
to Much time with My own troubles which may appear to you Selfish but
like to let you know purticulurly how we are in every way

I need say nothing about the State of Trade as Mr Robertson has I think
told you about that[.] the like never was[.] Many Days you would think
from the appearance of the Street that it was Sabbath not a person Stirring
nor a creature to be Seen in a shope[.] you will also hear from him & Mr
Stubs about the Ministers who has Seceded from the Established Church[.]
I need say nothing about that[.] You wish to know what Deaths and
Marriages has taken place Since[.] I am sorry to inform you that Since I
wrote you last that Mary Studthart [Stoddart?] has left this world and left a
young infant after her[.] She Married and died of her first Child[.] I dont
know what her Husband was and Mrs Robertson lost last Child died about
two months ago[.] you know She had two dead here before you went
away[.] She then went to Edenburgh [Edinburgh] where John died[.] She
came home to her own House last Summer with Thomas her only Surviving
child and he died of a few weeks illness about two Months ago it Mrs

Thomas Robertson I mean She desired me to give her best regards to you[.] She is I trust an eminent Cristian and quite resigned to the will of God[.] She has been most attentive to me during my protracted illness[.] Capt Sinclair of the Margrate lost his wife of a few days illness about 4 months ago[.] O that we may be always on our guard and be enabled to live every day as it were our last and Seek to lay up our treasure in Heaven knowing that every thing here is fading and transitory but O dear Brother in the time of Health we are too ready to keep it at a distance. –

You also wish to know who is Married[.] I am sure you will be surprised when I tell you that your Old Friend Miss Nivan was Married to Wm Isbister or you will I think know him better by Stenus [Stenness] William in the seventh of Nov last[.] there are no other Marriages that you would be any way interested in[.] Mrs Ann Isbister and her Mother Desires to be remembered to you and Miss Graham[.] Miss Dunnet is quite well now[.] you will ere now have My letter Cuntaing an account of Jean Clouston Death[.] her Mother is Still alive and very friendly now and I make no deferance[.] I had a letter from Isabela about a fourth night ago[.] I understand that She Says if I would send for her She would come home but dear Brother how Can I Send for her[.] I Can do nothing fore her and besides how can She think that I Could Send for her[.] the night She left the House and went to Mrs Fleats I would Sacrifised any thing to her to have Stopt but She would not so much as bid me good bye[.] when I think of it I Cant refrain from tears but I have no bad feeling to her but I Cant forget it[.] it is a great Mercy to her that She has none but herself to think of[.] you know it was about Catharin that She first quariled with me so I am very glad She has found a little of what I complained off but Dear Brother dont think that I say this with the intention of lowering her in your esteem tho I would be very sorry to do that[.] nothing would give me more pleasure than to find that an affacionate feelling was established between us and if She would come home and be agreeable it would be great Comfort to Me as I am Sometimes extremely dull among my own and the Childrens Bad health but when there is nothing to be done how can I encourage her[.] Ships of the very best are doing nothing trade of all kinds I may say is completly at a Stand[.] Nothing for Straw platting which was a great help[.] as for Lodgers a private Family has no Chance So that I could not Send for any one except I Could do Something fore them[.] if it had not been for you what would I and mine have been[.] My Dear Brother when I began this letter I intended sending it by the Hudsonbay Ships but David Robertson told me not to do it for that their were Ship going from London in Agust which would bring it much sooner to you and he desired to be remembered to you and tell you that he prevented me sending it by the Ships[.] I am afraid Dear Brother you have not got all the letter that I have wrote[.] I assure you I have ommited no oppertunity that I knew of[.] it is afourthnight Since I began this and Janet is a little better but the Complaint is not removed yet but I trust I must wait with patience and try to Submit to the will of My Heavenly Father who has Suported me hitherto[.] Constans is in Birsay[.] She was 2 nights with Cusin Mary and the rest of the time in Swana side [Swannay][.] She desired Me when She went away to give her kind love to you and say you must Com home and I assure you I am expecting you and will be much disapointed if you dont Come[.] Janet wishes to be remembered to you and bade me say that She intended have wrote you along letter but was not able[.] She Speaks Much about you and calls you her best earthly Friend her mother accepted [excepted]

My dear Brother I must conclude for I have nothing more worth telling you at this time[.] Mr Angus sends ther best wishes to you and Mrs Bowers Famely and Mrs Louttit ernestly wishing that the Lord may bless you and prosper you in all you undertakings and send you Safe to your Native Home is the earnest prayer of your ever affectionat Sister

Betsy Clouston

As well, a friend in London wrote discouraging news about the state of affairs in Stromness.

∽ Mr John Spence, Carpenter, Fort Vancouver, Columbia

London 29th Septr 1843

Dear Freind John

I received your very kind and Welcom Letter by the arrival of the Cowlitz which gave me great pleasure to hear from a old freind and you enjoying good health and happiness, I do asure you it gives me great pleasure to hear from one that I passed such a long time so agreable with and bring to remembrance times pased and, and, [repetition] gone. I have to be very thankfull for my lot[.] my place is agreable but being such a long time exposed to the fresh ear, and now to be in a closs place in the middle of the City of London, which makes My health reather quere some times but I have great reason to be thankfull[.] I have no reason to complain, Yes, John I am got settled at last, with a Wife and One Boy and Girl after my long wandering life and which I hope will gave me comfort, and I have no reason to repent[.] I would have wrot you before but I was afraid it would not come safe to hand, If you remain writ me and let me know how you are. If I can do any thing for you I shall do it with the greatest of pleasure or if you wish any articles sent out to you I shall be happy to serve you.

R. Wilson still remains at Y[ork] F[actory]. I have not had a letter this two years from him but by all accounts he is not over well satisfied with his place, but he is better to remain as long as ~~as~~ [crossed out] he can for I do asure you That times is very dull in Britain and particlar in Stromness, nothing doeing there but disputing about the Church, Must all the people is left the established Church and has built a new one and the same all over Scotland

My best wishes for your health and happiness

    I remain Yours Truly

      John Rendall

John Spence did not receive these letters because he was on his way home, arriving in London on the *Vancouver* in June 1844. In July he arrived in Stromness. However, he did not stay long. Perhaps, with his "Old Friend Miss Nivan" married, a sad sister overburdened with responsibilities, and a poor economic situation in the Orkneys, the place his sister calls his "Native Home" is not as attractive as it might be. Or perhaps he was swayed by the word of his friend, John Rendall, who also warned that "times is very dull . . . particlar in Stromness" and suggested that their friend Robert Wilson (entry 74) was better off staying with the HBC rather than returning. John left for the Columbia Department within a month of his arrival home, as a carpenter aboard the *Vancouver* headed for Fort Victoria. He never returned to Britain. After working aboard the coastal trading ships of the Company from 1845 to 1861, he retired in 1861 to Victoria, by then a bustling colony and the centre of Company trade. In 1863 he married Maria Robinson of Nanaimo, who had come out with her brother George Robinson, the man in charge of the mines. He died there in 1865. A funeral was held at his home on Superior Street and he was buried in the naval corner of Quadra Cemetery in Victoria. His will indicated how his conflicting loyalties were finally settled. He left bequests to his wife and Betsy's daughters, Janette and Christina, and money to churches in Kirkwall and Victoria.

17 THOMAS FRANCIS: *For the Sake of your only Surviveing Boy Joseph*

Ann Jackson's letter to Thomas Francis, to which she added her husband's name, reveals the vagaries of relationships with men who make their living at sea. Her report of some sailing men's misdeeds and neglect may well be an indirect way of reminding her friend that "your only Surviveing Boy Joseph . . . has had no one to See him Since you was in the river." That was in 1834, when Thomas left aboard the *Ganymede*, bound for the Columbia Department. Even before that, Thomas had not spent much time at home.

He first left in 1831 when he served as cook aboard the *Eagle,* not returning to England until 1834 in the visit referred to in the following letter.

～ For Thomas Francis, Cook of the Droyd [*Dryad*], North West Coast of America

Poplar January 14th 1836

Dear Friend

I take a nother Favourable Oppurtunity of writing to you hopeing this will find you Well as this Leves us all at Presant, I was very much disapointed at not haveing a Letter from you wen the Eagle Came home, I See Some of the men that Came home in her and they Said you ware very well wich i was very glad to hear for the Sake of your only Surviveing Boy Joseph[.] he grows a fine boy and gets on with his Learning very well, he dont forget his Farthe Francis[.] he says i am to give his Love to you and tell you to bring him a Bird hence, he has had no one to See him Since you was in the river, Mortimour [Mortimer] is dead and Ellen has not been Seen by aney one that i [k]now this 12 Months[.] i Should almost Suppose she is dead[.] M[r] Nowland is very well but in a great deal of trouble[.] I told you in a former Letter that he was Mate of the Earl of Hawkney's [Orkney's?] Pleasure yought [yacht] going to Napels[.] he was in her Six Months and Left her at Napels[.] it is Now 9 Months since and he has not got home[.] She thought he must ben Dead but She received a Letter from him 3 Months ago Saying he Shoud be home at Christmas but he has not Come yet[.] it is 9 months Since She had aney mony from him, you will be surprised to heare that M[rs] Scarth is Married again[.] She found out for Certain that Scarth was a Married Man and his wife living in Scotland. She has Married a Widower at Blackwall the Name of Littlefield[.] She apears very happy and Comfortable[.] Scarth never returned from India or wrote to her, M[r] and M[rs] Page desire ther kind Love to you and M[r] and M[rs] Richards[.] She is now Confined – M[rs] Holms desirs her Respects to you, and M[r] and M[rs] Mafounder and James, I am happy to Inform you that My Husband i[s] quite well and desirs his Respects to you[.] he i[s] Mate of the Soho now been about 6 Months[.] he is very Comfortable with Frazar[.] I have an Increase in my family Since you Left me[.] I have another Son a 11 Months old[.] My Robert is very delicate[.] he has been down in the Country with his Grandmothr about 4 Months[.] Poor Mrs Crowley is dead and Sarah Keeps the house on at Presant, if you Should have an Oppertunity of writeing before you come home we Should be very Glad to hear from you, M[rs] Corney did not behave very well to me[.] She Promised me wen She heard She would Let me now and she did not and i have ben there Several times and they always Say She is not at home but [I am] quite Convinced She was, though it was of very Little Consequence i did not want any thing of them only mearly to heare from you[.] I am sorry I have no more News to tell you but hopeing this will find you in Perfect health and hoping that God Almighty will Bring you Safe home in his own good time[.] My husband and Joseph Join with me in Love to you and Believe us ever to be your Sincear

Friends and Wellwishers Thomas & Ann Jackson

It seemed that the Jacksons, caregivers for Thomas's son, were having a hard time contacting the boy's father. They probably attempted to contact Mrs. Corney because Peter Corney was serving on the same ship as Thomas. The Hudson's Bay Company's London Committee had resolved, in a major departure from their usual practice, to allow Corney,

> to take his wife and four children out in the vessel to remain in that Country; his wife to mess with him at the Captain's table. The children in the steerage and that he be charged at and after every rote for three persons say 4s. 6d. per diem for the whole; further that they be no expence to the Company for their maintenance in the Country, it being understood that the Chief Factor in charge may engage Mrs. Corney in any capacity, for the education of the Natives or any other that she may be qualified for.

The unfortunate Peter Corney, however, had died on 31 August 1835, even before the ship had left British waters. Mrs. Corney may have been too overcome with her own problems to contact the Jacksons.

At the time this letter was written, Thomas was serving as cook aboard the *Dryad* stationed at Fort Vancouver. His last recorded service is as a seaman on the *Columbia* from 1836 to 1837, the ship that returned him to London in May 1837. At that time Thomas Jackson was probably reunited with his friend because a letter from Thomas Francis, addressed to the Company, is written from the district of Poplar, the same area in which the Jacksons lived. In his letter to the Company, Thomas petitioned for extra pay because "he was allowed no spirits or any kind of perquisite which as Cook he would have been allowed had he been on board" for the two years and five days he spent at Fort Vancouver between 1835 and 1837. No record has been located of his ever receiving compensation.

18 WILLIAM POUCHER: *You will think that you are quite forgot – and "become as a dead man clean out of mind"*

Sometimes, in reading letters, it seems a good thing that the intended recipient was able to live a little longer without knowing their contents. If

William Poucher, who had shipped out as a steward for Captain Darby aboard the *Eagle* in 1833, had received these letters, he would be forced to read his brother's detailed explanation – over two letters – of the dreadful end of their brother Joseph.

Wm Poucher, Hon Hudsons Bay Comp^y Service – Fort Vancouver, Colombia River, N.W. Coast of America, Feb. 10 1836, RP

the Vessel sails tomorrow
Sydenham Feb 10th 1836

　　Dear William
　　I fear that my long Silence in not writing to you before this will have been productive of great uneasiness with respect to your Money order (which I received safe tho a little informal)
　　I have not been able to learn any tidings about the sailing of the Hon Company Ships till this morning, I have trusted to Samuel for information as he is so frequent in the City but by some Mischance for which I cannot account he has allways missed the opportunity and it is only by mere chance that I have heard of the present –
　　My last informed you of the death of our poor Father – Joseph has now gone to his place of rest poor fellow let us hope that the mercy of the Almighty may have been extended to him[.] his sufferings have been very severe here[.] he died on the last of December 1835 – deserted by his Shameless Wife[.] I have not seen her since the Christmas of 1834 nor do I ever wish to see her again – but I will give you more particulars hereafter when I next write by Gods permission – I have the Satisfaction of feeling that I did my part as far as lay in my power and put the poor fellow decently in the Ground at the last –
　　Our poor Mother still lingers on – at John Barny[.] hers has been a life of Suffering and of woe[.] let us pray that the Almighty may grant her pardon & peace when he sees fit to take her to himself – the rest are as usual –
　　the informality I mentioned in your bill was your omitting to indorse it with your own Name – to me[.] it would have had to come back to you previous to being paid had not Mr Nix kindly entered into a guarantee to Indemnify the Hon Company from any loss by their pa[rt.]
　　I was under the Necessity of sending your letter to the Board for their inspection but I took care to erase what I thought might be construed to any disrespect to the Honble Company – hoping to hear from you when ever convenient I shall now conclude with prayers for your health & Welfare & a Safe return
　　& believe me to be your affectionate Brother

Richd Poucher
J. Nix Esq. Sydenham Kent

∼ Wm Poucher, Hon Hudsons Bay Comp^y Service, Fort Vancouver, Colombia River, N.W. Coast of America

Sydenham Feb 28 1836

Dear William

I am afraid that after the very long silence that has been observ'd towards you – you will think that you are quite forgot – and "become as a dead man clean out of mind" but such I do assure you is not the case, for tho such an immense distance intervenes betwixt us – it does not lessen the affection ever felt for you – and by your absence from your Native Land you have been spared the pain of witnessing the distress of a part of our Family – you may suppose that I am now alluding to poor Joseph[.] his has been a very pitiable case but now his earthly career is past now he has gone to his long home where the Wicked cease from troubling & where the weary are at rest[.] let us hope that the Almighty Father of Mercies has in his own good time remov'd him from this Scene of Woe and that he may have pronounced Pardon & forgiveness to his poor departed Soul thro the Merits & Media- tion of our Blessed Lord & Saviour Jesus Christ – for the last two years or in fact longer he has not been quite right tho I did not at first entertain that opinion – but from later experience such must have been the fact

Shortly after you left England I spoke to my last Master Mr Newman Smith in his behalf and he gave me a Note to the principal of the Pheonix Gas Manufactory on Bankside Southwark where he remain'd but a short time but during that time I was led to believe by his Vixen of a Wife that they were in an improving way with respect to personal Comfort and that there would be a change for the better which gave me great pleasure for as *I* was present at the time they were united for better or worse I consider it my duty to do what I could to add to their welfare but my hopes were soon destroyed[.] the poor creature being then in a State bordering on Lunacy was driven by the conduct of one who ought to have cherish'd him – to leave his work and that under circumstances which in a person of Sound Mind would have been most disgraceful – and which conduct caused much unpleasantness betwixt Mr S. & his Friends as allso towards myself – & by the base womans misrepresentations I was induced to believe that the faults all rested on the poor Fellow – which subsequent facts have prov'd were falsely laid to his charge – things went on till December 1834 when she was confined with a boy[.] I happend to call two or three days after by chance & saw her and as usual went away somewhat lighter in pocket[.] things

appeared to be very moderate & comfortable to what they had been as Mary was recommended to a friendly Society of ladies who were in the course of three Weeks were let into the secret of her behaviour & consequently withdrew their assistance & then the secret was out[.] she sent me word that the poor fellow had put a broker in the house but the fact was that she had remov'd what she thought fit & then told her landlord to seize the rest under the Idea that I would release them but the deception was then removed & as I refus'd so doing the poor fellow then under went a very distressing trial and in a state of Starvation untill Samuel & Mr Chart a person who lived opposite to where George Kinton did live in Kings Bench Walk they had a great deal of trouble to get him into St Georges where she remaind for a short time & then left him towards the Autumn[.] he was obliged to be sent to the County Lunatic Asylum where he died on the 30th of december and now I have given you the details of a small part of his suffering[.] I shall now conclude thanking you for the Money Order which you sent – but having wrote a short time back which I trust you will have recievd ere you get this
I remain your most affectionate Brother
  Richard Poucher
hoping you will write any opportunity that may afford –

   William's brother Samuel's short letter follows Richard's detailed missives and contains more depressing news.

Dear Brother, as Richard [h]as left a corner I have taken the oppertunity of it. Father and Joseph has died since you left home[.] Mother continues but poorly she is almost worn away to a shadow[.] I should not be surprised to hear of her death. Betty has been very bad lately one of the Window sashes fell on her head[.] she has given up but she still linguers here below, she is rather better[.] the rest of of us are tolerable well in health hoping you are the same[.] we are living on Brook Street West Square at 98. I conclude with our love to you, Hannah is pretty well as my self likewise from your Affectionate Brother
  S[amuel] Poucher

   It is interesting to note that the Company is consistent in its careful requirement of the fullest documentation possible for all its acts. It will not honour a bill (a permission to pay money owed by a man to another person) when the man has not signed the request, unless someone else guarantees the money. As well, the brother must send the letter in which William makes the request to London, for the Company officials' "inspection." Poucher's ill fortune did not end with the deaths of his father and Joseph, the news of his mother being "almost worn away to a shadow," and Betty's accident. A letter to the Company written after William returned home aboard the *Ganymede,* and therefore not among the undelivered letters, describes an injury to his wrist suffered on the trip home.

[13 November 1837]

Honoured Sir

Humbly hoping that you will pardon the liberty I take in addressing you Sir to state the Situation in which I am unfortunately placed – I had the honor of Serving on board the Hon. Company's Brig Eagle as Steward to Capt Darby – Sailing Dec.ʳ 1833 to Columbia River and continuing in the Hon Companys Service untill the Arrival of the Ganymede in March of the present year – On board of which Vessel Honoured Sir I unfortunately met with a severe injury to my Right Wrist which disabled me on the Voyage home – On the Ships Crew being paid-Off – I was admitted an Inn Patient at the Westminster Hospital where after Seven Weeks the Gentlemen told me that Amputation was all that could be done – but not feeling Satisfied, I was Recommended to Mʳ John Scott of Broad Street who on inspection gave me every hope of saving my hand & by that Gentleman's Kindness & Skill through the Blessing of Almighty God my hand has been restored from being a mass of dead Flesh to a perfectly healthy State – the wrist joint still remains very weak & will require a few months longer rest –

My Object Honᵈ Sir in Stating my case to you is humbly to ask if I may be permitted to petition the Hon Company's Committee if they could give me any temporary employment either as Ship Keeper or Messenger or any other employment that I could perform as I have no means at present of earning my Subsistance & I have been Endeavouring to obtain employ but have not been able to get any –

I trust that my Conduct whilst in the Companys Service was allways such as met with the approval of my Superiors

again humbly begging pardon for this intrusion

I am Honᵈ Sir

your very humble Servant

William Poucher

Sydenham Common, Kent

Nov 13ᵗʰ 1837

Poucher's injury had been treated at the hospital in Valparaiso, Chile, but remained a concern throughout the trip. In response to the letter in which he asked to return to the Company's service, he was told no work was available. Perhaps, despite his brother's careful erasure of what "might be construed to any disrespect to the Honble Company," his discontent was known through other sources. At any rate, his wrist must have healed enough to work, as the Company secretary noted "at Shorter's – Gardener" above the address and date on his letter.

19   FRANCIS JOSEPH HARDY: *Make Yourself independant as fast & as far as you can*

Francis Hardy left England as a seaman aboard the *Columbia* in 1835 and later served on the *Cadboro* and the *Lama*. The novels of the early nineteenth century make us familiar with the concerns expressed in the letter from his sister Louisa. Her preoccupations with courtship and marriage, as well as her ambivalence about the relationship between education and spinsterhood for young women, is typical of her class. Her frankness about the stupidity of Englishmen and her lighthearted joke that her brother "bring home a South American wife," however, reveal a slightly more assertive and risqué bantering than found in most genteel fictional heroines of the time. We also see here, as in many of these letters, the importance of sisters as advisers and authorities in the lives of their brothers. Louisa's instructions to Frank are peppered with "do not forget," "do not fail," and "keep from drink."

∾ Francis Hardy, Seaman, On Board the Columbia, Belonging to the Hudson Bay Company's Service

Innisgort [Inishgort, County Galway] Septr 22^d/36 [1836]

My dear Frank,
We were very much vexed that the letter and money we sent to London did not reach you in time, as my Mama came to Dublin at a great deal of expense and inconvenience to send it to you & you may judge our disappointment when the letter was returned with an account that you had sailed the day before it arrived. However I hope this will be more fortunate. We wrote to my Uncle & Aunt about you and they were kind enough to say they could have it forwarded by one of the Company's vessels. they got all this information for us from the person with whom you lodged in London & who spoke of you in the highest terms, She also said you went away in her debt but that you intended sending her an order for the amount whenever it was in your power, do not forget this — We are most anxious to hear how you like the service and Country you are in *so do not fail to write* by the *first Ship* that returns which we know will be early *next*

Spring. You will be glad to hear that my Father was removed to this place about two years and a half ago, and as a special favour has been granted the same salary as Mr Landies who contrary to his wishes is still in the same place. I have been here these three months and like it very well. I bought Mrs Young's Piano Forte so that we will have plenty of amusement for the winter nights. I left School last January to my great regret tho' Marianne says that if I had remained, I stood a fair chance of dying an old Maid which I can assure you she does not intend to do as I believe she has had a dozen proposals already amongst the rest Captn Wickham of Wexford, he said ~~he said~~ [crossed out] he was well acquainted with you and the Harrises. I suppose he mentioned this by way of recommendation. Tom Brown of Corryholly [Corryhallie, near Beauly, Ross and Cromarty] is at present on the carpet, he is very rich but she will not have him either, for he is neither tall nor smart enough for her fancy. There is a fine young man to be here at Christmas, measuring six feet two in his stoken vamps, who I think will succeed[.] My cousins are very well, going on in the same old way. We were very sorry that you did not know that my Uncle & Aunt were in London the same time you were there as it would have saved you a great deal of expense and would also have been Society for you. Tierney is still living here and your little Godson is dead. The "Chance" cutter has left this and the "Hawk" is come instead[.] there is a very trim man commanding it, as for the rest they are all a set of stupid English men, who only think of eating and drinking from Morning 'til Night. My Mama desires me to ask do you owe eight and six pence to Dan Hogarty? he says he lent it to you before you went on board the "Penelope." We did not like to pay him as we were not sure it was due, so *don't fail* to let us know when you write. We were very sorry to hear that [you] would not return for four years, be sure & tell us what time we may expect you home, as we cannot think you would go a[way] for such a length of time without letting us know. Write us a long letter & tell us how you are employed & how you like the Country. We are in hopes you will bring home a South American wife and make the natives of this place stare. And now dear Frank having told you all the news I can think of let me beg of you to keep from drink and all bad company and endeavour to form some respectable acquaintance[.] do this and there is no fear but you will prosper in life and tho' last not least to have the fear of God at heart as without this all is as nothing.

I must now close this and once more beg of you to mind all I have said to you on this subject and if it were but six lines write by the first opportunity or as often as you can. My Father was going to write but I thought I would tell you more news, as he is very much hurried preparing

for the Commissioners who are expected here in a few days. both he my
Mama and Marianne ~~in love~~ [crossed out] join in love and prayers for your
happiness with
Your affectionate Sister Louisa A. Hardy

[cross-written] Easton is as well and fat as ever.

   A letter from Francis's father, Henry, gives us an interesting picture of the
life of an Irish lighthouse keeper and of a family down on its luck, struggling
to maintain the values of the middle class. When Frank's father wrote to his
son after finally receiving word from him, the emphasis was still on the
importance of good and dutiful behaviour, but especially on the need for
financial success.

∾   Single Letter – Postage paid to London,
   For – Francis Joseph Hardy, Seaman on Board the Brig Lama, Columbia
   River, NWest Coast of South America,
   To the Care of The Hudsons Bay Company House, Fenchurch Street,
   London

   Old Head of Kinsale Light House, Kinsale – 18th May 1838

   My Dearest Frank
   I need hardly tell you that your Letter directed to Innisgort [Inishgort]
   and receieved by your Mother & Sister Louisa at that place some days ago
   – has indeed praise be to God been a heartfelt relief and pleasure to us all –
   for you Cannot imagine – how truly wretched – how miserably anxious we
   were all at not getting one line from you since the Letter you wrote to us
   from Mrs Chapman's New Gravel Lane London last on the eve of your
   sailing for South America – I answered that Letter im*medi*ately – and sent
   some Money in it to you and even for fear it might be too late your poor
   Mother went to Dublin to forward it properly – but the letter was returned
   to us together with the Money stating that you had sailed previous to the
   arrival of the Letter so there we were without knowing even the Name of
   your Ship or absolutely where you were gone to – till we got your Aunt &
   Uncle Hawley to hunt out Mrs Chapman – & from her we learned that you
   had gone to South America – in the Ship Columbia – NWest Companys
   Service to remain abroad for 5 years – Well then we waited till after Louisa
   Came down to us when your Uncle & Aunt enquired again – & Louisa –
   wrote you a Letter which I hope you received tho, very likely not as your
   Uncle and Aunt did not get us your proper address – at least not the same
   exactly as that We have got Now – but thanks be to God at last we have

heard from you and that you are well and doing well – I was appointed
Princpal Light Keeper here – early last March – and as we were very badly
prepared for the Change – I was obliged to come off in a great hurry (as
you know Mr Halpin does not give much time) along with your Sister
Maryanne – and leave your Mother and Louisa in Innisgort [Inishgort] –
untill we are able to muster up Money enough to pay off what we owe in
Westport – & defray their travelling expences into the Bargain – as the
Change Came so sudden we Could not be well prepared for it – Your
Mother & Louisa are in Innisgort Light House which is now Kept by a M^r
Hocker – who has a Wife & very large Family[.] I succeeded Him here –
and this is a capital good Mainland Station & no People can be Kinder
than they are both here and in Kinsale to myself and Maryanne Since our
arrival (the 14th March last) but still We can feel no happiness without
your Mother & Louisa who with the Blessing of God we *now* expect
immediately – and then indeed we will please God be able to enjoy
ourselves once more together round our Fire Side and drink your health
and taste by anticipation the pleasure of your return and having you again
under the same Roof with us my dearest Frank – Your Mother tells Me (for
she did not send me your Letter) that you are doing well – & that you will
as soon as you make enough of money return home to us – I need not tell
you how this rejoices us – and now let me Beseech you for the love of God
my dearest Frank to make all you can – *Without* money there is Nothing to
be got in *this* World & *with* money everything – how happy would We be
even if We had but enough to take a small Farm – & retire from the
anxieties which are ever attendant on a precarious Public Employment –
out of which you may be turned at any Moment at the Despotic will of
Your Superiors – but I trust the Almighty has something good in Store for
us and that we are not allways to be Crowed over by a set of Heartless
Relatives – Louisa came to us now nearly two years ago – poor Girl her
health suffered Much from Confinement in Dublin[.] she Your Mother and
Maryanne are Now quite well – you would hardly know your two sisters
they are fine good Girls – Your Uncle & Aunt Hawley are very well I
believe[.] they reside at 19 Princes Square Kensington Cross London – Your
Cousin Hardys are grown very old and the Older the *Worse* – Eliza has
completly adapted. Young Bayley Keeps a Horse – & servant &c &c for
him – & did not give Maryanne one shilling when we saw her as we passed
thro' Dublin – We have the same to say of Harriet – in Short *Nothing
whatsoever* is to be expected of them & they won't forgive Louisa because
she does not go out *Governess*! – No Frank I will see them to Old Nick
before I let her do that – as long as I can earn a Morsel of Independant
Bread for My Family – Who knows – May be we might with Gods Blessing

be better off than themselves yet – Gen¹ Freeman is dead – left all to Bell Nuttal & not one farthing to anyone else. John Hardy – died – last March – left one son & two Daugters – Henry Hardy died in Trinidad 12 Months ago – He died a Batchelor – and whatever Money he had he did not remember – Me – Old Radcliffe is dead – poor Myles Brae is dead – Nicholas Byrne – with two of his Sisters & I beleve also Old Byrne of Ballybroch is dead [crossed out] are dead – Catherine Norton & Her Husband as usual – John & Bess (your Aunt Bess- Brae) in Dublin – Bess in some small Employment – and We – Maryanne & I received more good nature from Her than from those who were able to afford it – I know of Nothing more worth telling you or that indeed you would care one straw about – No More than my self and I assure you my dear Frank I am quite disgusted with the world – but your Letter my dear Fellow – has Cheered up my spirits – there are now but 3 *Male* Hardys of us in the world Vidzᵗ you and I & John Hardys son who is a sickly Cat of a Fellow I hear – so mind yourself & perhaps my dearest Frank you Might be the Head of the entire yet – *above all things* do not ever forget the worship that is due to the good & great almighty God – without that all we can do of ourselves is of no use – I forgot to tell you that your old Captain Kirk is dead – My dearest Frank for the love of God Mind the advice I have given you in this letter[.] Worship God and Make Yourself independant as fast & as far as you can – Oh! how that will rejoice – your Poor Mother[.] the very thoughts of seeing you soon & happy again is a renewal of her Existence – Accept all our warmest loves 10000 times – & my Dearest Frank that the Almighty God in his infinite Mercy may keep & protect you & restore you to us safe and sound well & happy is the Constant prayer of Us all – Ever my dear Frank your affectionate Father

    Henry Wᵐ Hardy

Henry's reference to debts and the inconvenient family arrangements in his new lighthouse no doubt made financial advice a priority. His determination to keep Louisa home and not have her work as a governess seemed to assert a family value from more prosperous times, one familiar to us through novels such as *Jane Eyre,* which reveal the risks inherent in the position of governess. Many middle-class fathers with witty, accomplished daughters did not want to place them in positions in which their virtue might be compromised. Implicit and explicit in this letter is a strong message to Francis that much depends on his doing well.

    The family's concern about Francis's drinking is shown to be not without justification by a coincident occurrence, in February 1836, when Francis and a companion, Thomas Wheeler, "returned on board drunk & commenced abusing the crew & commanding officer." Wheeler was discharged from the *Columbia*. How Hardy avoided this fate is unknown but, in April 1836, he was discharged into the *Cadboro*. Although Frank never read his father's advice to "Make Yourself independant as fast & as far as you can," he did make himself independent in August 1837 by deserting his ship when it was docked in Hawai'i. The restrained language recorded by a Company official on his father's letter reads: "not in Columbia. Left HBCos service." We do not know where Francis Hardy went from Hawai'i, but in both 1838 and 1839 his father Henry was still writing to the Company asking to have letters forwarded to his son. By 1839 the father was no longer at the lighthouse in Kinsale but wrote his letter on 10 July from No. 11 Elliott Place, Dublin. On 12 July 1839 the Company secretary wrote back that Francis Joseph Hardy had deserted in "Woahoo" – Oahu, Hawai'i – and returned the father's letter. With both father and son relocated, it would have been even more difficult for them to find each other. Without a son's support, it would have been hard for the family to maintain middle-class status. Louisa may well have been forced to become a governess.

20 GEORGE PRATTENT: *Anne entreats becheeses and implores you will not consider it necessary to remain longer*

As second mate, first on the *Nereide* and then the *Columbia,* George Prattent had completed one long journey from London to the west coast between 1833 and 1835 and was one week into a second trip when chief mate Peter Corney died and George became chief mate. However, an incident occurred at the Sandwich Islands in which Captain Darby accused Prattent of drunkenness. Prattent in turn accused the captain of trading furs independently of the Company. At his own request, Prattent was transferred to the *Beaver* to return to the Columbia Department. He faced three charges, the first of which was that he had been drunk on duty several times, although one witness said he "never saw him unable to walk the Decks, or bereft of judgement merely elevated, not drunk." He was also accused of "leaving the Deck and turning into bed, leaving the Deck in charge of one of the men, and sometimes in charge of one of the apprentices Edwin Rye, quite a lad, until it was time to wash the decks." And finally, Darby accused him of "at Woahoo, being continually on shore neglecting his duty on board, and out of the Ship for 48 hours, not able to come on board from intoxication." Prattent denied the charges and called for a court of inquiry, which convened on 3 May 1836 at Fort Vancouver, presided over by five Company officers. The first charge was not proven, the second was proven, and the captain withdrew the first and third counts of the third charge, but Prattent admitted that he had been absent without permission for thirty-six hours. In May 1836 he was dismissed for intoxication and was sent down to Fort George (Astoria, Oregon) to await the return ship. In late October Prattent requested a cabin on the return trip home and asked that Chief Factor John McLoughlin "take into consideration the length of time I have been at this Fort losing both time and experience, and hope you will conceive six Months at Fort George sufficient punishment for the two Charges brought against me."

Meanwhile, back in England, George seemed to be facing more trouble, as his sister-in-law's letter indicated. His wife, Anne, whom he had married secretly, was facing dire circumstances that began just after George left her.

For Mr G. Prattent Columbia,
care of Mr Smith, Hudsons Bay House, Fenchurch Street, London

Chelsea Feb 27th 1837

My Dear dear Prattent
I fear you have expected a letter long since and am sorry to say we have always been so unfortunate as to miss the opportunity of a Ship going to Columbia, however Anne has this day seen Mr Smith (which you will be very much surprized to hear but I have a long tale to tell) and he has promised to forward a letter this week, and now for my story. In the first place I must tell you that immediately after your departure your poor Anne was seized with a most dangerous fever which has terminated, I had almost said, worse than was anticipated but thank God her life was saved. – Previous to her illness she was obliged to declare her marriage owing to some deeds she was wanted to sign, which business could not be transacted as her signature is of no use now – well poor Anne has suffered more than I can attempt to describe, the violence of the fever caused the Bones of the right Elbow joint to unite, bones, flesh, ligature and indeed every internal part of the arm has become stiff and fixed so as entirely to prevent the use of the arm. she was attack one week after you left England and has been ever since under Mr Gaskell's care; he has done all in his power and treated her in the kindest manner, everything has been done that could be thought of, every trouble and expense that our limited means would permit to restore to health and render her arm serviceable but apparently until very lately without effect, with the blessing of Providence if we can still procure Mr Gaskell's attendance we have hopes that her arm will yet be restored although not for a very long time. The second part of my story is, that, when Alick heard that Anne and you were married he was absolutely furious[.] at first he affected to disbelieve it but when he found it was indeed true his rage knew no bounds, of course they do not speak now.

Frank came home las[t] May (1836) when he was made acquainted with the *Horrid* affair, you may imagine what Anne had to contend with[.] I am sorry to say scarcely a day passed without some fresh insult, nothing but the hope of your speedy return could else supported, under the pain and misery she went through[.] She would have left home but had not the means to procure an asylum, driven to a state of desperation she has this day made application to the Hudson's Bay House for £50 to enable her to pay Mr Gaskell part of his bill and remain here as Alick is determined to take Mama from London despite the urgent necessity there is for Anne remaining [cross-written] under Mr Gaskell's care some time longer. She hopes and trusts that you will believe that nothing but dire necessity would compell her to this step but as the restoration of her arm depends on the plan adopted being persued and which very few Surgeons will undertake (every other day she undergoes an operation to have the joint disunited and the danger is in breaking the bone in the wrong place). She is sure you will not mind the expense of her remaining particularly as she can the moment you return said money by disposing of her reversions in trust in Mamma property if it is necessary. If she gets the money it is settled that Mamma leave her and I behind rest assured she shall want for no comfort or attendance that I can procure her[.] I shall continue as I have done for the last twelve month to support myself therefore shall be not much expense to her and will do everything in my power for her wellfare and happiness.

Frank has been appointed to a ship since Oct (36) and was at Plymouth four months on boar the Scorpian Brig, but has since been appointed to the Vessel 74 at Lisbon[.] when at Plymouth he sent us very little news[.] indeed he will neither write nor speak to me as [he] says I connived at the *deceitful transaction*[.] you will be surprized and sorry to here that your friend Agustus Scott is no more[.] He died of Consumption six or eight months since[.] Amelia is going to be married to a master in the navy[.] Pen is still Pen Scott. M^rs F Silling our worthy Aunt is dead and a son and a daughter married. Nancy Merchant has unfortunately got connected with one of the fiddling tailors belonging to the Little Chaple and her parents have turned her to doors.

John Gidley says Eliza has turned out a compleat Blackguard but I do not believe that, coming from such a quarter. Anne sends ten thousand thousand kisses and deeply regrets that she cannot write herself but you must consider this as her letter not mine as I am writing from her dic[ta]tion[.] She prays that you are as well and happy as when you last wrote although I assure you that was a most heart breaking letter and entirely destroyed the hope she formed of seeing you back by the Columbia. The Gas has not yet arrived consequently I have not sent my letter[.] I am look out very anxiously as she is expected in a few days. Anne entreats becheeses and implores you will not consider it necessary to remain longer because she has applied for the money she may not even get and if she does as I before mentioned can always make it up at your ret[urn]

[cover, lower left] We called on Gibbons the other day he was exceedingly kind and said if he had not met with a severe Loss he would have assisted [cover, lower right] Anne himself – Anne desires me to say she is more than half in love with old Mr Smith and could scarcely prevent herself giving him half an oz he was so kind –
[upper right, cross-written] I have scarcely left myself room to say from myself that I earnestly beg you will embrace the first opportunity of coming to England[.] our dear mother's health is very much broken and should any thing occur what a doubtful state Anne would be placed in [cover, upper left] Mamma and myself join in wishing you every happiness and a speedy return and believe me your truly affectionate sister G.M. Coull

Poor Anne is suffering, both from the anger of her family at her secret marriage and from the painful and disabling affliction of her elbow. In a letter to the Company, Dr. Gaskell diagnosed it as "severe Bilious Remittant Fever which endangered her life – it has left her right elbow anchylosed." This infection, pyogenic arthritis, could come on as a complication of other ailments such as pneumonia, a gall bladder infection, or gonorrhoea, and the only treatment at the time was manipulation of the grossly distorted joint. Anne's letter with the doctor's certificate and proof of her marriage on 18 August 1835 in the parish of St. Paul, Shadwell, resulted in the Company secretary, the careful but kindly William Smith, allowing £20 of the £50 requested to be dispensed to the bride.

Meanwhile, after the court of inquiry convened by Chief Factor McLoughlin had dismissed Prattent, McLoughlin nevertheless allowed George his full pay to November 1836 and passage home to England aboard the *Columbia,* which arrived in London on 1 May 1837. His wife would probably know nothing of his problems, since her sister, writing on her behalf, mentions a letter they received in which he speaks of being well and happy.

When he arrived back in England, George Prattent pursued his case with the Company. A letter of 14 May 1837 thanked the Company for its kindness to his wife, and complained that he had been abused by Captain Darby and the inquiry process, claiming that the witnesses were "John Coon Second Mate, then in his [Darby's] pay [see John Coon's story, entry 28], J^{no} Coldicot, his [Darby's] own apprentice, and Wm Lucas (A.B.) [able seaman]. This man who had been in confinement during our stay at Woahoo & who

Capt Darby knew to be my most inveterate Enemy, having been Shipmates with me in H.M Ship Melville w[h]ere he had been punished in consequence of a report having been made by me regarding him." On Monday morning, 15 May 1837 he requested an audience with Company officials and was granted one on the following Wednesday but the letter was returned unde-livered on 19 May. Whatever satisfaction he did or did not receive from the Company, George was once more writing to them on 28 October of the same year to complain that Darby did not return his watch. The Company's reply was that he must approach Captain Darby, then residing with friends at Cookham, Berkshire, if he wished to gain knowledge of his watch. And with this response the Company record and our knowledge of the turbulent life of George Prattent, ends. Prattent might have taken some satisfaction in knowing that Darby had also been dismissed from the Company's service. Darby wrote a letter to William Heath (entry 29), in which he indicated that he intended to get as far away as possible from the scenes of recent unhappi-ness for himself and his wife by heading to Sydney, Australia – but that, in May 1838, Prattent was still "on the shelf waiting."

21   CHARLES BAKER: *I ham very much Sopriced of you not Riting to me Sooner*

Charles Baker had been on the west coast for four years as a seaman, first aboard the *Eagle* and then the *Lama*. He was serving on the *Columbia* when his wife of ten years wrote of her relief after finally receiving a letter from her long-absent husband. Mary's brief reference to being "in Service" so that she can support the children may explain what appears to the modern reader as a tone of anger barely disguised under the surprise in this letter. If she held the usual position of a "maid of all work," her day would begin at five or six o'clock in the morning and include myriad chores, from trimming the lamps and making preserves, through cleaning everything from chamber pots to fireplaces, as well as waiting on the ladies of the family and serving at meals. If the maidservant had any time out from serving, cleaning, and cooking before her day was over at ten or eleven o'clock at night, she was expected to read her Bible and behave herself.

Mʳ Charles Baker on Bord of the Brig Lamer [*Lama*], fort vanCouvor, Columbia River, North West Coast of america March 4ᵗʰ

March 4ᵗʰ 1837 [Old Bell Lane, Holburn]

   Dear Husband
   I Red your Letter With the Much Pleashur But I Was very Sorrey to heare of you Bean so Bad But I ham Quite Well thank God for it but my

Youngist Child is But verry Porley and it is 2 Years a Go since i have Seen
Eling upon a count on Been in Service and I ham Stil in Service now and
Doing very Well[.] What keeps me Back is to have to Pay for the Child and
I have Kist ArayBell [Arabella?] for you as for Eling i Cannot and Gets a
fine Girl thank God But I ham very much Sopriced of you not Riting to
me Sooner and I have not heard from your Mother for Some Time and I
hope that you Will Send me Some Money as Sone as you Can for I Want it
very Bad and for not hearing from you so I thought that you Was Dead
from your Affec[tiona]te Wife Mary Baker Old Bell Lane, Holborn

Mary would have missed her children (John, baptized in 1830, and Elizabeth, in 1835), since a woman in service could not bring her children to live
with her, and would see them only on rare afternoons off and only if the child
were kept by people close to her place of work. Visits to young children any
distance from the place of service were not considered a good excuse for
absence from the job in the 1830s and younger children, such as Mary's
daughter, could be at considerable risk if no close relative were available to
check on their care. Mary's letter never reached Charles because he was on
his way back to London on the *Columbia* in 1837. We can only guess at his
reception when he arrived home.

22 THOMAS LORKIN: *You are sailing to almost all ports*

Thomas Lorkin was thirty-one years old and an experienced sailor when he
joined the Hudson's Bay Company's service in 1835. Working as a seaman
aboard the *Columbia* on its London to Columbia route in 1835-6 did not
encourage him to stay in the district. He joined the *Lama*'s crew for the
return voyage only four months after his arrival. A flurry of letters – from his
cousin and sweetheart, Bessy Chapman, his two sisters, and a brother-in-law
– follow Bessy's receipt of a letter from Thomas almost two years after he
departed on the ship *Columbia* in 1835. From his family's concern for his religious health, we can assume it was not a happy letter. Although the family –
particularly the brother-in-law he has never met – were all very sure that the
danger in which he has put his soul is the cause of his discontent and that
their detailed advice will cure him, Bessy's refusal to "marry a man that lives
in one country and me in a nother," surely would offer another serious blow
to his earthly happiness if he ever received the news. The address Bessy used,
"Fort Anchovey, Collambia" instead of Fort Vancouver, underlines how
unfamiliar she was with her cousin's whereabouts.

↣ Thomas Lorkin, Seaman, Fort Anchovey, Collambia

London July 2 1837

Dear cousin

I received a letter from you in May and am verry glad to her that you are well – I am likewise[.] Much obliged to you for the Books you sent –

But I have not received them Mrs B [h]as got them I have not yet seen them So I cannot tell you what I think of them. I am verry sorry you did not see your Brother John for poor Fanny has been expecting to hear from him and she has not[.] I do asure you she has anougt to do to keep her self and Child and now she is growing a great girl and some Expence to keep her but she has not yet to thank her Father for any thing she has recived[.] I hope you will not think any more a bout me for I have quite made up my mind not to marry a man that lives in one country and me in a nother[.] your Money is quite Safe and will be given to you at your returne but to no one else[.] Fanney receive it for you and has got the care of it[.] your jacket likewise she has got[.] Louisa is married she has enclosed a letter for you[.] Mr Tracy is dead he died a bout three months ago[.] your Father is quite well and all your friends

Fanney Joins With me in Love to you I remain your
Affectionate cousin B.A. Chapman

Especially interesting is brother-in-law Charles's diagnosis of how homesickness can lead to moral turpitude.

↣ 20 Princes Square, St Geo East, London

[2 July 1837]

Dear Brother

Permit me to address you for the first time as such, but I must in the first place explain who I am and am happy in informing you that I am your Brother in law having married your Sister Louisa[.] we were married on the 3 of December 1836 at which time we were both living at Norwood but left it last Christmas[.] We are now keeping a Boy & Girls School in the Sunday Schools belonging at Pell Street chapel, & I hope we are likely to do well in them[.] And it is at the request of Louisa that I now take up my pen to write to you, the reason why she wished me to write is Bessy Chapman recieved your letter a short time ago which we have had the priviledge of seeing[.] we were glad to hear of your being in good health, but more happy to hear of the anxiety which you manifested about your

souls salvation but felt some concerns that you did not find comfort[.]
good health is a very great blessing, but what is the health of the body to
the salvation of the soul[?] Our bodies will soon die our souls will never
die, time will soon be over eternity will never be over and in a few years
~~will~~ [crossed out] we shall be launched into this great ocean we shall leave
the shore of this world but if we are not saved we shall never find another;
I am not surprised at your not being happy, for how can you whilst God is
angry with you, but thank God you may be[.] you say the sails of sin are
enclosed so fast around your heart that you think you can never get them
unfurled but God the Holy Ghost can unfurl them for you because you say
that you have been miserable for years, but it is perhaps you have not
sought in the right way to be made happy & without this you may be
miserable for years longer. I think I can picture in my mind something like
the state of mind you are in without you are made happy since you sent
Bessey's letter, & I will try to tell you how it is why sometimes when you
are by yourself you feel very unhappy you begin to think about home, and
you think about Bessy, and then you think that you are here all alone and
can see none of your friends and then you think about your sins that you
have committed, & how God is angry with you and what will become of
you in another world and that makes you unhappy, well then perhaps you
say to yourself I am determined to break of my sins I wont get drunk
anymore, nor I wont swear anymore, I wont break the sabbath any more,
but I will say my prayers and try to be good, well I think I can see you
knell down with these good resolutions & prey to God & you feel little
happier, but next time you go ashore your comrades appear to be all alive
& perhaps they will be going to get a glass and they will rally round you &
pressure to go have one glass just one glass they say theirs no harm having a
glass it does good, & if you wont go they will rally you about being
methodist[.] you at first feel reluctant but with persuading you go thinking
when you go that you wont stop long[.] well you get one glass but then
they will persuade you to have another and then another[.] conscience
some times tells you that you are doing wrong but however you take
another till the liquor gets into your head & then you are as anxious to
stop as any one else and you can hear or sing what you call the jovial song,
you sink into a state of intoxication[.] again your former resolutions are all
broken and you seem to be ten times worse than ever, and when you get to
yourself again you feel worse, you feel more unhappy, and you are ready to
fear that you will never be better[.] well now I doubt not but this has been
the case hundreds of times And you are ready to enquire O wretched man
that I am who shall deliver me from the body of this death. Now as I have
been in the same ci[r]cumstances I will try to direct you, and first you are

seeking wrong perhaps you are seeking for power to over come sin before
you get your past sins forgiven, how you must pray for God to forgive your
past sins first and then when God forgives them he will give you power
over sin, and then second you are perhaps striving to save yourself instead
of coming unto God through Jesus Christ, how we have sinned against
God we have broken his law and we cannot be saved by keeping that law
now it is broken, well then you say we must repent. But repentance does
not satisfy God for breaking his law what must we do then why we could
not save ourselves, but Jesus Christ came from heaven to save us, died to
satisfy God for us breaking his law and then he went to heaven after he had
risen again and lives there to pray for you and me. But then you ask is God
willing to save us yes For God parted with his son for this very purpose
See Roms 8.32, and John 3.16[.] Do you further object look at the great
promises Isaiah 55 Chap 1-7 verses ff. every one that thirsteth, how
delightful, and then Matt 11 Chap 28 verse and Revelation 22 Chap 17
verse, do you complain that none are so bad as you are, but then if you
look at 1 Timothy 1 Chap 15 verse you will see he came to save sinners &
even the chief of sinners, he came to seek and to save those that were
lowly[.] Do you still suppose that you are to great a sinner to be saved or
that sin is so fast entwined around your heart that you cannot shake it of.
See Heb 7.25. Well but you say you do not know how to come unto God
aright, but see James 1 Chap 5 verse, do you enquire whether God will hear
such a sinner or not, Yes if you are asking him to save you he will, See John
14 v 13 & 15 v 16, and Luke 11 Chap & 1 to 13 verses & Matt 21.22 and
many more that I might direct your attention to but seek for them See Acts
2 v 21 & Rom 10, 13, But then again we must ask in faith and if we exercise
faith on the Lord Jesus Christ we shall be saved See Acts 16 v 31 ~~Matt~~
[crossed out] Mark 9 v 23, 11 Chap 24 vrs John 6 v 29, 11 Chap 40 vrs Acts
13-39 Rom 3 v 24.25, 26 verses & 10 Chap. 9 1 Tim 4.10 and many more,
And if we do not bleive we shall be lost Mark 16 Chap 16 verse, now you
must strive to get into some secret place tell the Lord all about your misery
pray for the Holy Spirit to assist you, you cannot be saved without it, and
God has promised to give it to those who ask for it if ye being evil know
how to give good gifts unto your children how much more will God give
his holy spirit to those who ask him, Jacob prayed with the Lord all night
and one half of the time perhaps his thigh was out of joint but in the
morning God blessed him, happy are they whom God blesses, my dear
Brother I often think about you when I am praying though I have never
seen you, O how happy I should be if I was to hear of your being made
happy, I was once a great sinner & God saved me & there is the same grace
for ~~me~~ [crossed out] you as there ~~is~~ [crossed out] was for ~~you~~ [crossed out]

me[.] you perhaps just feel as if you was wrecked and about to finish but
Jesus Christ has brought the life boat[.] ask God to help you into the life
boat pray & pray till you feel the spirit of God come down & soften you
heart[.] come unto God to be saved just as you are if you strive to make
your self better you will only make yourself worse, ~~all~~ [crossed out] always
remember this it is God that saves you whilst at the same time we should
remember that God will not save us if we do not ask him. I have written
you a long letter but I hope you will excuse I should be very happy if you
would write me a letter I shall be happy to see you if you live to come to
London, and till then I pray God to bless your soul to lead you into the
way of truth & to show you his great salvation, I shall now leave room for
Louisa & Sister Bonallack
   So I remain
     Your Affectionate Brother
       Charles Barrowcliff

Sister Louisa writes of her new status as a respectably married woman.

[cross-written] My dear Thos You will be surprised I daresay on the receipt
of this letter little expecting your Sister Louisa after all her adventures to
get married[.] I find I have not waited one day too long[.] I now look back
& see what I have been preserved from, how many are the snares which
have been broken by an invisible almighty hand & here I am as a bird
escaped from the snare of the fowler[.] I have often thought of those lines
of the Poet "In *deep astonishment* I stand & ask the reason why *I see it
now*[."] I trust this union will prove my soul's salvation & what would it
have profitted me if I had gained the whole world & lost my own Soul[.]
Dear Thos I am glad to find that Salvation is the chief topic of your letter
to Bessy[.] I trust our prayers for you have been heard poor & imperfect as
they have been & before this I would hope the Lord has pardoned your
sins & make you happy[.] I heard a sermon last night that made me so by
the powerful application of the Holy Spirit[.] As Moses lifted up the
Serpent in the Wilderness, so the Son of God was lifted up & Sinners
invited entreated exhorted & commanded to look up and be saved & the
Lord in infinite mercy helped me (so deeply stung with sin) to look at Him
with an eye of faith & in a moment my dear brother he *saved me*[.] I could
hardly believe His compassion could be so soon extended; a look without a
word[.] Oh can I ever doubt his willingness again[.] never doubt it my dear
brother I have so long dishonored Him by disbelieving His will, doubting
His willingness to Save[.] I think I can now look death in the face devested
of its terrors, when I thought of it before "The monster brandishing his

sting appeared & *hell* was *close behind* [."] Oh that the Lord may help me to
live to his praise my few remaining years & to tell to the praise and glory of
His grace what He has done for my Soul[.] I'm glad to hear you say you are
tired of your company[.] I think you will try to have as little of it as possible
& get out of it at every opportunity. Be much in private Prayer & the Lord
will hear & answer you[.] since He has heard *me never despair*[.] We all
pray for you[.] We are told the Kingdom of heaven suffereth violence &
the violent take it by force[.] Strive to enter in, wishing *alone* will not do[.]
Write again & tell us all your feelings[.] we feel deeply interested for you[.]
when you come home we shall at all times be most happy to see you[.] M^rs
B [Ann Bonallack] will tell you a little news if she will perhaps & so I will
conclude by subcribing myself your affect[tionate] sister Louisa Barrowcliff

[on cover] I am happy to say My father is quite well[.] he is living now
with Mrs Tracy at Witham[.] He left Norwood before I was married to go
there on account of poor Mr Tracy's health[.] I am truly sorry to inform
you that he is since dead I think it was in February. Once more farewell
L.B.

The letter from "M^rs B" continued in the deeply religious tone the family
had adopted with Thomas.

∾ My dear Brother
    As your Brother & Sister Borrowcliff have left a little space for me to fill
up I feel a pleasure in so doing though as I have not seen your letter I can
scarcely tell how to answer it ~~enough~~ [crossed out] but I can learn thus
much that you appear to be anxiously inquiring "What must I do to be
saved,["] You say you have for a long time been miserable and would be
glad to know that your sins are pardoned, I do not wonder at your anxiety.
Heaven or Hell awaits on every breath but remember that "while the lamp
holds out to burn the vilest sinner may return and the Lord himself has
promised to cast out none that come unto him," go to him therefore and
cast your self at his feet and let the language of you heart be, here I am
Lord a fit object for the eye of thy mercy, plead the merrits of Jesus' blood
the language of the little hymn that perhaps you learned when young will
suit your case "Remember all the dying pains that my Redeemer felt, And
let his blood wash out my stains and answer for my guilt,["] However
guilty you feel yourself let it not hinder you from going[.] remember that
even David prayed pardon mine iniquity for it is great, thus making the
greatness of his guilt a reason why it should be pardoned, The Lord has
said by his word "A new heart will I give you and a right spirit will I put

within you,["] plead his own promise and continue to pray for a new heart till you feel assured that the Lord has answered you, be assured we do not forget to pray for you, may we be enabled to pray in faith, And now I must say a word to you as it regards Bessey who I suppose is about to give up all idea of ever being your wife and though this may be a triall to you at first I have no doubt you will at last see it is all for the best, for should the Lord be pleased to bring into the happy liberty of the gospel you would find no companion in her in your way to Zion and in many other respects I think she is not calculated to make you happy though she may [be a] good wife if she met with a man whose temper and disposition suit hers, and I trust that the Lord will direct you in the choice of one with whom you may spend many happy years if your life is spared. Mr Bonallack desires to be kindly remembered to you[.] I am happy to say that we and our children are all quite well since you left England[.] I have another *little boy* now about five months old, George and William have likewise each of them got another *boy* and you Sister Tracy is become a GrandMama as Sarah whom I think you know is married has also got a *little boy.* We have lately heard from Emily[.] she was quite very desirous of seeing some part of her family and some times indulging a hope that she may some day see you as you are sailing to almost all ports, I must now conclude[.] accept my kind love and believe me
Your affectionate Sister
  Ann Bonallack

Some of the heavily instructive tone of this family's letters may well be owing to the behaviour of another brother, John, who, according to Bessy, has left behind poor Fanny and a growing daughter who has received nothing from her father. Thomas Lorkin's confession that he is – in his sister Louisa's words – tired of his own company found a different expression than any of his relatives imagined. Lorkin deserted (or possibly was dismissed) during the *Lama*'s stopover at Hawai'i in 1837, never receiving his sisters' urgings to come to the Lord, his brother-in-law's detailed sermon of correction, nor his cousin Bessy's rejection. From our perspective as first readers of these letters, he seems to be answering the rhetorical question his sister Ann formulated – What must I do to be saved? – in a manner that would certainly surprise his sister. Men who left their ships at Hawai'i did not necessarily get saved from a life on the high seas. Often they were recruited by other ships and could end up anywhere in the world. Thomas's story must remain without closure for us, although we might be tempted to imagine what the scene would be if he returned to London to meet the judgment of his newly religious sister and her articulately instructive husband. Perhaps his sister's observation was right, and he kept sailing to almost all ports, far from those who would save him.

23   DAVID NEIL: *I should like that you could be employed as an Officer & not have to drudge as a common Seaman*

David Neil left London in August 1835 as a seaman on the *Columbia*. The family in Edinburgh, Scotland, received a letter from him written in November 1837, after he had been a year and a half in the Columbia Department. His brothers, hopeful that he would return home, wrote of a fairly prosperous life in a growing Edinburgh economy and seemed anxious that their brother should do better than "drudge as a common Seaman."

Mʳ David Neil, Seaman On Board the Brig Lama, Columbia River, North West Coast of America,
To be forwarded by The Hudson's Bay Coʸ, 4 Fenchurch Street London

Edinburgh 31 Gilmore Place 21ˢᵗ July 1837

My dear David,
I had been long looking for a Letter from you when I received yours dated 9 Novʳ 1836. It must have been delayed in the conveyance or the voyage must be longer than I had thought. I rejoice to know that you are well & that your term of service is drawing to a close as I should like that you could be employed as an Officer & not have to drudge as a common Seaman.
You will no doubt be anxious to know the changes that have taken place in your absence – Betsey is now the Mother of five children all girls. Is[abell]ᵃ was married about fifteen months since to a ~~clergy~~ [crossed out] young Clergyman Mʳ Harwood who is Minister of the Unitarian Congregation of Bridport. – He is a young man of first rate talents and acquirements & is likely to rise in his profession – She had a Daughter lately ~~which~~ [crossed out] who is to be named Isabella Neil. – She could not have been more happily married. – Your Aunt Mʳˢ Ross died in the month of February last. Rachel Ramage is married to a Mʳ George Henderson a postmaster in Edinburgh. – She according to the Will Succeeds to one half of the property and our family to the other. – The share will be but small, as the property has of late years been much depreciated in value, the rents having fallen to one half of what they were – but still it will be something. – I should like much that you were in Edinburgh that you might see us all. – Tom has been acting as a Clerk with me for some years past – I am thinking of establishing him in business for himself soon, but am difficulted as to the line in which

he should start. – Euphemia Wilhelmina Tom and myself are living in a
nice little house at Gilmore Place, and are all very comfortable and happy.
– Agnes is in partnership with a Miss Wilson as a Dressmaker. – She visits
us frequently. – She generally dines with us on Sundays and we spend a
very pleasant afternoon. – Agnes is a most excellent girl, and we are all very
much attached to her. – Mr Smith has taken Hope Parkend House where
he has a fine Garden & resides with his Sisters & Nephew & Nieces. – M^r
Hutchison lives in Clyde Street in a House above our Office[.] None of us
are yet married. – Mr Bradfute your old Master is dead, and Walker has I
understand been assumed as a partner in the business by Mr Aitken – This
will make him for life. –

I hope you read whenever you have an opportunity & Keep ~~for~~ [crossed
out] steady. – I must leave anything else I would say until I see you which I
hope may not be long – Tom will write under me & cross this Letter. – Write
immediately on receipt or as soon as you can, as I assure you it will gratify
us all to hear of your welfare. – With warmest wishes for your happiness –
    Believe me
        My dear David
            Your affectionate Brother
                Robt. Neil

Thomas's letter begins under and is cross-written over Robert's.

  ∾   My Dear David,
    From what Robert has said above you will observe he has given you all
the news of our circle; but I cannot allow the letter to be sent off without
writing a few lines in remembrance of one who has always had a warm
heart towards you. – You will no doubt be surprised to learn that I have left
the Tobacco line. – It was in consequence of bad health but I am thankful
that I have entirely recovered. – When you return to Edinburgh (which
will not be long I hope) you will be perfectly surprised at the changes that
have taken place – nothing but elegant shops, Bridges, and new roads in all
quarters of the Town; and besides there is a Pier and Harbour building a
little above Trinity for the purpose of allowing large vessels to come in and
when finished the Town of Leith may be [cross-written in red ink] advertised
for sale as it will be the means of taking all the vessels from that Port in
consequence of the Heavy Port dues and a deficiency of Water –

It will be very gratifying for you to know that Isabella is so well married
and that the remaining few are living happily together – Nothing will give
us more pleasure than your return from such a long absence – Robert is
wearying very much to see you – You say you will be home in about two

years but I fain hope that it may be sooner that you may have an opportunity of getting into a Vessel as an officer. – Margaret has had six children by the old gentlemen but one is dead. – Your old Shop-mate Learmonth has left here for New South Wales. Old Mrs Foran is dead and a great many more of our friends. – I must now close as I have exhausted all the news. – Do write every opportunity and let us know how you are and so soon as you arrive in London write immediately and let us know what conveyance you will take in coming to Scotland. – Euphemia Whilmina and Agnes join in kind love towards you. – I will write you soon and give you any further particulars which may occur. – God bless and protect you my Dear David and believe me to be
 Ever Your affectionate Brother
  Thos Neil

P.S. Robert requests me to state that it will be as well to let the Indenture be in Mr Pirie's hands until you come home. – Adieu again my Dear Brother TN

 David was not to receive his brothers' calls to come home. After serving as a lowly seaman on the *Lama* and *Cadboro,* as well as the *Columbia,* David Neil was on a routine coastal trading mission aboard the *Cadboro* on the California Coast when he and a Hawaiian seaman, Henry Napuko, decided to take their chances in the Spanish-speaking part of North America by deserting on 1 October 1837 at San Francisco on the way to Monterey. This was a decade before the Americans captured the port during the Mexican-American war and before the gold rush, but the city on the bay was already an attractive and bustling place to live. With its Spanish mission, its ranchero culture, and the visits of ships from many countries, it may have made an attractive alternative to life aboard a Company trading ship. Or perhaps it was a convenient port from which to leave on a different ship.

24 CHARLES HUMPHREYS: *I have spent a life of Care and Woe*

Charles Humphreys's mother, Margaret, was a widow in her sixties when she wrote to her twenty-seven-year-old son Charles. To support herself, she had leased a house in 1836 to use as a hospital for twenty-six scurvy-ridden whalers, the survivors of a disaster where twenty ships had become crushed in the Arctic ice. Of her thirteen children, the third boy, Robert, had died as a child and, as mentioned in the letters, her daughter Mary Dunn had recently died leaving a family of small children. Margaret's surviving sons were scattered in all directions, as the necessity of earning a living took them far from their home in Orkney. In this letter several are mentioned by name: Thomas, in an apothecary shop in Halifax; John, a sailor on a brief stop in London; and James, a doctor in Mexico. Other sons, Robert Stewart and Alexander (in New Orleans) are mentioned in a later letter. Unnamed sons are referred to more generally in warning Charles not to be like "some of your Brothers [who] ruined them selves by their Extravigance and keeping Company with those how loved their Bottle." Margaret had obviously had trouble with sons in the past and was in no mood to mince words.

Mr Charles Humphreys at Mrs Millers, 54 Lucas Street, Commercial Road, London

Stromness 13 Novr 1837

Dear Son,
   I now take the liberty of addressing you as I must confess my astonishment at not hearing from you again, incase there should be any Mistake in the post offices, as far as I can think I have not given any offence and the Malacholy subject which my letter was on I consider demanded ane answer; you are aware what a Shock and depression of Spirits this must have made on me and the only consolation, I hade in View was that of my Dear Charles if it pleased the almighty to send him safe home to me he would Condole with me and I could unbossom all my griefs to him but (ah) weak Woman that I am is there any Confidence to be put in the arm of Flesh[?] God is pleased to Confer preferment and Honours on you but Remember it is only to try what use you will make of it and should you waste all your earnings with extravigant Company and loose your reputation what pleasure will this afford to your Mind at the last, you are well aware what I have undergone I have in the first place brought up a large family and the only hope that was left was that some of them might doe me good when old age came on and their Comforting letters Cheer my drooping spirits[.] I have spent a life of Care and Woe when there was none of my family come to the Years of discretion or able to judge either for them selves or for me and now are they to desert me when I am unfit to doe any thing for my self[?] I have not earned one shilling this four months and hade it not been Thomas how hase sent me I should been ill of, those of my family how cannot spare me any thing I doe not look for it but I still think I am entitled to their love and attention[.] you have never thought it worth your notice to inquire how I have got such a long dreary time over for since your detainment in Hudson bay[.] I am not able to say how poorly I have been, when John arrived from America I wrote him of his Sisters Death but he did not think it worth his while to

return any answer[.] how unatureall, I doe not think he hade ever read my
letter[.] I dare say he was in a fever untill he got all his money spent and
then I suppose when his pocket was empty he was forced to go home to
his Father in laws[.] surely the righteous and just God will punish such
Conduct, it is now nearly four weeks since I received your few lines and for
this last three weeks we have called every Mail that arrived expecting there
would be a letter for us[.] I was much afraid that you hade been in bad
health as I certainlly thought nothing else would have prevented your
writing[.] I cannot Imagin how you could enjoy your self with Comfort
and not wish to know how your Mother was situated[.] I never once Could
have ~~imagined~~ [replaced by] Expected this of you[.] I hope you have not
over run your accounts at York factory[.] if you have it will not doe long
and well. I expect you will see your Brother John[.] I have a great deal to
Communicate to you but as you dont seem to be much interested it would
be needless to trouble you[.] let me know if you have heard from Mr Dunn
and how the Children are. I have not heard of him or from him only when
I got word of my Marys Death[.] how I doe lament for the dear little
Children and how sorry to think I am not in Circumstance to take little
Marg^t –

Now My Dear Son doe not Spurn at a Mothers advice[.] be sober and
Carefull keep good Company think what you are about and doe not
plunge yourself in trouble[.] mind how some of your Brothers ruined them
selves by their Extravigance and keeping Company with those how loved
their Bottle[.] Beware of this evil as it will soon Creep on and betray you
into disgrace, and Sin, and bring you to ane untimely end[.] doe not forget
God he over rules all events and it is by his unerring wisdom that we
should be directed in all our ways[.] if we ask his guidance in sincerity he
will bestow it on us and any evil propensity that is lurking about us he
will root it out[.] I need not ask you to Come home as I suppose this is
not your intention[.] you are More at liberty where you are then under a
Mothers eye. May the Almighty Conduct you and direct all your lawfull
Ways and it shall ever be the prayer of ane affectionate Mother for your
well fare and happieness till Death

from a Mother   Marg^t Humphrey
to her son

I hope you will write your Dear Brother Thomas and give him all the news
of your Voyage[.] he was verry anxious poor fellow for your wellfare[.]
Direct Apothecaries Hall Halifax Nova Scotia[.] he will be Most happy to
hear from you[.] there is no word of poor James which Ocasion many a
bitter thought MH –

Her sadness, her "Shock and depression of Spirits" at the death of her daughter Mary, who was only twenty-nine, the lack of communication from her son John, and her inability to earn a living might indeed cause the anger and frustration in Margaret's letter, even to a son who *has* written her just a few weeks previously to tell her of his preferments and honours. She seemed to take no pleasure in the happy event she must have known about: Charles's promotion to master of the *Eagle,* which sailed to Hudson Bay the year before. The Company's London secretary had written to Margaret on 15 December 1836, telling her the *Eagle* had been detained over the winter in Hudson Bay, so Margaret would have known why her son was absent for so long.

Charles first served with the Company as a seaman on the *Prince of Wales* in 1833-4, was promoted to first mate in April 1834 and served on two summer trips into Hudson Bay in that position before being appointed to master of the *Eagle* in 1836, at the young age of twenty-six. His service on the Hudson Bay route had not been easy and his promotion was a sign of how well he had handled a difficult situation. On his 1833 voyage, his ship was caught in ice and had to winter at Charlton Island. The captain and the first mate both died and Charles was promoted to first mate. On his return he was put in command of the *Eagle,* before he had even taken his master's examinations and, on a return trip to Hudson Bay, he was stranded on the rocks off Button Islands, near the entrance to Hudson Strait, and reached York Factory too late to return home until the next year – when the ship limped home taking on five millimetres (two inches) of water per hour. A stressful bailing operation with the constant fear of storms would have been part of such a risk-filled journey home.

Her son's success seemed to be no comfort to Margaret in her depression. He was detained in London to be examined at the Naval Academy in Navigation and Nautical Astronomy, at which he was found to be perfectly conversant, then immediately sent on board the *Columbia* as master departing for the west coast in the very month Margaret wrote her letter. He would be away until the spring of 1839, captaining a ship in unfamiliar waters.

Charles's mother, anchored in her own misery, had little positive to say about his progress in life or indeed about his difficulties. She referred to his brother Thomas, who would seem to have been a son more conscious of responsibility since he had sent money home to his mother – although not accompanied by a letter. Thomas did, however, take time to write to Charles.

❧ Cap\ Charles Humphrey, London
Care of M\rs Miller, 44 Lucas Street, Commercial Road, L[ondon]

Halifax Nova Scotia Dec\m 29\th 1837–

My Dear Charles

As an opportunity presents its-self at present (by a Capt Burwick of the Orkneys) I deem it necessary to put Pen to Paper- for I am afraid you are begining to think by this time that I have nearely forgot you. its not so. every moment that the mind is unemployed I am thinking upon you – and with that satisfaction which sooths the mind into a state of entire tranquillity – for I am convinced – that unless your conduct been Constituent to that of your situation it would not have been given you. I am allso convinced that a mans attainiments is not of himself and that there are an object which he values above the rest – this object being of a divine nature and that he will keep advancing both in the knowledge of business here below and allso towards his souls perfection in the world to come. Its true trials and afflictions are sent – but not for the purpose of making a man lower in this World – it is I verily belive, My Dear Brother, to bring him into an entire subjection and conformity – showing at the same time that this was an evil existing to be overcome – and in *your* late *Trials* look upon them as such – and may he who has the power sanctify all our afflictions. I suppose you have heard of our Sister (Marys) death – and that she died leaving us that hope – that she will again rise in glory, O! That our end may be like this – such Refined Consolation to all connected – I hope Dear Charles that poor Mother who has hade the most will reap accordingly. Time will not permit me at present to say much more – as the Vessel is about to Sail. I am sorry to say that my health is very precarious – My Constitution seems as it were broke down – Cloose confinement I belive is the cause and deep study which I never was accustomed to – and which is unavoiadable. The Establishment I conduct is very large – the Am^t of Stock in generail is not less than Five Thousand Pounds – so you may conjecture what anxiety will attend a few days hence (if well) will place me differently in that I then shall be an equal Partner (the first of 1838.) –

I now must draw to a conclusion, My Dear Brother, and O! if it were to please the allmighty god that we should but meet once again. I think that a reanimation would take place – but if its otherways decreed – may we meet in glory hereafter. All that I will say to you is this – keep at all times if possiable a cleare conscience – for it is the first that *Tells*.

Your
    Affectionate
        Brother
Thos Humphrey

Would you be good enough as to let Mother know that I sent hear a Little ~~of~~ [crossed out] Money – not having time to write a Letter with it.

I should feel very much obliged if you would write me when time and circumstance will allow asuring you it will ever be thankfuly rec^d. TH

Thomas's letter was sympathetic but he seemed as much absorbed by his responsibilities in the apothecary's shop and his own state of health, as his mother seemed absorbed in her miseries. A short letter from brother John in London, on the back page of brother Thomas's letter and written shortly after the letter arrived in London in May 1838, indicated a missed meeting between him and Charles.

Dear Charles
You will excuse me for breaking your letter oppen being from Thomas I thought it would not met with your displeasure
I was very sorry I did not see you before you sailed I was lying in long reach [in the Thames, near Gravesend] when you passed[.] I was not aware that you was going to Columbia or I should have seen you[.] I came with the steam boat on the Tusday after you sailed and was very much hurt that I did not see you[.] I have nothing particluar to say as you will have letters from all[.] I wish you my enjoy your health well and a prosperas voyage and soon be back
    your affectionate Brother
    John Humphrey

In May 1838 Charles brought his vessel safely around Cape Horn to the Sandwich Islands without any opportunity to send word back by another ship. He crossed the dangerous bar of the Columbia and on to Fort Vancouver later that month. A woman, who was his landlady in London and who seemed to have been well acquainted with his private life, wrote to tell him the latest news of his family and sailor friends.

Capt Humphrey

London May^th 28 1838

Dear freind I embrese the present uprtunity as it is the only on[e] that I have haid since your Departer from her[e][.] you will I have no Dopt be glad to he[a]r from old freinds & from home[.] I haid a letter from your Mother the other Day[.] she was then well[.] your Brother ~~Tho~~ [crossed out] John is in London at present[.] he is well[.] he is to Wret to you by this uprtunity[.] I haid a Capt Bowrook her from amaricad [America] with a letter from your Brothers wich I shale enclose in this paceges[.] you will have letters from orkney & Newes that will not be very agreble I mene

respecting the young leaday that you Corspond with[.] She Mared last
winter to Mr Andrew Moory [Murray?][.] I have no Dout bot the newes
will be a tryel to you bot I hope that it will be for your profit[.] you mos
looke upone it as from that suprem being that hais ben your freind & your
geed [guide] you a most have your owen[.] Thomas wood is maried to the
second Daughter of Docter Allen[.] I am tould ther is 25 yers Desfornce in
ther age[.] I had Mr Clouston her yesterDay[.] he Deisers his respects to
you & to say that the Company haid maid him a present of £10 Pounds for
extra work in the Eagle[.] he is going to Mai[n]land as ther is ben a gret
Dele of sickenes in London this winter[.] Mr Croy is haid the small pox &
much marked[.] Jessy Huray is haid them but not much marked[.] M^rs
Laughton bured her little Neese last week[.] My Brother is ben in my
House sicke all the winter bot is now gust [just] welle & is this Day Joind
the Preince of Wells [Prince of Wales] Capt Royel [Royal] Commands
her[.] Mr Reid is stile second meet [mate][.] Mr Westren is ben at hom & is
seiled for the sam voyage again[.] I haid a letter from my husbund on
Chrumistmus Day[.] he had then sumc oile[.] Capt. Laughton is Not as yet
arivd[.] My sistrs Joines me in respets to you[.] Mr Driver is very powerly[.]
My Margaret sends hur love to you[.] she is geting fast on with her gramer
& siffering [ciphering][.] I have hard nothing of Mr Dune [Dunn] letly
[lately] bot I hope to se him in London soune[.] Dear Sur I Conclud this
wishing for your helth & safty shall be the prayer of your seincer freind
    Margaret Miller

    Margaret Miller's mention of the marriage of "the young leaday that you
Corspond with" suggests that there were more good reasons for Charles to
feel unwelcome in Britain when the time came to return. At any rate, by September 1838, Margaret Humphreys knew where her son was and wrote to
him again – this time more gently, as she called him her "kind and lovely
Son."

Capt Charles Humphreys, Honourable HBCo^ys Barque Columbia,
Collumbia River,
Care Willm Smith Esqr, Hudson B^y House, London

Stromness 1st Septr 1838–

    My Dear Son
    I hope and trust in almighty God long before you receive this you will
have arrived at your destined port in safety and that you and your ships
Company is all well and happy and I trust by keeping good order in your
Vessel you will not allow them to impose on your good nature[.] I hope my

dear son you will be Cautious and gaurd against those people you have
gone among as they are not to trust and at a time when you least expect
they may doe you injury – the Natives I mean but my hope is placed in
God alone for the preservation and safety of your most Dear and Valueable
person[.] it is only from a few of my once Numerous family that I expect
any Comfort from, those how are left me would bestow it Could their
Circumstance allow and I trust by a sober steady well regulated life you will
be blessed by your God and held in respect by your Bretheren of Man,
what a Sweet Consolation will this afford to your own mind and a peace
that the World Cannot give nor take away. My lovely son take a Mothers
advice doe not neglect your duty to your Heavenly Father and he will
afford you relief in all your distreses[.] doe not weary on account of your
long Voyage, Nine Months hase now past and I hop that a good and
Gracious father will help you to bear with hope and patience your long
absence from your Native Country[.] I shall ever pray may peace be within
her walls and prosperity within her pallaces[.] they shall prosper that love
her[.] I will seek they peace O God[.] no doubt the time hase appeard long
and dreary to me since you went away but the gleam of hope that is
kindled in my Breast with a firm belief in a most kind and gracious Father
assures me he will protect and preserve his own people and bring them in
Saftey through their greatest trouble[.] my kind and lovely Son what
Comfort this brings to a longing mother to be I hope in the full assurance
that Christ will stick Closer by you then a Brother if you love and fear
him – I have not hade any word from Tho⁵ Since you left England[.] it is
not I am sure through any neglect but I think from a great pressure of
Bussieness. John poor man is well and gone to archangel[.] your Sister Jean
and her family is in good health and Mʳ Dunn and his Dear little Motherless
infants are well may the almighty be their friend and guid them in the
paths of Virtue. I am sorry to say there is no accounts of your Brother
James[.] I am afraid it hase been ane evil Hour and unlucy Step for him
when he left Halifax- and I have had a letter from Alexander from New
Orleans he was in good health and making a living[.] Your Brother Robᵗ is
away Just now at the Herring fishing but it does not appear to be successfull

   the present Crop all over England and Scotland is verry backward and
provisions of every sort is on the rise but whey should we Complain God is
ever kind and will bring about for our Comfort many unforseen mercees[.]
we are in good health bless God and doing the best we can and if I only
knew you were well I would be Contented[.] I have taken the earliest
opportunity of writing you by one of the Coʸˢ ships going out to Collumbea
which I hope you will write me by the earliest opportunity and send it by

the Co^ys letters as I think it will be the safest way. My Dear Tom hase been verry attentive to me[.] I wish the almighty may bless you Both[.] my Son my dear Son I love you[.] it is with tears of love I write you this letter and the kind respect of a Mother[.] may it please God to bless you with every Christian grace and Virtue that adorns a follower of Jesus Christ and may you prove a Worthy Member of Society this shall ever be the prayer of a kind Mother – be faithfull in all the trust Committed to you be faithfull untill death and Christ shall give the a Crown of life[.] My Darling Son Remember you have ane account to give to God of your deeds done in the Body[.] he hase been pleased so far to prosper you in your undertakings and to try you to see what good use you will make of all his blessings therefore embazel nothing[.] accept of my most Cordial love and affections and I ever will remain your kind and affectionate Mother while Margt Humphrey

Ca^pt Charles Humphrey of the Barque Collumbia [*Columbia*], Collumbia River

P.S. I hope you will miss no opportunity in Writing me with all particulars – Yours M H –

The extremity of Margaret's depression had moderated in the year since her daughter's death, perhaps because of her firm religious faith. Her words to her son show her to be hopeful that, with God's help, things would work out for all of her children. Yet her longing was still intense. Picturing her situation takes an act of the imagination on our part in an era when we have come to expect that parents will not rely on their children for their support in old age. In our time, when several means of instant communication are available to mothers whose sons do not take time to keep in touch, we have to imagine the frustrations and fears that Margaret had concerning her many sons. The widow Margaret, at sixty-five years, was seemingly alone much of the time and then had to worry about John, who had left for the dangerous voyage north to Archangel, Thomas, who still had not written, Robert, who had gone to the herring fishery, Alexander in New Orleans, and Charles on the other side of the world. Records show that her son James, a medical doctor, also moved around a fair bit: first to Halifax, then to serve in the war in Mexico, and finally to Boston. She complained that he did not keep in touch with his mother. Such a mother is likely to imagine terrible fates befalling her sons. Margaret, it seems, had moved from worrying about Charles's personal faults to the fear that he would be injured by the Aboriginal peoples in the

Columbia Department, a not unrealistic worry, since men had died in such confrontations. In fact, in 1827 a party that went ashore from the *Cadboro* to get water at Cape Lazlo on the east coast of Vancouver Island was attacked and Edward Driver of Kirkwall, in the Orkneys, was killed. The story of this man's death ten years previously would certainly be known in Orkney.

Charles Humphreys's fate was to be quite different but tragic in another way. For a time, he remained as master of the barque *Columbia,* plying the route between London and the Columbia Department. He must have married in the summer of 1842, because Company records show a request for £60 per annum for Mrs. C. Humphreys, to be paid quarterly (see Rea story, entry 44, for reference to Mrs. Humphreys). Chief Factor John McLoughlin agreed to allow him to bring his wife into the country. However, his mother's earlier concerns about his character were not unfounded, as there were complaints of his leadership ability that the Company asked him to answer during his stopover in London in 1842. In 1840 his first mate, William Heath, had refused duty (see entry 29), men had deserted, and he had had other problems to contend with. He wrote a private letter to Richard Drew, the Company committee member responsible for shipping concerns, to describe a strange incident involving a relative of George Simpson, Governor in North America for the Hudson's Bay Company:

> I have done myself the satisfaction of replying to the charges made against me which I believe is principally owing to the reports of M^r A[emilius] Simpson, Who, When Supercargo on the California Voyage behaved very unbecoming. We had no peace with him, He cut the Stewards head by throwing Glasses at him and also my face which was done by throwing his Watch at me after the Glasses was removed, in truth, he went on deck naked & Commenced dancing among the Crew. I made a Complaint to M^r McLoughlin who said no more than that he was sorry to hear of two officers quarrel in the same service.

It might well be the politic thing not to call too much attention to the behaviour of a relative of a governor of the Company, as McLoughlin, if not Humphreys, would well know. Meanwhile Charles had written a more public letter to Drew in his own defence, without naming Simpson, stating that "if i am ill tempered & Changeable I feel extremely sorry for it . . . [but] I met many Just causes of Provocation. I acknowledge having been twice intoxicated since a Master Mariner in the Hon. Co's Service, on both occasions after a safe arrival at Woahoo."

Charles Humphreys was reappointed as captain of the *Columbia* until 1844, when he became master of the *Beaver,* the Company's steamship on the coastal service. This appointment proved to be a very unfortunate one.

Charles's own letter to the Company two years later, in August 1846, details his side of the story:

> In obedience to your request I beg leave with great deference to detail to you more particularly the circumstances which give rise to my giving up command of the Hon. Hudson's Bay Company Steamer Beaver stationed on the N.W. Coast of America.
>
> As far back as September 1842 I left London on my passage to Columbia River in Command of the ship Columbia and arrived at Fort Vancouver on the 2 May 1843 and continued coasting in that Vessal until November 1844 when I was removed from said Ship by the express verbal instructions of Chief Factor McLoughlin, on the condition and understanding that I was to resume the Command of the Cowlitz and on this understanding I delivered up to him the Ships papers. Two days afterwards I received contrary instructions from C[hief] F[actor] McLoughlin to proceed to [Fort] Nisqually and take charge of the Steamer Beaver and after demonstrating with him as to the impropriety of his giving these instructions in opposition to previous orders I notwithstanding immediately proceeded to Nisqually (in terms of a letter of instructions of date 5 November 1844) to take charge of the Steamer, but finding the Mate who was to act under me Mr. Latt[ey], had been discharged two years previously from the Columbia then under my Command, for disobedience of orders and highly improper conduct, for having threatened the lives of some of the Crew[,] I had some hesitation in proceeding with him without another Officer being appointed, but in order to facilitate Matters I wa[i]ved all opposition and proceeded to Fort Simpson where I arrived on the 20 January 1845 and considered it my duty from the riotous and improper conduct of the Mate during the passage northward to discharge him from the Steamer and having then received another letter of instructions from Mr Work of date 5 February 1845 to proceed forthwith to Sitka and from that period the 25 September I had the sole charge and responsibility of trading with the Indians, who in all their transactions were treacherous and required to be strictly watched, without the Assistance or aid of any Subordinate Officer whatever. In consequence of which I found my health so much impaired by excessive labour and fatigue that ease was esentially necessary for the preservative of my life.
>
> It was these circumstances and from the dangerous state of our health, and the unpleasant way in which I was placed in consequence of what I have stated that I was compelled to give up Command and return home.

What Charles's letter does not mention is that, by 1845, his superior Chief Trader John Work had begun to notice significant changes in him. Not only was his physical health a problem but his mental health was also in doubt.

Company officials were concerned enough to relieve him of his command of the *Beaver*, even though he had traded successfully and his accounts were in order. There may be some question of the Company's responsibility for Humphreys's situation. As he himself noted, he "complain[ed] to Mr Work frequently respecting my situation without avail although there was a Sea-faring Officer at hand [to take Lattey's place], until at length my health became as ill as it well could be and under such feelings I was compelled to give up Command." John Work was right to suspect Humphreys's mental health. On the way back to Britain as a passenger on the *Cowlitz* Charles attempted suicide by taking laudanum, a tincture of opium. Like his mother, Charles seemed to have suffered from depression to an extreme degree, but it is important to note that he always did his job, keeping records and continuing trading, throughout his crisis.

Not only did mother and son share a similar emotional disposition, but both also wrote cogent letters of appeal to the Company. After Charles came home, Margaret wrote in November 1846 to Company Secretary William Smith. She had written to Smith three times before, in 1841, worried about her son's whereabouts, and again in May and June 1842, concerned about his safety. In these letters she did not fail to remind Smith that her "poor son is my Sole dependance and support, in this world." In 1846 she took up her pen to defend her son's reputation and work:

> I beg Most respectfully to Solicit your favourable attention to the Case of My son Charles Humphreys lately in the Service of the Honourable Hudson Bay Company [.] he hase been Compelled on account of bad health to come home in the Meantime, and the dangerous nature of the employment he was engaged in being in the Command of a Steamer going from place to place on the N W Coast of America in Search of furs among Savage tribes of Indians without ane officer of any kind to assist him, if under these Circumstances he hase done Wrong in leaving the employment I trust you will be pleased to excuse the necessity under which he conceived himself Compelled to act as he hase done, and have the kindness to exercise your patronage in order to get him again taken into the employment of the Company[.] my reason for asking this favour is because I not only flatter my self that upon Investigation you will find a Sufficient Justification for my Sons procedure but because I am a poor widow and in a great measure dependant upon the assistance which my son can afford me, ane aid which he cannot give when he is out of employment[.] trusting that this Communication from a Mother will be favourably received and attended to and as it hase pleased your Heavenly father to Confer great Honours on you here in this World I pray he may have a Crown of Glory Laid up for you in heaven as a reward for being the friend of the Fatherless and Widow.

Hudson's Bay House on Fenchurch Street in 1854, the address to which so many of the letters were directed, and where they were preserved when they could not be delivered.

The barque *Vancouver* rounding Cape Disappointment at the mouth of the Columbia River in September 1845.

Fort George (formerly Astoria, in present-day Oregon) at the mouth of the Columbia River had been the headquarters of the Columbia Department from 1821 to 1825, but by 1845 it was a small outlook post.

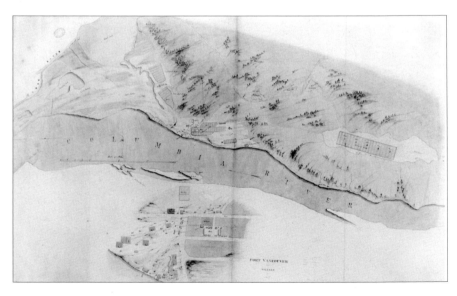

Situated a treacherous sail up the Columbia River, Fort Vancouver, in present-day Washington state, served as headquarters of the Columbia Department from 1825 to 1849. This map depicts the establishment in 1846.

By 1846, the year the boundary was established at the forty-ninth parallel of latitude, Fort Vancouver was a substantial settlement.

[AUGUST 26, 1848.

VANCOUVER ISLAND.—THE HUDSON BAY COMPANY'S ESTABLISHMENT.

The year after this drawing appeared in the *Illustrated London News,* 26 August 1848, Fort Victoria on Vancouver Island became the headquarters of the Columbia Department.

The port of Honolulu on Oahu in the Sandwich Islands (Hawai'i) was a meeting place for ships from around the world and a destination for salmon and timber from the Company's operations on the west coast.

Fort Nisqually and the Nisqually farm of the Puget's Sound Agricultural Company, on the shortest route between Fort Victoria and Fort Vancouver, was the destination for many of the men represented in these letters.

Fort Rupert, on the north coast of Vancouver Island, was the remote location of the Company's first attempt to develop coal mines in 1849, shown here in 1866.

By 1852 the Company had turned to Nanaimo as the focus of its coal-mining operations. Here the *Beaver*, the first steamship on the coast, is depicted aground at low tide on 20 May 1858.

The *Princess Royal* carried miners under George Robinson to the coal mines at Nanaimo. The last of the seamen mentioned (Robert Wilson, entry 74) was aboard this ship in 1854, the date this was painted.

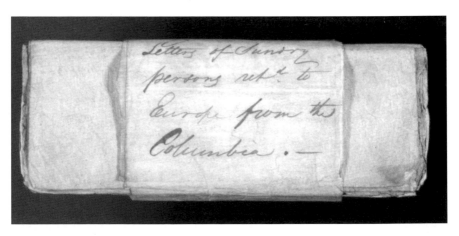

The "Sundry letters" wrapper that once enclosed the undelivered letters.

James Blackie in his 1832 letter from Fort Vancouver to his sister in London, took the occasion to propose marriage to his friend Kitty (entry 5).

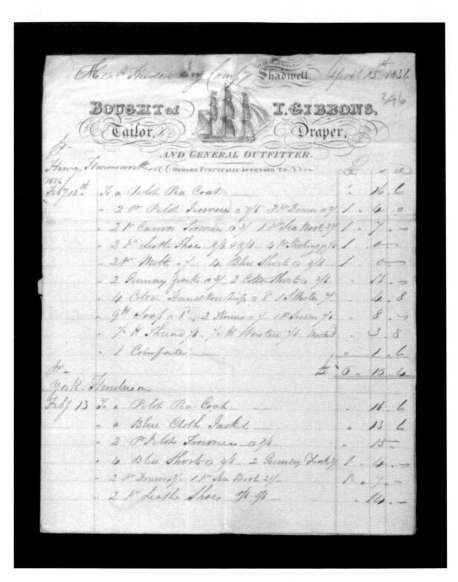

This tailor order lists the outfit supplied to Henry Harmsworth for his work with the Company on his last trip to the coast (entry 13).

John Spence, an Orcadian, wrote in 1835 from the *Prince Rupert* anchored at York Factory to inquire about Margaret, his "old lady," at Fort Vancouver (entry 16).

This cross-written letter to George Prattent illustrates how a single sheet of paper could be used to hold the maximum amount of news (entry 20).

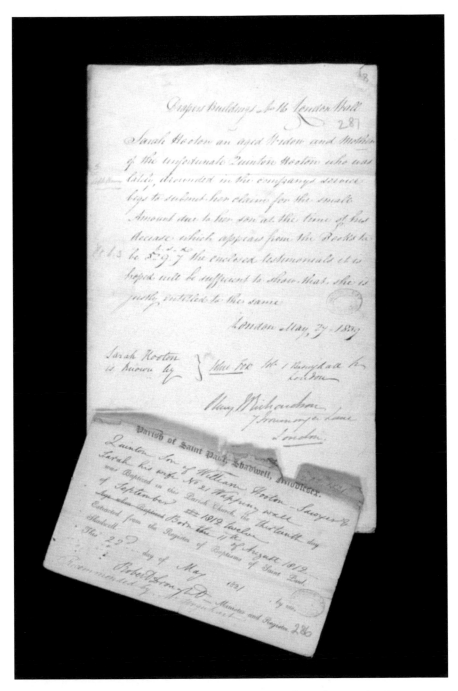

Mrs Hooten, from London, sent her dead son's baptismal certificate to the Company in order to claim the small amount due to him, a mere £5 6s. 3d. by the Company secretary's calculations (entry 26).

In 1838 Thomas Heath wrote of the good fishing and local gossip to his brother William (entry 29).

Several of the letters from Margaret Simpson to her husband, James, written in 1842 and 1849 from Kincardine, Scotland (entry 37).

Bromley September 19th 1847

My Dear Brother I write these
few lines hoping to find you quite
well as it leaves me at present
Dear Brother How do you like

the sea Dear Brother do you think
I improve in my writing Dear Brother
I should be very glad to see you
When I come to sea I shall not
come as a common sailor but be a
captain at once Dear Brother I
have been were you have not
been Dear Brother I have been
in a whales belley So no more
from your affectionate Brother

EDWARD WALLIS

HUDSON'S BAY COMPANY

In 1847 young Edward Wallis wrote to his brother of his plans to follow him to sea (entry 54).

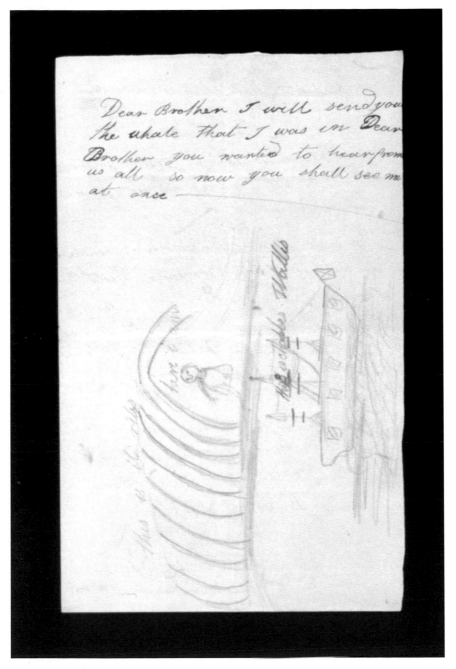

Edward Wallis drew a picture of himself enclosed by the ribs of a whale, and of his brother Charles in the crow's nest of his ship, the *Columbia* (entry 54).

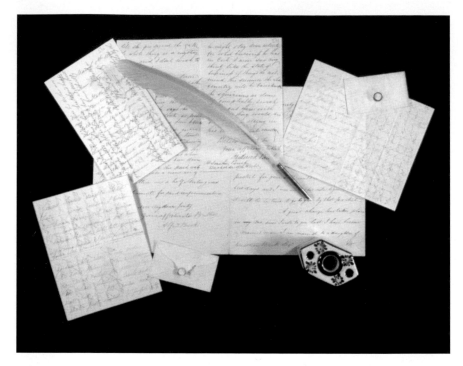

A few of the seventeen letters written in 1844 and 1848 by the very literate Buck family of Cork, Ireland, to young Jonathan, whose brother addressed him on the "Backside of the World" (entry 47).

Neither Margaret's appeal to the Company's sense of responsibility for putting her son in a bad situation, nor her appeal on behalf of the fatherless, nor her oft-repeated reasoning that a poor widow deserves some consideration, had much effect on the Company.

In October 1846 Charles sought a job in the Oriental Navigation Company but failed to receive employment. He had written to the Company asking for a reference, but there is no record of such a reference being given. At age thirty-six, Charles had begun a meteoric rise in the Company service. Given a great deal of responsibility at a very young age, and driven by difficult circumstances and his own insecurities, at mid-life he found himself exhausted and plagued by an impossible workload, to which suicide must have seemed, for a moment, the only solution. But there seems to have been little forgiveness on the part of his employers for a stress-related illness that they may have helped to cause; the idea of a potentially suicidal master was a risk they were unwilling to take. We know nothing more of Charles Humphreys. The only other fact we know for certain is that his mother Margaret was still working, as a midwife, in the 1851 Stromness Census. By then she would have been seventy-eight years old. Margaret, like her son Charles, did indeed have a life of care and woe.

25   WILLIAM RIDLER: *Every wish was Gratified except seeing of you*

William Ridler was a seaman and gunner on the *Nereide* when he left London on 13 February 1836. He served on the same ship for a year on the west coast after his arrival on 26 August 1836, but all was not well on the *Nereide*. On 31 May 1837, just as the ship was ready to sail to Fort Simpson, Nass, with trading goods, the entire crew went to Chief Factor John McLoughlin, the highest authority on the west coast, to complain about their captain, David Home. Reading the official correspondence regarding this incident gives us insight into the lives of the men aboard the Company ships. Chief Trader James Douglas, second-in-command to McLoughlin, wrote to Governor George Simpson describing the incident:

> At this urgent moment we were informed of a lawless combination of the crew, who, almost, to a man, refused to serve under Captain Home, on the ground of alleged severity & excessive duty, a circumstance which occasioned a vexatious delay of 17 days. At the request of Captain Home the complaints advanced by the disaffected crew were heard & their several depositions, on oath, taken, but they completely failed in establishing any grievance worthy of attention, and, in fact, their several charges were so unsupported by evidence either direct or circumstantial that no Court in England would have entertained them for a

moment. A moderate course was pursued by Dr McLoughlin, who felt justly alarmed lest the spirit of insubordination should extend itself to the crews of the other vessels the *Lama* & *Cadboro* then nearly ready for sea; and thereby the business of the whole Naval Department be at a stand.

The crew did not return to work when McLoughlin gave in to one of their minor demands. They decided to hold out for their major goal, a new master. McLoughlin had them confined in irons and fed on prisoner rations. By 14 June most of the crew had given in and, in a letter to London, John McLoughlin describes the extreme measures he felt he had to take with the remaining mutineers:

> On the 14th I went on board the *Nereide,* and . . . ordered John Lucas and John Jarvis to be brought before me, and on refusing to return to their Duty, had a Dozen lashes given to each one of them. On the 15th I went again on board . . . At first Lucas and Jarvis refused to return to their Duty; the Crew on being ordered up, came to me, and asked if I was going to Flog these men again, in a way between pleading and menacing; I told them they were called to see what was done, that we did not bring men to the country to Flog them, but to perform certain Duties, and if they would not do their Duty by fair means, we would try if other means would not do, as I was determined they would do their Duty; During this conversation, the Captain with the Two Officers Messrs Dodd & Lattie were busy taking the Two men to the Rigging, but when they saw themselves going to be tied up, they said they would return to their duty, and I ordered them to be released, and since then they have all done their duty well. Before leaving the Nereide, after all the crew returned to their duty, I ordered Wm. Redlur [Ridler] the Boatswain to be reduced to a Foremast man, for refusing to make a Cat [a whip] when ordered to do so by Mr. Dodd chief mate, to whome he replied it was a thing he never had done, or would do.

William Ridler, as boatswain, had disobeyed a direct order, and he suffered for his disobedience. In spite of the Company's preference to avoid corporal punishment, the officers sometimes resorted to force on the west coast where men were often tempted to desert or defy orders and were not easy to replace. After this incident, Ridler joined the *Columbia* as boatswain. A year after her brother's demotion, Ridler's sister writes a letter with news that would not be likely to raise his spirits. The black-bordered paper would have announced the nature of its contents, had he received the letter.

⮀ William Ridler, Columbia

Gravesend May 20th 1838

> Dear Brother
> This comes with my kind love to you Hoping it will find you in good
> health As it leaves us at present[.] I write to inform You of the death of
> your Mother[.] She died The 18 of last december after being Confined To
> her bed Ten months[.] every wish was Gratified except seeing of you even
> by having Your likeness buried with her[.] We received Your letter last April
> Twelve months and was Sorry to hear you was so ill[.] we have been Rather
> Unfortunate by the long illness of Mother but I am happy to say she
> wanted for Nothing for it was Mould's whole Study[.] he Paid for her
> Funeral as freely as if it had been His own Mother[.] I hope we shall meet
> once More That we can Talk Things over[.] When you write direct to 16
> Windmill St as we As we [repetition] have made A Change I hope for[.]
> We applied to the Hutson bay company And they sent the letter out, M^r
> Adams Is dead and [I] understand That he left nothing For the girls, We
> hope we shall hear from You as soon as possible as the last returns The
> Hutson bay company had from you Was in June, we Join our love Me
> Mould and Sarah
> So no more at present
> From your Affectionate
> Sister P Mould

His sister's concern that she has had only one letter, one that told of his
poor health, and her worry that the last information the Company had of
him was in June 1837 indicate the state of uncertainty about the fate of their
loved ones that many families felt. This time that worry was justified. At the
moment his sister was writing, William had been dead for four months. Not
long after his mother was buried without even his "likeness," thwarted of her
dying wish to see her son, William drowned with four others crossing the
Columbia River on 26 January 1838. Ironically, the hated Captain Home was
among those who drowned with Ridler. The Company received a letter from
Ridler's widow, Mary, on 6 November 1838, by which time she had learned
of his death. Unable to write the letter herself, she signed it with her mark
and, at the secretary's request, sent a sworn declaration indicating that her
marriage had taken place at Portsmouth on 1 July 1822. She had received no
money from him since he had sailed and was then "a widow without any
other means of support than my own labour [and] consequently in great distress." It was her hope that this declaration – witnessed by a Justice of the

Peace and certified by baker William Beard, Gravesend, and grocer John James Starbuck – would open the purse strings of the Hudson's Bay Company. On 14 November, the Company secretary asked her to look in, so that she could get some money. She must have been comforted when she was handed the sum of £19 7s. 10d., a small fortune to a destitute widow and the equivalent of almost one year of her husband's wages.

26   QUINTON HOOTEN: *I am very unesy about you*

Like William Ridler, Quinton Hooten sailed as a seaman on the *Nereide* out of London in 1836, and, as his mother's letter indicates, had only written home once in three years. It was not unusual for mothers to be uneasy about more than one son, as Sarah is. The economic conditions she described on the home front sometimes sent whole families of sons into the employ of various overseas ventures.

∿   For Quinton Hooton on Board the Ship Nerenede [*Nereide*] at Columbia

November 27 1838 London

My Dear son
   this comes Whith My kind Love to you Hoping this Will Find you in Good Health as it Leaves us all at preasent[.] Dear son i am very unesy about you for We have only had one Letter since you Been Gone[.] Dear son your Brothers and sisters sends ther kind Love to you All But your Brother Fredrick and im We know Nothing About for We have Not heard frome him since you Been gone Which Makes Me very uneasy[.] Dear son your Brother phillip is Married again and has got another Boy Which Makes Four Boys And them all Quite Well and your Brother Leonard is Doing very Well and your sister Mary as got Married to a young Man a Box and packing case Maker the Name is Lawson and thay Both send ther Love and We should Like to see you once More and send us Word How Long you think you shall Be Before you come home for i am Getting old and i May Not Live for ever But i should Like to see you and your Brother fredrick once More then i shall Be happy[.] Dear son M^r and Mrs Tovey is Much as usual and thay Live ~~have~~ [crossed out] in No 18 foxses Lane know and Mrs Barry is Dead and he has Left Betsy And your cousin Macdonald and her two Daughters send ther kind Lov to you and thay are Quite Well at present[.] Exther [Esther] Gower sends her kind Love to you and she is growing a very fine young Woman But We have Look out a good Many Nice young Woman and ther all a going to Waite to see you first for i Remember you

said that you should get Married When you come home But i understand their going to be a War and times are very Bad in London and every think is very Dear and Nothing to Do for Men and What ther is to Do is paid for so Bad that poor people cant scarce Live so No More at present From your affectionate Mother Mrs Hooton Please to Direct for Mrs Hooton at Mrs Russell N° 16 Drapers Building London Wall opposite Finsbury curcus city

The many nice young women who were waiting to see Quinton when he might have returned home to choose a bride would have had to look elsewhere. Long before his mother's letter – full of her desire to see her absent sons once more – reached Fort Vancouver, Quinton was dead. In late May 1837 he had been one of the sailors who went on strike against the treatment of Captain Home on board the *Nereide* (see William Ridler, entry 25). He had been put on prisoner rations of bread and water, but avoided the lash and the punishment of receiving only one cup of grog a day by returning to duty. By January 1838 he and three other crewmen shared a watery grave with their captain. In a letter to Governor George Simpson, Chief Trader James Douglas described the incident:

I have now to enter upon a most painful subject the melancholy death of Captain Home and four seamen of the Nereide[']s crew who were drowned; on the 26th of January last in crossing this River in the ship's Long Boat from Red Bluff where the vessel was anchored, to Fort George [Astoria, Oregon]. The weather was moderate when they left the vessel and they were seen running under a press of sail in the direction of Tongue Point until concealed from view by the intervention of a slight snow shower, When the weather cleared up, the Boat could no where be seen, a circumstance that passed unoticed at the time; but on the following day the protracted absence of the Party excited some uneasiness. The attention of Mr Lattie, one of the Officers on board was attracted by an unusual object appearing about mid channel, which on examination, was found to be the Mast head of the absent Boat: lying there submerged, with every rope fast and every sail extended, as if the boat had been suddenly overset by a violent gust of wind leaving the unfortunate crew no time to ease the sheets, or take other measures for their safety and they were probably hurried into their watery grave without a struggle.

By May 1839 Sarah Hooten had learned of her son's sad fate and sent in his baptismal certificate and a letter signed by John Fox and Henry Richardson certifying her claim to his account of £5 9s. 7d., revised to £5 6s. 3d. by the punctilious Company secretary.

27 JOHN WILMOT: *Hop that you Will not think of stoping in a contry that maks*
    miserabell wile you have a freand in World

John Wilmot also left London aboard the *Nereide* in 1836 and, after two years'
absence, his sister's letter was full of worry about the unhappiness he expressed in his letter, which she had just received. Evidence shows Wilmot had
very good reason to be unhappy, since he is recorded as one of the sailors put
in irons for participating in the strike from 31 May to 10 June 1837 (see
William Ridler, entry 25).

~ For John Wilbner, From Mr Scotts Kingsland, Went Out in the Ship
   Neriad to Columbia River

May 21 ^1838

   Dear Brother
   this Comes with my kind Love and James and the Children and are
   much disppointed at you not revcieve our Last Leter sent on November 27
   1836[.] i received a Leter on May 21 1838 an was Much Heart to Hear that
   you ware so yn happey an hop that you Will not think of stoping in a
   contry that maks miserabell wile you have a freand in World[.] Dear
   Brother your Leteres is so short your first Letter sed that your ship mate
   wad call an Tell me all about you and Cantrey but he never Cam near me
   at tall[.] i fell much heart to think that you should think you ware forgot[.]
   i pray to God for your safe Returne[.] owat a hapey meting we shall have[.]
   James is doing well in trade[.] Emen [Emma?] as Left Cranes[.] i have got
   her a Good place and hop she will be a comfort for you wen you return[.]
   dear Brother i receved ½ Pay for 3 Munth wich wos £3 Pound and was told
   that Hudsons Bay Hous house paid no more tell tha heard from you[.] i
   tell you in Case you should leve the ship befor your times his ~~you~~ [crossed
   out] yp[.] old Connor is ~~dead~~ [crossed out] Dead and old mankey dide
   with the Brane fever and Lays in Pla[i]stow Garden after a Long ilness wich
   you may get my Long leter Before you sey this Leter[.] Pray John dont for
   God sake give up to Drink Because your un hapey[.] i hop this will with
   love &c the Larst time Sea will see you[.] John Dont forget to write a Long
   Leter wen you Get this as i shall Be uncomfortabell tell i hear from you
   agane[.] i shall write agane in 3 Months[.] Dear John i have nothing to tell
   you at presant more than i have don
       Mr Scott and all the Famley Wish your Safe Returne and all the Lettel
   Children sends you A Kiss
       Pray Dont Lat your ship mates see this Leter as i am not well wen i write
   as i am a shemed of it

your Dear Sister
Elizabeth Scott
and Brother James

PS I Goe everey 3 Months to your Crews for a Leter

[on the cover] Preserve me O God for in the[e] do i Put m[y] trust

John Wilmot escaped the fate of his mates William Ridler and Quinton Hooten (entries 25 and 26) and came home a year later. He served as a seaman on the *Columbia*'s return voyage in 1838-9, thus missing his sister's letter. Despite his former troubles under Captain Home, he must have had a clean record otherwise, since the Company rehired him. Perhaps his "miserabell" experiences had not turned him to drink as his sister worried it would. He departed again on the *Columbia* in 1840 and stayed on as a seaman until 1845, making two more return voyages.

28 JOHN COON: *Ples god you get this leter Saf*

John Coon began service with the Company on 15 September 1832, when he went to the Columbia Department aboard the *Ganymede* as a seaman. Once on the coast he served aboard the *Lama* from 18 July 1833 to 10 November 1834, when he worked the return trip to London aboard the *Eagle,* arriving in London 6 June 1835. He did the London-Columbia-London route twice more between 1835 and 1839. This letter was from a woman who seemed to have been more than her signature of "sincer friend" might indicate. Despite her difficulties with spelling, Ellenor's desire to receive some reply to her letter from her "der Coun" was intense and a bit forlorn after her miscarriage. Her reference to the "dounes," is to "The Downs," a good anchorage on the English Channel off the town of Deal. This was usually the last stop a ship made, waiting for a favourable wind before heading out to sea. The fact that Ellenor wished she had gone there with John – his last opportunity to take up his place aboard ship – is another indication that the two were lovers.

For Jhoun Coun, Boson on bord of the Cullombere, Capten houmifres, Coullombere river
[readdressed by Company secretary] John Coone, Boatswain on board the Columbia, Capt Humphries, Columbia River

london aprell the 22 1838

My der

Frind this Comes with My kind love to you hoping that thes fiou [few] liends [lines] will find you in good thellth [health] as it leves Me bout [but] very porley at presint for My der Coun i have had a vrey havey MisCarrey [miscarriage] bout thank god i ham a geting beter noy [now.] Bout as for aney oun doun the pond i have not hered [heard] nor sen [seen] aneything of non of Harr[a]y and My der Coun when i left you i wich [wish] i had a gon to the dounes [Downs] with you for it Cost Me as Mooch [much] befro [before] i got houp [up] to london for all the pots [post] wagon[.] i sent you a leter to the downs bout i dount sopose you got it or helse you wudd have a sent Me a anser to it and My der Coun ples god you get this leter Saf[e.] i hope you will Send Me anser to it and let Me no if you are a going to Stope out for 3 cheres [years] and when you rite to Me drect [direct] for Ellenor Smith no 4 Wallburg Street sent gorigis in the est [St. George's in the East.] so god belles [bless] you til ples god i see [you][.] so no Mor at present from your sincer friend and well wisher till dette Ellenor Smith

We cannot know if Ellenor was reunited with her "der Coun" but we can speculate about when the two were together before the letter was written. Coon's layovers in London occurred between 5 June and 24 August 1835 and between 2 May and 18 November 1837. The miscarriage and letter would both have been after this last sojourn. Coon arrived back in London from his last voyage to the Columbia Department on 21 May 1839. This letter would have been on its way out when he was coming home. The only further knowledge we have of John Coon is that William Green collected his wages for him on 31 August 1839, as Coon was unwell and unfit for duty.

29 WILLIAM HEATH: *A pleasantly situated cottage with a porch in front covered with ivy wherein you might smoke your pipe to solace the Evening of your days*

William Heath began his service with the Company as a young second mate of twenty-two, leaving London on the *Ganymede.* The voyage to the Columbia Department lasted from 15 September 1832 to 1 May 1833, and he narrowly escaped drowning when he fell from the rope ladder by which he was climbing from the rigging to the maintop (Tolmie 1963, 152-5). He was promoted to first mate aboard the *Vancouver* when he reached the west coast and subsequently lost all his property (worth £70 by his account) when that ship was wrecked (see Alexander Duncan story, entry 14). He transferred in 1834 to the *Cadboro,* and did not return to London until 12 May 1837.

In 1836 William Burris, a seaman, had described William Heath as "drunk as a Beast" (Burley 1997, 177). On his return voyage, as first mate aboard the *Columbia,* Heath refused duty – perhaps while drunk – and was replaced by Charles Chitty at Oahu. In May 1837 Heath wrote to the Company, reminding them of his loyal service and the testimonials of former captains Alexander Duncan and William Eales; he asked to receive his back pay and to be considered eligible for future employment. He was employed again, and by 18 November 1837 he was again headed west as first mate on the *Columbia* in what would prove to be a two-year round trip, which brought him again to London on 21 May 1839. In the meantime he would have missed four letters that followed him on the 1838 ship out, letters from brother Thomas and sisters Fanny and Ellen, as well as the following letter from former captain William Darby in London. Darby refers to several officers of the Company serving on the west coast, including Chief Factor McLoughlin and Chief Trader Douglas. The new commander to whom Darby referred is Captain Humphreys (entry 24).

Mr W. Heath, Ship Columbia, Columbia River, North West Coast of America

London May 24 1838

Dear Heath

I am rather surprised at not hearing from your Brother since you left England about that five pounds you had of me just before you sailed[.] after waiting some 3 Months I wrote to him but received no answer to my letter[.] should you not be comeing home I will thank you to send me an order for it on the Company which you can easily procure from them out there or request Mr Smith by letter to him to pay me and charge it to your Account. Bolton [Henry Edward Boulton] is Chief Mate in the Prince of Wales with Royal, I am going out to Sydney, and I believe I have got Eales a Staith[e] Master [wharf master] Situation at Stoc[k]ton in North, a shore Berth, and a house to live in[.] Handly is come home and is now on the shelf waiting (Prattent Do [ditto]) and I believe quite hard up. please to remember me to Capt Home McNeil Brotchie and all the other Naval men I know in the Service[.] if you have an opportunity I shall be happy to hear from and see you also when you return[.] all your Friends at Wycomb[e] I believe are quite well[.] when you come home I shall be living close to Maidenhead only ½ mile or less from the Town[.] we have left Cookham[.] should you see Mr Walker you may ask him for the Money for that Watch he had of me the price was £8.8s[.] should the Doctor McLoughlin be at the Fort give my compliments to him & Douglas, Work, McLeod, Cowie,

Allen, Ray, in fact all that I know not forgetting the Clergiman and Wife [the Rev. Herbert Beaver]. if you can will you bring me home a pair of Horns[.] ask Doctor Tolmie to send me a pair for my house

How do you get on with your new Comman[d]er[?] I hope quite well[.] now mind you write to me and when you come home come and see me at North Town near Maidenhead and there write to me[.] I shall always be happy to hear from you now[.] farewell from
   yours Truly
   W Darby

William Darby had been dismissed as captain in 1837 along with George Prattent (entry 20) and in Thomas Heath's letter that follows, we learn that he was trying for a ship to Australia. No doubt he was trying to settle his affairs in England before he set off. Darby's letter brings up a subject which, like William Heath's refusal of duty, does not bode well for his future. Heath's debt is not unusual and it is certainly small considering the estate that – as we learn in the next letters – William is to inherit. That he left it unattended might not sit well in a sailing community where news of bad behaviour spreads fast, and where William Heath already had one a black mark against him.

To better understand the family letters that follow – as richly reflective of the social scene of the country gentry as a Jane Austen novel – it helps to know some of the people. William Heath had several siblings, including those who were older – Joseph Thomas, Thomas Mason, John (Jack), and Ellen – as well as Fanny, a year younger. No mention is made of Emma (born 1808) or Jane (Jennie) (born 1813), although Jennie was alive when the letters were written (McDonald 1979, 84). William's father Joseph died in 1837, but his mother, who wrote and taught music in Henley, was mentioned in Ellen's letter. There are a number of references to the settlement of an estate. George Faithorn is Fanny's fiancée and a physician, and the Mr. Smith referred to is the Company secretary who saved these letters when they could not be delivered. Mr. John Dashwood is the local landlord from whom the family leased one of the farms. "Old Parr" refers to a man who was said to have been born in 1483 and died in 1635 at the age of 152. In 1563 at eighty, he married and had a son and a daughter, both of whom died young. The first letter is from brother Thomas, who offered a delightful, if sometimes crude, glimpse into the life of a class of people to whom good sport fishing was as important as the changes in the Corn Laws. His humour – revealed in his comments that "what is blood without cash" and "We ought to go to Heaven with three or four Parsons in the Family" – indicate where Thomas stands on serious subjects such as marriage and religion.

ꙮ Mr William Heath

Mill End Farm October ~~14~~ [overwritten by] 17th 1838

Dear William –

Mr Smith informs us the Ships sail for the N.W. Coast on the 19th so I commence my letter early in order that I may recollect all the news my memory can furnish me with. In the first place I must tell you I have taken Mill End Farm on a Lease from Mr John Dashwood & Jack has taken Fryars Farm. Our new lease commences from next October but we separated last August & I must say I feel highly satisfied with the arrangement. The weather for the Harvest has been highly satisfactory & the crops exceedingly fine. The rick yard is completely filled & likewise the Barns. The price of wheat owing to a general deficiency in the crops has been great – alarmingly so I should say – as the Public are bitterly complaining & petitioning the Legislature to remove the Tax (or at any rate to alter) the existing state of the corn Laws. We have had the duty on Foreign wheat at the lowest 1^s. Altho' the importation was great amounting to Thirteen hundred thousand quarters but a very slight depression was created in the market. The general feeling seems to be that we must have wheat very high the ensuing summer.

The Mallards Court business is to be finally settled on the 1st Decr next[.] Your share I should say would be about 440£[.] I should strongly recommend its being invested in your name in the Public Funds as it will then be available at a days notice in case you might need it which I hope may not be the case as with the saving of a few more hundreds you might realize your wished for object of a pleasantly situated cottage with a porch in front covered with ivy wherein you might smoke your pipe to solace the Evening of your days. I am so strongly possessed with the practicability of realizing these hopes that I do sincerely believe it is in the power of any man with a proper regard to economy to accomplish such views. Wm Smith has visited us twice within the last two months the first time he came was in the month of August he amused himself with throwing the bait into the Waters in the Park but the devil a fish did he catch – he wanted you there to explain the mystery of the art to him. On his last visit he shot the gun off I believe about 20 times Killing Oh ye Gods! one Pheasant! I do not shoot this Season, my intention is to hunt [.] I have been out once this Season my horse carried me remarkably well. The girls I suppose have told you that Geo Faithorn is practising at Chesham[.] an excellent change it is for him – indeed I have no doubt he will realize a good fortune there. There is some chance now for Fanny[.] I hear they will be married within 12 months – I have had a narrow escape lately old Boy with a neice of my

Friend Windows[.] I had a great inclination at one time to make proposals to her. But after all what is blood without some cash? She is a very nice ladylike girl educated in France &c &c. but none the better for that. Talking of marriages who the devil do you suppose is spliced now? no less a Person – God save the Queen! than our Friend William Faithorn!!! You and I must hold up our heads now my Lad[.] I shall not despair until I attain the age of Old Parr One hundred & fifty. I have not heard whether the boy (for one is born) is to be taken with the Father & Mother round the Country as a Public spectacle: or has it at present transpired whether he is all head & body & no legs. This is by no means improbable & a damned lucky thing it would be were it so – as there would then be some chance of supporting it in an easy gentlemanly & respectable manner. I am going to walk this morning with Mr Dashwood to see him & a party pheasant shooting[.] I expect I shall regret not having taken out my certificate. however I can take the Keepers gun. They call you the otter in this neighbourhood the devil a fish have you left below the saw mill in the Park. There will be some chance now for the trout – speaking of that fish Fryer caught one this season weighing *8 lbs* & the old Brute was Goth enough to pickle it. I should have liked to pickle *him* & then smoke dry him. The most severe winter that has been experienced in this Country for the last 50 years occurred the last & what is still more extraordinary a man of the name of Murphy had predicted it 6 months before stating the particular days the frost would last when it would break up & the coldest day &c. – It created a great sensation at the time but his future prognostications were not realized.

I have heard nothing lately of the Masons[.] Harry I believe has entered the Church & Arthur is studying for it. We ought to go to Heaven with three or four Parsons in the Family. When you write to us inform me of your shooting your prospects & whether you want any thing I can forward which shall be punctually attended to – but above all things write as frequently as you can. I must now conclude with a Brothers best wishes for your success health & happiness believe me Dr William

Your affectionate Brother

Thos Mason Heath

The sisters offered more polite but still humorous and satiric views of the social scene. Both sisters were preoccupied with how appropriate appearances make the man, as indicated in their jokes about Robert Hayward's hair. Sister Ellen began with some neighbourhood gossip.

Mill End Oct – 15th 1838

My dear William I was quite happy to hear from William Smith that you had reached *Wahoo* [Oahu] or one of the Sandwich Islands in safety. At first I felt surprised that we had received no kind of intelligence from [you] but he said that no letters had arrived and that the vessels only spoke which fully accounted for your silence – We all continue just in the same quiet state as when you left no weddings, nothing at all of a stirring nature though old Jack seems fully determined to splice himself as soon as he possibly can. I suppose Tom has told you that he rents Fryers farm he spends almost all his time up there only returning to sleep and pay his usual visits to the Mill – The Mallard's Court concern is at last decided but we must sacrifice about three hundred pounds but I am sure you will agree with me that to lose only that is nothing in comparison with the chance of its remaining twelve years in Chancery – Fanny of course will give you a full true and particular account of the practice George Faithorne has taken at Chesham – Ellen stayed with us about three weeks[.] She could not bear to leave us but was obliged to go to town to take care of William's house during the confinement of his *wife*[.] He is actually Married and had been so some time before we knew anything about it and has a very smart little boy. She is a good sort of a little Woman and I like her from her great attention to her husband[.] She seems to watch every wish and he is equally attentive to her[.] The only fault is that they are a little too loving – The old Admiral has been very ill for some weeks we make Puddings or Broth for him almost every day – The complaint is a fever which has carried off several of our old neighbours Poor Betsey Phelps among the number[.] She was buried today[.] She has left a Baby only three weeks old behind her[.] M[rs] Fastnedge is in a great deal of trouble about it on account of the children but her husband was such a brute that it is really not much to be lamented – Henry Fastnedge took a wife to himself last Christmas day without the knowledge of any one. he contrived to keep it secret for about six weeks – I think it is not all improbable that Ellen Heath at the Grove will be married before long to William Chown he spends most of his Sundays there. We had heard the report for some time before we believed but I think now [cross-written] there is very little doubt of the truth of it- We had a famous harvest this year the barns and rickyard are as full as they very well can be[.] Tom succeeded uncommonly well better than some of our neighbours. M[r] Dashwood had a rick of hay burnt he estimated the loss at above a hundred pounds[.] he is very civil and obliges us with Frank

occasionally. It appears that we shall agree very well with them as our Land
Lords. Bob Hayward has sold all his property at Watlington he had spent
rather more than he ought and found it the only plan – I should not be
surprised if he lives in part of George's house at Chesham – His hair has
not been cut for some months and in dry weather hangs in ringlets about
his back of course if the day be damp it looks as if he had some pairs of
bows hung round his neck. No one can laugh or pursuade him out of it he
is most stupid for he makes himself a laughing stock let him go where he
may[.] John bought the bedstead furniture and blankets &c of the room in
which you slept – he has likewise purchased several articles of household
use which looks a little like settling. Tom has had a slight attack of love
lately. The lady was a niece of Mʳ Windows. she has now returned home
and his affection has I think abated with her absence[.] You know he is
often a little touched[.] Mama goes on much the same at Henley she has
no scholars but has published two songs which have paid her about forty
pounds. – She is very much noticed by the gentry there. – All the children
are well Harry is with us and Charles goes to school at Mʳ Ayres he gets on
famously with his drawing but is rather stupid with almost every thing
else – How I wish you were here to assist us in demolishing some potatoes
and red herrings though I dare say you will almost laugh at the idea now
you are in the land of broiled wild ducks &c &c. I must conclude my dear
William as Fanny wishes to write on the other side of this sheet. God bless
you & believe me my dear Old fellow your affectionate
     Sister Ellen –

Fanny is the next sibling to write.

     My dear William
     I know you will like to see sister *Fan's* hand writing even tho she has
nothing to tell you fresh, Tom, Ellen, and I are writing all the news of all
kinds. I am still Fanny Heath as you will see by my signature but suppose
when next I see you it will be changed. George has taken a very excellent
practice at Chesham he likes it much and is likely to make a very handsome
income, he has taken a very handsome house and pays £60 a year for it, for
the present there is some idea of Robert Hayward leasing with him, you
know Roberts bald head, well the little hair he has is suffered to grow long
and hang down on his coat and intends having it made into a sham for a
lady[.] [cross-written] did you ever know such a silly fellow, he is quite a
fright, tho of course he thinks himself being charming, and has the vanity
to suppose all the girls are in love with him. I had a letter from your flame

E. Faithorne a day or two since[.] She sends her love to you, She is gone to town to stay at her brother's whose wife has a boy[.] I think very much of you dear Will and often wish to see you[.] I hope we shall have letters from you soon telling us you are well and happy and will soon be Captain. I shall be quite proud to have C^tn Heath as my brother. I have been staying with Mr Brooksbank at Totenham for a month he was very kind I think you once met him here and he liked you much. I have a little bit of news [below address] to tell that will make you laugh; What do you think of Tom in love! it is the fact. Mr Window has had a niece staying with him and we thought Tom was vastly attentive and had taken a great fancy to *Mr Windows* [above address] when at last it appears that it is *Harriette not Richard* that takes him to Fingest two or three times a week and Alas, she is now no longer there for him to see but is gone home and poor Tom [cross-written around address] left here in the dumps. You I know will pity him as you know what it is to be crossed in love. – I dare say you are got the better of yours, the salt water has washed it away[.] Jack is still as attentive as ever at the Mill[.] He talks of being married[.] His brother in law has a son. I mean Mr Gillet[.] I must now dear Will say good bye good night God bless you and believe me your affectionate Sister

    Fanny

In a final letter, written after another milder winter has passed, brother Tom indicated that things were going well with the estate. Tom had lost none of his humour, as he made fun of the sex life of others, as in his first letter, and lets us know that William's letters have had similar *double entendres*. William's share of the inherited estate was noted.

Mr Wm Heath,
[in another hand] Fort Vancouver or elsewhere

Mill End Farm. February. 17th 1839 –

    Dear William, –
    I was in London last week Endeavouring to make arrangements for the Settlement of the Mallards Court Estate & Succeeded as far as the annexed statement. There has been paid on your account to Rumsey [£]378.11.7. & [£]84. 1. 8 remains to be paid on the settlement of Chipps farm by Sir J^no Dashwood which will be settled in the course of 14 days from the present time. With the sum of forty pounds 14/8 ceded on each of our parts to Admiral Barker the whole affair will be arranged much better so than thrown into Chancery. For you know as well as I do that there are sharks on shore as

well as between the Tropics & I vow to God I think the latter are less
ravenous than the former. You will see by this that you will be in the clear
receipt from this source of at least *450£.* stating for instance that the
Expenses amount to the remaining [£]12 .13 .3. As you have appointed Joe to
act as your Agent I shall recommend him to invest this sum in the funds for
you. However to show you more clearly I will copy Rumsey's statement on
the other side for you altho it will occupy a considerable portion of my paper.

   I had almost forgotten to tell you I was apprized of the sailing of the
H.B.Cᵒ ships by Mʳ Smith at whose house I spent the evening when in
Town. He has had (I really believe) a most narrow escape from one of the
worst attacks of gout he has ever suffered under. You will find him on your
arrival (to adopt the language of the turf) very *gummy* & very *groggy* –
Darby (I met him at Maidenhead[)] is trying for a ship to Australia he has
been out of commission ever since Your departure. Now for home news –
Old Jack will be buckled to the next Saturday that dawns[.] I would give a
5£ note to witness the *opening scene* but I have no doubt the theatricals will
be *private* so that those only will have a chance to view who get behind the
curtain. You are aware how we always quizzed him for hanging an *arse*
behind – I am very much out in my calculation of events if he does not
alter the character of *things* & be hung a devilish deal more *before.* However
I should think as you Sailors say "she will prove a good Pilot & will lead
him safe into the Harbour of *Conception.*["] Inform us in your reply to
this if you have ever navigated in those parts how the *currents* run – the
soundings &c &c &c &c &c – What do you mean "*by the deep nine*"
I suppose *inches.* I'll drop this subject = *inches* will do. perhaps it may mean
feet. Now I have safely & snugly housed old Jack. I must tell you Fanny is
likewise going to be spliced. The day is fixed 5 weeks from the present time.
I was with Joe for a fortnight after Xmas[.] We licked all our competitors in
shooting & were offered to be backed by a sporting man there against any
two brothers in England. I must not say more of that otherwise you will
think me vain but it is really the fact. We have had a *remarkably* mild
winter & the sping unless a sudden check occurs will be particularly early.
The wheat plants (of which alone we can now speak) are looking well & as
far as we can Judge a fair prospect of productiveness. I must now my Dʳ
Wᵐ take my leave of you. The girls desire their best love to you & believe
me my Dʳ Wᵐ with the warmest wishes for your health prosperity & happiness your sincere & affecᵗᵉ Bʳ

   Thoˢ Mason Heath

PS. You see by this statement of Rumsey's you have to receive [£]462.13.3.

Dr Wm Heath in account with Ex^{ors} of T. Mason Esqr. C^r.

To ⅙ p^r. Paym^t to Adm^l Barker.	40.14.8	1839	
To ⅙ " value of Chipps retained till the Settlement –	84.1.8	Feb 8 Legacy.	400.00
504.10.3		Int. Decr 1838 to Feb. 1839	103.7.11
To Balance	124.16.4		
	378.11.7		
	503. 7.11		£503.7.11

William Heath served with the Company until 1846, but it was not all smooth sailing and his problems were not all washed away by salt water, as his sister had hoped his feelings of unrequited love had been. He came only twice to London between 1839 and 1846, once in 1839 and again in 1843. In 1840 he ran into difficulties with his new master, Charles Humphreys (entry 24), who in his October report to William Smith tells of Heath's questionable, even dangerous, behaviour:

After the Ship was loaded with Lumber and had proceeded down the Columbia River nearly as low as "Fort George" [Astoria, Oregon] Mr Heath openly refused Duty and also to proceed to Sea in the Vessel. An exchange took place with him and Mr Lattie the mate of the Honble C^o's Schooner Cadboro then laying of[f] "Fort George" which was effected by Mr Alex^r Simpson Supercargo of the Columbia. In proceeding down the [Columbia] River I was principally guided by Mr Heath's advice respecting the Navigation of the River but having got on the ground Several times I became more cautious on Account of the rise and the fall of tide, and also of having a Crowded Deck load Consisting of Spars, Beams, Planks and Boards, for the Sandwich Island Market. When passing thro' a narrow Channel on the one Side of which the Sands are rather dangerous I asked the Second Officer's opinion as to its position which So much offended Mr Heath that he refused duty and at that time without any other cause.

William Heath served on the *Cadboro,* the *Beaver,* and the *Cowlitz* but was never promoted to captain, as his sister Fanny had predicted. As late as 1845 one of the captains on the coast, W.H. McNeill, wrote to Sir George Simpson that "you well know Sir what a precious set some of our Officers out here are, Lattie is on shore at Fort Simpson, turned out of the Steamer for habitual drunkeness[,] Sangster pulls hard on the bottle and Heath I am sorry to say has been very much given to it of late also." Heath's last letter to the Company, on the progress of his 1846 voyage home, described the successful landing of the cargo, despite problems with the *Cowlitz* "being weak in her water ways as in stormy weather considerable quantities of water found its way through." Although his letter indicates no awareness that he has a problem, the entries in the *Cowlitz* log convinced the Company of his difficulties with drinking, and when he declined to bring forth evidence to disprove the charges, he was dismissed from the Company service for intoxication following his arrival in London on 27 June 1846.

But that was not the end of the Heath family's interest in the Pacific Northwest. Joseph, who had once won shooting competitions with Thomas, had gone out to the Columbia Department on their brother William's recommendation in 1843. But it was not good prospects alone that took Joseph to the coast. In Thomas's second letter he had mentioned that Joseph had been entrusted with investing William's inheritance. The patrimony of Joseph, William, and the others, however, went to pay Joseph's gambling and horse-racing debts. Joseph had been sent where he could do less damage, setting up as a settler and farmer with the Puget's Sound Agricultural Company at Steilacum, near Fort Nisqually (Tacoma, Washington) in the Oregon Territory, with his brother Thomas providing the £1,000 bond required as security. The Company was trying to establish its employees on as much land as possible, in part to bolster British claims, but more realistically to establish some defendable claim to properties under American law once the land transfer took place. The Company was also changing its trading direction to put itself in a position to supply provisions for its own operations and those of the Russian American Company. Joseph set to work with the determination to do well on his mixed farm, with sheep the main concern. (For an account of Joseph's banishment, see McDonald 1979, 6-7.)

Retired to England, William Heath wrote on 14 August 1847 to Sir John Henry Pelly at the Company, asking for passage to join his brother Joseph. The letter contains a report from Thomas describing William's change of temperament and dropping of "other vicious habits." The Company refused passage. William Heath wrote once more to the Company, one year later, asking for a certificate attesting to his abilities as a navigator and seaman, probably in preparation for starting over with another trading company. The Company recorded no answer to the letter. Throughout this time, his brother Joseph recorded his concern for "poor old Will" in his journal (McDonald 1979, 123, 150, 157). It seems that William had not found happiness in "a pleasantly situated cottage with a porch in front covered in ivy" and was not content to smoke his pipe "to solace the Evening of [his] days," as Thomas had once predicted.

On 7 March 1849 Joseph Heath died, after years of health problems, at Fort Nisqually in what was by then the US territory of Oregon. His symptoms were listed as indigestion, swollen legs, and chest pains. He died in debt but, when everything was sold off and the evaluation made two years later, the Heath brothers and sisters received a total of not quite £300 for Joseph's "moiety" (McDonald 1979, 170-2). This did not entirely discourage the family on settlement on the west coast, as Thomas Heath wrote to the Company asking for information on the colony that the Company had established on Vancouver Island and was sent the Company prospectus. William Heath probably did not sail the seas again, since he was listed as a farmer at Mill End Farm in the farm directory of the day. After 1869 his name does not appear in that publication.

30 GEORGE GORDON: *Just the Same as if you was transported*

George Gordon, of Wales, was hired as a seaman for the maiden voyage of the *Beaver,* the Company's first steamship. The ship left London as a sailing vessel on 29 August 1835 and arrived at the Columbia Department on 29 February 1836. George's father wrote to him with bad news.

～ George Gordon Beaver Steamer seaman, Fort Van Cover Columbia River or else where –
To be left at the H.B.C.House – Fenchurch street, London

Neyland 19th of august 1838

Dear Son in great Sorrow I inform you of the Death of your Brother John after a most Severe illness of eighteen weeks confinement[.] he died the twenty fourth of this May and we buiried him on the twenty ninth[.] he was verry ill for two before he died but 18 weeks before he died his suffering was beyond all telling[.] he Died of a decline and he had all means tryd for him Dockters far and near[.] he had taken all kind of medcine for two years and five months he drank gallons of brandy and port wine but all for no Service[.] when it came to the last he had a most Dreadfull coff for sixteen months and spit up all his inside[.] he wore to nothing but Deaths pickture[.] I suppose there was never such a frame seen[.] your Mother was eighteen weeks and never took of her clothes[.] he had every thing he had a wish for far and near while he was while he was [repetition] in this world[.] he was alive when we had your last letter and

he was overjoyd to hear from you before he left this world and he tryed to
Read your letter but his eyes was gone to weak to look on it and he cryed
and and [repetition] said he Should never See you again in this world and
he said when you have the next Letter from his brother George you will say
poor John was here when you had the last[.] he was always talking about
you and Joshua and saying he should never see either of you again in this
world but he hoped you would meet him in heaven[.] he told to tell you
and Joshua when you heard of his Death never to curse nor sweare any
more nor do any thing wrong but always to Remember you must die as
well as your brother[.] he was many weeks verry desireous to leave this
world and telling every body to pray for him to go from here that he knew
he should be happy if he could but die[.] he was [erased] I dont think any
body sufferd for 18 weeks so much as he did[.] he was verry patient and had
a great faith in the blood of christ and would often call on the Lord to
Receve him[.] you must know our trouble is beyond telling[.] he was
grown a fine young man and Just out of his time and got in the yard but he
was but there six months[.] he was above six feet high he growd much like
you and James is growing fast after him[.] Charels is grown a fine lad[.]
they be grown two young men[.] they be both with Mr Scurlock[.] now
Charels got three years to serve and James got five[.] we are Sorry you was
not here to bear part of our trouble[.] your mother hopes to See you once
again but she is a fraid she never will[.] Joshua is Married since last [crossed
out] January [18]37 and lives in Wexford[.] he have one child and is
foreman of a yard there[.] he was not at his brothers funirel it was to late
when he had the Letter but he is in great trouble about John[.] he had not
Seen him for three years before he died[.] we are all in great trouble here
about John but we trust he is he is [repetition] happay[.] I could never tell
you all about him untill we can see you in which we trust and hope you
[erased] in god you will come home once again[.] your Mother looks on it
Just the Same as if you was transported[.] Well [erased] we was Glad to
hear from you[.] I answerd your Letter and I hope you have had it[.] May
god keep and prserve you untill we see you again[.] poor old Charley
Childs have been dead this 19 months and Nancy Childs went to London
and died this May and betcy thomas and a great Many of your old
acquaintences is ded since you have been gone[.] Dear Son if you will come
home you are young you could be a Shipwrite it or you could go to Schooll[.]
we would do all in our power for you[.] old Nelly and Molly Lewis dead an
John Lawrence was Dround in Lakin hill[.] you would hardly know your
old place[.] hobbs point is a fine pier and the Packets Comes there from
waterford[.] Dear Son acceppt of all our Love[.] May god bless you[.] we
hope to see you again[.] from your affectionate friends and father

William Gaddarn Neyland near Pembroke Dock, Pembroke Shire south
Wales

[below cover] mind to Rite to us every optunity [crossed out] oppetunity
and come home as Soon as you can

The alcohol used to combat John's consumption (tuberculosis) was part of
many medicinal treatments in the nineteenth century. William Gordon
seems to be a man anxious to have his children all at home in Wales now that
he has lost one son so tragically. He will soon have George with him, but
under circumstances he could not imagine. By the time his father wrote this
letter, Gordon was in trouble on the west coast for his part in a mutiny
aboard the *Beaver*. Perhaps if George had received his brother's last advice,
"Never to curse nor sweare any more nor do any thing wrong," he might
have been more measured in his reaction to what was a very difficult situation aboard the *Beaver*. The ship was commanded by William H. McNeill
from Boston. When the Company purchased the brig *Lama* from its Boston
owners in Honolulu in 1832, they got McNeill as part of the deal. Although
corporal punishment was disapproved by the London Committee, it was
difficult to control in the remote Columbia Department. There were complaints about McNeill as an abusive leader. He had numerous successes with
the Company later in his career, but the mutiny on the *Beaver* was not one
of them. The ship and crew were spending the winter of 1837-8 in Fort Simpson, Nass, for repairs, and one evening McNeill was called away while the
mate was doling out the pint of rum and water rations that each crewman
received daily. It seems his assistants were too generous with the rum as, later
that night, the men became unruly. McNeill ordered them back aboard the
vessel and they refused, swearing at their captain, who "lost patience and
chastized them, severely, on the spot, with his cane . . . The following day two
of the Stokers were flogged with 24 lashes." Soon the entire crew, with the
exception of the two mates, boatswain, and woodcutters, mutinied. Chief
Trader John Work "yielded to their justifiable demands so far as to assume
the command of the vessel himself, when order was restored on board, and
all hands promptly returned to duty" with McNeill aboard as a passenger.
After the vessel's arrival at Fort Nisqually, John Work, McNeill, and Chief
Engineer Arthur argued their case to Chief Trader James Douglas at Fort
Vancouver. McNeill was restored to his command against Arthur's protests.
Although the seamen seemed ready to mutiny again, all except for three
seamen – William Wilson, James Starling, and George Gordon – eventually
submitted to McNeill's and the Company's authority. The three rebels were
returned to Fort Vancouver, where Douglas confined them in irons until he

could question them. When they still refused to return to duty he struck their names from the pay list, then sent them to outposts as "prisoners at large doing no duty, with the option of bread and water diet, or the common rations allowed servants of the place." They were without pay from 27 March 1838 until they entered the crew of the *Columbia* in November.

Despite the sense we get from George Gordon's father's letter that his son had a quick temper and a saucy tongue in the past, George's stubborn resistance against McNeill may well have had some just cause. Years later, on 25 June 1851, when James Douglas was in charge of Fort Victoria, he wrote to G.B. Roberts with considerable frustration that "William McNeill is not wanted here, and ought to be sent to Vancouver or any where you please, but here." McNeill certainly had a bad reputation among his men aboard the *Beaver*. The following letter from a friend, written 22 October 1838, shows that the gossip was circulating back home. His friend commiserated with George about his master, a "Monster" who was making his life "Miserable." At the time he expressed these emotions George might well have agreed with his mother that he was living in conditions that were as bad as being transported to a penal colony.

~ Mʳ George Gordon, Beaver Steamer, Columbia River

London October the 22. 1838

Dear George
I received your Welcome Letter the 18 of this month and truly welcome it was for I began to think you had quite forgotten us thinking of the lapse of time that has intervened since you parted from us but the long lookd for came at last and has the old saying better late than never[.] I must not scold you for your long silence considering it has come at last but we where all truly sorry to hear of you being so truly Miserable but it his a long lane that has no turning[.] let us hope your pilgrimage on that wretched Coast will not be so long has you fear and always bear in mind you have Friends that with Joy will welcome the Wanderers return[.] surely the Almighty will not suffer such a Vile Wretch has you have Described to pollute the earth long with his presence[.] such a Monster I cannot call him Man makes human nature shudder for believe me however he may scoff he has a terrible account to settle for so tortureing Mankind[.] but enough of him now and please God you return in safety[.] we must endeavour by kindness to make up for your long Exile[.] we was agreeblely surprised to see James Dick thinking you was not far behind but to make up for our Disappointment he said you would be soon back he thougt perhaps by the next Ship but we could get no particulars from him only there had been a

misunderstanding and he was very thankful to profit by it and get away[.]
he has made one Voyage to Sydney since and been Home about 4
Months[.] I am sorry to say he has been in the Hospital some time with a
very bad attack of the Gout but is now getting better[.] he Desires to be
rememberd to you and all his Shipmates[.] my Mother his much the same
has usual[.] I see no Differance in her and hopes to live to Dance with you
a reel to the tune of the Dancing Dog[.] William saild last week for the
Cape and from there to some part of India[.] I am afraid it will be a long
Voyage but please God to restore him[.] I am content for the hope of
return takes the Sting from Adieu[.] Louisa his much the same has ever no
Family yet and Betsy still single and living at the Fox but I am sorry to say
we have lost my Poor Sister she has been Dead this six Months, her end
was very Sudden and has left a Large Family to feel her loss, Sinclair his
still and old Batchelor[.] we expect him home every Day from the Black
Sea, and tho last not least Jessy[.] She is still single and waiting for you[.]
she thanks you for your present and says when you return she will give you
Two, Clarke still enjoys his pint and pipe the same has ever[.] we have
never heard any think of Leman since last I wrote and Irvin is Mate of a
fine Ship and gone away for Nine Months[.] I think now I have sent you
all the particulars of every body you know and hoping you will never let an
oppurtunity slip of sending to us and I promise faithly on my part to do
the same[.] my Mother Desires to be kindly Rememberd to you has does
Louisa, Betsy, Jessy and Clarke and receive the same from your ever sincere
Freind A. Randall
hoping to hear from you soon or else see you Adieu

It is interesting to note that another sailor, James Dick, had refused to talk
about the particulars of the mutiny, perhaps wisely avoiding the attachment
of his name to rumours about the incident. By the time the letters from
George's father and friend arrived in the Columbia Department, George
would have arrived home to face the death of his brother and the many questions about his conduct. He was sent home on the *Columbia,* leaving Fort
Vancouver on 11 November 1838 and arriving in London on 21 May 1839.
With the speed of men who believe in their own innocence, on 31 May he
and the other two recalcitrant men sent a letter to the Company, describing
their hardships under McNeill. They claimed that the captain often "wished
that he should like to see a bloody Row For and Aft so that he might blow
some of our brains out [and] constantly advised M[r] Scarborough our Chief
Officer to knock our bloody brains out with a handspike if we look[d] black."
The three men claimed that "from his threats & brutal usuage we was obliged
to refuse his Command for the safety of our lives." Their appeal fell on deaf

ears, and there is no record of George Gordon working for the Company after this time.

31 GEORGE WILLIAM BARTON: *It is a long time to look forward to*

At about the age of fourteen, in November 1830, George Barton left London aboard the *Ganymede* listed as a ship's boy, to begin his twelve-year career with the Company. He was one of the Greenwich apprentices who took their schooling at the Royal Hospital school and went on to apprenticeships in the navy or merchant ships (see James Dowden Buck, entry 32). He worked aboard the *Vancouver* and the *Dryad* in the Columbia Department until he completed his apprenticeship on the return voyage to London aboard the *Dryad,* arriving on 10 April 1836. He was hired on at the end of his apprenticeship as second mate aboard the *Eagle* for its summer voyage into Hudson Bay. During this voyage he was credited with helping to free the vessel from ice, as described in the following memorial sent to the Company:

> The Memorial of Robert Stewart Able Seaman of the Brig Eagle of N° 5
> Philpot St Com^l Road
> Sheweth
>   That the Brig during the last Voyage, on her entrance into Hudsons Straits became blocked in between the Ice, and thrown on her side, her perilous situation was such that the Captain and all the Crew abandoned her, except your Memorialist and the Second Mate (Mr Barton) when after 40 hours endurance of severe hardship, they providentially succeeded in getting her off, and with great difficulty, took in the Captain a[nd] Crew off the Ice.

As soon as the voyage home from Hudson Bay was completed the following year, George embarked on the *Columbia* on 18 November 1837 on a return trip to the Columbia Department. George met Maria Ridley, either through her brother James, another Greenwich apprentice, or through earlier contact at "Mr. Ridley's Hospital" in Greenwich where the boys got their schooling. Her letter indicates that she considered herself to be his intended and she wrote, hoping he would not stay the full five years planned because "it is a long time to look forward to."

~ Mr Barton Mate of the Cloumbia at Clumbia River

[23(?) August(?) 1838]

>   my Dear George
>   I have writen to you the first opertunity I have had of sending out to

you And I hope it will find you in good health likewise my Brother james[.] you can tell my Brother james that I have been to Portsmouth And Aunt And uncle sends their kind love to him[.] I received your kind letter from Gravesend in November 1837. your Brother samuel And his wife came over one day to see his intended sisterlaw has he said and I have been over to his house And to your Aunts once since that and they were all quiet well[.] I saw your Mother the last time she went to Hudson bay house[.] you talked to me of staying out more you are 5 years but I hope you will alter your mind before that time for it is a long time to look forward to but still I shall keep my promise And I hope you will Do the same[.] i hope when you come home you will bring me home some fur. I have made up my mind that you will[.] I had allmost forgoten but I supose your sweet heart And your little Child was very glad to see again And I supose james family was as glad to see him[.] I must tell you that james Osburn has been to see us once since you have been gone[.] I was very much Disappointed at your not coming home the next night for I had got A small present for you but I must keep it untill I see you again[.] Mr And Mrs Douglas And betsy sends their kind love to And hopes your Are quiet well as they Are all At present

Mr And Mrs forest sends their kind respects to you[.] jane is at home At present And Mary And Betsy janes sisters has got A fine girl each of them so now I hope they are happy[.] I supose I you will send home every opertunity that you have As I shall Do the same[.] I dare say if you get this letter you will not be Able to make it out[.] you know I told you when you was home [that] I was no writer And now I have proved it but you must excuse it and by the next time I write to you I hope you will be able to understand it better[.] I must now conclude with my kind love to you and remain yours most

Affectionately   Thursday
Maria Ridley   september [August?] 23[?] 1838
[In 1838, 23 August was a Thursday, while 23 September was a Sunday. Either the day or the month is inaccurate.]

It may surprise present-day readers to see the tolerance Maria shows for George's Aboriginal wife and child – whom she called his "sweet heart And your little Child" – in North America. Perhaps, since her brother also had such a family, it was apparent to her that many of these men would exercise their sexual liberty regardless of social mores at home. Given the lack of recognition accorded such unions by English standards, and the distance of the other life a man might lead so far away, Maria may have felt no threat to her status. However, her claim that she "had allmost forgoten" – as if she was bringing up the subject as an afterthought – seems a bit more casual than might have been the case. Perhaps she had not yet completely committed her heart to him, as she surely did when he arrived home for the summer of 1839. Records show that they married by 1840 and had a child by 1842. George was on a two-way voyage on the *Columbia* when this letter was written and missed the letter because he was returning home aboard that ship, arriving on 21 May 1839. He also missed letters from his mother and his brother that were sent at the same time as Maria's.

ᔔ Mr George Barton, On Bord the Columbia, Northwest America

Poplar Oct[r] 10th 1838

My Dear Son

I embrace this oppertunity of informing you that I am in as good a state of Health as can be expected hopeing in God this May find you in Health, Strength and prosperity and that you will so Continue till I have the plea-sure of Seeing again –

Your Brother Samuel is out at the West Indies, and Richard went a Voy-age to Quibac [Quebec] and back to Whitbay [Whitby] and from there he hase gon to Petersburg at £2 per month – your Sister Harrete poor girle is at present well but She is far from enjoying a general good state of health; your Grandfather and Grandmother is Still alive and well but very feable

I left the house in Regent Street and now resides near Stepn[e]y Church in a small house of less rent. I do as well as I can – I have a great deal to say but will defare till I have [t]he happiness to See you

I have no further to say; May God prosper and protect you

Is the sincere wish of

D[r] Son

your Affectionate Mother

Olive Barton

PS If there is an oppertunity please write and let me know how you are

ᔔ Mr G W Barton, 2nd Officer on board of the H Bay Ship Columbia, Columbia or elsewhere

[31 October 1838] N° 16 James Street E F Road

Dear Brother

I take this favourable Opportunity of writing these few lines to you hoping to find you in good health as it leaves me at present thank god for it[.] I have been out to Hudsons Bay in the Prince Rupert and now at home[.] I Expected to come out 2 Mate of the Vancover but I was not at Home quiet soon enough to Join her. I am quiet well but my Daughter is very ill[.] Mrs Barton is quiet well and sends her love to you.

This is all I have to say at Present.

I Remain your Most Dutiful

    Brother SR Barton

31st/10/38

Please to send an answer by the Next Ship

These family letters indicate the scope of British trade as well as the progress of the colonial enterprise by the late 1830s. With voyages to the Caribbean, Quebec, St. Petersburg, and Hudson Bay, this family is scattered in many directions.

On 18 September 1839 – and probably by then married to Maria – George embarked once more on the *Columbia,* stayed on the west coast for the year 1840-1, and returned aboard the same ship, arriving on 7 July 1842. His service ends there, perhaps because of a disagreement with Chief Factor McLoughlin. He wrote on 21 July 1842 claiming pay since he was ordered by the chief factor to take his "Chest and bedding and procede to England in the *Columbia*"; when he asked in "what capacity [McLoughlin told him that] Captn Humphrey's had got his officers and my services would not be required but that my Salary was to go on as before." His duties on the voyage home were listed as "sundry duties." The Company obviously decided to await official word from McLoughlin on the pay issue, because Barton wrote a more assertive letter on 24 August, asking that they "refer to Captn Humphrey, he will confirm this Statement as to the understanding that my Wages would continue independantly of which I was employed all the voyage home in Serving out the Provisions and Sundry other duties considering myself bound to perform any duty he directed me to do." He added a special appeal: "Being out of employment and haveing a Wife and Child it will be a greivous loss and inconvenience to me to await a reference to the Governor a period of so many months particularly as Captn Humphreys can vouch as to the understanding as well as state I was employed all the voyage home." Although Captain Drew, the ship's husband on the London Committee, informed the Company secretary that Barton had no legitimate claim, the Company offered £10. This would have been far less than Barton would have expected for his seven months work on the voyage home. However, we might assume that George Barton, with his skills and accomplishments, probably went on to support his English family despite his disappointment with the Company.

Barton's plea for his money on account of his family seemed somewhat ironic in retrospect, considering he actually has two families. How his other family in the Columbia Department might have fared is questionable. If his country wife had come from an Aboriginal family in close proximity, she may have gone back to them, where her child would be accepted as well. If she was of the Chinook people she may well have come into her marriage with slaves to work for her and considerable status in her own community. If she was Métis, she may have had a father of some standing in the fur trade, in which case she might well be looked after. On the other hand, if she was one of a number of Fort Vancouver women with no male relatives of substance, her future might well be dependent on forming an alliance with another Company man.

Barton left just at the historical moment when life was getting difficult for Aboriginal wives in general. The old Company customs were changing, partially because of George Simpson's policies, and "For a time the structure of fur-trade society was badly shaken. Suicides, abortions, and even infanticides by apprehensive country wives were not unknown" (Brown 1980, 149-50; quoted in Hussey 1991, 270). One abandoned wife was described by Chief Trader Francis Heron in 1835 as standing "on the beach [with] babe in her arms both weeping . . . The brute was as unconcerned at the parting . . . as if he was only taking a few hours excursion" (Hussey 1991). Even though in 1837 Chief Factor John McLoughlin was known to have actually whipped a man who was attempting to abandon his child unsupported, he was at pains to assure the London directors in 1838 that only a few women – a Company ward, a widow, and three wives of old servants – were receiving rations from the Company stores. The support of a wife and child was a man's responsibility, and we have no idea what arrangements, if any, George Barton made. His Aboriginal wife would certainly have a long time to look forward to without the father of her child.

32   JAMES DOWDEN BUCK: *We long to see you*

On 3 November 1830 James D. Buck was among five boys apprenticed to the *Ganymede,* along with Edward Rye, George Barber Roberts, James Henry Ridley, and Henry Harmsworth (entry 13). Their pay was to be £8 per annum for each of the first two years, £10 for the third and fourth, £12 for the fifth and sixth, and £15 for the seventh. At age fifteen James Buck went with the other apprentices to the Columbia Department aboard the *Ganymede,* leaving on 16 November 1830. As early as 4 January 1830 the Company Secretary William Smith and Captain Minors had attended the Royal Hospital at Greenwich and bound eight apprentices for seven years each to go out to the

Columbia on the brig *Dryad.* To comply with the regulations of the school, they gave bonds to the Commissioners of Greenwich Hospital "for the due fulfillment of the agreements entered into with each of the said Apprentices." It was anticipated, since the school educated boys for service at sea, that they would make useful servants on the Pacific coast. In turn, the Company was to supply "a proper supply of good warm clothing ... and every other necessary" and place them under the senior naval officer, who was cautioned to treat them with kindness, pay attention to their instruction, and take care with their morals.

James Buck stayed on for eight years working as an apprentice seaman aboard the *Cadboro, Vancouver,* and *Lama.* His parents, Richard and Elizabeth, worried a great deal about their young lad as there are records of them contacting the Company on three occasions for news of their son. By January 1838 they were very concerned because James had stayed beyond his time, and William Smith, the Company secretary, agreed to forward "a single sheet letter" overland in February. By October 1838 his parents were sending another letter, full of concern and longing for the traveller's return.

Weymouth October twenty-eight 1838, W. Smith Esqr Hudson Bay House, 3 Fenchurch S^t, London
[redirected by the Company secretary] For James Dowden Buck, Ship Nereid, Columbia River [with a note "If James Dowden Buck has quitted the Service to be returned in next Packet to the HBHouse"]

Weymouth Octr 28th 1838

My Dear Son
We are the Second time greatly Disappointed in not seeing you[.] we have wrote to Mr Smith[.] he said in his answer that you will come ~~house~~ [crossed out] home in the first Ship that will leave the establishment so my dear Son I hope the Almighty will still protect you and give you a safe voyge home to england again[.] once more we long to see you indeed it is a long time since we see you[.] we was happy to hear that you was well as Bless God it leaves us at present[.] your brother Richard is in the tartar Cutter and is quite hearty thank God for it[.] we shall have much to talk about when we see you[.] we have not heard from Ann for some time she was well then[.] my dear Child you must excuse me not writing more for I am going to get this letter frank^d, and I must be there by 12 Oclock[.] please to excuse blunders for I am in a great hurry. your mother Joins with me in love to you from your loving Father and Mother Richard & Elizth Buck –

[in his mother's hand] my Dear I longs to see indeed
    your dear mother

Indeed, James had stayed past his apprentice time but not by choice. When
his parents were sending the overland "single sheet," he was writing from the
Columbia River to his parents (dated 25 January 1838) and to Mr. Deane, the
clerk of cheque at the hospital where he had received his education.

To the Clerk of Cheque
Copy P.C. LeGeyt, Cl[erk] of the Cheque

Todds Bay Columbia River Ship Nereide Feb. 9th 1838

    Sir
    As I was bound apprentice in your presence in the year 1830 to the
Hudson's Bay Company for the term of 7 years I now take the liberty to
write a few lines to you as I consider myself very much imposed upon. I
have been confined to this part of the world ever since we first arrived to it
– I have often applied to the Governor for a passage to England. He told
me I should go if he could make it convenient. The same afternoon H.W.
Harmsworth received orders to join the "Sumatra." After I had done work
I went to the Governor [McLoughlin] again and all the satisfaction I could
get was a Shove down a flight of steps which nearly broke my neck. On the
22 of December last I applied to M[r] Douglas the Clerk at Fort Vancouver
for my Indentures. He told me they were not in this country. He likewise
told me on the 1st June last that I was £10.16s.0 in debt to the Company
and the accounts made up to the 1st February 1838 I should be £5 in debt
and although I was in debt so much I could receive any clothing whatever
from the Store. He then told me that I had been on A.B. Seamans Wages
since the first of June last. I then told him that I could not understand in
what manner I could now be in debt. We are now bound to Woahoo
[Oahu] one of the Sandwich Islands and I must apply to the British
Consul for a passage to England. Which would be quite contrary to my
inclinations if I could obtain it in any other manner
    Sir
        I remain your most
            Obedient Servant
        James Dowden Buck

A similar letter to his parents had inspired his father's anguished letter to
Company Secretary William Smith, dated 22 October 1838. He stated that
his son was "being detained there like a Prisoner. – I shall feel obliged by your

giving me all the information in your power on the above, as I feel quite uneasy as a Parent for the welfare of my son." Judging by their subsequent letter, the undelivered one quoted above, the Company secretary's reply seems to have reassured them. And, true to his word, James had left on the next ship, embarking on 11 November 1838 as second mate aboard the *Columbia,* a nice promotion to end his service. When he arrived in England on 21 May 1839, having missed this last worried letter from his parents, he would have something to show for his eight years away. He would have grown from a boy to a man of twenty-four and he had qualified himself to work on any vessel as a seaman and even as an officer.

Despite his parents' worries, James seems to have been able to survive quite well on his own and records indicate he also knew what was due him. He again wrote, this time to the Company, on 28 May 1839, to complain, "[I] had the misfortune to lose all my clothes with the schooner vancouver [the ship was wrecked in 1834]. I consider it very hard that I should be in debt at the expiration of the said term, arising from being obliged to get a fresh stock to make good what had been lost. Now this was deducted out of my wages amounting to about 12 Pounds." After the intervention of the clerk of cheque, Company Secretary William Smith made a note that the true amount charged was £11 7s., and defended the debit with a detailed explanation. Still, he reimbursed Buck £5 for his loss. But James Buck was not the only apprentice to complain, and the Company soon discontinued their experiment with this class of recruit.

33 WILLIAM GREEN: *A Piece of Work by & by*

In March 1834 William Green transferred from another vessel to the Company's *Dryad* while it was engaged in the Columbia trade at Oahu. He served on the coast, going to England in 1836, then returning to the Pacific northwest with his brother Charles on the *Columbia* in 1837. This letter addressed to him and to his brother Charles did not reach them because William was returning home aboard the *Columbia,* which arrived in London on 21 May 1839. Charles seems not to have been with his brother by this time, contrary to the family's information.

For William Green, Seaman, On board the ship, Columbia Capt[n]

London Nov[r] 3rd 1838

Dear William & Charles
I take the oppertunty of Wrighting to you A few lines to you [crossed out] Hopeing to find you well as Leaves us at Preseant[.] Robert Gay his

been home[.] I have Seen him & he sends his best Respects to you & Wishes you well & should like to se you[.] I Call^d on your Sister Mary but she was not at home at the old Place[.] Betsy Whitehead his been away from her Husband six Months but know his Made it up a gain[.] they are very Comfortable again now, She has loss her last Child since she been with him – the Girls his Left Margret sarah Brocket his got a shop in the Chandler line[.] Margret his got another Girl she his Christned after her aunt Elizabeth Forman

I Came down to Greavesend on the Day Saturday that You Sail^d[.] in Afternoon Half Past 3 Oclock took a boat but you was away[.] wee stop all Night down there[.] I Received your Letter from the Downs stating that I was to Receive Three Pounds Ten Shillings but he his not Gave me only One Pound till he Heres from you [.] I Read of the Vessell spoken of Sandwich Islands, My Mother & Sister his very well & Still In the old Place[.] Elizabeth W. Sends her Love to you[.] We Expects Gordon Home in May[.] we have had a letter from him & he was taken for a Soldgier in Canada Last Christmas but Discharge in May last

Robert Gay heard at China that you was Transported but he said that it was another William Green & Not you
Dear William
Direct as before to G. Jones, Cooper
N°5 Wellclose Square London Docks

So No More at Pressant from your Friend
G. & N Jones
My Little Children are Gitting on Fameous[.] Large George & Little George Jones sends there Love to you Both

Saturday Morning ¼ Pass ten Oclock
Novr 3th 1838

one year served out of Five
[written across the page] ~~We~~ [replaced by] I Expect there will be a Piece of Work by & by Here with Russiar

It is interesting to see the new worries that are becoming typical of families and friends of men working away from home in an expanding imperial economy of the late 1830s. George Jones writes of Gordon, in Canada, who was "taken for a Soldgier," possibly drafted to suppress the rebellions there in 1837-8, and mentions the kind of rumour that must have struck dread in many hearts, the possibility that a loved one had been transported to one of the penal colonies. Fortunately, the rumour, one that came all the way from China via another friend, is untrue. Despite the hint that there would be "a Piece of Work by & by," William did not stay in England long after his May arrival. By 18 September 1839 he had left again on the *Columbia* and served on her until, by order of Governor George Simpson in 1841, he was removed to the *Cowlitz*. He served as a steward on this ship as well as on the *Vancouver* and the *Beaver*, until 1846, when he returned to England and left the Company's service. The Company continued to carry £5 owing him on its accounts through 1847 and 1848, a considerable amount to leave uncollected. Green must have known about collecting back pay, since a fellow worker, John Coon, and his commanding officer Charles Humphreys (see their undelivered letters, entries 28 and 24, respectively) had sent him to collect extra pay due them on two occasions.

34   WILLIAM MARTINDELL: *I hope you will not be perswaded to stop but come home the first oppirtunity you have*

Charlotta Martindell's son William, from Plaistow (now within London), was enlisted as a fourteen-year-old apprentice by John Henry Pelly, Governor of the Hudson's Bay Company, who sent him and his father to sign an indenture with the Company in May 1838. His first voyage was a five-month return trip to Hudson Bay on the *Prince of Wales*. Within a month of finishing that voyage, he left on the *Vancouver* for the Columbia service in November of the same year. He had been a year in the district when his mother wrote to him.

~   William Martindell, Board Hudson's Bay Company [crossed out], Columbia River [crossed out], Trinity [crossed out] Fort Vancouver, Hudson's Bay House, London

[Plaistow] May 31. 1840

My Dear Son
    I received your letter soon after the ship arrived and was in hopes instead of seeing a letter I should have seen you[.] notwithstanding you pretty letter afforded me great consolation[.] I cannot describe my anxiaty for you[.] My dear boy I am happy to hear you had a safe and pleasant Voiage likewise to hear you are so happy and Comfortable[.] you will recollect you have served two years of your time[.] I shall hope with the blesings of God to see you home next May[.] I sent a letter out for you by little Collins which I dare say you have received before this time if you have seen him[.] I dare say you have heard of you Father and the severe illness that he had

he was in Consumption thank God[.] my dear boy I Cannot say wee had a
very pleasant Chismas for that was the time your Father was laying very Ill
but thank God I am doing pretty well[.] I was in hopes my dear boy that
the ship would not have gorn out quite so soon[.] I am expecting to present
you with a brother or sister every day[.] do not my dear boy make your self
unhappy about us I am doing quite as well as I can expect[.] I cannot till
you my dear boy how thankful I feal to Mr Pelly for treating you with so
much kindness[.] by your account I really call it Fatherly kindness likewise
to the Captain and all you have around you[.] be a good boy and hope
with the blessing of God you will have a safe Voyage home[.] I feal very
anxious to see you[.] now my dear boy I do not know that I have any thing
more very particular to till you[.] your brothers & sisters all sends there
kind love to you and hope they will soon see you[.] now my dear boy I
must conclude with my kind love to you wishing you all the health and
happiness this world can afford and believe me to be
　　your affectionate
　　　and ever dear
　　　　Mother
　　　　Charlotta Martindell
PS Your Grandmother's & Grandfather Uncles & Aunts send ther kind
love to you[.] Edger his gorn out and I hope you will not be perswaded to
stop but come home the first oppirtunity you have
Plaistow

　　Charlotta probably did get her wish to see her son home next May, as he
returned aboard the *Vancouver* in the spring of 1841. However, his apprenticeship took him back to the Columbia Department and records show a
twelve-year career with the Company. After finishing his apprenticeship he
served on the company ships *Columbia, Cadboro,* and *Mary Dare* as a seaman
from 1845 to 1850. On 20 February 1847 he joined Robert Dunbar, Joseph
Horne, Lewis F. Murray, and Robert Webster in refusing to take the *Cadboro*
to sea out of Fort Victoria if the chief officer, William Alexander Mouat,
remained on board. The ship's log kept by Captain James Scarborough
records the incident. The men were warned to be careful, but their complaints must have had a foundation because, when the man in charge of Fort
Victoria, Roderick Finlayson, refused accommodation to Mouat, the master
put Mouat off duty and sent him to Fort George (Astoria, Oregon) in the
Henry, where he acted as a pilot for the Columbia River bar and later was
master in the American vessel *Sacramento.* Martindell and the other men
then returned to work.
　　After thirteen years of service and only two recorded visits back to

England (including the 1841 trip), William Martindell deserted in 1850. His desertion was really a decision, typical of a number of men, to become part of the permanent settlement of what would become the American northwest. He appeared in the 1850 Census as a labourer at Nisqually (Tacoma, Washington), and by 1851 he had settled on a claim of 130 hectares (320 acres) in Pacific County, Washington. There his life ended abruptly on 28 June 1858 when, at thirty-four years of age, he was shot and killed by Joseph Duprey. Sent in irons to Vancouver, Washington, Duprey jumped overboard at a point below Willamette Falls on the Columbia River; his heavily manacled hands and feet pulled him under water and he drowned.

35 JAMES SANGSTER: *Could I have beleived it possible when you left me in 1831 that you would never put pen to paper for nine years*

James Sangster, born in Port Glasgow, Scotland, entered the Company's service as a "boy" in 1827. By 1831 he had become a seaman aboard the *Eagle,* the same ship he had served on for two previous long trips from London to the Columbia Department and back. His movement up in the ranks was steady. He became second mate on the *Vancouver* in 1833 and transferred to the *Cadboro* in 1835. He was promoted to first mate on the *Lama* in 1837 and served in the same capacity aboard the *Beaver* from 1838 to 1839, at which time he was promoted to captain of that vessel. When his mother wrote to him in 1840 she knew nothing of his success, since he has "never put pen to paper for nine years." The dynamics of a society in which the family is the principal source of all social benefits, and the only safety net for people without independent incomes, is well illustrated in her letter.

Mr James Sangster, ~~Columbia River~~ [crossed out], Hudson's Bay House, London

Bow Common June 1840

My Dear James
I again take the Oppertunity of writing you by the Hudson Bay ships to shew you how ever much you neglect me that my Love and Affection is still the same and ever will be[.] could I have beleived it possible when you left me in 1831 that you would never put pen to paper for nine years (for I do not call the order you sent me a Letter)[.] if you would writ and give a reason for your remaining such a number of years I should be perfectly happy if it were for your good which you know is not the case for every one steps over your over your [repetition] Head[.] I am told that the mate of Neried is down for a Command before you (so the Capt of her told your

Uncle Bargrie) and he has not been twelve years in there Imploy as you
have been[.] but if you have no wish upon your own account and wish to
rise no higher it is your Dutey to look to your mother in her *Old age*[.] I
am now 60 ~~years of~~ [crossed out] and am unable to do needlwork as used
to do and how can I live upon £10 a year which you know is all I have[.]
your Sister Mary is Comfortably married but Mʳ Shand thinks it is your
Duty to assist me so between the two I may starve[.] Mary befor she was
married allways assisted me a little[.] now she says it is not in her power[.]
Tom dous a great deal for me but it is impossible that he can Keep me and
a Sick Sister for Elsa has been at home for this last Eighteen months and
God only knowes if she will ever be able to do for herself[.] I wrot last year
to you for £30 which I fully expected you would have sent[.] if you recolect
when you went away you wish'd (at least so *you said*) to leave me a note for
£1 pr month[.] you may count how much that would have come too and if
you are any Richer then if you had done it[.] I make inquirey at every one
that comes, from Columbia River[.] one will say you are saveing money
another that you spend it all (wh[ich] I cannot see how you can do it)[.]
Capt Humpries [Humphreys] said you had saved a £100 and if that is the
case you ought to be ashamed of yourself for you ought to have saved as
much as have bought a share of a ship and then you are sure of a Command
when you come home[.] let me beg and entret of you to come home for
you are Idlin away the Prime of your life and will become of you[r] [cross-
written] old age[.] God Bless you my Dear Boy[.] Elsa joins in kind Love
   your affection[ate]
   Mother
      M Sangster

   This compelling letter may leave us feeling sorry for the son, whose
mother scolded his lack of progress, and for the mother, who receives no
word from her son for nine years. Certainly, Mrs. Sangster's needlework
would not have provided a chance to save for her old age, and her residence
in the Maritime Houses in Bow Common would indicate that she was the
needy widow of a seaman. By the time his mother wrote to him, James Sangster had become the master of the *Beaver* but she obviously did not know
this. The promotion was a brief one as his trip back to London on the *Vancouver* during 1840-1 was as first mate. It was during this time that he missed
his mother's letter. The day before he left London he wrote to the Company
asking to return to England where "promotion was more rapid," perhaps in
response to his sense, like his mother's, that "every one steps over your ... Head."
After going back to the Columbia Department as first mate on the *Vancouver*
in 1841, however, he never returned to England. He did rise, however, to

become master of the *Cadboro* in 1848 and then the *Una* from 1849 to 1851, with a brief stint as pilot of the steam sloop HMS *Driver* at Fort Nisqually in 1849. During this period he was known to be inclined to drink; in 1842 Governor Simpson said that "Sangster . . . has been and I believe still is a confirmed drunkard" and in 1845 Captain McNeill asserted that Sangster "pulls hard on the bottle."

Between 1847 and 1855 James Sangster's mother sent four letters, written in various hands, to the Company all asking for money and mentioning only one letter from him, in 1844. He retired in 1851 to Victoria where he worked as pilot, harbourmaster, postmaster, and collector of customs. In 1855 he sent word with Captain Mouat that his mother should be looked after, but added that "as to writing her, he had bin so long in not doing so that he could not do it now." When his mother and sister Elsa wrote to the Company in September 1855, however, they were informed that he had withdrawn his entire account. In the same year Sangster was listed as holding about eight hectares (twenty or more acres) of land in the Victoria area. He retired from his various jobs because of ill health in July 1858 and, in October, he committed suicide. If his mother was still alive, she would have been seventy-seven at the time of her son's death and would have been his heir.

36 JAMES ADAMS: *Young Bill Gets a big Chap And says you must Bring im a Bear to pla with*

James Adams of London embarked on the *Cowlitz* as a seaman on 24 August 1840. A year or more after his departure, his aunt Mary Ann Bishop wrote to tell him the news from home. Her letter is typical of many writers whose aim was to tell as much as possible of the lives of family and friends using the least paper possible, paper and postage of more than one page being an expensive commodity for a working-class family. Aunt Mary made no attempt to separate good news from bad, private news from public happenings: the birth of a prince and the expectation of a birth in the family are given equal space. Mary's letter, written to a nephew who would understand such references as Kate's "Beads and Rings from tom" – could it have meant an engagement to marry? – leaves us to imagine the lives of the thirteen people mentioned in the short space of this letter.

∾ James Adams, Seaman on Board the Cowletts

London November 10 1841

> Dear James
> I take the hopertunity of Adressing you with a few Lines hopeing it will

find you quit[e] well as it Leaves us all at present[.] We Receved that mony
Last November from Gorbbins[.] Harry as Got a very Good plase on
tham[e]s st[.] Kate is at home[.] she Got her Beads and Rings from tom
About 2 mounths ago[.] your Aunt Betsey is dead About 3 mounths[.]
Nick Kayton is marrid and All most Got 1 Little one to the [word
scratched out]

    the Armary in the tower was Burnt the 30[th] of Last mounth and all the
Arms destroid[.] her Magesty was Confined with a prince the 9th of this
mounth[.] Cousin ~~Mary~~ [crossed out] Mary sends her Love you and says
you must bring her A Long thing home with you[.] Old Kayton wont
Leave of smoaking[.] farther sends is Respects to you[.] young Bill Gets a
big Chap And says you must Bring im a Bear to pla with

    Kate & Harry and we all Long to see you

      So no more at present

        from your Affectnot

          Aunt Mary Ann Bishop

10 Herods place

James Adams, the attentive nephew who sent home money to his family
in the autumn of 1840, never received his aunt's November 1841 reply. He
would never see his friend Nick Kayton's new child or bring the "Long thing"
to his cousin Mary or the bear to young Bill. He drowned at Fort Vancouver
on 1 April 1841. At nine o'clock that day he and Robert Pelly were scraping
the bends (the wales or crooked timbers that make up the sides of the ship)
when the ladder they were on broke and both fell overboard. Chief Mate
Charles Dodd described the rescue attempt: "with the assistance of the Cadboro's boat we succeeded in picking up Pelly but Adams had sunk to rise to
[no] more. We procured a net from the Fort and Grapnels from the other
Vessels and used every endeavour to find the body without success."

37 JAMES SIMPSON: *Thow we are fare saperated one from each I hope our
    harts will never be sapareted*

James Simpson signed on as a ship's carpenter with the Hudson's Bay Company on 5 November 1838 and left for the Columbia Department on the *Vancouver* on 6 November. He had married Margaret Walker in Dunfermline,
Fife, in Scotland on 5 January of the same year. They had nine months
together in their Kincardine home, before he left for three years' service on
the west coast, first on the *Vancouver,* then on the *Cadboro* and the *Beaver.*
James's son was born in February 1839, three months after his father's departure.

Margaret wrote to a Mrs. Anderson at 9 Leith Street, Commercial Row, asking her to continue to collect the half-pay that James had arranged for her to have, telling her correspondent that "I have no other thing to depend upon in my husbands absence." Margaret's letter to James, after nearly four years of absence, was filled with her loneliness.

To Mr James Simpson, Ship Carpenter – Columbia River,
To the care of William Smith Esqr, Hudson's Bay House, London

Kincardine 202th [22] Augest 1842

Dear Husband
i recived your long wiched for letter and was truely happy to hear of you being well altho it was nearly one year deated back[.] i reacived it on 8th of Juely and yours was wrote on the 28 of Juely 1841[.] many a time i thought if i had recived no letter from you that i would rather chouse the Lord to taken me to himself than been in a state of dispare[.] –
i was truely hapy to hear that you had recived too of my letters – i was very soory to hear of you being so porely with the fiver and ago [ague] and I at such a distance from you[.] it has been so ordained that we are to be far seaperated one from each other that we do not hear one anether compleaints nor bare one anether burdons but dear husband wee must cast our cars and our troubles upon that God who is able to deliver us out of six troubles yea and out out [repetition] of seven. Dear what valous our life hear to a long and a endless eterenty let us be laing up stores in Heaven that when wee met thare we never shal part agin[.] you say you had given in your waring to the governer to leave this year[.] i hope eranestly that you may for many a time i think shall that time never come when we may once meet again – i stated in my letter that i wrote in April this year that i drew the 30 pounds from the banck on the 31 of March this year so i have paid every one thar ane and furnished a plain room withe the balance so if I have no mony wee have no deatt – I am quiet well and hopes you are the sam but i expect you will be left befor this can reach you[.] our littel Soon has been very porely with the ruch fever but we may thank the lord that he is beeter again for i may say he is all my company[.] he is 3 years and 6 months old now and many a time he says to me Mother i have not got a Father yet like the other boides has – your Father and Mother and sisters and J Muray [Murray] sends thar kind love to you[.] my Mother and sisters sends thare love to you[.] our sister Christian sends her respects to you that she has [ano]ther Son[.] i think she is to [have] Childrene for us all – we have [not received] her new only thar was newes cam last week about the Death of Robert Meckeljohn

[Meiklejohn] that his Mate Gorge Lormer had throning him over bord[.]
he has been examined but his trial is not com on yet

    I have no more to anounce

  at presant but reamins your loving Wife till

    Death Margaret Simpson

    Besides missing Margaret's letter because of his return to London aboard
the *Cowlitz* in 1843, James also missed paying the debt mentioned in the following letter. Simpson owed a considerable amount and George Abernethy,
the accountant of the Methodist Mission and later the first governor of Oregon, 1845-9, wrote on behalf of Dr. Richmond, the Methodist missionary at
Nisqually, in hope of collecting the debt.

Mʳ James Simpson, Carpenter of the Company's Bque Cowlitz, care of the
Secretary of Hon Hudsons Bay Co, 3 Fenchurch St, London

Willamette 18 March 1843

    Dear Sir

    Dʳ J.P. Richmond formerly stationed at Nesqually handed me a draft
drawn as follows Viz

John Mᶜ Laughlin Esq

    Sir $46 –

    Please to pay Dʳ J.P. Richmond on order the sum of forty six dollars for
value received and charge to the account of

nov 6 – 1841   James Simpson

    I presented the draft to Dʳ McLaughlin [McLoughlin] shortly after I
received it from Dʳ Richmond and he informed me that you had left the
country and that there was no money in his hands belonging to you and he
could not pay it. Will you please on receipt of this pay the amount with
Interest from 20 March 1843 as we pay Interest from that date @ 5 P Cent
into the Hudson's Bay Cᵒ to be credited to the Methodist Mission on the
Vancouver Books

    and oblige

      Dear Sir

      Your obedᵗ Servant

      Geo. Abernethy

Mʳ Jas. Simpson

Should the Secretary of the H.B.Cᵒ. not be willing to receive this amount
please send it to me in silver by their vessel

James Simpson may have heeded his wife's desire to have him at home, as he did not enlist with the Company again until 1848, although he may have served on other ships. In 1848 he went once more to the west coast on the *Columbia,* leaving September 12, and arriving at Fort Victoria on 16 March 1849. Margaret wrote to tell him news of his son, Archibald, the little boy of the previous letter, and Christian, their daughter, born while her father was at home, as well as to announce the arrival of a new daughter.

   Mr James Simpson, on board the Barque Columbia, Captn Cooper, Columbia river

Kincardine Jun the 26 1849

My Dear James

I am happy to hear of another oppertunity I have of writing you to let you know of all our well beigiens trusting in God that this will find you in the same[.] it has pleased the Lord to add another Child to our charge[.] I was safe delivered of a Daughter on the 24 of Feberury[.] she is a fine active Child tha all think you have been in good umer when you have got her[.] dear we may thank the Lord she is all write fore I had many a thought[.] you well know wat I mean by that[.] her name is Margaret[.] I have removed Archbald to Mst Buchanan Chool as I thought he was doing very little good at Mst Willson[.] Christian is a stout girl[.] I intend sending her of to Chool on Monday first[.] I receve my monthely money pointedley. your Father and Mother are in thare ordenery way but still the old crie thare is nothing doing hear. Duncan and his Famely saild from Glasgow on the 8 of Aprile fore New Yourk[.] your sister went of with a sore heart[.] thare house was sold 100 20 pounds the 3 of its velaw [value.] thare furniture was all sold at a publick rope [raup or auction][.] tha ware as mean when tha went of as when tha came home so I do not think we will Miss them[.] I Mury [Murray] is no weeter tha have got out the Licince and doing well[.] tha are the only Famely it will Miss herr. James Coutts is still at home and canot get a ship thare is neither work nore ships fore any one hear he has been at home 10 months and my Brother John 7 months[.] I am very soory to relate to you about the Death of my Brother Charls and William Wallker[.] tha joined a Brig at Glasgow bound fore Napels the one Master and the other Mate and Walter Walker 2 Mate[.] tha went a shore on Arkley Banks on the 27 of Feberury[.] tha put down one Boat trieng to safe thare lifes and it fild with water and went down and tha had lanched the other and after all was in the Boat only Wallker and the Cock and Charls[,] the Peanter [painter, or rope] brock and left them on the Wreck and thare was not the smalest Bit of her to be seen[.] the next morning

Wallter Wallker and the rest of the Crow was picted up and brought to London[.] Dear James we get many warings to be preparing fore Death o that we ware at all times ready[.] thes last 8 days thare was old Robert Gipson [Gibson?] and John Scotland and I Finely all at Curch the one sabeth and in thare grave the next[.] thar is nothing new here[.] Jane Hutten was mured on Alaxander Gray the last week

    I have no more to anounce only I hope you will not lose one opertunity of writing me fore you know my thoughts are never at rest thinking about you and I have got a good Charge at home now

      I have no more to sae

but reamins yous loving wife till

    Death Margaret Simpson

Margaret's news of James's sister Ann provides our information on the emigration to the United States of Alexander Duncan (entry 14). Given our knowledge of the Duncans from reading Ann's letters, it is interesting to see her sister-in-law's judgment that Ann went with a sore heart and that the couple were as miserly when they went as when they had last come home, so the remaining family was unlikely to miss them. Perhaps Margaret's bitter remark resulted from the family attitude to herself. Or perhaps it was influenced by the fact that she had just lost her own brother at sea and was even more nervous about her husband's absence and, as a result, less generous toward his family. However, by the time she wrote the next month to reiterate her news after she had heard of the *Columbia* reaching its destination, she had moderated her view of the Duncans somewhat and seemed then to be more concerned about how abruptly she and James parted.

Mr James Simpson on board the Barque "Columbia", Captn Cooper, Columbia river

Kincardine Juely th 16 1849

    My Dear James

    I hard by Mst Anderson on the 8 of Jun that the Clumbia arived all well on the 6th of Feberury wich I was very happy of[.] I think you would have no oppertunity of writing me ore I would have recived a letter but I live in hope that I will recive one in September. dear I wrote you in May and gave you all the newes wich you will recive[.] I state them over again in fear you should not recive it[.] I was safe deliverd of a Daughter on the 24 of Feberury[.] she is a nise active Child I hope she will be a Blessing to us both – your Father and Mother are in thare ordenry way but still the old Cry thare is nothing doing[.] Cpt Duncan and all his Famely is safe arived

out at New York all well[.] tha ware as frindely when tha went away as
when you cam home so you well mind I think – your sister Margaret has
got out the License and she is quiet high now[.] I Mury [Murray] is no
better[.] the rest of our frinds are all well[.] I also sated about my Brother
Charls and William Wallker Death[.] tha ware lost on the 27 of Feberury
with a Vesell belong to Glasgow bound for Napels & the unserteny of time
and the warnings we get every day[.] dear many is the time I sat hear and
think on the raped way we parted from each other[.] I hope our metting
will not be like our parting[.] Mary Hutton is parted from her husband
never to met in this World she died on Sunday last after a short illness[.]
the Childrene and I are well Chrisian is of to Choll and Archbald is stout
fellow getting[.] I hope this will find you in god health dear you must
excuse me the Babe is trubelsom and my Sister Christian and her Famely is
come frome Glasgow whill I am writing yo to stope 2 or 3 days[.] I have no
more to anounce but reamins your loving and afectionet wife
Margaret Simpson

Margaret wrote two more letters to James during 1849. Although they add
some news to the contents of the other letters, they are perhaps more interesting in charting Margaret's changing attitudes.

Mr James Simpson, Carpenter on board of the Columbia, Columbia river,
& care of the Hudson Bay Coy in London

Kincardine Oct the 12 1849

My Dear James
I recived your kind letter on the 6 of Sept deted the 25 of April and has
read it over and over[.] I am truely happy to hear that you are in good
health[.] you seem to think that I had soon fore got you but belive me dear
James thare is not one houre in the day but you are the most of all my
thoughts[.] you say thare is temping wages to go to Caleforne [California]
but I am content with the mone[y] you have[.] tha all sea hear that tha are
dieing like roten shep out thare so I think thare Gold dust will not be of
much use. dear this is the 4th letter I have wrote you I hope you have
recived som of them[.] I stated all about Margaret s birth and my Brother
Charls death and all the newes[.] the Childrine and I are quiet well[.]
Margaret is nise stout Child[.] she is 7 months old now[.] it is long time to
loke foret to before she can be embresed with a Father kiss but thare is one
year of it past[.] Christian is geting nisele on at the Chol[.] Archbald is
geting on with the conting he is in to bills a parsels[.] your father and
Mother are quiet well and all the rest of our friends[.] dea Colric [cholera]

has been very bad in this country it is round and round us but it has not com in to our small vilege yet[.] thar wase 5 hundred died in Gre[e]nock thes last 2 months o many is the waring we get to be ready. thare is no more acounts of Duncan and his famely since thar arivel out at New york[.] James Couts is away to Amareke about 2 month ago and Robert Gray saild fore Bombie [Bombay] 2 weks ago[.] thare is nothing new here it is like a toun to let[.] dear be sure and write every opertunety you know fore a letter frome you is like a healing Balsam to a severe wond[.] I have no more to anounce but reamins your loving and affectionet wife Margaret Simpson

when you write again say how Mast Mitchel is if he is still with you

[on cover] I receve my month pay reguler

∿ Mr James Simpson on board the "Barque Columbia," Columbia river, To the Hudson Bay House, London

Kincardine December 17th 1849

My Dear James
I hear by Mst A[nderson] thare is a Ship to sail this weck and I take the oppertunity of writing you to let you know how we all are[.] the Childrine and I are all well onlly Margaret has a large belling under her eye wich gives me a deal of truble and thought[.] dear I hope this will find you well[.] I mentioned in my last leter that I recived a letter from you wich I was very happy of[.] your Father and Mother are in thare ordenry way and all our other Friends[.] tha are geting few in number now[.] my uncell Walter Walker Died at Corck [Cork] on the 7 of November with Deasentery [dysentery][.] thare was a letter from C^pt Duncan last weck and he has bought a large Farm about 7 Hundred miles from New York and all the pleanshing on it and Catell[.] tha think tha will make a fortune fore life now[.] dear I wich you could find a peace of Calfornie [California] Gold out thare that we might live together fore life fore we must be alawas saperated fore the sake of our living[.] I am still reciving the monthly mony[.] dear you must truie and mind to fill your Bed with Feathers and stufe it well fore you know you have 2 Daughters to set of[f] now. when you write say if you think you will be kept all your time out fore I think it is a long time to loke foret to[.] thare is little news hear only Robert Hotton has got another wife with a Criple leg[.] she is a Mury [Murray] of Window Hill[.] I have had a viset frome Wallkers Widow[.] she appears to be very lonly[.] she has a nise Child much like his self[.] Mis Masttern has had a Child about a month ago and has giving it to my Brother Charls

wich causes much thougt if he had been a life to answerd fore himself[.] it brings his death all anew again[.] dear thow we are fare saperated one from each I hope our harts will never be sapareted[.] when you write say if you are still aboard the same ship and how you are coming on with Mat Mitchel[l]. dear I have now more to anounce but reamins your loving Wife till death Margaret Simpson

While Margaret had obviously been thinking of James constantly and writing to him regularly, James, who had received no letters, worried that she had forgotten him. James's mention, in a letter he wrote from the Columbia Department, of the possibility of going to the California gold rush, was at first received with some chagrin by Margaret, who assured him that she is "content with the mone[y] you have." By the latter letter, she was wishing that he "could find a peace of Calfornie Gold out thare that we might live together fore life." There seems to be envy of the Duncans, who may have left with sore hearts but now may "make a fortune fore life" in America. No matter how her opinions changed, the hope she expressed in her July 1849 letter that "our metting will not be like our parting" remains constant in her wish that "thow we are fare saperated one from each I hope our harts will never be sapareted."

James Simpson missed all these letters because he had left the west coast on 1 November 1849 aboard the *Columbia,* which arrived in London on 17 April 1850. By 3 June he was aboard the *Prince Rupert* as carpenter, bound for York Factory. We do not know if he had any communication with Margaret during the brief six weeks he had between voyages. He returned that fall with the *Prince Rupert,* which arrived back in London on 7 October, and there is no further record of his serving with the Company. Perhaps he went home. Perhaps he enlisted with another company. We can hope that Margaret and James were reunited and the children got their chance to know their father.

38 EDWIN ROBERTS: *We have been tosted about quite plenty*

Edwin Roberts of Liverpool, England, served from 1840 to 1845 as a seaman aboard the *Cowlitz,* a ship that sailed outward to the Columbia Department in 1840-1, back to London in 1842-3 and out again, leaving London on 23 September 1843 and arriving at Fort Victoria on 24 March 1844. He missed this letter sent in 1842 but may have received news of the family during his London layover in the summer of 1843. Edwin's brother, or perhaps brother-in-law, a lace manufacturer in Liverpool, told of his own economic woes but is singular in that he relayed absolutely no news of the women of the family and friendship group, except indirectly. As he had had two children who had died since Edwin had left, we may assume that Jones's wife was, possibly, Edwin's sister.

◡ Mr E Roberts on Board of the Barque Cowslip, Marriner, Fort Vancover, Columbia River, NW America

Liverpool 19 Byron Street October 25th 1842

Dear Edwin,
    I duly recieved your letter dated March 16 this day and am sorry to find you will be so long before you come home but am very happy to hear you are in good health and hope you will continue so and I must beg of you when you arrive to come right to me as you now will have a comfortable home to come to. I have recieved a letter from Sydney [possibly a person, or a reference to an unnamed couple or family who had emigrated to Sydney, Australia] about a month since and the[y] are in good health but from there letter I should say are but badly off as the wish me to send them 10 pounds. Trade as been I know very bad there but is now much better[.] I have been doing but badly since I last wrote to you[.] I had 3 retail shops and was doing a very good Buisiness in them But I had some very heavy losses[.] I lost on one occasion 800 pounds and again 200 more and so on for this last 6 months untill such like losses compeled me to stop payment which I did 2 months since and was made a Bankrupt but I have no got over it all and am carrying on my Buisiness as usual but have given up all my shops but this one which is a Little fortune for me[.] I have had 2 Children since you was in England but both are dead[.] one I called after you and you see I have had my Trouble but now all is quite right again[.] I am in the best of health and have been[.] I have not seen Henry lately but he his in the same place and doing very well[.] I have not seen my uncle this 12 months but I believe he his in the Town[.] We have had a very Bad Fire in Liverpool burning about 20 wharehouses and 30 Houses besides stables and property to the amount of near 900 Thousand pounds and 10 or 12 people kiled[.] The shipping trade is very bad here at present men are shipping for 2 pounds and 2 pounds 5/- Month I suppose it was never worse in fact all Trades are alike here at present[.] I do not know if my letters come to hand as I think the direction is not sufficient[.] I think James and Thomas will be back here very soon that is if the can get money to bring them[.] at all events it will now be in my power to put you all in a different way of getting a living and one rother more comfortable. and so let us hope for the best and hope the good is to come last as I think we

have been tosted about quite plenty f[or] young folkes[.] I have recieved my money from Mrs Balls 2 days after you where 21 and James and yours will be paid you when you come to L[iver]pool. I send you all the news I have and hope the next you send you will bring yourself and as paddy said thats a Blunder and Believe me dear Edwin till then your affectionete Brother

> SW Jones
> Lace Manufacturer
> 19 Byron Street
> Liverpool

Edwin Roberts's career with the Company extended beyond his *Cowlitz* service. After two years as a seaman on the *Beaver,* in 1846 he became a boatswain on the *Columbia* and was promoted in 1848 to second mate. Roberts signed Captain Duncan's protest (a legal document outlining the circumstances of damage to a ship) when the *Columbia* ran into trouble on the way from Fort Langley (present-day Langley, British Columbia) to the port of Victoria on 8 October 1847. It stated that, when "towing down the Straits of Juan de Fuca in a calm the Vessel was caught by a strong tide, [which eventually] swept the vessel broadside on the rocks and dragged her along them about 20 fathoms when she swung clear." The *Columbia* had arrived in harbour "making water at the rate of 4½ inches every 12 hours." In 1849, after five years of successful west coast service, he deserted with nine other men (including William Murray, entry 54) somewhere on the California coast where the fever of the gold rush was mounting. He is reported to have joined an American party travelling to the gold fields.

39 JOHN CRELLY: *You have a quick temper and you ought to gard it*

John Crelly's mother's letter from Stenston, Scotland, is one of the best illustrations of the ways in which the interdependent nature of family was sorely tested by the expansion of Britain as a trading nation and an empire. This mother had three sons far from home: John, who served as a seaman aboard the *Cowlitz* after leaving some other unnamed ship that was not a Company vessel; Peter, who has been away at sea for fourteen months without a word home; and James, who under an assumed name, seems to have fared the worst, falling to "drink [and] bad company" in London. With three ablebodied adult sons, a mother of that time might reasonably have expected some financial help from them in times of family hardship. It would seem that no such help was forthcoming very soon.

∾ John Crelly, Mariner on Board the Barque Cowlits, Care William Smith
Esqre, Hudson Bay House London

Stenston May the 10 [1843]

   My Dear Son I receved your kind and welcome letter and is verey happy
to hear that you are in the land of the living and in good health for I have
been looking long for a letter from you for I got the one you sent when
you left the Ship and you may consider what condition I have been in
since[.] Dear Son your friends hear is all in good health only my self I have
been poorly this long tim for I was greatly troubled about you and Peter[.]
I have got no word from him since the month of Agust and I am afraid he
is not in life or he would have wrot me and for you brother James I cannot
tel you anay thing about him[.] I had a letter from him out of London in
March last but it was not his own hand writ and he said he was well and
new arrived from a man of war and he wanted our answer and I sent him
three but I never got an answer from him[.] I will gave you his addres and
try and find out wher he is gon till but he is going under the name of
James Wilson[.] Dear Son I hope that you will not be so foolish about
London as he was but leave it as soon as you get clear of the ship and you
will get cheapest home and com with the tram to Liverpool and com with
one of the steam boats to Glasgow[.] and if you do not com home writ me
when you come ther and if I ame abel I will go and see you and take
stockings and drawers to you and the rest of you clothes and let me know
if you nead blankets[.] Dear Son I hope you will not take no drink and
kep of bad com[pan]y you see what it has done to your brother James[.]
come out of London as quick as you can for I have broken my heart about
him to think he has forsaken me as he has don but I trust in god that you
will not forsake me as he has don and god will reward you for it again[.]
the 13th of this month your brother Peter will be fourteen months saild[.] he
is out in the Nepal of Gre[e]nock but he could get no monthly money
left to me[.] it has mad me the warse of[.] if I had got stoping in my
owen haues my owen money would have done me but I have been with
you Grandfather since you went away for he can see to read none this
twelmonth[.] I have still kep my houes in the town[.] I well depend on you
to writ to me as soon as you recev this and I hope that you will take your
mothers adves and leave London and be cose you sister Marey is in
Glasgow and go ther for she will be happy to see you[.] I think if I once
seed you it would almost I vow en me for I neva thought to hear word of
you again as you left the ship[.] Dear Son you have a quick temper and you
ought to gard it[.] you Ant Sarah left the Bantills last martimas poorely in

health and Sally dead is maried and Willam is maried on a London lady[.]
you must go and see her[.] you friends hear sends their kind love to you
and is verey happy to hear frome you[.] you sister address is John Stewart,
Baleson lane back Lane No 22 Anderson Glasgow[.] the last letter address
I had for James is Mrs Walker Narey now black Wall[.] you must [let]
yourself be know to Willam deads wif and tell her you are coming hom
and if she has aney word to send to you Ants that you will bring it[.]
Mrs Willam Dead thamus [Thames] Street Rotherwithe [Rotherhithe]
London[.] Dear Son I hope if you see the Captain in Glasgow do not mind
him uniles you turn more troubel youself[.] no more at present but remens
you affectd mother till Death Janet Crelly
your sister Sarah sends her kind love to you and she hopes you have som
neo thing for her
I hope you will try and find out wher yore brother is gone till[.] I have not
apeney till put on with it

    Janet's concern with her own economic ills, once she could not count
on her sons to contribute to the family's support, was overshadowed by her
concern for John's physical and spiritual well-being. She also feared that his
"quick temper" would prove his worst danger if he should meet with "the
Captain in Glasgow." Perhaps John's last letter gave details of why he left his
former captain and ship. Janet knew that it would be trouble for her son if
his temper were given occasion to undo him. From her expectation of his
coming home, we can assume that John must have indicated that he had
joined the *Cowlitz* to return home. He arrived in London aboard that ship
on 9 May 1842, leaving the ship and the Company's service the next day. We
do not know if Janet was able to find her son to supply him with stockings
and drawers, as well as her good advice.

40 ARNOLD [JOHN?] NICHOLS: *Nothing will give equal satisfaction of seeing you*

Records show that a "John Nichols" left London in 1839 on board the Hudson's Bay Company's ship *Columbia* and arrived home on the *Cowlitz* on 9
May 1843. Sometimes men signed up under other names, making the difficult lines of communication even more tortuous. In this case, it seems that
Arnold Nichols may have signed up under his brother John's name. This letter also makes us aware that not only was delivery of letters from England a
problem but men's letters to their parents often went astray. The experience
of the Nichols – their sons scattered abroad – also reflects the effect on families of Britain's growing overseas trade in the 1840s.

∾ Arnold Nichols, on board the Barque Cowlits, to the care of Wm Smith Esqr, Hudson bay house, London

Millbrooke May 11 – 1843

Dear Son

It cannot but give us unspeakable comfort after so long a time to hear from you once more, your letter of the 7 is safe arrived and we sincerely hope your expectations of seeing us in ten or twelve days will be accomplished for nothing will give equal satisfaction of seeing you. The last account we received from you was by Robt Brown about 9 or 10 months since who informed us that he had seen you in America but as to the letters you mention of having wrote we have received none, but thank God we have now the news of your arrival in England and hope soon to be favoured with your presence, – As it regards our family concerns which you enquire after are chiefly as follows – your sister Herriot is married with a Henry Anderson in Jubilee Street Plymouth N° 24, you will probably have to pass her door when you come to Plymouth and your presence will give her great satisfaction. Pearce and John are now living with me, John is a widower but Pearce is unmarried; Wiliam I am sorry to say is no more he died on the Coast of Africa on the 12 May last – Thomas is at Sea in the Gorgon steamer and Mary lives at Wembury and is married to Willm Mitchell, this is briefly the outline of family pedigree but on our meeting which we look forward to with much pleasure we shall be able to converse fully on family information – Thank God I am still living but from Age and infirmity cannot boast of good health, still am thankful that I am so well as I am and spared I hope once more to see you after so many years absence and not knowing if you was living or not –. You will find us at Millbrook and hope no[thing] will prevent your coming for we shall all anxiouly await your arrival and receive you with great pleasure, for the present I conclude with the kind loves of your Brothers, Sister and families and belive me to remain

Your most aff^t Mother

Martha Nichols

Please to answer this by the return of post and let us know if possible which way you will come And your Brother John will be there to meet you

The letter bears the remark, "No such person on board the Cowlitz." Perhaps Arnold missed his mother's note because, if he had signed up as "John," his shipmates had not recognized him by the name "Arnold." After his many failed attempts to communicate with his family, he may have been on his way home. Or it is possible that he had found another ship and was outward bound, robbing his mother of her satisfaction yet again.

41 ISAAC R. CHRISTOPHER: *Tis a great thing to see a good Religous Saylor – and not adrunking fool*

Isaac R. Christopher left England in September 1841 aboard the *Vancouver* and was serving as a seaman on the *Cadboro,* engaged in its coastal duties in the Columbia Department, at the time his mother wrote these two letters. From internal evidence it is obvious that she has dated them wrongly and that the letter of 13 May was written before that of 12 May. Their mailing dates would also support reversing the order of the letters. A Mary Bardwell – who, as we learn at the end of the 13 May letter, is Isaac's sweetheart – had written to Isaac's mother giving her a London address for her son: "Fort Vanedriver, To the Care of Mr Smith Esqr, st Fenchurch N° 4, London." Not realizing that this is the Company's head office, Isaac's mother assumed that her son was back in England and she directed him to hurry with speed home to an ailing family – but not before he has checked on his sister's situation. Fanny would seem to have been in service with "Cap[tain] Handessen" (possibly Anderson or Henderson).

◠ Mr Christopher, Fort Vanedriver [Vancouver], To the Care of Mr Smith Esqr, st Fenchurch N° 4 London, with speed

May th 13 1843

My dear Child
I Receved a letter from Miss Mary Bardwell and was very glad to hear that you are well and you are come so near as London[.] I hope my dear Child you will let nothing hinder you to come home to see us[.] your Father and sister Martha is very bad[.] I hope you will come home at once[.] I know you will, if you are steady you dont want for money, I am hear in Market to day, and would leave no time slip as your sister fanny is in London[.] she Arived in London last monday and is but going to stop for a short time in London[.] I do not know her Directions in London[.] she was home seeing us for 5 weeks and went from Pater in the queens yot [yacht] calld Victoria Albert, she is now in the East Indea Dock, now my dear you may well know how glad your poor sister will be to see you now go so Respectable as you can to the east indea Dock and inquire for Cap Handessen or Harier the steward [possibly John Harrier, then steward on the *Cowlitz,* entry 48] and tell them you are Fanny Christophers Brother and you will be glad if you could find her out[.] I hope you will do the best you can and find her out[.] she will be so glad to see you, and write me along letter and tell me when you are coming home[.] you may well know

how glad we shall be to see you[.] your sweetheart was very kind to write to me[.] your Brother Caleb is gone to sea with Capt Griffiths[.] I shall say no more as I shall be waiting every day to see you so no more from your Mother

I thought to come to London when you you [repetition] come there to see you but my mony is to short or else I certainly would[.] I am wishing to see you[.] if you had half the desire to see me you would soon be home and I hope you will

What a frustration it must have been to think her son was so near and not actually know where he was! Another letter, however, makes Mrs. Christopher realize that she was foolish to take the London address as a sign that her son was back in England. We learn more of Fanny, who was as much a cause of concern as was Isaac. His life, far from home, was not one that his mother could easily have imagined; however, she could probably more easily have imagined a multitude of threats to her daughter, Fanny. If Fanny were in service, the most difficult part of her life would have been the gruelling work from dawn to dusk, a life as rigorous as her brother's life at sea.

∾ Mr I. Christopher, Columbia River, Care of W. Smith Esqr, Fenchurch Street, London

Jerusalem May ^th12 1843

My Dear Child
I Recieved your letter yestarday with great Joy, and am very glad to hear that you are alive and well, tis the only comfort I have to hear from you[.] I had aletter before the 20 of October[.] I am glad you have not forgot me[.] tis my greatest wish is to see you once while I am in this world[.] the Lord only knows whither I shall or no, I think you will come if you are steady and live and that I hope you are for I think you cant forget what we be by idleness, I am afraid that we shall be forced to be in the Union house – your Father is gone a sorry Old man and full of infirmities[.] I dont think he will live long[.] he is very bad now not able to do any thing and I am not much better– I had a letter from Shields the same day I had yours from Mrs Mary Bardwell[.] she was very kind to tell me she heard from you and desired me to write to her which I shall Do now, she gave me your Adress and I was so foolish to think you was in London – I wrote you a letter at once, I dont know will you have it or not – your poor Sister Fanny was Just gone to London she had been home for five weeks seeing us, and I wrote to her at once to tell her you was in London – but to her great disapointment she could not find you[.] I think there would been great Joy if you could a

met – she is living in the same place but the family was gone to London and she went there to meet them – she is a very steady Respectable Girl she is drest like a lady she is mostly drest in silk and her vail but she have got very bad health and very thin[.] she is very kind to me she helps me all that is in her power I am going to write to her – to write to you[.] poor Caleb is gone to sea with Capt Griffiths he went in February – I have not saw him since[.] Martha is home she takes in sowing [sewing.] she is grown a woma[n] and her sister have well rigd her of Joshua and Evan is in schoo[l.] Evan says when the wind blows I dont know where your poor Boy is now Mother the wind is blowing on him – Nathan Davies is gone out to America to Ohio[.] he wen[t] in last April not knowing any one[.] his poor Mother is in a deal of trouble about him[.] they wishes you could meet him he is a very Religous young man and very tall and Smart[.] twas his own will to go – the times is gone very bad here[.] them that was doing well – is very poor now – and no hopes of better[.] the Lord knows what we shall meet – your Grand mother wondered you never gave your love to her[.] she with your Uncles and Aunts and Cousins and Brothers and Sister Joins in love with your Father and me, and may the Lord bless you and give you grace and every comfort and may you come great in this world and become as Joseph was to his brethren

[upside down] I hope you makes much of your Bible and that will teach you to be wise tis a great thing to see a good Religous Saylor – and not adrunking fool[.] can you mind them good saylors that was here and what floks of people went to hear them praying, I hope the Lord will look on you now in your youth very slippery paths without a great Guide

now my dear Isaac I hope you will write soon and write along letter and leave me know when you think to come home to see me and what wages you gets and what are you doing away so long and is very warm of[f] there I did there is never no rain there [.] let me know all the news, so no more

from your mother

The observation that Fanny "is drest like a lady . . . in silk and . . . vail but have got very bad health and [is] very thin," explained why his mother wanted Isaac to see his sister: she may well have been worried that the environment of London – often seen in the nineteenth century as much more corrupt than other locations – might indeed have been bad for her Fanny. Meanwhile, there was more to worry about at home, with Isaac's father near death and "poor Caleb . . . gone to sea." This mother, like many of all classes, understood that part of her role was that of religious counsellor. Her hopes for her son's life were cast in religious images, as she wished he would become "as Joseph was to his brethren," a kindly caretaker. For us as readers, her religious sentiments may seem ironically suitable, as she wrote from Jerusalem. Her fears were also present as she urged him not to become "adrunking fool" but, rather, one of the good sailors who pray and read their Bible regularly.

Company records show that Isaac returned to England on 10 June 1844, aboard the *Vancouver,* probably about the time his mothers' letters reached Fort Vancouver. We do not know the fates of Fanny and Isaac or of their mother. Perhaps Isaac shipped out again to another part of the world, as many a returning sailor did. If he had saved a little money, perhaps he did go home to Jerusalem to see his mother, or perhaps he wrote to her after seeing his sister.

42 THOMAS STOREY: *Since I wrote this first part of my letter I feel more settled*

Thomas Storey had served with the Company since 1838 as a seaman aboard the *Vancouver.* Ann Storey's letter to her brother from Stoke Newington (now in London) reveals the precarious life led by women who earned their living in service, especially if any cloud of scandal hung over them. Sometimes a single young woman's efforts to retrieve her character after having had a child did not succeed. Ann seems to have suffered for her slip both within and outside her family and, in her letter to Thomas, she noted her many changes since her brother had left home.

Thoˢ Storey, on Board the Barque Vancouver, Fort Vancouver, Columbia River, Sent by the Barque Cowlits

Stoke Nevington Friday May 26ᵗʰ 1843

My Dear Brother
I was much pleased at receiving a letter from you and hearing that you had arrived safe and well and that you had a pleasant voyage[.] I received your letter on the 10ᵗʰ of May, dated the 3ᵈ of November[.] I sent you a long letter last March twelve month but I find you had not received it when you wrote this but it was a very long one. there has been many changes and up and down since you left home. Mʳˢ Tanners home and happiness is all broke up and through Henry having a loan from a society which his mother Bound herself down to be answerable for the money but that is above a twelve month ago she has left Pell Street all that time and they have took the other security and she is hourly expecting the officers to take her Body[.] I called on her the day after I received your letter and she was much pleased to hear from you and told me that I was to write for her and myself to. and as to myself there has been a great change with me[.]

when I wrote you my letter I expressed myself to be very comfortable
which was the case at that time although I had many reproaches and
unkindnesses to put up which did for the sake of my dear child. but I am
no longer Servant of Mrs Tallon. I have been treated in the most base cruel
manner and every Body in the neighbourhood cries out shame of her[.] she
gave me warning to leave her on the Tuesday about I think the ninth of
December Last and turned me out the next day without a shilling to help
myself after been with her nine years and a half. I felt her treatment severly.
I must leave the rest till I see you if God should spare our lives[.] I have
been at home four months the first two months I went out and earnt a few
shillings where I could but since that I have got into constant work. Its true
it cost too much but still it is a dependence eight shilling a week and
eighteen penc beside brings it to nine and sixpence a we[ek] and I think
that will keep and my child from want. the person I am working for lived
with Mrs Tallon or properly speaking worked for her nine years before me.
She knows more of her character than I do myself. She not only turned me
out pennyless but she tried to hinder me getting my Bread. she has been
everywhere she thought I had a friend scandaliseing me and setting them
against me even to Emma Macfarlane who was my dearest friend I had that
could spend a happy hour or two with, she has been to them and told all
about the child. and I know not for why except one thing she had a young
man at work in the stoare the with her for three month who she was very
partial to and because we got acquainted with she was afraid she should
loose me and because I did not Break it of she parted with[.] now this is
the only offence that I gave. for since you have left I can defy any one to
say ought against my character I have strove to the utmost to retrieve it and
I hope when you come home you will find striving in a steady upright
manner to get a living. the person I am working for is the little lady
opposite to Mrs Tallon. I am happier with her than I ever was with the
other[.] I come home to my meals and sleep at home. Mother still works
for Mrs Peglor. but she gets very ill able the infirmities of age is creeping on
her[.] I wish it was in my Power to keep her but I cannot. Caroline is still
with us but since you left we have had her at home to keep for she has had
a chap keeping her company for a year a half and has proved to be a
married man and that unsettled her for any place. she has now got a week
or two but [crossed out] work this summer but it will not last I am afraid
and one suiter but he is a very gay young man under 20 but an excellent
companion for you when you come home he longs to see you. we have not
heard any thing of father since you left. we have moved from the house left
us at but when you come home if you come to Mrs Lydamonts opposite to
Mrs Tallon you will find me tho I must tell you with my heart full that

since I have been at home Mother has behave in a most shameful manner
to me. nay indeed worse that the brute rea[c]tion I can say that since I have
at home I have not had one hour comfort for she makes me out the vilest
of the vile although I am study her to get many little necessary and clothes
for to apper comfortable more so than she has been for some years but I
cannot dwel upon this any more till I see you. when you come home when
you get to grevesend [Gravesend] if you writ to me I will come down to
gravesend and meet you[.] I shall look forward for the time and you see my
letter is full that I can say no more hoping this find you well and happy
when you return. I hope sincerely you find all comfortable I shall endeavour
as it lays in my p[owe]r it to be in so believe me Dearest Brother love your
affectionate sister Ann Story

at Mrs Lydamonts Staymaker opposite the dispensary high street Stoke
nevington
the house we used to live in was so shaky we could not stop so we have got
a comfortable little hous with good piece of garden and every convenience[.]
it is in the street opposite to where we live first and we have got I believe a
comfortable lodger with us since I wrote this first part of my letter I feel
more settled or else I meant to have taken a move and have been by myself
but I wish to be all the help to mother that I can for I can assure you that
nine and six pence comes in very sweet of a Saturday to go to market
therfore I think the least Mother can do is to be a little civil to me which I
am sure she has not ever been that since I have been at home but I must
leave all the rest till I see you hoping that you will find things more comfortable than you have ever done I will try my utmost to have our home
more comfortable so that I think you may cheer up and look forward with
more pleasure than you have before[.] carrolein has not even been to town
since you left without me and upon the whole her thoughts do not seem
inclination towards any thing found in her before[.] since I have been at
home I have no had a word amiss with if she will but avoid that is all I
want or I have ended my long letter[.] we all unite in kind love to you
likewise Mrs Tanner and family desire to be kindly remember[.] Mary is
married and betsy I think will soon be[.] William and henry are still at home
     from your affectionate sister
     Ann Storey
Our direction is Union Street High Street

     Ann's letter – written on the back of a letter dated 17 November 1836 from
Emma Hogben ordering stays from Mrs. Tallon, Ann's former employer – is
a rich source of knowledge about the social conditions for ordinary people

who have fallen on bad times. Mrs. Tanner may pay for her debts with imprisonment, and Ann herself was turned out penniless without references after nine years with the same employer. Even Ann's own family had not shown support and compassion, judging from her comments on her mother's harsh criticism. But by the time she wrote the second part of her letter, she feels more settled about her situation, hoping that her brother's homecoming will make up for her mother's disapproval. The letter to which Ann referred as not received by her brother in 1842 was not among the Company's undelivered letters, so perhaps he did receive her long letter after he had written to his sister. Storey left the Company's service after his return home on the *Vancouver* in 1844. Perhaps Ann had an opportunity to "come down to gravesend and meet" the one person she felt might still have been on her side.

43 JOHN OXLEY: *I have now My dearest John, a most painful communication to make to you*

John Oxley served as second mate on the *Vancouver* from 1841 to 1844. After she finished the long journey around Cape Horn, the ship was engaged in the Columbia service, trading along the coast for a year before beginning her return voyage. The two letters from John's brother in May and August 1843, in response to John's letter to their mother, give us a glimpse into the activities of a young, gainfully employed, London bachelor who was as much interested in the public world of fashionable news – from the birth of a princess to experiments in flight – as he was in the activities of family and friends.

Mr John Oxley, Ship Vancouver, Columbia River, via Hudsons Bay

Baltic Coffee House London May 28th /43 [1843]

Dear John,
It was with much pleasure I read your letter to Mother, which she receivd on the 15th I am happy to hear you are quite well, it appears the Columbian climate agrees with you, as so does the English with us at home, we are all quite well, with the exception of Mother who sometimes complains but that must be expected, from the illness she has been labouring under for so long a time. – Aunt has just returned from Liverpool, where she has been staying for two months with M^r & Mrs Viner who are quite well, they often enquire after you. – I was at home this morning, both Mother and Aunt decline writing this time as I am doing so, Aunt say she will be sure to give you a long letter the first opportunity. George was

at home he is quite well, they all desire their kind love to you. Uncle
Groves intends writing to you, not this time I think, he is not aware of the
ships sailing so soon, which I learn is on the first of next month, Aunt
Groves is quite well, and all the rest but Harry, who has been very ill for
some time, so ill indeed that at one time he was not expected to live, I need
not tell you that they desire their love. – Captⁿ Wilson sailed for Tobaga
[Tobago] last month, he has taken Alfred Bell with him, do you think he
will like it? some little difference between a comfortable home and a sailors
life, I should think. – I am still at the Baltic you see, with every likelihood
of stoping, we are in a deuce of a mess here, repairing the house, and
making alterations throughout, you must know I have had a rise in my tip,
fifteen bob a week a week [repetition] now jack, very agreeable, what do
you say?. –

The Thames Tunnell [crossed out] was opened last month by a grand
procession, which formed on the Surr[e]y side, and proceeded under to the
opposite one, and returned as the Times newspaper discribes as looking
very timid and much paler than when they started, it certainly must be
confessed that the walls themselves were in a *cold sweat,* but however the
public seem to be more courageous than those who opened it, if we may
judge from the numbers that have passed under upwards of 500,000 at one
penny each,

– Another great wonder is about to be started shortly, an Aireal Machine
something in the shape of a Bulloon, with wings, it is to go with such
rapidity that it will start from the top of the Monument at 8 in the morning,
and proceed to France to take up passengers, and then proceed to the
Pyrimids of Egipt [Egypt] to take dinner, start again and arrive at China in
time for a strong cup of Bohie [Bohea, a black tea]. – I will tell you a little
fasionable news now, the Queen was confined last month with another
Princess. The Duke of Sussex died a short time ago he is very much regretted. –

You talk of coming to England to get into buisness, every thing is very
bad here just now, every body is complaining about trade being bad,
therefore I think it would be a bad *speck,* as you have got a good birth I
should advise you to keep it.

– As to getting a wife for you, I can assure they do not require much
looking after, there are plenty both ready and willing, though I cannot
answer for the quality, but I flatter myself I shall be able to put that idea
out of you head altogeter when you come to England, the which you may
be sure I am looking forward to with much pleasure – I think I have told
you all the news now, you cannot complain about the lenght of my letter at
all events, you may depend I shall take every opportunity of writing, and
shall expect you will do the same in return.

All frinds join with me
    in kind love to you
        and believe I Remain
      Your Affectionate Brother
        WC Oxley
To John Oxley
Ship Vancouver
Columbia River

Mr John Oxley, Ship Vancouver, Columbia River

Baltic Coffee House London Augt 19th/43 [1843]

Dear John,

I think you will not have any reason to complain of my not having written to you, you must confess I have kept up a regular correspondence, they make me *letter writer general* to the family. – I was home this morning, Aunt says she hopes you will not think it negligent of her, not writing as she promised, for being so very much engaged at the present she has really not time, but desired me to give you her kindest love, & tell you she will not miss the next opportunity; when she will give you all particulars. – Mother also sends her kind love & hopes you are quite well, she is not so well as we *could wish,* the hot weather does not agree with her. George was at home he likewise sends his love; he was at home yesterday morning,– owing to an explosion in Fetter Lane at a fire work manufactory, at which six poor creatures have lost their lives; he thought he had better go down and let them know he was not blown up too. We had a dreadful fire on Friday night at Toppings wharf, the damage done is very considerable, St Olive's [Olave's] Church is completely gutted, with a number of houses: on the same night there were no less than 7 fires in the Metropolis, the number lately has been quite alarming. The weather is very hot indeed in London, although not exceeding last Xmas day with you, when the Sun melted the pitch out of the seams of the ship. – We thought of you on your birth day; & drunk you health, with many happy returns of the day. –

It seems a tremendous time since I heard from you, quite an age, I wish we could a little oftener, be sure & not loose an opportunity, this letter will come by the Cowlitz. – I saw Uncle Groves on Friday Evening; he say if he can possibly find time he will write to you this time, Aunt is quite well they both desire to be remembered to you, Harry has got quite round again. –

Captain Wilson has not returned yet, but is expected shortly, we have had letters from Alfred, who is quite well, & says he likes the Sea amazeingly. I saw Mr Bell yesterday he has been very queer lately, but is better now. Aunt Bell is quite well, as also are all the *little Bells,* they often enquire after you, if I were to reap over all the inquire's after you I should fill a sheet which is quite unnessasary, therefore suffice it to say that all friends constantly inquire very kindly respecting your welfare.

I have now a little bad news to tell you, you remember M^r & Mrs Hulbert of course, the poor old Gentleman was taken ill and died quite suddenly about a fortnight since. Mrs Hulbert is very much distressed you may suppose, Mrs Trimbrell was down on Monday week and brought the news, I know you like to know all, therefore I tell you every thing, I went to Gravesend on Sunday week, & spent a very pleasant day, George was with me & a friend, I had a great treat a short time ago our housekeeper got me a number of tickets, we went to the colleceum [coliseum] the Adelade Gallery and other places, & in the evening to the Theatre, George was with me, we very seldom go out without each other, where one goes the other is sure to go to. I often wish you was at home to go with us, but never mind *old Chap,* it [crosswise] is with much pleasure I am looking forward to your return, when I hope you will feel the benifit of so long a voyage, (in your pocket I mean). I think I have done justice to this sheet, I dont know what you will think, therefore I must conclude, with the hopes of hearing from you soon. – I remain

My Dear Brother
Yours Affectionatly
    WC Oxley
P.S. I find I have filled up too much so I must put it in another sheet.

Six months later, John's aunt wrote a more difficult letter, one that reminds us of the central place women played not only in their immediate families but often in their extended families of nieces and nephews.

Mr Oxley, Ship Vancouver, Captn Duncan, Columbia River

21. Jamaica Row, Bermondsey, March 2nd/44 [1844]

My dearest John,
I hope you have not thought it unkind my not writing to you before this – but you know how much my time is always engaged – and I trust that will be sufficient excuse – and knowing your dear Mother's punctuality in writing and her anxiety to give you all the News – that she left but little for me to communicate.

The last Letter we received from you was on the 11th of May /43. and dated Octr 30th /42 (which was the second you had written) informing us you were then at Fort George [Astoria, Oregon] – and that the Vancouver

was coming to England the following Year – you then thought of going to
Oahu or California – we have been looking most anxiously for one the last
few Months – William has written two since we received yours – one in
May – the other in August /43 – which I hope you have received

I will commence my letter from the early part of last year /43 in Feb^y[.]
Mr Venn had an advantageous situation offered him at Liverpool – which
he accepted – & Mrs Venn feeling a great deal at parting with her Family –
invited me to accompany them to stay a short time – I at first hesitated
fearing your dear Mother might feel uncomfortable at my being such a
distance from her – but She told me she thought it would be very unkind
if I did not go. – as Mrs Venn was such a kind friend – and that if she felt
ill – or wished my return I could come home immediately – and that I
might go more comfortable I accompanied her to Mr Callaways and he
then told me she was as well as she had been the last three years – & that I
might go – as I could get home in a day should it be necessary for me to
return – and your Aunt Groves kindly promised me that should your dear
Mother be ill – she would stay with her untill I could get home – I have
now My dearest John, a most painful communication to make to you –
one – equally painful for me to relate – as it will be for you to receive – but
which I trust you will bear with fortitude – but I will return to the time I
left London for Liverpool – I remained there 10 Weeks during which time
I received constant communication from home – Your dear Mother wrote
frequently ~~the~~ [crossed out] sometimes complaining of being poorly – at
other times ~~of~~ [crossed out] much better – The second week in May I
received a letter from your Aunt Groves telling me your dear Mother
complained of pains in her Limbs – and she advised her to have Medical
advice on the spot – as the Medicine Mr Callaway prescribed did not
appear to give her any relief – and that it would be better for me to return
home. Immediately I received the letter I left Liverpool the same even^g
travelled all night – and reached home at 7 o Clock the next Morning – I
found your dear Mother better than I expected but it was the pleasure and
excitement of seeing me – & she continued, we hoped, getting better for a
fortnight – (Mr Bunker & Dr Crutch attending her) but afterwards occasionally kept her bed 'till July – and became gradually worse untill the 1st of
Sept^r /43 – when she breathed her last – You May judge (My dear John) the
Trouble & Affliction both your Brothers and Myself were in for her loss –
also your Aunt & Uncle Groves[.] Your Aunt was with me at the time and
by her kindness helped to soften our Affliction – Her dear Remains were
Interred at Rotherhithe with your Father & Brother Henry – and followed
to the Grave by your Brothers George & William; your Uncle Groves,
Cousin George, Mr Newham & Mr Reeve

I will now My dear John enter into particulars the recollection of which is most distressing to Me. – your dear Mother was quite aware of her danger for some time – as she often spoke of it and told me it was the greatest comfort to her – My being with her – as she could communicate every thought to me & frequently told me in what Manner she wished Me to act – and one day when William was at home she said she had something she wished to communicate – that she should have liked George to be present – but feared perhaps she might leave it too long – she then said that from the weak state she was in, she felt she could not long be with us – and that when it pleased the Almighty to call her, she wished me to take her place – to be a second Mother to you all which she said she was sure I would – (as I had always taken the greatest interest in your Welfare from your earliest years) which I promised over and over again & which I will faithfully perform as far as lays in my power – She also said that as the Sum she had to leave was small – namely – 165 Pounds in the 3 Pr Cent Consols – that if she made a Will it would be attended with an expence – and also – if I was obliged to Administer – that it was her intention to give Me a Power of Attorney to have that Sum transfered into my hands – as she knew I should require a portion of it to meet Expences – and I should also require some for George – as she wished me to do the same for him as she had done – To find him in Clothing, Washing &c untill he was out of his Time – and that I was to take from the Sum she had transfered into my hands to do so – and also expressed a wish for me to keep a Home for you all, that you might be United (which was her most anxious wish) and that there might be a home for you when you returned, as she frequently spoke of you during her illness – I assure you I feel your dear Mother's loss most severely – I have not only [lost a] kind & affectionate Sister – but also My Companion – my Adviser and my greatest Comfort – but we must submit to the "Will of the Almighty disposer of Events – who gives or takes away as he thinks fit" – one great consolation to me is that I was enabled to attend to all her comforts during her long illness – I feel very lonely sometimes – your Aunt Groves kindly wishes me to reside with them – but I have thought of you when you return, as I should be obliged to move again as the distance would be too great for you – I have carefully looked over all your Papers – according to your dear Mother's wish & find the Memorandums as she told me – and what is due to you I will pay you on your return – she also spoke of a remittance you intended sending home – if you have done so – or intend doing it – you may depend on my placing it in the Savings Bank immediately I receive it – that it may produce Interest.

I must now tell you in what manner I have arranged – as [you] know

(My dear John) my circumstances will not enable me to pay all the Rent – which is £9 a Year – William has kindly offered to take his Third – I will pay my third – and George's third I must take from the money placed in my hands – (which I am sure you will not object too) untill he is out of his time, when he will be doing something for himself – which I assure you he looks most anxiously for – we are still at the old place 21 Jamaica Row Bermondsey –

I have received all the Bills this Christmas the expence of your dear Mother's Interment is £14-17-6 – Medical Attendance £9-9-3 – Inscription on the Tomb Stone £2-17-6 – George's expences for six months for Clothing, Washing, his third of the rent – & six pence a week pocket money – (which your dear Mother always allowed him £7-1-6 – which is altogether £34-5-9, which I have taken from the £165 and intend paying next week – and after this I shall only require money for George's Clothing, Washing, &c which I must take from the Funds – and you may depend (my dear John), I shall do my best to reserve as much as possible for you all as it is always acceptable, and I shall keep a correct account for your inspection on your return

We are all looking most anxiously for a Letter from you this Spring – and hope we shall not be disappointed – You warned in your last you did [not] know whether you should return in the Vancouver or not – how much as I should like to see you I would advise you if you are comfortable not to leave untill your time has expired – as everything is very dull particularly in the Shipping – Poor Captn Stratford has been out of Employ the last 12 Months – and cannot yet meet with anything

Do write as often as you can, as it will be the greatest comfort to us all, to know how you are going on – and we all look forward with the greatest pleasure to your return as half the 5 years has expired and Believe Me, My dear John, nothing shall be wanting on my part when you return to make your Home as happy as I can – that you may not feel your loss so severely.

I shall write you by every Vessel that goes out – as I make frequent enquiries at the Office about you – and should have written by the Brothers, which sailed last Sept^r, but being in so much Trouble I did not hear of it 'till it was too late – and William understood that the one he wrote by in August, would be the last that would sail that year. – I must now conclude, I shall have an opportunity in my next of telling you of the kindness of all our Friends (particularly of your Aunt Bell and Aunt Groves) during your dear Mother's long illness. – George and William are quite well, and are still at their old places. very comfortable. and desire their kindest love to you. also your Aunt and Uncle Groves – and all your cousins, and all Friends desire to be kindly remembered to you

God bless you (My dear John) and with every kind wish for your Health and Happiness. Believe Me Your Affectionate Aunt
    M.A. Groves
[written across the cover] P.S. Direct to me still at your Uncle Groves – and let me impress on your Mind once more to write as often as you can – I hope Mr Sangster [entry 35] is quite well – Make my kind regards to him. M.A.

    John's aunt could never quite bring herself to describe the actual death of his mother, the painful communication perhaps being too difficult. However, Mrs. Groves did give a careful accounting of John's and his brothers' money, as well as the financial and practical decisions she had to make for them after their mother's death. Her letter reveals a very different side of the lives of ordinary people than does his brother's letters. The Company added to Mrs. Groves's letter these notations concerning John Oxley's whereabouts: "returned to England p HBC° B^que *Vancouver* from Columbia Autumn 1843" and "Left the Service at S[andwich]. Islands [Hawai'i] in Jany 1844." Without knowledge of his mother's death, nor of his aunt's careful management of his funds, John Oxley had decided not to continue the long voyage home to London. The trading stopover in Hawai'i was always a difficult one for the Company, as it risked losing crew to other ships, often American, that offered men better money. As an experienced second mate, John Oxley might have been offered a promotion as well as increased pay. This was something that had been denied to him in the Company: records showed that, when Alexander Lattie was dismissed from his position of first mate of the *Vancouver*, Oxley was not considered capable of acting in his place. His discontent may well have led to his request for a discharge at Honolulu, as he had "no inclination at present to revisit England." He had, however, signed over his entire account to his mother, Harriet, not knowing that she had died many months earlier. Mary Ann Groves, as her sister Harriet's executor, was able to get guarantors in the person of James Bell and Robert Newham, to collect the sum of £36 1s. 6d. from the Hudson's Bay Company to add to her sister's estate for the care of the family.
    Once outside the Company, a man disappears from its records and from our research base. But this did not mean that he disappeared for his family. A loyal letter writer like John Oxley would probably have taken the first opportunity to write to his family and tell them of his new situation, and in time he would have received news of his mother's death. However, if a man had a wish to, it would have been easy to drop out of a past life and start a new one, without ties and responsibilities. As it happens, John Oxley returned to London and, in June 1845, he is on record as approving the

Hudson's Bay Company's actions in assigning his salary to his aunt. Whether he remained near his family or left again to the Pacific Northwest coast where his brother thought "the Columbian climate" agreed with him we do not know.

44 FREDERICK W. REA: *The other girls are rubbing up my memory while I write that all there is to tell, may be told*

Emma Rea wrote on behalf of her father to tell her brother Frederick news of family and friends. This polished literary account gives us a vivid glimpse into English domestic life, beginning with her father's words but soon entirely in Emma's voice. There is an abundance of personal news from both parties, Emma alone giving news of no less than twenty-two people with the help of the "other girls rubbing up my memory." The Humphreys referred to are Captain Charles Humphreys and his wife (see entry 24).

Mʳ Fredᶜ Rea, H.H.B.C. Ship Columbia, Fort Vancouver

Parrock St [London] Aug. 12ᵗʰ 1843

Dear Fred

As my Father dictates instead of writing to you I will begin with his part of the letter first, and tell you all that he wishes to say, he begins with. – "We have never received any thing from you since the letter dated near the Line[."] we are quite satisfied however that you are not to blame on that score as nothing has been received by the Hudsons Bay Company or any body else not even Mʳˢ Humphreys who spent a few days with us after we last wrote and again about a week since just before we left Park Lodge for Gravesend. she is a most delightful companion[.] we are all very much attached to her and hope when we return to Blackheath to have her amongst us again[.] Tell Captⁿ Humphreys we feel greatly obliged to him for his kindness in writing to us by the same conveyance that brought your letter[.] it seemed to show that you and he are on good terms which is very gratifying to us as much depends on his friendly feeling towards you which we doubt not you did everthing in your power to deserve. – I am sorry I cannot give you a better account of the Austins'[:] Edward has been a bankrupt, Bob is out of employment and Park Villa is about to be sold also, so God knows what will become of their poor mother. – And now dear Fred I must try to collect what news I can of a lighter and more trifling nature. In the first place Anna Maria has gone to spend a month in Huddersfield with Isabel[.] the other girls are rubbing up my memory while I write that all there is to tell, may be told, Isabel kept us in expectation for some time of becoming a mother but has at last disapointed us after rather a serious illness[.] this is deeply regretted by all particularly her husband and she felt it severely. Charles Campbell is articled to a lawyer you remember he was only a clerk before. Jane Riddle is married to a Master in the navy whose name is Pettey and John Riddle to Miss Mackenzie[.] we have not heard from Edward Rea since we wrote to you nor from Webb who has gone to Ireland where there have been riots looking very like a rebellion[.] we were misinformed when we told you he had gone to India it was a false report[.] Eliza has paid her promised visit to Miss Bragg without you which she very much regretted but she was determined to fulfil her promise before you returned so that you shall not quiz her any more about it[.] she made numerous enquiries about old friends[.] John Cox wished to enter the army but this not suiting his family he enlisted as a common soldier and is now abroad, poor little Easton went to sea and was drowned. Edward Smith my old favourite is dead[.] Louisa Triquette your old *flame* has grown a very fine girl and is now finishing her education in France[.] Miss Bragg still remembers you as one of her favourite boys and earnestly expressed a wish to see you again[.] Mr Raven has got the cottage for a long time so that when you return your meeting with us will not be there. Park Lodge is let for nine months and that is the reason we are at Gravesend[.] our stay here is uncertain we may leave in a fortnight or stay for months. Stone is going to live in the Bathhouse it is now being made habitable and makes a very pretty cottage[.] it will be very pleasant for us because he will take care of the boat while we are absent which by the by old Roth contemplated sending for but I think my father shamed him out of such meanness. I suppose you will have heard of Captn Drew's death[.] he was unfortunately drowned while on a survey[.] the vessel I believe was run down by a steamer[.] this is bad news[.] I should [cross-written] think his nephew will regret his loss. We have heard lately that Pim is quite well and Amy they have sent to the Adelaide orphan school. Old Brocklebank is dead and Westcomb Park is to be sold. little Muff is still alive and well, we have made an addition to our stock of pets in the form of a little sleeper [dormouse] which we nurse like a kitten[.] I must not forget before I conclude to tell you that when Mrs Humphreys is with us we have such long chats about you Captn Humphreys and the Columbia[.] Oh dear Fred you cannot tell how we long to see you it seems years since we parted[.] may God bless and preserve you our dearest and only brother and send you in safety back to us – with the united love and good wishes of my father mother and all the girls believe me dear Fred –

Your very affect sister

Emma E Rea

Turn over

P.S. Direct your letters for the future to my Fathers Agents Cox and son
44 Hutton Garden London – I believe the same direction was given to you
in our last letter which was written in March but as foreign letters are so
uncertain you may not have received it. do write us a long letter and give
us a long description of your ship Captain and Mess mates – Rosa wishes
to know if your whiskers have begun to grow yet and whether her prophecy
has come to pass that your figure will resemble that of Weaver[.] Yeomans
were quite well when we last saw them and wished to be remembered
to you

It is interesting to readers of these undelivered letters to see that the
family had entertained Captain Humphreys's wife at Park Lodge in Blackheath. Considering the unhappiness we see in Charles Humphreys's history,
this letter offers a happier glimpse of his life – a wife who was a delightful
companion and a captain who was both kind and considerate to a humble
seaman and his family. There seemed to be a personal connection between
the family and the Humphreys that would have been unusual between a
sailor and his commanding officer. Rea's family was similarly well connected
to naval news and had the story of Captain Richard Drew's death. Drew, who
was mentioned in other stories, was the member of the Company's London
Committee who handled marine affairs. The Company notation on this letter reads "Returned to England." Frederick Rea served as a seaman on the
Columbia's voyage to the west coast in 1842-3 under Humphreys's command
and briefly as a boatswain on the *Vancouver* in 1843, and came back the same
year on the *Vancouver* as an ordinary seaman, arriving in London in the
spring of 1844.

45 WILLIAM CARRACK: *There is nothing on Earth so dear to me as you*

As second officer on the *Cowlitz,* William Carrack would have had a different on-board experience than the average seaman. Instead of sleeping below
deck in the damp fo'c'sle he would have been housed in the aft cabins above
deck. This area was cramped but comfortable, with an occasional chance for
privacy. Although mates worked hard – serving as the captain's deputy in
charge of the daily supervision of the crew as well as taking their share of the
regularly rotating four-hour watches – they did eat comparatively well, with
a full service dinner served by the ship's steward. As William's mother's letters
indicate, he was part of a seafaring culture that had friends on voyages to
places such as Genoa and Trieste. The presence of four of five letters – the
fifth is referred to in Elizabeth's 29 August 1844 letter – allows us a fairly wide
view into the working middle-class world of the Carracks, in which we see

how important to William's career opportunities was the mentorship of Sir John – most probably John Henry Pelly, member of the board and the governor of the entire Company for thirty years. Elizabeth's knowledge of the details of sea trade gives us a glimpse into the busy world of the ports of London and southern England, as well as showing us its dangers. In her first two letters, one virtually repeating the information of the other, we see the kind of precautions those in the know took to try to ensure that their mail got through.

∾ Mr Carrack H.B.C.^s Ship (Cowlitz), Columbia River

London Nov^br 13th – 1843

Dear Son
I am very sorry my Letter did not reach Torbay in time for you to get it[.] Sir John returned it to me on the Monday after you was gone saying you had only saild A few Hours before it came down[.] I was glad to hear of your being quite well when you Left[.] I hope you have been so ever since and that the cold Climate has not affected you,

I hope you did not suffer from that severe gale that Happened on the Monday Night after you saild[.] great numbers of Vessels and lives where lost round the coast, I received the Letter with the Mony Order quite safe it was duly paid to me the same morning at the Post Office[.] I am very thankfull for it as I have been able to pay my rent much sooner than I Otherwise could have done[.] I was also very glad to hear that Sir John had given you some mony for your own use[.] I am sure you wanted it stoping so long in the Channel[.] it was a great Blessing you met with such a Friend[.] I hope the young Gentleman & you are both well & happy together & that he likes the Profession he has chose[.] give my respects to him[.] I have recived A letter from Sir John telling me the Brothers will be ready for Sea in few days[.] he advises me to send two Letters as he says he shall do so in case one should be Lost[.] one he incloses for me to A Gentleman at Cowes I suppose to be sent by some one of the Ships Officers the other in the Companys bag, R[ichar]^d Brodie calld on Friday Oct^br 20th he desired to be remembered to you[.] he did not bring any Letters but wished to tell you when I wrote that he was going to sail the next day in the Thames as second Mate bound for Genoa [Italy][.] the Masters name is Spencer[.] I forgot to ask any thing about the Mate[.] his Brother was gone in the Urchin I do not think he told me in what Capacity[.] you will be very much surprised at hearing that all your Anxiaty and Trouble was lost in trying to seperate E^d Maune & Bennet as thay are both with Capt Rutherford in the Urchin which saild on the Saturday three days

after you Left London in Ballast for Yarmouth to take in Cargo for Ancona
[Italy][.] Maune was bound apprentice to Capt – Rutherford Richard did
not know if Bennet was or not[.] thay saild from Yarmouth Oct^{br} 1st[.] Capt
Robson has got a cargo for Trieste[.] I beleave he has not saild yet[.] I think
this is all the news I have for you now about the seafareing Poeple, when
you write which I know every Opertunety you have you will tell me exactly
how you feel in your mind if you are happy[.] I hope you are[.] there is
nothing will bring so much peace and happyness as endevouring in all
things to do the will of God then you will be sure to do your Duty to all
men and be an example to all around you[.] my ernest prayer is that the
Lord may Strenthen and Bless you in all undertakeings or situations you
may be Placed in,

Mrs Comber sends her best respects to you she is quite well,

my dear Child I have no more to say at Presant only that I am well and
as Comfortable as I can expect to be, I shall write another letter in a day or
two[.] I have no doubt but you will get them both, from your ever

Affectinate Mother

Eliz[abe]th Carrack

Mr Carrack 2nd Officer, Barque Cowlitz, Columbia River

London Nov^{ber} 16th – 1843

Dear Son

this is the 2nd Letter I am writeing to come by the Ship Brothers as Sir
John adviced to do so for fear one should be lost[.] I have enclosed one to
him as he said he would forward it for me[.] this I am going to send to
Cowes myself[.] I must repeat the same in this letter as is writen in the
Other in case you should not get them both[.] I hope you will[.] I am
sorry my Letter did not reach Torbay in time for you to get it[.] Sir John
returned it to me on the Monday next after you saild saying it came down
only a few Hours after you was gone[.] I am very glad to hear you was
quite well and hope you have been so ever since and that the change of
Climate has not affected you, I hope you did not suffer from that severe
Storm which Happend on the Monday Night next after you saild[.] great
Numbers of Vessels and Lives were lost round the Coast, I received the
Letter with the mony order safe[.] it was duly Paid me the same Morning
at the Post Office[.] I am very thankfull for it as I have been able to pay my
rent much soooner than I Otherwise could have done[.] R[ic]^h[ar]^d Brodie
calld on Friday Oct^{br} 20th[.] he desired to be remembered to you[.] he did
not bring any Letters but when I wrote wished me to tell you that he was
going to sail the next day as 2nd Mate in the Thames bound for Genoa the

Masters Name is Spensor[.] I forgot to ask any thing about the mate[.] his Brother was gone in the Urchin he did not tell me in what Capacity[.] you will be very much surprised at hearing that all your Anxiaty & Trouble was lost in trying to seperate Ed^rd Maune & Bennet as thay are both with Capt Rutherford in the Urchin which saild on saturday three days after you left London in Ballast for Yarmouth to take in Cargo for Ancona[.] Maune was bound aprentice to Cap^tn Rutherford[.] Richard did not know if Bennet was or not[.] thay saild from Yarmouth Oct^br 1st – Cap^tn Robson has got A Cargo for Trieste, Sir Johns late Housekeeper Mrs May came to see me Nov^ber 13th for the first time she is A nice Comfortable Elderly woman[.] Sir John was so kind as to send a pound of Tea by her[.] you are aware it was very exceptable how kind and thoutfull it is of him[.] if you write to him you must thank him as it is on your account

my dear Child I know you will write as soon as Possible[.] do tell me all Particulars as to your Health & spirits and all your Adventures how you liked the Cold wheather, I hope the young Gentleman and you are quite well and happy together[.] you must give my respects to him, I have seen your Aunt Cooke & Miss Smith thay desired to be remembered to you, Mrs Comber sends her best respects to you she is well, my Dear Child I think I must Conclude as I have nothing Particalur to say more only that I am quite well and Comfortable as I can expect to be, may God Bless and preserve you is the sincere prayer of your ever Affectinate

Mother Eliz^th Carrack

Elizabeth's concern with not only William's physical safety but also his moral and religious safety, was typical of many mothers of the era who believed that their prayers were essential to a child's safety. In her next letter, she told William that she had arranged for additional public prayers to be said for him. She would appear to have been one of the evangelistic Methodists, judging by the content of her letters and the later one from church elder Thomas Brown. For his part, William had behaved as a dutiful son should by arranging for his mother to receive her rent money.

∾ Mr Carrack, 2nd Officer HBC Barque Cowlitz, Columbia River

London March 7th – 1844

Dear Son

I was very much Pleased to here you were spoken with in November and all well[.] I hope you have been so ever since and have had A Plesant Voyage and also that the Lad speaks of your kindness to him which I know you will Continue as far as lays in your Power, I suppose you had not time to

Write me A few lines[.] I hope you will get this Letter and the two I sent
by the Brothers as I wish you to know exactly how I am going on[.] I hope
you are quite well and happy, my Health is very good at Present indeed it is
better than it has been for some time past, I have not any News to send
you this time as all I know about the Shiping and the Boys I have sent in
the last two Letters[.] all things seem about the same as when you left up
to this time, I am going to take this letter to the Office when I expect to
Receive my mony for the Fourth time and A great Blessing it is and when
I think that it is through your Labour and Persevereance my Dear Child
that I receive it I feel it as A double Blessing for great are the Promises to
Dutyfull Children therefore I know you will have your Reward, both in
this World and that which is to come, my dear Child do not Omit any
Opportunety of sending A few lines as the time already seems long since
you went away[.] I desire to wait with Patiance hopeing & Beleaveing
that I shall hear from you as soon as Possible for although we are so far
seperated in Body wee are Present in Spirit[.] I can say safely that you are
always upermost in my mind[.] there is nothing on Earth so dear to me as
you[.] I never fail dayly to commit you to the Lord that you may be
Preserved in Body Soul & Spirit from all the snares of the World the flesh
and the devil, you know God tell us in his Word that he will hear when
Sinners Confess there sins unto him and forgive them therefore I have
Confidance that my sins are forgiven me and that my Prayers will be heard
for you and you will be Preserved and Prepared for the coming of the Lord,
my dear Child take heed to your ways and be carefull for we must not Sin
that Grace may abound[.] do not omit to confess your sins unto God and
pray for him to keep you for you know not for what wise purpose you are
sent there for it may be that your example is to be a great Blessing to those
that are with you[.] O it is so Delightfull to know that you are Prayed for
Morning & Evening in the Church but most especially on Sunday in the
Holy Communion Service When Mr Miller prays for all that are traveling
or that are in distant or remote parts of the Earth that Crave an interest in
the Prayers of the Church[.] I have no Doubt you do[.] when you write tell
him you do[.] open your mind freely to him[.] he has the care of your soul
on his Heart you are one of his flock, write A Letter to Mr Miller & enclose
for me one[.] you had better not send any more the first time[.] I have no
thoughts of Leaveing the House at Presant[.] Mrs Comber sends her best
respects to you she is quite well, My Dear Child I cnnot think of any thing
more I have to say to you now only that I send my Love to you and may
God bless you
 from your Affectionate Mother
  E Carrack

Elizabeth understood religious life as a series of commitments – almost contractual arrangements – between humans and the deity. As we see in her next letter, she viewed her prayers, public prayers from the church, and the correct behaviour of her son as part of a continuum in which God "has said he will Reward dutyfull Children both in this World & that which is to come."

〜 M[r] Will[m] Carrack, second Officer on board H.B.C[os] Barque Cowlitz, ~~Columbia River~~ [crossed out]
Hudson's Bay House, London [inserted later]

London August 29[th] 1844

Dear Son
I am thankfull to have another Opportunity of writeing to you[.] this is the fifth Letter I have sent hopeing you will get them all[.] this comes p[e]r the Vancouver, I hope you are quite well and happy and that the Voyage has been A Plesant one also that your Health has not been Effectd in any way, I desire to Praise God that I am in good Health & have faith that he will Bless and preserve you and that I shall hear from you soon as I know you will write if Possible, I am still in Mount St I have no Idea of Leaveing it at Presant[.] I continue to Receive the mony regular and do receive it with great Plesure knowing that God will Bless you for it[.] he is faithfull to his Promise, he has said he will Reward dutyfull Children both in this World & that which is to come[.] Sir John keeps his word he writes to me every time theres any chance of writeing to you and will the moment he hears any thing, in my last Letter I told you what I had heard concerning the loss of the Urchin[.] I have not been able to gather much more, only that she ran ashore near Brindisi [Italy] and went over on her side and was A totel wreck, thay saved nothing but there Lives[.] after many hardships thay got safe to England, but did not stop long, R[ichar]d Brodie was not with them he was in the Thames which Arived home about the same time from Leghorn, Cap[t] Rutherford has bought the Thames & gone out to Trieste again[.] M[rs] Rutherford and her sister are gone with him, Bennett cald once but could not stop but A few minutes as also did R[d] Brodie[.] thay did not know then what thay were going to do[.] Bennett thought he was not going with his Uncle but he did as James Brodie Cald the Night before thay saild and left word that himself his Brother Bennett & Maun were all going with Cap[t] Rutherford[.] he said it would be very uncertain when thay should return as it was Cap[t] Rutherfords intention if he chould not get A Cargo for London to trade out there for some time[.] thay nether of them brought any Letters for you if thay had I should have sent them

but desired when I wrote that I would give there best respects to you &
hoped you was well

Mrs Comber sends her respects to you, I hope Sir Johns relation is quite
well[.] remember me to him, now my dear Child I must conclude by
saying that I send my Love to you & all the Blessings that A Mother can
give, I commit you in to the Hands of him that is able to keep you and will
if you put your trust in him as I beleave you do,

do not fail to write to me every Opportunity that if I cannot see you I
may hear from you[.] it will be A Comfort to your Affectionate

Mother Eliz^th Carrack

Elizabeth's attempts to project spiritual protection to her child was perhaps
intensified by her knowledge of how dangerous life on the high seas could be,
as she pondered the total wreck of the *Urchin,* but was comforted by the fact
that the crew had been saved. Her knowledge of the physical and spiritual
dangers her son faced may have made Elizabeth grateful that a church elder
joined her in the religious instruction of her son in the next letter. Thomas
Brown urged William not to wait until he got back "to where there is a Place
of Worship, and to a Land where God is acknowledged" to study his Bible
and do his religious duty.

❧ To Mr William Carrick, 2nd Officer on board the HBCo Barque Cowlitz,
~~Columbia River~~ [crossed out]
Hudson's Bay House, London

London 1st September 1844

My dear Brother

As the Elder over you in the Lord I gladly avail myself of this opportunity of writing and I trust that this letter will find you in health of body
and in peace of mind, following out your duties in quietness of being
assured that you are labouring in that part of Gods creation that in His
Providence it hath pleased Him to call you. For it is only the consciousness
of this that will give quietness of mind. Your soul naturally pants after the
water brooks – and like David – when driven from His Sanctuary by
Absolam [Absalom] – under which banishment he wrote the 42 Psalm you
feel the desolation of not being able to appear, with the Saints – before
God. Nevertheless you will derive great comfort on reflecting that in our
midst – all who travel by Land and by Water – and morning and evening –
held up daily – before God. You know those sacred hours – from 6 to 7 in
the M[orn]ing & 5 to 6 in the ev[en]ing. So that, no matter in what way
you are occupied as a Seaman – you as a Member of Christ – are ever, in

the unity of the Body, before Him. And you will understand this, your
priveledge, more distinctly – on referring to 39 Exodus 8 to 21 verse –
where, is set forth the 12 Stones, a stone for a tribe of Children of Israel set
in the Brest Plate – which was borne by Aaron, the high Priest Morng and
Eving, into the Holy̶s̶t̶ [crossed out] Place in the Tabernacle Leviticus 6. 6
to 8. Now Aaron was a type of Our Great High Priest Jesus Christ – who
has gone into the Holiest of *all* (see Hebrews) and having us all upon His
heart – He ever liveth to make intercession for us. And as the will of God is
to be done in the Earth as it is in Heaven – so now, as you have seen with
your own eyes and heard with your own ears when amongst us, – here is
daily Intercession made by the Church, and Jesus the Head of the Church
gathers it up – and we are represented by One – even by our Lord Jesus
constantly in the Heavens. The contemplation of this glorious reality will
fill your mind with gratitude love and praise – And be thankfull – be
thankful – be full of thankfullness to God who hath loved *you* and washed
you with His own blood – not that we may go to wallow in the sin of this
world – but that, being washed, we may ever keep near to Him and walk
with Him. Your safety depends on your nourishing the Grace of God you
have received. And you can do this by keeping, in your spirit with us
around the Altar – You believe in the "Communion of Saints" – realize it
by putting your spirit forth in practice. The Apostle Paul exercised himself
in his office of Apostle in this way see Colossians Chap 2 – verses 1-5. Your
body is bound in your profession – and half this world rolls between us –
but your spirit is free – is not hindered by distance or by time and will
roam where your desires lead it. If therefore your heart be ever laid in the
hand of God, the spirit of God will ever be present with you, comforting
you and filling you with peace. And if it be not so – if thro' the snares of
this wicked world – and the weakness of our sinful nature – you should fall
from this peace – do not despair. Do not *wait* until you get back to where
there is a Place of Worship, and to a Land where God is acknowledged as
in this land – but flee to the Blood of the Lamb – see 51 Psalm, 1ˢᵗ Epistle of
John 1ˢᵗ Chap – Gospel John 3 – 14 – 22. Confess your fault – see the peace
of God in "the blood of peace" – and be not afraid to lay hold upon it. Yea
again – and again even should you fall away. I am not supposing that you
must fall – or will fall b̶u̶t̶ [crossed out] for if you will keep the blood of the
Lamb before your eyes (by faith) and the "Hope of Glory" before you (see 1
John 3 Chap – 1 – to 3 verses) you shall not fall. Should it please God to
call your lot in a command – however small – endeavour to gather those
under you to the Worship of Almighty God on the Lord's Day – the
Service in the Church of England prayer book will best help you in this

matter for our own Book is not understood by any but those gatherings. And now unto Him who is able to keep you from falling – do I commend you / Jude 24ᵗʰ.

    Peace be with you. Amen
      Yours faithfully
      Thoˢ Brown
Mʳ Carrick
[cover] PS You will find the daily Lessons & Psalms in the Church Prayer Book – a very beneficial source of meditation – and if you were only to keep one verse in mind daily it will be very helpful to you in keeping idle thoughts and idle conversation away from you TB

Neither his mother's loving letters telling him that "nothing on Earth is as dear to me as you" nor his church elder's religious advice were to save William Carrack. He drowned on the voyage to the Columbia Department, on 4 February 1844, one month after passing the Horn of South America and a few days past Juan Fernandez Island. Drowning at sea was not a frequent occurrence – estimates have been made that, between 1821 and 1850, 4 percent of Company men at sea drowned (Wilson 1997, 39) – but being swept overboard or having an accidental slip was a possibility. The comments in the ship's log, however, indicate that William Carrack did not drown accidentally:

At 6/30 [p.m.] Mʳ Carrick the 2ⁿᵈ Officer at this time threw himself overboard. A boat was immediately lowered and every possible endeavour made to recover him but unhappily without effect. He had a few minutes previously delivered a letter to L. Birch apprentice addressing his mother which will be forwarded her with the first dispatches. There is strong reason to believe that he had been drinking Spirits and from the evidence of the Carpenter, Boatswain and Birch who confirm the opinion, such is ascertained to have been the case. There is also every reason to believe from previous observations that for a long time he had not been in a sound state of mind. [signed] Wᵐ Heath 1ˢᵗ Officer J.T. Heath Passenger [see William Heath, entry 29].

Someone has put a pencil line through this passage and has written: "Who wrote this. Such a transaction should have been certified by the Court." On 8 February at five o'clock in the afternoon, the log records: "Sold the effects of the late Mʳ Carrick to the Crew" and another pencil annotation reads: "The Amᵗ should be stated AW." If the person making these comments was Alexander Weynton, the member of the London Committee with special responsibility for shipping, he would have made them after he joined the Committee on 22 January 1845 and before his death in 1847. It appears that the Company decided to suppress the suggestion of suicide. The letters written by Elizabeth in August and Thomas Brown in September 1844 have been annotated by the London office of the Company with the words "drowned on voyage out from England p Cowlitz 1843/44."

Sometime between the last letter in September 1844 and April 1845, Elizabeth must have learned of her son's death, possibly through the letter that was forwarded to her by the apprentice, Birch, who may have been the "young gentleman" related to Sir John. She petitioned the Company for support in a letter dated 15 April and, on 16 April, the London Committee ordered that she receive £10 with the caution that "as you have no claim on the Company no future application for relief can be attended to." She wrote back to thank the Company for its donation and acknowledge "that I the more especially feel their humane generosity being fully aware that I have no claim upon them." On 13 June 1845 the Company paid £54 to the Merchant Seaman's Office, the sum of the results of the sale of Carrack's effects (which brought in £60 6s.) and his wages for seven and a half months (£31 10s.) – its original information was that he had died on 25 February– after his advance (£8 8s.) and expenditures (£29 8s.) had been subtracted.

46 DANIEL HOPKIRK: *If you Now'd the trubel and the anxtey We Dow have on your ackount I thinck you Would Com home*

Daniel Hopkirk's father had little expectation that his son would read the lines he wrote but felt that he must at least try to reach him, if only to give his son his new address.

～ Daniel Hopkirk, Seaman, London to the Care of S Smith a Sqyer [Esquire], Near the hudson Bay house, N° unnoing [number unknown], ~~By Lime St Square~~ [crossed out]

Liverpool Fabrury 14 [1844]

My Dear Soun
If you Should Be So Louckey to get this Few Lines From Your Father it Will Be More then I Expet But I Pray God You May as I Dow Not Nou hou to or Whean tou Find you and May God Bless you if you are a Live But o My Dear Boy if you Now'd the trubel and the anxtey We Dow have on your ackount I thinck you Would Com home[.] Dow Com home as Sowen as you Can and Sea your Power Mother Be For it is tow Late[.] o Com if you have Not a Peney or the Seckend Shirt to your Back and it Will Repay ous For all our trubels[.] I Shall Not Right Mouch But Pray to God

Night and Day ~~Foar~~ [crossed out] For your once More hapy Return to
your home and May the Lord Draw your Mind to Dow So is the Pray of
your Loven Father
    James Hopkirk
I ham Bording With M^rs F Kline if you Should get this Leter Right to hur

Posted in February 1844, from a father who sent his blessing to a son whose
absence had caused much trouble and anxiety, this letter did not reach
Daniel because he was on his way home. After spending three years as a seaman on the *Vancouver,* he would have arrived in England by mid-June 1844.
Perhaps the prayers that his father offered up night and day were rewarded
and Daniel did come to Liverpool to see his ailing mother.

47 JONATHAN BUCK: *Was not Alfy's marriage funny?*

We know more about Jonathan Buck than about most sailors, because of
our contact with a descendant of the Bucks, the family's prominence in the
art world, and the large number of letters from this very articulate family. A
cherished son of widow Harriet Buck of Cork, Ireland, Jonathan was named
for his grandfather and great-grandfather, silversmiths and jewellers in
Limerick and Cork since the early 1700s. His father, Frederick Buck, a successful miniaturist, had died in 1840, at the age of at least seventy years. Both
Frederick and his brother Adam were miniature portraitists, creating paintings on ivory mounted in elaborate gold cases, a profession that fitted well
with their father's jewellery business. Adam Buck (1759-1833) pursued his
career in London, but Frederick stayed in Cork and provided a very popular
service to this bustling port. W.G. Strickland's biographical dictionary of
Irish artists describes his work: "During the Peninsula war, when Cork was a
busy port of embarkation of troops, Buck had so many orders for portraits
of officers and others going to the seat of war that he kept a supply of partly-
painted ivories to which he added the heads and the regimental facings, etc.,
when his customers gave him hurried sittings" (1912, 123). But his renderings
of locals were also popular, according to Rosemary ffolliott: "For a span of at
least thirty years – from about 1785 to at least 1815 – anybody in Co. Cork
who had any pretension to social consequence sat for their miniature to Frederick Buck" (1975, 15). Evaluations of his work have been highly critical,
including comments that his numerous miniatures were "poor in quality,
hard in outline, and badly drawn and modelled" (Strickland 1912, 123) and
that "he developed a terrible trick of drawing all sitters with what was first a
crouch but which steadily degenerated into what can best be described as an
elongated shoulder" (ffolliott 1975, 21). Nevertheless, his resulting substantial

income had allowed Frederick to purchase land and, from 1796, he had been busily involved in land transactions. In 1852 Mrs. Harriet Buck, his widow and Jonathan's mother, held 40 hectares (100 acres), her husband's cousin Samuel 52 hectares (129 acres), and Miss Frances Buck 14 hectares (35 acres) at Curra, 19 kilometres (12 miles) south of Cork – a considerable amount of valuable property in Ireland at that time.

At her husband Frederick's death in 1840, Harriet was left with at least eight children from her marriage with Frederick Buck, at least one issue of her 1806 marriage with William Craig, and at least three of her husband's children from his 1796 marriage with Eliza Reily. Her main concern was to settle these children around her. The young women had to be settled with good marriages, and the necessity of getting the young men established in an occupation meant that some had to be trained for positions in business or on the family's land. Two of the sons appear to have inherited their father's skill with drawing and were employed with the railway and other public works. At least three, including Jonathan, were launched on a seafaring career.

When Jonathan left the family in 1842 to travel to the Columbia River, he had probably already been at sea as an apprentice, since he began as a second mate on the Hudson's Bay Company's ship *Columbia*. The family had only the vaguest notion where he was headed: letters were addressed variously to the Columbia River, Hudson Bay, Arctic Regions, and the "Backside of the world." Much to his family's delight, Jonathan had written two letters after his arrival on the coast and before he left on a trip to California. The package of letters that his mother gathered together in 1844 included one from his brother Adam that had missed the previous packet as well as others from herself, his sister Harrietta, and his brothers John, Alfred, and Sidney. Henry Buck – referred to as "Mr Buck" in the letter, with whom Jonathan's brothers Adam and later Alfred were apprenticed after their father's death – was in charge of public works and was building the Limerick and Waterford Railway in 1844. Although they shared the name "Buck," which was uncommon in Ireland, we have found no indication of whether or how the families were related.

～ Jonathan Buck, from Adam

Athlone 6th Septem^r 1844

My dear Jonty
I received information a few days since from Mother that there was an opportunity of sending a parcel to you and that I might avail myself of it and write, of this you may be sure I am very glad – the opportunities are so very few that they are precious. –

I derived great pleasure from the perusal of your letters dated at Fort Vancouver 5ᵗʰ Octʳ N̶o̶v̶ᵣ̶ [crossed out] & 21ˢᵗ Novʳ 1843, they were sent to me to read[.] I think on the whole you must have had a good voyage or else you are bashful in telling of the bad weather you encountered. –

I am to leave Athlone to morrow after a residence here of two years and 5 months[.] Mʳ Buck & family are removing so that I and the other apprentices must follow Head quarters [.] the reason of this change is that the works on the lower part of the River have been completed & those up farther are now only begun and Mʳ Buck has to be stationed in the centre of his district – we are going to Drumsna about 40 miles above Athlone on the Shannon –

I have been at home once since I joined – about this time last year for a month – when returning, Mʳˢ Long and I went to the Lakes of Killarney & from that up the Lower Shannon to Limerick she then returned home and I proceeded up the Shannon to Athlone – I am trying to get home for about 3 months this winter[.] if I accomplish this I will then remain 3 months longer with Mʳ Buck in the spring and after that accept any employment that I can procure – I hope we will be able to see one another the next time you come home – I should think you are a good deal more comfortable a̶t̶ [crossed out] in one of the vessels of the Company than you would be in a common Merchant Man there is so much more regularity on board them and we were always kept regular – I just now remember that to-morrow morning 7ᵗʰ September is that on which our Father died. – I have no more news to tell I think, mine is particular news you must depend on those at home for general news – I hope there is no fear that you will run away with one of those she Indians that you gave such a glowing and flattering account of. –

I remain

My dear Jonty

Your affectionate Brother

Adam Buck

Mʳ. Jonathan Buck

In her later letter, Jonathan's mother was anxious to recount the state of the extended family. The family mentioned included Samuel and Elizabeth, children of Frederick Buck's first marriage. Samuel's family of ten lived near the village of Belgooly in the country at Curra. Samuel's sister Elizabeth had married Robert Olden, a tallow maker, in 1814 and had borne seventeen children. Harriet, Frederick's second wife, was adjusting to her second widowhood. Although the records available do not indicate children from her 1806 marriage to William Craig, it is likely that the child she mentions as "my

William" was from that marriage. The package of letters to "Jonty" prepared at the end of 1844 was addressed to:

∾ Mr Jonathan Buck, on board The Honble Hudson's Bay Company's Ship
Columbia, Columbia River, or elsewhere
[in another hand] To the care of the Company's Office Fenchurch Street,
London
Hudson's Bay House, London

Mardyke [Cork] 4 Decr 3 – 1844

My Darling Jonty

Not a line for 12 long months the difficulty of communication is dreadful but in the letter I got you mentioned you were going on a six months voyage to the Coast of California which in some degree accounts for my not hearing, if you are on your way home of course this will never reach you, but I will continue to write until I know. I need not tell you with what anxiety I await some account from you now, as I expect it will tell whether I may see you in March or April, or not for 2½ long Years more[.] May he who Commands the Winds and Waves preserve and keep you, and enable you to cast your anchor of security within the veil linking it to the cross of him who is a refuge from the Storm even that Saviour who is ready to receive all who come to him and Sanctify and Save.

I suppose the Boys will each tell their own story Fred at Jones, John at Savages [a bookshop], Adam still serving his time[.] at present he is on one of the numerous railways intended to be made in Ireland[.] whether what he is earning goes to his Master or himself I do not yet know[.] I send you a letter of his which came for the last Packet too late[.] They are all well in the country 10 children there now, we have been on and off there all the Summer, The Oldens are living in the handsome brick house on the North Mall[.] Business Flourishing with them as usual[.] Mrs Olden now pretty well recovered her loss[.] in fact we are all Thank God well and if the Nasty incumbrances were paid off our little Property would be very comfortable but I can never be thankful enough for being as I am. – Mrs Burnet not M^r B was in Cork this summer much interested about you as usual[.] I have every confidence in you that you will not disappoint them by acting in any way that would bring disgrace on their recommendation of you, You are now my dear child arrived at a time of life to form a character[.] May you My dear boy establish one begun in the Fear of God ~~and~~ [crossed out] and leaning on that foundation *Purity Integrity* and *Sobriety* be respectable in time and happy in eternity[.] I also hope you are prudent about your

Money Matters always I hope if Spared keeping a settlement at home in view[.] Would you like to Farm part of Curra[?] I would like you all settled about me[.] I may perhaps be spared to have that happiness[.] even my poor William like the Prodigal Son may make one of the Number[.] his letters are satisfactory but is at present in a very unwholesome part of India Seinde[.] and now my darling child Farewell[.] May God bless preserve and Keep you is the daily and nightly prayer of

Your ever affectionate Mother H. Buck

Jonathan's younger brothers and his sister Harrietta joined to send greetings to their absent brother. Besides the family members, a number of friends enter the picture. The Connells may have been related to John Connell, a portrait painter of the period. The Knowles had a house called "Oatlands" that was near Samuel Buck's house, "Curra," which would explain the close friendship of Freddy Buck and Charley Knowles.

~ Jonathan Buck Esq

Cork December 6th 1844

My Dear Jonty
Wide Awake Here
I just sit down to write a few lines to you as Mamma tells me she is going to send you a packet of letters. you cant expect a very long epistle as I am quite tired of scribling all day at Mr Savages[.] I suppose you will feel rather surprized when I say at Mr Savages because I was Intended for Mr Ridings before you went away but things have changed here since. Mr Ridings failed about a year after you went away and I was handed over to Mr Savages. we are all quite well here I cant exactly say for Adam for it is nearly a month since we heard the last news. he was on the Limerick and Waterford Railway with 6/- a week however I suppose he is so buisy he had not time to write. Fred or otherwise Fuz or Buz is quite well. The Oldens are now living at the North Mall they have great fun there every night. they have come there since Mr Oldens death which happened about nine months since. We had great Boat Races here this summer and a Horse Race a few days since at Rathcoony. Batty is in town I was there Last night and saw very good acting[.] Mr Harper the American Acter sung several songs with his banjow it was very good indeed[.] they are all quite well in the Country[.] Freddy is a great sportsman he sent in a lot of Curlew the other day and two brace of Wild Duck. he and Charley Knowles are great Chums[.] Duckey is in town with us her[e] going Miss Connells School.

Sam has 9 children now I dont exactly know whether we will have any
more[.] I must now close as the two Boys are going to stick in a few words.
hoping that you are well with the Blessing of God
  Remain your affectionate
  Brother John Buck

Dear Jonty
  I am just going too write you a few lines not to let us forget each other
my eyes are rather sore this short time back and you cannot expect much
from me. The men were in from the country a few days ago with corn and
on their way home got drunk and lost some of the things[.] Fred sent out a
packet to Mr Daunt by them which was fortunately not lost[.] a strange
man took home the horses who was drunk and when the door was opened
fell on doty. I cannot tell you any more news at present   A[lfred] Buck

Dear Jonty
  I take this pen into my hand not to let us forget each other[.] I have no
room to tell you any news[.] hoping that you are in good health
  I remain Truly yours
    S[idney] Buck

Dec. 6th 1844

  My Dear Jonty
  Mamma & Johnny have written you such long letters that they have left
me little or nothing to say. However all is new to you let it be ever so old to
us and I am sure will be acceptable to you[.] Thank God we are all well,
both in town & country in the enjoyment of many blessings[.] All the
Oldens are also quite well[.] Lizzy thinks herself ill and has been staying for
the last few weeks at an Hydropathic establishment at Blarney of which D^r
Barter is the proprietor[.] She was attending poor Allan Macdonnell who
has died of consumption. – Mary Olden is in London on a visit[.] The
Connells all very well – Mrs Osborne and her young son are at home at
present[.] Edward is gone on a 6 months voyage he is to call at Cork for
her on his return & proceed to Liverpool the place of his destination, he
went over to America as first mate but he has now got the command of a
vessel. –
  For the last 6 weeks I was in the country[.] I had not been well for a
long time but – feel quite well since my return[.] Freddy & Charles
Knowles are great friends the[y] go fishing & shooting together[.] you
would not know the children they are so much grown[.] Ducky is in town

with us going to school at the Connell's. – The country is a good deal
changed as regards its inhabitants. – Captain & Mrs Knowles are dead M^r
& Mrs Millefont – Mr Atkins & a great many others[.] Mrs Creigh (Isabella
Millefont that was) lives in their old house, all the young have taken the
place of the old. – Adam is on the Railways and is expected home to
Christmas. I wish you were to be here but soon now we hope to see you[.]
If you can get birds for stuffing bring all you can in the way of curiosities[.]
Bob Olden often gives me a stuffed bird[.] Faithy sends her love to you. I
must now conclude with assurances of sincere affection
  I remain Your aff[ectionat]^e Sister Harrietta

  This package of letters was sent back to Hudson's Bay House undelivered,
as Jonathan had left to return to London before the letters arrived on the
coast. After his arrival back in London in May 1845, he no doubt found time
to return home and see his family face to face. This visit with family would
have been short-lived, however, as he departed for the Columbia Department again in October 1845. After his arrival back on the coast, he again
stayed for a year, working on the *Beaver* as well as the *Columbia*. Many in the
extended family who were mentioned in the 1844 letters contributed letters
to the 1848 packet. The Buck and Olden nieces seemed particularly fond of
their uncle and expressed their affection along with the family news. The
compelling news that formed a thread running through the 1848 letters is the
story of Alfy's marriage to the daughter of his employer, Henry Buck. Elizabeth's daughter Adelaide Constance, then sixteen, wrote the first letter.

∾ J. Buck Esq, Hudson bay, North America

22 January [1848] [Inishannon]

  My dearest Johnty
  Since last I wrote to you many changes have taken place on this side
of the globe but I can safely say not one change has taken place in my
affections for my beloved Uncle. We have this long time been expecting to
hear of or from you and it was only and it was three days ago since Andrew
brought us word there were letters going for you must know We have left
town this year and are living near Innishannon if you know where that
celebrated town lies[.] our deme[s]ne is called Rock Castle[.] it is something
in the style of the Little Island but much handsomer and larger[.] the water
comes up to the grass [cross-written] garden[.] the river is not very wide[.]
it looks splendid on a stormy day when ships are coming up[.] We have
beautiful bowers and seats cut in the rocks and in short just suited to
people of romantic minds. I have had a great dissapointment lately in a

love affair with the Honourable, though I must say dishonourable, Henry Bernard[.] he and Lord Bandon called to visit one day about six months ago[.] the moment I saw him I set the eyes of my affection on him[.] I thought he returned my love ~~and~~ [crossed out] (O and Henry why didst thou deceive me[?)] I can say no more[.] he married General Turners daughter – Is not that a grand romance[?] I would not know Henry if I saw him as I never laid my eyes on him but twice[.] I suppose Harriet will tell you about Alfys being married – I will finish ~~on~~ [crossed out] foolish scribble as I am as great a fool as ever your Affection[ate] Adelaide Olden

While Adelaide mentions Alfy's marriage, she was much more interested in their new home and in her own romantic fantasy of a liaison with Henry Bernard, son of Lord Bandon of nearby Castle Bernard. During the 1847 famine near Cork, Lord Bandon, with an annual income in rents of £30,000, subscribed a slender £10 to the soup kitchen, much to the disapproval of the suffering populace (Somerville-Large 1995, 181). Still, the possible link to a titled gentleman carried a certain cachet with the impressionable Adey.

In the next letter, sister Harrietta provided vital details of Alfy's marriage, although cousin Sammy's scandalous silence about his fate gets equal billing. Bob and George Olden were listed as veterinary surgeons in the 1844-5 and 1856 Cork directories and were probably the men for whom Liz was about to keep house in Ballyshannon.

꩜ Jonathan Buck

February 8th/48 [1848]

My dear Jonty

I sit down to write to you hoping however that you may be at home with us before our packet reaches America. We are all beginning to long for your return – yet when we look around us & and see every thing nearly the same as when you left it is almost impossible to think so long a time has elapsed – Indeed we have great reason to be thankful that our family (and all connected with us) has been preserved during the awful year that is past. Fever raged throughout the whole country, amongst rich & poor alike but thank God with the exception of George Olden we all escaped[.] he had a fever & a long & tedious illness after it. –

The most important piece of news that we have to communicate has been mentioned by every one that has written to you I suppose – Namely Alfy's marriage with Miss Fanny Buck, M[r] Buck's daughter. Alfy has been

with him for more than a year & he is now married & settled with M^r
Buck in Boyle. Just think what an age he has brought the cares of life on
himself at he is *19 & she 16*[.] Mama faltered a great deal about it at first &
Fred was quite mad & all the rest of the boys were greatly amused[.] None
of them would believe it at first. –

Sydney left London about a month or six weeks ago for Ascension
Island[.] he expects to be away for a year[.] Mrs Barnet [Burnet?] is as
fond of him as ever. She says he will be the handsomest of the family –
Yesterday we got an account that Sammy was in Dublin[.] He went to
America this time last year with emigrants[.] the fever got into the ship &
Captain mate & almost all the men & passengers died of it & nothing
could be heard of Sammy. after a long time we found out that the ship
came home & left him in hospital & we were afraid he had shared the fate
of the rest – for he never wrote a line & it was by chance they heard yesterday that the ship was in Dublin – Freddy is in Bantry under Mr Frealy the
County Surveyor Adam is in Tipperary on the Waterford & Limerick
railines. – Johny at Mr Perrin's insurance office & Fred as usual at Jones.
no marriages taking place at all. Liz is going to keep house for Bob at
Ballyshannon where he & George are to live[.] Andrew has been sleeping
at the house ever since his Mother went to Rock Castle[.] We are thinking
of moving from our present abode but we have not taken a house yet[.]
The Feltons are also leaving their house – [cross-written] The Manions are
all quite well, Jimmy at College & Nobie at Fermoy Brewery with M^r
Kirkman – The Adams at Sundays are also quite well – We are all good
friends again – Mary you know is married to Mr Gibbs & lives with her
father & mother – Sydney Olden went to China last April & has not since
been heard of – Ellen Connell is gone to New Zealand to be married to
Richard Ridings & Mary Jane Sullivan went in the same ship to be
married to Sam King – Hannah is gone to Liverpool to live with Anne
& Edward who are settled there[.] he has the command of a steamer
between Liverpool & Donigal so we have lost them from Cork. We miss
them very much. – Willie is a fine boy[.] now – I think I have exhausted
my stock of news & must now conclude and believe me dear Jonty your
affectionate sister
   Harrietta

Another niece, Samuel's daughter Henrietta, wrote from Curra. Perhaps
her distance from the furor in Cork made her comments on Alfy's marriage
more restrained. Understandably, her brother's whereabouts caused her more
concern.

◈ Jonathan Buck

Curra Feby 21/48 [1848]

excuse all mistakes as it is late –

My Dearest Jonty

I sit down to scrible a few lines to you though far off; I d [crossed out] it's not what I have to say but [crossed out] to you I am sure you will find it a treat so far off you will get so many notes that I will say, will not be much. I need say nothing about Alfy's marriage for I suppose you will hear that from every one that writes. I think I ought to be ashamed of myself; he has made quite an old woman of me he being 7 months younger. But twenty is not to[o] young to despair

Had I known there was a package going to you, in time I would have a note from Fred but I did not know of it untill two days before and he is situated so far from home that I could not get it before a week. He has been living in Bantry for the last six monthes; and in Bandon for the twelve monthe before. As for Sammy we have not heard one word for a long time[.] he will be left for J [crossed out] St Johns a year in March and have not heard since but once in the summer the Vessel came home but he was left in America ill of fever and a sore leg and not one word since[.] Well as for Miss Doaty she is growen quite a young woman much larger every way than myself and all the others getting on in size pretty fair. Mama and Dada quite well but a few of the black hairs changing into grey[.] the[y] desires [crossed out] their kindest loves to you as does also Master John, and I thinke he should have written to you himself; but I am not so bad I will be a good niece – I wonder will the time be far distant when I will have the unspeakable happiness of seeing my beloved Uncle for I long once [crossed out] wonce more to have a tumble in the haystacks as we had many a pleas-ant time before – I think now – I have said a great deal and maybe to[o] much but trusting to the forgiveness of my Uncle I will conclude with all here wishing their loves to you and accept the same from your affectionate

Niece Henrietta Buck

The paper upside down no matter for that –

Emily Olden introduces an intriguing sidelight on the question of mar-riage, and on Jonathan's prospects in particular.

◈ J. Buck Esqʳ, Hudsons bay, North America

Rock Castle, Innishannon February 23ᵈ 1848

My dearest Johnty

I was very much disappointed at not receiving a few lines or even a message from you the last time you wrote but I suppose "out of sight – out of mind" is your maxim but it is not mine therefore I pardon your laziness and again favour you with one of my elegant epistles

of course you heard that we left the North Mall and are living two miles beyond Innishannon in a very pretty place. it is rather lonesome[.] we have not any neighbours nearer than two miles and are not intimate with any[.] A formal visit now and then is all the intercourse we have with them[.] There is a very nice place within about three minutes walk of us belonging to a gentleman who has a large fortune and large family and two wives both living in the house with him, one married to him and the other not[.] the ladies agree very well. The married one called on us but we did not return her visit[.] nobody speaks to any of the family[.] Liz has been in Dublin for her health which is a little improved. She is going to Dr Barters next week

Our men have just done fishing, you must know the Bandon river runs just before the house and we have a salmon net with which we catch lots of Salmon in the summer – the season has only begun – and we have not yet caught anything, We are so much out of the world here that I have not a word of news to tell you – [cross-written] it is three months since Cork saw my face – we never go outside our ground except to Church. Was not Alfy's marriage funny[?] You must not follow his example or I shall be jealous[.] how is my Sandwich Aunt[?] everything here is just as you left it except that there are a great many merchants broke[.] All here send you their love[.] write to me soon and think of me often. I remain dearest Johnty

ever your Loving and affectionate

Emily Montague Olden

When are you coming home I wish you would come soon as I want to have some fun with you, Adey, or as she now calls herself the Lovely Constantia has met with several disappointments in love[.] the most distressing was her affair de coeur with the Earl of Bandon's youngest the honourable Henry Bernard[.] she will confide her sorrows to you in her note.

Could it be that Jonathan had mentioned an alliance with someone from the Sandwich Islands? This would explain Emily's mention of her "Sandwich aunt." We are not to know, and neither are we to learn any more of the affairs of Alfy's sudden marriage in the next letter, from Liz Olden, who seems oblivious to the excitement of either Alfy's or Sammy's actions, unless her first sentence is intended to be ironic. She seems more concerned with her health and her upcoming return visit to Dr. Barter's hydropathic cure, which she had already tried in 1844. Her fascination with the railways in Kingstown (now Dun Laoghaire, pronounced Dun Leary), and especially with the unusual "atmospheric," reminds us of how new technology was affecting everyday life.

〰 Jonathan Buck esq. Arctic Regions

Rock Castle, Innishannon February 23 1848

My beloved Uncle
You will perceive by the letters of your other nieces that nothing very surprising has occurred in the family since we last had the pleasure of seeing you – As for myself I am fortunate enough to be able to report a considerable change for the better in my health – owing in a great measure to an expedition which I took to Dublin in the autumn[.] I spent some time in Kingstown enjoying the fine sea breezes. as I had never seen a railway before I was greatly gratified with beholding the operations of the two which are at work at Kingstown the locomotion and atmospheric – the latter is very curious – it leads to Dalkey a place not very beautiful in itself – but from the heights above it the view is splendid –
as it was no less than eight years since I was in Dublin before, and I had been nearly all that time ailing it was quite new life to me to look about me again and I became so much enlivened that I have continued so ever since[.] I have no very clear idea where you are at present[.] I hope not any where likely to take off your nose or ears by means of frost- I hope you will come home before we leave this place that is in two years. it is the pleasantest and prettiest place we have ever had, I think you would prefer it to "the *Island*" – I saw your friend Miss Bessie Magrath in Dublin – she is looking changed and is grown very fat – [cross-written] I also enjoyed the occasional society of the Boy Dick other wise Dick Davies whom I think you Know – the dear boy is in College where he is in process of transmutating into a parson. – The girls here are longing for you to come back – they say they never had a good romping match since you left them.
good by Dear Jonty
believe me always your affect[ionate] niece
Liz

In their 1848 letters, Jonathan's brothers were more circumspect than Harrietta or Emily in their comments about Alfy's marriage. Their remarks indicate that they were no longer greatly amused and by then seemed to resent the actions of their older brother rather than having found Alfy's marriage as funny as had niece Emily. The brothers were more forthcoming on the fate of the ruffian Sammy in a cautionary tale no doubt intended as a warning to the distant Jonathan. Frederick's reference to the "squireens" gave his opinion on the effect of the famine on the small landowners that, as a class, were particularly badly affected.

∾ Mr Jonathan Buck

Cork Feby 26th/1848

My Dear Jonty

The mother saying there was an oppirtunity of sending a letter to you I avail myself of it.

From the number of letters and notes I see for you I think you must be pretty well informed of all that has happened in this part of the world[.] of course mother has told you all about Alfreds unfortunate marriage[.] she never told a word of it to us till she produced the cake[.] the whole thing is a mystery to me and I dont wish to think of it

Sam was in town to day[.] he came to see the mate of Sammy['s] ship[.] she is in Dublin and will be home the first fair wind. he says he is as fat and stout as possible the ruffian has been 6 weeks in Dublin and never wrote, nor all the time he was sick in N America,

Jones is much in the same state he was when you left[.] he has been down to Kinnure this past week[.] he might stay down entirely for what business he has in Cork[.] I never saw any thing like the state of business[.] if things do not mend this summer the whole country will be banckrupt[.] the squireens ar[e] done up compleatly, I wish I was out ~~there~~ [crossed out] with you[.] any thing would be better than staying in this unfortunate country,

    Believe me to be
        Your affctionate Brother
            Frederick Buck
Mr Jonathan Buck   Backside of the World

The next letter, from brother John, contains the first reference to events outside the close family circle, with mention of the revolution in France. His mention of the robbery by the *Modeste* refers to the British ship that spent some time on the west coast of North America.

∾ Jonathan Buck Esq, Barque Columbia, Columbia river or elsewhere

March 1st 1848

My Dear Jonty

I take this opportunity of writing to you hoping that you are in a good state of health now as also when this will reach you.

I will now proceed to give you some account of the strange things that
are passing in this quarter of the Globe, Anthony Savage has given up his
book Shop in Patrick Street, it is now in the possession of Messrs Bradford
& Co. I have left that line of business entirely[.] I am now in a bloody old
Insurance Office on the South Mall. I have very dull times of it ~~now~~
[crossed out] all the Boys being gone away but Adam ~~& me~~ [crossed out].
Sidney left about 2 Months ago for Ascension Island and the Vessel was to
go round the Horn to Valpara[i]so so you will not be so very distant from
one another. Sammy has arrived in the Old Governor Douglas in Dublin[.]
she went out last Spring with passengers to New York and was one of the
Vessels the great mortality by Fever occurred in. Sam was left in the
Hospital sick when she left that City, and she has made a second trip now
and brought him (as well as some others that were also left there) home.
You will no doubt find in some of your letters an account of the *Marriage*
of Alfred to the Daughter of Henry Buck Esq. it was rather a strange
transaction[.] the Bridegroom is going on 20 the Bride 16 years something like an Indian Marriage I think. before this will reach you will have
an account of the Revolution in France[.] the King has abdicated the
Throne & run nobody knows where as also several other personages of
importance[.] Guizot the Minister is in the hands of the People and ere
now his head off. I suppose this will bring about a War which (although
they make all professions of Peace) the Annexing of Belgium to the French
dominions (the King of which has also cut) will not be looked on peaceably
by all the other powers so that I may be able to get something to do in a
Military line. There is no starvation in this Country now the Winter has
now passed over without any deaths by starvation which was not the case
this time 12 Months and the People in the Country are now setting potatoes
in as great a quantity as ever. I hope the War If such arises will have no
effect on the trade of the Company in that quarter, and that you will not
run any risks by it. Andrew Olden has [cross-written] just arrived from
Rock Castle where his Mother now resides and unites with me in love
health and happiness to you. I now close hoping to have a letter from
you soon and that you will also be home shortly
    & Believe me
    Your ever Affectionate Brother
      John Buck
Jonathan Buck Esq
P.S. The D^r desires me to tell you not to forget the collection of curiosities
altho you were robbed by the Modeste.

In the next letter, Faithy – apparently an older half-sister – dismissed Alfy's marriage with the words "crim – con," referring to a "criminal conversation" or "criminal connection" normally used in association with adultery. Perhaps Faith was implying that Fanny was pregnant; Alfy and his wife did have a daughter named Anne, but we have not yet found reference to the date of her birth. Faithy, however, was far more interested in her own marriage prospects than in those of either brother.

❧ March 1ˢᵗ [1848]

dearest Jonty

I suppose all the news that I could tell you has been written by other friends. I have but little of any importance to say. I suppose you read of all the starvation our country endured[.] every one has suffered[.] your humble servant is seldom exempt from suffering[.] my tenant is beginning the last year to pay very badly[.] well this is dismel talk for a careless sailor who has no thought about any thing – What do you think but I fell in love with a Portagay Capᵗ[.] the boys would not have him at all for me, but I expect will bring me home a fine *middle aged* fellow that does not *snore* because I'm as bad a sleeper as ever[.] he must be a rich Capᵗ[.] I suppose they have all mentioned Master Alfys doings crim – con you may be sure, Johnny has got some foolish notion into his head of going to America[.] None of the Miss Oldens married yet, nor the Miss Bucks of Curra[.] Bell is very well enjoys wonderful health and sight[.] why dont you ever write[?] I saw one letter you wrote and you had the audacity not to mention my name[.] Sidney Olden went to china and has not been heard of this year and a half[.] Sammy had the fever in Quebec and never wrote a line since[.] they dont know is he dead or alive[.] our own poor Sydney I'm told is very well off as respects a good Capᵗ. I'm looking forward with great pleasure to see you soon and to get a kiss from my dear *troublesome Jonty*[.] dont forget *presents* and *curiosities*[.] dont give them to the Burnets or the Morrisons[.] Miss Harriett is not married yet[.] she very seldom comes to see me[.] if I was rich and had a grand house how attentive the family would be. I hope you read your Bible and have the fear of God in your heart Farewell your loving sister
[cross-written] Faithy

In her second letter Jonathan's mother, Harriet, was more concerned about getting word from her son. But she did take time to lament the consequences of sending her son Alfred off to Henry Buck's.

～ Jonathan Buck, Columbia River

4 Mardyke [Cork] March 1ˢᵗ 1848

My darling though far distant Child
With such a Package from So many of the Family I am sure I can have
no news to tell you, but to bear my Testimony to the Protecting and
Providing Care of a *Faithful* God, through a Season of unparralled
Suffering, Disease, and death, I have borne my Share of Loss with I May
Say every member of the community of which I form apart, but I and
mine have had Food and raiment and what few Families have to Say been
preserved in Health and strength in the midst of disease and death, "bless
the Lord oh my Soul and all that is within me bless his Holy Name"[.]
May his preserving care of you my dear Child induce you to cast your self
Body *Soul* and Spirit on him who is able to Save to the uttermost all who
come to him by Faith, Foolish very very foolish Alfreds marriage has given
and is giving me much uneasiness, but circumstances rendered any thing
but consent impossible[.] he is now unemployed and I Suppose must be a
dependent on Mʳ Buck his £16 a year will go a short way on his Family it
is all I can do for him[.] ̶h̶i̶s̶ [crossed out] he writes himself that he has
brought a heavy weight on himself but Gods help he himself will support
the Load, his engineering instruments and outfit altogether cost me over
£40 – 14 months ago when going to Mʳ Bucks, I little foresaw the result,
we have but the one short note from you since you left[.] why do you not
have a letter written ready or rather a short Journal which by adding a line
when opportunity offered would be so satisfactory to get[.] the ̶M̶o̶d̶e̶s̶t̶e̶
[crossed out] Modeste is come home[.] I am sure one of the officers would
have thrown a letter in the Post on returning if given to him[.] Foster
thoughts of home and of your poor Mother[.] God protect and preserve
you my darling child to a happy meeting
y[ou]ʳ affec[tiona]ᵗᵉ Mother H. Buck

The last word was left to Alfred himself, who seems a little chastened by
the fuss that his actions have created.

～ Jonathan Buck Esquire, H.H.B.C.'s Barque Columbia, Columbia river or
Elsewhere,
[printed on envelope] "On Her Majesty's Service", "Office of Public Works
Dublin"

County of Roscommon, Boyle. March 2ⁿᵈ 1848

My dear Jonty. –

I received a note from mama ~~on~~ [crossed out] yesterday in which she said that the spring packet for your ship would be starting in a few days and I now write this note to you hoping it will be in time to go to you by that packet. –

A great change has taken place in ~~my~~ [crossed out] me since I wrote to you last[.] I have become a married man. I am married to a daughter of Mʳ Buck to whom Adam served his time and with whom I have been for this last year and nearly half. she is not 17 years of age yet but is very knowing (not at all girlish I mean). –

There has been a great diminution in the expenditure of the Board of Works this last year. all the money which was expended on the Relief Works has greatly crippled them and they have got into dreadful disgrace with the Treasury in consequence of the very lax manner in which they kept their money accounts. the entire management of the accounts was left (in the Shannon Commission department of the Board) to a man named Mason who was so clever that since the year 1841 he contrived to keep his books in such a manner as to appear correct ~~and to tally with the Book of payments which was kept in the Bank~~ [crossed out]. he returned an amount of £9000 or thereabouts as being in the ~~National~~ [crossed out] Bank of Ireland to the credit of the Commissioners, but his leg having been broken last summer he was obliged to remain absent from his duty for some time and the person who got charge of his books during his absence seeing something suspicious in them enquired in the bank balance they had of the Shannon Commission funds[.] to his amazement he was informed that there was only about £1000. the Commissioners having been informed of this circumstance Mason was brought before them on his last leg the second having been amputated when there was sufficient evidence produced to have him confined in Newgate.

Mason was tried afterwards for forgery and acquitted and secondly he was tried for embezzlement & found guilty and sentenced to be transported for 7 years. –

I am at present off pay assisting my father in law who is employed in inspecting the improvements proposed to be made on the estates of different persons under a recent act of Parliament whereby one million and a half Sterling was voted by Parliament for said improvements. –

ever my dear Jonty

Your affectionate Brother

Alfred Buck

The long description of the Mason affair may have been a transparent attempt by Alfred to divert attention from his own peccadilloes. Harriet wrote a final note as she hurriedly bundled off the packet to catch the out-ward bound ship.

〜 Mr Jonathan Buck, on board The Honble Hudsons Bay Companys Barque Columbia, Columbia River, or elsewhere, care of The Companys Office, Fenchurch Street, London

[4 March 1848]

> Dear Jonty
> I have written to Adam twice for a letter for you and have got no answer and am afraid to delay the letters for fear of being too late ever your affect[ionate]
> Mother H. Buck

Jonathan had deserted at the Sandwich Islands in April 1847, long before the package arrived on the coast in the fall of 1848. The Hudson's Bay Company was not aware of his whereabouts and returned the letters to their London headquarters. If he was joining a lover in Hawai'i, the alliance does not seem to have lasted. He appeared in 1849 as a settler in Willamette in the Oregon Territory, being listed as a single lumberman in the US Census for Clatsop County in 1850; records in Ireland, however, indicated that he died at the gold diggings in California in 1850. The consternation and grief among the various members of the family is easy to imagine. How the yearning nieces coped with their loss is not certain, although, according to family records, Adelaide married Longfield Davis. What with Alfred's troubles and Jonathan's death, Harriet's declining years might not have been as happy as she had imagined with her children all settled about her on neighbouring farms. Perhaps she had a portrait of Jonathan by her late husband to keep his memory alive.

48 JOHN HARRIER: *You have no Baby to see when you come home ... but I hope at your return to make you happy with one*

When his wife wrote her love letter with a lock of her hair enclosed, John Harrier had been away from home for two years, having left London in September 1843 as steward aboard the *Cowlitz*.

〜 Mr Harrier, Steward of Ship Cowlitz, Hudson's Bay Company, Columbia River, North America

Brixton June 5th 1845

My Beloved Husband

I have within this last ten Days received 2 Letters from you and I think the last was written first but I cannot understand them[.] in one you thalk of comming home in June[.] that is this Month and should you come this letter will fall into some other hands and I must write it accordingly[.] now My Dear Husband should you get this letter I hope it will find you about to return to your home again and forever as I hope by the Blessing of god you and I are to remain together after this for it is time we began to look after a home and to provide for the Days that are coming[.] I was sorry to find from one of your letters you had been ill on the voyage out but I hope My Beloved one you are well as the other Letter says looking well and stout[.] I am very poorley with a cold now and I have suffered greatly this last winter[.] we have had a very cold & long one[.] father as been very ill also but I am happy to state they are all much better now and send ther kindest love to you[.] James is not Married yet he is waiting untill you return[.] David did not go to sydney for his Wife would not go[.] they have 2 children a girl and Boy[.] they all send ther love[.] John as Been in Business for him self some time[.] they have only 2 children[.] they also send thire love to you[.] I hope you have get love anough without mine but I supose you would rather have mine than all the rest together[.] My Dear Husband you say a ship called the Brothers came out without a letter for you but I sent one by that ship Last Augist and I have written 5 letters to you since you left England and I have not let one oppertunity pass withougth writting to you and I hope you have had them and know by this time that you have no Baby to see when you come home[.] but I hope you are as anxious to come as if thier was one litle you and I ougtt to thank god for it as we are situated at the present but I hope at your return to make you happy with one if not we must be content withougtt[.] you know by this time how I am situated[.] I am thankful to say I only whant you and a comfortable home of mine own to make me one of the happiest Woman on Earth[.] I hope My Dear Husband you will not stay longer than the 2 years[.] I have made up my mind too waite that time contented[.] should you stay any longer I shall be very Disapointed[.] I Do not care how soon you come only do not stay Longer[.] I hope you will let me know as soon as you can what ship you are coming in and about what time you expect to be hear that I might be ready against you come[.] I told you in a letter some time ago that Mrs Kerwin is ded also poor Henery Plew[.] susan sends her love to you but she Do not entend to write to be your 2^d for if she can get the Man in the mind she will be Maried soon[.] I whent to see Mrs Fleuer the other Day and she is allways very kind and longs to see you home again[.] she hopes you will stay then[.] Miss Fleuerr as been very ill again[.] I am glad to state my love I have had 4 letters from you since you left England[.] I had one in New years Day at 8 oclock in the Morning and what a present it was[.] I hav the one with the Lock of your Beautiful hair Maney thanks for it[.] I am glad to find it as not turned grey yet[.] I will send you one of my ringletts for i have a plenty of them[.] I have had my tooth out that yoused to ache so I am not troubled now with that[.] I am looking much the same as when you left me[.] I often go to see Mrs Brocking[.] they are the same as ever[.] Mr Rundall as been thier since we left[.] for some time I did not see him[.] he is gone to sydney again[.] Mr Horace Fleuer is expected home by christmas[.] for some time Mrs Fleuer as not any more children yet the are all grown very much and Fine looking like there Father[.] John Drinys child is ded[.] they are keeping a Beer shope and Doing very well I hear

My Dear Husband you say how often you think of your home and those sweet sundays we spent together yes and I to how long for them to come again[.] I hope we shall make better youse of them than we did then[.] I hope you Do remember the sabbath Day and keep it holy for we can serve god aney were or at any time[.] your little Wife Do not forget to ask her Heavenly Father to keep and guide you in her Daily prayers and I hope you pray to god to keep me[.] I long my Beloved one for your return that we might serve god tteguther and I hope our end will be that of happiness[.] only think what a Dreadful thing it would be for you and I to be calld to give an account for all our past sins – withougtt gods forgiveness[.] I long for to have you to kneel Down by my side and thier to ask god to forgive the sins of our past life[.] My Dear Husband I often Dream you are at home and we are so happy[.] I wonder if you will ever see me again on Earth or not[.] if not I hope we shall meet in Heaven never more to part then

I must conclude with every ones kindest love to you and I hope to see you vry soon[.] Mother prays to see you again[.] this is the 10 Day of June 1845 you have been gone 1 year and nine months almost now and [upside down] I hope you will be home next year[.] your affectionate Wife Marey Ann Harrier
I am going to take this to the office to Morn[in]g but I Do not know when it will leave England

Although she wrote the letter conscious that others might read it, Mary Ann could not mask her pain that John Harrier would have no baby when he came home, perhaps indicating a miscarriage or dashed hopes of pregnancy. She seemed to be apprehensive about how John would receive the news and anxious that he return as soon as possible. Her husband was probably just as anxious to leave. In the fall of 1844 while the *Cowlitz* was on its coastal trip to Sitka, Captain McNeill – suspicious of Harrier's services as steward – "broke the after storeroom out which had been in his charge, found five boxes of raisins emptied by rats and a quantity of new Tin ware greatly damaged also a quantity of new knives and forks under his immediate eye in the pantry." Captain McNeill put Harrier aboard the *Cadboro,* headed back to Fort Vancouver, with the instruction to Captain Scarborough that, "if he goes to work on board the *Cadboro* and gives you satisfaction his wages will go on[;] if not he will receive no pay during the time he remains idle." John Harrier left for England on the *Cowlitz* in the fall of 1845 and did not serve with the Company again. A little more than a year after writing her letter, Mary Ann would have had her beloved husband home, ready to make him happy with a child or be "content withoughtt."

49 ABRAHAM NORGATE: *If no one els wont have you I will as soon as ever you come home*

Abraham Norgate had left England as a seaman aboard the *Vancouver* in 1841, serving afterward aboard the *Columbia* and the *Cadboro* in the west coast service. Young Ann Norgate wrote this letter to her uncle on behalf of his mother and father, to tell him the good and bad news, especially of all the marriages in this large family. Abraham seems to have been unusually communicative, having sent two letters as well as a present, and his efforts were appreciated by his family.

꙰ Mr Abraham Norgate on board the Barque Columbia, Fort Vancouver, Columbia River N.Wd Coast of America
[outer cover] Mr Abraham Norgate, Hudson Bay Company No 4 Fenchurch Street, London

Yarmouth June 7th 1845

Ever Dear Son
    I now take up my pen to address these few lines to you hopping to find you in good helth as thank God it leavs us all at present[.] we received your kind and welcom letters and was verry happy and glad to hear from you but shood have been happy to have seen you if it had been so as we could for we thought verry much abought seeing of you[.] we received your 2 lettors and the present and I hope the Lord will reward you for it as it came verry exceptable as they talk abought taking the house from us since you have been gon[.] they have olmost all of them got married for your Sister Marry Ann is Married and have got a fine boy and har husband joins

with har in sending their kind love to you and your sister Elisar [Eliza] is
Married hand have got a Doughter but it is a verry poor little thing and har
husband joins with har in sending their kind love to you and brother James
is married to Marry Mack and they are both quite well and send their kind
love to you so that is oll the Marrages in our family[.] your Brother William
and his wife and Doughter Ann are oll quite well and send their kind love
to you your brother John and his wife and his 5 children are oll quite well
and send their kind love to you and your Brother charles is quite well but
he remains single as yet but we suppose he will nut be long before he is
married but he keep his place yet and but he send his kind love to you[.]
your Brother Eliger [Elijah] is entred on Board of man of wor and he is
quite well and send his kind love to you your Brother Jerry is quite well
and send his kind love to you but he say he do nut know wen he shall see
you for he say he should be at sea he hope before next year for he is full
bent to go[.] Your father joins with me in sending our kind love to you[.]
now we have told you abought oll your Brothers and sister but we oll hope
you will keep your self single untill you return for we suppose you will nut
git Married to none of the forrigeners for poor Riar strike say she will
waight for you if no one els do nut as she had nut your Brother james[.]
your old friend john Amison is Dead so you will nut see him when you
return and your old friend james Gower is Married to Miss tate and have
got 2 children and lissa [Lisa?] Coe is married to tom Bane and poor Tom
smith is Drownded in a pond of Mr Macks[.] your Brother jarry [Jerry?]
was swiming with him at the time and james smith is gon for a soldier and
poor james Lubbock was agoing to be married to 2 or 3 Diferent people
but when they got almost to church and then the girls wood nut have
him[.] I came to yarmouth impurpose to let your Brother William and
Elisar know of it and your Niece Ann Rote it and she say that if you do but
keep single untill you return we will be both Married on one day for if we
cant make you a wife no other way wee will buy you a ginger Bread [one]
so when you are tiard of [her] you can bight har head of[f] but if no one
els wont have you I will as soon as ever you come home for I am plenty big
anuf and I dear say I am as toll as you for I am 5 foot hight so now I conclude with our kind love to you I remain your loving Father and Mother
and loving Niece untill Death us do part
Ann Norget yarmouth aged 15 years

From the context, we can assume that the gift was money, which might
have forestalled the taking of the house from the family. Ann's flirtatious
humour at the end of the letter indicates that at fifteen a young woman

evidently felt herself ready for marriage in a family and district where marriage seems the order of the day. Because Abraham had left the coast on the *Cowlitz* in December 1845, arriving in England in late June 1846, he missed this letter, sent by a ship that probably crossed his path. He would have had to wait until he was home in Yarmouth to hear all the news, including marriage proposals.

50 JAMES JOHNSON: *Thousands of tears have I shed for you*

James served as a seaman on the *Vancouver,* leaving London in early September 1844. The letter to which his mother Mary referred must have been written in October, about one month before the ship reached Cape Horn, as it was dated eight months previous to hers. Why she had received it so late, we cannot know. Mary's 1845 letter indicates that it had become common for families not only to know of men working in a variety of places abroad but to have relatives emigrating to places as distant as New Zealand – unlike letters in the 1830s.

James Johnstone, App[renti]ᶜᵉ, Ship Vancouver, Columbia River

[22 and 23 June 1845] [Ilford, Essex] Sunday June 22ᵗʰ 1845

My dearest Boy

With joy I recieved your Letter yesterday and am most happy to hear when it left you, you was well and happy, God grant you may continue so, I began to think the time very long, I cannot express the pleasure we all feel at your being happy, Thousands of tears have I shed for you, but I now shall feel more contented. We are all pretty well at present – Your Uncle Edwin has another little Girl named mary – Ned does not forget you[.] when we ask him where you are he says gone to sea. Emma and Eliza desire thier best love to you, Emma is going to a place next week, she is going to live in that new House in the Orchard – Your poor Uncle William Died at new Zealand March 1844[.] he had only arrived there 12 days[.] we never had heard from him once untill we heard he was dead, the news arrived to us in October last[.] it has been a very great grief to us all, he had recovered his health, entirely[.] he died in a fit under a tree where he had set down to rest from fateague[.] he was quite sensible but could not speak, it was a dreadful thing[.] he was alone when first taken, his family are all well but badly off – John was Married 15ᵗʰ of last October but I am sorry to tell you poor Ruth died in Febuary, she was never well after she married[.] I was with her when she died, she died with rheumaticks in the bowels, poor

John was dreadfully cut up but is better now, he is lodging at Marion's again, They had a house two doors from Thorn's beautifully furnish'd – she is buried in Stratford Church yard– They were married at Leyton Church – Your Uncle and Aunt, myself, Emma and Eliza met them there, saw them married and return'd to Marrion's to dine, and a splended dinner and dessert we had, we all dear Jem regretted your absence much, poor Ruth spoke of you often – She was a very nice young woman, but I hope she is better off

Monday 23ᵗʰ I have just return'd from the Union[.] your Aunt Julia desires her love to you – We all pray that we shall have a happy meeting here on earth has I hope in Heaven, I hope my dear Boy you do not forget to pray to your God and my God, I constantly pray of him to watch over you, and preserve you from the perils of the deep, from sickness and that you may be spared, and all that are now left of us be spar'd to meet again on earth, but my dear Jem, without his will nothing can be done, and I think the perils you have to encounter at sea, ought the more to induce you to pray to him[.] John Simmonds, return'd home, after eleven months absence, but I am sorry to say not reclaim'd[.] he is a bad boy and has been had before Mʳ Gibson for stealing plants from the Missionary School, his father was obliged to pay or he would have been sent to Ilford jail – our neighbours all seem very glad I have heard from you, and all desire to be remembered to you, you do not say in your Letter how long you are likely to be gone, I hope not for five years, Your Uncle Edwin call'd at the Hudson's Bay House last week, they have heard nothing yet of the Vancouver, I hope I shall soon hear from you again, as it is six [crossed out] eight months since the date of your Letter, pray write to me every chance you get, I was at Waltham Abbey about a month since, I saw Mʳ and Mʳˢ Beard they was surprised at hearing you was gone to sea, I have never heard any thing of your Aunt Jemima or any of them since you have been gone – Mʳˢ Baker of West Ham Abbey is dead and Buried, John tells me there is another Boy gone from the Factory to America by the name of Vine, he used to work in the loft with you, Captain Pelly is gone to Maderia [Madeira] for three years, and now my dear Jem I think I have told you all the news I can muster[.] I shall therefore conclude hopeing this may reach you safe and find you well and happy –

   God bless you my dearest Boy
     And believe me to be
       Your Truly Affectionate Mother
       Mary Johnson

Give my respects to the young Man who was so kind as to write me the
Letter I first had from you

Mary's dearest boy, the object of "thousands of tears," would generate even
more. James drowned at Fort Vancouver on 2 April 1845, only a month and
a half after his arrival in the Columbia Department – giving his death an
eerie echo of his uncle's death in New Zealand just twelve days after arriving
there. By the time Mary had received his only letter telling her he was well
and happy, he had been dead almost three months.

51 WILLIAM SMITH: *You will be near your old Friends the Yankees*

William Smith took one trip to the Columbia Department, sailing from
London on the *Mary Dare* in November 1846 and arriving on the coast on 23
May 1847. He returned on the *Columbia,* leaving the coast on 10 November
1847 and arriving in London on 22 May 1848.

⌒ Mʳ Wᵐ Smith, On board the Hudson Bay Company's Brig Mary Dare,
Sandwich Islands

6, Ocean Street, Stepney 4ᵗʰ April, 1847. –

My dear William,
I wrote you on the 10th ult[imo (last month)] in answer to your's of the
1ˢᵗ Janʸ dated at Sea, in which you stated that you liked your vessel and we
hope, with the Blessings of Almighty God that you may prosper in your
Voyage, for it is wonderful what may be accomplished by a steady
perseverance and good conduct, so much so that you will turn about and
wonder how it could arrive. – Tomlinson is still here and I am afraid he
will find it out that he has staid too long ashore. – Dixon & Sister are well
as well as your Brother and Mʳ & Mʳˢ Morris' children – they were much
pleased on hearing of your Letter and look forward to your happy return. –
We have not heard from James lately – I suppose on account of the late Dʳ
Lubbock's Death, as no doubt he must come in for a share of his Practice
which was extensive. – Dʳ Tawke who was James' colleague at the Despensary
will be elected to the vacancy in the Norfolk & Norwich Hospital. – I sent
you three newpapers by the Post office but your Company told me that none
would be allowed to accompany this letter, or otherwise I should have
forwarded some. – I addressed your Letter Mʳ Wᵐ Smith, on board the
Hudson Bay Company's Brig Mary Dare, Sandwich Islands, but I understand
it is probable that you will be at Columbia, if so, you will be near your old

Friends the Yankees – your Mother thank God remains much as you left her, as well as myself, and should our lives be spared – we shall expect to see you come home a happy and prosperous Man[.] All your family join us in sending their Love and believe us to remain

    Your affectionate Parents

      E & J.G.

P.S. You have escaped one of the most tedious and unpleasant Winters in my recollection. – Both your Mother & myself have felt the Effects – It is now breaking up a little but still very cold. –

By 1847 the Oregon Treaty signed by Britain and the United States, which ceded British claims to the lands south of the forty-ninth parallel, was one year old. William Smith's father seems to be aware of the new politics of the region when he referred to his son being "near your old Friends the Yankees." After the border was determined, the Company moved its headquarters to Fort Victoria on Vancouver Island, and Fort Vancouver later became a US army post. Delivery may have been complicated by his change of ship and by his common name, as there was another William Smith on the ship on his return journey.

52 JOHN WATKIN: *She hopes you will soon come home to turn her Mangle*

The remark by Mary Hayes that her brother John Watkin's letter of 3 August 1846 did not reach her until July 1847 underlines how long delivery to and from the Columbia Department could take. That she had expected their last letter, dated April 1846, to arrive on the coast before August shows the lack of information available to some families concerning the very long route mail had to take and the delays waiting for vessels bound for the west coast. This letter is one of the minority of letters that mentions a payout of money to a sister.

❧ John Watkin, Barque Columbia, Columbia river or elsewhere

London September 6/1847

    Dear Brother

    We did not Receive your Letter ~~untill~~ [crossed out] Dated August 3/46 untill july 1847 But it was with Great Pleasure we Receveed it for we felt very Anixous to heare from you[.] we sent you a Letter in the Month of April 1846 through the Hudson Bay House But we was Doughting weather you Received it or not as you did not mention aBout it in your Letter[.] we sent to your Granmother Who is still Living to Let her know that we had

heard from you an Likwise to your Sister Ellen[.] they was very Glad to
heare from you and that you was quiet Well[.] your poor old Grandmother
fails very much[.] She as Got quiet Blind[.] your sister El[l]en his still with
her[.] your sister Ellen as had a son since you was away But it only Lived
six weeks But she is about to Be confind a Gain[.] her husBand is Gone on
a voyage to Gurnsey [Guernsey] an Jersey[.] we have Got two children
ourselves they Both are quiet well and Likewise ourselves[.] Dear Brother
we hope this will find you the same[.] I Received your Letters that you sent
me from Gravsend and the Downs and Likwise an Order for the Money
from the Hudson Bay House which I went and Receved for six Months
that is from December 1845 untill May 1846 which I feel very much
Obliged to you for it[.] I hope please God to spare you to Arive safe home
to England so that we shall have the pleasure of seeing Each other againe[.]
as for poor Grandmother I do not suppose you will have the pleasure of
seeing her againe as she is failing very much[.] the Govener of Greenwich
Hospitall is Dead and Likewise Sir Richard Dobson the Late surgoen of
Greenwich Hospitall[.] the old Houses in yure street is all pulled Down for
the Railway[.] But Little Careloine Taylor says she hopes you will soon
come home to turn her Mangle and she desire me to send her Love to
you[.] so now Dear Brother we conclude with our

    Affectionate Love to you
    Robert and Mary Hayes
Direct for Robert Hayes
At Messrs Simpkin & Co, Booksellers Stationers Court, Ludgate Hill
London

With a loving sister and the possibility of Caroline Taylor waiting for her
mangle (a hand-turned wringer for washing) to be turned, it is perhaps not
surprising that John Watkin completed only one return voyage as a seaman
with the Company, arriving in London in May 1848 aboard the *Columbia*.
Since his training had probably been at the Greenwich Hospital – his sister
mentions the school twice – which specialized in turning out qualified seamen, it is likely that he went on to serve on other ships.

53 CHARLES WALLIS: *How do yo like the sea?*

Charles Wallis left England in 1842 as an apprentice sailor on the *Diamond*,
a chartered barque under Captain Fowler, and transferred to the *Columbia*
when he arrived on the coast. He was back in England between May
and October 1845, when he no doubt caught up on family news before he
left again on the *Columbia* on 4 October. His father and mother enclosed

letters gathered from the rest of the family, all written between 17 and 19
September 1847.

∿ Charles Wallis, apprentice to the Hudson's Bay Company, Columbia River,
North America

Bromley September 19th 1847

My Dear Son
With Great Pleasure We received your Kind Letter But at the same time
was very sorry to hear you had such an unplesant voyage out with the
Captain[.] We was glad to hear you was happy when you wrote to us[.] We
received your Letter the 13th of July 1847[.] I hope you had the Letters we
wrote to you[.] I suppose you have seen Bob Lawrence before this[.] He
Could tell you all the Particulars of Bromley[.] Mr Lawrence have let his
house to Mr Darling[.] he now Lieve next Door to the Mulberry tree[.]
Mr Lawrence old house is going to be a beer shop
I have no occasion to give you much account of susannah and maryann
as you have a Letter from them[.] I dont Know whether I shall have one
from george for you[.] I have wrote to him[.] he have left ware he was[.]
he is now at Bishop Startford But Prehaps only for a Little time[.] Louisa
married to Bob Lawrence Brother George[.] the[y] Lieve at the Bottom of
our street next to the Beer shop –

My Dear son
your mother think it is of no use to send you shoes or jewes harps as it is
quite Likely you would not have them as it is quite uncearting when you
Come home[.] I asked Mr Smith whether you would be at home next
year[.] he says that is quite uncerting
we have had a great deal of illness But thanks be to God we are all Pretty
well at this time, you told your Brother we could take your Money that was
due to you But we have never asked for it although with so much illness we
should have Been very glad of it we will Let it be untill you Come home
which I hope Please God you will return home safe and that he will spare
our Lives till we see you again[.] mary ann is very Comfortable[.] she is
married to George Nevett at Brentwood[.] she was not married to George
More[.] she was married the 30 of november 1846 at Hackney Church[.]
Louisa was married the 2nd of July 1846[.] I think we shall have susannah
married before your return[.] Mr and Mrs Grehan Mrs Pitchford Daughter
are gone to Live In Ireland[.] Mrs Edward Pitchford have got a very fine
Boy[.] Mr Edward have Been very ill

Dear son

Robert Partridge is gone out again[.] John is not going any more[.] they are all a very Bad Lot[.] they have tryed to Injure us all they Can But they Can do no good in what they have tryed at[.] it is all becorse your Mother take in a Little dress making as well as they do and she is ready to hang us for it[.] she have send Letters to Mrs Pitchford to try to get me out there But she Cannot do it[.] John Portridge told your mother he would Knock her to Piecies[.] your mother said she wish you had Been at home you would have showed him the water and Put him into it[.] your Brother James have not Been at home yet we expect him at home within a week or two[.] his first voyage was to Constantinople and Back to Glasscow [Glasgow] in Scotland his 2nd voyage to west India and Back to Liverpool his 3rd voyage to Brazill south america and Back to Hamburge his 4th voyage to Quebeck north america[.] we Expect him to come to London this time[.] it will make a Long voyage all togather –

Dear son

Captain winton [Captain Alexander Weynton, a member of the London Committee] have Been dead a Long time[.] Richard Pelly is in his Place for a time[.] old appleby is at Mrs Pitchfords yet[.] I think I told you that John Henery is going to be a Priest[.] alfred is at the Factory[.] Miss Catherine is gone to Ireland with Mrs Grehen[.] I told you of the deaths of sarah and william in my Last Letter[.] Edward and Elizabeth and Emma and arthur are all quite well[.] Edward is Geting a very good seallor[.] John Good sends his respect to you and a great many to numerious to mention all Sends there Kind respects to you, you did not say any thing about Mrs Martingale's son [see William Martindell, entry 34] and he did not send her a Letter[.] she is very uneasy about him[.] he ought to have sent her a Letter as Every Parent feel anxious to here from there Children, and if Children do not Love there Parents how can they expect that there havenly Father will Love them, and watch over them and Protect them in all there troubles, if there is any means at any time send us a Letter[.] Please to excuse me saying any more at this time and accept this with our most Kindest Love
From your most affectionate
Father and Mother J. & S. Wallis

The packet includes a brief note from his sister Susannah.

∾ Southend Septr 17th/47 [1847]

My dearest Brother
With much Pleasure I received your kind [letter] and was glad to hear
that you are quite well thank God[.] this leaves me quite well at Present[.]
I had a letter from home this morning they were all quite well

My dear Brother
you said in your letter I was to Have your Watch Guard ready[.] it will
be quite ready by the time you come home[.] I am making one now[.] I
wish you would be home as soon as that will be finished

My dear Brother
I have written before this[.] I hope you have received it[.] there is not
much news at Present to tell[.] you said you supposed louisa was married[.]
she is Mrs Lawrence now and mary ann is Mrs Nevitt but Poor old Sukey is
still an old maid so my dear Charley they have not all changed there name
there is still one Miss Wallis[.] when you write to me direct for me at
home[.] my time is short now so I must conclude with my Kind love And
Belivere me my dear Charley to remain
your ever Affectionte sister Susannah

Mary Ann Nevitt included a handbill for her husband's business as a dealer
in marine stores on Back Street, Brentwood, addressed "To Servants and
Housekeepers in general." It served to introduce details of his business
collecting rags, clothes, and other refuse, and also emphasized her newly
acquired respectability.

∾ Brentwood Sept 17th 47 [1847]

dear Brother
I take the oppertunity of wrighting theas few lines to you hoping to find
you in good helth as it leaves me and my husband at presant[.] dear
Brother I have alterd my situation sins you came to see me befor for now I
am married to George Nevet [Nevitt] and I am very happy and comfort-
ablely situatid[.] you know my husband very well indeed[.] it is the young
[man] that used to carry coffee on the common[.] when you knew him he
wore a paten ring under one of is feet[.] Dear Brother he is all the better
for that for he is very kind to me[.] he never said wrong I do[.] dear
Elizabeth is with me for a holiday and sends her kind love to you[.] dear

Brother my husband sends his kind love to you and hops he shall have the Pleasure of seeing you when you returne home for he offen talks about you when you used to come to Brentwood with me and we used to send you to the horse and groom to get a pint of beer against we got there

dear Brother you must save all your old close [clothes] for me
so now I must conclude with our kind love to you from your affectionate Brother and sister
G[eorge] & M[ary Ann] Nevett

Another sister, Elizabeth, added a brief note on the bottom of Mary Ann's letter.

dear Brother
this comes with my kind love to you from your
affectionate sister
Elizabeth Wallis

Having a brother serving as an apprentice on a ship bound for the west coast of a distant continent could fire the imagination of those at home, as it did for Edward, Charles's younger brother.

Bromley September 19th 1847

My Dear Brother I write these few lines hoping to find you quite well as it leaves me at present[.] Dear Brother How do yo like the sea[?] Dear Brother do you think I improve my writing[?] Dear Bro I should be very glad to see you[.] When I come to sea I shall not come as a common salior but be a captain at once[.] Dear Brother I have been were you have not been[.] Dear Brother I have Been in a whales belley[.] So no more from your effectionate Brother   EDWARD WALLIS –

Dear Brother I will send you the whale that I was in[.] Dear Brother you wanted to hear from us all so now you shall see me at once – [Here Edward included a drawing of himself inside a whale, with the labels "This is the ribs" and "here i am," and a ship with stick figures in the crow's nest labelled "this is charles wallis."]

Sister Louisa dashed off a note to her brother while her father waited to pack up the letters.

[19 September 1847]

My Dear Brother
Acording to your wishes I with pleasure take upp my pen to write a few Lines to you which I hope will find you quite well and happy[.] Dear Brother you said I was to save you a pece of weding cake but it will be so stale you will not Like it so when you reseve this note you must ask the Captain to let you come and take tea with me and than I will have a stuning Cake Like you had at Pedleys[.] my address Mrs Lawrence next to the royal oak Bromley[.] dont forget to ask and I will Come and meet you[.] My Dear Brother I Cannot say aney more as father is waiting to pack them up[.] So good bye Dear Brother make hast home
  from your affectionate
    Sister Louisa L[awrence]

Perhaps it is just as well that his parents did not send Charles the "shoes or jewes harp" he had requested, since he missed the family letters, which took a curiously circuitous route overland from eastern Canada through Kingston, Holland Landing, Penetanguishene, and on to George Simpson McTavish's care at Sault Ste. Marie, arriving there by 1849. Even if it had arrived on the coast, Charles Wallis would have missed it since, in November 1847, he left for home after two long return voyages in his six years of apprenticeship. After his arrival in London in late May 1848, he did not serve again with the Company. Perhaps his troubles with his captain, Alexander Duncan (entry 14), mentioned in his parents' letter, prevented him from returning to the Company.

54 WILLIAM MURRAY: *It is my earnest wish that I may see you before I die*

The increasing worry of a mother with more than one son at sea is conveyed in these two letters to William Murray, one written six months after he left as a seaman on the *Columbia,* and the other a year later.

William Murray, Seaman on Bord Columbia

Aberdeen 23 aprill 1849

My dear son
I am happy in having this oppertunity of writing you but my ever dear son I cannot describe what my fellings concerning you are[.] to think I have so little oppertunity of hearing from you for such a length of time[.] often do I think where my dear william is[.] I was very sorry you did not

get your Brothers letters[.] they were returned again but I Sincerly hope that god will preserve you and send you safe home to me again it is my earnest prayer to god on your behalf[.] I hope my dear william you will seek god for your self and he will never leave nor for sake you[.] I was like wise sorry you did not get your Cloths[.] I sent them all but they were two late[.] I was much disapointed for I purchased some cloths which would been very comfortable for you but they were returned Back to me[.] my dear William your mony was very acceptable to me but beleive me I would been more happy for one sight of your self[.] I have received all yor letters since ever you left london but I am sorry that you have got none from me[.] your sister Margaret got a Boy and a girl 8 days after you left which are Both doing well[.] she has her Best love to you[.] her husband is never returned yet but she expects word dayly from him[.] I have had no word from your Brother Robert since ever you went away[.] Burnet has his Best love to you[.] hes still trades Between London and inverness[.] dear son I hope you will take care of your self[.] do every thing in your Power to preserve your health in these sickly climes they are often dangerous[.] may god preserve you that is able for he has promised to be a Father to the Fatherless[.] I trust you will rely on that[.] your name son is growing a fine Boy and sends his love to you like wise little Jance sends her love to her uncle[.] she is very useful to her mother with the twins and Joseph is growing a nice Boy at the school[.] I have no more to say but I hope the Blessing of god and your Widow mother will ever be with you where ever you go

    I remain your Faithful affectionate mother
    Susan Murray McReady
address to me as before
No 8 link street

    In her first letter, Susan was merely frustrated that the clothing and letters she had sent to her son have come back to her, because they were too late to catch up with him before his departure. Since she had received letters from William, she was not too worried. A year later her mind was much troubled, not only about William but also about son Robert, who had been unaccounted for in the last year. On 26 February 1850 she had written to the Company asking for information on her son "William Murray-McReady on board the Colombas," assuring them that "by letting me know by return of Post you will greatly oblidge his Poor Widow mother." Although the secretary noted on her letter that William had deserted to California in 1849, the information was either not sent to or not received by Susan, and she wrote once more to her son through the Company.

∾ William Murray McReady on Bord the Columbas

Aber[dee]ⁿ April 4 1850

   My Dear Son
   I again take the oppertunity of writing you hoping Sincerly that this will
find you in good health[.] I have been lying all this winter in bad health
and my mind has been as much troubled as my Body concerning you[.] I
never was so weared in my life to hear from you[.] this is the 3ᵈ letter I have
wrote you with out receiving an answer[.] your Brother Burnet is well and
sends his kind love to you like wise your Sister Margaret and her family
espicaly your name son William[.] I have not received any word from your
brother Robert this twelve months and I cannot tell wheather he be dead
or alive and my dear william I hope nothing will hinder you from answering
this letter for by course of nature my dear son you will not have your aged
mother long to write to[.] you will write me when ever you receive this and
may god bless guide and direct you in all your ways and I hope as soon as
you can get liberty you will Come home and see me[.] your Brother in law
Robert Mills was at home 7 months ago and is at Eden just now[.] it is my
earnest wish that I may see you before I die[.] I Pray god to Bless you my
dear william and preserve you is the earnest wish of your ever affectionate
Mother
      Susan McReady
   Address to me 8 Link st
      Aberdeen

   We do not know whether Susan received word from her son or got her
earnest wish to see him after he had deserted to California at the height of
the gold rush fever. No further Company record of him has been found.

55 WILLIAM BLAIR: *I would not give a sight of you for all the gold in Caliafornie*

Janet Clairmont longed for her loyal son, William Blair, who had kept in
touch during his service as a seaman. He was first on the *Columbia* on its
1845-6 voyage out to the coast and his mother had contacted the Company
in August 1846, ten months after its departure, to find out if he was alive and
well. She was reassured, but by March 1847 she had David Hill write on her
behalf since "there has, as yet, been no Letters from him." Shortly after,
another reassuring letter was sent by the Company secretary to state that
William had transferred to the *Mary Dare* on the coast. Finally, in May 1849,
his mother received letters from her son that informed her of this change,
and she sent off this missive.

〜 To William Blaire, Seaman on bore the Brige Mary Dare

Montrose 25 June 1849

Dear Son I received bothe the lettrs in the month of May[.] I was very unwel when I recevied them but thanks be to god I am well againe and fit for my worke againe working the saime as when you left me but not so abile now[.] I am very weried for a Sight of you now I would not give a sight of you for all the gold in Caliafornie [California][.] I hope you will try and get home as Son as posabil[.] I am still in Mr Rollint house very weriet for my Sun[.] I would have sent you out word long bee fore this time but I was allwise expecting you home[.] I have all ways as shilings of your monie yet bee fore I went I think you will Sun bee home[.] I think I need not aske anie monie[.] I have been very sparing working hard[.] Mr Mill Deide in the Month of aprile and a great number of our aqintines is gon[.] Mrs Bibie hase her best Respects to you[.] James is puling away in the hobart, all ways they have ben kind frinds to me[.] gorg is stil at the Debefort [Deptford?] enquring for you[.] Elisbeth Dicker is all ways enquring a bout you[.] Margreat her Daughter is Never married yet[.] I have Received all the lettrs you have Sent me and I hope you will ccuse me for not having wun from me since[.] Margreat Rollan is married to wun Joseph Church water man in london[.] she is away from us long ago[.] los[e] now [no] time in writing if you ar not Coming home[.] I expect you will bee the first word your Self[.] no mor at present but I remaine your affectionat mother Janet Clairmont

Janet's mention of the gold in California was unwittingly ironic, considering that her son deserted from the *Mary Dare* on 20 August 1849 while at Fort Victoria. At that time, the temptation was great for seamen to jump ship and James Douglas, now chief factor at Fort Victoria, expressed his fears to the London Committee that "we live in hourly apprehension of seeing the Company's vessels altogether deserted in consequences of the enormous pay given to seamen, in Calefornia." It is quite possible that men who deserted joined other ships and found a way of contacting their families. Our contact with them ends, however, when they ceased to be associated with the Company.

56 THOMAS PEREGRINE LEWIS: *Be thoughtful and careful of your character & constitution for if you once make a breach nothing that you can do will so firmly reinstate you in the opinion of your Patron*

Along with telling their son the sad news of his sister's death, Emma and Thomas Lewis are each diligent in separately instructing Thomas junior in the proper behaviour of a young apprentice. Thomas Peregrine Lewis had left England in 1845 aboard the *Columbia* and had completed one round trip when he arrived back in May 1848. His delighted father wrote to the Company on 24 May asking how long his son's ship would be in port and suggesting that he come home by the next steamer leaving Bristol. On 26 August, his father notified the Company secretary that Thomas was on his way back to the ship by "the first direct opportunity ... since receiving your summons." He also asked for a position for his seventeen-year-old son Harry, requesting "the favor and privilege of sleeping & messing in the half Deck" and adding that his "only object in wishing the latter is that he may be less exposed to contamination, when he has had some experience he will be better able to contend with it." Thomas junior was on another voyage when the following letters were sent by the Company's ship *Cowlitz*, four years into his six-year apprenticeship.

[on outer envelope] Mr Thos P. Lewis, H.B. Barque Columbia, Columbia River, N.A p^r [per] Cowlitz.
[on inner envelope] Mr Thomas P. Lewis, Barque Columbia, Columbia River, N.A.

Milford (Pembroke, Wales) July 14 – 1849

My dear Tom
    I need scarcely tell you how happy your letter made us to hear of your safety & good health – long my dear son may you enjoy the inestimable gift of health without it life is a blank – a heavy road – since you left home we have been called on to experience a very sad bereavement – your poor sister Emma is dead after an illness of three months[.] Mr Drew called it a Galloping Consumption[.] I dare say you will fret when you hear of her death – it has been a most severe trial to me[.] it was more accutely felt in consequence of poor Harrys departure. he shipped on board a barque bound out to Calis [Calais] apprenticed for four years – we have had three letters from him since he left in all of which he affectionately remembers my dear son Tom – he appears quite satisfied with the sea & well he is for had he remained at home this winter I fear it would have gone hard with him in regard to maintenance much less clothing – as your Father's circumstances appear most discouraging – indeed I do not know where it will end[.] trade is quite at a stand here but the crops of hay &c are likely to be more abundant this summer than last – I trust your lot will be cast in brighter soil[.] steadiness & perseverance will do wonders – both of which I hope you will follow[.] not only make money honestly but take care of it – no lot can be harder than a sailors – but they are very *foolish* in spending

hard earned money – your Father will send you a long letter of particulars but I think you do not like to receive or send long ones yours are always short & sweet but I am content to hear you are well – time will roll on as it has done before when we shall be looking out for you it may be years if ever we all meet again as we did last year – death has made a sad inroad in our family two dead since you left poor Tom Propert survived dear Emma five days – he was worn to a shade a melancholy spectacle[.] William still carries the Contest he has won two prizes again this term[.] he is quite well as are all the family – your Uncle George I lament to say is in dread of parting with his little blessing as you used to call him little George is very ill[.] your Grandmother, Aunts & Uncles are much alike as when you left with the exception of being a *year* older – I have lost another [cross-written] tooth which gives me a more sage look & if my life is spared much longer I think they will all depart. The Children are growing very much especially Georgina. She promises to be tall[.] dear Emma grew very fast & was considered to be a lovely girl – I daily miss her she was so good & steady[.] I have nothing to say to interest you further.

    may God protect & bless my dear son
      prays your fond & affectionate
        Mother
        Emma Lewis

Milford (Pembroke, Wales) 18 July 1849

    My dearest Tom

    The Cowlitz being about to sail for N.W. Coast I avail myself of the opportunity of writing to you by her and could wish I had no bad news to communicate to you but such is the will of an alwise Providence & we must submit to it[.] Your poor dear sister Emma who was when you left home so apparently in perfect health is now no more[.] she was taken from us on the 21 March after four months rapid consumption – she died exceedingly happy & her thoughts during her last moments dwelt much on you and Harry – it has left a sad blank to your dear mother as you know she was her constant companion therefore she feel the void more[.] I wrote you by the Ascweth [Asquith] which I hope you received from M^{essrs} Phillips & Ogden – I am sure you must find this acquaintance very desirable that you avail yourself as much as possible of it. I also wrote you by Harpooner[.] when you write next let me know if you received them. We were delighted to receive yours announcing your safe arrival at the Islands and I hope in this your prospects of promotion have been realised – and I am very sanguine you will render yourself every way deserving of such great responsibility – I am persuaded that with the change of situation you will be thoughtful and careful of your character & constitution for if you once make a breach nothing that you can do will so firmly reinstate you in the opinion of your Patron and all hopes of further promotion in that quarter will be thrown away wherein if you restore my hopes you have the brightest prospects before you & with the Governors good wishes you will soon become your own man after having the usual time as 2nd & 1st mate[.] do apply yourself continually to your navigation as on your correctness in that will depend your passing your examinations at the Trinity Board – for that will now be undisputable[.] now do let me beg of you to write us a long letter giving Aus [crossed out] the whole particular of your prospects for this voyage the state of your health[.] Mrs Owens has received a letter from Mr Rook which satisfies as to the fate of her son. We are now looking forward to the happiness of seeing poor Harry in about three weeks time if his life be spared[.] We have had three long letters from him – he is reconciled to his fate from dire necessity – as there was nothing on shore for him to do – he is in an excellent employ & if he has his health I have no doubt will soon be well off[.] times have been so very bad here for the last five months that we are almost a general wreck[.] the carpenters are all out of work & starving and so the whole Kingdom is in the same state[.] I have only had £5.10.0 store rent during the time – I have not yet been able to pay Capn Allen or Hewley as you may judge how much we are straightened & I trust my dear boy that you will make much of every penny and not squandered any foolishly away for a moments plea-sure – I still hold on the farm and things look very promising up to this time[.] the potatoes are excellent and quite a treat[.] Bob Pringle is dead – the Cholera is raging very fatally in Strethyr [Strathaird?] Neath Bristol &c &c I trust the Almighty will spare us from the scourge. Georgina Pury & Katrine are all well & send their love & lots of Kisses. George Williams is gone to Cardigan as Comptroller of Customs[.] he is likely to remain there for some years[.] Hannah is not yet gone there to live she expects an increase shortly – all your old Friends are well[.] your mama has written you a letter & will tell you all the news I have omitted & that you may enjoy every health & happiness ever prays

Your affectionate Father

Thos J. Lewis

It seems that Thomas had been a good son, writing home his short and sweet letters, and his father is sanguine about his chances for promotion. Thomas had missed this letter on his journey home, and after his arrival in the spring of 1850 he asked that his indentures, although unexpired, be cancelled and he be appointed as second mate to one of the Company's vessels. The Company did not accept this suggestion, and he left on the *Prince Rupert* for a summer trip to Hudson Bay, still listed as an apprentice. However, records show no further employment with the Company. Despite a letter in 1851 from his father asking that he be taken on "provided he has a chance for promotion," the Company replied that there was no position available. Perhaps his father's warning was a real concern, and there was some breach in behaviour that left his character in question. The laconic ship's logs give no indication of a problem.

57 GEORGE HILDRED: *They send their love to you and a thousand kisses every night and morning when they say their prayers*

George Hildred's wife, Elizabeth, at home with three children – one born since her husband's departure for the west coast – wrote to tell him of her financial situation and to give news of a birth and a death in the family.

Mʳ Geo Hildred, Carpindor on Board the Ship Fife Shire, Vancovers Island, North West Coast America

[Hull] 1ˢᵗ March 1850

My dear Husband
It is with very great pleasure that I now write these few lines to you[.] I have received three kind letters from you which gave me great satisfaction. I was delighted to find by your letters that you were quite well and pretty comfortable and had I known how to have sent a letter to you I should have done so long ago for I know that you would have been very happy to have heard how we all were. You have no doubt received my letter which I sent by the Flashire. My money has been stoped for 3 months so Uncle wrote when we received your letter stating that you were in the Ship and comfortable so they have sent me one months half pay but said nothing about the other two months which are due so my Uncle wrote again and asked them what they meant[.] we have not had our answer yet but we are expecting one every day. I got safe over my confinement[.] it is a little girl[.] they call it Cariline but you would see all particulars in my last letter. George and Mary Anne grow two fine children and they talk about every day they have great deal to tell you[.] they were very much pleased with the kisses you sent them[.] they send their love to you and a thousand kisses every night and morning when they say their prayers[.] they pray that

you may return safe home. Mother and brother Robert have ben over to Hull[.] they were pretty well and send their love to you. You will be very sorry to hear that poor little James is dead[.] he died on the 5 of last April[.] it will soon be a year since this mournful event took place. We all felt it very much and still continue to do so. Uncle felt it very much. Your Mother and Sisters send their love to you and they as well we all are long-ing for your safe return. Aunt Uncle & cousins send their love to you and will be glad to see you home once more. Work is very slack in Hull. I continue midlin and the hope of soon seeing you cheers me up. I felt it very much when my money was stopped but Uncle & Aunt were very kind to me so I have got on so far. Accept my love[.] I think the time long[.] Please to write as soon as possible.

  Mrs Bolton [Boulton] sends her love to her Husband and she has not written because she thought her Husband would have left for London
     I remain
        Your Loving Wife
           Elizabeth Hildred
God bless you

   Although his wife addressed him on the *Fifeshire,* George Hildred was serving as a carpenter at £5 per month on a long journey aboard the *Albion* – first to Sydney, Australia, then to the west coast of North America. On his way to San Francisco on 22 April 1850, George became a deserter along with sixteen other men, including Second Mate William Boulton, whose wife inquired after him through Elizabeth. By the time Elizabeth wrote to George that her money had been stopped, he may well have been in the gold fields. His children's prayers for their father might indeed have been needed if he had entered the uncertain life of panning for gold. But as a carpenter he may well have made money during the boom in building that accompanied the gold field activity. If so, he may have relieved the poverty that would certainly have been Elizabeth's fate without her husband's money from the Company.

58 JOHN BRACEBRIDGE: *Beware of the black girls*

Despite the rigours of life far from home in Britain at the turn of the half-century, men like John Bracebridge were lucky in some ways: they avoided the bad economic times and the cholera epidemics described in these letters.

~ John Bracebridge Seaman, Hudson Bay Companys Barque Cowlitz,
Columbia River or elsewhere

Poplar October 31ˢᵗ 1849

Dear Brother

This letter comes with my kind love to you hoping it will find you in
good health and spirits[.] I am happy to tell you that we are all quite well
in health[.] Father and Mother are quite well they both send their love to
you[.] Ted has not gone away as yet – I don't expect he will go this year[.]
he sends his respects to you[.] Thomas and Mary ann are quite well[.] they
do not forget you[.] they are continually speaking about you and want to
know when you are coming home[.] they very often have a row about you
they want to know who has got the best right to you[.] I have wrote 2
letters to your Mother but I have received but one answer from her[.] they
were both well when I heard from them[.] we received one letter from you
from Deal[.] when you went we expected we should have heard from you
again but I hope it will not be long untill we hear from you[.] there has
been great many died with the Cholera since you left London[.] Mrs
Lathams Mother died with a few hours illness[.] I am sorry to have to tell
you of the Death of little Maryann Kelly we sent her away from us[.] she
only lived 3 weeks after she left[.] there is a great many that you know has
died but Thank God we all escaped from it[.] I went to the office the first
Thursday in last month[.] they did not ask any questions[.] we are all very
much obliged to you for doing as you have done[.] I am going again to
morrow to the office there is no trouble in getting the money[.] sophy has
gone to place again 5 weeks ago she is quite well[.] I hope you will not
neglect writing to us at every opportunity for we shall be most happy to
hear from you[.] work is very bad at present there is scarcely any one at
work present[.] when you write let us know where we are to write to[.] I
should write moe to you but I do not know whethere you will get or not
but I have more to tell you when I hear from you[.] Maryan Gorman is
married a month after you went[.] I am quite as well as can be expected
but if it is a boy it shall be named after you

No more at present from your
Affectionate Sister B. McCarthy

Beware of the black girls[.] your Ginger dont look so well as when you
were at home

John's mother and his stepfather, John Zealand, wrote in response to what
appears to be a complaint that John had made about them.

∾ John Bracebridge Seaman Hudson Bay Company Barque Cowlitz North
America

London Nov 30/49 [1849]

My Dear son
It tis with pleasure I have the oppertunity of sending you these few lines
hoping they may find you as well as they leave us at present on bord now
ling [lying] in the pool at London[.] we boath was at kellyes yesterday and
expects Mrs Maccarthey [John's sister] on bord to tea to morrow and they
tould us all thay knowed about you but we did not see your intended wife
and sehe was not very well pleased because she was not sent for, we have
not much newe to send[.] all your relations is very well[.] your ant Kemp is
quiet fat but all very much disapointed of you not coming home this sumer
as well as us but I hope and trust you well have a plesanter voyage and com
home to your satsfaction this time so that you will not have the voyage to
blame to keep you away but if you have the chance to rite send us word
when you expect to com to England as I think we shall see you this time,
for I doant intend to rite much as my letters give ofence so when I see you
I can speak for myself if ever I have the oppertunity but I somtimes think I
never shall but if this you be 3 or 4 years as you have sind [signed] for you
will wish you seen your Mother befor you whent away but if you doant
think so your Mother would have liked to see you[.] if she had droped of
when you was at London you would not have thought it was all a lie or an
excus as you did[.] ~~for~~ [crossed out] I shaul not be surprised at her droping
of very suden sum of these times for she is very ill at times but you will
think uponet sum day when it tis to Late but I hope God will pro[te]ct you
and bring you safe home
we have nothing more paretular to say this time[.] I expect by the time you
com home I shall either have a biger vesal or els no one at all so you need
not expect to find us any diferant then when you last sa[w] me
   no more at present from your affectinate Mother
   and me your ever well wisher
      John Zealand

The fact that John Zealand signed himself John Bracebridge's well-wisher
did not keep him from cautioning his distant stepson that he may be sorry
later in life for neglecting (or avoiding) his family. On the other hand, perhaps he merely added his name to a letter written mainly by John's mother.
A month after her first letter, John's sister wrote about the family's concern
regarding a young woman, Sophy, whose status is uncertain, possibly the
intended wife referred to in the previous letter.

~ John Bracebridge Seaman, Hudson Bay Companys Barque Cowlitz, North America

Poplar December 6 1849

Dear Brother

I take the opportunity of writing these few lines to you hoping they will find you in good health[.] I am happy to tell you that we are all quite well in health[.] Ted has gone to Sea[.] he went the 25 of last month to Sydney[.] he does not expect to be away more than 10 months[.] work was very bad so he thought he had better go away[.] Father is doing a little at present[.] Mr Zealand came up 3 weeks ago he is quite well[.] your Mother came up a fortnight yesterday she spent 2 days with us[.] she is quite well she told me to tell you that she never was comfortable in her life as she is at present[.] we told Sophys Mother when your Mother came last sundy week but she said it was no use of sending for sophey for she could not get out[.] she told us that we could send your Mother to her if we liked[.] we asked your Mother if she would go but she said she would not[.] she said that the girl was a stranger to her[.] you mentioned nothing about her when you wrote to her[.] I shall not say anything untill we see one another which I hope will not be more 18 months at the furthest[.] Tom and Maryann are both well[.] they donot forget you[.] your Mother was quite pleased with them both to think that they talked so much about you[.] they both told her the name of the ship you was in and were you was goine[.] Tom is her favourite[.] we spent Tuesday very comfortable together[.] I have got a letter from your Mother which I am going to post with this one[.] Dear Brother Tom going to the office this morning[.] we are very much obliged to you for doing as you have done[.] we will get the last money in March[.] we shall be very happy to hear from you which I hope will not be long[.] I hope you will write at every opportunity[.] Father and Mother both send their love to you[.] Mary and Martin was married last Monday week[.] they are loving up stairs[.] they old man has gone away[.] Tom and Mary ann both send they love to you[.] I hope you will take care of yourself and keep from the black girls[.] I wish you a merry Christmas anda happy new year[.] I have more to say when I hear from you.

No more at present from your Affictionate
Sister B McCarthy

John's sister and mother both seem concerned about the status of the young woman named Sophy and await his presence in England to clear things up. That would not have happened, as John Bracebridge, seaman aboard the *Cowlitz,* was discharged on 27 January 1850 by order of the British

Consul at the Sandwich Islands after "using threatening and abusive language to the Captain." He left without having received his sister's warning
that he "beware of the black girls." He seems to have escaped the imprisonment
that was the fate of his fellow crew members as deserters (see the story of
William Dean, George Mouat, and George Micklefield, in entries 59, 61, and
62, respectively). Bracebridge, however, probably did not escape the tempta-
tions of the numerous grog shops and hotels that dotted the busy port of
Honolulu. Unless he was hired by another ship headed for England, it might
have been some time before he faced his family and friends back home.

59 WILLIAM DEAN: *It seems as though you had never Been home*

On 8 October 1846 William Dean left London aboard the *Cowlitz* as a young
teenaged apprentice and served on that vessel until 19 May 1849. He left on
his second voyage on 4 August 1849 and his sister and brother-in-law wrote
to him on "the last day but one in another year," to tell him the good and
bad news from home.

~ William Dean, On Board the Barque Cowlitz, N. America

December 30 [1849]

   My ever dear Brother
   I now sit down this the last day but one in another year to address a few
lines to you trusting by the blessing off our heavenly father you are almost
to your Journeys end[.] I hope you have not had much rough weather[.]
theire as been numbers off ships lost this year but I hope you are Spared
alive from a watery Grave[.] I often think off you When I look at my dear
littl Boy[.] he grows nicely and begin to say daddaw and chattr in his little
way[.] Father is quite wel I am thankful to say[.] mother remains about the
same – her hip gets Weaker she can not sit up much But I think she may
lay a Great While[.] Aunt as been sadly[.] I thought she would have laid up
but thank god she is better[.] you wished me to say how father Was off for
money[.] very bad and he as had such misfortune with two houses wich is a
deal out off his way but I hope he will scratch through this Winter but he
is indeed a man off much trouble[.] the Apples fetch scarse any thing[.] the
destress in theis part is schocking indeed. Grandmother is still alive and as
tiresome as ever she was[.] Robert as left Jenners this week and gone home
as father as no money to pay a man and he and George cannot do it all[.]
I shall be thankful to see the summer again as It tis a great trouble to me to
see them so destressed[.] we had hoped to have had a letter before this but
none as come but I hope all is well with you and the ships company[.]

I often think off the Captain Lady poor thing such a long voige[.] William Keble is quite well he is fatter now as 40 Pounds a year[.] I have not had a letter but once since you have been gone from emma[.] Bob Wenborn as been at home ever Since you left at least about a month after and he is not to go out with this ship[.] it seems as though you had never Been home[.] Remember us all to Lawrence and the steward and mate[.] I hope you are all comfortabl[.] Father and mother desire the very best love to theire dear boy[.] The boys and all freinds Join in best and kindest love to you and Except off a Sisters kin love and many Prayers for your happeness Your affectionate Broth[er] and sister J. & C.

The intriguing reference to the "Captain Lady" would seem to indicate that Captain Alexander John Weynton took his wife on the long trip to the coast, but we have not yet found confirmation of this fact in the Company's records. Although unusual, it was not unheard of; in a diary entry for 15 July 1836, Levi Chamberlain at the mission house in Honolulu noted that "The Captain of the Nereide [Robert Royal] is we learn accompanied by his lady." William's sister probably hoped that, if the *Cowlitz* captain's wife was onboard, she would show maternal care toward her young brother while he was so far from home.

After William's brief summer in England, it may well have seemed to his family as if he had never been home – and it might have been a long time before the Dean family saw him again. He and Bob Lawrence (mentioned in the letter) were among five members of the crew who left the ship when the *Cowlitz* stopped at Honolulu in February 1850. British Consul William Miller, who was called on to settle their fate, described the situation to R.C. Wyllie, the Hawaiian minister of foreign relations, in a letter dated 2 February 1850:

> The crew of the Hudson's Bay Company's Barque "Cowlitz" of 391 Tons burden, now in this Port, on her way from London to Vancouver's Island, with a valuable Cargo, and a large quantity of Gunpowder on board, having refused to weigh anchor, or proceed any further on the Voyage, unless their Wages be doubled, a Month's paid in advance, and New Articles of Agreement drawn out and signed, and every effort on my part to bring these men to a proper sense of their duty having failed, I am under the necessity of soliciting the Intervention and Assistance of the Sandwich Island's Authorities in the matter.
>
> The Crew all signed regular Ships' Articles, previously to sailing from London, to serve for a period not exceeding five years. I have mustered them on board, and having heard what they had to say I feel fully persuaded that they have no cause of complaint whatsoever.

I therefore suggest, and indeed solicit, that such Men of the Cowlitz' Crew who still persist in refusing to proceed to Sea, be imprisoned, in the securest manner possible, in the Fort, until one of Her Majesty's Ships of War, daily expected, arrive at Honolulu, the Agents of the Cowlitz, of course, being responsible for attendant Costs and Charges.

I need scarcely add, in conclusion, how extremely pernicious it might be to the good order & tranquility of this Port, especially under the present existing circumstances with regard to Seamen in general, if such conduct as that displayed by the crew of the "Cowlitz" did not meet with prompt and energetic Rebuke.

The same day, the master of the *Cowlitz* was invited to "Point out to the Marshal of the Hawaiian Islands such Individuals of his Crew as he may deem it expedient to have confined in Irons or otherwise, in the Fort." The apprentices were confined on board ship, and fifteen men were recommended to be held at the fort in irons. Two days later, however, the consul was obliged to complain that "unless the unruly seamen of the 'Cowlitz' be confined in Irons, in the securest manner possible, they cannot, it seems, be safely prevented from deserting, or occasionally absenting themselves from the Fort." Since they were not placed in irons, "the apprentices & some of the other men on board the 'Cowlitz' have this morning shewn themselves a more refractory disposition than before." Wyllie replied that "the want of irons, was the reason why the Sheriff had not carried out your request ... & that he will put these men in irons, so soon as he can procure them." Some of the seamen "came to ask the Captain pardon and was sorry for what they had said willing to do their best to get the vessel to Victoria," so they were released out of irons on 5 February 1850. When the ship arrived at Fort Victoria, with a crew complemented by Hawaiians, Chief Factor James Douglas described the situation to Company Secretary Archibald Barclay in a letter dated 3 April 1850:

The B[ar]que *Cowlitz* from England, arrived in this Port on the 17th Inst. Having been 40 days out from the Sandwich Island's where I am sorry to say, she was deserted by nearly the whole of the ship's company. The first defection was of five seamen, who ran from the ship a few days after her arrival at Honolulu; the ten remaining seamen and three apprentices did not exactly follow their example in deserting the ship; but their conduct was almost equally bad, as they refused to work on the terms for which they had signed, and demanded a month's pay in advance, having previously taken up the balance due on the voyage, and when that indulgence was denied, it being suspected, on good ground's that they intended to desert after receiving the money, they one and all, refused to work, and set the Master and Officers at defiance.

The case was then referred to Consul General Miller, who put the apprentices into confinement on board, and removed the seamen to the Native Fort, to be confined there at the Company's expense, until transferred to one of Her Majesty's ship's. That appears to be the severest punishment he can inflict on refractory seamen, and it is practically of no advantage as a protection to ship owner's. It proved so, in the instance of the *Cowlitz,* deserted, by nearly all her crew in a foreign Port where they could not be replaced. Besides the detention of the ship, the company is put to the further expense of supporting the delinquents until discharged from the Fort it is evident that no actual advantage but rather the reverse was derived from the presence and interposition of the Consul who is not armed with sufficient power to enforce obedience in cases of mutiny, on board of merchant ships. I am happy to say that Captain Weynton speak's in the highest terms of the conduct of his Officers, M^r [Joseph] Miller, [John] Swanston, and [John Logan] Sinclair, and also of the Boatswain [Jeremiah McCarthy, entry 60], Carpenter, Cook and Steward who remained faithful to their engagements.

The seamen on being questioned by General Miller as to their treatment on board, said they had no complaint to make on that score; their disgraceful conduct may therefore be entirely ascribed to visions of Calefornia floating on their minds. Captain Weynton was finally obliged to complete his complement, with Sandwich Islander's and managed to bring the *Cowlitz* safely into this Port, but since his arrival here, he appear's to have strong objection's against putting to sea again with the same crew, and I, consequently anticipate, much trouble with this vessel, as seamen cannot be had at any price in this quarter.

The Brig *Mary Dare,* was also abandoned, at Honolulu, by all her crew, except the Carpenter and Cook and was, from that cause, detained several weeks in harbour, and nine day's after the departure of the *Cowlitz,* as Captain Scarborough refused to leave Port with a complement of Sandwich Islander's.

She was at last manned by six of the *Cowlitz's* men who were induced by the hope's of freedom and good pay, say 20 Dollar's a month to ship by her. There is no means of controuling seamen in any part of the Pacific, adjacent to Calefornia and they cannot be trusted even when receiving the highest rate of Calefornia pay, lately 150, but now 80 Dollars a month an expense which no regular business can afford.

William Dean did not stay repentant very long, however. In a letter dated 6 April 1850, Chief Factor James Douglas noted that he had run off with several of the crew, with the intention of making their way to the gold fields of California. By the time his sister wrote to him, he might well have been on another adventure, in search of riches far from home. (See also the stories of Jeremiah McCarthy, George Mouat, and George Micklefield in entries 60, 61, and 62, respectively.)

60   JEREMIAH MCCARTHY: *I hope you may get some account of Owen from some of the American Whealers should you fall in with any*

In his two undelivered letters, Jeremiah McCarthy's father, Florence, wrote of his sons, who were all over the world, even off whaling on the high seas. He sent his first letter by the *Prince Rupert* to York Factory and overland to the "North West Coast."

∾   For Jer^h McCarthy Seaman on Board the Cowlitz, Columbia river, North West Coast of America

London March 1st 1850

   Dr Son
   I embrace this opportunity of leting you know that I rec^d a letter the 25th Feby from your Brothers[.] Charley is in the Elphinstone Felix was very bad but was nearly well again when Charley wrote the letter from Eden on the 26th Decr last[.] he likes India very well but says Dr Father I often wished myself at home with you[.] they expects to be back to Bombay in about 6 Months time[.] I have left Mother Kill about 2 months ago[.] I live with your Uncle Jer^h we all enjoy good health at present thanks be to God I hope this will find you in the same[.] your Uncle rec^d a letter from Ellen about a month ago she was well in health then and behaved well to her Father she sent him £8.0.0. [crossed out] to buy a boat to go on the river to sell Beer[.] he has not heard from Flory those 2 Months[.] your Aunt Mary is well in health and in the same place still –
   I rec^d a Sovereign from James Hays on your account[.] Patrick made a voyage to Petersburg when he was out of his time another or 2 in the coal trade[.] I do not think he is much the better of it[.] he do not seem to have much Clothes or to care much for them[.] Jack is just the same as usual[.] I hope you will Ans^r this the first opportunity[.] I have not heard anything of the others I fear I never will[.] provisions is very cheap but work of all sorts very slack[.] no more at present from your affectionate Father
   Florence McCarthy

   This father seemed to be resourceful in keeping track of his sons, noting that he read in the newspaper of the safe arrival of the *Cowlitz* at Victoria. The newspapers, which depended heavily on private sources for the latest news, often received word before anxious family members.

∾ For Jer^h McCarthy Seaman on Board the Cowlitz, Columbia river, North
West Coast of America

July 25th 1850

Dr Son
   this is to inform you that I rec^d two letters from your Brothers Felix &
Charles[.] in the first it mentioned Felix was ill that was dated 26th December
back Bay Eden the next the 26th of April they were all well then[.] I have
wrot 2 letters to them Ans^rs to those I rec^d. I have wrote one to you before
this the time of the Prince rupert Sailing in that I mentioned leaving
Mother Kill at Christmas last[.] I have not seen her since[.] I hope I never
will as long as God spares my eye sight[.] your Brother Patrick is gone to
Quebec in a large Brig belonging to Sunderland[.] he has been in her since
he was out of his time[.] we have delightful weather here and the prospect
of the most Plentiful harvest all over the united Kingdom and Europe at
large[.] all sorts of provisions is plentiful & cheap but work is scarce and
badly paid for[.] I hope you may get some account of Owen from some of
the American Whealers should you fall in with any[.] as for Florence I give
him up altogather[.] I hope it might prove otherwise[.] John is still at
Allens the same old thing[.] it gave me pleasure to see your ship & the
Norman Scot [*Norman Morison*] mentioned in the paper arriving at Victoria
the latter part of March[.] I hope this will find you and all hands well as it
leaves me and all your friends and relatives at present thanks be to God[.] I
have got a room to myself in the same house with your Uncle Jer^h[.] he has
given up coal work and got a purl boat[.] Ellen sent sent [repetition] him
£8. I think he will be able to get a living
   I rec^d £1 of James Hays from you[.] your Cousin Florence was home
about March last[.] he is gone in a schooner up the straits on a trading voyage[.] I *hope you will Ans^r this* as soon as possible
no more at present from your affectionate Father
   Florence McCarthy
N.B. Since writing the above we have buried old aunt Martin

By the time these letters were sent, Jeremiah was on his way home. He
served with the Company as a seaman – one round trip from 1844 to 1846 on
the *Vancouver* and *Cowlitz* and a summer trip in 1848 on the *Prince Rupert* to
Hudson Bay. In 1849 he joined the *Cowlitz* as a boatswain and sailed on 4
August 1849 for the coast, where he drew praise from Captain Weynton as
one of the few members of the crew who did not join the deserting seamen
at Honolulu in February 1850 (see William Dean, entry 59). Jeremiah continued in the Company's employ for the return voyage of the *Cowlitz* but

took his discharge in October 1850 at Oahu, Hawai'i. With sons Charlie and Felix in India, Patrick in Quebec, and the younger Florence seemingly not in communication with the family, Florence senior would have had only John near home and perhaps his two daughters Mary and Margaret, although they were not mentioned in the letter. He was anxious to hear news of Owen, employed in the whaling industry, and hoped that Jeremiah might have been able to get news of his brother from the American whalers. This working-class family would not be untypical in the 1850s, as hard times at home and growing employment in overseas shipping and fishing ventures scattered families all over the world.

61 GEORGE MOUAT: *There is many Chinges in the world ... But still there is sorow in the world*

George Mouat had left London on 4 August 1849, serving as a seaman aboard the *Cowlitz,* bound for the coast. Gilbert Mouat wrote to his brother to tell him to keep his faith as the "one thing neidfull" in a world of sorrows.

George Mouat, Seaman, HBC⁰ˢ Service, Fort Victoria, Vancouver's Island

Leith Agust 14th 1850

Dear Brother I take the opertunity of inform you that we are all in the Land of the living as yet[.] only Charls wife she is ded and Mothir is still alive and we are all about the same as when we Left Echother [each other] altho there is many Chinges in the world[.] there is war Betwin Denmark and Germiny Bot all other Pleaces are at Peace But still there is sorow in the world[.] the Colora [cholera] took away Good many thousands frome the world Bot it never Came to Shetland[.] Bot there is truble there fore there is Grate want in Shetland for Last year was not Good and Cropes was Bad so the money you Left to Mother Came in Good time altho I only God the Last of it is a short time ago[.] Charls hase one Child ded since this wife died which Leves him two and urlsa our Sister Came to keep his house and when she Came would not take Charge[.] But I Most inform you that the abestant [absent] is sin [soon] forgot[.] whin I Came to Mrs Mouat to inquire for the name of your ship there was non[e] in the house that Could tell me Eany about you or the name of the Shipe So I had to aply at the hutsons Bay house fore information Concirning you dear Brother & I hope you well Remamber the one thing neidfull is your Eternal Stite your niver ding [dying] soull[.] Look to the Blood of a redimer [our Redeemer] and see if it is to Be spilt in veean [vain] fore you[.] I hope george you will not for git the one thing neidfull[.] dear george I have to

inform you that I have got another Daughter and name is Elisabeth[.] so
I most Clos with all our Cind Love to you so no more at Present Bot
Remans your Dear Brother
    till death Gilbert Mouat
[crosswise] I hope you will send ane answr as sun as you Cane to me[.]
Direct as Befor Couper st 47 nort Leith

Although George Mouat did not receive these reports of death and disease
from Shetland, perhaps he was seeking a less sorrowful world. He left the
Company's employment by deserting on 31 January 1850 during the *Cowlitz's*
stop at Hawai'i. He may have been one of those incarcerated in the jail at
Honolulu (see William Dean, entry 59). He might have been attracted by the
better-paying employment aboard an American ship, where he might have
earned up to US$80 a month compared to the Company's £2 ($10).

62 GEORGE MICKLEFIELD: *I hop wen you receve this you will rite*

Mary Ann Rose wrote to her son, George Micklefield, who had left England
in August 1849 on the *Cowlitz*, serving as a seaman.

  George Micklefield, Seaman, Ship Cowlitz

December 1 1850

    My Dear son i now take the pleshure of riteing these few to you hoping
to find you in good helth as i am very unwell at preasent[.] i rite to inform
that your sister metilda was put to bed on 23 of march and was in good
helth tel the 1th of June[.] she took ill on the same day and went in a
galloping comptsumption and the little girl took bad on 24th of July and
died on the 5 of august and your poor sister died on 24 of october after
lingring 4 months and 24 days[.] she wished for me to take her home to die
for to be bured in same grave with her sister so she was bured on the 30 of
october at limehouse as she wiched[.] your uncle William is ded and
bured[.] your brother John is well and in the countrey at preasent[.] miss
yardley is remurred [remarried.] your brother Willi[a]m is well and so is
your sister mary and your sister sarah i expect to be confined a bout nexe
Janeurey for she is very porley at preasent[.] the children is all well at
preasent[.] my dear son i have not receved no letter sence your bin gorn a
way from you[.] your Brother and sisters sends thair love to you[.] i hop
wen you receve this you will rite for the owners told me that you could in
the ships that come home from thair to london
    so no More at Preasent from your loving Mother Mary Ann Rose

Besides the deaths she had just endured, Mary Ann would have had to wait to know where her son was. Unless he found a way to write to her from prison, she would not have discovered his whereabouts for some time. Company records show that he deserted in Hawai'i in February 1850 and, unlike the other seamen, who were released within a few days, he was imprisoned for 100 days, until 13 May 1850. The Company was required to pay US$100 for his prison board and expenses, much to the chagrin of Hudson's Bay Company officials. (See also the stories of William Dean, Jeremiah McCarthy, and George Mouat in entries 59, 60, and 61, respectively.)

63   JOHN THOMPSON: *I have just come off the Race course and not very Sober*

As a seaman on the *Norman Morison*'s 1849 voyage, John Thompson was still on the west coast when his brother James wrote in response to John's letter home.

~ John Thomson, Ship Norman Morrison, Vancovers Island, Care of the Honble Hudson Bay Company

Carlisle (Cumberland) 5 July 1850

Dear
Brother I have just this minute seen your letter to my Sister and you can Scarcely imagine the Pleasure it gave to both my Brother William and me to see it, as we thought you dead or something had happend you, our Father is still alive and well in health his arm is now Powerless but he has not taken any hurt as I think the family has all had a look to him and has tryed to keep him Comfortable[.] he promised to be here this week to see Carlisle Races but has not come[.] I hope you will write soon and let us know how and where you are, our Father enclosed your letter in one to me and he thinks so much of yours that I have to be carefull in sending it back again to him now[.] I hope you will write to me as soon as you get this[.] it is a long time since I saw you and you never did send me a letter[.] you might for once try if you could, it is not worth my while entering into any Particulars as we are all well thank god[.] that will be as much as you want to know and I have just come off the Race course and not very Sober[.] I hope you will excuse my bad write but my feellings are good[.] I Remain Dear
   John you[r] affectionate
      Brother James Thompson

This letter went undelivered because John was on his way home when it arrived at its destination. In contrast to his brother, John was unlikely to have been able to afford trips to the races with the comforts of alcohol. He was one of a number of crew members of the *Norman Morison* dissatisfied with their wages, among many other complaints on that trip (see Francis Mannock, Charles Lobb, and George and James Wishart, entries 64, 65, 66).

On 11 May 1850, Albert Hale, Charles Lobb, and the two Wisharts were missing at six o'clock in the morning and at half past one in the afternoon, the eleven remaining seamen, including John Thompson, refused to man the windlass until the four men were replaced. Because of the difficulties in getting out of Victoria Harbour, Chief Factor James Douglas decided he could not risk losing the wind and tide, and ordered the men to the fo'c'sle as prisoners, taking the additional precaution of ordering each of the three officers to load a pair of pistols and two muskets and remain in the after cabin. By 14 May the imprisoned men were replaced by some of the emigrant labourers (see the stories of George and Henry Horne, and William Ross in entries 103, 104, and 105, respectively). Later, calling the confined men to the quarterdeck, Douglas was "willing to look over [their refusal of duty] upon condition of good behaviour in future" when they agreed to return to work.

On 27 February 1851, after travelling to Fort Simpson, Nass, and New Archangel (Sitka, Alaska), the *Norman Morison* returned to England. There, John Thompson was among a dozen crew members who signed a petition notifying the Company that James Douglas, the chief factor at Vancouver Island and soon to be governor of Vancouver Island, had promised a £25 gratuity for good conduct. At that time, when desertions were rampant and American ships were offering much better wages, the Company had a number of labour problems to resolve as well as this particular thorn. John Thompson and the petition writers were at least still serving their masters. The fates of some of the other crew members are narrated in the following entries.

64 FRANCIS MANNOCK: *I hope you will take care of yourself and not fall in the Water*

Francis Mannock entered the Company's service as an apprentice aboard the *Prince Rupert* on its 1839 trip to Hudson Bay. His father, who had once been master of the ship, had died in 1833. One son, William, was employed in the Company ships in 1836 and, in 1839, their mother successfully petitioned the Company for a place for Francis. Between 1840 and 1844, Francis continued the yearly trips to Hudson Bay on the *Prince Albert*. By 1849 he was a seaman aboard the *Norman Morison* on its voyage to Victoria. His wife wrote to him in July 1850 while he was at sea.

〰 Francies Mannock, Seaman on bord the Norman Morrison, North West
Cost America

July 31. 1850

Dear Husband
I have embraced the early oppertunity of writting to you trusting this
will find you in good health as I am present only that I feel very lonely
without you and indeed I am thinking hourly of your returne[.] I did think
I should have heard from you when some of the rest heard[.] I have not
had any money since the month of June[.] I have removed to 21 Cleveland
St Mile End Road[.] your Sisters and Brothers is all quite [well] at present[.] My Dear your Sister Jesey has opend a school at Marys and Edward
has got a situation in London and William has garn Captain of the Prince
Rupert and one thing more to say I have that is I hope you will take care
of yourself and not fall in the Water[.] my Dear I must conclude with all
Sinceres desiars of a Loveing Wife to Frank Mannock
   Beleve me my thoughs is ever with you
   so no more from your affectionate
      Wife E Manock
PS trusting to god you will not make your stay eney longger then you can
help and you may come home safe good buy god Bless you

Although safe from the drowning his wife worried about, Francis had been
involved in an incident with other members of the unhappy *Norman Morison*
crew. On 24 February 1850, some of the men discontent with their wages refused to go to prayers. When he and other men returned to their duties without further disobedience, Captain Wishart ordered their grog and lime juice
(for protection against scurvy) to be served. According to the mate, George
Holland, several sailors – including Mannock, William Johnston, and James
Wishart (entry 66) – "refused to take their grog; this being reported by me
to Captain Wishart he ordered that those men alone who took it should have
it in future." The next day, the Captain again offered the scurvy medicine
and grog ration: "in consequence of bad weather Captain Wishart gave the
men another opportunity of taking their grog when it was again refused by
those who refused to receive it yesterday with the exception of Francis
Mannock." The captain's main source of concern over their refusal seems to
have been their protest rather than any health concern.
   Back on the straight and narrow path of obedience to his superiors, Mannock went on to serve on the Company's ship *Otter,* once more leaving his
wife in 1852 and staying on the west coast until 1855. He died aboard the *Otter*

on 23 July while it was at Esquimalt. He was buried at Victoria on 3 August 1855. If he had begun his seafaring life as an apprentice in his mid-teens, he would have been only in his early thirties when he died, without fulfilling his wife's wish that he "come home safe."

65   CHARLES LOBB: *May the lord bless keep and preserve you free from every evil and safe from every danger*

Three months after he left England, Judith Lobb missed her son Charles, who had left London on 13 October 1849 as a seaman on the *Norman Morison*. She had written to the London Committee on 12 January 1850, asking how to get in touch with him. The Company secretary replied to Judith's Landport, England, address, telling her that a letter for anyone on the *Norman Morison* could be sent to Hudson's Bay House, where the Company would forward it when the opportunity arose. In early July, Judith wrote to her son.

For Chas Lobb, Seaman on board the ship "Norman Morrison" (D.D. Wishart Master), Vancouver's Island, NW coast of America

july 7 – 18.50 [1850]

my dear Son
     I received your kind and welcom letter the thord of this month the day that your father took his money and I was just come home with it ready to die with trouble how I should pay my way for he was rogue enough to keep A sovering [sovereign] out of his money wich if I had the hole of it I could scarcely show my face to Mr print only look at the family and your letter the[y] charged two shillings for but my dear it done me good to hear from you but I was surprized at your not letting me know how you was sitiuated for I should like to know wether you was comfortable or not and wether you was in a hot climate or a cold one[.] my dear wen you write again doo send me all perticklers about your self for I long to know[.] my dear I received your letter wen you was in deal and that was A satisfaction to me to hear from you[.] my dear I was glad to find you was well as I hope this will still find you and as it leaves all our family pretty well except my self but I ham very unwell but I hope the lord will spear me that I may have the happiness of seing your dear face again for that is my sincere desire[.] god bless your dear heart I wish I could see you now[.] ~~my der you do~~ [crossed out] william has got A board order to be entered in the dock yard but I believe it will be A long time before there will be any entry[.] he stills works with his father but if he could get A shure place to work out a

gate I believe he would marry carroline directly but every thing is very dead here no work for no one old or young[.] jack hunter was discharged out of the dock yard and now he is got back again to be employd for a few months only herriot is still living with me poor girl but I ham sorry to say she still goes with him[.] she is gone with him to dinner to day[.] my dear you have never been out of my thoughts since you have been gone and indeed all of us alike we are continualy talking about you[.] george alves is on board of the conflict steamer at lisbon[.] he said he is misserable for he never was in such A ship in all his life for the are to work from five in the morning till seven at night[.] now my dear I hope that you are steady and taking care of your self I should like to know wat you are on board now[.] my dear I have one favour to ask you that is if you will oblidge me to send me A pound or two it will greatly relieve me and I shall never forget your kindness[.] all the family sends their kind love to you[.] william sends his kind love to you and except [accept] the same yourself from your affectionate mother[.] may the lord bless keep and preserve you free from every evil and safe from every danger is the sincere prayers of your affectionate mother

   Judith Lobb

With a husband who did not always share his pay, Judith missed her son financially as well as emotionally. The son about whom the family was continually talking and who was never out of his mother's thoughts was going through his own particular hell at the time his mother wrote this letter. On 11 May 1850 Charles had deserted his ship in Victoria Harbour with three other seamen (see also George and James Wishart story, entry 66). He had boarded the *England,* a non-Company ship fresh from San Francisco and the gold fields, bound for Fort Rupert (near present-day Port Hardy) to collect coal from the Company mines. The *England* arrived at Fort Rupert in June, and the sailors and captain mixed with the fort people and talked of the opportunities in California. Only when the *Beaver* arrived on 27 June did Dr. Helmcken receive a request from Governor Blanshard, governor of the new colony of Vancouver Island, to act as a justice of the peace, along with the information that Company deserters were now aboard the *England.* Helmcken summarized their fate in a letter to James Douglas almost a year later:

A canoe of Newittians [Nahwitti men from near Fort Rupert] had been out hunting: returning home they fell in with three white men upon a small island in the straits: these men had a small Canoe with them: The Newittians approached and the white men who were unarmed warned them off: one of them taking an axe and flourishing it at them. The Newittians however, went nearer, with the intention it is said of giving them to eat and to take them where the other deserters (miners) were hidden, when a white man took a stone, flung it into the canoe and broke it. Immediately upon this the Indians fired, killing two, the third ran into the bush, was pursued and in a short time was shot also. They now stripped the bodies and had thrown one into the sea with stones tied to his feet and were preparing to do the same with the others, when another canoe arrived and advised them not to do so. Upon this they hid the other two and went home.

Charles was one of these three men. The men might have survived threatening a group of Aboriginal people with an axe but not the destruction of a canoe – the equivalent of destroying a man's livelihood. (Compare another version of these events in the James and George Wishart story, entry 66.)

Chief Factor James Douglas reported the deaths of the murdered men, including Charles Lobb, in a letter dated 5 October 1850, and Governor Blanshard wrote to the Colonial Office with his own version of the affair on 18 August 1850. The Company wrote in May 1851 to reassure Robert Pyke, the concerned father of three boys on the ship, that Caleb, Jonas, and William Pyke were not among the dead. Charles Lobb's family, however, does not seem to have been informed, as – more than two years after his death – his mother Judith Lobb wrote to the Company asking for his whereabouts.

November 21st – 52 [1852]

Jinblemen pardon me for the liberty I have taken but I have a son on board the norman morison by the name of charles Lobb and I have received but one letter from him since he has been gone that is 3 years last october and I ham very uneasy about him for I do not know wether he is dead or alive[.] jentle men you will much oblige me to let me know how soon the ship will be home and whether if I send a letter to you you will be so kind as to forward it as soon as an opportunity offers and in so doing you will much oblige your humble servent Judith Lobb
living at N° 13 landport street landport

This letter bears the Company secretary's endorsement "ans^d Nov. 23" and the notation "Out per N Morison 13 June 1849. Deserted from the ship 11 May 1850." It is not clear why his death was not noted, as the actual reply of 23 November has not been found. We do not know when Judith Lobb finally heard of the death of the son she had hoped would be safe from every danger.

66 GEORGE AND JAMES WISHART: *I was happy to hear that you had such a fine Run out and every thing well*

Brothers George and James Wishart were seamen aboard the *Norman Morison* that carried so many of the first immigrants to the new colony at Fort Victoria in 1849. Their parents wrote to them after receiving word of their "fine Run out."

∾ To George or James Wishart, on board the Ship Norman Morison Captain Wishart, Fort Victoria, Vancouvers Island

~~Augt 29~~th~~ [crossed out] September 2th 1850

Dear Sons
I write you these few lines to Lett you no that we ar all well at present thank God. and I hope this will find you boath in good health and all the Ships Compney and I hope you ~~in~~ [crossed out] ar all adgreable with each other[.] I received your Kind Letter on the 3th of July and I was happy to hear that you had such a fine Run out and every thing well, mother sends hir kind Love to you bouth[.] Richard & Gane [Jane] Send thire love to you[.] John sends his love to you, Robort Came home son after you lift and he did not behave very well[.] he was in London a bout 3 Months and he only come home twice

you must excuse me for giving you such a short Letter[.] I have only seen Godfrey twice sinc you left[.] I Believe they ar all wel[.] Mrs and Sargent Robbie sends thire Kind love to you. I hope you will write by the Ships as the Leave the Island and I will write by the Ships that Leaves London[.] Robart I Beleave have gon to Mad[r]as[.] the next Litter I write you may expect to Get Sum thing better[.] the next Ship you disered me to writ by the Colimbia but She as up for Seal. but I took the first Ship after I received your letter[.] the over Land Letters ar two Shillings that a half more then from India[.] I canot Say what the Ship Charge[.] all that I had to do was to take it to the office and put in a box so you can lett me no next litter[.] I expect that will be by the Norman Morison for She is Expectd next Ship. Mr Clanch disers to be rembred to you, give my kind love to Mr Holland & Mr Sinclar [Sinclair] Captain Wishart and all the Ship Compney[.] I was sory hear that you Had the Smal pox on board but I was happy to here that it was no wors. Mother is much the Same with her Hand[.] Gane is Still the Same working at her neddle. I will conclouse by washing you both well and happey

your truley affectenet Father & Mother
  J Wishart 7 Nottingham place York St.
  Commercial Road East
    London

Although the brothers gave their parents the impression that all was well, James had been in a bit of trouble in February as part of the crew forming the port watch, which had refused to attend prayers. A week later, he was one of eleven seamen who refused to take their grog and lime juice (see the stories of Francis Mannock and Charles Lobb, entries 64 and 65). When the *Norman Morison* got to Fort Victoria in May, both Wishart brothers deserted when the commercial vessel *England,* on its way to Fort Rupert for a cargo of coal, stopped at Victoria.

Dr. Helmcken, the newly appointed magistrate, reported that George left the *England* with Charles Lobb and A.F. Hale (alias Fred Watkins) when he heard in late June that Helmcken and Captain Dodd of the *Beaver* were arriving to apprehend them. According to Helmcken, the three deserters intended to join the ship once it had left the harbour so that they could proceed to the gold rush. George met the same fate as Lobb and Watkins (entry 65).

Charley Beardmore, an apprentice clerk from Fort Rupert, described his attempt to recover the bodies, accompanied by an the fort interpreter, Linecous, and four Bella-Bella men:

½ past 12 [on 12 July 1850] arrived at Shushale Harbour [Shushartie Bay?], where I found Barque England Captain Brown, anchored. Being on my route to a hostile tribe, I was thoroughly armed and when I went alongside the barque, being invited on board I of course had my arms about me. Captain Brown gave me some dinner, I asked what he took the deserters on board his ship for at Fort Victoria, he said, did not know it till outside and that they reported themselves left there by a ship (this was a decided lie) as Captain Brown knew no ship was lying at Fort Victoria save the C^{os}; accused him of trading Sea Otters, did not deny it, only said if his ship was going to be searched, could and would pitch them overboard, accused him of giving a passage to the Miners, did not deny it, abused the Co^y much, asked a description of the deserters and he told me their alias vizt Charley [Lobb], Fred Watkins and George Wishart. The 4th man a deserter [James Wishart] was still on board his Ship. At ½ past 2 Oclock started & arrived at the Neweettee village about 7 Oclock. They all attacked me with Guns and Spears, but I showed none in return and they witheld fire. I told them I came to smoke and talk & not to fight, they then invited me in the lodge & I sat down – I asked them had they killed the men; they said, Yes, I asked, How Many: they said 3, and they, the white men, broke their Canoe with a stone first: I then told them, they knew that I would pay for the Canoe if they came and told me, and that they should not have killed the men; they said the men were slaves, hiding from their own people & bad men & they did not think I would pay for their Canoe & therefore their hearts being bad they shot them. I offered two Blankets first, then 4, to give me the dead bodies, they told me of two of them, but the third they would not tell me where to get it as it was in the sea, they were so very stubborn about it, that it gave rise to a suspicion that the third was not dead, but sold for a slave and gone North. They would not go with me, as they were afraid of Browns ship, but described the place. I demanded how it occurred; they said two of them were out in a canoe, and saw these men on a small Island, they went to them and as they approached Fred Watkins fluorished a small axe at them and told them to keep off, they did not but offered them food, when one of them took up a big stone, pitched into the canoe and smashed it; the Indians instantly fired and killed two and then followed the other one into the bush & shot him also. Stripped them and had already pitched Fred Watkins into the sea, when 2 more of their tribe came up and recommended them not to drown the other two bodies as they might be required, they then put George Wishart in a hollow tree, the other alongside stretched out and covered with brush. They had their Clothes. I slept the night in the Newittee Camp.

Saturday 13th July. Early started to look after the dead bodies & bury them, went up the Straits and met Brown beating out, invited me on board & the 2nd Mate flung me a line, but when I proceeded to mount the side, the 1st Mate Cadbu took a rifle & presented it to me & swore to shoot me if I came up with a pistol on me, I told him I had none, he told me I might come up; I told him I would go aboard no such cut throat ship. Captain Brown sheered over to the starboard side; then followed a volley of abuse & pointing of Guns from nearly all hands. Damned me, my mate, M[r] Blenkinsop & Masters, swore I had killed the men (I at the time being near Fort Victoria) told me to clear off out of those seas or they would shoot me; one man jumped up, I am James Wishart you bugger you killed my brother. I'll jump down and take revenge, (I invited him to do so) I'll sail about for 20 years, but what I'll take revenge, the damned Co[y] is done for, I'll teach you to kill Englishmen, the damned fort has nothing but Kanakas and damned Canadians; you an Englishman, but only half a one, an Englishman's bastard – I told my Indians to get ready their guns & if they fired, to fire at the 1st mate and Captain in return. I sheered off and asked the Captain did he wish to send a Sailor to recognise the bodies, he declined and I sheered off to do my duty. About 3 miles from Shushate on the right side of the Straits lay 2 small Islands, at low water only one island & on the northern one lay the bodies & occurred the murder. I followed the plan of the Indians & soon found the bodies, Charly not disfigured & straight out, George Wishart all of a heap in a hollow tree, bleeding and covered with blood, I took him out and stretched him out and as the bodies were fresh, I thought the D^r and Magistrate might wish to see them, so covered them carefully up & set off home, where I arrived at 8 P.M. ...

N.B. On Monday 15th Dr Helmckin proceeded to the place and brought the two bodies to the Fort on Tuesday 16th and they were buried with due ceremony.

Once the bodies were recovered and buried at the fort, James Wishart left on the *England,* bound for California. He did not, as far as we know, carry out his threat of revenge. The Company, however, suffered as a result of the incident. In March 1851 Chief Factor James Douglas asked Dr. Helmcken what he had put in his official communications that would have led Governor Blanshard to report to the Colonial Office that "the three men who had deserted from the Company's Service had been murdered by the natives, and that the Officers of the Company are accused by the whole inhabitants of having instigated them to this massacre, by offers of reward for the delivery of the deserters dead or alive." Helmcken replied that this was a mere fabrication and explained the circumstances:

A great many men having deserted, Mr Blenkinsop one morning finding others had disappeared was somewhat enraged and declared he would have them back again, with this intention he hired canoes and Indians to go and search the coast in order to find their lurking place: promising to pay blankets if they discovered them hidden anywhere. I stood by him at the time, and did not hear any word mentioned about bringing them back dead or alive ... These canoes never left the harbour, and the Indians never went in search of them, because we learned that the missing men ran away in the Massachusets, this circumstance took place about three weeks before the melancholy massacre.

His report and the rumours of Company complicity in the deaths led Governor Blanshard to visit Fort Rupert on the corvette *Daedalus* on 1 October. He demanded that those responsible be brought to justice. Three armed boats found the Aboriginal camp that had been visited by Charley Beardmore deserted. On the governor's request, Captain George Grenville Wellesley's men from the *Daedalus* destroyed the camp's cedar houses by setting them on fire. Blanshard continued his pursuit. In July 1851, a year after the event, HMS *Daphne,* with eighteen guns and a force of sixty men, went to where the Nahwitti had retreated and again destroyed their deserted houses, canoes, and other property. Four Nahwitti were killed and two wounded. Finally, in September, James Douglas was able to report that "a party of Neweetis [Nahwitti] came along side of the Mary Dare, after she sailed from Fort Rupert, and exhibited the mangled remains, of two human bodies, in one of their canoes, which they reported to be two of the murderers, and they stated that the third would also soon meet his fate at their hands." The Company suffered the revenge of a damaged reputation and deteriorated relations with the Aboriginal peoples that lasted long after the incident.

Information about such events often arrived in a garbled form to relatives back home. When the father of three other seamen, Robert Pyke, had inquired about his sons on hearing that three boys from the *Norman Morison* had been killed, he was told that both James and George Wishart had died. Whether the Wisharts heard the news of George's death from their angry son James or through the Company, we do not know. The "fine Run" that the Wishart family had taken pleasure in at the beginning of their sons' adventures had turned into a tragedy for them, the Company, and west coast Aboriginal peoples.

67 SAMUEL PEPPER: *We have had the Geogrifry and traced the place and saw the Fort and it said the Island was 300 miles long*

Samuel Pepper was a seaman on the *Norman Morison* on its voyage departing England in the fall of 1849. Arriving in Victoria in April 1850 he was transferred to the *Beaver*. His mother wrote in October to tell of family news and express the family's curiosity about Vancouver Island.

❧ Samuel Pepper, On Board the Hutson Bay Company Ship Normon Morrison, DD Wishart Master, Vancoves Island, NWAmerica

[2 October 1850, Lymington, Hampshire]

My ever dear Son

I now take up my Pen to write you hoping with the blessing of God it may reach you and find you in the enjoyment of health and streanth wich is one of Gods c[h]oisest blesings upon us wile we are hear below[.] my dear Samuel my health is not so good as it have been but thank God i am better than I have been and can occopy the Armchair and I am happy to tel you that your dear Father enjoy his health verey wel and has shot 3 widgen in September and desire his kindest love and hope you wil be spared to come home and shote with him: your Brother John is gone to Dimchurch in Kent with a Commishon he has been gone about 2 Months and he is verey Comfortable but he did not like it at first to leave it was like leveing home and before he left he desired wen I rote to remeber him kindly to you and dear Samuel your sister Elizebeth is much the same as ever not verey strong but she has a verey pretty littel Girl indeed now a twelfmonth old[.] John grow a fine stout boy Howgego is verey wel and they both desire thar kindest love and say how much they should like to see you

and now my dear son for a littel news[.] your Sister Hannah is Maried to Mr Jones[.] he stil belong to the Active Cutter and she is gone to Newhaven to live and we have herd from her and she write verey comfortable indeed[.] she lodges with Mr Combs a boot maker[.] Jones had 10 days leve and came from Newhaven to our house and was Maried on Harriets Birthday the 4 of September[.] Harriet was 18 years old and we injoyed our selfs as wel as we could but verey different to Elizebeths you gone and John gone and I would not have straingth so we had no one but old Mrs Lorace [Lawrence?] and Luesa Cole beside our own family[.] we all talked about you and wished you and John was with us and we shold want no more but my dear Samuel we must hope it is all for the Best[.] God orders all things and I hope it wil be for your good in the end I am shure[.] I often think of you and beg of God to guide and protect you in a Foreign land and bring you back in safety to us onse moore[.] I forgot to say wc all like Jones verey wel he is verey steady and clean looking young Man[.] they were married at Milford Capple [Chapel] and Harriet and Father went with them[.] Hannah desired me before she left wen I rote to give her kindest love to you and hope you might be spared to come home and see herr[.] Harriet send her kinddest love to you she is verey wel and such a fine young girl[.] she beat them all[.] Marry grow a fine girl and often talks of you[.] James is quite as tall as John Howgego and grow so much like you that we often call him Sam[.] he say sometimes he wil go down to the Neadels [Needles] in the littel boat and fetch you from that Brig only he must stop and mind his Mother[.] he has a grate spirit[.] we often talk about you to him so he may not forget you[.] my dear S[am] you must write a long letter the next time and let us know wat you do and how you live and wether you stop at one place[.] we have a man at Milford that has been there in a man of War[.] he say there is beuteful Potatoes but I suppose not so far in as you are but you must tel wether tis Cold or warm[.] we have had the Geogrifry and traced the place and saw the Fort and it said the Island was 300 miles long[.] dear Samuel wen you rite beshure you put the date then you shal know how long the letter is coming[.] dear Samuel you wished to know were Petre Manson he is out in the West indes for 2 years and he told us he would stop out if he had the chance and James Manson went out in a ship laden with Coal to the East Indies but the Ship caught fire and they pumpt for long time to keep her a float but at last they were Obliged to leave her and he is out a broad now[.] O I forgot to tel you that Lt Gray is Dead that was on board the Active wen you was[.] he ran the Cutter against Newhaven Peer and nocked her Bows in and had a cort of inquire on him and some said he was Dismised from the servise but he died direcly after[.] Jones helped to carry him to the Grave and he said there was not one sober afterwards[.] they had a real spre so you see he did not reign long after you left[.] they have had 2 or 3 sins [Ensigns?] and Jones say they were worse than Gray[.] this is the first day of Lymington fair the 2 of October[.] I should have rote before but i stopt til i could tel you all the news[.] I do not think of any thing More to tel you but we all join in our kindest love and best wishes for your welfare

pray God to bless you is the prayer

of your affectionate Mother and Father

H Pepper and J Pepper

                    Mr Pepper Hurst Castle Near Lymington Hampshier England

When this letter was written, full of news of other men's adventures in the sea trade, Samuel was having an adventure of his own. On 9 June 1850 he deserted at Fort Victoria with a Hawaiian woodcutter named Namotto and two stokers, Jean Baptiste Dechamp and Jean Baptiste Kanatakonda. They left during the night, taking all their effects except their sea chests. They probably left Vancouver Island aboard another vessel since they would not be very successful trying to find work on the island itself owing to the Company's control of commerce there.

68   THOMAS WALSH: *Only for your Aunt that Gets the Little washing we . . .*
       would not Be to gathr

Mary Walsh wrote to her brother Thomas the year after he sailed on the *Norman Morison* as a seaman, to tell him of the devastation of deaths, partings, and economic hardship that this Irish family has suffered since his departure.

～ Thomas Walsh, Fort Victoria, Vancouvers Island, N West Coast of America

Drogheda 21 june 1852

    Dear Brother

    I Received your Letter this day and I am very Happy to find that you are Doing so well[.] Dear Brother you wish to Know the Particulars About your fathers Death[.] I am Sorry for to have To tell you[.] He Died on the 27 July 1849 and your Poor Mother About 3 weeks After which was and is a very Great Loss to us. Mary Darby died also Died a short time after which

Left us worse – Pat. Left the Lady Florrens [Florence?] on the Last year of his Time and went out to Africa[.] the Black fever Came on the Crew and 15 of them died and we hear Pat was the Second Man It took and he was Buried In the Sand Banks[.] the vessel Came Home to Liverpool and I got A Letter Requesting me to Go over and So I did And all I Got was £1.1.10 out of all His Wages. In Consequence of your Grandmother Long Life And Is Still Liveing your Uncle John Has very Kindly Sent us Some relief which only For It we would Be very Badly off[.] your Uncle John Is Liveing In New york, America[.] He Lives at Number 419 West Street. New York[.] And Now Tomy do not for Get writing To Him and return Him your Best Thanks for His Goodness Towards your Grand mothe and your Brothers and Sisters For He wishes to Know Where you are and where you would Be Trading to for He can receive your Letters from any Part[.] you Should not for Get to AcKnowlege Him for wen He Heard of our Loss He did not for Get us and If It was not for Him we would Be Straying on the World[.] John Left the Mill of 27th March Last And Got No work since So he went to Sea on the Pelican this day week so we are Badly of Just now and only for your Aunt that Gets the Little washing we Co [crossed out] would not Be to gathr[.] Now Myself Is In the Mill Earning Littel or Nothing your Two sisters is in the Convent School you Poor old Grand Mother sends Her Love and Blessing to you Hoping you will not For Get Her as She Never wanted more[.] your Aunt Mary is Still with us (And Same for Catren) Also your Two Little Sisters May and Alice Sends Their Lov to you and all your old Acquantances[.] No more at Present from yor Truly And Affection Sister
  Mary Walsh
O Dear Brothe If It is in your Power at all where you are do not For Get to Have mo [crossed out] Mass offered for the Eternal repose of your Poor Father And Mother Souls
May the Lord Have Mer[c]y On their Souls –
  M. W

Mary would have one more departure to add to the growing list of family members not contributing to keeping the family together: Thomas himself. He deserted his ship at the Queen Charlotte Islands, perhaps a victim of the gold-rush fever that was then bringing thousands of men northward from California, to the Fraser River and inland, and even as far north as the remote coastal islands. A Company-ordered investigation of the rumours of gold had been going on as early as 1850, when a "rich specimen embedded in white quartz" was found, and in 1851 when a rich vein was discovered at Mitchell Harbour. Governor James Douglas reported that "Dr. Kennedy thinks that the said 58 lbs. [26 kilograms] of ore will yield 6 lb. [2.75 kilograms] of pure Gold." However, the Company could not keep six American vessels, each with forty to fifty miners, from rushing northward as well. For a while, the usually quiet Queen Charlotte Islands, inhabited by Haida, would become a space contested by the Company and the Americans, before attention moved on to some other dreams of golden riches. It was during this period that Thomas Walsh disappeared from his ship and from the Company records.

69   ALFRED A. MOSS: *If you ar gon as long or longer than you except you will*
       find a son oar a daughter i can not tell wich wating to see you

Alfred Moss joined the crew of the *Norman Morison* in London for its 1852-3 return voyage. His wife wrote to him in October 1852 to tell him news of her pregnancy.

Alfried Moss, On Board the Norman Morrison, Vancoves Island, North West coast of America

october 7 1852

   my Derest frad i now sett down to rite a few lines to you with a very very [repetition] hart thainking what a long time it will be before i gat any anser to this latter but i now you will rite as sune as you can[.] my dear frad i miss you more and more and i fail so lonsom with out you but i hope it will not bee for long[.] i have got som news to tall you my dear frad i hope you will not bee gon so long as you except but if you ar gon as long or longer than you except you will find a son oar a daughter i can not tell wich wating to see you and if you have got any name that you should like you mite sand me ward in your letter i should like you to pake a name for our bab[.] place god that should lave [live][.] my dear frad i have bee[n] very all [ill] wase fost [forced] to live [leave] my wark but thank god i ham batter than i wase and i go to wark now for you know that i muste wark[.] i have not got any of Jays monny but that is satled martin have got is 13 pounds 9^s and he would not pay yours because you ad not sined your name to a stamp papar and he sad if you ad only pott your name to the bottom of that pappar he would have paid me but never mind my dear he say it will bee save anofe till you sine your name to a stamp pappar[.] my dear frad you need not feer but what i shall gat don for whan i ham taken all if you ar not home but i hope you will be home befor than[.] dear frad your brother martin as been at wark ever sence you have been gon and she is not got to bad yet and that time i wase so all she cud not come to see me thought she wase in the row i thought it very on kind of har for whan i

ham able i go and run about after har but i toked it to be that she thought
i ad not yet anny thang to gave har so she would not come to see me but
my derest frad if place god we should love to see each eithar we shall have a
~~home~~ [crossed out] house and home[.] i know my dear you dow not want
me to tall you to take care of your monny you will dow that for the sake of
me and your babe

my dear frad your hant Barnet is very all[.] both of tham sands thare
loves to you and tom moss and his wife my morther and saster my brother
willam and is wife martin and all of tham sand thare loves to you[.] my
brother James is a atorne now[.] my dearest frad I hope these few lines will
mate you in god halth as thay lave me batter[.] my dear i fill very timed
[timid] to the changes that is going to take plase but i pope [hope] you will
rite as sune as you gat this letter[.] you ar sure my dear frad that i shall you
think the time long to hare from[.] i pope my dear you will brang me some
thing home to show me you thougth of me whan you wase away[.] my
dear we ad a latter from my brothar Johan last sunday and he his arrived in
london and he is shiped on aboard of a marchman [merchantman] bound
to bombay and he sand his love to you so no more from

    your afactad wife Sarah moos x x x x x

      thase ar all for you x x x x x x

John Betts of Yarmouth also inquired on 9 April 1853 about Alfred Moss
in a letter addressed to the Company assistant secretary, William Gregory
Smith, son of the late William Smith. Alfred may have seen his wife and
become acquainted with their new child soon after arriving home at the end
of July 1853. If so, he would have had an even greater motivation to get every
penny he could when he signed the petition claiming an unpaid gratuity of
£12 10s. from the Company in August 1853. The petitioners admitted that
they had refused duty but defended their action:

> As regards our refusing duty on the 9th March all that we can say is that we did
> so on account of the ship being short-handed [three men, Joseph Sinnett,
> Thomas Hawkins and James Austen, had deserted and the first mate, Nugent,
> and the third mate, Stewart, had left without leave on March 7], and all that
> we requested on that day was that we should receive either the wages of those
> men who had left us, or that an equivalent number of *seamen* be sent in their
> stead. The £5 Gratuity offered, in our own foolish idea, was not adequate to
> the wages which those men would have received, therefore we refused it, but
> we trust that this will be looked over. It is unnecessary to say that we are all
> greatly disappointed and we sincerely hope that you will lend a favourable
> hand to enable us to receive it.

Chief Factor James Douglas's account of the incident differed significantly. While he had sent the original of his account with the *Norman Morison,* a duplicate was sent by a different route and had arrived on 23 May 1853:

> The crew of the 'Norman Morison' came to a strike at the last moment, and in the most shameless manner, demanded a Gratuity of £12.10 a man before they would move the Ship, even though she was then aground, in the entrance of the Harbour.
>
> There was no alternative on our part but submitting to their demands, as we could not replace them, and it would have been unwise to detain the ship longer in the country. We will I fear always be exposed to such demands, while seamen's wages continue so high on this coast, the present rate of pay being 40 dollars a month [approximately £8, compared to the £24 per annum that Moss had signed for]. This gratuity is entered upon the ship's articles.

Although Douglas criticized the way in which the men had gained the gratuity, he acknowledged that it had been promised. The sum was paid.

70   GEORGE NAUNTON: *If you write to me from Vancouvers try & collect a little interesting matter respecting the Island, its history, produce, &c*

Robert Naunton wrote to his son George on his third trip to the west coast on the *Norman Morison,* and five years into George's apprenticeship. He had hoped to send some newspapers but, guessing that his son might not receive them before his departure from the Columbia Department, Robert successfully converts his own letter into a newspaper. There is news of everything from the Duke of Wellington's funeral – an event of extraordinary national importance in Britain – and the death of Daniel Webster, to local embezzlements and the destructive floods in England. This father's letter brings together the personal, the local, the national, and the international to give a vivid portrait of the world through the eyes of an Englishman from Ipswich in late 1852.

꩜   George Naunton, Hudsons Bay Company's Ship "Norman Morison," Fort Victoria, Vancouvers Island
[in another hand] Via Panama

[1-10 December 1852] Ipswich December 1/52 (Wednesday)

Dear George,
I have after a long delay, made up my mind to commence a letter to you, just to let you know a small portion of what is going on in this part of the

World & what have been going on since you left, but I hardly know how to begin, in the first place you will be glad to know we are all quite well & sincerely trust you are the same, we have been anxiously watching every paper we could get hold of to see if your Craft had been spoken with but have never seen or heard a word[.] on Monday I wrote to Mr Smith to ask him, this Morning I rec^d his reply to say the Norman Morison had sent no communication since her departure in August last but the H.B.C. would dispatch another vessel to Vancouvers Island some time next month (his letter being dated Nov 30th) & that an opportunity would then offer itself to send out this letter or Newspapers but considering the start you have got in all probability you will have left before she arrived so I shall abandon the idea of sending by that source. you must therefore content yourself with recieving a letter only.

I must tell you the all absorbing topic of conversation for the last 2 months have been our great national calamity, the loss of one of the greatest Generals that the World ever saw in no less a person than the Duke of Wellington who was staying at Walmer Castle, his official residence as Warden of the Cinque Ports[.] he sat up till ½ past 11 on the Even^g of the 12th of Sept^r (an hour & half over his usual time) & conversed cheerfully all the time, his valet calling him the next morn^g at ¼ past instead of 6 as usual when the Duke breathed with some difficulty, which gradually increased, his Medical attendants were immediately summoned, at about 8 O'clock his Son, Lord Chas Wellesley with the Surgeon's permission, prepared some Tea & asked him if he would take a little, the Duke replied, "Yes, if you please" which were the last words he ever spoke, he had a succession of convulsive fits, & never after rallied, about ¼ past 3 his pulse had ceased to beat. a mirror was held to his mouth, the polished surface remained undim^d & the Great Commander had departed without a struggle, or even a sigh, to mark the exact moment when the vital spark was extinguished, as such died the (once) noble, & mighty, Duke of Wellington, the intelligence spread like wild fire all over the Kingdom, flags were hoisted half mast high on vessels &, Cathedral Bells were toll^d, & dumb peals, wer[e] rung all over the Kingdom and one and all, seemed to mourn the loss of one, he whom we owe our homes, & our liberties, his body laid in state at Walmer Castle till the 10th of Nov^r, when on that Even^g, it was removed by special train to Chelsea Hospital, & laid in state there till the 17th in the Even^g it was removed to the Horse Guards for the night when at 7 o'clock on the morn^g of the 10th it was placed on a magnificient Car, built for the purpose & drawn by 12 of the finest black horses, that could be found, the funeral was a public one, & exceeded in grandeur, everything ever yet seen, there were detatchm^ts from every Reg^t in the service, & almost every Band, & deputations from almost every nation in Europe, (viz) Spain, Russia, Prussia, Portugal, the Netherlands, Hanover &c it is impossible to convey to you any discription, of the extraordinary & solemn grandeur, of the whole affair, attended as it was, by all the nobles in the Land, all the Military, Naval, cival [civil] & clerical, authorities, officers of state, &c &c, it started from the Hor[s]e Guards, up Constitution Hill, Piccadilly, St. Jermain's St, Pall Mall, Charing Cross, Strand, Fleet St, to St. Pauls, and there burried by the side of Nelson, "The greatest Military, by the side of one of the greatest Naval Chiefs, that ever reflected lustre on the annals of the history of England", I have given you an outline, but shall preserve a Newspaper till your return, America, has likewise lost one of her greatest men, Daniel Webster, who died on Octr 24th which the Yankees regard as a great National loss as a Senator, there has been very great & destructive Floods, in the counties of Nottinghamshire, Devonshire, Herefordshire, Oxfordshire, & many other counties, which have done a vast amount of damage, whole Towns have actually been sub-merged, that in a very great many houses the water has reached to the cieling of the ground floor, & families have been oblig^d to run up stairs to save themselves, & have food &c conveyed to them by Boats. Bridges have been washed away, Railway Arches, & embankments, washed down, & Tunnels destroyed, & the traffic on many of the lines stop^d. some of the Turnpikes flooded some as much as 4 or 5 feet deep. Horses, Cattle, Sheep &c have been drowned & seen floating about in all directions, in Leicestershire, on the Midland Railway, at a place call the Crow Mills Viaduct, six of the arches of 20 feet span each were washed away destroying both lines of Rails for a length of 150 ft leaving a complete Chasm of that width, in fact it has caused an incalculable amount of damage, both to Houses & Land, many Mills & factories (in consequence of having had their machinery flooded) have been stop^d & a great number thrown out of employment, many Towns have been put into utter darkness, the Tops of the Gasometers only having been seen above water, there have hardly been one fine day in Novr but often it has rained for several days & nights together, such a month of wet, as have not been known within the memory of man, now I think it is time for a little home news, Willm Hutchinson has been a voyage to the North, with his Uncle, it was a rather rough passage, so he was cured the first dressing, I saw him the other day at his desk in his fathers office, I asked him if he liked that better than going aloft in a stiff NorthEaster, he said he had had quite enough of the Sea so I suppose he will settle to his fathers business, I see by the "Liverpool Courier", the "Blackwall" was spoken with Octr 2nd in Lat. 13 N, Lon. 24 W. they must have been pretty close to you, I am sorry to tell you, the papers announce a report from the

committee of the Ips[wic]ʰ Museum, that they are in debt between £400
& £500 & unless succor come soon they should be compelled (although
reluctantly) to sell off! I think it is all owing to Mʳ. Geo Rainsome, who has
sadly disgraced himself, by committing one of the most henious offences
that man can be guilty of. A committe (composed of all the leading
connected with the Museum & the town) met, to consider the affair, &
evidence, & facts produced, which convinced the Comᵗᵉ that no doubt
remained of his guilt, so it was unanimously resolved not to countenence
him in any way, until he could establish his innocence, & which he has not
done at the present time, nor has he made any attempt, that I can hear of,
so how truly it may now be said, that, "he is despised & rejected of men",
how keenly must he feel his degraded & disgracful position, once the pride
& admiration of all the Great, Good, & Philanthropic men (I may say) in
the World, how painfully has he forfieted that good esteem once possessed
by the virtuous, & benevolent, what pain & misery, it has brought upon
himself & family, his outward appearance clearly shows the anguish of the
heart, I had occasion to speak to him once since you left & at once saw
such an alteration that greatly astonished me, instead of a cheerful, robust,
& happy countenance, I saw a pale, dejected, & emaciated one, he is very
seldom seen only by his immediate friends, he has put off his business, & I
hear he intends leaving the country, here is an example which will teach us
how we ought always to be on our guard, against the sins by which we are
continually surrounded, & how firm ought we to be in our resolution, to
resist temptation, to spare us the painful reflection of "how sorry I am that
have done so & so, I wish I had known the misery it has caused me" &c,
but a great deal of evil may be averted if we endeavour to imbibe the
principles of religion, but I trust you know the worth of a good name &
character, not to require any warning or caution from me for if it please
God to spare you, I look forward with hope & pride that you will realise all
our most sanguine expectations, if you write to me from Vancouvers try &
collect a little interesting matter respecting the Island, its history, produce,
&c, if convenient bring a variety, of Shrubs, flowers, minerals &c if
interesting, but do not inconvenience yourself, startling accᵗˢ reach us from
the diggings at Australia & California, a vast & extensive tract of Land has
been discovered by an American expedition beyond California. The french
people have created Louis Napoleon "Emperor" of france, they have an
immence Army & Navy & ready at a minutes notice which has caused
much Alarm in England to know what it all means, so they are turning
earnest attention to our "National Defences", we have already 10 powerful
line of Battle Ships fitted with the screw propeller, & 10 more are to be
ready as soon as possible, as well as Ships of other lines, 5000 Sea men are

to be added to the Navy, with a proportionate addition to the Marines,
2000 artillerymen, 1000 horses, & 200 field guns with carriages &
equipment for the army, the fortifications are to have additional heavy
& efficient cannon ammunition &c fit for immediate service, 50.000,
Militiamen have been enrolled & have been up for 21 days drill, have
acquited themselves very satisfactorily, they are now disbanded, but are
likely to be called up again shortly, the Tory Government are still in office
& the Chancellor of the Excheqer has delivered his Budget, he propose
to reduce the duties on the nescessaries of life, reduce the burdens on
agriculture, & the Shipping interest, but he propose to extend the income
& property, & house Tax, to make up the deficiency of the revenue, M^r
H.J. Bristo has got married since you left, & all are living with the Old
Gentleman in Jacket St. Mrs Fisher was down about a month since, she is
much the same, poor old Mr Seaman met with a serious accident on the
day of the Duke's funeral, he was walking on the causeway on the Tower
ditches, it was dark, he mistook the steps & fel[l] from the top into the
road & broke his thigh in 2 places, 2 ribs, & his collar bone, so that it
protruded through the skin, he was taken home, & the doctors pronounced
the case fatal, but to the astonishment of all he has been gradually mending,
& is expected to get about again, he was born about the same day as the
late Duke of Wellington, we have had a great stir & turn-out at the Post
office, a systematic robbery has been going on for a long time, the government
Inspector was sent down & in course of time discovered all, laid traps &
caught 3 of the clerks Fred K. Sheldrake of Carr St. was one, Collins, was
another, & Brummitt the other, the first 2 are out on very heavy bail, all
are to be tried at the Assizes next March, it is expected they will all be
transported, their places are filled by others[.] I see by the papers Capt.
Inglefield R.N. of the Screw discovery Comp^ys Steamer 'Isabel' who has
been in search of Sir John Franklin, but have not seen anything of the
Missing expedition (Forward to first page)
[cross-written] he made a very lengthened report to the Admiralty of his
observations geographical sketches &c he seems to have gone further than
any other, Northward, he discovered several small Islands, Inlets &c he
says, "sailing northward, I reach^d Cape Atholl Augt 23 being calm I steamed
round the bay close in shore, I proceeded against a heavy gale from the
N.W. & after being blown back 3 times we entered Whale sounds, 25 miles
inside this opening in the coast a settlement of natives was observed &
visited, they were strong, healthy, & vigorous, as any I have seen on the
coast. I found a steel knife blade with "B. Wilson, cast steel" marked on the
blade, an all tin canister & some rope, I dssh^d [dashed] for Smiths sound,

I reached Cape Alexander on the 28th under sail & steam, we had no sooner fairly opend the sound than I involuntarily exclaimed "this must lead into the great Polynesia of the Russians" I could but admit on my own mind that a great Sea was beyond, the strait mark[d] so narrow on our charts I found to be 36 miles across. it seemed more of a genial clime, the sides of Cape Alexander itself being streaked with bright green grasses & moss, I went on to the N.W. and a high range of mountains terminated the Western shore on a bluff, which I termed "Victoriahead", here the outline of the coast ceased for though I reached at noon of the 27th the Lat. 78.20. nothing could be seen but loose ice," so after encountering most severe gales it appears he was obliged to return to England, he speak[s] highly of the high pressure steam power, afterwards he concluded by saying "my large chart being now finished, with the track round Baffin Bay & the discoveries I have made (comprising 600 miles of the new coast line) correctly laid down, I do now enclose the eye sketch alluded to, but shall take the earliest opportunity of waiting on their lordships with the same & numerous sketches of the unknown coasts I have explored, I think the report must be a very important one, I think I must soon conclude I am almost afraid I have driven off writing too late, but trust you will recieve it all right," Nixon is rather queer just now with his old complaints he is getting on very well, he has begun French, he desires his kindest love to you, your Grandfather & Grandmother are much as usual. M[rs] Frostick is dead, he is going to leave his farm, St. Peters Foundry is completely burned down, the fire is supposed to have been the work of an incendiary, it was happlily confined to the premises or it would have been a serious affair. Horace Kindred is expected home soon his father had a letter from him from Ceylon, your uncle & aunt Nettleship are quite well much disappointed at not seeing you to say good bye. thay desire their kind love, & Willey, mother, aunt Elisa, Rob[t] & myself join in kind love & wishing you a happy & prosperous voyage & safe return, with the blessing of God

    I remain your Affectionate Father

      Rob[t] Naunton

      Dec[r] 10th

[cross-written] reports have reached us that a great many lives have been lost by the floods, in one town as many as 3 inquests were held in one day & a great many Cattle, Sheep, & pigs have been seen floating about in all directions, I cannot think of any more now, we have not yet changed our residence[.] there were several people killed by the excitement caused by the Duke of Wellington lying in state at Chelsea, the crowd to gain admission was terrific, some were in the crowd five or six hours waiting for their turn,

moving only an inch or 2 at a time, in a crowd of several thousand, that
they were completely suffocated, there was only one on the day of the
funeral & that was a man fell of[f] the top of Drummonds Bank,

    Good bye & god bless you, RN.

    think of the Sarsasparilla

George Naunton missed this letter – even though it was sent by the Isthmus of Panama to speed its delivery – because he was on his way home. Even
if he had received his father's requests, it might have been hard for an apprentice seaman to gather and store a collection of flora and minerals, considering the cramped quarters on board ship. He may, however, have been able to
store enough knowledge of the new places he had visited to satisfy his father's
curiosity about the interesting matters of distant lands.

71 THOMAS HOLMAN: *I dread the interval between this & an answer to it,*
    our anxiety will be so great

In his letter of application to the Hudson's Bay Company, Thomas Holman
described his considerable experience on board ship. He was hired and in
1850 became first mate aboard the newly purchased Company brigantine
Una, bound for the Columbia Department to replace the *Mary Dare.* The
ship arrived at Fort Victoria in June 1850. Thomas's sister, J.E. Holman,
writes him often – we have five undelivered letters in all – and her articulate
and detailed descriptions of family affairs offer an insight into the lives of
working middle-class people in mid-century. Her first letter was written on
Christmas Day, one year after her brother left.

～ For Mr Holman, Hudson's Bay Company Service, Fort Victoria,
Vancouvers Island

Bridges Cottage Harbledown Christmas Day [25 December] 1850 –

    My Dear Brother,

    It gave us all very great pleasure to recieve a letter from you sooner than
we expected as it was but little more than 3 months from the date – I
should have answered it immediately but have been waiting in hopes of
being able to give a better account of our Brother, in that I am however
disappointed for we recieved a letter from him this Morning to say he had
not yet succeeded in getting a Berth & he really did not know when he
should[.] You will be surprised when I tell you he has not had anything to
do since you have been away[.] In March he came home ill, stay'd a fortnight
when he was obliged to return to London on receiveing a summons from M^r

Ives who enter'd a action against him for Money due to him from Charles
& which Charley thought would balance a debt due to him from Mr Ives,
but that would not stand good in Law one debt could not be set against
another, therefore it is being now paid by Monthly instalments & I hope
God will let me live long enough to outset it all[.] I get abundance of work
& this last few weeks have been better able to labour – though in a very
feeble state of health at present, am better than some few months ago when
I did not expect ever to read a letter from you or write one to you, But to
return to poor Charley after this Business was settled he cam[e] down again
in June ill with Ague but in a Months time he got very hearty & returned
again to old Mrs Judges & ever since has been looking out for a Berth &
cannot yet succeed in getting one[.] oh you would not think what a
Trouble it is for I am sure he is in want. we none of us can keep him from
it being so entangled with the other business I can do but little for him
poor fellow, if it was not for that I could help him a good bit[.] Dady &
Mother have withdrawn from what you left in the Savings Bank first £5
to pay Charley what you owed him, & 10£ to pay down when Mr Ives
Business was settled[.] it shall be replaced again if possible & poor Charley
promised me he would pay 30s p^r month towards it if please God he could
get a Berth[.] Now all this Dear Tom I tell you in confidence as I ought not
perhaps to have named it only I feel that you will pity our unfortunate
Brother & should I be removed by death before fulfiling my engagement
you will I know settle it for me & that will be a relief to my Mind to think
of – Now I must tell you of a few bereavements since you left England[.]
first of all our poor Old Uncle Mr Nicholls died 8th of January in the
present year & a fortnight afterwards his Son George died[.] The poor Old
Gent drop[p]ed down in a fit the Saturday after Christmas day as he was
dressing himself in the Morning, he lived about a week but never recovered
the use of his limbs or his faculties[.] his Mind was gone entirely – We
wrote to inform George of the fact & he came down when to our great
surprise he appear'd to be in the last stage of consumption & so it prov'd,
Edwin came down to accompany his Father back to London, it was very
providential for us he did so for poor George only lived a fortnight
afterwards

Now I have a sad event to relate of poor Henry Holman at Ramsgate[.]
he had been in a poor state of health for some few months & it appear'd to
affect his intellect for shocking to tell in the early part of June he made off
with himself in the Night, – His poor Old Father call'd him in the Morning
& then went to carry out a Grist, on his return not finding Henry down
stairs he call'd him again, & receiveing no answer went up to his Bedroom
& there found the poor unhappy Boy had destroy'd his own life[.] You can

suppose what a shock it was to his Father, indeed to all the family & they
have not yet got the better of it, poor Old Uncle lives quite alone now[.]
Mrs Bayly wishes him so much to come & live entirely with her but hitherto has not been able to prevail upon him to do so,

 You will think dear Tom that June was an eventful Month & so indeed it
was, for in the same poor Edward Dunkin died[.] You will remember they
had left Harbledown & took a farm at Chilham, it was a larger concern &
requir'd more capital to carry on the business than he poor fellow had
reckoned upon, consequently he worked too hard & from Christmas till
his Death was in a poor state of health[.] his Widow with her little family
of 3 remain there still & she is in hopes poor dear of being able to get a
living, but it is a bad business for a Woman to have the management of,
she is such a nice gentle creature that I trust she will meet with friends who
will assist her all they can for she is too far off for Edwards family to be of
use to her much as they wish it, Henry Dunkin is married & living in M^r
West's little Cottage[.] C Dunn has bought an annuity with her little
property she poor girl thought so much off, & is Lodging at Canterbury
she took two or 3 different places as servant but she did not find herself
comfortable[.] she thought she was to[o] old for Service so has given it up
all together, if not too Old poor Girl she had been too much indulged by
her poor Father to like service again[.] Now I have to tell you of a Death
that I in common with others have most keenly felt[.] my much loved J.E.
Dunkin died also in June & was Buried on the very day your letter to
Father was dated on the 27th[.] oh my Brother that was a Blow indeed to
me; you know a little of her kind and tender care of me, but oh you knew
not half, I look around me now in vain to find her equal, for never in this
cold hearted clime shall I ever meet with such another friend, her illness
was Inflamation & diseased Lungs, but her death was indeed most happy
& I sometimes forget my sorrow for her loss in the joyful anticipation of
soon meeting her again, in that better World w[h]ere Sin & sorrow are
alike unknown, Poor M^r & M^{rs} J Dunkin still mourn for their Child; to
day has been a trying one to them, Bless the sweet Girl she told them ere
she was taken away that they ~~should~~ [crossed out] must take me as their
child when she was gone but oh I never could make up their loss; or be to
them what she was in Duty & Affection; Sarah Ann is gone to live Ladys
maid at Lady Greys so that only Polly & George is at home; He growing a
nice youth but lost in Jenny the Sister he loved the best of all,

 Our uncle J. Holman at Canterbury is now recovering from a serious
illness & last week walked up here again[.] he is new Grandpapa! John's
little Boy is about 6 months Old & is also named John; Aunt & all the
family are well[.] Mary Ann is living as Shopwoman at a Drapers in

Ramsgate; & Jane Maria at a Drapers in Herne Bay, they are all at home
for their Christmas holiday & seem a very good, & very happy family,
Charley is Shopman at Mr Paynes draper in Canterbury so they are all
pretty much of a Trade – old Mr Bunel is dead, also Old Mr Hearn &
Granny Hawkins, William Anderson went to Hamershorn to see Aunt
Betty in the Summer she is very hearty indeed[.] All our Whitstable &
Sarr[e] friends are going on about as usual & I think you will be tired of
my detailed account of persons & things, so I must draw to a conclusion
hopeing you will not too nicely criticise my letter, I hope too you will my
Belov'd Brother write as often & as much as you can[.] our parents get very
infirm & trouble has made their spirits weak so that a letter occasionally
from you will do them good as well as me[.] they both desire their very
kind Love to you & hope you are really comfortable were you are, but
with me they lament your being shut out from every
[on cover] thing that would tend to remind you that this world is not our
home[.] but my Brother will not forget there is another state for which we
must prepare & therefore frame his life according; I that have so much to
remind me of the fact, too oft forget I am an accountable being & have
need of the advice dearest Jenny gave her loved ones when she said to them
"do not grieve when I am gone but read your Bible Love & Serve Your
Saviour & then you'll come to me." Bless her it is as though I see & hear
her now[.] Happy are we dear Tom to hear you say you are not inclined for
the diggings, why really the accounts of their goings on in California are
quite horrifying, Love of Gold appears to transform men into Fiends, tell
me when you write if I shall send you any news papers or any thing else,
Oh my Brother & are we not to look for you home again for a long period;
tell me how long you think; I should like to have some time to think of
meeting again even in this World, Now I must say Good bye & with
Charleys love united to mine & that of all friends Believe me my Dearest
Brother We remain
your Truly affectionate Sister JE Holman

Besides the news of debts and deaths, including a suicide, we get a sense
of women's work from this and Miss Holman's other long letters. Women of
Miss Holman's class not only cared for the household and the sick but earned
their own keep as well. Miss Holman's skill at needlework or "fancy work" (as
she called it in a later letter), brought her an abundance of work. Friends
Mary Ann (perhaps a cousin) and Jane were shop women with drapers; C.
Dunn had tried to work in domestic service but had failed because her father
had "too much indulged" her and she was not able to maintain the demanding
dawn-to-after-dark hours and exhausting duties of a servant. As well, Edward

Dunkin's widow, with three children, seemed to be trying to maintain her husband's farm, although she might not succeed as "it is a bad business for a Woman to have the management of." Miss Holman herself, with the help of money from brother Thomas's account, was trying to pay off brother Charley's debt in spite of the "other business" that she does not specify. Charley could not find a job, and she feared for the family's future.

Miss Holman's relief at the end of her letter that Thomas is not "inclined for the diggings" reminds us of the gold fever that had captured the imaginations and lives of many men (and some women), and of the worry that this gave to those back home. In April 1851 Miss Holman wrote the hardest news of all to her brother.

5th April 1851 Bridges Cottages, Harbledown nr Canterbury, Kent

My dearest Brother,

It has been no easy task to me to summon up resolution sufficient to enable me to write to you – Heretofore it has always been a pleasant task but now most painful, I say this by way of preface to the heavy tidings I would in some measure prepare you for hearing

It is of our Father, our dear & tender Father I now must speak, why do I say our Father[?] Alas my Brother we have no earthly Father now he is departed[.] he is gone, Yes gone to Heaven never more will he welcome you to your earthly home but I trust he will to your & his Heavenly home, when a few short years at the most are pass'd away we shall all meet again never more to be seperated, Still I have always indulged the hope of our meeting again even here & when he has sometimes said I shall never see poor Old Tom in this world again I have always replied that is more than we can tell[.] So it is he would say but I am getting an Old Man you know dear girl I cannot expect to live till his return, Bless him, Bless him he was right & I was wrong – I thought it a little singular that Christmas night was the first begining of the final breaking up of his sytem, He walked on that day down to Old Mrs Dunkins with a letter to post for Charles, Sarah seeing him so feeble offer'd to take it to Mr Pilchers & he stayed with the old Lady whilst she went[.] when he came home he seemed quite tired out not poorly through the night however he was very restless which was unsual for him, A week pass'd away when he complain'd of feeling so weak & had not so good appetite as usual, We sent for Mr Reid who prescribed for him & said he would be all right in a few days there was nothing to be alarmed at, so we hoped the Medicine would take the desir'd effect[.] instead of that however he seemed to lose strength dear creature & he could eat but little his thirst appear'd to be insatiable drink drink [repetition] cold water nothing he relished like it his dear Tongue became so coated & black still he suffer'd very little pain except in his Bowels at times until about 3 weeks after Christmas when his Bowels became very obstinate & we gave him repeated dose's of Castor Oil before they would Act, After that they were as troublesome the other way which we fear'd would weaken him still more[.] Yet Mr Reid kept telling poor Mother that Dady would be better in a little time & so he went on so gradually failing getting so tired of all his little nourishments that he could not take them[.] he first of all used to take only his breakfast in bed & get up directly after then he would lay till 10 oclock, then 11, then Just come down in time to see us have a dinner for bless him he could not make one himself then he lay a bed till 2 or 3 oclock which was the time he came down on Sunday the first of February[.] he had the cold shivers so sadly when he got up & went To Bed about 6 very ill[.] at 12 oclock I had always taken him some little refreshment before I went to bed[.] on that night I found him quite delirous though he had been sleeping from the time he took his Oil of supper[.] when Mother went to bed at 9, I was then for the first time alarmed & so was poor Mother[.] the next day I wrote to tell Charley I feared he was worse than the Docter thought him as he merely told us certainly he was not so well[.] Tuesday he seemed a little better but did not get up either Monday or that day[.] on Wensday we did not consider him worse but when Mr Reid came he said how badly dear daddy drew his breath[.] oh Sir I said it is nothing so bad as on Monday[.] well he said he must sound him[.] he did so & then bled him copiously kept telling me not to distress my self & then told poor Mother & me that Inflamation of the Lungs had come on & it was his duty to say that from his Age & present state of weakness he feared there was but little hope of recovery[.] He however would do all that he could for him[.] when I went to our Belov'd Father afterwards he put his dear arms around my Neck & said do not do not [repetition] grieve my child But we must part[.] that Man knows I am near my end or he would not ble[e]d me[.] That night he had a large blister on the next day 10 Leeches & another blister beside Mustard Poultices[.] the disease was by these means subdued & on the following Wensday Mr Reid said it was entirely removed but he was sinking[.] Oh my Lov'd Brother I wish I could describe minutely his last days but unless you had seen you could not form any idea of his perfect resignation to the Divine Will[.] oh so *patient* so *loving meek & gentle*[.] it was indeed beautiful to see him he was indeed prepar'd & meet for that Heaven he enter'd on Saturday the 15 of February[.] He died without a struggle at least he fell asleep in Jesus for Death it could not be call'd[.] He was Buried on the 24th[.] Charles came down to the Funeral[.] he has not yet a ship, I should have written to you before this but I wish'd to know about poor Mothers Pension & we have to day heard that they have granted her £25 pr annum So my dear Brother you may rest assur'd that our remaining Parent will not want for any thing; I trust we shall be able to remain here at present & as I have had constant employment at fancy work it will be a shame if I cannot supply my own little wants[.] I have written to know if Mr Ives will forgive me the remainder of Charleys debt to him as it is impossible for me to continue the payment at £1 a Month at present[.] You well know my dear Brother what our daddy was to us & therefore can Judge of our cause for Sorrow but still we do not Sorrow as those without hope of meeting again where death shall all be done away & we shall part no more

[crosswise] Our dear Mother & myself are as well as can be expected[.] you must accept our united & Kindest Love & Believe me to Be Your Only

    Affectionate Sister

    J E Holman

If this reaches you dear Tom do write & as often as you can after. Our Uncle John Holman is in a poor state of Health all our friends are so good & kind to us (all are well), I beg you will excuse all errors[.] did you get my other letter[?]

The long description of the treatment of the father not only portrays the still-typical treatments of bleeding and poultices but also indicates for us that, in every century, doctors can have successful treatments – as the disease here was subdued – but nevertheless lose the patient. Miss Holman's continuing concern with the family finances made her delay writing of their father's death until she could also write that their mother would be receiving a pension. She assured her brother that she would also help support herself, as "employment at fancy work ... [would] supply [her] own little wants."

Ironically, soon after she wrote this letter Thomas himself was confined to bed, unfit for duty, in June 1851. By October 1851 Thomas was well enough to sail on the *Una* for a six-month trip as far north as the Queen Charlotte Islands. At the same time, his sister wrote to him, relieved to have received a letter even though it told of his illness, but worried that he was not receiving her letters.

~ For Mr Holman, Hudson's Bay Company Service, Fort Victoria, Vancouvers Island, N.W. Coast of America

4th October 1851 Bridges Cottages's, Harbledown, n^r Canterbury

    My Belov'd Brother

    We recieved your letter this day bearing date 3rd February and most

keenly have dear Mother & I felt that he who shar'd alike our Joys &
sorrows was no longer with us, Oh my Brother you have no doubt 'ere this
recieved the mournful intelligence of our dear Father's death, Precious
Parent, the grief which we to day have felt at hearing of your illness he
cannot feel, No grief, no pain, or woe where he now dwells, but all is peace
without allay & happiness which knows no interruption, Long and
anxiously have poor Mother & myself been looking out for a letter from
you but this must surely have been delay'd as it is just 8 months & a day
from the date to the time of recieving

Our dear Father was out in his reckoning as to the time you would be
away from Vancouver Island, for he repeatedly said Your Letters would be
there Long before you got back from the Sandwich Islands whither you were
going when you wrote to him the 27th of June 1850[.] Now we find from
your letter to day that you were back & expecting an answer long before it
reached you, & that adds to our sorrow on your account, so much so indeed
that we long for the wings of the dove that we could not only fly to nurse
& attend you if still it is needful, but also to speak a few words instead of
trusting to time & uncertainty as to *when* or *whether* you recieve this,

My dearest Tom if there is a mail from England once a month is there
also one to England? if so do write I entreat you when you get this, or if
you are unable to do so get some other person to write for you, I dread the
interval between this & an answer to it, our anxiety will be so great, But
Patience & Prayer must be & will be, our only remedy, Our poor dear
daddy so often said it was just the Climate to suit you; Bless him he would
have felt disappointed to hear your health had fail'd

When you are sufficiently recovered I hope & Mother hopes you will
leave there & come home, it may be that the climate does not agree with
you & if it does the distance is so great that it is terrible not to be able to
see or to hear from you for so long a time, did you know that Uncle John
Holman has been a sufferer with the Liver complaint for some few Years,
& I think it is about 10 years ago that he was so very bad with it none of
his friends thought he could possibley recover, but here he is now 'tho very
feeble poor Man & failing greatly,

However knowing the bad state he was in so long inspires me with hope
as to your recovery; Oh, my Brother I dare not think the contrary, 'tho I
know & feel that God cannot do but what is right, Yet to think that my
daddy is gone, poor Mother it is not to [be] expected from her age will be
long with us, & to lose you who I more than ever cling to now. Must I
who have been so rich in Parents & Brothers Love become all at once so
poor so stripped of all, may God of His Mercy forbid it & *I do, I must
Hope* that He will,

All are going on about as they were when I last wrote, Mother is quite a wonder her health & spirits both better than we could ever expected they would be under our heavy bereavement, we purpose remaining in the Old Cottage at present, it is you know lower rented than the Houses in Canterbury & we are loth to leave the place so dear to us, where every thing reminds us of our departed one & of bygone happy days,

Poor Charley sailed the 1ˢᵗ of May for Valpar[a]iso in the ship James Armstrong[.] he is gone 2ⁿᵈ Mate, and we hope & trust he will be comfortable[.] it is a 12 or 14 months voyage. He told us that very like he might see or hear of you out there[.] is there any chance of it do you suppose?

Old Mʳˢ Judge has been very ill since he left but was better when we last heard, Do you dear Tom be sure & write I ask again & if please you are restor'd as I trust you are 'tho it is I know a tedious complaint; can we send you any thing if you stay there, I will get a Book for you with an account of the Great exhibition which has been the general theme of conversation & object of pursuit to all persons rich or poor for the last 6 months, (Not includeing dear Mother & self)[.] I am thankful to say I have not wanted for work since daddy has been gone away, and I have hitherto found that as my day, so has been my strength 'tho very feeble at times it has never quite failed[.] Our Belov'd Mother desires me to give her kindest Love to you, All our friends desire me to make their kind remembrance whenever I write, May The Lord Bless You My Dearest Brother & permit us to hear a better account of you in your next letter[.] Believe me to be your Truly affectionate Sister J E Holman

It must have come as a great relief to the family that poor Charley has finally got a place on a ship; the relief, however, was mixed with anxiety at the difficulty of communication. Thomas's first letter arrived in only three months; by 1851, monthly mail delivery had been made possible by sending mail across the Isthmus of Panama and connecting with the many ships plying the waters off the west coast of North America. However, this letter was marked "missent to Hobarttown," a route that would have delayed it considerably. By then his sister and mother wanted Thomas to come home. Miss Holman wrote again a month later, after receiving his "3ʳᵈ letter to our dear dear Father" and realizing that he had received none of her letters and did not yet know of their father's death nine months before.

〜 M[r] Holman, Hudson's Bay Companys Service, Fort Victoria, Vancouvers Island, N.W. Coast of America

14th November 1851 Bridges Cottage, Harbledown n[r] Canterbury, Kent

My dearest Brother,

We have this day recieved your 3rd letter to our dear dear Father & you will more easily Judge than I describe the mix'd feelings of pleasure & pain it was welcomed with, Yes my lov'd Brother it was indeed most welcome to us, to us that are left, as doubtless before this time you are aware as our dear Mother & her who never expected to know the loss of a Parent, but alas the dreadful *reality* has been experienced by me, And our Heavenly Father knows it is my desire to bow in meek submission to His Wise & Holy Will, But I must not dwell upon the melancholy theme My former letters have made you acquainted with the mournful fact, oh my Brother my Brother it is just 9 months tomorrow that you & I & Charley have been Fatherless & when I remember how M[r] Reid & other friends apprehended that the blow would lay me too in the Grave, I can but wonder & adore the goodness of God who has supported me under it & made me in the absence of my Brothers the [an ink blot obscures a word here] only prop & stay of our dear kind Mother, –

I cannot tell you how very very thankful we are to hear you were a little better when writing on the 1st of September, than you were in February 3rd – which was the date of the letter we recieved on the 4th of October[.] we do hope by Gods Blessing you have continued better to this time & will 'ere long be restor'd to your usual health[.] It appears that you do not suppose the climate has ought to do with your illness but indeed I should fear it has, if so, as I said before so say I now again pray pray do not remain there, I think dear Tom you never have been strong enough to bear the change of climate[.] surely if you came home something of a situation in the customs or some other might be obtained[.] at all events it would not be right to stop out were you are if there is a probability of your haveing better health in your own native land, Oh health sweet sweet health! All California's Gold if I possessed it gladly would I give for the purchase of that greatest earthly blessing for me & mine[.] We are now sadly perplexed about the letters I have written to you[.] the 2 first certainly ought to have arrived at the Island by the time you were writing your last[.] I hope & trust that you recieved them by the Mail you were expecting in a few days, I have to day sent to the general Post Office in Canterbury to ask if there was any other way of forwarding a letter to you more speedy & sure than by posting at their office, The Post Master assures me that no better way is open to me, & he cannot account for the others delay but that there was

no neglect on his part he is very certain[.] Should it please God to restore
you to health & you stay w[h]ere you are some time longer would it not be
a good opportunity to send to you by one of the Companys Ships? As any
thing you wanted that we could get would reach you in that way[.] I hope
dear Tom you will not scruple to let us know if you do, for we are so highly
favoured with kind friends who think it no trouble to assist us in any thing
so that 'tho our Belov'd Father is no longer with us we should find no
difficulty whatever in procureing whatever you require

And happy should we be to do so, I cannot express what we have felt &
still feel on your account[.] It has been a year of Trial to each of us but
yourself in particular must have had need of patience to endure, not only
bodily suffering but anxiety of mind, oh I do hope there is no cause for it
now yet if it should unfortunately be the case at any future time that letters
are delay'd Never Never allow the thought to intrude that you are forgotten
by us, you must indeed account for the omission in every way but that, it is
true I am at the best but a poor scribe & at the worst a very bad one, still you
may depend upon an answer to yours at all times, & oftener if you wish it

In case my former letters should be lost I had better tell you over
again what friends have been removed by death &c &c they are our poor
Old Uncle W.N. also his Son George, my much loved Friend & Cousin
Jane Ellen Dunkin also her Uncle Edward Dunkin, Henry Holman at
Ramsgate, & of Neighbours they are old Mr Birnie, Captain Archer the
first died in his chair whilst writing a letter to his Son John who is
Chaplain of a Ship at Gibraltar, old Mr Hearn, Old Mrs Page, & Dame
Young, all of whom you will I think remember are also dead, The only
little stranger I have to tell of is John Holmans Son & heir, also Henry
Dunkins, he is living in Mr West's little Cottage & the Old Lady with
Sarah remain in their own[.] the old duchess has had a good crop of Hops
this year & sold them for a good price Mr John has likewise done the same,
both himself & Mrs John also the old Lady & Sarah indeed I ought to say
all of the family that know you have at different times desired me to give
their Love & good wishes to you whenever I wrote, Uncle & Aunt John
with their Boys & Girls desire the same, Also our Cousins at Sarr[e] &
Ramsgate[.] all are I believe going on about the same as usual except M^r
John Mascall & he goes on worse than ever, You know I think that Tom
at Sarr[e] has built both Hannah & Mary his Sisters a Cottage adjoining the
Mill which our poor Old Uncle W.H. used to call his own but it now
belongs to Tom at Sarr[e] & William Mascall Hires it of him, it appears that
J Mascall had borrowed money of some persons & told them the Mill

belong'd to him also the Cottages & a great deal more but when the creditors became aware of his deception they put an execution in the house & all their things were sold for the 3rd time[.] he owed 4 Hundred Pounds which they knew of & they expect they do not know all[.] he has not been home since the sad affair & the poor woman is truly miserable, Oh Tom dear Boy light indeed are our troubles to hers but I have for the last Month been very anxious about our poor Old Mother she has been so ill & quite laid by for that time, Now Mr Reid gives me great encouragement for he thinks her in a fair way of recovery & she really is a great deal better[.] she has had inflamation which threw itself out in her body first like a bad scald which gradually came to a wound[.] Cold Poultices day & night have been applied & happy am I to say the wounds are now healed[.] her appetite is exceeding good & so is her rest at night[.] Mr Reid has taken his leave of us & I do think she is likely to be better than she was before this illness[.] God is indeed Kind not to take her from me yet[.] we are so comfortable together could not be more so we find a rich supply of all necessaries Ah & every comfort which can be possessed is ours[.] I must now conclude with dear Mothers & my own kindest Love hoping you will write to us every oppertunity & that we may hear better accounts of your health
Believe us to be your Truly Affectionate
    Mother & Sister C & J E Holman
[written in the margins] Am sorry to find my letter to [you] so blotted but you will excuse. when you write please to say if you have recieved the 4 letters I have written. I told you that Charley sailed in the James Armstrong for Valpar[a]iso on the 1st of May

We can sense Miss Holman's growing worry as, with her father's death, her mother having suffered a serious illness, and Charles and Thomas both far away, she was the "only prop & stay of our dear kind Mother." The depths of her feelings may be revealed in what appear to be tear stains that blot the letter on the first page. At the same time as this letter was written, her brother Thomas's life was at risk also. In May 1851 John Work had unsuccessfully investigated Englefield Bay and Cape Henry after some Aboriginal people had brought gold to trade at Fort Simpson, Nass, the year before. In the summer Work had returned with Captain McNeill and Captain Mitchell of the *Una,* remaining five days but finding nothing. In October the *Una* returned and Thomas, who had recovered his health, was on board. Captain W.H. McNeill reported the *Una*'s adventure to the colony's governor, James Douglas, on 20 November 1851:

We commenced blasting the Rock at the old place. We commenced in a Vein of Quartz and were very successful, the rock proved to be rich with Gold ... We followed the vein and found it deeply impregnated with Gold ... We found it in four different places in Mitchell's Harbour but had no time to examine it. – I am sorry to inform you that we were obliged to leave off blasting and quit the place for Fort Simpson, on account of the annoyance we experienced from the natives. They arrived in large numbers, say 30 Canoes and were much pleased to see us on our first arrival. When they saw us blasting and turning out the Gold in such large quantities they became excited and commenced depredations on us stealing the tools, and taking at least one half of the Gold that was thrown out by a blast they would be concealed until the report was heard, and then make a rush for the Gold, a regular scramble between them and our men would take place, they would take our men by the legs and hold them away from the Gold, some blows were struck on these occasions. The Indians drew their knives on our men often. – The men who were at work at the vein became completely tired, and disgusted at their proceedings, and came to me on three different occasions and told me that they would not remain any longer to work the Gold. – That their time was lost to them as the natives took one half of the Gold thrown out by the blast, and blood would be shed if they continued to work at the diggin[g]s. That our force was not strong or large enough to work and fight also. – They were aware they could not work on shore after hostilities had commenced therefore I made up my mind to leave the place, and proceed to this place [Fort Simpson].

He recommended a force of at least eighty if they returned and recommended ways to discourage the men from trading on their own. On 25 December 1851, the *Una* was driven onshore at Neah Bay (Juan de Fuca Strait) and was burned to the water line by Aboriginal people. By 16 January 1852 the incident was reported in the *Portland Weekly Oregonian* and the news spread quickly, with Lloyds reporting it in England in May 1852. The families in England must have had unnecessary worry, since the newspaper report stated that the crew was taken prisoner for two months by the Aboriginal people. In fact, they had been rescued immediately by the crew of the *Susan Sturges* – and the Aboriginal plunderers had been punished by their chief. Rather, it was the passengers and crew of the *Georgianna* who had experienced two months as prisoners of the Haida after running aground on the east side of the Queen Charlotte Islands.

Not knowing anything of her brother's peril, Miss Holman wrote again in May 1852, still in hope of hearing from him by the *Norman Morison,* which she had been told would be the next Company ship to arrive.

〜 via the United States,
Mr Holman, Hudson Bay Companys Service, Fort Victoria Vancouvers
Island, NW Coast of America, Oregon

5th May 1852

[letterhead drawing] "Canterbury from Harbledown," Goulden, Publisher,
Canterbury, Engraved by Mould and Tod

May 5th 1852 Bridges Cottage, Harbledown, Near Canterbury

My Belov'd Brother
Both Mother & myself have been for some few weeks past looking
moste anxiously for a letter from you[.] how glad we shall be to hear how
you are but no remedy have we but patience & soon I trust we shall get
tidings[.] I should have sent another letter to you before but was in hopes
one of your Company's ships would have started by this time from London
to Vancouvers Island, we have not been able to ascertain the time that one
would go until now, we applied to Mr Daniells at Whitstable to make the
necessary enquiry at the H.B. C{s} House in London; as he was not going
for some time himself he refer'd me to his nephew Baker who resides in
London, I wrote to him accordingly, but never recieved any answer, then
I requested our Cousin Henry Nicholls to go & ask the question, he went
but got no answer, as a last resource I wrote to the Secretary as I supposed
there was one & now have recieved a very satisfactory reply; He informs us
that the "first vessel for your Island will leave London the end of July &
whatever we wish to send to you can be forwarded by that ship"[.] it is at
the least 7 or 8 weeks since I wrote but they did not it is probable know
until now the exact time of her sailing and we do feel it very kind of Mr
Secretary for not forgetting our request, Now should we be spared & your
health permits you to remain there any time longer, we shall not again be
so perplexed as we know how to get information without troubling any
one, We are so in hopes of hearing from you by the Norway [Norman]
Morrison which will arrive I should expect before long, sometimes poor
Mother & I say we should not be surprised if you are comeing home in her
& I really think we have almost persuaded ourselves that such is the case &
if it might be the means under God of reestablishing your health it surely
cannot be wrong of us to wish it may be so,
I have just completed your Shirts & hope they will fit you very nicely,
Mother has made the flannel ones, & knitted you 2 pairs of Worsted Stock-
ing's such thick warm ones, to be sure, I wish I could tell what you would
like best for 'tho you may get your wants supplied out there by others

I flatter myself you would feel most pleasure in wearing what came from
our own sweet home; Yes my loved Brother it is sweet home still, although
its *bright Sun* is *set in the grave* & rendered it unlike what once it was, Yet
faith's strong eye can look *above* the *vacant chair,* & *beyond* the *cold dark
grave,* teaching us not to sorrow as those without hope, & enableing us to
enjoy with calm & thankful hearts the many many blessings we still can
call our own, Tis just a month to day since we recieved a letter from our
dear Brother who we expected would be home by this time, but we find it
may be 6 months longer ere he returns, He wrote in Jan^ry from Arica on
the Coast of Peru, The James Armstrong did not go to Valpar[a]iso as he
wrote us when he sailed from the Downs 12 months ago, he had been
expecting they would get a Freight for England but had not done so at the
time he wrote, the Ship was employed he said carrying hay to different
places[.] he was pretty comfortable & had enjoyed very good health ever
since he left us, You shall have his Letter with your parcel by & by; Uncle
John Holman has been up to day[.] he is very feeble & shaky much more
so than our dear Father ever was, a few weeks back he had a return of
spitting blood to an excess, Mr Reid did not think he could possibly
recover & is quite astonished to see him now but poor Man I do not think
his recovery will be permanent, his Son John is living next door to him the
house between Aunt Hope's & his Father & Mother's, poor little Mr Bax
has lost his eye sight & is now quite blind, Young John has bought his life
& that is the reason for his comeing into that house as it was part of his
Uncle Toms property; Young Tom is gone to London for a year or two for
improvement in the Millwrights business – Charles is gone to Maidstone
shopman in a more extensive Drapery businss than Mr Payne's at Canterbury,
Jane Maria is Shopwoman at Charley's old place at Herne Bay & Mary
Ann is the same at a drapers in Ramsgate, Lizzy is her Mother's maid at
home but in such delicate health they are fearful she is consumptive but
I hope they may be wrong[.] They are such a happy united family that the
removal of one of its members by death would be keenly felt by all, M^rs
Wm Mascall is staying at Mr Dunkins & desires her kind love to you[.] she
is looking so stout & well but her husband is as little as ever; John Mascall
was at Deal staying for 5 or 6 months after the execution was put in his
house but is at home again now, I think I told you in a former letter what
trouble he has occassioned the family & his wife[.] the Debts which he
acknowledged amounted to upwards of £400 & in what way he can have
made of[f] with the money is a mystery to all And himself, Mr Holman at
Sarr bought the Furniture in again & have got it made over to himself for
John had given bills of sale on his goods to 2 or 3 different persons, M^r &
Mrs Holman have not been up to St Lawrence since John has been home

again & poor Hannah is so simple as to think they are slighting her[.] it is
quite a grief to her but it is only that worthless man's misconduct they are
resenting & it is a pity Hannah allows her peace & comfort to be inter-
rupted by it[.] he is now going to pay 2s 6d in the pound at least his wife
& Hannah will pay it for he has not a shilling to call his own

what do you think of our good friend Mr Crawford going out a
Missionary[?] he left England in Jan^ry last for Jerusulem[.] his Wife &
Children with one of his sisters went out with him, his health is so very
feeble that well as I wish the cause I cannot think that he was called upon
to give up home & friends to encounter the proba[b]le hardship of his
Mission but certainly he thought otherwise[.] He is a Truly good man &
such are much needed in our own highly favour'd land, No tidings as yet
of poor Sir John Franklin[.] there are more vessels lately gone out to search
for him, his Lady will not give him up neither do many others but our dear
Father did before he died so that I should think they must surely be all lost
before now

Aunt Betty Anderson is dead, & William being heir to her little property
of between 3 & 400 £ makes him a few degrees higher than before[.] I do
not think the poor Chap will attain to her or his Fathers Age for he is far
from being healthy or strong, he is subject to Influenza Cold's & hoarseness
which leaves him very weak particularily on the Chest, M^rs A is very
hearty[.] They both of them frequently enquire after you indeed so do all
our friends, relations, & aquaintance; M^r & Mrs J. Dunkin are quite well &
so are their children, George & Sally are such great man & woman you
would hardly think they were the same you left as boy & girl[.] Sarah Ann
is still in Mr Edens family[.] he poor man has long been afflicted with
Paraly's [paralysis] quite unable to walk or dress himself & is I suppose worn
to a shadow, Old Mrs Dunkin has been ill again but is now recovering[.]
The poor Old Ladys mind is much the same as ever always in trouble of
some sort & yet wishing to have the lease of her life renewed[.] poor M^rs
Edward will leave her farm at Mich[a]elmas & William thinks to lease it as
he is heartily sick & tired of keeping the Plough[.] Henry has lost his little
boy & a happy thing too as M^rs [Tayulden or Iqulden?] would say; good
kind Sarah rubs on with her poor Mother but is constantly suffering more
or less with that sad complaint of the Liver, Our Beloved Mother sends her
best love & wishes to hear from you before long[.] I cannot tell how much
we wish it or how often you are the subject of our thoughts & conversation[.]
we have neither of us been quite well of late but the spring of the year is
very trying to every one & we can but feel thankful to be so well as we
are[.] I hope you will excuse all imperfections & accept the endeared love
of your Truly affectionate Sister J E Holman

All our friends at Harbledown, Canterbury, Sarr [e], Ramsgate, St Lawrence, & St Peters always when I see them beg their kind love to be given to you

Miss Holman's mention of the continuing search for the Franklin party, lost in 1847 in the Arctic during the effort to find a Northwest Passage, reminds us that all families of sailors would have been very aware – through news of such a famous ongoing event – of how hazardous a profession their men were engaged in. Thomas Holman was one of the lucky ones, surviving the wreck of the *Una*. Having experienced illness and shipwreck within several months, he decided to come home, sailing on 16 January 1852 as a passenger on the *Norman Morison*, which arrived in London in June 1852, just a month after the last letter. His mother was right when she said she "should not be surprised if you are coming home in her." The long intervals between letters that Thomas Holman's sister dreaded so much would be over, at least for a time. His service with the Hudson's Bay Company ended with his trip home in 1852-3.

72 THOMAS MORROW: *I heard of all your hardships before I had your Letter*

Thomas Morrow was an apprentice aboard the *Una* when it was driven on the rocks and burnt at Neah Bay on the south coast of Juan de Fuca Strait on Christmas Day 1851 (see Thomas Holman story, entry 71). By the time his sister wrote in October, she had read all about her brother's hardships in the newspapers. She seemed to be more caught up with news of her own, however: the emergence of their sister from a convent life.

〜 T. Morrow, on Board the Una, Fort Victoria, Vancouvers Island

6 Somerset B^ds Walcat, Bath October 19th 52 [1852]

My Dear Brother
you must excuse me for not answering your kind Letter before[.] for some months past we have been thinking of giving up our Business as we do not find it answer[.] Humphries Lad got A situation as Clerk down in the Orange Grove[.] we thought at first of going to Australia but I could not fancy being on the water so long; I have lots of news to tell you[.] I heard of all your hardships before I had your Letter; from the News Paper[.] never mind Tom so as your life is spared. I gave your letter to Mother[.] she seemed very much Displeased at your not writing to her[.] she is pretty well but as usual often grumbling she is not in service; Mrs Pelly is *Dead* she was only ill A little more than A week[.] her Husband is still in India – when

you write again you must tell me all about the Gold you have found: The people here are Gold mad thousands going to try their Luck in Australia[.] my Dearie and self are pretty well[.] you must make haste home to see your little Nephew he is such A Darling and so healthy I am quite sure you will love him he prays every night for Uncle Tom. now I suppose I shall supprise you by telling you that Agnes is out of the Convent and like yourself put all her Roman views under her feet[.] you can just fancy how bitter Mother is against her[.] she tried hard to keep the poor girl in that *worse* than prison all her life but I got her out by Scheming unknown to Mother[.] she does not know untill this day how she came out[.] the poor girl looked more dead than alive; she has been in Bath 9 Months and is now quite well happy and steady and is looking forward some day to be Married[.] there is A young fellow looking after her[.] she shall not have any one without my Consent[.] she has been greatly belied and I Believe Mother hates her[.] I must tell you that Dr Crow [Cran?] has been suspended for getting to Close to the girls; be careful and dont do the same they are Dangerous Articles best at A Distance[.] Mother regrets your having lost the Watch[.] she sends her kind love to you[.] dont get to[o] fond of Women and pray when you write which I hope will be soon Direct as before[.] Agnes sends her very kind love so does my Dearie and hopes you will take care of your self[.] we all want to see you very much indeed[.] say in your next when you are likly to come home[.] write soon[.] God bless you my Dearest Tom with best Love I remain your very Affectionate Sister Mary Humphries

Agnes added her own assurance that she was "out of [her] prison safe and sound."

⁓ My Dear Brother
I suppose you will be surprised to hear from me[.] I shall only send my very kind love to you this time as Mary has written a long letter to you but in a month I will write and tell you all the news[.] I am out of my prison safe and sound and only want to see you to complete my happiness[.] I shall conclude with a 1000 kisses and as much love as the ship will carry from your affectionate Sister
Agnes Morrow

Mary Humphries minced no words regarding her conflict with her mother, assuring Thomas, who had already forsaken Catholicism, that sister Agnes is out of her nunnery "prison" and has put "all her Roman views under her feet." Her report to Thomas of their mother's reaction to the news of the *Una* disaster – that she "regrets your having lost the Watch" – and the fact that Tom wrote to his sister rather than their mother, suggests that Mary has effectively taken over as mother of the family. In that capacity, she had no intention of letting Agnes marry inappropriately and also warned Thomas away from women.

Mary is not the only family member capable of direct action to solve a problem. After the *Una* shipwreck, Thomas was assigned to the *Recovery,* which was helping to set up the Company's gold mine at Mitchell Harbour (see Thomas Walsh, entry 68). The men who worked the mine received no pay but were issued tools and blasting powder and could keep half the gold they produced. As an apprentice seaman, Thomas would probably not have been eligible for this opportunity and, with so many American entrepreneurs arriving, it must have been galling not to be part of the action. On 1 November 1852, Thomas deserted with two other men, William Hudson and Edward James. He, like Agnes, had found a way to escape his hardships.

73 JAMES M. PHILLIPS: *Pay respect to your Officers. – Keep from strong liquors. – Write as often as ever you can*

On 20 August 1852, when the *Norman Morison* left London on its third and final trip for the Hudson's Bay Company, James Phillips was aboard as a landsman. Most of the landsmen's time on this trip was spent "drawing and knotting yarns" – producing the threads used to make up a strand of rope. James's cousin writes to him with the kind of best wishes and hopes that many families sent to their young men overseas.

~ James Phillips, Ship Norman Morison, Vancouvers

Decr 23rd 1852

Dear James

I have taken the opportunity of sending you a few lines by the kind hand of Your old Officer. Grandmother is very well and desires that you should know it; she hopes, with all the rest of us that you are perfectly happy in your new situation, and that you can agree with your shipmates. Fred^k Brown has got leave for a fortnight for his christmas Hollidays, and he says he likes the service very much and is perfectly happy. – Aunt Betsy is not married yet, and still lives in Queen St Oxford Street. She is very well. – Selina is a little better than she was, and desires her love to you. – Amelia is not married yet. – The Old Duke of Wellington was buried on the 18th of November, and none of us went to witness the sight but Mother, it was a grand sight, he was buried at St Paul's Church. We are all pretty well and hope you are the same. – and prosperous. – Pay respect to your Officers. – Keep from strong liquors. – Write as often as ever you can, and be sure to let us know when you are on your passage homeward. – It is no use wishing you a Merry Christmas, because it will be all over before this reaches you, but we hope you have had one. –

from Your Affect^e Cousin
James Beard

After serving on the *Norman Morison* from its January 1853 arrival in Vancouver to its departure in March, James was home again on 1 August. He must have lived up to the advice in his cousin's undelivered letter and been respectful to his officers as well as kept from strong liquors, for we have discovered no record of his doing otherwise.

74   ROBERT WILSON: *And I Trusted that you Robert Would Asisted her With a Little Money*

Robert Wilson, a seaman aboard the Company's new ship, the *Princess Royal*, went out to Fort Victoria on 6 June 1854. Also on this voyage were the miners destined for the Nanaimo coal mines under George Robinson – men who are remembered as the founders of that community. Robert arrived on 23 November at Esquimalt with the miners after a speedy but difficult journey of "death, misery and dissatisfaction." He remained with the ship and left Victoria two months later in January 1855. The return trip took less than five months, arriving in London 25 May 1855. His uncle wrote reminding him of his duty to support his mother.

To Robert Wilson Seaman On Board the Honourable Hudson Bay Company Ship Princess Royal, Captn Wishart Bound for Columbia, St. Catharine Dock or Else Where, London

Stromness June 5th 1854

Dear Neaphew
We Received Your Letter on the Morning of this Day Dated May 29th And was verry Much Surprised that you Did not Write when you Arived and Give us Direction Where we would find you[.] had it not Been Margaret Alen We would not have Known of your Arival untill Mr James Brown Came home[.] we Received the Letter Directed to your Brother William and they Wrote you the Answer[.] We your Uncle and Aunt is No Dout Going Down Hill[.] I have Turned 70 Years and She is Not very Far

Behind me[.] Your Mother is Still verry Feble and Needs Great Asistanc[.] Some one must be Continually Attending on her And I Trusted that you Robert Would Asisted her With a Little Money and then God Would Prosper you and you Would Be Onley Doing your Duty as a Son[.] Believe me I am Writting You now What I Think is your Duty For their is none Instructing me[.] I hope this Will find you Well And I Wish you a Pleasent Voyage So no More at Present. We Remain yours James and Barbra Wilson Write when you Receive this

From the letter, it appears that Robert had been away and that, before he had shipped out again, he had written to his family telling them where he was bound. Although only a week had passed since he wrote, the return letter would not be fast enough to reach Robert. He left the day after his uncle's letter was written, reaching London almost two weeks later. Someone made an extraordinary effort to find Robert, as the letter bears the notations: "Not known in St. Katherines Docks," "Try London Docks," "Not in London Dock," "East Indian Dock," "Not in the East India Dock," "Not in West India Dock," "Not in Commercial Dock or Surrey Canal." His ship had already set sail. By 1854, with Britain's empire and sea trade ever growing, there were many ships and places to which a man who wanted to might disappear. The letter was finally readdressed, "try Hudson Bay Company," where it remained to become part of this archive of undelivered letters.

Letters to Voyageurs

The fur-trade *voyageurs* who powered the canoes across the continent from Montreal to west of the Rocky Mountains were part of a continuous tradition stretching back to the seventeenth century. The hiring practices, terms of employment, work conditions, and patterns of daily life differed very little under the French, the North West and XY companies, and the Hudson's Bay Company. These men entered the trade to earn money to support their families on the farms along the St. Lawrence River, but they were also attracted to a life where the personal attributes of strength and courage were valued far from the social restrictions of religious farming communities. Yet, despite a public perception that the fur trade offered relatively broad personal freedom, the contracts laid out strict terms of employment: loyalty and obedience in exchange for food, clothing, and wages.

Three of the six *voyageurs* represented here were from Maskinongé, a small village on the north shore of the St. Lawrence River between Montreal and Trois-Rivières, that for generations had been supplying men to the fur trade as *engagés* (men working under contract to a fur-trade entrepreneur). They signed on as young men, leaving their homes and families for the distant and sparsely inhabited parts of the continent. Often they made their homes in the west and did not return, or came back after many years to a society that had become alien to them.

The frequent mentions of letters received demonstrate that some of the men were able to write, or at least to dictate letters. In fact, we have included a letter from a *voyageur* himself. Since the writing in his letter is quite regular, but the *voyageur* signed his contracts with an X, he may not have taken pen in hand personally; the thoughts and wishes expressed, however, would seem to be his. Few of these letters have survived, but it is apparent that many were written. Most would have reached and been read by the intended recipients and, once they had served their purpose, would have been discarded. But occasionally the system failed. The undelivered letters written to six *voyageurs* serving west of the Rocky Mountains fall into the sample documented in this volume.

The ranks of the fur trade included officers with managerial responsibilities and servants or working men. In the North West Company, the predecessor to the Hudson's Bay Company in the Columbia trade, the officer in charge of a post was referred to as the *bourgeois*. This term was continued by the French-Canadian *voyageurs* even after the Hudson's Bay Company and the North West Company united in 1821 when the English language predominated for business. The *voyageurs* crossed the continent from Lachine to west of the Rocky Mountains, holding positions named for their place in the canoe: *milieu* (middleman) for the unskilled, and *gouvernail* or *boute* (steersman) and *devant* (bowsman) for the more experienced. By 1830 the Company accounts were kept in English currency, although the letters mention livres, Spanish dollars, and French louis as well as the English pounds, shillings, and pence. Pay for these men ranged from £18 for inexperienced *milieux* to £26 for those with more years of service.

For delivery of parcels, letters, and gossip, family depended on the frequent Company expeditions between the west and home. One of the names most often mentioned was Joseph Morin, a recruiter for the Hudson's Bay Company, who worked in the Maskinongé region. He had travelled to the west on a contract in 1827, before returning to scour the village and environs for strong young men and to accompany them as a "goer and comer." Others mentioned were Henri Lacharité and Pierre Leclerc, as well as the unreliable Martin referred to in the letter to John McKay. For those on a farm in Lower Canada, the best news was the imminent return of a loved one from *le pays d'en haut* (the Upper Country), a term from French colonial times that was applied to the much larger region following the expansion west to the Pacific.

75 JOSEPH GRENIER: *Have you forgotten us and have you completely lost the memory of our tenderness to you in your youth?*

In 1815, at about eighteen years of age, Joseph Grenier had joined the North West Company bound for the Columbia Department as an inexperienced *milieu*. In 1818, after his three years of experience, he was promoted to a *devant*. On the merger of the North West and Hudson's Bay companies in 1821, he continued his work as a freeman, not under contract but serving when required. From 1824 to 1830 he was a middleman on Snake Country expeditions under Peter Skene Ogden, in the area bounded on the west by the Columbia River, on the south by the Spanish territories, on the east by the Missouri River, and on the north by the territories of Saskatchewan tribes. Their travels took them through Oregon, Idaho, and parts of Montana and Utah in 1824-5, when Joseph travelled with his gun, two horses, and four traps. In 1826-7 they travelled into northern California. Joseph's parents had not heard from their long-absent son since 1826 and, in their anxiety to reach him, they wrote three letters in April 1831. The first letter, carried by Henri Lacharité, was not among the undelivered letters but the second, entrusted to Pierre Leclerc, was.

∾ Monsieur Joseph Grinier, dans les Pays dans [d'en] Haut

Ruisseau des Chênes Avril 1831

  Mon cher fils
  je metes la main à la plume pour ma deuxieme lettre que je tenvoye une par Lacharité et celles ici par pierre Leclaire crainte que ma peremière ne se rand pas[.] je Reste dans l'espérance que ~~mon dieu~~ [crossed out] tu receveras cette present lettre et je te prie en grâce de ne point nous Enbandonnez pour toujour de tems [t'en] Revenir le plus vite que tu pouras parce que nous somme biens vieux et nous vous derions [voudrions] biens te voire avant que de ~~mourir~~ [crossed out] mourrire[.] revient donc Mon cher Joseph nous te receverons, les bras oûvert, nous panssons Continuellement a toi mon cher Enfans et nous ne manquons pas de prièr Dieu qu'il te conserve et quil te ramenne en core une fois voire ton peauvre vieux père et mère qui ont biens vérsé des larmes pour toi et qui en verse Continuellement Mais suivant les nouvelle que nous avons reçus nous Croions de te revoir bien vite
  Je fenis Chère Joseph en te Priant de tams [t'en] revenir cette année et nous ne manquerons pas de priers Dieu pour la ~~conversa~~ [crossed out] conservations De ta Santé et nous te donnons notre St Bénédiction en tembrassant [t'embrassant] Mille et mille foi ton tendre père et mère jusqu'a la mort
  Joseph et Marie Grinier
Tous tes Oncles & tantes et frères et Soeur tams brasse [t'embrassent] de tous de leur coeur et te Souhaite une bonne Sansté et espère de te revoir biens Vite
  Adieu Cher Joseph
  Je sui ton père
  Joseph Grinier

Mr. Joseph Grenier in the "Pays d'en haut" [Upper Country]

Ruisseau des Chênes April 1831

My dear son

I take my pen in hand for the second letter that I am sending you, one with Lacharité and this one with Pierre Leclaire, for fear that my first won't arrive. I continue to hope that you will receive this letter and I entreat you not to abandon us forever. Come back as soon as you can because we are quite old and we are anxious to see you before we die, so come back, my dear Joseph, we will receive you with open arms. We think of you constantly, my dear child, and we will not fail to pray to God that He will keep you safe and lead you back again to see your poor old father and mother who have shed many tears for you and continue to shed them constantly. But according to the news we have received, we think that we will see you again soon.

I conclude, dear Joseph, in begging you to come back home this year and we continue to pray that God will preserve your health and we give you our holy benediction, embracing you thousands and thousands of times. Your affectionate father and mother till death

Joseph and Marie Grenier

All your uncles and aunts and brothers and sister embrace you with all their heart and wish you good health and hope to see you again very soon.

Goodbye dear Joseph,

I am your father

Joseph Grenier

By 20 April a third letter was sent containing more entreaties to return. His grandmother, Antoinette Marchand Sicard, was particularly anxious to see him before she died.

A Monsieur Joseph Grinier, a la Coulomierre

Ruisseau des Chènes 20ᵉ Avril 1831

Mon cher fils

s'est pour ma troisième lettre que je tems voye [t'envoie] de pui [depuis] que j'ai Reçus ta lettre voila cinq ans[.] c'est la [là] la dernièr de tes nouvelle Excepté que Lacharite ma raporté des nouvelle de toi[.] je ta sur [t'assure] Cher Enfant que tu nous cause beaucoupe d'ennui et de chagrin sur nos vieu jour de voir notre cher Enfan que nous avons tems [tant] eu de peine à Ellevé et croyant avoir du Soulagement et la consolation de lui et a present de le voir si Elloignée[.] Cher Enfan nous atû [as-tu] oublier et a tu perdu

le Souvenir de notre tendress enver toi dans ta jeunesse[?] Croi moi Cher
Joseph, moi et ta peauvre mère te Disirons bein de te revoir en cor [encore]
une foi a vant [avant] que de mourrir parce que si tu ne dessent [descends]
pas bien vite tu pouroit bien pas nous voir vivant parce que nous tasurons
que nos peauvre cheveux on biens blanchie de pui que tes [t'es] partie
d'avec nous[.] Prand donc courage revien don nous voir Encor une foi nous
te recevrons les bras oûvert et ton arrivée pouroit petaitre bien nous faire
vivre ~~qu'el~~ [crossed out] quelques année de plus par la joi que tu nous
Causcrai dc tc rcvoir et ta peauvre Grande mère Sicard qui est agé apresent
de Quatrevingt Neuf ans[.] Elle dit toujour quelle demande à Dieu de te
revoir devant que de mourire et Elle tams brasse biens et Ell prie Dieu pour
toi que Dieu te fase Connoitre le Devoir que tu doit a ton cher Père et
Mère[.] Cher Enfant si Dieu te fait la grâce de tems [t'en] revenir je te prie
une foi que tu se ras [seras] a Montreal tu ~~poun~~ [crossed out] pouras
Embarqué a bord du b[atime]nt a feu pour te mener a Sorel et une foie a
Sorel tu te feras amener au Grand Yamaskas et la tu trouveras bien etoû je
reste[.] je Reste au ruisscau dcschèncs

    Cher Enfan nous fenisson moi et ta Mère en tams brassant [t'embrassant] du
profond De notre coeur et nous te Donnons notre St. Bénediction et nous
obliron pas de prier dieu pour toi qui te fasse la grace de revenir En bonsanté

    Tous tes frères et Soeurs et Oncls et tantes tambrass bien et te fond bien
leur Compliment

        Je Suis ton père jusqu'a la mort
        Joseph Grinier

To Mr. Joseph Grenier in the Columbia

Ruisseau des Chênes 20th April 1831

    My dear son

    This is the third letter that I am sending you since I received your letter
five years ago. That was the last we heard of you, except for the news that
Lacharité told me about you. I assure you, dear child, that you cause us a
great deal of worry and concern in our old age to see our dear child that we
took so much trouble to raise and believing that he would give us care and
consolation and now to see him so far away. Dear child, have you forgotten
us and have you completely lost the memory of our tenderness to you in
your youth? Believe me, dear Joseph, I and your poor mother want very
much to see you once again before we die because if you do not come
home quickly, you could well not see us alive because we assure you that
our hair has gone quite white since you left us. So take courage, come
home and see us again. We will receive you with open arms and your

arrival could well help us to live a few years longer because of the joy that you would give us and your poor grandmother Sicard who is now eighty-nine years old. She always says that she asks God to see you before she dies and she embraces you and prays God for you that God will help you to recognize the duty that you owe to your dear mother and father. Dear son, if God grants you the grace to come back, once you are at Montreal you could board a steamboat to take you to Sorel and once in Sorel you can get to Grand Yamaska and there you will easily find where I live. I live at Ruisseau des Chênes.

Dear child, we end, your mother and I, in embracing you from the depths of our heart and we give you our holy benediction and we will not forget to pray to God for you that He will grant you the favour to come back in good health.

All your brothers and sisters and uncles and aunts embrace you and send their compliments,

I am your father till death

Joseph Grenier

Only the second and third letters were returned to London to be filed in the Company secretary's office but neither would have reached their son. On 3 July 1830, long before this letter was written and started its long overland journey from Lower Canada to Fort Vancouver on the west coast, Joseph Grenier had drowned along with eight of his fellow countrymen. The incident was described by James Hargrave:

This misfortune occurred at a place where our Boats passed and repassed every year since the Columbia Trade is established and was never considered to be a place of danger, the Brigade this year happened to meet Mr. Ogden half an hour after the accident and went up in perfect safety. In fact, the accident proceeded from the people getting allarmed and loosing their presence of mind, a whirlpool caught the Boat and instead of the men springing to their paddles to pull her out they dropt them and she went down by the stern.

Peter Skene Ogden himself gave a more dramatic and complete account:

It was in the summer of 1830 that I arrived at the Dalles [falls on the Columbia River above Fort Vancouver] on my return to Vancouver, after an absence of eleven months, spent in scouring the prairies in quest of beaver. I had a small party of trappers under my command, and having left our horses at Walla Walla, where a crazy boat had been furnished us, we had reached thus far on our descent, without an accident of any moment, and in eager anticipation of a speedy restoration to our friends. Exhilerated by such a prospect, the natural vivacity of the Canadian voyageurs, increased to ten times its usual vigour ... The heat was intense; and though the breakfast hour was gone by, the stench of putrifying salmon was so overpowering, that I resolved on proceeding a few miles lower down, before taking my morning repast. Accordingly the men were directed to push off and prepare for this important event of the day, at a spot indicated, while I resolved to saunter downward by land. Little did I then anticipate the sequel. Scarcely had I set out, when the men put forth and began steering in an oblique direction across the stream, in order to avoid a string of whirlpools that for a short distance impeded the direct navigation; and as the boat shot majestically onwards, I half repented my resolution of walking, envying the swan-like ease with which she appeared to descend, so contrasted with my own fatiguing progress. Suddenly, however, the way of the boat was checked; so abruptly, too, that the rowers were nearly thrown from their seats. Recovering their equilibrium, they bent to their oars with redoubled energy, but the craft yielded nought to their endeavours. The incipient gyrations of a huge whirlpool at the same instant began to be felt, holding the boat within its influence. The vortex was rapidly forming, and the air was filled with a confused murmur, high above which might be heard the hoarse voice of the bowsman, shouting "Ramez, ramez, ou nous sommes pais [possibly péris]!" [could be translated as "Row, row or we shall perish!"] The danger became momentarily more imminent; there was no longer any doubt of the sad mischance which had befallen them, for yielding to its fatal attraction, the boat glided, at first slowly, into the whirling vortex; its prow rising fearfully as the pitiless waters hurried it round with increasing velocity.

Is it surprising that I grew dizzy and faint as I gazed, until at length one wild, long cry warned me that all was over, and suddenly restored my senses to their activity? Alas! To what purpose, save an overpowering sense of grief, was the restoration of my faculties of thought!

Utterly incapable of rendering assistance to my drowning companions, I stood a helpless spectator of the scene. The spot where the boat had disappeared, no longer offered any mark whereby to note the sad catastrophe that had even now occurred there, the vortex was filled up, and its very site was no longer distinguishable; for awhile it was more like a dream than a real occurrence, so little vestige appeared of the life-struggles which had just taken place. A few minutes more, and the paddles, sitting-poles, and various other articles of a buoyant nature, were cast up in all directions around, while here and there, a struggling victim was discoverable, hopelessly endeavouring to evade the fate that awaited him. One by one they disappeared, drawn down by the lesser vortices that continually formed, and again as speedily filled up, in the environs of the catastrophe. After a brief interval, nought was to be distinguished but the now mournful rushing of the waters, and I sat down with the consciousness of being left, in the fullest sense, alone. ([Ogden] 1853, 165-9)

By 1832 Joseph Grenier's father wrote another letter, this time to the Hudson's Bay Company's Montreal offices and so not among the undelivered letters.

Au Bureau des Bourgeois des pays d'en haut à la chine ou à Montreal
[in another hand] rec[eive]d 11th

Ruisseaux des Chènes Township D'Upton 5 Fevrier 1832

Messieurs de la société je madresse avous en vous Suppliant de bien vouloire me donner des nouvelle de mon Garçon, qui est a votre Service de pui [depuis] l'annéé 1815, je sais bien que la premiere annéé il à été hiverné a la rivier de la Colombier, d'arier la Montagne de Roche, et l'an 1830 il sétoit encor la [là] Comme chasseur libre, et son nom est Joseph Grinier, voyla cinq mois que jai apprie qu'il esttoit mort voyla pourquoi Messieurs que je madresse a vous pour savoir ci cela est vrai et je vous prie bien de m'endonner des connaissance, si c'est une Effet de votre bonté et en le faisant vous me rétirerez d'une grand inquiétude de Sur mes vieux jours
    Messieurs je rest avec les plus grand réspects qui vous son due
        Votre Serviteur
        Joseph Grinier
    Père de Joseph Grinier
    qui est où qui a été a votre Service

To the Office of the Bourgeois of the Upper Country at Lachine or at Montreal
[in another hand] rec[eive]d 11th

Ruisseau des Chênes, Upton Township, 5 February 1832

Gentlemen of the Society, I address you humbly requesting that you give me news of my son, who has been in your service since 1815. I know that the first year he wintered at the Columbia River, beyond the Rocky Mountains, and in the year 1830 he was still there as a free hunter, and his name is Joseph Grenier. It has been five months since I learned that he was dead. That is why, gentlemen, I address you to know if it is true, and I beg you to give me any information, if you would be so kind, and in doing this you would lift a great burden from me in my old age,
    Gentlemen, I remain with the greatest respect that is due to you,
        Your servant
        Joseph Grenier
    Father of Joseph Grenier
    Who is or who was in your service

No letterbooks for Montreal survive for that date but calculations in the margin show "£25.9.9 – £8.18.9 = £16.11.0," which may indicate the money that the Montreal office thought was due the father. However, investigation in the Columbia accounts reveals there was another heir. Joseph Grenier had married Thérèse Spokane, a woman of the Spokane tribe, according to the custom of the country. She and their young daughter, Marie-Anne, gradually spent the credit due to Joseph Grenier. By 1839 the account was empty and Thérèse married Joseph (Pierre?) Cournoyer, a new provider for herself and her children from two previous marriages. The Company had an established practice of dispensing funds of deceased employees for the needs of their Aboriginal families so that they would not become dependent on the Company. With payments being made to Joseph's widow and family, nothing remained for the grieving family back in Ruisseau des Chênes, who may have been completely unaware of Joseph's family in the west.

76 JOHN MONGLE: *I assure you that nothing can delay my return once my time
     is up*

John Mongle (also known as Jean Monde) first joined the North West Company in 1816 at about fifteen years of age, and signed another contract in 1821 when the Hudson's Bay Company and the North West Company united. Just two years after marrying his second wife, Mongle decided to part with his wife and child to rejoin the Hudson's Bay Company in 1829. No doubt he was driven by a desire to make more money to support his growing family. Because of his previous experience, he was able to secure an appointment as a *boute*.

In her letter, written by a helpful scribe, Marie emphasized the need she had for her husband, not only for his companionship but also for the monetary support he could provide.

∾   a Jhon Mongall, Hudson bay

Maskinongé le 20 Avril 1830

Cher Epoux
La présente t['] apprendra que je suis en bonne santé Grace a dieu et je souhaite que la Presente ~~Vous~~ [crossed out] te trouve jouissant du même bonheur ~~et je souhaite~~ [crossed out]
tu ne doute cher Epoux que depuis ton Départ et que j['] ay passé des jour ennuyans depuis que tu est partie[!] enfin je ne feroit ta Discription de Mes inquiétude[s,] soit en seulement Persuadé[.] je n['] ait Rien de nouveau a te [dire] excepté que L['] anné Derniére a été bien dure et que le peu

d'argent que tu m[']a envoyer ~~mais~~ [crossed out] m[']a été bien favorable et
si tu peu m[']assisté encore tu me fera bien plaisir et je te prie de ~~Noil~~ [crossed
out] ne pas Retardé ton Retour et j[']espert que tu Reviendra au bout de
ton tems et cela me marquera que je ~~nespey~~ [crossed out] suis toujour ton
epouse[.] Recoit nos complimen[ts] de la part de ton beau frére Belisle et ta
soeur son epouse les quelle te salue et t[']ambrasse ainsi que tous les Gens
de l[']androit[.] enfin je n[']ait pas Recue les 15 franc que tu avois laissé a
chàtlin ainsi que le bled sarazin de charlette Belisle[;] il ne veut pas me les
donné[.] J'ay passé l[']ivert [l'hiver] ~~enplu~~ [crossed out] sans Misere Malgré
tout les tourment que tu ne doit pas douté – je n[']oublie pas toujour de
Prier dieu pour ta conservation et j[']espert que mes voeux seront exausé[.]
enfin Rien de plus nouveau a t[']apprendre excepté que ta soeur et ton beau
frére et tout leur Maisonne t[']ambrasse de tout leur coeur[.] enfin Recoit
les plus tendre Ambrassement d[']une epouse qui te cherir [chérit] (ainsi
que Mon petit Garcon) et qui n[']aspir [espère] que le Moment de te Revoir
personnelement pour te Marqué exterieurement ce que le papier ne peu que
supporté[.] enfin Adieu jusqu[']a ton Retour[.] je me dis Pour la vie ton
epouse fidelle

    Marie St jermin Epouse de Jhon Mongall
ton beau frére Belisle te prie de donnér au blanc Belisle tout ces Respect
ainsi que de son Epouse et il lui accorde sa Benediction et lui souhaite
toute sorte de bonne prosperité[.] Si tu peu m[']anvoyer quelque pair de
soullier ce me soilagera [soulagera]

To John Mongle, Hudson Bay

Maskinongé, 20 April 1830

    Dear Husband
    This is to let you know that I am in good health, thanks be to God, and
I hope that this finds you enjoying the same good fortune.
    You must not doubt, dear husband, that since your departure, I have
passed wearisome days since you have been gone. I will not describe my
worries, only you can be sure of them. I have nothing new to tell you
except that the last year has been very difficult and that the little money
that you sent me has been very helpful and if you can assist again you
would give me great pleasure and I pray do not delay your return and I
hope that you will come back at the end of your time and that will indicate
to me that I am still your wife. Receive our greetings on the part of your
brother-in-law Belisle and your sister, his wife, who greet you and embrace
you as do all the people in the neighbourhood. Finally, I have not received
the 15 francs that you left with Châtelain or the buckwheat from Charles

Belisle. He does not want to give them to me. I passed the winter without
misery in spite of all the torments, which you can imagine. I do not forget
to pray constantly for your preservation and I hope that my wishes will
be granted. So, no more news to tell you except that your sister and
brother-in-law and their whole household embrace you with all their
heart. So receive the most tender embrace from a wife who loves you (as
does my little son) and who waits only for the moment to see you again in
person to demonstrate to you what paper can only suggest. So goodbye
until your return. I will always be your loyal wife,

Marie St. Germain, Wife of John Mongle
Your brother-in-law Belisle asks you to give Blanc [Pierre?] Belisle all his
respects along with those of his wife and to convey his benediction and to
wish him every form of prosperity. If you could send me some pairs of
shoes this would assist me.

Marie's interest in receiving a few pairs of shoes was repeated in some of
the other letters to *voyageurs* (see Félix Lebrun and John McKay stories,
entries 78 and 80). These would have been moccasins, the sale of which
seems to have provided a welcome source of revenue for the families.

Months later Marie would have received a letter from her husband. Only
a week before she had sent her letter, he had an educated co-worker, possibly
Payette, who signed the postscript, record his longing to be with his wife.

Madame Marie St Garmain, Paroisse Maskinongé

Fort Colville 12 davril 1830

Ma tres cher Epousse

Cest avec boucoup d'annuit que j'ai attandu L'occasions qui Se presante
Par les voyageur[s] qui vont a Moreal [Montreal], pour vous informé
L[']état de de [repetition] Ma Santé qui est tres bonne Grace a Dieu
jusqu[']o [au] presant. Dieu veuille que La presante lettre vous trouve jouissant du meme bonneur [bonheur], je croit qui [qu'il] N'est Rien de plus
sansible que d'etre Separé du Person aussi cher que Son Epousse[.] aussite
je vous assur que Rien ne peut Retardé Mon retoure apres mon tems finis.
Je seroit flatte de Savoir si vous avez Recu ma lettre L'autonne derniere Par
Pierre Delard, et par cete meme Raison Si vous avez Recu La lettre vous
M'enformerez si vous avez Retirez 3 Louis au Bureaux de la Compagni[e]
de la Bay Douson [Baie d'Hudson], et si vous l[']avez Recu Marqué Moi le
dans votre lettre en Ser fin que je puisse en tenir Compte et j'ai Laissez
pour vous, entre les main[s] de Mr Chattelin 12½ chelins pour vous
reMetre[.] enformé moi Si vous les avez Recu[.] je ne puis pas vous en

n['']anvoyez Cete Ané en Considération que mon Compt N'est pas ecite [icitte] et le Bourgois ne peut pas le fair sans voir Mon Compte. Mais vous pouvez ettre Sur pour L'anné prochaine car je vais prandre Mes precaution d'avance[.] je seroit flaté de Savoir Si vous ette enCor a la meme Place out je vous ait Laissez et si par Cas vous n'ette pas Sorti je seroit contant que vous puissez Restez jusqu['']a mon retoure. Le metre [maître] de La Maison ne perdras pas cest peine a mon retour des Soin qu['']il L'aura prit de vous. Mes Respect a mes Soeur et belSoeur, et tout ceux qu['']il s'informeront de Moi, en vous Souhaitant une perfaite Santé et que Dieu vous conserve en n['']atandant le Plaissir de vous voir

Je sui votre affectione et tendre epoux

John Mongle

Mr Pierre Bruneau m['']avais donné une Lettre pour Mr Kittson mais j'a eut le Mal'heur de La pirir en Chemin et par Cete Rayson [raison] il se trouve ausi avancé comme Moi votre Amis Payette

Marie St Germain, Maskinongé

Mrs. Marie St. Germain, Maskinongé Parish

Fort Colvile, 12 April 1830

My very dear Wife

It is with a deep longing that I awaited the occasion which presents itself by the voyageurs going to Montreal, to let you know the state of my health, which is very good so far, thanks be to God. I pray God that the present letter will find you enjoying the same happiness, I think that there is nothing more painful than to be separated from someone as dear as a wife, Also I assure you that nothing can delay my return once my time is up. I would be obliged to know whether you received my letter last autumn by Pierre Delard, and at the same time if you received the letter please tell me if you have withdrawn 3 louis from the offices of the Hudson's Bay Company, and if you have received it please let me know in your letter so that I can take it into consideration, and I left for you, in the hands of Mr. Châtelain, 12½ shillings to give you. Let me know if you received it. I cannot send you any this year since my account is not here and the bourgeois cannot do it without seeing my account. But you can be sure for next year because I will take my precautions early on. I would be obliged to know if you are still in the same place where I left you and if by any chance you have not left, I would be pleased if you could stay until my return. On my return, the master of the house will be compensated for the pains he will have taken in your care. My respects to my sister

and sister-in-law, and all those who ask for me, wishing you perfect
health and that God preserves you while waiting for the pleasure of
seeing you

   I am your affectionate and tender spouse
      John Mongle
   Mr. Pierre Bruneau gave me a letter for Mr. Kittson but I had the bad
   luck to lose it on the way and for that reason he is just as informed as I
   am. Your friend Payette
Marie St. Germain, Maskinongé

By early 1832 Marie had heard rumours that her husband was dead and
wrote to the Company for confirmation. She included the letter from her
husband as proof of her claim to his estate. It may be that the Company's
records, which showed his name as "Jean Monde," delayed the official news
from reaching her ears sooner. This time the letter was written by a less
skilled hand, perhaps by Marie herself, and it reached its destination.

[postal mark] Berthier 13 Jan, (rec'd 14th)
au Burau de L'honoraBle Compagnie de la Bay hudson, LaChine, Montréal

Maskinongé, 13 Janvier 1832

   Messieurs
   Comme voyla plusieur Fois que j[']ai entandu dire que john mongle
Mon marie et [est] déCédé au service de LhonoraBle Compagné de la Bay
hudson et que monsieur Morin m[']a fait dire dernierement qu[']il ettoit
noyer, j[']ai prie la liBerté de m[']adresser a vos honneurs Comme etant
malade et dans une grande miserre à la remerCie de tout le monde pour
[crossed out] C'est Ce quil m[']oblige de prier vos honneurs d[']avoir la
Bonté d[']examiner Les Compte pour voir s[']ils lui revient quelquechose a
seul fin de pouvoir me soulager et en meme temps pour prier humBlement
vos honneurs d[']avoir quelque egard a ma miserre[.] pour marque de la
vérite j[']ai mie devant vos honneurs une lettre que j[']ai reCu de lui en
1830 qui prouve que je suis veritablement que gerais [crossed out] son
épouse et en [mê]metemps je prient vos honneurs d[']avoir la Bonté de
m[']éCrire Ce qui en est pour savoir s[']il est mort ou vivant et d[']avoir
La Charité de Franchire la lettre de réponse voyant que je suis inCapaBle
de la retirez Messieurs je suis avec respect votre humBle servante
Marie S^{t} garmin epouse de john mongle Maskinongé
a L[']honorable Compagné de la Bay hudson

[postal mark] Berthier 13 Jan., (rec'd 14th)
To the office of the honourable Hudson's Bay Company, Lachine,
Montréal

Maskinongé, 13 January 1832

  Gentlemen
  Since I have heard many times that my husband John Mongle died in
the service of the honourable Hudson's Bay Company, and Mr. Morin
recently sent me the information that he drowned, I have taken the liberty
to address your honours, since I am sick and in great misery, under
obligation to everyone, which is what obliges me to ask your honours to
have the goodness to examine the accounts to see whether something is
owed to him, with the sole purpose of assisting me and at the same time to
beg your honours to have some regard for my misery. As an indication of
the truth [of my claim] I have placed before your honours a letter which
I received from him in 1830 which proves that I am truly his wife and at
the same time I beg your honours to have the goodness to write me what is
the situation so I will know if he is dead or alive and to have the charity to
pay for the letter of reply since I am not able to pay to receive it.
  Gentlemen, I am, with respect, your humble servant
  Marie St. Germain, wife of John Mongle, Maskinongé
  To the honourable Hudson's Bay Company

  During his time at Fort Colvile (Colville, Washington), John had made
himself useful repairing the bastions, taking down the windmill, and leading
various construction parties. On 25 October 1830 he and four other men
from the post had joined John Harriott and the Express in four heavily laden
boats that were "not over too well manned owing to the want of good
boutes." On 29 October, William Kittson, in charge at Fort Colvile, noted:
"Four of our men that accompanied the Express boat arrived from Okinagan, with the most unpleasant news of seven men drowned on their way
down below the little Okinagan dalles [falls]. Six of these poor unfortunates
were new comers from Canada, and the other was a most useful man of this
District by name Jean Monde. In addition to the above great loss several
pieces of provisions and leather were also cast away." Six months after the
couple had each sent off their letters, John was dead and unable to provide
for Marie and their son. In spite of his confidence that "nothing can delay
my return once my time is up," the treacherous waters of the Columbia River
had prevented him from joining his anxious family in Maskinongé (see also
Olivier St. Pierre and Félix Lebrun stories, entries 77 and 78, respectively).

77 OLIVIER ST. PIERRE: *The cruel misery that you endured in those miserable regions*

Olivier St. Pierre was about twenty-four years old when he came out to the Columbia in 1830 as a *milieu*. He wrote on 6 and 26 July 1830 and his letters were not reassuring to the family back home in Trois-Rivières. His wife, Eléonore Duplessis, whom he had married on 15 October 1827, wrote a letter full of concern, expressing her longing for an early reunion with her dear husband.

∽ Monsieur Olivier St Pierre, voyageur au font de la maire

trois rivière 28 Mars 1831

Mon Chere Marÿ

J'ai recu ta Lettre Datee du 6 de juliette *1830* qui m'a Caussez boucoup de Chagrin de scavoire La Cruel misere que tu endurais dans Ces miserables endroit[.] J['] ai ausi recu ta Lettre Datée du 26 ausi de Juliette dans lequelle tu ne me marques Point tems [tant] de Misere Mais Cela ne ma Point Consolez Car je scai tres bien et me figure bien la misere que tu a souffert depuis ce tem[p]s la[.] a Chere Marÿ je ne Croÿ Pas que tu doute de ma Peine et de mon annui [ennui] et de mon inquietude[.] sÿ je navais Pas Craint Les reproche Jamais je naurais Consentie a ton Depart. Je nest [n'ai] aucune Consolation – toujour dans la Peine et Lannui[.] Plus je vie et Plus je manui et Plus ma Peine est Grande[.] Cante [Quand] je Pensse quil faut que je ~~pens~~ [crossed out] Passe encore deux ans sans avoire le Plessire [plaisir] de te voire je m['] en deespere [desespère] que ce tems sera Long mais infin il faut que je me Conforme a La Volontez de Dieu et vive dans Lesperance que tu viendra ausitot ton tem[p]s fini[.] ah Chere Marÿ que rien ne t['] en enpeche de venire rejoindre une tendre Epouse qui ne vie que pour toi, Mon Chere Olivier, ma lettre me Laisse en assez bonne Santéz Grace a Dieu et je soihaite de tout mon Coeur qu['] elle te trouve en bonne Santéz[.] Ce sont mes voeux et Prierres addressez aux tout Puissant tout Les jour infin [à fin] quil te Conserve et me fasse la Grace de te ramenere a moi[.] tache donc Chere mary de menagere autant quil te sera Possible infin de ne Point tendeptere [t'endetter] et que tu Puise revenire ausitot ton tems fini[.] Je suis toujour residente Chez jos morise jusqua Present, a mes Propre depend [dépenses][.] j['] ai eu la Chance davoire toujour de L['] ouvrage[.] avec Les 5 Loui[s] que tu m['] a envoÿez Pour n['] etre aux depend de Personne quo [qu'aux] Mien[.] J['] ai recu Les 5 Loui[s] que tu m['] a envoÿez a la fin de Novembre[.] tout tes freres et

Souers jouise d[']une bonne Santez et te font Leurs Compliments, ainsi que
Papa et Maman et mes freres et ma souer et bel souer te soihaite une bonne
santez et te font Leurs Compliments et serai tout Content sÿ tu etais ici
avec nous[.] J[']ai de Nouveaux a t[']aprendre que Dollé Precour est Mariez
avec Lariviere du 15 de Novembre, et ausi ton amÿ Abraham est Mariez
avec Caliste [H]amlin du 28 Novembre et ausi Esther Dugre Mariez avec le
veuf frere Cormier le 14 de janvier *1831* et ausi olivier Barbinat mariez avec
toutou Placé[.] tu scara Pour triste Nouvelle que ta Pauvre Morisson est
devant Dieu elle est Decedée dans le mois de Maÿ[.] tu scara ausi que
Baulac qui a Desertez davec vous autres na eu Pour toute Punition que un
mois de Prison et rendre Largent quil aves [avait] recu[.] Chere marÿ tu me
marque dans ta derneir Lettre que sÿ je nest [n'ai] Point assez de 5 Loui[s]
de te le marquere et que tu menvoyera Plus mais Je Prefere que tu menvoÿe
encore moin Pluto [plutôt] que de dendebter la et que tu ne Puis Pas
revenire[.] ma misere ne sera Point sÿ [si] Grande ici Comme la tienne[.]
tache de faire en sorte de ne Point dendebter la infin de tanrevenir ausitot
ton tems fini – tout Parent et amÿ te soihaite une bonne santez et te font
Leurs Compliments[.] Chere marÿ je fini en esperant de tes Nouvelle Par
ecri ausitot quil sera Possible[.] recoi Les enbrassements dune tendre et
fidelle Epouse Nelleÿ St. Pierre

Mr. Olivier St. Pierre, Voyageur at the ends of the sea

Trois-Rivières 28 March 1831

My Dear Husband

I received your letter dated 6 July 1830, which caused me a great deal of
grief to know the cruel misery that you endured in those miserable regions.
I also received your letter dated the 26th, also of July, in which you did not
report as much misery, but that did not console me at all because I know
very well and I can well imagine the misery that you have suffered since
that time. O dear husband, I do not believe that you doubt my own pain
and anxiety and uneasiness. If I hadn't feared reproach I would never have
consented to your departure. I have no consolation and am always in pain
and anxiety. The longer I live, the more I worry and the greater is my pain.
When I think that I must pass two more years without having the pleasure
of seeing you, I despair that the time will be long, but in the end I must
bend to the will of God and live in hope that you will come home as soon
as your time is up. O dear husband, let nothing prevent you from coming
to rejoin a loving wife who lives only for you. My dear Olivier, my letter
leaves me in pretty good health, thanks be to God, and I hope with all my
heart that it finds you in good health. These are my wishes and prayers

addressed to the Almighty every day, that He will protect you and grant me the favour of leading you home again to me. Try then, dear husband, to save as much as possible so you will never go into debt so that you can come back when your time is up. I am still living at present with Joseph Maurice at my own expense. I have had the good fortune to still have work, along with the 5 louis that you sent me so I would never have to be dependent on anyone other than myself. I received the 5 louis that you sent me at the end of November. All your brothers and sisters enjoy very good health and send their greetings, as do Papa and Mama and my brothers and my sister and sister-in-law wish you good health and send their greetings and all will be happy when you are here with us. I have some news to tell you, that Dollé Précourt has been married to Larivière since 15 November and also your friend Abraham [Pierre-Jean] married Calixte Hamelin 28 [actually 22] November and also Esther Dugré married the widower [Pierre] Cormier 14 [actually 17] January 1831 and also Olivier Barbinat married Toutou Placé. You should know for sad news that poor Morison is in the presence of God, she died in the month of May. You should also know that Beaulac, who deserted from your crew, had for full punishment only one month in jail and the return of the money he was paid. Dear husband, you say in your letter that if I don't have enough with the 5 louis that you will send more, but I prefer that you send me less rather than indebt yourself so that you can't come back. My misery will never be so great here as yours. Try to arrange things so as never to indebt yourself there so you can come back as soon as your time is up. All your relatives and friends wish you good health and send their compliments. Dear husband I end hoping to hear your written news as soon as possible. Receive the embraces of a loving and faithful wife, Nelly St. Pierre

Nelly's comments on the deserter, Beaulac, point to the difficulties that the Hudson's Bay Company had at this time in obtaining and keeping men. In 1830 François Boucher and Joseph Morin were busy recruiting in Maskinongé and their letters to James Keith in the Company's Montreal office reveal the challenges they encountered. Two men who had deserted the year before were arrested in April but one escaped across the Chenaille du Nord road, a winter road over frozen water that was less than about 1.5 metres (4.5 feet) deep at the time, and "could not be taken." The other man avoided prison because he was "a minor under the care of his Tutor, who did not consent to his Engagement." The best deal that Boucher could get was to have the Company's advances paid back by the tutor. By the end of May, Boucher had heard from the magistrate that the worst punishment two other deserters would get was to "be kept in gaol for a fortnight and after the only recourse is by Civil action against them, which would be of very little advantage." By the middle of June one deserter had a certificate of illness, and three others were at work on the Lachine or the Rideau canals. In spite of a great deal of effort, none of the men was punished. The Company could only try to recover expenses and get the men to replace themselves with able-bodied recruits.

Heriette Duplessis added to her sister Nelly's letter her own incentive in an attempt to encourage Olivier to make a hasty return.

～ Mon Chere olivier vous scaurez que je ne suis Pas encore mariez[.] je vous avez Promis de vous attendre Pour mes Noces et je Croy bien vous attendre ausi ce sera Pour votre arrivez[.] votre affectionez bel souer heriette Duplessis

My dear Olivier, You will know that I am not yet married. I promised you that I would wait for you for my wedding and I believe I will wait as long as it takes for your arrival. Your affectionate sister-in-law Heriette Duplessis

Unfortunately, the cruellest misery that Olivier would endure in what his wife termed "those miserable regions" was death. On 25 October 1830, he drowned in the Columbia River along with five of his companions who were just arriving in the west, and one man who had come the year before. (See also the stories of John Mongle and Félix Lebrun, entries 76 and 78, repectively.) The incident was described in a letter from the chief factor at Fort Vancouver, John McLoughlin, to the Company's governor and committee in London:

Mr. Harriott arrived here on the morning of the 2nd Inst. and I am sorry to state had the misfortune to lose seven men drowned in a Rapid below Okanagun Dalles; the place has been always considered sufficiently safe to run with loaded Boats, in this instance there were four Boats in company, the three first past safe and were allowing themselves merely to drift with the current till the fourth came up as by getting in a whirlpool she had fallen a little behind. But the next Rapid is so nigh the one the Boat wrecked in that the three first were in it before they saw the wrecked Boat which was drifting along with two men on the bottom of it; the first Boats immediately put ashore and the men dispersed themselves along the beach to see if they could give assistance, but to no purpose as they saw none of the crew except the two in the Bottom of the Boat who were saved, and the Steersman who had jumped out of her and swam ashore.

Whether or not Nelly was able to live on in Joseph Maurice's home, she would have had even more reason to regret that she did not protest more vigorously against Olivier's decision to leave her.

78 FÉLIX LEBRUN: *When you come back we can come to an agreement
between us*

Félix Lebrun was almost twenty-three years old when he went out in 1830,
with a number of others from Maskinongé, as a *milieu* to the Columbia
Department in the Hudson's Bay Company's service. He had written to his
family on his arrival and his letter was delivered when Henri Lacharité
returned in the fall. Félix had described his trip out as a pleasant one, unlike
John Mongle's a year earlier and Olivier St. Pierre's the same year (entries 76
and 77, respectively).

Monsieur Felix Lebrun, à la Coulombière

Masquinongé 19 avril 1831

    Chère frère
    Nous avons eiu [eu] le plaisir de recevoir ta lettre lautonne dernière
par Monsieur Henry Lacharité Ce qui nous à fait beaucoup de plaisir
d'apprendre par ta lettre que tu jouissait d'une par faite santé, et que tu
avait fait une monté heureuse ce qui nous afait aussi bien du plaisir car
pense que papa et maman était bien en peine de toi de te voir partir pour
aller aussi loin, ainsi nous te souhaitons une parfaite santé et que tu te
comporte toujours comme un honnéte homme [undeciphered word
crossed out] et nous Espérons que tu conservera ton butin, et nous
Espérons de te voir au bout de tes trois ans, et je tapprend que jai
embandonné ma cléricature, et je part au commencement de mai pour
m'en aller resté Commis à québec chez Monsieur Eugène Trudeau, et je n'ai
rien de nouveau à tapprendre que nous jouissons tout d'une parfaite Santé,
et toute la famille se joignent toute amoi pour te faire leurs humble respect,
et je tapprenderez que Capitaine est en famille d'une belle fille, et elle est
agé de huit mois, et elle petit [crossed out] est grosse et grasse et elle est
bien eveillé, et le petit Garçon de Louis est mort le vingt de juillet dernier,
et nous avons rien de nouveau à tapprendre, papa et maman jouisse d'une
bonne santé et il se joignent amoi pour te faire leur respects,
    ton tendre frère
    David Lebrun
N.B. et nous avons pas reçu aucune nouvelle de moise que par ta lettre,
Magdeleine et St Pierre te font bien leur respect – DL
N.B. nous avons reçue par Henry Lacharité les souliers que tu nous à
Envoyé et nous en avons donné une paire à Louis Paquin tel que tu nous à
Ecrit, et mademoiselle Leclaire est ici présente et elle te fait bien ses respect,
et nous avons donné une paire de soulier à St Pierre Comme tu lavait dit à

Henry, et papa te donne sa Bénédiction et il souhaite que tu te comporte
toujours bien, et si tu nous Ecrit cette autonne, Écrit nous si tu as réçue de
largent de Francois Ayot, car il nous à dit qu'il t'avait donné cinq piastres et
dit nous si tu en à reçu oui ou non car il ne veut pas payer, et nous osons
pas le poursuivre mais Ecrit nous si tu as reçu de largent de lui nous le
poursuivrons pas quau retour de ta lettre, et ne cache rien si tu en à
reçu dit le,   D.L.

Mr. Félix Lebrun, in the Columbia

Maskinongé 19 April 1831

   Dear brother
   We had the pleasure of receiving your letter last autumn through Mr.
Henri Lacharité, and it gave us a great deal of pleasure to learn by your
letter that you enjoyed perfect health and that you had a good trip, which
made us very happy because you can imagine how worried Papa and Mama
were to see you leave to go so far away, so we wish you perfect health and
that you will always act like an honest man and we hope that you will keep
your booty and we hope you will bring it back at the end of your three
years, and I must let you know that I have abandoned my clerical training,
and I am leaving at the beginning of May to go to stay in Quebec as a clerk
at Mr. Eugène Trudeau's and I have nothing new to tell you except that we
all enjoy perfect health and the whole family joins with me in sending their
humble respects and I will let you know that Capitaine has a beautiful
daughter and she is eight months old and she is big and fat and well
brought up and Louis's little boy died the twentieth of July and we have
nothing new to tell you, Papa and Mama enjoy good health and they join
me in paying you their respects,
   Your affectionate brother
   David Lebrun
N.B. and we have received no news of Moise except by your letter,
Magdeleine and St. Pierre send you their regards – DL
N.B. We received the shoes you sent us by Henri Lacharité and we have
given a pair to Louis Paquin just as you wrote, and Miss Leclaire [Leclerc?]
is here and she sends her respects and we have given a pair of shoes to St.
Pierre as you said to Henri and Papa gives you his blessings and he hopes
that you will always behave well, and if you write to us this autumn write
whether you received money from François Ayot, because he said that he
gave you five dollars and tell us whether you received it or not because he
does not want to pay and we do not want to pursue it but write us if you

received the money from him. We will not pursue it until your return letter, and do not hide anything, if you received it say so, D.L.

In the next letter to Félix Lebrun, we have a glimpse of the challenges the *voyageurs* faced in managing their affairs of the heart.

A Mʳ felix LeBrun, voiageur, Dans dans la coulombier

Mas Kinongé Le 20 avril – 1831

Cher amie

Las presante ais pour t[']aprendre que je sui an [en] pare fétte [parfait] santé[.] jes pere [j'espère] que La pre sante [présente] te trouvéra de meme[.] popait [papa et] mamans ainsie que la famille te fon [font] dais [des] Compliment[.] je nais [n'ai] de nouvelle a taprandre [t'apprendre] que le plaisir de te revoir[.] â lé gare [à l'égard] de ce que tu m[']avais promie que tu soulagerai paupas [papa], tu ne l[']a pas fait mais comme je me trouve dans une grande nésésité j[']espere que tu pansera amois [moi] et que tu nousBlira [n'oubliras] pas de manvoiez [m'envoyer] ce que tu m[']avais promis et can [quand] tu re vinderas [reviendras] nous s[']arangeron Bien tous Lais [les] deux[.] tu métera [mettras] sa antre [entre] Lais [les] main de maurains [Morin][.] tache de ne pas mouBliez [m'oublier] je sui et seré [serai] toujours tonnamie [ton amie]

Daviede sigard

To Mr. Félix Lebrun, Voyageur in the Columbia

Maskinongé, 20 April 1831

Dear Friend

This is to let you know that I am in perfect health. I hope this finds you the same. Papa and Mama and the family send their greetings. I don't have any news to tell you, only the pleasure of seeing you again. In regard to what you promised me, that you would reassure Papa, you didn't do it, but because I find myself in great need, I hope that you will think of me and that you will not forget to send me what you promised and when you come back we can come to an agreement between us. You can put it in the hands of Morin. Try not to forget me. I am and always will be your friend,

Davide Sigard

If Davide Sigard's "grande nésésité" was more than financial need – perhaps it was even a pregnancy – she would wait in vain for help from

Félix. He could send neither money nor an explanation to her father. On 25 October 1830, not long after Henri Lacharité had left for Lower Canada with news of the successful trip out, Félix drowned in the Columbia River with seven others, including his fellow newcomer Olivier St Pierre and Fort Colvile labourer Jean Mongle (entries 77 and 76, respectively).

79 HERCULE LEBRUN: *You asked Mother to buy back the piece of land held by Louis Paquin. We bought it immediately*

Hercule (Louis-Hercule) Lebrun left his home in Maskinongé in the spring of 1830 to be a *voyageur* in the fur trade. Also among the new recruits taking the long trip across the continent was his cousin Félix Lebrun (entry 78). He would have laughed heartily if he had received the following whimsical letter from his nephew, Olivier Fizette. Not discouraged by a lack of news, Olivier laboriously wrote a warm letter to his beloved uncle for whom he had such good feelings. Through his letter, some of the petty grievances of a small town come vividly to life.

∾ Mʳ Hercul LeBrun, à la Coulombière

Maskinongé le 12 Mars 1831

Cher oncle
Les occasions sont si favorable que je ne puis m'enpécher de técrire; Ce n'est pas pour le grand nombre de nouvelles que j'ai a t'apprendre mais C'est seulement pour renouveller les bonnes amitiés que nous avons eus ensemble durant le tems que nous avons résidé pendant que tu étois en Canadas[.] La plus grande nouvelle que j'ai a te marquer C'est que tous le monde ont le nez au milieu du visages tous les maisons sont debouts et ont leur cheminés, les haches sont au bout de leur manches et les Chiens et chats ont la queues derier[.] Bigre a l'oeil plus Croche qu'a lardinaire, la pinepache fume dans la queue de sa pipe elle est engribouille avec josé dunard elle veut le faire pendre au bout de sa cheminé
Je crois que Cela est assez pour te faire rire[.] ma grande mére na pas perdu son sommeille. Papa et maman sont très bienportants et te font bien leur Compliments[.] aucune mortalité n'a été dans notre famille. Anastasie et Catherine se joignent a moi pour te saluer. Je demeure an attendant ton retour
Ton affectioné neuveux
Olivier Fizette

Mary Ann Harrier sent her husband, John, one of her many ringlets after receiving a lock of his "Beautiful hair," which she was glad to see had not yet turned grey (entry 48).

J.E. Holman, when she wrote to her brother Thomas in 1852, chose letterhead to remind him of their home in Harbledown (entry 71).

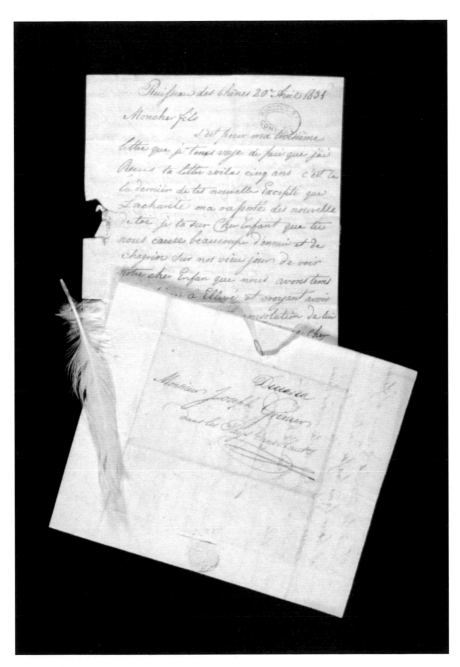

Two of the three letters written in 1831 by Joseph Grenier's father to his *voyageur* son, as well as the yellow feather enclosed, rest with the "undelivered letters" with the notation "Deceased" added in the hand of the Company secretary (entry 75).

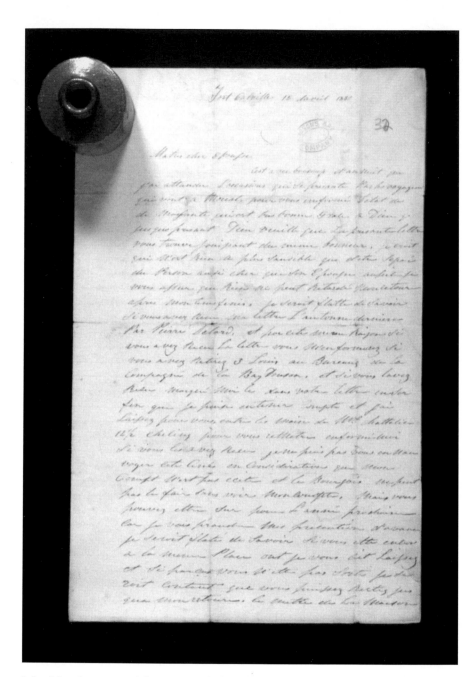

John Mongle sent word from Fort Colvile to his wife in Maskinongé, describing how much he missed her (entry 76).

Mary Macdonald sent her sweetheart, Allan McIsaac, a lock of her hair, though she did not have time to fulfill her promise to write her letter in blood (entry 87).

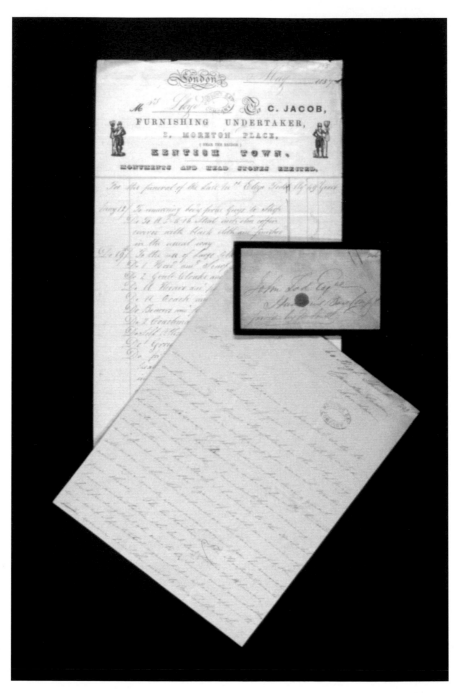

In 1857 Jane Lloyd, a friend of his wife in England, sent John Tod the sad news of Eliza Tod's death and the bill for her funeral expenses (entry 92).

Portrait of Chief Trader John Tod, shown with his books and a distinguished bearing (entry 92).

Mrs. John Tod, née Eliza Waugh (entry 92).

Sophia Lolo, the fourth Mrs. John Tod (entry 92).

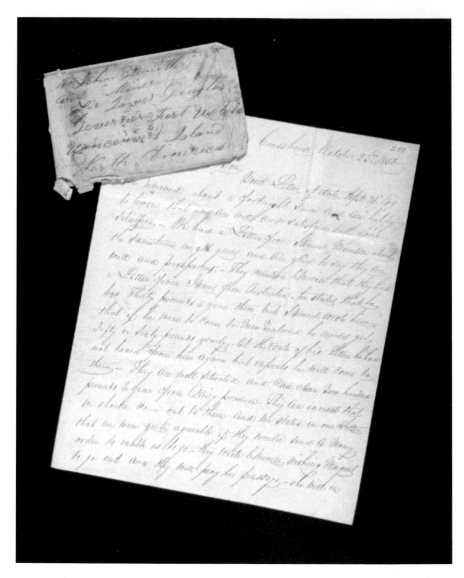

James and Agnes, parents of John Smith, one of the miners who deserted at Fort Rupert, wrote in 1850 of the many destinations for emigrants (entry 94).

The parents and girlfriend of farm labourer John Shadrach Blundell wrote letters in 1850 addressed to "Van-Covers Island" (entry 96).

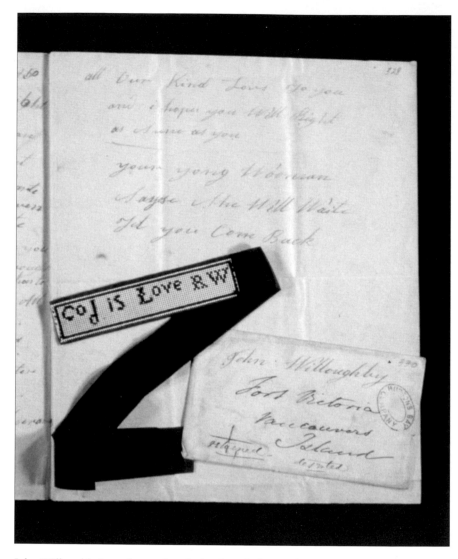

John Willoughby's mother enclosed a bookmark that read "God is Love" in her husband's letter to their absent son (entry 97).

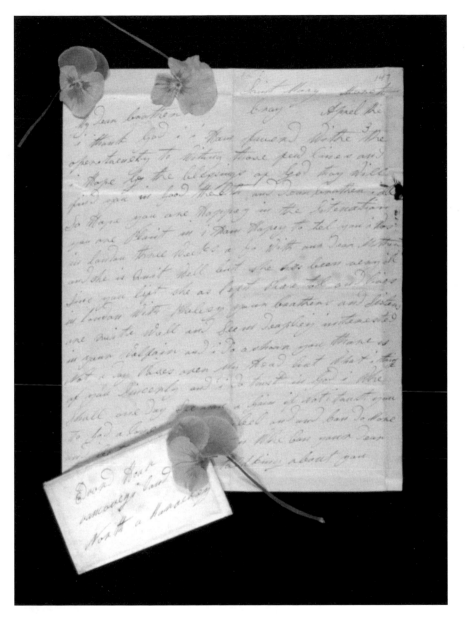

Sister Sarah's letter never reached Edward Hoare. He later deserted at Nisqually (entry 98).

In 1850, the passionate Anne Watters reminded Henry Horne of their time together in her garret in Kirkwall, Orkney. She worked hard at filling her large piece of paper (entry 104).

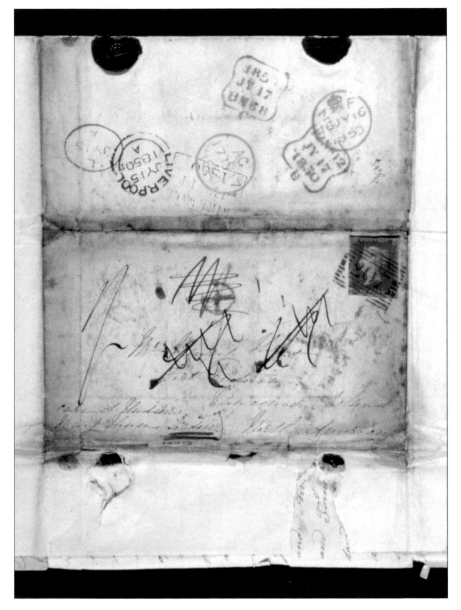

The cover of Anne's letter shows the many cancellations required and the recently introduced one-penny stamp (entry 104).

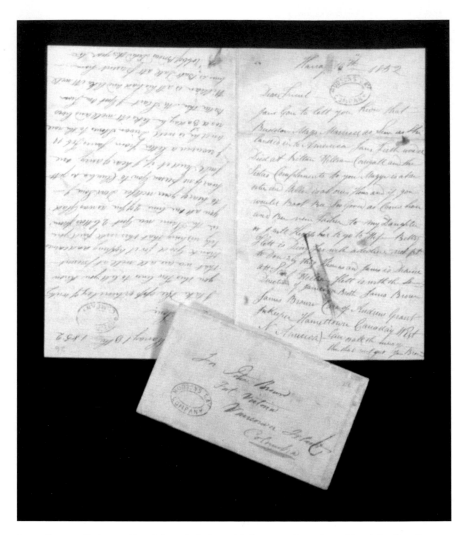

Peter Brown died near Fort Victoria before this letter, written by a friend for Peter's father, James, arrived. The friend attempted to separate her part of the letter by reversing the page when recording the father's words (entry 105).

Mr. Hercule Lebrun in the Columbia

Maskinongé, 12 March 1831

Dear Uncle

I cannot let this favourable opportunity pass without writing to you. It is not because of the amount of news that I have to tell, but just to renew the good relations we enjoyed during the time we lived together while you were in the Canadas. The most important piece of news I have is that everyone has a nose in the middle of their face, all the houses are standing and have chimneys, the hatchets are at the ends of their handles, and the cats and dogs all have tails behind. Bigré's eye is more crooked than ever. "La pinepache" smokes the stem of her pipe and is fighting with José Dunard. She wants to hang him from the top of her chimney.

I think that should be enough to make you laugh. My grandmother has not lost her sleep. Father and Mother are very well and send their greetings to you. No death has taken place in our family. Anastasie and Catherine join with me in greetings. I continue to await your return.

Your affectionate nephew,
Olivier Fizette

In contrast to his nephew's letter, the one from Hercule's eldest brother was all business. Thanks to the delivery services rendered by Joseph Morin, the family had received a letter, some money, and some curiosities from Hercule. Their mother had followed the instructions received in his letter and had used the money he sent to buy land. In fact, she wanted him to send even more money to buy the adjoining piece of land.

~ Monsieur Hercule LeBrun, voyageur, Rivière Colombia, Faveur de Mr Joseph Morin

Maskinongé ce 18eme avril 1831

Chèr frère

Je profite de la Bonne occasion de Mr Joseph Morin Cest pour te faire assavoir de mes nouvelles ainsi que ceux de la famille quels sont très bonne Dieu Mercie, et je souhaite que celle ci te trouve dans le pareille étât quel me laisse, Cher frère J'ose me flatté que tu dessendera aussitôt ton tems finis Car tu ne doute nullement que nous nous Ennuions Beaucoup de toi et nous t'attendont a grande hâte; nous avons reçu ta lettre du 10 Juillet 1830 qui nous a fait Beaucoup de plaisir t'apprendre le Comportement de ton voyage [insert: "qu'il a été très heureux"] et nous prions Dieu pourqu'il te conserve durant ton absence. nous avons aussi reçu quarante piastres d'espagnes de Mr Joseph Morin dont tu priait bien maman de vouloir retirrer ta part de terre que Louis Paquin Jouissait[.] nous l'avons retirrer immédiattement[.] nous avons reçu cinq paire de soulier moux et Cinq plume. maman désirerais bien ci cela t'était possible de lui envoyer 450 livres pour retirrer la part de terre que Moyse a vendu a Paquin dans la terre de chemin qui adjoint ta part pour la retirrer en ton nom et elle ne voudrait pas que tu t'endetterait au bourgeois pour en envoyer, nous avons satisfait Mr Eugène Trudeau pour ce que tu lui devait[.] nous avons aussi fait dire deux basses messes que tu demandait. Moyse voyage dans les chantiez Comme à l'ordinaire, Chs Fortier est gros marchand a St Léon et Louis Belmard est aussi marchand dans la maison de Mr Latourelle. David Lebrun est sorti de chez M^r St Antoine et moi je [crossed out] jy suis encore actuellement, aucune mortalité a t'apprendre, Rien d'autre Chose à t'apprendre tous tes parans et amis jouissent de bonne santé et je [crossed out] se joignent à moi pour t'assurer de leur meilleur amitié, nous avons un très beau poulin de l'année derrière et jespère que s'est toi qui le dontera[.] maman dort toujours à l'ordinaire[.] Félix est résidant à la maison et moy[se] lui a vendu ce qu'il avait et a présent il n'a pu rien du tout, je t'apprend que Emilie Vertefeuille est marié avec Pierre Peltier Cordonnier, Je te prie de me croire pour la vie[.] Je finis en te souhaitant toute sorte de bonne prosperité, je suis

    ton affectionné frère

    Ch^s M^tor Lebrun

    Clerc Notaire

Mr Hercule Lebrun, Colombia

Mr. Hercule Lebrun, voyageur, Columbia River, via Mr. Joseph Morin

Maskinongé, 18 April 1831

    Dear Brother

    I am taking advantage of the occasion presented by Mr. Joseph Morin to let you know my news and the family's, which is all good, thanks be to God, and I hope that this finds you in the same state that it leaves me. Dear brother, I dare to flatter myself that you will return as soon as your time is up because you cannot doubt that we miss you a great deal and wait impatiently for your return. We received your letter dated 10 July 1830 and it gave us great pleasure to learn that your trip was a good one and we are praying to God that He will keep you during your absence. We also received the forty Spanish dollars from Mr. Joseph Morin with which you asked Mother to buy back the piece of land held by Louis Paquin. We bought it immediately. We received five pairs of moccasins and five feathers [or possibly pens]. Mother wonders whether it is possible for you to send her 450 livres to purchase the parcel of land that Moise sold to Paquin that is in the road allowance next to your parcel so she can buy it in your name. She wouldn't want you to become indebted to your bourgeois in order to send it. We have paid Mr. Eugene Trudeau what you owed him. We have also had the two low masses said that you asked for. Moise travels around the lumber shanties as usual. Charles Fortier is an important merchant in St. Léon and Louis Belmare is also a merchant in Mr. Latourelle's place. David Lebrun left Mr. St Antoine's and I am still there. No deaths to tell you about and nothing else to tell you. All the relatives and friends enjoy good health and join with me to assure you of their best wishes. We have a very good young horse from last year, and I hope it is you who will break it. Mother sleeps normally. Félix lives at home and Moise has sold him all he has and now has nothing left. I must tell you that Emilie Vertefeuille married Pierre Peltier, shoemaker. Pray believe me for life, I end in wishing you good health, prosperity, I am

> Your affectionate brother
> Charles M^{tor} Lebrun
> Apprentice Notary

[To] Mr. Hercule Lebrun, Columbia

The 450 livres that his mother requested would have been a year's wages when £1 equalled 26⅔ Montreal livres. Unfortunately, Hercule did not receive either of the letters, nor his mother's request for money. It appears that the Company confused him with his cousin Félix, since the note on the letter read "deceased." In fact, he did not die but returned to Canada in 1833 and appeared on the Montreal pay list for 1833-4. His nephew would have been disappointed when he decided to return to the coast in 1845, taking a claim near the centre of the French prairie in 1849 and living his life as a US citizen, far from his family along the St. Lawrence River.

80 JOHN MCKAY: *I was anxious to know whether the trip had destroyed your health, but it seems not*

John McKay joined the Hudson's Bay Company as a *milieu* in 1832 at the age of twenty and set off on the long journey to the Columbia Department. A year later his friend wrote to send news and ask for money.

∿ Monsieur Jhan McKisse, Le Mer

York [St-Cuthbert] 12 avril *1833*

Mon cher enfant

Comme nous toublions point je prend plésir de técrire cette létre pour t'apprandre de nos nouvelle[.] nous Somme tous en bonne santé et nous éspéranrons que cette létre te trouve de même[.] j'ai été inquiete de savoir sie le voiyége tavais auté de la santé Mais il paroit que noms [non][.] je te remercy de la bonté de nous avoir envoisy les soulier et un tabliéz & par Martin Mais Ce Monsieur Sans disgrécé la pâte il na pas voulus les donné que les deux pere [paires] de soulier qui sont pas montrable pour être vilin[.] probablement Ce n'ai pas Seuse [ceux] que tu nous à envoiyéz[.] nenvois rien par lui[.] j'aime mieux que tu en profite Mais par monʳ Morin[.] Comme tu le proposais de nous envoiyéz de larjens tache de faire ton possible pour Menenvoiyéz tu Mobligera boucoup[.] Cest à quoi je Mattant[.] ton poulin est bien gras et bien portems nen soit pas inquiete jai Soint de tous Comme jespere te voir Comme tu me le promest que tu me trom[p]era pas nous t[']atendons

ton amie engelique prend la liberté de ce joindre à moi pour te faire Sést Meilleur amitié auses te dire qu[']el[le] ne t[']a pas oublier une instens depuis ton dépars aspère le momens de te voir elle te souaite une bonne sante

Fémé et ton firjousl [filleul] éndre t[']enbrasse bien[.] il perle souvent de toi insie [ainsi] que toute la famille et chez ton oncle fauteux parens et amie te fon tous leur Conpliments

Ma petite fille te fait bien Ses Conplimen moi et ma femme nous te fesons bien nos Conpliment

je suis et Ceré toute ma vie ton amie, endré blais

judique te souaite un bon voiage paradiz et sa femme te font leur Conpliment et tous les Seuse qui te connaise

Mr. John McKay, the sea

York [St. Cuthbert] 12 April 1833

My dear child

Because we do not forget you, I take pleasure in writing this letter to give you our news. We are all in good health and we hope this letter finds you the same. I was anxious to know whether the trip had destroyed your health, but it seems not. Thank you for your kindness in sending the shoes and apron etcetera with Martin, but this disgrace of a man wanted to give us only two pair of shoes which were not presentable because they are badly made. Probably they were not the ones you sent. Don't send anything else with him. I would rather that you profited, but with Mr. Morin. Since you suggested sending us money, try to do your best to send it to me, I would be much obliged, it is just what I need. Your young horse is fat and well, don't worry. I am taking care of everything because I hope to see you as you promised that you would not deceive me, we are expecting you.

Your friend Angélique takes the liberty of joining with me to send her love and also to tell you that she has never forgotten you one instant since you left and she is waiting for the moment when she sees you again. She wishes you good health.

Fémé and your godson André send their love. He often speaks of you as does the whole family and your uncle Fauteux's family, relatives and friends send their greetings.

My little daughter sends her greetings, I and my wife send you our greetings.

I am and will be all my life your friend, André Blais
Judique wishes you a good trip. Paradis and his wife send their compliments along with all who know you.

In spite of being tricked by Martin with worthless shoes – unsaleable moccasins – André still hopes to make a good deal for his friend if John could send shoes through the more reliable Joseph Morin. (Compare the Hercule Lebrun story, entry 79.) His main message, however, was for John to send money. John McKay never received the letter – perhaps the unusual spelling of his name (McKisse) on the cover confused the Company officers and prevented delivery. He did return to Canada in 1835 to join his family and friends and to get the news firsthand.

Letters to Men
at the Posts

The undelivered letters kept so carefully by the Hudson's Bay Company do not include very many addressed to regular employees of the continental fur trade. As these men were usually long-term employees, who rarely deserted to find other work or left in the middle of their contracts, their whereabouts were not often in doubt and their personal mail usually reached them. Letters to them from Europe normally arrived in North America – as did the men themselves – across the north Atlantic Ocean through Hudson Bay to York Factory rather than by the south Atlantic route around Cape Horn to the Pacific Ocean. Columbia Department postings that required travel with the fur brigades by way of the river routes and mountain passes, however, effectively separated the men from the east by distance and time, and the chance of mail not reaching them was greater.

The letters to these men show concerns similar to those in many other undelivered letters. In a few cases, because of the longer career spans of the Company men, we have more information about their lives and are able of offer more detailed narratives, such as the tale of Chief Factor John Tod and his several wives. As Orkneymen are as plentiful in this sample as they were in the regular ranks of the Company's employees, we have been able to access the excellent records of these island people to offer information on their lives after they left the Company service. The last three stories involve men who made the transition from commerce to settlement and who came to look on the west coast as home. Despite the small size of this sample of letters to Company men, they represent a wide range of company employees, from labourers to the founder of Fort Victoria, James Douglas – the man who was both an officer of the Hudson's Bay Company and governor of Vancouver Island and British Columbia.

81 WILLIAM JOHNSTON: *She is Waiting for your return*

William Johnston's father and sister, writing to him in 1834 and again a full year later, seemed to be unaware of the fact that William had crossed the continent to the Columbia Department. Their letter was addressed to York Factory in Hudson Bay – the Company's main supply point for the continental fur trade – which was thousands of kilometres east and north of where he served in the Columbia Department. William was hired as a labourer at York Factory in 1833 and went overland as a middleman with the brigade, to serve in the Columbia trade. The words "inland or Else-where" in their address cover half a continent. Many Orkney families were familiar with the Company's voyages into Hudson Bay; as William had entered the Company's service by that route, York Factory may have seemed the logical place for William's family to send their letters even though they may have known that he was headed inland. Both letters indicated the severe economic conditions that were the impetus behind many a man's decision to ship out to North America.

William Johnston, a servant to the Hudsons bay Company inland or Else-where, York-Factory

Kirkwal[l] Jun the 15 1834

Dear Son I tak this oper tunity to let you know that I am living yet but how long lord knows but your frend Jannet is dead[.] She died in the first of march on the 8 day and I was obleaged to to [repetition] Sel my watch to get har buried and it did not do then and I got your leter and george al at one time which was 4 and sixpence[.] their is one hundred and fifty as I hear that is dead hear Since new years day as I hear a great death hear indeed and an[n] and betty is to put letter to you and the whol family of Sav[e]ro[c]k Sends their Compliments to you and robert tullock and thomas flet[t] desires to be Remembred to you be Caus you did remember him in yours and betty bad me to send to you for one of your grand fidles but She is to wreat to you harSelf and ann and I have nothing to Say but you wil hear mor news or all that I Can give you[.] times is very dul at present and it wil be dul me al my time but Still my life must have alitle Suply[.] I have nothing mor to Say at present but I Still remains your father till death Hugh Johnston

When father Hugh remarked that he had to sell his watch to bury William's friend Janet, his son would certainly know how desperate things were at home. His sister Betsy's letter, written a year later, also went undelivered.

∽ To William Johnston, York Factory, Inland or elswhere

Kirkwall Jun 16ᵗʰ 1835

    Dear and Loving Brother

    I take this upportunity of writing you this few lines to let you know that I am in Good health at present thank God for it hoping this will find you the same – Dear brother I am but Poorly off at present my father is growing feeble he is not able to Work and I am not fit to hold the house but we must or b[e]li[e]ve to the hand of Profidence and fear God. And I hope so do you for it is him and him only that can sustain us. Dear Brother never forget that God is seeing you though you are far from me – Oh fear him in your heart and keep his Commandments and never for Get him and he will never forget you – Search the word of God and there you will [find] a Savour that will take you to himself if you will follow him – O William follow Christ with A Pure heart Seek the Lord while he may be found call upon while he is near let your heart Cleave unto Christ never forget him – Dear brother I was sory to hear that you did not like the country it may be dull but we cannot help it – let your Bible be your companion every day and remember what is said in it[.] Dear Brother remember me and I will remember you – never forget me. Dear brother, my Sister ann is still in Service – Shee is well at present – I have not much news to send you just now – but only Thomas Flett is Got married and is worth above A 100 Pounds – he is married with Elisabath Wishard [Wishart] – and is set up Marchant for himself – and Robert tullock is still with Mʳ Shearer's Shop he sends his Compliements to you – Along with Mʳ and Mʳˢ and also Ann Shearer's – and your frie[n]d William Clouston is listed for a soldier[.] he sends his Compliements to you – he is down here at Present listing men – and is a fine young man – Your brother Thomas is Got a daughter since he came home from America – and he is well and his wife[.] Your friend George he bron [Hebron] is no more. his Daughter Barbra sends her kind love to you – along with her Mothers – Your friend James Ewin's Tailor sends his best respectes to you and that he is well- Dear brother we are courting and that throng at present he is a fine lad and doing well – he has plenty of work – Dear brother all that I have said to you at Present never forget God

    I add no more at Present

      But remains yours for ever Betsy Johnston

Dear brother i did not remember to tell you that Barbra Coming [Cumming] is Got married with John Muir the Millers son they married this last winter[.] they have Got no family yet but it will be Coming soon – James and Cathring commin [Cumming] is not maried yet nor no word of it –

their love to you[.] Amelia Greig Sendes her best respects to you – and bids you mind on old times – along with her fathers and Mothers[.] william Couplan is Got married to Margret Flett – and also William Marwick is married – but there is no word of A man to your friend Barbra Hebron – She is Waiting for your return –

Sister Betsy's advice to let the Bible be his companion in fighting the dull employment in a strange country, her reminder that God is "seeing you though you are far from me," along with her news of other men's worth would have reminded William of the standards of moral conduct the family expected. She also likely intended to encourage him to gain some economic worth before he returned. Nevertheless the details of how other people were getting on with their lives back home must have made many men reflect on their lonely service in the new world.

William Johnston never found out that Barbara Hebron was waiting for his return since, the very summer his sister wrote urging him to fear God and carry on, he drowned at Fort George (present-day Prince George, British Columbia) on the Fraser River on 7 July 1835. His father would have to add him to the count of the people who had died that year, including the 150 in Kirkwall. But it was not until much later that Hugh was to know of his son's fate, probably because there were at least two William Johnstons, also Orkneymen, in the Columbia Department. Hugh wrote to the Company in December 1839 when he heard reports that his son had drowned: "You will do a poor man a particular favour if you will inform me what the Hon[ble] Company know of my son, and if there be any thing due him that it be remitted to me, as I am in great necessity." He received a reply that there were two men by that name and there was no remark against either of them. For the Company no news was good news. The news of the death should have come long before this time: as early as the spring arrivals of 1836 or at the very least by spring 1837. In September 1840 in response to yet another of Hugh's inquiries – his having received "verbal reports from different quarters" – the Company confirmed the death. The Company secretary asked for a certificate from a minister and a church elder to confirm that Hugh was the next of kin and that his son had died unmarried, before the father could claim the £10 10s. 4d. owed William in wages.

82 GEORGE LINTON: *Should it be the case that you should be angry with me do not let it be known that I asked such a thing*

George Linton began service in 1818 at the age of twenty-one as an apprentice clerk with the North West Company in the Athabasca District (now northern Alberta). He continued in that capacity three years later, when the Hudson's Bay Company took over the North West Company trade. He served at Fort Pelly in the Swan River District (in present-day Saskatchewan) and Fort Edmonton before being promoted in 1829 to clerk in charge at Fort Assiniboine, in present-day Saskatchewan. In 1832 Governor George Simpson described him in his typical blunt style as: "An Englishman (Londoner) about 36 Years of Age, has been 13 years in the Country. A stout strong square built fellow who would have made a very good figure in the 'Prize Ring' being an excellent bruiser; has a good deal of the Manner of a man accustomed to live by his Wits, and I suspect is out of a bad nest. A low Knowing Kind of fellow who is neither a good Clerk nor Trader. Useful however in many respects, but fully paid at £100 p. Annum. Has no prospect of advancement." Linton was a clerk in the New Caledonia District in what would become British Columbia, posted at Fort George on the Fraser River, when his sister wrote to him in early 1834 with the hope that he will help her to buy a house.

To the Honourable Hudsons Bay Company London to be forwarded
To Mr George Linton, Honourable Hudsons Bay Company, Hudsons Bay

March 2 1834

Dear George
You will prehaps think by this Letter that I beginning make applycation for the Support of my family but I can asure you it is not the case I have within myself some few Pounds which I have but these Several months and the use I was intending them to be put to was in purchasing a House but not making the Sum any more this while I am a fraid that I shall be obliged to alter my intention and pondering in my mind what way I would do for the best, thought I would Summon up a resolution and ask you if you would join with me in getting one, I will send you the papers of it and then you will not be I hope a loser by me but rent is a devouring or rather an eating thing and keeps me back[.] Houses here are very Cheap to purches but still brings the rent[.] try and do it for me and I shall be as thankful as if you had made me a present of it. Arthur knows nothing of this so should I not be favoured with what I have asked he can not laugh at me. I hope you are well I hope also you will excuse so much waste paper but the family ar not well except our little boy Called George Linton Douglas. I will take the house in your Name but I Canot say any more, but remain your affectionate
    Sister H.A. Douglas
if you send an answer direct for me Teacher Dalmellington, Scotland tell me how I am to act with respect to the Posting of your Letters –

I hope my dear George you will pardon me for the question or rather the favour asked of you by me but as I have no flattering nature to me you must take it as it is, it is the truth. I might have done better perhaps had I not have asked it but should it be the case that you should be angry with me do not let it be known that I asked such a thing.

You will see a number of errors likely but I have not been so fortunate as Betsy or you. all the Education ever I received was one year but I Now my deficency and inproved myself in all thing that I this day am Mistress of. I had no Person to go to but to the Lord to unbosom all my grief or make known my wants. I long for that day on which I may say Come into my bosom my Brother
adieu my [word scratched out]
Education: From Miss Watts Brixtan Surry

Linton's widowed mother was also seeking his assistance. Elizabeth Linton wrote four times to William Smith, the Company secretary, from Woolwich and later from Mr. Blandford's near the dockyard gate. In a formal petition in December 1836 she states that she is "Eighty years of age and quite without assistance and incapable of earning anything and that her Son did last year send her £25 to keep her from want and also express'd his intention by Letter of doing so yearly." In her March 1837 letter she again told Smith that she cannot work. Some money must have been advanced at that time, for she wrote again in July 1837 thanking the Company and asking for a little more, telling Smith "my money is gone to one shilling." A speedy reply from Smith acknowledged her letter and stated that he could offer her only £10 until "further measures are taken." These measures were necessary as a result of the death of George Linton in a drowning accident on 8 November 1835 on a rapid of the Fraser River between Fort George and Fort Alexandria (now Prince George and Alexandria, British Columbia). Archibald McDonald described the fate of Linton and his fellow travellers: "That poor Gentleman with his interpreter Westrape, their 2 wives & 4 children were drowned in Fraser R. last Novr on their way down to [Alexander] Fisher's in two small bark canoes" (Cole, ed. 2001, 113). As William Smith, the Company secretary, explained to Linton's mother, her son had left "some property in the Company[']s hands, fully sufficient, if he has not left a family, to make you comfortable for the remainder of your days; instructions have been sent to ascertain this point and as soon as an answer is received I will again write you."

The Company had become very careful, when disposing of deceased employees' property, to discover whether they were survived by Aboriginal wives and children. Company officials had inherited numerous problems of this nature as a result of the rather lax practices of the North West Company. The Company had established a policy to prevent a family at a trading post from seeking supplies, as it had when the Company employee was able to support it. In delaying the disposition of Linton's estate until he discovered that the man, his interpreter, and both their families had drowned in the accident, Smith was following this policy. As it turned out, Elizabeth Linton was granted letters of administration for her son's entire estate, a considerable £338 19s. 1d. As administrator of his estate, Elizabeth may well have given her daughter money for a house, if the sister once more worked up the courage to ask.

Two and a half years after George's death, in March 1838, the widow of Toule Whates told a very different story about George's "accidental" death to Alexander Fisher, who was in charge at Fort Alexandria. She had fled from her village to the fort in fear of her life after her own husband's death:

14 March 1838: I have a conversation with Toule whates Widow and she states that the deceased Linton and Family with Westyappe [the interpreter] and family were all murderd by Cheelquette & sons – Except Cousie & Toule whate who were not present at the time. It happen'd thus. The deceased Linton encamped a small distance below Cheelquettes Lodge about 30 or 40 Yards and slept there[.] that Westyappe early in the morning purchas'd a Dog from Kow na yelle but that the Indians was not satisfied with the payment and asked for more[.] that at this time the deceased Linton was on the eve of starting from his encampment[.] that Westyappe told the Ind[ia]n that he had paid enough for the Dog & at once killed the Dog to embark him [Westyappe] in the Canoe, that Kowna yelle said so you have killd my Dog well you shall die like my Dog too, and fired his Gun at Westyappe which kill'd him, that deceased Linton was in the act of taking hold of his Gun when Kow na yelle took another Gun from an Ind[ia]n standing by him and shot the deceased Linton also, that his Eldest Daughter seeing her Father drop run to him, then all the Ind[ia]ns fird at the deceased Linton and his Daughter was kill'd, that the Deceased Lintons Wife caught hold of her youngest child and made an attempt to run off with it, that Tzil tzie ran after her and ripped her open with a Dague and kill'd the Child with the Butt end of his Gun. by this time Westyappe's Wife had got into the Indian Lodges[.] that Est lay went after her into the Lodge and kill'd her with his Dague that after killing all of them, they were all thrown into the River and also all the property that Cheelquette said do not keep any of the property or else you will be found out, but still some little things was kept, that they washed the place where any Blood was spilt and also split the Canoe in two to make the whites believe that they were drowned. The next day Cheelquette dispatched one of his sons la Tete Grise or Est lay to

Cousyies & Toule whates Lodge to tell the News and what had taken place, where this old Woman Toule whates Wife was & then & there she heard from Est lay what she now Relates – She also adds that after her Husbands Death (Toule whate) that the Ind[ia]ns intended to kill her, that a Woman one of her friends told her to run off[.] that she heard the Ind[ia]ns talking to such purport & she immediately started hid herself in a Hole and always travelled by night & hid in the day and never made a Fire until she reached Quesnels River – Names of the Indians at the Murder – Cheelquette, Kow na yelle, Tzil tzii, Yeskai chen nâ, Est lay or Tctc Grize, Yate luss, Ozate zil this last was encamped about 100 y[ar]ds from the others & when he heard the firing run to it but all were dead by the time he got there[.]

No record has been found that this disturbing version of her son's death was passed on to Elizabeth Linton, if she was still living. Nor have we found that the Company took any action, let alone a campaign of the scale that the 1852 killing of Peter Brown by Cowichan occasioned in the Vancouver Island colony (entry 109) or the campaign following the 1850 murders of Lobb and Wishart by Nahwittee (entries 65 and 66).

83   JAMES DICKSON: *I Advise you and tak my advise and dont take a wife in thatt Cuntry for they are plenty hom*

James Dickson entered the Company service in 1825 at the age of thirty-eight. His family had supplied blacksmiths in Feolquoy, Harray, Orkney since the 1600s and he followed in this family trade, first at Rupert's River, then at Moose Factory in James Bay. Although no record has been found of a trip home, he and Jean Flett were listed in Orkney as parents of a son baptized in 1831. He travelled home in 1834 to see his family before leaving in 1835 to serve as a blacksmith at Fort Vancouver. An undelivered letter from his brother-in-law two years later tells of the poor working conditions in Orkney, suggesting a possible reason why James entered the Company's service so late in life. William Corrigall's motivation in telling James not to marry a woman in North America – we have to assume that Jean had died – reminds us that taking a "country wife" had, by the nineteenth century, become a frequent occurrence for Company employees.

To Mr James Dickson, Blacksmith York, Columbia River ore Els wher

Jun 6 th 1843

Dear Brother I take the oppertunity of writing to you to lett you know thatt I am In a State of good helth att present and my father and Sisters

alsoo hooping thatt this will find you in the Same and to lett you know how times is att hom[.] I would Surpris ther is noo work for pletters [plaiters: women who wove straw for making straw bonnets] att all and men nothing to dow[.] ther is plenty of wuman att hom[.] I Advise you and tak my advise and dont take a wife in thatt Cuntry for they are plenty hom and iff you dow itt Itt is nothing in this Cuntry that Shew Can dow[.] Dear Brother you're a[u]nt Mudy [Medy Heddle married James Firth] is deed this bowr [voar or spring] and thank good [God] fore all his mercies[.] You Sent to James Corrigall for a Stand of Cloth you might lett me known of itt[.] Suppos your father is nigh to the wind I was noot Caran[.] I shall tell you who married[.] William Borrowick and Margrat Flett in Narston [Knarston] and William Hourston and Betsy Rinnet William Morrison and Mary Louttit Neteltar and Thomas Isbister and Margaret Kirkness of Moan that is all thatt is married in Harrey [Harray] the year Butt plenty Curtan [courting][.] William Dickson and William Linklater is Hoom all the Sumer and has nothing to dow[.] the Herring fishing is all most done[.] rite me and lett know if a man Can Save ought wher you are or nott for hee Can Save nothing hom att all[.] I remain your Brother tell death
  William Corrigall

   The remark that William Corrigall should have been informed about James Dickson ordering cloth from James Corrigall, possibly a relative, shows how family frictions travelled across the ocean in the letters. In the following letters, James's sister Christian, who had married into the Isbister family, included angry words about their brother. She reported that William was an example of how the nearest relations "often times … is most unjust," in what would appear to be a disagreement about money. But before we can learn more of the family problems, the Isbisters turn to public news. The reference to church disputes is not casual, as all of Scotland was at that time caught up in "The Great Disruption" in the Presbyterian Church. The British Parliament had approved a bill in 1712 that allowed wealthy landowners to appoint ministers of local churches and effectively left the congregations to be controlled by moderates, thereby excluding the Evangelicals, a Calvinist group that nevertheless remained a powerful force in the Scottish church. As historian T.M. Devine observes, this bill "struck at the heart of one of the key principles of Presbyterianism, in which ministers were supposed to be selected by the local church communities" (Divine 1999, 73). By the General Assembly of the Church of Scotland on 18 May 1843, tension between the factions reached the breaking point and the Evangelicals decided to leave the established church to form the Free Church of Scotland. We can see by the following letter that the disruption is being felt at the grass roots level of the church. The history of this fracture is complex, often dividing families much as a civil war would. The Isbister letter indicated that "it would take sheets of paper to Contain all about" this important change in religious life in Scotland.

∾ James Dickson, Blacksmith, Fort Vancouver, Columbia River or Elsewhere, Hudsonsbay

Harray 12th June 1843

   Dear Brother with pleasure we inform you that we have received 3 letters 1st July last 2nd at Martimess by the Ships the last one about the 12th of May[.] hapy to see in your last letter you was well in health as we all are at pressent thank god for all mercies bestowed

   Now to answer the Contents of those letters[.] you sent a power to us as we received safe also a Box as likly we have writen before that we received. your orders was the Box to me your sister, the skins to Tho[s] the other articles according to your order. we feel much oblidged to you for your kindness to us. as to public Burdens such as afects property we have payed[.] as for M[r] Blyth poor man he has been long unwell with a Stomach & Nervus Compliant[.] for this long time would not speak to any person to receive Money when gon from Harray to his manse[.] many stands in unsetled state with him by reason of his health[.] he never asks, which no doubt will not be well for some, I went to setle with him found the truth as was formerly told that he was not able to Converse and setle[.] Now he is South and likly may never return[.] Certainly aman will be appointed by him which we will atend to you[.] you sent a Bill by the Fall of £13 according to your orders you may depend, as for the Ballence you May depend it will be taken care of for you – you also alowed me one pound[.] M[a]y you long and prosper for your kind affection[.] if speared I will remember you for the same[.] as for William our Brother you know the neighest relations often times if unfer is most unjust[.] he is deceived us very much being so to us as he was[.] we did not think he would proved so as the mouth of the public takes such advantage upon relations in being Expert to force payment when due in so disagreable always thought it would proved better

   As for the public news of the County

   1st The Ministers of the Establishment[:] great disputes is among them[.] about 600 of them through the Established Church of scotland is left their Churches because the Law would not submit to them[.] they wished to have all power to themselves which the Law would not submit too[.] we hope providence may bring good out of it in the end[.] M[r] Malcolm is left

or about to leave his manse and Churches is making ready to flit to
Grandon[.] Mr Blyth is another[.] Mr Lirmon in stromness his friends is
building a Church for him in stromness[.] Mr Petrie second Minister in
Kirkwall one Mr White a helper to Mr Blyth at first was a minister North
Ronaldsay is Come out[.] Mr Clouston Sandwick first said he would Come
out but stopt in also said sundries more returned back they wish still to
labour like disenters in their parishes[.] they Petitioned from Court to
Court up to the Queen then the Law was read against them[.] other
Ministers will be sent down to there Churches[.] they have agreed with M^r
Mason to grant them his Churches to preach in untill they get Churches
for themselves[.] great displeasure between those that have gon out and
those that are stoping All Calling those that are stoping Thieves &
Robers that have Climb over the wall[.] they have made out a fund by
superscription of £240.000[.] it would take sheets of paper to Contain
all about them.

2nd There was a Mr Bell that Mr Blyth agreed after Mr White[.] he was
over us for about 2½ years a good man then left us in a suddent and
away for Hobbart Town in Vandemans land [Van Dieman's Land, or
Tasmania][.] since these 3 years there is great Orruptions been in Harray –
Although Mr Blyth agreed with us to find us a good asistant the Lords
supper year about in our parish he never fulfiled he promised a sabbath
school which was fulfilled Famely vizit never till last year[.] Wished to get
rid of Harray as he found no profit by the Helper. He Mr Clouston & M^r
Malcolm asured us to try for a disjunction of the Parishes they would
assure us Mr Bell would return back[.] a meeting was called in the Church
the Three minister present had all been were they told us it would been
both easy and glorious a party of us mistrusted their speach[.] they got a
majorety not in a proper manner then no sooner they Petitioned to
Dundas to grant Harray to another [man] of their Choise unknown to
us[.] he was so Honourable he would not without the Parish wish[.] they
went to the Court of Session to force a disjunction still as our eyes opened
we stood off as it [. . .] a runious for a small Parish wished to [. . .] Mr Blyth
to his bargain seeing them so opresive with their manses[.] Mr Clouston
declined when he saw the state of all things said had he [known] in the
beginning as he did in the end sho[uld have] never insisted[.] George smith
hapned to be one of the Committee a man that neither regarded his own
pocket nor the Parish Continued active with Mr Malcolm and our school
master thinking to obtain the porochial school that had to be along with
the manse[.] a Runious thing also th[e] porochial Teachers applying for £50
a year [. . .] state Houses a garden of a ⅓ of an acre of the medium ground

of the Parish all the Heritors had to furnish[.] now Consider ye what that would done to the Parish[.] then at Last them [. . .] got in a Confussion themselves we wrot Lord Dundas accordingly[.] he Considered the [good] of the Parish very well found the best way way [repetition] to Collect all and pay the Expence incured as he was willing to pay his proportion the same[.] both Parishes is agreed too but I cannot just now tell your proportion it will likly be I supose be about within a pound[.] Considerably I have with great trouble engaged to help on this letter being in a ver bad state of health with a stomach Complint It is a very bad Complint likely death will be the period so welcome be his will in mercy[.] I am hapy to write you respecting your boy[.] he imitates much of yourself with an obligding turn[.] a promising boy sinsible and ready[.] he was last winter at our Chamber as schollar to my William which gave me a full oppertunity to know the Contents in full[.] the boy will give you satisfaction[.] I would feel hapy to seen you[.] our Fathers was about an eage and died about an eage[.] it appears I am not to be speared so long[.] had I been as formerly I would [send? write?] you much more news as I am yours affectionatly Jas Is[bister]

  Now Dear Brother we Conclude your letter being thankfuly for [the] kindness you have shown and hopes we will be speared to meet[.] we are hapy to find you got over that kind of Fever[.] this is very dull times in the Orkneys especialy in horses no demand at all[.] we are happy to say stock & stour and Crops very well as we ought to be thankful as we are your Brother & sister till death

  Tho⁵ & Christian Isbister

  It is interesting, after such a lengthy discussion of public affairs, to see the letter return to family matters in reporting on the education of James's son, who has been left in the care of the Isbisters. What may seem an abrupt change from the public to the private, may not have seemed so to the correspondents, as both church and family economies and politics were intimately joined in the small tightly knit communities of Orkney. In a separate letter, Christian addressed her brother about her concerns for his son James, whom she is raising and who had the measles. Christian begged that he not be taken from her, as she had developed a mother's love for him. This concern was a prelude to letting James senior know that a major argument had broken out in the family over who would inherit if James and his son should die. This argument, which recorded a negative characterization of a relative, has been deleted from the letter at the request of descendants in Orkney, where community memory is still a factor in daily life even after more than 150 years.

~ Harray 16 of June ~~12ᵗʰ~~ [crossed out] 1843

   Dear Brother James Dickson I write this few lines to let you know that
we are all three in good health at present thank god for it earnestly wishing
this may find you the Same[.] Dear Brother it is the terriblest time now
that ever we beheld on acount of Religon[.] 20 for one is holding the new
way[.] their was ameting held at the Church on tusday last[.] it is fully
determined a church is to be Built Just abouve the well of Brough[.] the
ofer was made this year if not Embraced this year it never was any Chance
again[.] their is no Expence but as people please to give[.] their was a fast
yesterday no entrance in the church as usual Master Clouston Came and
Stoped it[.] he went in and very few with him[.] Master garson [John
Garson, a native of Sandwick, assistant to Mr. Blyth] preached under the
church yard dike agreat Congreation with him[.] he is to preach in Harray
Birsay and Sandwick as oft as he Can[.] he is a fine preacher[.] now their is
many Ministers Comming down very Soon every one will have their
Choise[.] now it is the law in the church of Scotland now which we hold
now Christ is the head of our Church and we deny goverment to be the
head of the church[.] Dear Brother I think that James is this day efected
with the measles I hope in god it will not be hard on him[.] you may
depend with amothers heart I will take Care of him[.] he is Dear to us as
achild and will be as long as I live[.] I hope you will not take Dear James
from me it would hurt me very much[.] he is my Companion and thank
god is growing agood Scolar[.] he was wishing very earnestly to wrote you I
hope you will not be angry for he was not able for his head but he is agood
writer[.] I hope he will writ your next letter[.] William Corrigal of Midhouse
[Harray] Sibea Corigal nerth biging [North Bigging, Harray] Maried this
year[,] William Mer[r]iman Mary Loutted [Loutit] Nettlor [Netlar] Mared[,]
William Borwick Brough Margret Flett Nisteban [Nistaben] Narston
[Knarston] Married[,] William Hourston and Betty Kennet in Corston is
Married[,] Thomas Isbister in Rus[s]land now is Married with Margret
Kirkness of Moan Brough his third marreags that is all that Married in
Harray this year[.] John Firth of Wasdale [Firth] Married with Catherine
Linklater in Settler [Setter?] now Bellonging to innerton [Innertown]
Stromnes[s][.] Thomas Wilson our Cusin is Married this yeare with Betsy
Heddel Daughter of William Heddel Stromness George Smith Burried two
Daughters within amonth and James Smith Burried his oldest Daughter
and his youngest Son this year[.] Thomas Johnston died in Summer
Churlot is gone Back to Netltar again[.] Maxine Corrigal in gorn died this
year and Betty Redlan[d] is beried this day and old Charly Flett in

Caperhouse died in winter[.] Betty has the house and William the Mill of Sabaston [Sabiston] that he Bought[.] old James Flett Lineath died this year they are got the mill from James for 28 years by Subtilty

...

we were expecting you home this year[.] we thought very long when you did not Come home[.] I thank you Dear Brother for your Rich presents to me[.] I am Sory I Cannot Recompence you being so fare away[.] god bless you both Soul and Body for your goodness to me[.] James is growing very big and afine looking boy[.] he is going to Samuel Hourstons School and is doing very well[.] he is agood many Rules in his Count Book and is well beloved with master and mistress and his School boys that is agreat pleasure to me[.] his master gives us good Comfort he was very hard till the last year[.] I am Sory that he is not able to writ you[.] be not discomfitted on his acount every one is had good masles[.] I ad no more at present but Remains

your Loving Sister till Death   Christian Dickson

These letters indicate how complex family life can become when a landowner and father left home for an extended time. A final letter from James Robertson, husband of James Dickson's sister Helen, was more concerned with immediate economic loses and how his brother-in-law might react than with church doctrine. However, the Robertsons are also concerned with little James.

~ Mr James Dickson, Black Smith, Clumbeay forte vancovor or Elsewher

June the 19 1843

Dear Brother – I take this oppertunity of writin you to leatt you know that we ar all in good healty thank god for it hoping that this will find you the Seam[.] Dear Brother I receved your letter and was hapy to hear Thate you was well hopin Still to Se you if God will[.] ~~Dar~~ [crossed out] Dear Brothar I am Come [to] a los of – £50 pound Stirlin withe my Brothar[.] David and I had to pay thate Soum or go to the lar [law][.] Consistin the property Thate I gote efter me uncel David war to go on The pors roll and Came it befor the Court of Cesion and I had to pay to the mase and kirk the Som of £22 pound Stirlin and I have had a hard tim you may know and I am had 8 Children and and [repetition] – 7 – in life and your neam Daughtar is Gate preming [premium or prize] for Beng the Best ritar of all The lases that was ate the Scoul[.] Dear Brothar it is a hard tim on me for Scouling and servants the hous Bige and Childrin small as yeat

Dear Brothar I am note Be holden to any Boute to you and If you hade note Ben more a frend or my Brothar I Ben worse[.] Dear Brothar on acount of thate trubel I am not Gote you payed as yeate Bout I am note Behoulden to man Boute you and the Lord grante his Greas [Grace] to do what is rite and anust [honest] with all our delings for our time in this world is pasin and hope we was frends and well Be as long as we live in this wold and I wish we may mete hapy in the next wold dear Brothar

James your Son is grown op big and Coms to se me along with his ante and I am Glead to se him as he heave boute fewe frends I regard him for Your Seak and from Old Friendshipe and mey gos ther and ses them on lines I hope You will ~~note~~ [crossed out] note Be hard withe me as I hope this is me hard as ~~the~~ [crossed out] him

Dar Brothar I have no mor to say

But remians yur

Dar Brothar and Sister

Tell Death

James Robertson

Hellen Dickson

Records show that James Dickson missed these disturbing letters because he was on his way home, working as a seaman on the *Vancouver,* which arrived in London in October 1844. Debts and feuds, both private and public, would be part of his lot as an Orkneyman when he got home. He would also discover, as affirmed in these letters, that his son James was growing up to be "agood Scolar" and "well beloved."

84 WILLIAM SWANSTON: *If you have any though[t] fore os*

William Swanston, named after his father, was born in 1819. His father had joined the Hudson's Bay Company in 1812 and had married the daughter of Joseph Brown, a Company employee, and his Aboriginal wife; together they raised a large family of eight children. He stayed until his death at Moose Factory in 1865, as did many who married into the Métis community. Young William and two of his brothers, Joseph and John, followed their father with a career in the Company, as did several of their half-brothers.

William junior became a sailor on the sloop *Union* at the age of fifteen in 1835, the year after his older sister, Elizabeth, had married Andrew Linklater. The couple, who had left Moose Factory for Orkney in 1839, wrote an undelivered letter to him. In 1841 William junior had crossed the continent to the west coast to serve as a slooper in the Thompson River District. The Linklaters addressed William at "Columbia Ore else where" and counted on

Archibald Barclay, now Company secretary at the Hudson's Bay House in London, to know where to send his mail.

∽ Willem Swanston, Columbia Ore else where, care of Archibald Barclay Esqr, Hudson Bay House, London

Hirrey [Harray] Narston Janeray the 3/1844

    Dire Brother I tak this opertuney of wretin this fue lines to let you know that we all wile [well] in h[ea]lt[h] At present thank God fore it houping that this will find you in the Same as it leves us[.] bot I think that you are foregot os[.] you could Sent alter [a letter] to us bot we Dount know whare you was[.] we have Sent a letter the yare that you went of[f] and soume thinges More bot I sepose you gout non[e] of that[.] bot I houpe if you ricive thes letter I houpe that you wille Send wone to os If you have any though[t] fore os bot if you have Non Never Mind it bot your Sister is very Soray that Shou Canot hire from you[.] and If you cane tele os about Jofes [Joseph] and John your Brothes let os know how the[y] Coumcnon if you cann and let them know abot os[.] hir is my cind love to you ale if you riciv this letter and littel Kathren & Ann & Elizabeth litle Willem your name Son Cind Complementes to you and you Brothes[.] I have Bin at the Stretes [Straits] the last yare and Got 7 fish [whales] and Got youn ["yun" meaning "that"] Shipe Stoved and came home with a pice of Sillskine [sealskin] Niled [nailed] on hare Bottem[.] Nou Dire Brother I have Got No More Newes ot let [to tell] you of tile I ricive a cind letter from you and then I will Send Sum things[.] I do Find your ould Swirthert is come to london with Willem Tulok [Tulloch] and the[y] are Stopen [stopping] ther[.] hi is a plice Man

    and Elizabeth Mour She is Coume home with Gorg Mowad [Mowat or Mouat] in Sanwa[.] Nou Dire Brothers we are fare parted a we May Met aGaine and me Never God noes bot we Dont know yeat Bot God by with you and fore Ever amen

    Nou Dire Brother I ad no More at present Stile remend you Dir brother and Sister till Dith

    Andrew Linklater

    and Elizabeth Linklater

and if you wret to os you can drek [direct] hare to Andrew Linklater, Harry Narston Orckney

At the time this letter was written, all three Swanston boys were on the west coast and Andrew and Elizabeth Linklater inquired about all of them. Joseph had initially gone to the Company's California agency as an apprentice but soon was a middleman there and then a slooper at Fort Vancouver; by the 1845-6 outfit year, however, he had been discharged at California, apparently preferring his prospects there. Their brother John had gone to the Columbia Department in 1842 as an apprentice sailor on the *Cadboro* and served on the coast on the *Vancouver, Columbia, Cowlitz, Beaver, Mary Dare, Otter, Labouchere,* and *Enterprise* until his death in 1872. William's career, however, was not as long or as favoured. He would never have to know that his old sweetheart was living at London with a policeman named William Tulloch, since he drowned at The Dalles (the Columbia River rapids upstream from Fort Vancouver) in July 1843. Chief Factor John McLoughlin described the incident in his letter dated 2 August 1843: "Since I last wrote you, the Brigade has been to this place, and in going up, one of the Boats, I am sorry to say, was swamped in a whirlpool, most of the party in her lost, and one of the men, named Arcouet, drowned – and another, Swanson, his setting pole slipped, he fell out of the boat into the water, and never appeared again." In a later letter, dated 15 November 1843, he provided a few more details:

> I am pained to be obliged to inform you, that a Boat was lost at the Dalles of the Columbia, by which accident one man was drowned, and a day after, another was unfortunately drowned by falling overboard, while using the setting pole in a rapid, his pole slipped, he fell in the water, and never rose again, his body was found some time after, and it would appear from a deep wound on the forehead, that in falling, his head struck upon the rocks, and the severity of the blow had stunned, and rendered him incapable of making any effort to save himself.

News of his death had not yet reached home almost six months later, when his relatives wrote to him. By a coincidence of fate, William's brother-in-law, Andrew Linklater, also drowned. His death was in Houseby Loch in Birsay in 1860 when he was returning home after a farm sale.

85 ALEXANDER MORISON AND MURDOCH MCLEOD: *If you are in life*

By the 1840s men from the Isle of Lewis (in the Outer Hebrides on the northwest coast of Scotland), such as Alexander Morison and Murdoch McLeod, were supplementing the Company's traditional Orkney employees. Alexander Morison had left for York Factory on a Company supply ship, the *Prince Rupert,* in 1840 and had crossed the continent the next year. Murdoch McLeod had served as a labourer at York Factory and in the Saskatchewan District for two years, from 1832-4, before going by the overland route to work as labourer and middleman in Fort Vancouver for many years.

This letter to Alexander Morison from his father, John Morison, included one from his sister-in-law Ann to her brother Murdoch McLeod. (Ann was the wife of Alexander's brother John.) The family was not sure if Murdoch McLeod – who in 1845 had been away for thirteen years – was still alive, and they had received word that he had been hurt. In early June, these families wrote to call their men home as soon as possible. These urgent calls for men to come home and help their families keep their livelihoods gives us a dramatic sense of the enormous time and distance involved in communication between Britain and the Columbia Department. The letters, mailed in Stornoway, the principal town of the Isle of Lewis, would have travelled on the Company ship that called at that port to hire labourers for the fur trade. After arrival in York Factory at Hudson Bay, the letters would then have travelled the long route across the continent to reach the men.

Alexander Morison, Labourer Columbia River, Care of Honble H Bay House, London

Branahu[i]e 8th June 1845

My Dear Son

We Received your Kind letter Last wiek with we were happy to See that you were in good Steat of helth[.] we also Received an order for Four pounds which we received very Safe from the Bank of Stornoway we rejoice to see that you thought of assisting us in our Latter Days[.] we hope you will soon be thinking of coming home to your own country and to see your poor parents and your frinds. they are not pleased at you for not leting them Know in this letter how is Murdoch Mc Leod from Shather [Shader] because you said Before he got a hurt[.] your frinds are all in helth but John your brother has lost a child last winter[.] he has gotten another Boy since and he is called after your name[.] we are Keeping the land yet hoping you will come and take possession of it[.] we wrote you in the winter time but we see from this letter you have not gotten it. we hope when your time is served with the company that nothing will be the means of Keeping you from coming to see us all[.] we hope you will write us if you get this letter

we all Join in our love to you

we Remain your affectionate parents

John Morison

⮜ To Alex^r Morison
[crosswise] dear Alexander if Murd^h is in life you will send him this other
part of the letter

To Murdoch McLeod from John your [Alexander Morison's brother's] wife

Melbost 9th June 1845

    Dear Murdoch
if you are in life we are longing to hear from you, for since we heard that
your helth Broke we do not know what to say and not getting any word
from you or about you[.] your poor Mother is Keeping to hold the Lands
thinking you will come and take possession of it and if you are in life and if
you got halth she is very needfull that you would send hir somthing if you
are in halth we hope you will come home for it is very easy for a person to
get plenty of work in the Island because there is plenty of work Doing in
the Island by the new propritor[.] we also trust if this came to your hand
you will not make eny delay in writing us how you are[.] we Join in our
love to you
    I Remain your sister
     till Death
       Ann Morison

    Ann's comment that their "Mother is Keeping to hold the Lands" in the
hope that Murdoch would return – similar to John Morison's comment –
indicates that able-bodied men are needed to work the land or the families
will be in worse financial condition.
    Alexander Morison and Murdoch McLeod, who had been suffering from
health problems at the time Alexander had written to his family, were both
still very much alive when these letters were written. Alexander left to go east
across the continent to York Factory in the spring of 1846, thereby missing
the mail. When he returned home after six years with the Company, he married, on 28 December 1846, Ann McLeod – a woman with the same name as
his brother John's wife. This Ann McLeod came from Knock and she died in
1854, leaving him with two children. He later married Isabella Montgomery,
with whom he had three more children. He did stay at home on the Isle of
Lewis and farmed, as his father had hoped, dying there in 1897.
    It appears that Murdoch McLeod also had two wives, although the name
was a common one and the records may refer to different men. A letter written to the Company on 12 December 1846, from Colin Leitch of Stornoway
indicated that a Murdoch McLeod had left behind a wife with three children;
after the children had been abandoned by that wife for another man, they

had been supported by the parish. In response to the parochial board's request for help through Leitch, the Company secretary made a note to the effect that McLeod had a credit of £37 7s. 8d. at the Vancouver depot at that time. When the Murdoch McLeod related to Alexander Morison arrived home from the west coast at the end of his seventeen years of service with the Company, he married Kristy (Christian) McLeod on 4 December 1849. Kristy survived Murdoch, who died in the early 1850s; she remarried and had two daughters, one in 1857 and another in 1861. We have found no evidence that this Murdoch McLeod sought to support the children referred to by Leitch.

86   ANGUS McDONALD: *I am keeping the house and every thing as you sae in hops to see yourself soon*

Angus McDonald of the parish of Markethill, Stornoway, Isle of Lewis, signed on as a Company labourer on 17 June 1841. He sailed to York Factory on the *Prince Rupert* and travelled overland to work in the Columbia Department in 1842. He served at Fort Victoria from 1843 to 1845, then for a year at the Company's farm at Nisqually. In his five short years he served in three of the Company's major administrative posts – York Factory, Fort Vancouver, and Fort Victoria – as well as the very different atmosphere of one of the Puget's Sound Agricultural Company's farms. His farming activities from 20 January until he left on 11 March 1846 included cutting up and rolling aside trees, cleaning oats by wind, dressing shingles, sawing boards for the roof of a big house and the store, roofing, acting as protection for Joseph Heath (entry 29) against "marauding Indians," "delving" (digging) a garden, thrashing peas, squaring wood for a barn, erecting a calf shed and making a park for milch cows around it, coopering beef casks, and getting oak wood for wheels (Dickey 1989). His father wrote to tell him that the family was expecting him home soon.

Care of the Honble HBC° London, Fenchurch Streer
Angus McDonald, Labourer, Fort Victoria, Hudsons Bay

Old Market hill by Stornoway Feb[ruar]y 16 1846

My Dear Son
I received your kind letter last November with £5 St[erlin]g which gives me great pleasure to se[e] that you are in health also that you are greatfull to mind of your Parents. I am keeping the house and every thing as you sae in hops to see yourself soon & I hope you will not Bind yourself more there But that you will come home this year[.] if you intend to come you

need not Bring much Clothes more than a shift or two for cloths are cheap
here than there for you must take care of your earning as well as you can[.]
I thought of writing before now but I was advised not to write tell now. I
do not expect to write you this year Because I expect yourself home But if
you don't come you will write me and send me some help for your mother
altho she is living she canot help me much[.] your fiends are all in health
except Mal[col]^m who was in Campbellton & your grand father[.]
I conclude with kind love to you.

    While I remain your affectionate
        father Murdo MacDonald
Your mother join in love with me to you and all friends
    Mur MacDonald

    In the spring of 1846 – while his father's letter was on its way to him –
Angus made the long trip back across the continent with the express brigade
that took returning men and mail to York Factory. From there he took
the Company's ship, the *Prince Rupert,* back home, avoiding the longer trip
around the Horn of South America. By the 1851 Census, Angus had rejoined
his parents, Murdo and Margaret, and had married Margaret from Uig. His
earnings from his five-year contract with the Hudson's Bay Company would
have helped support his aging parents and provided a good start for his new
family.

87 ALLAN MACISAAC: *Mind you and dond marry one that is out there and I*
     will not marry one that is here till you come

When Allan MacIsaac came out to York Factory in the fall of 1849, he went
immediately overland to serve as a labourer in the Columbia Department,
first inland and later at the Vancouver depot. His sweetheart, Mary Mac-
Donald, must have received word from him, as in her undelivered letter she
mentioned hearing that he had been ill and addressed her letter to the
Columbia River District. She was living with her mother, Mary, a forty-five-
year-old widow, and her older sister, Peggy, and younger siblings, Donald,
Janet, and Lexy.

  Allan MacIsac, Laberer Columbia river, Care of H.B.C.hous, London

Stornoway 1 october 1851

    Dear allan I took the opportunity of writing you this few loins to let you
know that I am in Good helth hopping this Will find you the same[.] I
wase verry sorry that you did not tell me whether you Got the letter that I

sent you or no[.] I wase verry sorry when we hard that you took the fever
and we new that you would be verry bad[.] we new that there would be no
one to th attend you[.] you here that Girls are Geeting married but I did
not marry yet till you come[.] dear allan if you are to me as I am to you
that will do[.] mind you and dond marry one that is out there and I will
not marry one that is here till you come[.] mudena Campbell is a widow
sinc you went[.] dear allan I forgot the little lie that you told me[.] that
wase not the worst of it but the way you went[.] the crop is verry Good the
year as yet the patotes is not so bad the year[.] I wase verry sorry that I did
not Get the letter I wrote you if you did not Get it[.] I hard that James
macIver friends is verry well and I am verry Glad to here that there is one
frone with you[.] I hop tho you are not hearing a minister that you are not
forgeting that there is a God[.] dear love tho I am here I am there[.] my
mother sents her best respects to you and she is verry Glad to here that you
Got petter of the fever and she hopes that she will be boilling you weeding
yet[.] I wase so bussy that i did not wait to write you with blood put I
hoop that is fore no difference[.] dear lov I will be to you ase Good as I
promised tho I write you this Know I am Going to write you [whe]n the
wrest will write[.] [whe]ther you have the old time in mind or not I have
and so long I wase wthout ~~writing to~~ [crossed out] hearing from you then
were near to Go out of my mind put when I Got your letter I minded on
them[.] my mother sents her best respects to you and Donald my brother
an murdena Campbell and her mother and all my frends an peggy mac
leod and mind whenever you Get this letter mind and write and nil mac
Kay sents his best respects to you an all his family is well and he is working
with the sapers[.] I have no more to say at present but your trew love till
death mary macdonald

Mary must have decided that she could not keep her promise to wait, as
in 1853 she married Donald Matheson from Gravir on the Isle of Lewis.
Perhaps her promise to Allan seemed as impractical as her romantic notion
of writing in blood. Or perhaps the romantic fling of a Catholic Uist lad –
Allan was unlikely to have been a Protestant, from the overwhelmingly
Catholic community in Uist – with a Protestant Stornoway girl during the
days before the ship sailed for North America was not a solid start to a lasting relationship.

MacIsaac was discharged from his labourer's job in 1853. He may have
intended to settle in the Oregon Department, as he had a balance of £42 10s.
on the Vancouver books that he did not withdraw all at once. By 1856 his balance was down to just under £9. There are at least two possible endings to
the story of Allan MacIsaac. Perhaps he eventually went home to his own

parish, South Uist in the Outer Hebrides. An Allan McIsaac appeared in the 1851 Census living with his unmarried sisters – it is possible that the sisters entered his name, although absent – and a man by that name died in South Uist, unmarried, in 1893. Another possibility is that he was the Allan MacIsaac referred to as an "old servant" of the Hudson's Bay Company who drowned at New Westminster "by slipping from the guards" of the steamer *Governor Douglas* while drunk. Either way, he did not make up for the "little lie" or join the close family of Mary MacDonald.

88   HUGH MOUAT: *Your Mother is but tendar and very lonsom for yow alway and hopes that yow will come home at the eand of your contrake if the lord spares yow to serv the time*

Hugh Mouat joined the Company in December 1850, coming out on the annual ship to York Factory in the fall of 1851 as a labourer and travelling overland to work at Fort Vancouver. Letters were sent from home at the time of the year when Scots celebrate Hogmanay and try to be the first visitor in neighbouring homes. Such letters – like the one below – were filled with the many activities of the extended kin and friendship groups of Orkney. Hugh's friend, John Inkster, was most concerned with keeping him up to date on the marriageable women.

∾ Mr Hugh Mouat, Fort Vancouver Or else where, Columbia, Care of Secretary of the Honourable Hudson's Bay Company

December 31 1851

   Dear brother I take the plasant opurtunity of writing you this fiw lines to let you know that we are all in good health at prasant thank god for his mercies hoping and earnestly wishing this will find you the same[.] your uncle of e[y]nhallow and his wife and famely is well as yet we should be thankful for his mercies one and all of us[.] James Inkster my brother went of[f] last march he went of to shields and engaged their with a baroque bound for quebec[.] he was a voyage their and back to shields again and then he left the ship[.] he was about a week their engaged with a brig going up the mediterranean a 6 month voyage[.] your mother and sisters is all well and Cirstinu is maried this winter and we have all got a weding at inisgar [Innister?][.] there was not many people at it all the people of cogar [Koogrew?] Jane Flett and James Craigie of hatherhall [Heatherhall] your aunt of grain John Inkster and peter from that was all from e[y]nhallow[.] this winter there is ben alterations is in e[y]nhallow[.] this winter there is ben a fever en it is been in william mainlands house[.] Jennet mainland left

this world on sabbath night and william about 2 weeks after and it is been
in william louttits house and harrjut is left this this [repetition] world so we
have great reason to be very thantful that we are still spared a little longer
in this sinful world[.] that should be a warning to one and all of us how
uncertain our time is here[.] John mowat your brother is still unmarried
yet[.] he is finely well in health[.] James Inkster wife and family is in good
health at preasant thank god for it[.] John Inkster of pliverhall [Ploverhall]
is home this winter[.] young John Inkster of e[y]nhallow was at caithness
all the summer at the herring fishing and I had 3£ of wages[.] david and
william mainland was to[o] and I was in skeal [Skaill] in sanwick [Sand-
wick] all the harvest i had 30 s[hillings] of mony for the harvest and i have
been in gorn this two winters and Peter is in whis[.] Margaret Craigie is
still in gorn and she is finely well her mother and all her sisters thy all put
their kind compliments to you[.] margaret craigie of knarston she is not
married yet[.] she put her compliments to the[e][.] she has no sweethart
now atal simpson is still unmaried yet but he is not going to her at all –
John Cl[o]uston girl is always coming To us she was used to do[.] magnus
and bettsey and their mother is all well and magnus was at the herrin
fishing in burra[y][.] hugh craigie of Death [Deith] and isabella and mary
and John is all well at preasant[.] John Inkster and Jane craigie of gorn is
both in good health[.] James craigie of blackhamers [Blackhamar] and
barbara craigie of torbittail [Turbitail] is bucked [booked] but not
married[.] all her sisters is married but Jane elin an of seventyfiver isabella a
fine young lad in kirkwall – magnus cl[o]uston and John Inkster goes from
the house every night to the girls[.] a fine lightsome winter in wesbyster
[Wasbister][.] there is no fis[h] for John Cl[o]uston and hugh mowat[.] If
you see william craagie [Craigie] margaret's brother you will tell him to
send a letter for it is 2 years since they received one from him[.] John
craigie of hillion [Hullion] is married with sarah sinclair[.] John sinclair of
news [Newhouse?] is built a new house but he is not married[.] George
Leonard and margaret clouston is finely well and they have got another
daughter[.] James Leonard is home this winter[.] cecelia is finely well[.]
Margaret gibson flintersby is married this winter with James stenston a very
grand wedding all the pecks of the island[.] you will send home all the
news you ave if you got safe to calombia[.] I Have no more to say at
preasant what remains your dear friend John Inkster

   My Direction is
     Mr John Inkster
     E[y]nhallow to the care of M^r ~~Hug~~ [crossed out]
     Mr Hugh Charles Evie
     By kirkwall

Inkster was informative on whether female acquaintances were booked but not yet married, meaning that their intended fiancés had booked or arranged with a minister to have the banns of their marriage proclaimed in church. The "booking night" was an important one, because in an era before engagements it was the first indication that a marriage would take place.

The fact that John Inkster's brother, James, had within the previous year sailed to both Quebec and the Mediterranean, indicates the wide seafaring experience of the Orkneymen. They voyaged around the world but still liked to keep in touch with the doings of the folks back home. Hugh's brother, John, also wrote to wish him well on New Year's Day.

∾ Mr Hugh Mouat, Fort Vancouver, Or else where, Columbia, care of Secretary of the Honourable Hudson Bay Company, London

Instar [Innister] Rousay Janury the 1 1852

Dear and loving brother I Embrace this oppurinntunity to let you know that we are all well at presant thanks be to god for it[.] Earistly woshing that this few lins ~~yallaghe~~ [crossed out] find yow in the same[.] we recived your wallcome latter the 23 october and wase glade to har that you ware wall[.] we recived your 2 latters and the bill that yow sent bout the Mony is not dra[w]n yet[.] your sister cirsty is got Married this wonter to man his name is william lutted [Loutit] and thy stop in firt[h] in chambar at preesant[.] he blong to rendal[l] and James simson and Markret gibson flintury is Married and black hammery [Blackhamar] barbery cray [Barbara Crey] is Married[.] this wonter we hade very good harren fishing and fine crop and it bene a fine wontar what is past[.] I have no pertlager News at presant but that we are all on the usualy way as when yow lefte us and the people tow send thir cind love to yow and Margret corger sisey vakrey send thir cind love to yow[.] so loving brother your sistars an all the famely of our others house send thire kind love to yow wishes yow well and I ame gone to stope till yow come home and get shire of my widden yet[.] cirsty widden was at Instar [Innister] 20 day before I rite yow this latter a fine littele Markes.

So dear and loving bother your sistar Elisa [&] brother send thir cind love to yow and hopes that yow will sike the lard ware ever yow gow as he is to be found in all place[.] rembar ashes [Zacchaeus] when he was found clim up the sishomery [sycamore] tree sicking [seeking] Jasus and hopes that yow will Make the rote [root] of a tre your closet[.] dear brother my earnes prayer is for yow and I hope yow would pray for me so that if we niver Mate on earth we Miht all Mite at our father right hand[.] so bloveing

brother I am gone to klose this latter now with a few wards[.] your Mother
is but tendar and very lonsom for yow alway and hopes that yow will come
home at the eand of your contrake if the lord spares yow to serv the time

So loving brother yow will rembar your Mother And brother and sistars
Til dith
John Mowat

After being promoted to steward at the Vancouver depot in 1854, Hugh
Mouat was still at Fort Vancouver receiving wages in 1860, far from his "tendar and very lonsom" mother.

89   PETER IRVINE: *I hop that you will came hom son for i am sure they are non
     to me like you or ever will Be*

Peter Irvine came out to York Factory in 1850 and went overland as a labourer
in the Columbia Department. He was working at Fort Colvile by the time
these letters were sent. The first was from his parents, apparently written by
his sister Cris, full of news from family and friends in Lerwick, Shetland.

〜 Peter Irvine Labourer, Columbia River, Care of Archibald Barclay, Hudsons
Bay House, London

Lerwick 1th Feby 1852

Dear & loving Son
This Comes with our kindest love and best wishes to you hoping You
are well, and to let You know that we are all alive and Stiring about a litle
unless your poor Mother[.] She is just Cut up with with [repetition] the
rumothism So that She can only Come to the fire with the height of the
day but Can do nothing[.] She in particular sends her twenty Blessings &
gods Blessing to you for your Suport that you Sent her or else we hade not
been in the Body for want of Suport, if it hade not been your mercifull
heart that Sent us what you Sent, we Could not have been alive in this
place for you know the way of it it needs a daily income of Some way or
other, but may the Lord requite you & bless you aboundantly for so doing,
it is not in our power to requite you, but we hope you will be rewarded by
a higher power for our Sakes, we have no strange news to inform you of
only a poor year in Shetland of weather & deaths & a great deal of wrecks
in England – Lawrence Johnson & theoder Johnson of Setter is both dead
foreign but James Came home in harvest and is home yet, but theoders
dead news they have not heard yet, but Lawerce they Soon heard, for James

had the account with him[.] Magnus anderson of Clothan is no more[.] he
died going out another Voyage upon discovery, his father is dead & Burried
but he was a great poor

  what think you of Andrina of Clothan that is Married with Henery
Anderson of Ulsta, & theoder Johnson of Clothan with Barbra Sutherland
of Cuppaster [Copister] Just now and Joky anderson of Cupaster is a
widow for he thought to git her, Dear Son we gave the pound to your litle
Boy as you desired and it was acceptable[.] his mother & he was been lying
2 Months in the typas [typhus] fever and Lawrence was at thr knob – She
was very thankful of it, and Sends her best respects to you and wishes you
health & hapines for remembring the Child – but my Dear peter See and
git loose of Your task if possable and not Stop in such a dismal place if you
Can git free either by want of health or aplication, let us know if you
would wish to Come and we will aply to Doctor Cowie for a lease, for
Since we got your letter and heard from the place by other Men we ave
been quite unhapy, we sleep none thinking about *You*[.] we have never
Seen Andrew Since we Saw you but we have heard from him[.] he is out a
voyage at new oerleans his Second time[.] he was not well when he was at
liverpool in harvest[.] we Sometimes git a letter from John but nothing
else, he is at the Rock of Giblartle [Gibraltar] yet but he was thinking of
Coming to England this spring, Betty & litle John is with us, Dear son
when you write let us know if William yats [Yates or Tate?] be with you
and where you are and how you are, D[ea]ʳ Son we wrote you 2 Letters one
with the Montrial mail & 1 with the Ships[.] we are Sorry you got none, we
hope you will write us by the first oportunity for that will be a treasure to
us to hear of your life Spared, we are sory that you wrote mary philip for
She is been courting with Rob[er]ᵗ Bolt Since he Cam from greenland and
now he is left her & Courting Jannet Donalson[.] mary is a great fool – Dʳ
Brother I your sister Cris been Just out at Service one Quarter but hade to
Com home for the necessity of the house and intends to Stop till I See if
ever the Lord Sends you home to us that is my desire in this world, Margret is in Doctor Cowies but Still hase an eye towards the House, She is
going to git married to an old man David Nicolson, but I am going to stop
till you Com home to be best man to my weding[.] my Blessing & gods
blessing to you, and let me know if any thing Can be done for you or not
to git you free from yon place

  So Dear Son we all Conclude with our blessing and gods blessing ever
to atend you, Cirsty & May sends their blessing to you also Margret &
Betty sends theirs and every neighbour & welWisher sends theirs. Elspet
Sinclair sends her kind love to you She is not like to git Maried yet, And
rina Sutherland is in town and Sends her Blessing to you She is still

unmarried[.] they are Stoping in North mavirn [Northmavine] now, in Sandvoe West[.] Yell is a poor place now[.] Cirsty Blanu Blanu is got Maried to a good fortune and hase a Son[.] her people Sends their Blessing to you –

So hoping to hear from you again if the Lord Spares you, we ever remain your loving parents, John & C Irvine

The second letter is a more plaintive one from the much-maligned Mary Phillips, who considered herself to be Peter's lover.

To Peter Irvine Labourer, Columbia River, Care of Archibald Barclay Esqr, Hudsons Bay House, London

Larwick [Lerwick] 22 June 1852

My Dear and ever aff[ectionate] lover
i take the uportunit of writing you this fue lins to let you know that i am in good hal[t]h at Prasent and in hopes that this will find you in the same[.] My Dear you see that i am wrot you this fue lins to you altho you wold not writ to me[.] i wold like to knaw the rison that you did not writ to me the last time[.] i likent a latter when all the rast got ane But i got not from you an i am though great long for a latter ar ward fram you[.] i hop that you will writ me and let me know how you are and all your nuse[.] My Dear i am sory to hear that you Did not git the latters that i sant to you last time[.] i hop that you will came hom son for i am sure they are non to me like you or ever will Be[.] i am sure of that and you can belive it[.] when you com in my mind it makes me think long to think of all the old tims that iam sen in ous house[.] But naw it is all Dol [dull] naw fore our Roberd is away from us now and we thank him a gret mise out of the house and Andrew is at graland [Greenland?] an the saraw and we are liking him home now so y[ou] may think and cansider how Dol our hous is now[.] all My Cousens sendes there kind love to you and thare all wating for your wading and thear all liking him son[.] all our people sindes thare kind love to you and you can acexcapt [accept] of the same from your ever aff[ectionate] lover til Death Mary Phillips

A complex situation might await Peter if he went home: a sweetheart vowing that there "are non to me like you or ever will Be" – and whom his parents have attested has had at least one other beau and been condemned as "a great fool" – and another woman, whose child Peter had recognized as his own and sent money to support. As well, his parents yearned for his return, hinting that other girls, more suitable wives perhaps, were available. Irvine stayed at Colvile until 1856, when the simple word "left" in Company records indicated the end of his service with the Company. Whether he "left" to go home, or "left" to take up free land in Oregon or other enticing possibilities – as numerous Company servants did – we do not know. Why he did not claim the substantial £17 9s. left on his account remains a mystery: it was written off by the Company in 1860.

90   JOSEPH WILLIAM MCKAY: *I will be bound to state that ... few of the good things of this life go her way*

Joseph William McKay represents many of the dynamic and varied qualities that emerged in the descendants of the marriages between Company fur traders and Aboriginal women. William McKay and Mary Bunn, Joseph's parents, were themselves both children of such unions. Born at Rupert's House (present-day Waskaganish, Quebec) in 1829 and schooled at the Red River Academy, Joseph served for many years with the Company in the Oregon Territory and later in the colonies of Vancouver Island and British Columbia. His many-faceted interests in business and the welfare of Aboriginal peoples represent a wide involvement in the history of the Columbia Department, the Vancouver Island colony, and the province of British Columbia.

Arriving in Fort Vancouver in 1844 at age fifteen, Joseph was assigned to assist in naval reconnaissance, then transferred to Fort Victoria in 1846 where he helped with surveys. In 1848 he was appointed as a postmaster, the highest level to which Company employees born in North America could normally aspire. He worked in many capacities for the Company in the years that followed, but was especially successful at negotiating the Vancouver Island treaties with the Aboriginal peoples there. He explored the Cowichan and Comox valleys, started the Company's salmon fishery and sheep station on San Juan Island and the mining operations in Nanaimo. He wrote the letter below from Nanaimo in 1853 regarding a small inheritance he was to receive that involved shares in the Puget's Sound Agricultural Company, formed to facilitate the Company's development of the Vancouver Island colony and to supply provisions to the Russian American Company.

Joseph Bailey Esquire, Care of A. Barclay Esq., N° 4 Fenchurch Street, London

Nanaimo Coal Mines, Vancouvers Island, July 13th 1853

Joseph Bailey Esquire
   Sir
   I have just received advice from Mr William McKay enclosing your Communication to him dated from London June 3 1850 which contains

the information I required regarding a small bequest left me by Alexander Mckay deceased and which I much regret not having received before

It appears by your letter that the sum in question amounts to £48.5.6 of which my share is £24.2.9. In your Capacity as executor of Alexander M^ckays will you hold the said £48.5.6 on the plea that said estate is liable to Call from the Puget Sound Company on a share of £100 held by said Alexander McKay in said PSC° and of which share only £10 were paid in.

Will you inform me whether the aforesaid part share is included in the above sum of £48.5.6 or not if so Can you not include the said £10 or part share. in my share of the bequest and I will hold myself liable to the PSCompany for any future Calls on said share.

In the mean time can you not let the poor Widow Catherine McKay have her share of said bequest

I cannot give you any information as to her place of residence as I have not heard of her for the last 15 years. I will be bound to state that Wherever she is in the *Southern Department* few of the good things of *this life go her way*

In reference to security for said Calls from said Company on said share, I have not the sum of £90 in the funds of the HBC° at present as most of my spare Capital is invested in Various Speculations on Vancouvers Island. My Wordly possessions are however much more than equal to that amount and so long as I retain my health and present situation. I am confident that my draughts on the HBC° to any reasonable amount will always be duly honoured.

    I remain

      Yours Truly

        Joseph William M^ckay

Joseph's uncle, Alexander McKay, had died on 25 May 1842 at Migiskan in northwestern Quebec after "having kept his bed only a few days previous though unwell all spring." His widow, Catherine, appeared on the Company's Annuitant's list for Moose District from 1842 to 1865, earning about £5 per year and spending about the same amount until 1855, when a withdrawal of £13 brought her account down to about £4. By 1862 she had no further income and, in 1865, a debt of £7 3s. 2d. was transferred into the "Servants" Account. Perhaps because Joseph's letter in which he expressed his concern for his aunt's welfare went undelivered, no large sums were paid into her account, and she seems to have ended her days in debt.

MacKay's interest in widow Catherine is typical of his later interest in Aboriginal peoples, whose welfare was not heeded as the pressure to colonize and industrialize swept the region. After an active career as a Company man, and then as a businessman developing the natural resources of the region, he also became in the 1880s a federal government Indian agent, first for the Northwest Coast and later for the Kamloops and Okanagan agencies. He worked to share his stock-raising and agricultural skills with Aboriginal peoples, defend their land rights against the Canadian Pacific Railway and settlers, set up a industrial school near Kamloops, and personally inoculated more than 1,300 Aboriginal people against smallpox. Dividing his time in his later years between his business affairs, his political interests and work for the Indian Affairs department in British Columbia, he died in Victoria in 1900. In 1985 historians Peterson and Brown observed that the "history of the métis peoples runs deeper and more broadly across the North American landscape than has previously been acknowledged" (1985, 4). Joseph McKay's contributions certainly illustrate that assertion.

91 EDWIN KITTSON: *Your friends in this country are all well*

While most of the undelivered letters in this section are from relations of men in the lower ranks of the Company, the closing ones involve two very well-known Company men. James Douglas wrote the letter that follows to the young Edward Kittson, who was born at Fort Nisqually in 1840 and was therefore very young when his father William died at Fort Vancouver on 25 December 1841. James Douglas and John McLoughlin were Kittson's executors and took their roles seriously.

Douglas began as a North West Company clerk known for his "industry, punctuality, observance of the smallest detail, and a determination amidst the most pressing business to acquire knowledge of literature and history, politics and public affairs" (Ormsby 1972, 238). This did not mean he was always in control of his destiny. He was one of the most vehement young North West men in the struggle against the merger with the Hudson's Bay Company, even fighting a duel and making a show of appearing threatening at all opportunities. But once the union was accomplished, he buckled down to become a good trader and the best of Company men. Early on, despite his intelligent, hard-working nature, he was sometimes violent and often made enemies among Aboriginal people, being assaulted on more than one occasion. Fortunately his wife, Amelia Connolly, the daughter of a Company chief factor and his Cree wife, had more experience in Aboriginal customs. According to some accounts, she once had to rescue him from the knives of Carrier warriors intent on vengeance for a man Douglas had executed for murder. She managed the rescue through an age-old trading ploy: "She promised [Chief Kwah] ample restitution and then rushed upstairs and began throwing down trade goods to the crowd. This action diverted the Indians, and since the 'throwing' of gifts was a mark of deference according to Carrier custom, the Indians were placated and departed" (Van Kirk 1980, 113). When Douglas reached the rank of chief trader at Fort Vancouver, he had been for many years one of the men, along with his chief factor, John McLoughlin, who most affected the lives of the many men who are the subjects of this book.

He and McLoughlin – and their wives – often became caregivers and guardians for children of Company servants in need of protection. His letter to Edwin Kittson indicates a gentler side of Douglas, who, in his senior years when he was governor of Vancouver Island and later of British Columbia, was often seen by his contemporaries as rather distant and despotic.

Mʳ Edwin Kittson, Blue Style Academy, Greenwich,
Care of Wᵐ G. Smith Esqʳ London

Victoria Vancouvers Island 14ᵗʰ January 1857

My dear Edwin

I was very happy to hear of your welfare, through the receipt of your letter of which I forget the date, having mislaid it, and it unfortunately cannot, at this moment, be found.

I was however, much pleased, with the evident improvement, in the hand-writing, the diction and the whole appearance of the sheet. Your account of the school is very satisfactory, and I have no doubt if you are a good boy, that you will always receive the kindest treatment from your excellent Teachers. You must however study to please them, by the most assiduous attention to your studies; the strictest regard to truth and by being kind and obliging to all your companions.

Your friends in this country are all well expecially James who is growing fast, into a tall boy, and often speaks of you in terms of affection. Your mother and sister, now Mʳˢ St Clair, were well last I heard from the Columbia River. Mʳˢ Douglas, Mʳˢ Helmcken and all your other friends unite with me in affection and best wishes for you welfare.

My dear Edwin
Yours affectionately
James Douglas

Edwin's father, William Kittson, began his service as a North West Company employee after serving as a second lieutenant in the Voltigeurs Canadiens in the war against the Americans in 1812. William had a long career as a clerk, later serving in the Company under McLoughlin and Douglas in the Columbia Department, and he stayed at that rank all his life. Edwin's surviving siblings included Eloisa Jemima, who married William

Sinclair III – the "St. Clair" mentioned in Douglas's letter – and Jules and Pierre Charles, children from William's earlier marriage to Marie Walla Walla. The Mrs. Helmcken mentioned in the letter was Douglas's daughter Cecelia, who had married Dr. John Helmcken (see entry 66).

Governor Douglas was truly a "friend in this country" to the orphaned boy, since he took time from the affairs of the colony to reply to the letter of a young man studying in Greenwich. There, Edwin was learning the kind of skills that might make him eligible for employment with the Company or in the new colony – the future of Douglas and of many descendants of the Company's servants. Edwin's name appears in the 1858-9 sundry accounts receiving £20 in wages at Langley, possibly connected with the Fraser River gold rush; the following year only his debt appeared. His subsequent career has not been traced, although a Kittson descendant thinks that he created a line that now lives in Montana. The James whom Douglas mentioned in the letter was probably his own son. The Hudson's Bay Company Archives contains hundreds of Douglas's letters, reports, and other writings that testify to his role as a dominant figure in the fur trade but, as far as we know, this is the only one of his many letters that remained undelivered.

92   JOHN TOD: *I think in October she always anticipated a visit from you & her dear little Emma*

John Tod joined the Company in 1811 at age seventeen. He was promoted to clerk in 1814 and put in charge of Severn House (Ontario) the next year. After five years at Island Lake (Manitoba), he received a posting west of the Rockies in the New Caledonia District and spent nine years at McLeod's Lake. There he enjoyed a large library of books and the devotion of a young woman he called "the singing girl." He is reported as observing that without the books and the woman, he would have found the isolation of the "wretched place" insupportable (Wolfenden 1982).

In 1834 he was on his way home to Britain on leave on the *Prince Rupert* out of York Factory; on board, he met twenty-six-year-old Eliza Waugh, who was returning from a position as governess in the Red River colony. The shipboard romance put all thoughts of the singing girl – as well as two previous unions – out of John's head and the pair married when they reached England. They returned to Red River the next year, despite the fact that Eliza had not liked life in the settlement when she had lived there before. Not long after their arrival, she was showing signs of mental breakdown.

The couple went together to Island Lake, hundreds of kilometres up the Nelson River from York Factory. By this time they had a daughter, Emmeline Jean, and Eliza's behaviour had become so extreme that there was fear she might harm her. In 1837 Tod took his wife and child to England on the *Eagle* from York Factory. He left instructions that his son, James, by his first Aboriginal wife, be kept for four more years at Mr. Jones's school in Red River; but on their safe arrival in England he instructed that James be withdrawn and placed with his mother. All his support would go to Emmeline Jean, who was left under the protection of her great-aunt, Miss M. Greenshields, until of school age. Before returning to his west coast service, John Tod left his wife Eliza in Carmarthen, Wales, with her mother, Letitia Waugh, who wrote to the Company on 24 February 1838 with some anger about the situation:

> I beg leave to lay before you for your humane consideration, the unfortunate Case of my unhappy Daughter, now Mrs Todd, who, as is well known, accompanied the Rev^d M^r & Mrs Jones, at the particular solicitations of Mrs Jones and friends, to the Red River Settlement, Hudson's Bay, in the year 1830 [actually in 1829] – not only in a perfectly sound state of mind, but possessed of very considerable talents; and who has lately returned to me, to my indescribable misery, a confirmed Lunatic. The cause of her misfortune may possibly be known at the Settlement, but however that may be, no certain clue had been obtained to it here; and the Medical Gentlemen of this place recommend sending her to an Asylum; but that is utterly out of my power; and the sum allowed by Mr Todd for her support is very inadequate, more especially as she requires the constant attendance of a proper person to take care of her; and I am, therefore constrained to beg, if it should appear that it is not in Mr Todd's power sufficiently to provide for her, that you will be pleased kindly to deliberate on the subject, and grant such assistance as may alleviate her greatly to be deplored situation.

A doctor's certificate enclosed in Mrs. Waugh's letter attests to Eliza's "mental derangement" and the inability of Mrs. Waugh to provide for her, "being in very straitened circumstances with a large family unprovided for." John arranged to have half-yearly payments of £15 made to Eliza's mother and, through the intervention of Governor George Simpson, Eliza was eventually placed in an asylum at Guy's Hospital in London. John Tod wrote to Simpson in 1842 pleading that, what with responsibility for "two aged parents and four sisters on my hands," he could not afford the institutional costs of his wife. Simpson wrote to Guy's Hospital, arranging for Eliza to be taken in there as a "charitable" case because "notwithstanding all his labors & toils in this country of between 25 & 30 years [her husband] is still absolutely worse than penniless." In 1846 John wrote thanking Simpson for his "benevolent arrangement of [his] unhappy wife." Eleven years later a letter with a description of Eliza's death, enclosed in the black-bordered envelope customary for the times, was sent but never delivered to John Tod.

～ John Tod Esqre, Hudson's Bay Compy, forw'd by Mr Smith

[26 May 1857] 60 High Street, Camden Town, London

My Dr Mr Tod

It becomes my painful duty to announce the Death of your poor Wife Mrs Tod who expired at Guys Hospital on the 11th of May last[.] She had been suffering for several Weeks from a disease of the Kidneys producing great disturbance of her Brain &c which finally terminated in her death. Immediately on receiving intimation of her illness I hastened to the Hospital and found her in the Agony of death uncons[c]ious of all around her. She expired on the same night, the next day I made every arrangement for her removal from thence. The Authorities at the Hospital would have undertaken the last Sad duties of burial but finding that she was to be buried with several others in a mass I protested against it & at once offered to remove her[.] I then went to Mr Smith at the Hudsons Bay house saw him told him the whole of the circumstances & my intention of removing her. He very kindly heard my proposition approved of it and generously promised to assist me in fulfilling the last Sad duties to the remains of your poor wife. I had only a few weeks before lost an Aunt her funeral had cost me £20. I told Mr Smith and he then said that when I brought him the Bill He would do all he could for me. I did so & he very generously gave me £15. in the enclosed is the Bill which I beg to forward for your satisfaction. Her remain's was brought away to the undertakers House the day after her death & all arrangements made for the funeral, which was conducted most respectfully to her last resting place in Highgate Cemetery the Chief mourners were her Brothers John, Frank, & myself and should you ever revisit London & wish to learn the spot where your poor wife was buried you will find it at the above place with the following inscription of the Headstone: Sacred to the Memory of Mrs Eliza Tod wife of Mr John Tod of the Hudson's Bay Company who departed this life May 11th 1857 aged 49 years.

I regret very much I could not secure the wedding ring, it had been taken away from her 4 months before she died & no one at the Hospital can render any information how it disappeared. It must have been stolen from her for you might take anything from her but her ring was sacred no one should touch it[.] Poor Eliza for many years past her Brother John & myself has continued to visit her. We have always supplied her with many little necessaries, we never went empty handed we invariably found her very rational would engage with us in conversation on various subjects & her memory was as good as if nothing had ever disturbed it. She always asked after you at particular Periods of the Year. I think in October she

always anticipated a visit from you & her dear little Emma[.] I sincerely
hope Yourself & Daughter are quite well. I shall never forget the manner in
which she clung to me when I left her on board the Ship which was to
convey her away. I hope she & yourself are well in health[.] Mr J^no Waugh
with myself & Harry who was a child when you were with us (& who
writes this because my Eye sight is so bad) unite with me in Kind love
& with best wishes for your health & happiness

    I remain Dr Mr Tod

      Yours very truly

        Jane Lloyd

P.S. I shall be most happy to hear from you as soon as you can conveniently
approving of my best Efforts in behalf of your Poor Wife

[enclosed invoice]

London   May 1857

Mrs Lloyd   To C. JACOB,

FURNISHING UNDERTAKER,

3, MORETON PLACE,

(NEAR THE BRIDGE)

KENTISH TOWN.

MONUMENTS AND HEAD STONES ERECTED.

For the funeral of the Late Mrs Eliza Todd [crossed out] Ag^d 49 Years

May 12/	To removing body from Guys to Shop	
	D[itt]o To A 5^ft 8-16 Stout inch elm coffin covered with black cloth and finished in the usual way	
D[itt]o 19th/	To the use of Large silk trim^d velvet pall	
	D[itt]o 1 Hood and Scarf	
	D[itt]o 2 Gents Cloaks and crape hatbands	
	D[itt]o A Hears and pair of horses	
	D[itt]o A Coach and pair of horses Velvets &c	[£]22.10.0
	D[itt]o Bearers and pages in crape bands	
	D[itt]o 2 Coachman d[itt]o Cloaks and bands for d[itt]o	
	D[itt]o Self Attendance in silkband to highgate	
	D[itt]o Ground fees &c 12 ft	
	D[itt]o for Providing and fixing head Stone and foot D[itt]o with the inscription of the above painted and Letter^d black	

    Received C. Jacob

      May 26 1857

Jane Lloyd's reference to Eliza's anticipation of a visit from her husband and daughter, and her reminder of how little Emma had clung to her when she was conveyed by ship to be placed with relatives in Montreal, are perhaps meant to make a man who had never seen his wife since taking her home to her mother feel guilty. But John Tod's life in North America was not one on which Eliza's death would have much impact. By 1857 Tod was settled in Victoria. His father had gone there as a settler (Dickey 1989, entry for 6 November 1850), and John had joined him in November 1850, retiring from the Company's service in 1852. By 1857 he had been a member of the Legislative Council for six years and a respected citizen of Victoria. John was living with another wife, Sophia Lolo of the Thompson River post, his partner of many years with whom he had seven children. They were formally married in 1863 after news of Eliza's death eventually reached Victoria, and before their daughter Mary married.

Sophia and Eliza were only two of Tod's four wives. His first country wife was Catherine Birstone of the York Factory area, with whom he had a son James in about 1818, when Tod was twenty-four (Fuchs 2000). He also had at least one daughter by the "singing girl," probably "Mackoodzie, a Sickannie woman formerly with John Tod," who appears in the Outstanding Balances for 1834-5. There may also have been an affair with the wife of Andrew Wilson, a postmaster who served under Tod in the years just before Tod met Eliza. Wilson had been accused of drunkenness and dismissed by Tod in 1834, but in 1835 the Company council at Norway House reversed the decision, awarded Wilson his back pay of £40 and charged the money to Tod's account.

Despite considerable talent and service, John Tod never rose above the level of chief trader, perhaps because George Simpson felt he was "not generally liked" (Wolfenden 1982). After the problems of the Wilson affair and Eliza, Simpson may have hesitated to support him even though John had considerable success as a trader and possessed a talent for writing that was almost essential in a Company that depended on its employees' reports to keep up with its far-flung empire. In fact, in retirement John Tod wrote his memoirs, "Career of a Scotch boy" and, in letters later in life, presented himself as a spiritual man who loved his family. He lived with his wife Sophia on his Oak Bay farm in Victoria until his death in 1882.

Letters to Emigrant Labourers

During the period between 1846 and 1854 the Company was going through a transition, from an enterprise concerned with trading for furs to a company supplying a growing international traffic up and down the west coast. It was also undergoing economic diversification into mining, forestry, and the salmon fishery. As well, its long-time expertise with local conditions and the fact that it was the only British institution with a permanent west coast presence meant it would be acting as agent for the British crown in its effort to create a permanent settlement on the west coast. In 1846 the Oregon Treaty saw the end of the Company's hopes that the international border would be drawn down the Columbia River. Its main Pacific headquarters at Fort Vancouver now lay inside American Territory. Britain had agreed to extend the forty-ninth parallel to the ocean in exchange for US agreement that the border would then move south to contain Vancouver Island inside British possessions. Even though the Company was permitted to operate inside American territory, it began to prepare to move its headquarters to what would become Victoria on Vancouver Island.

Many new challenges lay ahead for the Company and particularly for the man who would carry the responsibility of the change of location, James Douglas. He had been, until 1846, Chief Factor John McLoughlin's second-in-command at Fort Vancouver. While McLoughlin chose to retire in the new Oregon Territory, where he became known as the "father of Oregon," it would be Douglas's destiny to establish the colony that would eventually become British Columbia. Between 1849, when Douglas transferred to Fort Victoria permanently and 1853 – during the time these letters were sent to labourers – he had to deal with many difficult situations. In those first years many things went wrong: desertions to the gold rushes – in California in

1849 and in the Queen Charlotte Islands in 1851 – as well as the rebellious actions of mine workers in Fort Rupert and the wreck of two of the Company's ships, the *Una* in 1851 and the *Vancouver* in 1853. In addition, after complaints by members of the British Parliament that Douglas's joint duties as temporary governor of the new colony and chief factor for the Company put him in conflicts of interest, Richard Blanshard, an inexperienced young lawyer, was sent out from Britain as governor. In the two years Blanshard spent in the new colony (1849 to 1851), he managed – almost single-handedly – to destroy the Company's long-standing good relations with Aboriginal peoples in the area (see George Wishart story, entry 66).

The real problem with the new colony lay not in Douglas's Company loyalties – or even in Blanshard's inexperience – but in the terms by which the Company, under the aegis of the British government in London, had set up the Vancouver Island colony. The idea was to replicate the social system in England, where a gentry class with enough money to buy land and hire labour owned large holdings on which agricultural labourers toiled, while the owners managed. Consequently, land was to be purchased at £1 per acre up to twenty acres (eight hectares) and purchases larger than that were to be of 100 acres (forty hectares) or more and could not be made without a land-owner agreeing to bring five single labourers or three married couples for each 100 acres purchased. Over time it was assumed that these labourers would become small freeholders – limited in this case to eight hectares unless they too could assemble enough capital to hire labourers. On the model then in effect in England, only landowners could vote, and only large landowners could hold political office. To make matters worse, those who did not own land would not be permitted to engage in entrepreneurial activity in the resource industries – mining, forestry, and fisheries – that were to become the true mainstays of the future colony.

For many reasons, including an abundance of rocky land, a shortage of labour, and cheaper – often free – land south of the border, the plan did not work in terms of building a colony although the Company did make money in the resource industries and fur trade. Despite Douglas's many ploys for evading the letter of the British government's law in his real desire to build a colony, the early years of the settlement depended on emigrants – mainly agricultural workers and colliers – sent out by the Company itself. These men were somewhat different both from the many sailors represented in the undelivered letters and from the Company men. Many represented here were recruited in the same district, Kent. They often knew each other and had firm goals for their ventures overseas: either making good money to take back to their lives in England, or else finding a place of settlement where they could own land. They shared a strong sense of independence and entitlement, often willing to risk disapproval and Company censure when they believed that they were not being treated as they expected. Only 641 were sent, some of whom died during the voyage or quickly deserted. As a result of these unfortunate conditions, letters to some of these emigrants were undelivered. Almost all the emigrant labourers in our sample did not receive their mail because they found conditions in the colony not to their liking and left as quickly as they could, for greener pastures or for home. In the meantime, their families – some of them hopeful that their relative's work in the new colony would lead to their own immigration – wrote letters that, because undelivered, have come through time to us.

93   JAMES ROSE: *I hop to be in america with you yet*

James Rose went out to the Columbia Department aboard the *Harpooner* in 1848. This was at the time when the Hudson's Bay Company was developing the colony on Vancouver Island, and Rose was employed as an engineer and a blacksmith at the Sooke River settlement near Victoria. Also settled at Sooke were such gentlemen settlers as the colourful Captain Walter Colquhoun Grant, not a working man but the owner of fourteen hectares of land where he built a log manor house. Grant attempted to pass himself off as a land surveyor, but was less than convincing when he got lost for five days on his way from Sooke to Victoria. Grant had recruited James Rose on the promise that he could purchase land at the end of his five-year contract with the Company.

Rose's brother Alexander wrote to tell him that the family had received his letter, written on his arrival at Victoria, and to let him know how things were going at home. The letter crossed the continent through Holland Landing and Penetanguishene in October and arrived at Oregon City about Christmas 1849, an astonishingly short three months, unless the Oregon City cancellation was made the following year when the letter was returned to England.

Mʳ James Rose, care of Sir James Douglas, Fort – Victoria, Vancouver's Island, North America

Nairn, Sept 19ᵗʰ 1849

Dear Brother

We received your most welcome letter on the 6ᵗʰ Sept. Dated June ᵗʰ3 and we were all very happy to hear from you and to know that you were enjoying perfit helth. – thank God this leaves us all enjoying the same blessing, our mother is not keeping very strong but she is always going about but it gave her great pleasure to hear from you for she thought she

would neaver hear from you, she sayes that if she could goe by land she
would travel to se you, we are verry anchous to know how you will be
situtated and what sort of food you get & what kind of people are the
natives, their is nothing particular to mention Just now but the cholora
[cholera] is reaging verry much in Inverness[.] their is a great number
dying every day but our friends have all escaped as yet, Duncan Ross wife
died since you left hear that is the publican in Nairn[.] She died in
child-bead-last spring. the Simpsons left Iornsides [Ironsides] soon after
yourselfe[.] thay had a reagular row &c – Sandy Simpson is married. Tom
your Brother is learning to be a carpenter east near dyke [near Nairn] and
he is liking the busness very well, James McIntosh the Butcher was
wondering very much that you did not mention anything of him in your
letter as him and you were so intimate, all hear have have [repetition]got
word except Thomas Munros Mother & She is very uneasy about him She
sends her compliments to you and hops that you will sind her shure word
what has hapened to him as she is shure their must have something
hapened to him when he did not write. their is three or four steamers calls
reagular at nairn now[.] Nairn is getting a verry stiry town[.] your Sister &
George Gauld has got married on the 15th of June[.] he hase taking this
house for another twelve months and your Mother Stops in the one room
and them in the other[.] thay are living very happy and comfortable and he
sends his Kind love to you as his Brother[.] he is always with Mr Sinclair
yet but he is intending to go to the south very soon, every thing hear is Just
moving on the same as when he was hear – the croop is looking Beatifully
their is a great crop of every thing hear – I am always with Mr Dalles yet
but I Intend leaving him in the first of next season I Intend going to the
South he is not yousing me as he should I am not getting my money from
him but with a griat dial [deal] of trouble.

James Cuthlard [Cutler?] & Lauchlan Hay sends their Compliments[.]
I must conclude as time will not permit and paper will not admit, we all
Joine in Sending our love to you

A[lexander] Rose

[inside envelope flap] you must sind more news in your letters as they are
so very dear

WRITE SOON

By April the family had heard from James Rose and knew of his location
in Sooke. The family was expecting him home, so it appears that he was
not convinced that working in the colony for five years before he could own

land was a good idea. His sister, a milliner, along with her new husband, a
carpenter, sent a letter in the same envelope with Alexander's next letter.

∾ By the American Mail [in another hand] Via Halifax, [and yet another
hand] Missent to London
Mr James Rose Engineer, Soak River Settlement, Vancouvers Island,
By Panama, North America

Nairn, April the 9 1850

Dear Friend
    we received your most Kind and welcom letter and we were so glad
that you were Keeping your health so well[.] thank God this leaves us all
enjoying the same blessing, we wear all verry much delighted with the
most interesting letter that you sent[.] the most of your aquentances had
a reading of the letter and thay were all verry much delighted with it and
Iornsides [Ironsides] most espeacally[.] he was the first that came hear, the
letter was not two hours in the house when he came up and the [crossed
out] he requested that his Kind love would be sent to you and to tell you
that he had two sones now and that you might mind on the fine spree that
you had at the first one. Your mother was quit[e] overjoyed when the letter
came and more espeacialy when she h[e]ard that you was coming home,
and she is to have a bottel of the best whiskey wating you on your ariaval,
your mother wishes to Know if you have put up a church yet and if you
have a minster or if you work Sunday and Sauterday[.] we were much
surprised that you did not menton aney thing about the other lads that
went out with you as their was Know [no] letter that came but yours,
William Fraser came down from auldearn [near Nairn] and he desired
us to menton in our letter to his son that thay were all quit[e] well, you
may tell William McDonald that his mother died in October last in a few
hours ilness, Mary Bane of Foynesfield is a widow her husband died about
a week after she had a young son so she is stoping in Foynesfield now, we
wish to know what time you received our letter and what way the letter
went and what the letters costs you from hear[.] we paid 2.s[hillings] for
each letter but we was taken in by the post office people hear[.] we got
word from the General post office that letters only costs 8D [pence] by sea
and 1.s[hilling] by land, we are going to send you some newspapers to hold
you out of longer[.] I supose you have not yet a printing establishment out
with you yet,
    Betsy has got a young Son on the 26 of march[.] we were married on the

15 of June[.] we are still remaining in 27 higt Street Nairn[.] your mother is stoping with us as when you left, I am working up at cawdor [near Nairn] at a free church that is going on their,

Your Mother and Betsy sends their Kind love to you and receive the same from me as Sandy [Alexander] is to write to you to[o], I add no more at presant but hops this will find you well and a safe return home,

your afectionate Brother and sister

G.E. Gauld

Despite Alexander's earlier assessment that "Nairn is getting a verry stiry town," James's brother is not content with his work and expresses the hope that he too can come to America to join him. This was becoming more possible since the colony had been established. Indeed, in August 1852 the *Norman Morison* brought 200 passengers to settle on Vancouver Island.

∾ Nairn April 9th 1850

Dear Brother

I now sit down to write a few lons to you to let you Know how I stand in sircumstances at present[.] I thought I would not be in Nairn till now as My Master is not paying as he should do but I cannot help it now but I hop to be in america with you yet and I wish how soon it may bee for I would like to go abroad and I think that Tom would like to go two[.] in case of your not getting our first letter I may tell you that he is learning to be a cartwright with a carpenter at dalvey nere Forres and he likes it very well[.] my mother says that if she would only get one fill of her eyes of you she would be satisfied[.] I hop you will soon be able to gratify her wishes in that point and I shal be happy to go and mek you abit of the rod[.] I shall now give you a few words on the line of provisions here[.] we dont get our tobacco so reasonable as you get yours nor yet our tea but we get all other provisions at a very reasonable price at present but when the male is plenty the Money is [s]carse[.] perhaps that is not the way with you but when the money is plenty with you a few £s would do good to is [us] so the money that you was speking of will be very exceptable and when you will be going to send it you will write a Letter before it stating when it will be so that we may be on the look out[.] by the time this reaches you I dont know if I will be in Nairn but you will have another letter frome in about a month[.] Dear Brother I am sory that I have not more news to give you at present but perhaps Ill have some more the next I write you, Ann Simpson is now married and so is sandy Simpson and he sends his best respects to you and so does Robt Fraser and not forgeting Robert Falconer

N.B I was in Inverness on the 7th of this month and saw all our frends there and they are all quite well excepting my poor old grand Mother[.] she is very week[.] I have no more to say at present[.] Brother Tom sends his Kind love to you and likewis I your

Affectionat

Brother A[lexander] Rose

good By

James neither stayed in Sooke nor went home to England. Company records indicate that he went to Oregon City in 1850. Why he and the two letters in the same city by December 1850 did not connect is unknown. Given the exclusivity of the settlement rules that the new Victoria colony (and the Company) had set up, which favoured gentleman farmers capable of providing their own labourers, perhaps James decided to take his chances in the United States. By 1851 his mother Margaret, a "scavenger's widow," was still living with her daughter, Betsy, Betsy's husband, George Gauld, and their one-year-old son Alexander, waiting in vain for James's return.

94 JOHN SMITH: *Happy to learn that you are well and satisfied with your Situation*

John Smith, aged twenty-five, was one of this first party of colliers that went out on the *Harpooner* with his wife and child in December 1848 to work in a Company mine on Vancouver Island. Although the Company had known of the existence of coal on Vancouver Island since 1835, it was only in 1848 that the London Committee, under pressure from Governor George Simpson, made an effort to exploit its mining potential. Fort Rupert was established on the northeast coast to act as a trading post and the centre of the coal mining operations. David Landale recruited the oversman (foreman) and journeymen miners in Ayrshire on specially drawn contracts that attempted to adapt the then-current practices in Scottish coalfields to the very different requirements of Vancouver Island. Landale wrote to the Company advising them to treat the Scottish miners with some respect:

> I trust you will be prepared for them and put them up comfortably until the ship sail – They will have to be treated mildly in the ship and if possible put under the orders of the Oversman, who knows their ways – It is to be kept in mind by the party in command, that these people have been in the habit of earning high wages, and on *piece work* – that is – they work hard, or easy, and when they liked, and they may take ill at first with the regularity of a ship. But – a little management will soon shew how to guide them, they are *very good men* of their kind.

Landale's letter gives us an insight into what may have gone wrong later at Fort Rupert. Company records tell us of a miners' rebellion against the fish diet – the Scots wanted oatmeal and the English wanted tea and sugar, as well. Landale's psychological assessment of what it takes to handle workmen used to a measure of freedom and independence may explain some of the discontent. Nevertheless, the first days' experience aboard ship may well have been acceptable to Smith himself, who wrote to his parents from Gravesend on 6 December 1848, aboard the *Harpooner,* anchored three kilometres (two miles) out. He assured them "we are all well and very comfortable" and goes on to explain how they will be able to get the money he has arranged for the Company to pay them, confident that the Company "will arrange it all satisfactorily." It would seem that discontent did grow during the voyage, however, as Captain Lewis Morice reported that the miners complained that they had been served inferior beef and had been "*roughly spoken* to without cause on many occasions."

The *Harpooner* docked at Fort Victoria with the miners: the Scottish oversman, John Muir, his wife and two children, and five other men of the Muir family; John McGregor with his wife and two children; and John Smith with his wife and child. They spent three months with little to do at Fort Victoria, and Douglas complained in August 1849 that he had to persuade them to go to Fort Rupert. Nevertheless, John wrote to his parents on 29 September 1849 to tell them he was satisfied with his situation. His parents replied a year later in a letter written for them in an educated hand.

∼ Mʳ John Smith, Miner, care Sir James Douglas, Governer, Fort Victoria, Vancouvers Island, North America

Crosshouse October 23ʳᵈ 1850

Dear Son

Your Letter of date Septʳ 29/49 we received about a fortnight since and are happy to learn that you are well and satisfied with your Situation. – We had a Letter from Samuel Manson about the same time we got yours and are glad to say they are well and prosperous; – They mention likewise that they had a Letter from James from Australia. he stated that he has Thirty pounds a year there, but Samuel wrote him, that if he were to come to New Zealand he would get Fifty or Sixty pounds yearly; – At the date of his Letter he had not heard from him again but expects he will come to them. – They are well situated and can clear two hundred pounds a year from Dairy produce. They are earnest that we should come out to them and we stated in our Letter that we were quite agreeable if they would send a money order to enable us to go. – they write likewise wishing Margaret to go out and they will pay her passage – she will in all likelyhood go in the Spring. – Wm Balloch likewise purposes going – possibly we may all meet there yet – We think when your engagement is expired you would do well to go there likewise but before doing so let us know. – We have received on your Letter from Gravesend Five pounds and Five pounds by the check you have sent us for which we return our grateful thanks. We had a Letter from William from Stranraer, he and family are well. – Mathew is at work there and residing with him. – We have seen Robert Muirs wife Boghead and delivered your message – there is a Letter from her to her Brother forwarded to you along with this. –

William Balloch is residing where he was. he and family are quite well. – Agnes and family are in good health as also our other friends. –

We are

    Dear Son

    Yours affectionately

  James & Agnes Smith

P.S. We sent you sometime ago a Letter & small parcel by Andrew Hunter Engine man who is coming out. The parcel is a Small present from ~~his~~ [crossed out] James' Grandmother to him

The whole of the Money you settled upon us was remitted by the Co^y to the Irvine Bank – and if you would send a cheque for the Balance of five pounds still lying it would be obliging in case we should go out to New Zealand in the spring or Summer – Write on receipt of this –

  J & A. S. –

The parents, like their son, have been looking into emigration and have decided on New Zealand, hoping that John will join them. But by the time they were writing their letter, John was one of the miners who had deserted at Fort Rupert in rebellion against their pay and conditions. Complaining that they were treated more like labourers than colliers, they had taken refuge aboard the British barque *England* not under the control of the Company. This was the ship that picked up the *Norman Morison* deserters in May 1850 (see Lobb and Wishart entries 65 and 66). Records show that women and children, the families of some of the Scottish miners, were among those fleeing. Of the Scottish miners who came with John Smith on the *Harpooner*, only John Muir, his wife, and youngest son stayed at the fort. It is likely that John Smith, like other discontented workers in the new colony, took advantage of the free land being offered in Oregon or continued to California aboard the *England*. (See also the stories of John Willoughby, entry 97, and Richard Whiffen, entry 101.) With such a common name, there was little chance to find the John Smith to whom this letter was addressed, and it was returned as undeliverable.

95 EDWARD PARROT AND RICHARD RIBBINS: *I do not know but the time this reaches you we may be all deed*

The girlfriends of Edward Parrot and Richard Ribbins wrote a joint letter to the two young men who had gone out with other emigrant labourers on the *Cowlitz* in 1849 with the expectation of working in the new colony at Victoria. (These young men were part of the large contingent recruited by Henry Hulse Berens from around his estate in Kent. The Berens family had a long history of association with the Company.) Their letter came in the same envelope as one from Richard's parents.

~ For Edward Parriot and Richard Ribbens, Forte Victoria, vancouver Island, North America

Bevington April 2nd 1850

Dear Edward and Richard
we have taken the oppertunety to rite these few lins to you wich I hope will find you boath Quite well as thank God it leavs us all at present thank God for it[.] Dear Edward I have Not Seen your Father Never Since you have bean gon but Father sane [seen] him once and Soaph[i]a was about the Same[.] your Father and Mother and Henry is all Quite well[.] Dear Edward you are not to forget to rite to Mr Feathestone for he often enQures after you and rite to us as Soon as you Can for the Seams Seems [repetition] so long since we herd from you[.] Mrs Petty and Mr Pety sends there kind love to you and hops that you will rite to them[.] Please to give all our kind loves to Jhon Durtnall and George and tell George that I Miss him on a Sunday Moare than a nough and I hope that you all will retturn home Safe at youre return from that Country[.] Edward your Brother Thomas is at Mr Brookers at Palls Cray [St. Paul's Cray][.] I have not Seen John Since you have bean gonn[.] Mother Says that you are to tell us all about your jurney and your Country when you rite and that will be as soon as you like for every day is as long as a weak to me[.] So No Moare Att Present From Your Affectnate Friend
J and C Page
~~March~~ [crossed out] April 2nd 1850

Richard's parents wrote from Ruxley, Kent, wondering if he would serve out his full five years or come home.

❧ Ruxley April 2 1850

Dear son this comes with all our kinde love to you hoping to find you in good health as thank God it leaves us all at present thank god for it[.] Dear son we begin to think it a long time sins that we see you now[.] i dont know how it will be before your five year is over and dear son thou[gh] you are a long way from us you are you are [repetition] under the same god as we are and Dear son i hope that you will rite to us the first Chance that you can for to let us know how you Get on and how you like your contry for this has been in a bad state this winter with a great many hear tho we must not find any fort [fault] ourselfs[.] we have got a fresh master M[r] Robart Allen and i like him verry well and your Brother Joseph and John is both in plases and James is at mitchum [Mitcham] yet[.] your Brothers and Sisters all gives there kind loves to you so now i must Conclude with your mothers and my kindest loves to you so know more at present from your ever loving father and mother John and Margrate Ribbens

A second letter from Edward Parrot's sweetheart was more intimate, as she worried about his possible unfaithfulness or even his death. She also specu- lated that she too might emigrate.

❧ For Edward Parrot vancouver Island North aMercia

Aprol [th] 2 1850

My Dear friend
I take the first opturnty of riting these few lines to you wich I hope will find you in good helth as I ham happy to say this leaves us at present but I do not know but the time this reaches you we may be all deed but I hope by the blessing of God we shill all live untill you return[.] it is a very long time to look fored fore I dersay you think the time long[.] if you do not the people over hear do I can ashure you[.] I think you had better ov stayd hear for it is as the song says there is a better time a coming boys and know I do think they have come at last fore provishon is very cheap know but I do not know how long they will last so.
My Dear Edward I hope you arived over quite safe and when you rite you must lett us know wether you recived the letters that we sent by the seckent ship ore not[.] I must tell you that I ham a agoning to leave M[r] Berens this mo[n]th and so you must no be surprsed if you shold see me over ther soon[.] I have told you in order that you might mak[e] redy fore

but you must not expect me untill you see me fore father and mother will
not leet me com not wile they are alive[.] I do not know what they wold do
if I was to leave then fore so long a time[.] they wold brake ther hearts
quite then they ar bad enuff know and they wold be worse then[.] I do not
know woich wold be the worst her ore me then[.] I dersay you think that
place very derferated from the old place[.] ther is nothing like old england i
think[.] i dersay you will be glad when the time comese for you to come
home unless you have got some nise young woman out there and if so i
supose you will get maried and settled ther fore life[.] I think you had but
little love or resp[ec]t fore any one you left behind[.] I did not think you
wold dow such a thing[.] I thought you had got more sence and not to say
any thingh about it untill you had encaged to go and people say that I was
the cause of your goning but I ham shure I do non know in what way[.] I
have not sen your mother nor father but I seen your Brother tom on
sunday an he was quite well[.] My Dear friend you must not fore git to
Rember me to all that I know perticaley to Richard Ribens[.] I hope he is
quite well[.] I hope that neder of you marked the mop goning over and I
shoud hope you wold not coming home[.] we long for you all to come
home to lett us know what sort of a place it is fore we have heard so may
tales about it that we do not know what sort of a place it is[.] some say it is
a very nice place and som say it is a very bad place but I sopose we shill
know if we should all live to meet each other wonse mor wich I hope we
shill[.] it is a very long tame to look forward fore but we must trust to
provendence[.] I sopose you do not git any aples ther as we do over hear or
frut of any kind[.] ther ar a great elecshon [election] since you left and I
dersay ther will be a grate deal more by the time you return[.] I hope you
ar all happy over ther[.] I often think of you and Richard and shold vey
much like to see you but it is in vain as yet I must wait fore a time[.] if any
of you are married you must tell us when you rite fore I can ashure you
that almost all of the people ar about hear and shislehurst [Chislehurst][.]
My dear friend the greens you planted fore me to tak to Cray and sell will
about be redy wen you come back fore you I dersay you will when you read
this you will wish you was hear selling them know[.] father and mother do
nothing but talk about you boath and often say wat a foolsh thing it was of
you all[.] you must not fore get to Rember me kinley to Gorge and John
durtnell and I hope they are quite well and happy[.] I hope you have some
fine wether ther we have Butfull over hear[.] Uncle Copper and Uncle petty
are about the same at present[.] I ham afraid they will not last untill you
return[.] poor Mrs Durtnell as been very ill since you left[.] I think it is fret-
ing so much[.] I do not think you will find Richard single when you return
fore he is thinking about it know or at least I think so[.] Mrs Wells is still At

the same place often talks about you and the dog[.] I think I must know
bring this short note to a Concludence at last an have nothing more to say
at present but beleave me to be yours ever
C and P

After the long voyage around Cape Horn, the *Cowlitz* stopped at the
Sandwich Islands where, on 27 January 1850, Edward was "unfortunately
drowned at the Sandwich Islands being unable to swim and having ventured
beyond his depth, while bathing in a fresh water pond in the valley of Nuana
[Kapena Pool, Nu'uanu Valley]. His remains were afterwards found and
entered in the public cemetery." His sweetheart had wondered if they might
all be dead by the time her letter reached him. By then he himself had been
dead for two months. His friend, Richard Ribbins, did not stay to work his
five-year contract but returned home as a seaman on the *Norman Morison*,
arriving in London in 1851.

96 JOHN SHADRACH BLUNDELL: *I hope you are Landed Safe and Like your*
      Emploment and meet with the Reception *as you* Expected

John Shadrach Blundell was also one of several men from Kent recruited as
emigrant labourers by Henry Berens. His sweetheart, who remembered "the
games we have had togerther" and wished that she too could travel, wrote in
hope that John was establishing himself in the new colony.

∾ John Shadrach Blundell Van-Covers Island North America

[St.] Pauls Cray Opral [April] 3 1850

My Dear Sharach
I have wrote this few Lines to you and glad of the oppertunity[.] M^r
Herney Berin [Berens] as been So Frind as to Let us know that a Ship is
Coming to you So with your Mother Consent I have written to you
I feel ~~serting~~ [crossed out] certain you would Like to hear from home[.]
your poor mother is but every poorley[.] She feel[s] your Lost graitly[.] I
hope she will be Spared to see you once moor
your falter with Jenney and Emema are well they Send thar *Love*
I am happy to Say I am quite well feel *dull* at times[.] I ~~we~~ [crossed out]
have not forgoten the games we have had togerther
I hope the day will Come when we may Be *happy* yet[.] by this time I
hope you are Landed Safe and Like your Emplo[y]ment and meet with the
Reception as you *Expected*
[St. Paul's] Cray is about the Same Every dull only the Streets are beenig

pave[d] with Stones[.] I have not much new to tell you only I should Like
to Come to you

joseph hills and Emma jr [h]as cut ther ~~Aquance~~ [crossed out]
Acquaintance

Dear Shad[rac]h I have been to London[.] your brothers and Sister are
all well[.] they will be glad to [hear] from you[.] I whent on Bord of 2 or 3
ships sence my stey in town[.] they wear going to different part of the
globe[.] I could not avoid wishing I could Embark[.] give my best Respect
to your companion ~~and~~ [crossed out] I hope you are happey ad so you will
tell me when you write[.] good bye a[n]d god bless you

I Remain
your truly
    E. Sandenford

John's mother was as anxious as his sweetheart to hear of his employment
and reception in the new world.

april 3 1850

My Dear Son this comes With my cind [kind] love to you hoping this
Will find you quite Well as it leves your father henery and emma all
midlen[.] as to myself i am not Very Well at the presant[.] do give our
cindest love to all the young men that Went out With you[.] i hope you
all got safe there and are all hapey to gether and like the plase[.] do pray
my Dear Shadey rite to us and tell us all about the plase and how you all
like it[.] tell us every pertclar [particular] a bout your pasage over Wether it
Was safe or smoth and how your health Was out and how it is now and
may the ever blessed god cep [keep] and persevr you all from all harm[.]
Do pray let me beg of you all to mind What you are a bout and cep [keep]
your selves stadey and think of home[.] Wee are so lo[ng]ing to hear from
you[.] mind you Wee cant forget you[.] Wee pore mothers do see each
other often to talk a bout you all[.] i hope the other ship as got safe to you
before this and i do hope you Will be happey all together[.] do give our
love to john philips to the samsons and yore Compney as Wel to mrs field
and husband and to all i know[.] i must tell you the times are bad here
now[.] your father and his mates are out of Work now[.] there Work as
bene short this Winter – they have got a little stripen to do when it gets
Warmer[.] my dear shadey do tell us What Work you do and What house
you live in and if you are all together and tell us if you are realey happey or
not[.] i hope you are all happey and like the plase and pepoele tow[.] pray
dont do any thing to get into trouble[.] may god bless you all and cep you

all from all trouble is the prayer of your ever loving and affication[at]e
mother – Jane Blundell
Joe hils best recepts [respects] to you all [I] hopes to see you all at cray
again
bless you all

John travelled all the way to the west coast on the *Cowlitz,* a voyage
delayed in Hawai'i when the crew deserted (see the stories of John Bracebridge, William Dean, Jeremiah McCarthy, George Mouat, and George
Micklefield, entries 58 to 62), and Edward Parrot (entry 95) drowned at Honolulu. John worked only seven months at Fort Victoria and Nanaimo before
calling it quits. He signed articles on 9 September 1850 and returned home
as a seaman on the *Norman Morison.* Like many others who came in those
first years of the new colony, he did not "meet with the *Reception*" he had
expected. He was paid off in London on 26 February 1851 and would have
faced going home to St. Paul's Cray to his sweetheart and, probably, unem-
ployment as well. The letter from his mother warning him of the bad times,
that his "father and his mates [were] out of Work" had missed John on his
journey home. Still, "Shadey" seems to have fared well, marrying a woman
named Ann from St. Mary's Cray and having four daughters baptized
between November 1855 and August 1864.

97 JOHN WILLOUGHBY: *Be Obedent To Them poot in a Thority Over you*

A number of the sixty emigrant labourers aboard the *Norman Morison* on the
1849-50 voyage to Vancouver Island, including John Willoughby, were destined for the remote Fort Rupert in the northeastern region of the island. The
fort was far from the relative civilization of the Victoria settlement. Letters
from his father and his brother indicated an interest not only in John's well-
being but also in the possibilities for settlement. In his father's April 1850
letter, John's mother slipped in a bookmark with the words "God is Love –
R. W." cross-stitched in blue with a long blue ribbon attached.

᠕ John Willoughby, Fort Victoria, Vancouvers Island

April 2 1850

Dear Sun
With plesher i Take my pen Too Wright a Line Too you [h]Oping you
[h]ave Bean preserved From Dangers So Grat Crosing That Grate Oshing
[ocean][.] my harte and Solde [h]as Besought The God of h[e]aven That he

Woolde Garde and protackte you and That his mersey ma[y] Beover you as
a Sheald [shield][.] i hope you will Be Brought Too Feare The Lord With
All your harte[.] With plesher i Tel you Tha[t] Whe are All Will Ah[ea]d
and Comfortbel[.] Tho[ma]s your Brother Got Clear of [h]is Trobel and
Joseph [h]as Bean in Worke All The Winter[.] your Brother James is Gone
in another Bridge [brig] and Gon[e] up The Stra[i]ts of Mederanean to
Alexander [Alexandria] after Corssi [Corsica][.]

    T. [or J.] Willoughby

all Our Kind Lovs To you and i hopes you Will Right as Sune as you [can][.]
your yong Wooman Sayse She Will Waite Til you Come Back

John's father's hope that his son had been preserved from dangers on
the great ocean proved true. The family heard of his safe arrival in a letter
received 17 July 1850, and in October his father wrote again.

∾ John Willouahby, Forth Victoroa, Vancouvea Iland, North maraca

[1 October 1850]

    Dear Sun i Receved your Kinde Leter on The 17 of July With Grat
plesher[.] i Felt Disapointed When The Outhers Letters Came That
Whe Did not [h]ave one[.] i Whos Glad Too hear you had a Good
vouige [voyage][.] i had a Grate maney Thought Abought you and poot up
maney prayers Too The God of haven For you That you might Git Safe
Landed and i Thinke The Lord he ansered my praers[.] i Hope Now you
are Safe Landed you Will Be Obedent To Them poot in aThority Over
you And kind and pesebele [peaceable] And That Will Go Best Thru
The World[.] Whe Receved a Letter From James in June he Whos in
Constantopale [Constantinople] in Turkey[.] he Thinks he Shell Be home
in October if alls Well[.] he Whos verey aynshos [anxious] Too know
Wether Whe had heared From you[.] my Thoughts is verey often among
The Woods Allmost Fansinge [fancying] i se you With your Long Gun
Shooting The Wilde Beast[.] i Hope When you Wright Agane you Will
Give us a more pertickler acount[.] your mother is Geathering For your
broather master Dunnel. master Folings and Dunnal Whas verey Glad Too
heare of you[.] Litel Daniel is hed Cow man at Cocmanines[.] your
Brother Joseph as Bean in Worke Ever since you ave Bean gone But i Feare
he Spends hise money as Faste as he Gits hit[.] Thomas Beat The Jews
compleat and keeps on Shop keeper[.] your Sister Ruth Stil Works in The
mill[.] i Worke at mister Colgates Orpington Mill[.] your Grand mother
and Tom son is in The unone [Union] Work house[.] Whe ave no Leter At
present From James But Expeckt him Back From Turkey verey Sune[.]

Henery Pyke and William Pyke is Bouth Drowned[.] your Brothey
Thomas Since i Wrot The First part of the Leter as Bean verey Bad in The
head Quit[e] Lost his senses But he his somthing Better now[.] i Conclude
With All Our kind Love Too yo[u] may The Lord Bless you
   no more From yours
      T. [or J.] Willoughby
        October 1

His brother also wrote, intent on emigrating.

~ John Willoughby, Fort Victoria, North America, Vancovers island, By
Hudson bay Campnay 1850, October 29

[29 October 1850] Deptford

   Dear Brother John
   After a Long absent from each other i set Down with grat plesure to
write these few Lines hopeing it Will find you quit well and happy as it
Leves me and Mrs Willoughby Quite well at present[.] Likewise my son
Thomas is growing very Well[.] Mrs Willoughby was confind on Oct 6
1850 with Daughter and it is going to be crison [christened] her on Next
Sunday Oct 27 it going to be crison Eliza Mary Willoughby[.] i had three
week illness my self in september Last i was obige to put my Milk walk in
to a man hand to serve my custmer[.] i hope i shall be able to get on better
now i h[a]ve got the wo[r]st of my tro[u]ble of[f] my back now exsept
£16 0.0 Rent i owe M^r P Buntor[.] he is very kind to me[.] there is very
Lettel Work about hear[.] i Dont think Joseph Will be Long before he is
married[.] [h]is young woman is Dowse at. Father he is Blest with plenty
Work he ought to feel very thank full he as got plenty Work[.] James is
been Laying in commerchel [Commercial] Docks two Week come From
turkey Loding with Leence Seed [linseed][.] the Ship he is in the Name is
Leven[.] i think he is Bound for West indes for suger[.] he said he will sail
to your island when he [h]as serve[d] [h]is time out if you will send me a
Full and True statement of the island and tell me whether i can b[u]y any
Land statement [crossed out] of the hudson bay compay and what price
per [a]cre[.] When you send me word i intend to see Mr Baring [Berens]
ask him For a For[e]man place to come out and to tell me whether there is
any other shiping come to that island and whether there are any other see
port Town near to your island and send me word What Distond the see
port Town is From your island and send me Word What is the best Good
to Bring out With me or if you want any think sent you by the ships if you
send me Word i will send it to you[.] i hope if you see a good Living on

that island you Will stop there[.] Thare is plenty starving in this part World[.]
you can [send] me Word What Kind Seed to Bring out with me send me
word Whether there is plenty cattel on the island[.] is [I was] in London
Docks the other day i see the hudson bay compnay putting grate deal of
ingine Worke in ship to Bring to your island in ship Torry [*Tory*] London
that is the Name of her[.] thay told me there was about 100 Fameiley come
out in the ship[.] i wish i was one of them[.] your young woman can Not
help young men Torking [talking] to her because they come to see her
Brother charles[.] i have Not see her Walk out with any one without her
Brother tuck [took] her out for Walk some time[.] there is a young man
with him some time take Walk they told me they was going to gig [dig] a
coal Mine on your island[.] Sarith Gregorys is confind with Daughter[.]
She as got a good place as Wet Nu[r]s[e] 10s per week[.] i hope you wont
forget to write me[.] answer by the First channce you have because is
intend to come out[.] i Remain with kindes Love to you Thomas
Willoughby No 27 hughes Field Deptford Kent

Interest in the new colony was obviously spreading as both brothers
Thomas and James were looking into coming out to settle. By the time
Thomas wrote in October 1850, however, brother John had been part of a
large-scale desertion from Fort Rupert. He certainly did not heed his father's
advice to be obedient to those put in authority over him but may have had
some cause for discontent. Several factors contributed to the unhappiness:
the mine's remote and rugged setting, the fish diet, combined with a fear of
the Aboriginal workers who had had the mining jobs before the European
labourers arrived and who had achieved remarkable success as miners. These
factors along with harsh punishment from the dreaded Captain McNeill
after a work strike, led to the desertion of a number of men, including John.
(See also the stories of John Smith, entry 94, and Richard Whiffen, entry
101.) When the British barque *England* arrived at the fort in June 1850, John
and others took the occasion to head to California.

98 EDWARD HOARE: *You Must Not do as you said you Wood Marry a Black girl*

Edward Hoare went out to the Columbia Department as a labourer on the
Norman Morison in 1849 bound for Fort Victoria, Vancouver Island. His sister wrote to him the next spring.

~ Edward Hoar, vancovey island, North a Marackey [America]

Saint Mary Cray Aprel the 3 [3 April 1850]

My dear brother
i thank God i Was faverd Withe the operetuenety to Withing those few
lines and i Hope by the blessings of God thay Will find you in Good thelth
and dear brother i all So Hope you are Happey in the Siteuation you are
Plaist in[.] i Ham Hapey to tel you i Was in london three Weeks a Go
With our dear Mother and she is Quit Well but she has been very ill Since
you lift she as left Plaxtol [Plaistow] and lives in london With Philiez[.]
your brothers and Sisters are quite Well and Seem deapley interested in
your Welfair and i do a shoar you thare is Not a day Pases over My Head
but What i think of you Sincerly and i do trust in God i Whe Shall one
day See you a Gain if Not i trust you to God a lone as he is abel and and
[repetition] Can do More and bether for you than Whe Can[.] your dear
Mother is a Wal Ways tallking about you and as been very Much Con-
serned a bout you[.] i Ham keeping Compney With Alfred turner ever Sinc
you left and he Sends his best love to you[.] your brother William is Got
Constant Work and is Quite Well[.] Henrey is Coming to london in
May[.] Richard and his family is Well[.] Lucey and Ann as been very ill but
thare are bether[.] i lo[d]g[e] Whare i did When you left and Mary and
Haret and all desire to be remberd to you[.] dear brother you Must excues
Me if thare is any think a have left out as i Wish to tel you every think that
you Wald Wish to know[.] if i Can i Will Wrigth you a longer letter
Wheen i Have Had a one from you[.] Now dear brother Mother and your
brothers and Sisters Join With our best and kindest love to you and Beleve
us to Remain loving frends
So Good by and God bless you un till Whe Hear from you
    your Sister Sarah Hoar
Remberer Me to all

Edward had been sent to Fort Nisqually, and its journal details the kind of
work that labourers such as he would have performed: melting fat for tallow,
preparing and cutting hides for cabraces, washing bands of lambs in tobacco
water, and working in the slaughterhouse (Dickey 1989). On 7 August 1850
word reached Nisqually that the deserters from the *Norman Morison* had
been killed after a run-in with some Aboriginal people (see George and James
Wishart story, entry 66). Edward's mother was quite right to be concerned
about him because of the danger from others as well as his own actions. On
16 September 1850, Edward was not at work after having got spirits from a
man named Charles, a settler at Nisqually Bottoms. After this incident he

was once more at typical activities for the farm: cleaning out large vats in the slaughterhouse to receive beef for salting down, working with some Aboriginal women who were "grubbing" (turning the ground) in a swamp, roofing a store, dressing a band of sheep, and threshing barley as well as maintaining a potato crop. On 15 October 1850 the journal notes:

> The Englishman Hore who arrived this year from England who has of late been very dissatisfied and gone very unwilling about his work, he this morning was no where to be found – it appears that last evening he left the Fort in company with a man who is engaged on board the Brig Orbit (now lying at the landing) taking with him his box of clothes etc. I myself went down this morning and assisted by Captn Fay thoroughly searched the Brig, but we could find no clue as to his whereabouts, he is not much loss to the Company being a worthless lazy fellow.

Four months later, on 6 February 1851, the journal records: "The Englishman Edwards off duty drinking and carousing with deserter Hoare and part of Orbit's crew who have been paid off." The *Orbit* sailed for Victoria on 13 February with a cargo of horses and cattle for Victoria, and by 27 February, news had come that the ship was "driven high and dry off Whitby Island." In 1851, on the other side of the globe, Edward's mother was still worrying about him.

∾   Edward hoar, victoria fort, vancouver island, North America
[in another hand] Care of Dr. Tolmie, Nisqually

St Marys Cray, July 8th 1851

My dear Son
thase few lins Coms with my kind love to you hopeing they will find you in good health as I am happy to say this leves all of us at Preasent thank god for it[.] dear Son Wen you Went away you Promised me you Wood get some one to Writ But I have mever Received any letter from you But I hope Wen you get this you Write Back to me as sune as Posable for I long to hear from you and to hear how you are geting[.] I hope you are happy and Comfortable[.] My dear Boy I have News to tell you and that is your sister Sarah Was Married last Sunday the 6 of July to Robert [crossed out] Alfried turner[.] he is Now in the Police in London[.] they Boath desire ther kind love to you and Wish you Ware Not so far away so that you Culd of had some of ther Weding Cake But it is to far to send you a Peace[.] you Must Not do as you said you Wood Marry a Black girl you must Come Back as sune as you Can and then I May have the Chance to

have a Peace of your Cake Wich if I do not as long as I Can see you Back again I do not Mind[.] I had a letter from your Brother William this morning[.] they are all Well Except one of his little girls[.] your Brother hennery is in London and he and his Wife and famly are all Well[.] he as two Children[.] your sister Elizebeth is Come home from scotland her husband as left his Place[.] they have five Children[.] Richard Jane Lucy and Pheby are all Well[.] Ann had the Misfortune to Brake her leg some time ago[.] it is not quite Well yet But her husband and little girl are quite Well[.] she is down hear With Me for a day or two[.] Hennerys last Child is a Boy his name is Edward after you[.] your old Mistress is now Confind With her Eight Child Mrs Evending I Meen

My dear son I said in the Beginning of my letter I had not Received a letter from you But I have one and hope to Receive a nother as sune as you get this and tell me all the News you Can and Wither you intend Coming Back as sune as ~~sune~~ [crossed out] your time is out[.] I hope you Will, I have No Moar News to tell you at Preasent so I must Conclude With My Best love I Remain

Your Affectionate Mother
Elizabeth Hoar

Her letter was forwarded to William Tolmie at Nisqually and on to Columbia City, Oregon Territory, but never caught up with Edward. We do not know whether Edward Hoar was aboard the *Orbit* in February 1851, nor do we know his fate.

99 WILLIAM BURGESS: *Your poor Father Has Been confin^d 10 week with the small pox*

After watching her husband suffer through smallpox, Sarah Burgess was anxious about her son, William, who had left in October 1849 on the *Norman Morison* as a labourer bound for the new west coast colony.

Fort Victoria, For William Burges, Vancouvers Island

Clapies Cottage St Mary Cray, April 3 1850

Dear Son william

This oportunity offers by favour of Mr Berrins [Berens] – for us to send our kind Love and good wishes to you wich we Hope by the time you receve it you will be at your journy End – wich I have no doubt has been attended with many troubles to you all – but my dear Boy I have to tell you of much trouble that has Befol hus at home – your poor Father Has

Been confin^d 10 week with the small pox[.] he took Bad about a fortnight after you wer gone – and very Bad he had it we never thought he would rise again – Now it pleased the Almighty God to restore him his Health again But my dear Billy – you would hardly know your poor old man – he is so alter^d – it was a hard trial for us Both and I have been bad ever since – my dear Boy my Greatest Anexety is to hear from you – But I much feer I shall not live long Enough to have that pleasure – I am allways thinking of you and we never sit down to our Sunday dinner but you are talkd of and I wish I could get at you with a Bit – But I hope God has protectd you in your perilous situation – you have often heard me speak of the dangers of the Sea and I know by the time you have Expeiranced many of them such a long passage is not gone through without we have had very heavy Gales here at home and Great Losses of Ships here in the Channel[.] poor Henry pike is lost and Susan pike is dead[.] Mrs Roberts has left the risen sun and lives in the Barrack where Mrs Holden did and phil Cooper has gone into the House[.] Mr Ayre put him in[.] Stephen has left Spearings and gone in with them and Kempe as got Stephens place – here is great Changes here but none for the Better – the foremen has all lower^d their men to ten shilling none give more – your father is still at Hammonds he has Been in the Barn ever since his Illness – he thrash^d the Lent Corn and peas – But the devil thrash^d all the wheat[.] Now my dear Boy I have given you all the accounts of home – I must give you our Love and good wishes toward your future prospects in Life[.] be alive to your own well doing – be willing and active to serve your Employers and try to give them Satisfation in whatever they may put you too – and you will find you will fare the Better[.] have Brotherly Love for those lads with you for you are all Brothers – if not from one Mother – you are all from one Soil – and that in a forieng Nation ought to Endear you to Each other[.] your father joins with me in Love and good advice to you and be sure write home soon as ever you can and tell us all you can about how you get on[.] get your most Inteligent writer to do it for you and reward him in the best manner you can – I wish you could write for yourself

uncles and Aunts are all well and sent their Love to you and your father and myself send you our Blessing and may God give you his also – Emma is very well but I think she has forgot poor Billy – for I hear she has got another young man

farwell my dear Boy and may you prosper and do well is the wishes of your Ever Loveing father and Mother

Thomas and Sarah Burges

Sarah stated that her husband Thomas took sick with smallpox two weeks after the ship left. An outbreak of the same disease aboard the *Norman Morison* occurred on 29 October 1849, nine days after it left port. William was separated from the other steerage passengers on 30 October and placed in the upper fo'c'sle with George Ball, the first victim. Eventually, there were seven cases of smallpox on the ship. Since the disease can have a three-week incubation period, William may well have caught the disease at the same time as his father and gone on board for the late fall departure without knowing that either of them had it. As smallpox can be spread through contact with clothing and blankets as well as through direct contact with an infected person, either William or George may have been the carrier of the disease on board the ship. Unlike his father, who was confined for only ten weeks, Sarah and Thomas's beloved son Billy never did rise again from his sick bed. He died early in the morning on 17 November, and twelve hours later the log noted "committed the body of William Burgess to the deep with the usual ceremonies" on his outward voyage. He was the only one of the smallpox sufferers on board to succumb to the disease.

100 GEORGE MILLER: *I hope and trust by the time you receive this letter you will be in a good place much better than ever you had in England*

George Miller left England in 1849 as an emigrant labourer on the *Norman Morison*. His passage was paid as part of his contract with Captain Grant, who established his ill-fated farm at Sooke (see the James Rose story, entry 93), based on the premise that Grant would bring out labourers in order to be eligible to purchase a larger parcel of land. George's mother hoped he would stay his full five years because economic opportunities in England were very poor. From her comments that they were "making a good deal of Powder for the Hudsons Bay Company," we learn that family members had been working for one of the gunpowder manufacturing mills that had sprung up near the Royal Gunpowder Magazines in Purfleet.

～ George Miller, Labourer, Fort Vancouver, Columbia River

Orange Tree place near Dartford Kent, May 28th 1850

My Dear George, I hope and trust by the time you receive this letter you will be in a good place much better than ever you had in England, My dear George up to the time I now write we have not been able to hear a word of the Ship you went out in, nor of you or any body on board of her, but we sincerely hope you have arrived at Vancouvers Island in good health and spirits, and we also hope you will write to us as soon as ever you can and tell us something about the Voyage, and as far as it lies in your power of the Country, and how you are situated, tell Henry Wain his Father and Mother are very anxious to hear from him[.] they often call here to know whether we have heard from you, but we hardly expect to hear from you yet, I should think you have scarcely arrived at your destination, but we are as anxious to hear from you, but of course we must wait patiently[.] I dare say you have not forgot us, I am glad to inform you that we are all situated much after the old style, Emma Ellen Betsey are all at service and Tommy works at the printing Grounds[.] we have only Billy at home now and he will soon be able to work

I suppose you will expect to hear a little account of the old Country but I can only say it is very much in the state you left it, plenty of men out of work although it is Summer time, we have been making a good deal of Powder for the Hudsons Bay Company this Spring, perhaps some of it may fall into your hands[.] if it does you will think of home but I hope you will not have cause to wish yourself in England again at least not before your five years have expired, we pay only 4½d or 5^d a loaf and 8^d or 9^d a gallon for flour, and our wages have not been lowered so that is a good thing but the farming men have had theirs lowerd[.] I am sorry to say I have nothing more particular to tell you at present but I hope you will write as soon as you can and then we will send an answer directly, so my Dear George hoping you are happy and content I remain your Affectionate Mother, your Father and Brothers and sisters send their kind love and good wishes for your prosperity, good bye till we hear from you

His brother added his greetings, keen to hear about the Victoria colony where he, too, hoped to settle.

Orange Tree Place 1850 May 29th

My Dear Brother
I hope you will not forget to Let me know the state of the Country and if you think I can do Better there then in England I Will come the next Ship and I Hope I shall hear that you are doing Better than ever you did[.] we are all very anxouis to hear from you and I hope if you have the Least chance you Will send word[.] Ann sends her kind love to you[.] I hav no more to say But remain your
Efficonate Brother
Henry Miller

The Miller family was keeping employed despite the poor times, with three daughters in domestic service, a son at the printing grounds, and family members working at preparing "Powder for the Hudsons Bay Company." When George Miller arrived in Victoria, almost anywhere else offered better opportunities for a labourer. Rapidly disliking working for Grant, he deserted. Colony governor James Douglas reported in his letter to the Company of 16 July 1850, that "Mr. Samuel Robertson apprentice Clerk, lately absconded from this place, in company of one of Captain Grant[']s labourers [George Miller] and is now believed to be in Nesgually [Nisqually]." According to a letter to Company governor George Simpson, Robertson was working as a "day labourer on the highways at Nisqually" but there is no mention of George Miller. In Nisqually, George would not have to work for five years before being eligible to purchase land, as he would had he stayed on the Vancouver Island colony. The new American territories were offering free land if a man fulfilled certain conditions of working the land – much as a later generation would be offered land on the Canadian prairies. There is no Nisqually journal for July 1850 when George deserted but, on 7 September 1850, three of Captain Grant's men returned to Nisqually from Vancouver "where they had in vain been seeking more profitable employment than is to be found in Vancouver's Island" (Dickey 1989). Two days later they proceeded back to Victoria. George seemed to be in search of the "much better" place that his mother wished for him.

101   RICHARD WHIFFEN: *As you had the Small Pox when a boy you was not afraid of that when your ship mates had it on board*

Richard Whiffen one of the many emigrant labourers on the 1849-50 trip of the *Norman Morison,* had written home to tell his sister that he had escaped a smallpox outbreak on board. His cousin Cecelia Welch wrote to him from rural England during a beautiful summer and enclosed a letter from his sister, Lydia, in order to save postage costs.

Richard Whiffen, forte Victoria, Vancouvers Island, North America, Hudsons Bay Company
[small yellow paper seals read "Search the Scriptures" and "Keep yourselves in the love of God"]

Mason Hill, Bromley Kent August 1st 1850

My Dear Couson
I am very thankful to hear you were landed safe and that your companion Peter Leach was still with you[.] i hope you are permitted to continue togather[.] I also hope you are comfortable and happy and in the enjoyment of good health that most essential of all Gods earthly

Blessings[.] i am thankful to say i am quite well at present[.] Dear Richard you will have some thing to pay for this letter as i find by inquiry we cannot pay all the Postage in England but i hope it will not cost you much[.] i shall be happy to hear from you whenever it is convenient and you feel inclined to write for i am anxious to hear how you are geting on and tell me how you spend your Sabbaths[.] have you any Minister or Missionary near you that you can get to hear but i am afraid not[.] I hope you are allowed your Sundays and that you will spend them in Prayer and the Study of Gods Holy Word[.] My Dear Couson do not let one day pass without seeking the blessing of God and the teaching of Gods Holy Spirit by earnest Prayer and make your Bible the daily rule and study of your life and in all your actions remember that the Eye of God is upon you and be careful to make God your Friend and then you need fear no evel[.] Dear Richard strive to live as you will wish you had lived when you come to Die namely in the fear of the Lord[.] if you have not already repented of your sins delay not another moment but come at once to the Saviour and confess your sins every one to him and Pray for the pardon of them and for Grace to go and sin no more and let all your Prayers be offered up in the name and through the merits of Jesus[.] i hope ~~you~~ [crossed out] you find that little Book entitled Come to Jesus a comfort to you[.] i am very fond of it my self[.] My Dear i was sorry to hear you lost your parcel after you left me but i am glad you replaced the book[.] i am going to enclose Lydias letter with this as they will then come under one expence[.] i think Lydia [h]as told you all the news[.] i hope we shall all be spared by Gods mercy to meet again in England in health and Hapincss[.] how pleased we shall all be to see you[.] i must now conclude with my kind love to you and may God Bless and keep you in all your ways for Jesus Christs sake I remain your
ever Affectionate Cousen
    Cecilia Welch

～ Starts Hill Farm, Farnborough August 1st. 1850

    My Dear Brother
    We was all so very glad to hear from you again also to hear that you accomplished your voyage without very many difficultys. As you had the Small Pox when a boy you was not afraid of that when your ship mates had it on board[.] I hope my dear you will try and make your self quite happy in what ever station you may be placed and try and do your duty to your uttermost for your employers as the 5 years will soon pass away and then should you feel disposed to return home again how happy we shall all meet again[.] My dear always put your trust in God and Pray to him in all

troubles and distress to help you through them as you have the same God their as at home[.] I must tell you we are going on as usual at Starts Hill[.] we have a nice lot of fruit this year except Greengages and Pears they are rather scarce and we are likly to have an abundant Harvest should it please God to send us a good time to gather it in[.] Uncles have got very fine Crops of wheat this year[.] I am sorry to hear that the desease is very bad in the Potatoes again this year about us[.] George sends is Love and so dose all your Sisters[.] they all live in the same places they did when you left home[.] my dear now for the newes First the Weddings[.] Mr Morgan and Miss Fox as got married and Edward Carvil and Miss Garth, T Dodd to Miss Janny Jones the Blacksmiths Daughter and Baker the Taylor to some one at Down[.] Now for the Deaths Poor Thommy Leach died the 3 of Jany so poor fellow he just see the new year come in[.] old Mr Carvil the Doctor fell down dead and poor Tomas Mitchell the Sawyer at Mr Stows was brought home bad one Saturday and was dead by the next Thursday and Seagars that married the Widow Arrows was found Dead in is Bed and Mr Calab Arrows as died of A decline and Mrs Winfeild is dead[.] We have yet another Doctor come to Farnborough to live he as taken Mr Morgans rooms at Giles so now we have 2 Doctors again[.] Betsy Packman is going to get married to one of the Smiths at Cutham and Edward Packman as got a son he married one Ann Smith[.] my dear I think that is all the news i have to tell you off at Present[.] I hear that there is another Ship load of Emegrants comeing over to you this Month[.] I shall try and send you another Letter by them[.] Please to give my kind respects to Peter and [cross-written] tell Him his mother and Brothers and Sisters all sends their kind Love to him and they are all quite well as present[.] all at home sends kindest Love to you hopeing this will find you in good Health as I am by the Blessings of God Happy to say this leaves us all at present from your ever affectionate Sister with
Love Lydia Whiffin

I must tell you I did not get my Letter untill a fortnight after the rest of the people got theirs[.] I began to think some thing had happened to you[.] They tell us at the Post at Bromley we cannot pay only 1 shilling towards this Letter they said you must pay some thing when you get it[.] we would have paid all the expence of it if we could have done so[.] In your next Letter please to let us know how much you had to pay for it[.] I hope you wont have much to pay[.] please to write again as soon as you can and let know all you can about the place[.]

    I have got a lot of Uncles left off I Think[.] I wish I could bring them over to you in abloon [a balloon] and so bring back a load of Salmon[.]

now I cannot think of any more so I hope God will bless you and send you Health Happy ness and Prosperity[.] I hope we shall one day meet again[.] I am well.

The Eldest of the Miss Percevals is also Dead now their is only one left

Richard worked at both the Company farm at Nisqually and at the ill-fated coal mine at Fort Rupert. On 18 June 1850 he deserted with Peter Leach (mentioned in his cousin's letter), John Willoughby (entry 97), John Smith (entry 94), and other labourers. He went aboard the *England,* which was bound for California. He did not, however, join the unlucky sailors who fled the ship for fear of being turned over to authorities – only to die after aggressive behaviour toward some Aboriginal people. (See the story of the Wishart brothers, entry 66.) Although Richard had been safe from smallpox, survived Fort Rupert, and made a successful escape from a dreary job, a note on the envelope of this letter read "supposed to be drowned at California" in 1851.

102   BENJAMIN WICKHAM: *Dear friend when i Saw your brouther i Could all most fancy it was you*

Elizabeth Petty, who wrote to Benjamin Wickham, a labourer who left England on the *Norman Morison* in 1849, might have been a sweetheart or simply a friend. Her concern for him, her thoughtful and friendly contacts with his family, the carefulness with which she had obviously read his letter home, her report on the "Children," and her reference to his help when she had "So much trubble," would seem to indicate an intimate relationship at least promised if not already committed between these two "dear friends." Perhaps her reticence to express her feelings more clearly was caused by her uncertainty as to whether he has yet learned to read and write and, therefore, whether someone else would see her words first.

For Bengaman Wickham, Fort Victoria Vancover Islan

Renald Smith, Orpington Sept 5.50 [1850]

Dear friend
with much Pleashour i Sit down to answar your kind Letter[.] i was so happay to hear that you arived Saif to your Jurney end and that you was so Conmfortable Setled and i hope you will remain So all the time you bean thear[.] i was very happay to hear that you was with the you[n]g men that went out in the first Ship[.] i hope you will remain with them[.] you Say that you bean So well in your helth[.] i hope that you will remain So[.] i very often think of you and i dearsay you doo of me[.] i often think of your

kindness to me when i was in So much trubble[.] dear friend i ham happay
to Say that i ham very will in my helth and so is all my famley[.] dear
friend i ham happay to tell you that edwin is Living with the fuller at east
hall[.] he went to the fullers the weak befor Christmas, he Lives in the
house[.] William is still at Mr Lains at Werke

dear friend your dear broather as bean to See me[.] they bean all quite
well[.] i gave them the Letter to read to them all and then he brought it
back to me again[.] he told me that they was all quite well[.] your Mother
and father allso wer mor very Sorray to hear of the to deaths that you
had[.] William bargas [Burgess] father had the Small Pox at the Saim time
that William had it[.] he was very much Cut up when he hard of it[.] dear
friend when i Saw your brouther i Could all most fancy it was you i was
Shour it was your brouther befor he told me it was he is So much Like
you[.] dear friend you told me when you went away that you wold Learn
to read and right[.] i hope that you doo and then you can read your bible[.]
i was Glad to hear that you had got a Minaster and a doctor[.] i hope you
will find every thing Coumfortable to the end of your time and if you
Should Live to See me again and i you wish i hope whe shall the time will
Soon Roll Round and if it Should Pleas the Lord i hope you will Return to
us Saif again and may his blessing rest upon you and Protect you and Lead
you all your time that you have to Stay

Dear friend Mr Lain and M^r dun and Mr Petty was very happay to hear
from you[.] they desire thar best Respects to you[.] they was Glad to hear
that you was happay and Conmfortable[.] dear friend i Should have roat to
you befor but i was not hat home when they Sent the others Letters[.] i
hope dear friend that you will right to me when the others right to thear
friends for you know that i Shall be very happay to hear from you at
any time[.] dear friend doant think any thing about wat Richard
[indecipherable] Said[.] you know what he is befor God is above all such
as him and it may fall to his Lott if not to be sarourend to Somthink else[.]
all the Children desired to be rememberd to you[.] they was happay to hear
from you[.] ewen goas to Worke at the mill[.] Poor Littell Gorge cried a
great deal about you and that day that you went away and he waked up in
the night and wonderd whear you was[.] dear friend hanah inglefield and
her husband desaird ther Respects to you[.] the Littell boy grows a nise boy
now[.] dear friend i ham happay to say that i gits Plenty of Worke to doo
and whe rub a long from day to day and i hope whe Shall Continue to doo
so With the Blesing of God

dear friend i often See your broather William[.] i hope my dear friend
that the Lord will keep you from gettn into any trubble While you bean
over thear[.] when you right to me again tell me what Wirke you bean

dooing and wheather you bean Still with the youg men that went out
first[.] doo right when you Can Send for i ham glad to hear from you and
i will Send to you as often as i Can[.] may the Lord bless you and keep you
from all harme is my Prayer for you[.] i remain your Effectionatley
Elizabeth Petty

dear friend my Mother desiadd to be Rememberd to you and alls My
Sisters and broathers[.] they was very happay to hear from you and they
hope you will be conmfortable

Elizabeth Petty

Despite having conveyed to his family that he was "Conmfortable Settled"
and had the civilized services of a "Minaster and a doctor," Benjamin – like
most labourers who went to the Victoria colony under the aegis of the Company – quickly found it not to his liking. But instead of being tempted by
gold fields in California or free land in Oregon, he must have had a good reason to choose home instead. He went back to England as a seaman aboard
the *Norman Morison* in September 1850, thus missing this letter from his
"dear friend."

103 GEORGE HORNE: *You prommised me five pounds for every tune that I
     learned on the Cordian*

Brothers George and Henry Horne were among the labourers who signed
up to go out to Fort Victoria on the *Norman Morison*. George's sweetheart,
Isabella Simpson of Orkney, wrote him two letters giving news from
home. Like many people of humble means writing to their faraway friends
and relatives, she reported that there was little employment worth coming
home to.

༄ Mʳ Georg Horn, Fort Victora, Vancouver's Island, north America, to the
care of the Hudsonbay house London

[Kirkwall] July 9 1850

Dear frend
I take this plesant opportunity ~~to let yo~~ [crossed out] of writing you this
few lines to let you know that we are all well at presant thank god for it
hoping and earnestly wishing this will find you in the same[.] I received
your very wellcome letter the 5ᵗʰ of July and was very happy to heare from
you once more[.] you say you once had pleisant times in Kirkwall you say
its away now whitch makes me and us all very un happy for fear that you
are not well appointed but if gods will I hope you and all of us will have as

happy times in Kirkwall again[.] all of us fel very dull for your kind com-
paney[.] my mother cryes when she thinks you ar not well apointed and
my father wishes you had been here yet[.] little bill is very sory for you and
has the pipe you give him[.] mary sinds kind love to you and tells you not
to fall in love with a indian[.] Dear Jorge I am very happy of the pritty
according that I got from you and you promised me a present if I could
play four tunes on the according but I went and learend it and I can play
on it very pritty so I am won the promise. –

Your father was here in Nov and give us his kind company to nights and
we ~~make~~ [crossed out] made your father very welcome in stad of yourself
and he earnestly wished me to come to Wick With him but I did not go
for I am expecting your sister here and I am to go over with her then[.]
your father told me your sister was well you never thought to hear of well
on earth[.] my ant sends her best respects too you and She is thinking very
long for you and hops to see you *with* when you come to Kirkwall[.] each
and all of us sends our kind lov to my uncle John and tell him that I am
thinking agrate delle of tonge [often] for him[.] So gorge sabiston sends his
kind love to you. george young is ben in the prison in wick for saying he
would stab a man[.] my Dear I hope you will excuse my bad rite for I had
no time for fear the offes would be shut or els I would given you mor[.] I
hav no mor to say at presant but I reman your true frend till Death
      Isabell Simpson

Three months later, after receiving what must have been an encouraging
letter from him, she wrote again.

Mr George Horn, Fort Victoria, Vancouver's Island, North America, to the
care of the Hudson Bay house, London

[Kirkwall] October 4 1850

Dear Sweatheart
I take thiss opportunity to write you this few lines to lett you know that
I received your very wellcome letter and wass very happy for to hear off
your being saffe arrived at your ports end and i am very happy to hear that
you like the place for ther is nothing doing here and your old friend
George Young sat up busness for him self in wastrey [Westray] but he only
stopped a very few weeks at it and he cut home to wick and was put in
prison their for his good manners and your old Aunt in Orphir is A widow
since you went awy and she is gott married again to an old man about 90
years off age and my sister mary is got A south Country painter for A
swetheart and I am afread that you will loss the wedding for she will be

married before you come home[.] my father and mother and Billy sends ther kind love to you and hopes that your in good health as thiss leaves us all in the same and we had A veisete of your father in Kirkwall the last winter and he gott your coat and trunk and he told me that he was going to tak your watch iff it should costt him five pounds[.] my Aunt sends her kind love to you and hopes for to see you home in her house again and give mary love to her uncle John and She hopes that he will show his generosity towards her for she is expecting that he will send something handsome home to her towards her wedding for it will be before he comes home and give him father and mothers and Aunt and Billy kind love hopping he is well and doing some good for himself for ther is nothing to do here for your [y crossed out] Brother george is lieying home doing nothing for him self or any body elles[.] you tell me that you had some happy days in kirkwall but I hope that you and me will have some happyer days in it yet when your spared to return back a gain for i hope that our happy days will only be to begin then it will be the time then but you will be taking some indinen wiffe ther so I am affried for to stope till you come home[.] And me for to stope till then and be disapointed and you told me you wass not altogether but I hope that you are gott alltogether now and you must send somthing handsome present for me for you prommised me five pounds for every tune that I learned on the Cordian for I have learned ever so many but it is getting done for I have been playing so much on it to keep anay longer for you and my mother wass very unwell when you went away but she is in good health now and she dos think very much long for you she is allways speaking about you and wishes that your time was out that she saw you once again

   the rose is red the vielots blue
   the honeys sweet and so are you
   if youll prove kind i[']ll prove true
   and after this i[']ll marry you
No more at present but remains your true lover
   Isabella Simpson

Despite writing to Isabella that he liked the place on first arrival, George accepted the opportunity to fill in for the many deserters from the crew of the *Norman Morison*, working his way home as a sailor on its return voyage. He might have had a hard time keeping his promise to pay Isabella £5 for the "ever so many" songs she had learned to play on the accordion.

104 HENRY HORNE: *O the gerret the lonsom Garret when ever i ame up i aly think i seay you up in it*

Henry's sweetheart, Anne Watters, did not expect to see him for four years after sending her first letter to him. Anne's letters to her beloved Henry were an intense mixture of yearning, jealousy, and fear of loss commingled with more weddings, courtships, and news of family than most letter writers can manage. All of this intensity was written phonetically, exactly the way Anne would have spoken it, and is more easily understood if read aloud.

[in another hand] Mr Henry Horne, Fort Victoria Vancouver Island, North America,
care of Hudson's Bay House London

Kirkwall July 9th 1850

My Deare
I reseved your veary walkemed leater on the sixe of Jul and i ame veary hapy to find by it that you ar wall as this leves me[.] this leves me the seme that is in the enjoyment of good helth thank God fore it hoping and earslend wising that this will find you the seame[.] you will be Astounesed to heare that my Brother hast got mared to Betsy Tealur [Taylor] and he is Away to hudson beay Abut sex Wekes after he mared and John Fleat [Flett] hase got mared to A strumes [Stromness] girl five wekes Agoe and he is away to hudson beay[.] i wase at none of thear marges because i wase [not] at home i wase into enburg [Edinburgh] it the time i wase to month A way geten the fitthens of the bonetes and the dresses[.] when i wse A way i wase at Glasgo[w] and at dundeay [Dundee] ant at strelen [Stirling] an at frehburey [Freeburn] ant at maney more plases and now i ame come home Abut sex wekes Agoe and i ame working up in the garret[.] O the gerret the lonsom Garret when ever i ame up i aly think i seay you up in it[.] O the Grret i wish you was heare besid me i woald be veary glead for i ame thinken veary long in to it[.] O the gerret fore i ame Afread that I will never get out of the [garret I] wish i never had goenet unto it fore the thought of the [garret ma]kes me think long for you[.] if you was heare be side me i wald not care but I hop that want be long till I will be out of the wearsom garret for if i ame spared I ame entened to goe Away veary sune to enburge [Edinburgh] Agene[.] my Father and Mother sendes theare kind love to you and Deana and my sister Jeane is to writ to you i hope that you wont beleve hare what she says Abut me[.] my Deare i hope that you will come home when your time is out[.] i will kep my word as long as i sead i hop that if you have last thoughtes of the promeses or repentenede i hope

that you will rite me Abut it fore as sune as i do I will write you Abut it
fore my hart and mind is stell towardse you if you are standing true to me
as you rote i ame doing the same fore thar is none on the earth that I leake
but you[.] Catren Ross sendes hare kind love to you hare and John Wards
is casten out and she is courten with A sealur his name is Tomes Reed A
veary nis young mane[.] Tomes Allan is courten with rebena Tealur
[Taylor][.] James Fleat [Flett] is not courten the nue with aney porsent he
is A veary prety young mane you wold not know hin now[.] Anry
[Henry] Leny is stopen in dearness [Deerness] he is courten Ann Omond[.]
John Omond is stell courten with Mary Burges[.] John is now set up A
shope in dearness[.] James Luted [Loutit] is courten with Ann Wilson[.]
James is gone Away veary sune[.] Willan Matson is courten with Leanny
Creare [Crerar?][.] John Melear went A way to enburge [Edinburgh] last
weake[.] Willam Sinkler [Sinclair] is not got mared yeat but he is stell
going with Anne Wase he is A Sealeare on the pargone [*Paragon*] fore this 8
month[.] Peter Sheare[r] is warken ou of the towne besid his mother[.] M^r
Clarke hase t[h]ree leades [lads] in his shope Maken [Malcolm] headle
[Heddle] and Maken green and John Shea from home[.] I reseved A leater
from Willan Murey [Murray] to you and it is with in the oure leater[.]
Willame Creay [Crey] that wase in hue Wood [Howwood?] hase got mared
to A Shore girle and Deaved [David] Gune [Gunn] hase gote mared to Jeane
Drever at the shore and Anry Manson e hase got mared to Anne Stone and
Tomes Everen hase got mared to Berly Carel[.] your cousen daved hase got
Another sone[.] your anty that stopes in oferg [Orphir?] mane deayed A fue
dease after you leaft kirkwall[.] your Sister elesebeth went Away to enburge
at Bellen to A please[.] your sister Anne is stoping with your anty and i seay
your Sister Catren in Strumes [Stromness] when i wase up with my
Brother[.] if you wase in Orkeny [Orkney] you wold geaty the fune[.] have
you gote A swethart whare you are[?] i supose you have got A hafe A
Dousen[.] i could have had A veary preaty sealeare fore wane to me if i had
leked but i will never as long ase you stand true to me[.] i hope if you are
not standing true to i hope that you will rite me Abute it fore i feare you
are got Another[.] you wold not know me now i ame so altered from what i
wase[.] i now sportes the veale and parsole and A gensen coulerd silk dres[.]
My Deare still keepe op thy hart fore time will ware Away it is now nine
montes sens you went Away and i ame stell keeping up my hart thinking
that we will see wane Another yeat[.] i hope it wonte be longe[.] i wish I
wase besibe you now i wold not geve it for aney thing if i hade it for you
guste up in the garret whare we have been togere maney A time[.] i wish we
had the gens [chance] Agene i would improved it beter[.] O My Deare it
regouses [rejoices] my hart that time is passing Away that we may see wane

Another Ageane if life and helth is spared[.] May God keep us both and
[de]llever us from evell and that he may spare us bouthe to met Ageane and
if we may not seay wane Anotheare heare on earth wan we met in heven
wheare we met to parte no more may the keper of resely [Israel] that never
slunbers nor sleep keep you O My Deare fore it is in and true him wheare
we see wane Another or no but we will hop that we will see wane
Another[.] O my Deeare O my Dearling i wish we ware to ger wane
deay it makes my hart to bet and my eay to wepe whene i think on you[.]
do you [remember] the least night you wase in kirkwall[.] i wase veary
so[rry to] se you so drunk but i hop you will refren it nou[.] [that] night i
thought my veary hart wold have splet with in [my] breest and when i
think on you yeat i could have been marred sins you went Away but I ame
puten trust in you what you sad before you went Away and i hope if you
are not to full fel your promiss i woll be vearry thankful to you if you wold
let me know[.] you were only true to me heare and now when we are fare
frome wane Another your mind may altur but remember writ me Abut it
fore my hart and mind is one you yet and ase sune as i ame entenday to for
get you I will rit you[.] O My Deare I wisish i wase Along with yo O you
with me[.] i hope we will be to ger yet fore my hart is still one you but if i
thought you wase for got me i wal soo[n] marey if you will breake up the
enge[ge]men[t]s but wile my hart betes in my brest i never will for geat
you[.] O stend true fore i ame doing it if I wosh you wase heare i could tell
you beteare i wise I was beside you[.] O my Deare when i reseved your
leater i could not helpe crying when i think on you[.] may god keep you
till i se you be sueare and writ eveary upetunity and i ame sure i will
do the sam
por Anne Watters
[written across top of the first page] my Deare Henry if you ware heare o
how hapy i wol ben[.] i hope you wont for geat poor Anne[.] me and
Catren Ross is coming to you if we could geat i wold crouse the roaren
mane fore you[.] O my Deare remember me O for A kess of your mue
cudle nennel nefe[.] my Deare if my sheat of peper ben larger I wold have
rot more[.] O remember poor Anne pore fore saken lover O henry my hare
and breast is sore whene i think one you[.] por Anne was very wanten[.]
Henry dont for get me
    Anne Watter

    What the "mue cudle nennel nefe" refers to is a bit of a mystery. Some of
those consulted in Orkney think that it might be Spanish; certainly "mue"
could be "muy," meaning "very." "Cudle" might be "cuddly" in English. In
Norwegian "mye" means "a precious sight of" and "nenne" is "have the heart

to." But in any case the message remains a secret between the lovers until someone solves this linguistic puzzle. Anne's next letter repeated some of the news.

[in another hand] Mr Henry Horne, Fort Victoria, Vancouver Island, North America,
care of the Hudson's Bay House, London

Kirkwall Ocob 12th 1850

Dear Henry

I now sit down with the greates of plesure to writ you this fue lines to lat you know that I am wall at present thank God for it and my enrsny deseary [earnest desire] is that this wil find you the same[.] My Dear O the long i have been thinken for you when you are so fare from me and fare from my home you will forgeat that evear you saw me and i will never seay you anay more My Dear beloved[.] O My Dear Your anty that stoped in grengoe [Grindigair?] is got mared Ageane with A man beloungen to rendel [Rendall][.] she wase A weadey [widow] About nine ~~weeks~~ [crossed out] month[.] your sister Anne stoped with hare till she mared and your sister elesbeth went to enburgh Abut five month Agoe and the leters that your Father sent you hase returned Abut A month Agoe[.] I dont know what wase the mater but my wane is not returneg yeat and i hope not[.] Catren Ross sendes hare kind love to you and bedes me ask you if you mind the time that you asked hare if she wase eagear for she remembers it yeat[.] she is corten with tomes reed A sealear and hare an helek is done with it[.] Jeames Luted [Loutit] is in leth [Leith] stopen in A shop in leth [blotted out] gearh get and Johy Melear is in enburgh [Edinburgh][.] Johy Omen and Meary Burges is steall courten and rebena wilson I beleve and Tome Alen is [s]trong at it[.] we have not got A leater from my brother sens he went A way but we expeten wane every post from him[.] I thought I wold have had A leater from you or nou but thear is none come yet[.] my Fathear and Mothear sendes thear kind love to you and Jean and Marget and Deana[.] My Deare i wish you wase beside me now[.] O could this leater spek my love it wold teal more or i cand hold the pene to writ[.] my Dear i have lost the hart of heare [hair] you give me to kep but i have the picture sefe yeat[.] if it could be posable that you could send A treat of your hear i wold be veary glead[.] I hard that i could geat A leater seant to you so i enbrased the optnity hopind that you will reseve it[.] my deare i hop that you want sleap [slip] aney oprtunity and i ame sure i wont fore whene i reseved your last leater none on the earth could have bean more hapeare

then I, I hop you are pasen your tiM theare as you did heare and i hop
that you are kepen op your heart for time will weare Away[.] it is wane
yeare and fore dease sins you left orkney[.] i hop my deare that you will
come home when your time is out fore years will sune pase Aweay if Life
and helth is spard[.] i hop you are stenden true to me fore i ame sure i
ame doen it to you[.] my Deare i hop you are not for got the promeses
you med to me and if you have repented it i hop you will be so kind and
writ and leat me know for as sune as i repent it i will writ you but I do not
repent it yeat[.] steal heape op your heare as i ame doen hopen to se you
sune[.] may God kepe you from All harm and delever you from all
dengers[.] Dear henry i hop that al thoe you have not the preveleges of
A gurge [church] thear or A minster as we have hear i hop and earnesly
preay that you may be capet [kept] in the right way for if you seak him
you will find heam yay if you toke the winges of the mornengen an flea to
the otre [utter] most end of the world thear dost his rit hend keap you[.]
my Dear I wis I wase besid you fore when I think on the pleasure we have
seane betenune [between] us both my Deare i hop that you and me will
sune met to part no more[.] I most now c[onc]lud[e] with my Best wistos

    I reamen your efectenly

      Anne F Watter

pleas writ when evear you cane O remembear me for i ame sure i will
remembear you

    O be sure and writ
    O writ
    O writ
    may God
    Kip you
    godd Beay

The Orkney community was used to these long absences of their men and,
although Anne seemed resigned, she was in an agony of yearning – especially
when she is up in the garret, waxing poetic for her Henry. She feared that he
may by then have had a dozen sweethearts. She has worried, too, about his
self-control, as he had been quite drunk on his last night in Kirkwall and she
suspected that this might also happen far from home. Orkneymen were
known for taking Aboriginal wives and Anne would surely have heard from
her friends Isabella and William Ross (see their letter to William Ross, entry
105) that her Henry was "to be appointed to the Shop after learning the languages of the Indians," so she might be even more worried about him cohab-
iting with an Aboriginal woman.

Anne Watters, however, would not have needed Henry to send her a tress of his hair, as she would soon have had him home in person. Like a number of others, he did not stay on the west coast. Along with his brother, George, Henry returned as a seaman on the *Norman Morison,* arriving in London in February 1851. Orkney records show that on 17 February 1852 Anne and Henry were wed in Kirkwall.

105 WILLIAM ROSS: *Keep yourself from being taken any notice of in respect of being any way in quarrels as it will break your contract agreement with Company and hurt your own Intrest*

His parents sent William Ross, an emigrant labourer aboard the *Norman Morison,* two letters filled with news of the close-knit Orkney kinship and friendship networks. Even the traditional Kirkwall mass football game on Christmas Day and New Year's Day, known to Orcadians as "The Ba," is reported. In it, the whole town joined in two huge teams, the "Uppies" and the "Doonies," each trying to get the ball to a opposite point along Broad Street, with the harbour as the goal of the "Doonies" (Tinch 1988, 140; Payne 1989, 68). In both letters the parents expressed concern about a fight William has had with another Orkneyman named Gillespie.

Mr William Ross, Drainer at Fort Victoria, Vancouvers Island, North America,
Care of the Hudson's Bay Company's House, London

Kirkwall 11 July 1850

Dear Son

We received your long looked for letter on Sauterday th6 instant and was happy to here by it that you were well and that you arived safe at your desired port, I thank God for it and you ought to remember to do the same seeing that he preserved your life while he might have cut you off in the small pox, as well as him that he took [William Burgess] therefor look to him at all times & ask his help and he will grant it to you, We are astonished the Gelispie [Gillespie] should turned out such a bad freind to you seeing what your father did for him But you father desired me to tell you that [you] need be in no fare [fear] of him or any one else if you do you[r] work and are Capible of doing it and be shure and try to please them that are over you and then you have nothing to fear[.] you Sister Jean had a Daughter three weeks after you went off and Alexander had a Daughter born to him the same week and Jean has Named her Daughter after you and Alexander calles his Daughter Margaret, your Brother Davids

Daughter is finely [finally] well and are Still in Firth But David has not
been doing Very little all winter for the work has but been little over all.
Since you left, you[r] father is Still doing a little but it is quit triffling he
has been in Sanday finishing the work that you left him with, Yon Old
Gossip David Gunn has married with one of Nicol Drevers Daughters[.]
John Flett, Effy Balintines [Ballantyne's] son has married Jannet Creelman
belonging to Stromness and he is gone to Hudson's Bay[.] William Waters,
has married Betty Taylor and he is gone to Hudsons Bay and William Ross,
Daniels' son is gone to hudsons Bay and Great Many more than has gone
any year yet and agreat many Went from Shetland and I believe that they
were two that went By the Hudson Bay ships that is going to Columbia to
your place[.] Jearm Eunson & his Wife sends there kind Compliments to
and hope that you are Well, George Moars best respects to you and he is
happy to here that you are well and got as an Overseer over the Drainers,
if Gelispie, be under you, he says you should Keep an eye over him in case
of his shyness, Thomas Barnnet went off from here about two months ago
with the Paragon but he has sent no word home yet and no body Knows
Whither he be gone to Sea or where he is[.] he was seen in Sheilds but not
since and his Aunt is very Greived about him[.] Francis Barnet is Doing
very little all winter and now he is Driving a Cart to *Captain Dash*[.] let
us know if they be any place of Worship where you are and by what
Profession it is and if you attend it and let us Know all that you can about
the place and the People and what way the employ themselves and how the
live in General and When ever you can see a chance of sending a letter do
it what ever way you can get one sent as we will always be Glad to here
from you, Mind Slip no oppertunity of writing us, May & Peter Yorston
Send their Compliments[.] Jean Moar, Sends her Compliments, Auntie
Barnett send her compliments to you and she hopes you are [well]. John
Clark Mr Fortesquoy Greive is leaving Fortisquoy and has taken the farmer
of Quoy Birstan [Quoyberstane]

~~Anny~~ [crossed out] Effy Balentynes [Ballantyne's] house was pulled
down about her and she had no place to get to and Bob made ~~A~~ [crossed
out] made a Tent and the people saw it on the Road as the[y] went to
Church and she is not to get leve to Go to the Gooddughter or then they
are going to turn them Both out, David, & Margaret & their Child Send
their Kind Compliments and they are well and if they be spared next time
you will get the word of another addition to their family, Alex^r & Jean &
Margaret send their Kind compliments to you and they Hope you are well,
Your Father and Alexander are working in Gairsay at present but it will
soon be done and they have no other on hand at present[.] Cathrine and
Isabella are still going to the School yet[.] their Kind love to you, &

Jeans Compliments to you and your name Daughter Willimena's[.] Ann
Watters is well and She and us all got our letters with the same post[.] her
Compliments to you and she hopes you will write when ever you can
see a chance, The Foot Ball went down the Street and Middle Tree of the
Bonefire[.] William Loutit has married and Bell Loutit that was in M^r
Borwicks, and I forgot to let you Know that William Waters was in Prison
a whole night & Day and William Ross for Stricking John Brodie in John
Taits Shop and they were fined Waters 15/- [shillings] and Ross 10/-
[shillings] each for the[y] paid the fine because they had to go to Stromness
to Join the Ships, Gilbert Foubister and Francis Barnet send their best
respects to you[.] Margaret Duncan's Compliments to you and she away
south to Service her Compliments, The Peats are coming home now and
the Crop is looking middling but the Potatoes are looking best this season
that they looked this soom years[.] There are no difference in the loan since
you left Only Mr William Bews is taken the House of Andrew Garrioch
and Captain Dash is Lodging with him[.] Miss Firth has got married to
Mr Gold of Grain Bank since you left home, Barbara Caldar and Thomas
Irvine Married here three ~~years~~ [crossed out] weeks agoe[.] Jean Moar's
Compliments to you the second time and she hopes you are well and she
hopes you will not take an Indian Woman for She hopes you will come
home and take her yet yourself as she say Says she is renewing her age like
the Eagle and she is getting as *prim* as (hansom) *Misline neddle*[.] Mr John
Tait Merchant died here very suddenly of Palsay[.] it continued with him
about nine days at it is made a great overturn, Robert Tullock and William
Spence has taken the Shop and Bought all the Shop goods and all other
things was rouped and the Shiping is Sold and the Heirs are gone to the
law about the Will[.] that is all at this time from your affectionate
Father & Mother William & Isabella Ross
Jean[']s Compliments to John Sibeston

[in another hand] Mind write as soon as ever you can and when ever you
see a chance whatever place from as we will like to here from you still,
Isabella Ross

∾ William Ross, Fort Victoria, Vancouvers Island, North America,
to the care of the Hon^r Hudson's Bay's House, London

Kirkwall 12 September 1850

Dear Son
    We received you welcome and long looked for letter and was extremely
glad to learn by it that you were well and had arived safe at your Desired

port and were likewise glad to learn by it that you had got to be an overseer of the Draining department and that Henry Horne was to be appointed to the Shop after learning the languages of the Indians and on the Other hand we were astonished at what you told us about Gilespie [Gillespie] that he was such a bad freind to you on the passage and likwise glad when we hard by your own words that you Stuck up to him and gave him a beating, it was just what he deserved, Now on the other hand I wish you to take care what company you Keep seeing you have got a prefarement and Keep yourself from being taken any notice of in respect of being any way in quarrels as it will break your contract agreement with Company and hurt your own Intrest and remember to read your Bible and if there be a place of Worship of any presbyterian sect that you can here the word of God explained go to it but if not Stop at home and read and meditate on your Bible.

The work in this Country is farely done there is Nothing to do at all[.] your Brother David has not a Stroke of work this whole Summer and at the same time he has got an addition to his family of a daughter (and her name is Margaret) and your Williamina is finely well and prattling a Speaking you would be taken up with her now, David got a share of his father in laws Land but it has not turned not [crossed out] out as he expected and he thought to have got out to you but he cannot for he is not belonging to Orkney[.] David and His Wife and Childeren send there Kind love to you and are sorry that had not been going along with this letter[.] Alex^r has been working with me at Gersay [Gairsay] and Holm this Summer but we are just about done and have no apperance of a job[.] Alexander and his Wife Sends there Kind love to you and wishes that you may be well as this leaves them and little Margaret at present, We sent you a letter as soon as we got your last letter and all the news that we Knew and if you have got her you will have it[.] we therefor just inform you that this night is Christian Dick of Scapa's Wedding night with a freeston cutter called James Herdman and there are bidden to the Wedding about one hundred and eighty people, but where they are to stow them we Know not except they go Butter and bread fashon and David Gunn Married as you will see in our last and about two months he had a Daughter and he was almost like to have been a Widower for his wife was very bad and went out of her mind so far that they were obliged to take and put the Child to a nurse but she has got better and is nursing it herself but I think that he has now [crossed out] no work Doing at present[.] your mother has nothing farther to say than she wishes you her earnest Blessing and Wishes the Lord may guide and Direct you in all your dowings and wherever you go, But she has Been very poorly this summer more so than formerly[.] I am telling you

again that your Sister Jean has a Daughter and She calls her Williamina and
Jean sends her Kind compliments to you and wishes you all prosperety and
Kathrine her love to you and she is going to the School, & Isabella sends
hers and she is going to the School likewise and Jean Moar sends her love
to you and she hopes you have not forgot your promise to come home and
Marrie her[.] Peter and May Yorston Send their Compliments hopeing that
you are well as this leaves them at the present time[.] Give my best respects
to Henry Horne and I hope as I heard from your letter that you had
agreed so well and stood by one another I hope you will continue so as
long as you continue in the Country[.] my Compliments to John Sibiston
[Sabiston] and Geo. Horne and I hope they will do well if God spare them
life[.] Dear William if there is any thing that you want let me Know what
it is and give me a Direction what way you wish me to send it and I shall
do the best in my power to get it and to send it[.] there has been three
letters wrote one when we wrote and two since by Henry Hornes father
and have been returned but Ours was not returned so it must be in the
Direction or else they would have gone as well as ours or then ours would
been returned also – The provisions here are very cheap but the work is
nothing in compare and therefore it makes the Provisions dear[.] Barley
meal is at 1/3 [1s. 3d.] for 17½ lb Oat meal 1/7 [1s. 7d.] & 1/8 [1s. 8d.] the
best South Country Meal Potatoes are offered at 2/- [2s.] and at 1/6 [1s. 6d.]
pr barrele taking 20 Barrels[.] – Kathrines compliments to Henry Horne
and she hopes he is keeping his health and is well and Ann Watters Compliments to you and she hopes you are well and liking the place[.] No more
from father & mother at this time W^m & Isabella Ross

[sideways along the edge of each page] George Moar sends his compliments
to William Ross and Henry Horne and he hope that they are well and he
was glad when he read about you noble stand with Gillespire [Gillespie]
and the Beating that you Gave him if he had been with you he would
helped you, Adue, G. Moar

   The Henry Horne mentioned several times in this second letter is the one
whose sweetheart missed him so much (entry 104).
   While both parents and friend George Moar support William's defence of
himself in giving Gillespie a beating, his parents hoped for more prudent
action in the future. They knew very well that the Company was a major
employer of Orkneymen and any black mark on a record could risk future
employment or, as they put it, "hurt [his] own Intrest." While no mention
of the fight appears in the ship's log, William Gillespie was listed as another
of the emigrant labourers; no doubt the dispute happened outside the view

of the ship's master or mate. William Ross, however, certainly fared better than the unfortunate William Gillespie. James Douglas described Gillespie's fate in a letter to Archibald Barclay, Company secretary, dated 15 May 1850:

> A quantity of Rum was sold by some party on board the *England* to the men and Indians of this settlement, who, in consequence, became so riotous and disorderly, particularly the men who arrived from England by the *Norman Morison* that, for the protection of the establishment, we were under the painful necessity of confining several of them in irons, and they are not yet all released from custody. Governor Blanshard, I am happy to say, approved and supported with his authority, the measures I suggested for the suppression of the riot. William Gillispie one of the labouring servants sent out by the *Norman Morison,* was unfortunately drowned on the 11th Inst, the day of the riot, having gone out with two others, in a small canoe, which he upset in a fit of intoxication. The men in company narrowly escaped a watery grave. The body of Gillispie was found and interred yesterday.

The luckier William Ross was recruited to replace the deserters, coming home as a seaman on the return trip of the *Norman Morison* along with his countrymen, the brothers George and Henry Horne. Although men by the same name – a common one – were employed later by the Company, it appears that this William Ross was not employed again.

106 WILLIAM RITCH: *For the five years wil wear bot i thenk them long anof*

William was one of several Orkney labourers recruited in 1850 by Edward Clouston on five-year contracts to the west coast. On the *Tory,* he shared a crowded cabin in steerage with five other young men: Wm. Stockand (twenty-one years), Wm. L. Guthrie (nineteen years), Wm. Garrioch (twenty years), Wm. Work (nineteen years), and Christopher Finlay (seventeen years). With four other Williams in such close quarters, last names must have been the order of the day in cabin number 6.

William Ritch's wife, Margaret Swordie, wrote hoping to reach him in London before he left on the Company's ship *Tory,* headed for Fort Victoria. Her letter, if read aloud, conveys the broad dialect used by Orcadian speakers in the past. Margaret's reference to Mary Marwick and Magnus Linklater "gost gons to be boket" probably refers to the "booking" when the man went to see the minister to arrange to have the banns of his marriage proclaimed in church. The "booking night" was an important one, because it was the first indication in an era before engagements that a marriage would take place. Margaret referred to another unfamiliar custom when she says that "lisia is feid weath the mother a twalmont": "feeing" was the term for hiring farm servants; there was a "feeing market" twice a year to which servants who wanted to change their place of employment could go for a contract for either six months or a "twalmont" (twelvemonth).

Mr William Ritch, Hudsons Bay House, London N° 4

Oct. 30 1850

   my dear lover I take this opertunety to rite the[e] this fue liens to leat you knoe that i ame in goude helth at present thank god for it and i have recived your t[w]o leters which i was verey glade of and it gave my mind much ease to knoe that you are wal for i coud not get sle[e]p for thinking one [on] the[e] til i got this letres and my sistes Ann and John Marment [Merriman?] is courting wich is ben several times at our hous since you went of[f] and he told me he was verey sorie that he did not come and folow the[e] apace ["a piece" or some distance] that last day at chorch and he seas [says] he shal be mereid [married] vere sown if she wil do it with him and Marey Morouck [Marwick] and Magnes Linkl[a]ter in moseter [Mossetter] is gost [just] gons to be boket [booked] as fare as i hear and i hear that your brother is not tinking much abou[t] his brother dith [death] and you Mother tock bad when she hard it bot it was not long til she was op bot she is not siad aniething of os [us] since bot i dont no how long she keps that way and shea was very ernes incwiring [inquiring] Margaret Mowat the nuse [news] frome you and i have bein at your Sisters wance sence you went of[f] and she was vere cind [kind] And they ware all wall and Andrew Spance [Spence] and Margaret Mowat wants to be remembred to you and they sade they are thinking very long fore you bot she bides you not to think long for the five years wil wear bot i thenk them long anof[.] James Flet[t] is not hom as yet and katren Johanston and Lisia Johnston wants tou be remembred to you and lisia is feid [feed] weath the mother a twalmont [twelvemonth] and i hed no word of any sepertation in the house as yet and all the wal wal [repetition] wising frings [friends] and nabers [neighbours] is very glade to hear goud nuse from the[e] and i have no more nuse at present to send the[e] bot we are alle weal at present hoping and erenestly wising to find you in the same and i wod be very glad if time coud aloue [allow] to rite me a fue lines be fore you left London and teal me the name of the Shipe that you are gone with and let me no whou [how] youre are for steal [still] reames [remains]

   you aficanet wif til death
   Margaret Swordie

William worked for two years at Fort Rupert before he left with many others for Nanaimo. Since he was a striker in the blacksmith shop and sometimes had to be wakened to fire up the bellows, he did not get glowing reports of his service at Nanaimo. Margaret's expectation that he would be away for a long time proved to be true. He stayed in the new colony and died in the Nanaimo hospital on 30 March 1888. According to his obituary in the *Nanaimo Free Press* he had been "one of the ablest and best educated men in the Hudson Bay Company's employ, but an inordinate desire for liquor soon wrecked a bright and noble intellect." In the 1881 Census he was living with forty-year-old unmarried Anne Ritch, born in British Columbia. What became of his "aficanet" wife Margaret Swordie has not yet been traced.

107 THOMAS CRAIGIE: *You have too hearts your own one and min*

Thomas Craigie went out at twenty years of age as an emigrant labourer on the *Tory* in 1850, recruited in Orkney by Edward Clouston. He shared cabin 2 with five other men: Edward Pike (eighteen years), Emanuel Wiles (twenty years), Richard Gibbs (twenty-one years), David Skea (twenty-seven years, the only fellow Orkneyman), and Robert Porter (eighteen years). He had an inauspicious start in Stromness when his luggage was "seized by a Sheriff Office for a debt of £1.9.1" and Clouston had been compelled "to step forward and relieve it, or what had been advanced would have been lost, as he could not proceed without his luggage." His sweetheart, Jean Flett, wrote to him at the time of his departure from London. Although the letter followed him and was postmarked in Olympia, Washington, it never found its way into the hands of its intended recipient.

∾ Mr Thomas Craigie, Hugans bay House, London [in another hand] Hudsons Bay House

Kirkwall the 4 Novembar 1850

My Dear Thomas
I have always pleasure in thinking upon you and I cannot rest one minut longar till I troubel you with this few lines[.] I am very happy to think that you have not forgot me[.] dear Thomas I received A letter from you on the 26 of Octobor and anothar on the forth of Novembar which I was very happy to receive[.] I am allso happy to hear that you ar engoying god helth and I earnestly hopp that this may find you the same again[.] dear Thomas I have thought very much long since you wee both parted but I think that I will think more yet before wee both meet again and for myself I think that it is impossabol that wee evar can meet but My dear Thomas if ~~us~~

[crossed out] wee should never meet on earth may wee both meet in heaven and then wee shall be both happy for eaver and eaver [.] – dear Thomas you say that you ar thinking very much long for uord from Orkney[.] I cannot say wheather it be for ourd from me or not but this I know that I have never been happy since you left Kirkwall and must gust say that I can naver be so happy again on earth for though lost to my sight yet to my mind you ar still dear[.] Thomas you said in your first lettar that if I would keep true to you that you would keep true to me but I gust mean to tell you the truth of my mind at first which is best I think both for you and me[.] you know perfectly well that I would not have asked you to writ me if I did not intend to keep true to you but although I have said so and would do so if you do not intend to do so you need not troubel yourself by writing if you do not intend to keep your uord and you may think that I am rong but I think lik maney more that I am quit right and I am speaking my mind and when you writ you must gust do the same[.] dear Thomas well may I say dear for you have been dear to me since wee last parted for whather you beleive me or not you ar navor out of my mind night or day for I naver thought upon your going till you was away yes away from me for eaver on this earth[.] My dear I can naver forget myself for gaving you nothing for A keepseck but the only thing that I can gave you now is my heart and it you had long before now so by that you have too hearts your own one and min[.] keep my one and gave me yours but perhaps I am saying to far for perhaps you have gaven your one to some one before now and if you have you cannot gave it again to me[.] dear Thomas I will be very glad if you can have time to writ me before you sail from London and let me know all your mind and if it is not in your mind to keep your word naver set it on paper that is not in your mind for if you do not intend to keep true to me I can get maried before 3 months gon but if you will only say that you will keep true their is none on earth that shall ever part us for although I was maried this night I could naver be happy with one on earth but you[.] dear Thomas I would have told you all this before you left Kirkwall but I thought that you would think that I was making A ly but as shure as I have to diy and God maid me I am telling you all the truth wheather you beleave me or not but time will till[.] dear thomas I have been in my Fathers house since the uadensday after you left Kirkwall for my foot and leg was that bad that I was Confind to my baid for tenn days with it and I was nave out till yesterday at the Church but thanks be unto God for his kindness to me for it is quit well now and no thanks to Willam Sharor [Shearer] for it[.] dear Thomas I have not much news to tell you of only James Kirkness was in ouar house on friday last and he was saying that he did not think that you was wrot to your folks yet

so I said that I did not think that their was aney uord from aney of you yet
but he said that som of you had sent uord whateaverway so thinks I to
miself thats taru for I got uord to[o] thank God or yet I think I would been
daid houever James told me that your sister Bettsy I think that is heir name
she is very anxious to see me but for all that she may nevr have the Chance
but if it Could do hair aney good I would travel to hair on the night and
all for your saek[.] My sister Jessie sends hair kind and warmest love to you
and that she will nave forget you in hair life[.] now My dear I earnestly hop
that you will nave forget me but writ me as soon as you receive this and lit
me know all your mind[.] I shall add no more at present but may the god
will of him that dwelt in the bush with moses and the peace of God which
passeth all undarstanding ever remain with you is the earnest wish of your
afectonat and Constant lovor
when you writ derect to Jean Flett
   to the Care of Robert Flett
     Musicianer Main Street
      Kirkwall

We do not know why Jean's confession of love never reached Thomas. He
worked on farms in Victoria and on the Esquimalt farm of the Puget's Sound
Agricultural Company, a farming operation affiliated with the Hudson's Bay
Company. There is no record of his going home to return the "heart" sent in
this undelivered letter. In 1870 he married Mary Ann Porter at St. Paul's
Anglican Church in Esquimalt, and died in Victoria on 18 June 1882 at the
age of fifty-two. It is possible that the letter was never forwarded from Washington Territory to Vancouver Island and was returned directly to London,
to wait 150 years for us to read of Jean Flett's unrequited love.

108 PHILIP COLE: *Great many poor going out now every year to different
     parts of the world*

Philip Cole applied to the Company in 1850 when it requested farm labourers who were "strong, healthy and of sober and industrious habits" to go out
to the Victoria colony. He had letters of support from two local farmers who
would later be successful suppliers of market garden produce to the London
market. G.L. Parrot wrote a letter that referred to Philip Cole's many acquaintances in the farm community. William Woodthrope of Purfleet stated
that Thomas Cole wishes "to go out with his brother – his family have always
lived in the neighbourhood and have all borne a respectable character."
Philip, aged twenty-three, shared steerage cabin 11 aboard the *Tory* in 1850
with his brother Thomas (thirty-five years), George Culley (twenty-five

years), and James Salcomb (twenty-two years). They were all recruited by Captain Richard Wilson Pelly, a former officer in the Royal Navy, fifth son of Sir John Henry Pelly, Governor of the Company and, after 1843, the member of the Company's London Committee acting as Ship's husband in charge of shipping activities. Philip's mother and his friend G.L. Parrot wrote letters to him in 1851, almost a year after his arrival in Victoria aboard the *Tory*.

∿ Philip Cole Labourer To the care of Sir James Douglas &c Fort Victoria Vancouver's Island N.W. America

Monday Decr 1 1851

My Dear Son
I recevd your Letter & was very thankfull to hear from you & also to hear that you was in the enjoyment of good health as thank the Lord this leaves us all at this time[.] I was afraid that I should neve have heard from you any more but thank God I have had the pleasure of hearing your letter read[.] I have heard from your Brother Sam I have had two Letters from him & thank God he is quite well[.] he is in the Steam Ship Alecto of the Coast of Africa & your Uncle William [crossed out] Thomas Warfut & his family is gone Out in to a forign County & his family & I exspect that your Sister Jane will go as soon as she Can get an Oppertunity as She is fully made up her mind to go so I never Shall [sideways] persuade her any more not to go[.] I have not heard from your Sister Mary for a long time but I beleave She is quite well[.] your Brother George is Left me thank God at Last he is gone to live in London[.] your Brother John & William is still Liveing with me[.] Work is very dull about us at this time[.] Jhon is out of work now[.] your Sister Sarah & Emma is with me & Jane is Liveing at Hare Street with Mr Lorance [Lawrence] at preasent[.] Mr Harris as left Rody & is gone to Live at Limehouse I have got their two Children at present but not for long[.] I am very sorry to Inform you that your Uncle Cole is as bad as he can be to be alive he is a Live & that is all he never can recover[.] I took your Letter to Mr Parrott & he was very glad to hear from you & also to hear that You was quite well & comfortable[.] I will send you all the News I possible Can[.] Mr Hill is going away from Wennington as he is arrested for rent & every thing is to be sold to pay[.] Mr Lee is dead that lived a gainst the Cherry Tree[.] William Werts & his wife is gone in to forign parts & so is Downhard & his Wife & son[.] Mark Gibbord Lives in Pamments house & Pamment Lives up in Mark Gibbord House a gainst the Church[.] Mrs Convoy is Maried again to the Foreman Gurkin that Lived with Mr Ingram at Mere Hall[.] Mr Webb as got 2 Children a daughter & a Son[.] poor Porterfield that used to Live at Mr Hill got killed

dead upon the Spot Last week was buried on Sunday[.] Matilda Berry is Still a widdow[.] poor Old m^r Seamen is dead & Buried[.] Mr West [sideways] Mr Hide & all the Neibours sends thir Best respects to you & wish you all the Blessings this World Can afford & your Brothers & Sisters Send thir kind Love to you & we are all of us vey sorry to think that your Brother Tom should be so vey uncomfortable a long with you & that it was his wish to be seperated from you after going away together but I hope that God will forgive him & I hope tha[t] he will Prosper & pray God Bless him is my earnest prayer[.] William Gibbins is dead[.] Jane Setting is maried Dennis Ashgull[.] we exspect that the Rail Road will go on[.] all your Old Mates send thir Best respets to you & was glad to hear from you[.] hope that you will right as soon as you receve this Letter & let us know all the particulars that you can as we like to hear from you[.] my Love to you & pray god bless you[.] I remain your Affectionate
    Mother Sarah Cole
Wennington

Sarah Cole's letter is one of those many mother's letters that lets us see how the nature of family life was changing in the face of economic necessity and the adventures and opportunities offered by colonial expansion. We learn that Philip's brother Thomas has not stuck with him and this disappointed Sarah as much as the fact that her daughter Jane was also threatening to emigrate. Before her letter was posted in Romford, Philip's friend G.L. Parrot added his own words of greeting.

Aveley. Decr 3^d 1851

    Dear Phill Cole
    Your Mother has just brought me up her letter to give to post at Rumford[.] I cannot let it go away without writing a few lines to tell you that we are all quite well & to say how pleased we are to hear that you are doing well in Vancouver's Island and also to ask whether we shall look out a *wife* for you & send out. What do you think of the girl at the gate? or Mrs King's daughter: I think though you had better lay by all the money you can get together & come back in a few years to old England & look out for a wife yourself. We are all going on in the same way as when you left. Robert & Balls & all the men are well[.] J. Aley looks after the sheep now. I have about 500. plenty of good turnips &c. I hope you will do well where you are. I do not see why you should not. There are a great many poor going out now every year to different parts of the world – Mr W. Joyner & family are on their way to Australia. There are nearly 300 Emigrants in his ship. All I must I say is keep sober & steady & you will be

sure to succeed if you are favoured with good health. Tom Room Came up
to the harvest this year & inquired much after you. They hardly lost a day
all the harvest & finished within the month. The Corn was good[.] I shall
be glad to hear from you all particulars of ye Country & remain your well
wisher

   GL Parrott

[cross-written on front page] Mr Scrivaner & Susan & all desire to be
remembered to you.

   Parrot's letter expresses the dominant feeling of many letters in this period,
that for poor people almost anywhere but Britain offers a chance to escape
their economic condition. Philip Cole stayed with the Company, however,
only until 1852; his name stayed on their books but with no wages entered for
another year. After 1853 he disappears from our view.

109   PETER BROWN: *If you would Boot Bee Soo Gooud as Com hom and Bee now
         Father to my daughter*

Peter Brown left Orkney in 1851 on the *Norman Morison*'s second voyage with
the intention to be a labourer in the west coast colony. Both his parents and
a female friend wanted him to come home but for different reasons.

✑ For Peter Brown, Fort Victoria, Vancouver Island, *Columbia*

Harray 19th [June?] 1852

   Dear Sone
   I take the oppertunitey of writing you this Few lines to lett you know
that wee are all well at present thank Good for it hopping and earnestly
wishing that this will find you in the Same[.] wee Goot 2 letters from you
att one time 2 of Jun as was Glad to hear of your wellfer[.] Dear Sone I
hear of no person Gon to Clumbia as yett[.] I will Send it if I hear of any
one[.] I received a letter from James Feb 11 and he is well Drivan Stones to
the race road 3 s[hillings] a day he liks itt well and lives Better then M^r
Scart[h][.] I Goot one From William is att his trad and liks itt well[.] times
is Butt Dull att present here[.] robb of Bordus [Boardhouse] dided this year
too[.] William Spence & Magnus Kirkness John Scott all off to America
this year[.] John Anderson and Mary the Sister and Bilse and the wife is
Gon to Astrilia [Australia] this year[.] Margaret Anderson was her[e] All
the winter and plenty of voars [springs] Gon ther the Courting only Began
this winter and marrun far more[.] If you want a wife you will Sind Hir
hom and lett hir Bee Sett a Side till you Come ore thils [else] you will nott

have any Chanse atall[.] the woman is plenty But nise a noff Still[.]
William Brown your Cusin is Gon to America this year Tow William Spence
Braka [Breckan?] young William
James Brown
Direction of James your broth[er] James Brown Care of Andrew Grant
Inkeeper Hameltown [Hamilton], Canaday [Canada] West, N America
Give us all the news of them that went out   James Brown

A woman friend wrote a letter upside down on the back of his father's.
Both letters are in the same handwriting.

❧ Harray 19th [June?] 1852

Dear Friend
I am Gon to lett you know that Buddan Mays Married as Sun as she
landed into America[.] Jams Firth was a Died at Bittan[.] William
Corrigal and the Sisters Complements to you[.] Maggi is above ostus and
Stella is at ours Hous and if you would Boot Bee Soo Gooud as Com hom
and Bee now Father to my daughter or I will Keepp her to yo[u] to Wife[.]
Bettsy Flett is Ding Fas [dying fast] with a decline not fit to Dou any
thing[.] Thomas and James is Draine att Scart[.] William flett is with the
Sea
I have nott Mutch to tell you but plenty Married and plenty Died[.] I
will tell youl all that married an Died first Magnus Kirkness Meg Sinclair
William Corrigal Helling Isbister Margaret Corrigall William Isbister Bilse
of Skipaw [Scapa?] Came[.] Corrigal Came hom and Married an of Gart a
daughter of Gorge of Garth Married this year Sar John and Maggie Manson
Gille Spence and Ane of C Johns Married[.] that is all that married[.] this
year Died Cirsten of evergone and Magge of Whenarcal Thomas Isbister
ruslan [Russland] Bothe the Peter Creys is Dead and the Mother all Dead[.]
Sins you went of Great alterations in ope pleas[.] John Scott James Dick
the [h]as Goot Dead letters From this year plenty Died and plenty Married
Bell rowland Cam home again to see Jans Silk Hesket but he was awa

It is interesting to see that neither parents nor woman friend were making
an absolute demand that he come home and meet parental duties. The
mother of the child offered him the option of coming home and being father
to her daughter or, if he was not willing, she would marry someone else and
take her daughter with her. His parents advised that, if he did not arrange
to have a wife "Sett a Side" he will not "have any Chanse atall."
These problems would not be a matter for Peter to decide. On 5 November

1852, while working as a shepherd at Lake Hill farm on Vancouver Island, he was shot to death. According to the testimony of a fellow shepherd, Aboriginal people were responsible for his death. Colony governor James Douglas wrote to the Company secretary the same day describing the circumstances of the death:

A foul and atrocious murder was this day committed by some parties unknown, though two Indians of the Cowegin [Cowichan] Tribe are strongly sus[pecte]d as being the authors of the crime, at one of the Company's sheep stations, about five miles distant from this place [Fort Victoria]. The unfortunate sufferer is one of the Company's Servants by name Peter Brown a native of Orkney, and a very steady well conducted young man who arrived in this country last year by the Norman Morison.

Two men and several Indian herdsmen were attached to that station, who alternately herded the sheep by day and watched the folds at night. James Skea his fellow shepherd, reports that four natives, 2 men and two women came to the station about 8 oClock this morning and entered the house in their usual quiet and friendly manner. Such visits being matters of daily occurrence excited no attention and Skea shortly after their arrival drove the sheep out to pasture leaving Brown and the Natives in the House. He returned to the station about mid-day and to his horror and surprise, discovered the lifeless remains of his fellow shepherd extended on the ground face downwards, a few yards from the House. The body was still warm and was surrounded by a pool of blood, and death had been evidently caused by two gunshot wonds one of which had penetrated the chest from the right side where the ball had entered, the other had taken effect on the left side about the region of the heart and must have caused almost instant death. The door of the House was open, and several articles of property were missing, including two Guns, and four Blankets, having been carried of[f] it is supposed, by the murderers. A firebag, Looking Glass, a wooden Comb and pipe of Indian manufacture, which they had evidently left behind in the hurry and alarm of their retreat were also found in and about the house, a fact which adds strength to the conviction, arising from the other circumstances observed, that the deed was committed by natives, and most probably those who stopped at the station in the morning. One of those parties is well known here, having been employed as a shepherd at that station, and I have no doubt we shall soon discover the real authors of the outrage; who it is supposed had no other motive than that of plunder.

Having just returned from the scene of the murder I have not had time to arrange any plan for bringing the criminals to justice, a matter absolutely necessary as an example to others. There is no reason to suppose that they had any accomplices, or were acting in concert with their Tribe. I propose in the first place despatching messengers to the Chiefs of the Cowegin Tribe tomorrow, to inform them of the foul deed that has been committed, and to demand the surrender of the Criminals, if, as suspected, they belong to the tribe. I shall also offer a reward for their discovery and apprehension, and should those measures fail in their object, I shall be under the painful necessity of sending a force to seize upon the murderers, in whatever place they may be found.

The great point in such cases is to avoid implicating the whole Tribe, in the guilt of individuals, and if we succeed in that object the parties will be brought to justice without much trouble or expense.

Her Majesty's Ship "Thetis" arrived here on the 16th October with orders to remain for the winter. In case of need I shall call upon Captain Kuper for assistance in settling that affair.

The killing of Peter Brown proved to be an occasion for James Douglas to establish the authority of his colonial government. Douglas had preferred diplomacy to direct action in the case of the 1850 deaths of the men at Fort Rupert, whose actions seemed to bring on their own fates. (See the description of these events in the Wisharts' story, entry 66.) John Phillip Reid (1999, 98) provides a rather critical analysis of Douglas's application of justice: "James Douglas, who killed more than one Indian manslayer in cold blood, took comfort in the fact that they were 'guilty,' boasting that when dealing with Indians he had 'invariably acted on the principle that it is inexpedient and unjust to hold *tribes* responsible for the acts of *individuals*.' He was wrong, of course. It was surely expedient, and perhaps even just, to hold Indians to their own legal standards." In the Brown case, Douglas had to call "upon Captain Kuper" to help in a wider search. On 4 January 1853 the accused were pursued with the *Beaver,* the *Recovery,* the boats of the *Thetis* in tow, a field force of 130 seamen and marines under the command of Lieutenant Sandom of HMS *Thetis,* along with eleven Métis "enlisted in the Colony for that service." Douglas wrote a detailed account to Company Secretary Archibald Barclay:

The Expedition anchored off the mouth of the Cowegin [Cowichan] River on the 6th, and I immediately dispatched messengers to the several Native Tribes, who live on the banks of that stream, with an invitation to meet me for the purpose of settling the difference which had led to my present visit; and at the same time to inform them, that in the event of their refusal to do so, I should be under the painful necessity, of assuming a hostile attitude, and marching the Force under my command into their country. I received their answer the same evening accepting the invitation, and expressing a wish to meet me the following day near the mouth of the River. The disembarkation of the Force, was made early the following morning, and we took post on a commanding position at the appointed place; fully armed and prepared for whatever might happen. In the course of two hours the Indians began to drop down the River in their war canoes, and landed a little above the position we occupied; and last of all arrived two large canoes crowded with the relatives and friends of the murderer, hideously painted, and evidently prepared to defend him to the last extremity, the criminal himself being amongst the number. On landing they made a furious rush towards the point which I occupied, a little in advance of the Force and their demeanour was altogether so hostile that the marines were with difficulty restrained from opening a fire upon them. When the first excitement had a little abated, the murderer was brought into my presence and I succeeded after a good deal of trouble, in taking him quietly into custody, and sent him a close prisoner on board the steam vessel. This capture having removed all cause of dispute, I assembled the Indians and spoke to them long and seriously on the subject of their relations with the Colony, and the rules which must govern their conduct in future. They expressed the utmost regret, for the misconduct of their countryman, and their desire to live on friendly terms with the Colony: and appeared much intimidated by the imposing Force before them. They left us in course of the afternoon in the best possible temper, and the Forces were immediately afterwards re-embarked, having fortunately concluded the days work, without firing a shot in anger; though several times, on the very point of coming to a serious rupture, which indeed could not have been prevented had the discipline of the troops been less perfect, and my orders not been rigidly enforced by Lieutenant Sandom, who, on all occasions, gave me the most hearty and cordial support. Having thus effected all that was desired at Cowegin, we proceeded towards Nanaimo and arrived there on the evening of the 9th. I pursued the same course, as at Cowegin, but found a decided reluctance, on the part of the Tribe to surrender the murderer; they however at length consented to deliver him into our hands; but on the day appointed they failed in their promise, and made an attempt to ransom his life by a payment of Furs. In consequence of that breach of faith, I took his father and another influential Indian into custody, in hopes of inducing them by that means, to bring in the criminal; my object being if possible to settle the difference without bloodshed and without assailing the tribe at large. After two days of the most anxious suspense it was again arranged that they should bring the criminal to the vessel, and he was accordingly brought to within half a mile of the anchorage; but on seeing me repair to the spot, he was landed and fled to the Woods. There, being then no alternative, except a recourse to coercive measures, without a positive loss of character, I ordered an immediate advance, towards the River, near the mouth of which the Nanaimo villages are situated. We accordingly pushed rapidly in that direction but from the shallowness of the water, the boats grounded about three quarters of a mile below the first village, where the troops were immediately landed, and we pushed rapidly towards it and before the Indians had recovered from their first consternation we succeeded in carrying the stockade, without firing a shot. We spent the night there, and the boats came up before morning. We then moved up the River, to the second village which we found nearly deserted, by its inhabitants who had fled, with their property, to the Woods. The murderer's father was Chief of this last village; consisting of many large houses and containing all their stock of Winter provisions. They were now completely in our power, and as soon as I could assemble a sufficient number of the inhabitants, I told them it was my intention to treat them as enemies unless they submitted to the demands of justice. We then learned that the murderer had left the River, and was concealed in the Woods, on the sea coast, about three miles distant. The Pinnace was immediately despatched with 16 sea men and nine half-whites towards that point, where his place of refuge was soon discovered, and after a long chase in the Woods, in which the half-whites took a principal part, the wretched man was finally captured, and taken on board the steamer "Beaver." The Force was withdrawn the same day from the River, without molesting or doing any damage whatever to the other Natives. The two criminals being now in our possession were brought to trial, and found guilty of murder, by a Jury, composed of the Officers present. They were sentenced to be hanged, and the execution took place in the presence of the whole tribe; the scene appearing to make a deep impression upon their minds and will I trust have the effect of restraining others from crime

I am happy to report that I found both the Cowegin and Nanaimo Tribes more amenable to reason than was supposed; the object of the Expedition having been brought to a satisfactory close under Providence, as much by the influence of the Company's name as by the force of intimidation. The surrender of a criminal as in the case of the Cowegin murderer without bloodshed by the most numerous and warlike tribe on Vancouver's Island, at the requisition of the Civil power, may be considered an epoch in the history of our Indian relations which augurs well for the future peace and prosperity of the Colony. This however could not have been affected without an exhibition of force. I feel much indebted to Lieut^nt Sandum for his perfect arrangements and for the admirable temper and forbearance exhibited by the Force under his command in circumstances more trying to brave men than actual conflict. The Officers and men have won my thanks not only by their steadiness and discipline, but also by their promptitude and alacrity in the field; and the half whites emulated their good example. The reflection that our success has been unstained by a single act of cruelty and that no blood has been shed except that of those who paid the just penalty for their crimes adds not a little to the satisfaction which I have derived from the result of this expedition.

It is interesting to note the different handling of this case compared with Governor Blanshard's action in the wake of the deaths in 1850 of A.F. Hale, Charles Lobb, and George Wishart (entry 66). At that time, Blanshard destroyed a whole village, houses, canoes, and property. For James Douglas, whose concern for the success of the Company was fast turning into a concern for the future of the colony that would be his home and his children's future, the outcome of this incident may well have been a "satisfaction," in that he felt he did justice. But as we have seen time and again in these letters, the concerns of folk at home in Europe were quite different. For those who cared about Peter Brown, there could be no "satisfaction," either for the family that wanted their son at home or for the woman who asked him if he would "Bee Soo Gooud as Com hom and Bee now Father to my daughter." For them, the episode was an ending. For those indigenous to and those settled as immigrants in the new world of Vancouver Island and the future country the colony will be a part of, the story was just beginning.

Conclusion

I n the present day the testimony of people in everyday life is becoming a
more prominent part of the narratives that tell us about the past. Such
testimonies are generally used to bring to life events and circumstances
that are already recognized as important to history. Memoirs, letters, diaries,
and other accounts that give witness to war, to political and economic
change, and to such events as large-scale massacres, can stand alone as testimonies that help make our ongoing historical narrative. Few of the subjects
in this book were close to such events and circumstances; their lives were
lived out behind the scenes of major events. And so this book is not a history
in the usual sense.

Neither is this book literature in the traditional sense. When letters
become part of the "literature and letters" canon of any culture, they are generally the personal accounts of very well educated and prominent citizens
whose writings show the same artistry as a literary product. From John
Donne's meditations to Anaïs Nin's diaries, such works are crafted and styled
to be literary products as well as personal testimony. In settler cultures such
as Canada, where no literary elite existed until the work of nation building
was well advanced, explorer and settler accounts can become validated as literary products. These accounts are usually by people who have some literary
accomplishment and/or some consciousness of the historical significance of
their activities. This is not generally true of the writers of these letters. And
yet, as editors we discovered that the effect of these letters as a group was to
increase our understanding of the history of mercantile and colonial expansion in the early nineteenth century and to give that sweeping change a
human face, or rather, many human faces. Through the words of diverse citizens living in the first half of the nineteenth century, these letters allow us to
read the literature of that period differently, as the letters expand the cast of
characters and situations given to us by the writers of that time.

In presenting so many letters in their full detail, we wanted to share something of the experience of working in archives. Many who work in archives speak about the special moment when, lifting their eyes from the documents, they are surprised to find themselves in the twenty-first century, where there are telephones, computers, traffic in the street outside – after they have been elsewhere, in another time, living other lives. This effect was not produced by the art of a skilled novelist, dramatist, or poet, but by the cumulative effect of the words of people who probably never dreamt that their writing would be preserved through time for future eyes.

When people who work in archives get together, a common discussion – usually framed by humour – centres on the addictive quality of the work. One begins with a fairly secure sense of a project to be accomplished, but as the documents expand the complexity of past events and lives, one finds oneself wanting to go on and on, well beyond the scope of one's original purpose for being there. It is as if the archive itself has come to life rather than being merely a place of research. Certainly, as the keeper of the Hudson's Bay Company Archives, Judith Beattie has had many occasions to observe and participate in searches in which the process of searching itself becomes more significant than the few scraps of evidence that may result. As a literary scholar, Helen Buss began her work in settler women's archives with the conviction that there were unheralded, yet accomplished, settler writers waiting to be discovered. She quickly found that so-called naïve accounts, lacking polish and linguistic complexity, can become more exciting than traditional literary texts. They seem to invite the reader to construct the story herself rather than live inside an already constructed world.

As editors, we wanted the readers to have some of the same reading experiences that we had when we first read the letters. For example, a number of the letters were written to men who were already dead but we did not know that on first reading. When research revealed the time and place and mode of death we felt a real sense of loss, as if we had known these men because, by the time we learned of their deaths, we were very familiar with the lives of the people who wrote to them, the marriages and births in their extended families, their parents' advice to them, their worries for them, and the desire of their loved ones to be reunited with them. To become familiar in these ways is to be like family, and we felt a sadness at their loss. We hope that the form of our narratives that introduce and comment on the letters leaves the reader free to feel the same involvement and, at the same time, find appropriate factual information to make the letters more readable. However, these stories remain open ended, a place to begin research and/or the creative act of imagining a story. We cannot offer closure to the stories these letters evoke.

"Closure" in an ironic word in this context, since the lack of closure is part of the fascination of these letters. The letter writers assumed that their reader would understand the multiple contexts of what is said, and therefore they leave out connectors and background detail that a good story would include. Instead of making the letters less interesting than the narratives of literature and history that do provide such contexts, the effect is often to stimulate the imagination. We are left to speculate, to puzzle and imagine the events before and after the letter. Personal letters have a further quality that stimulates the imagination: the fact that these letters were not addressed to us puts them in a special category of knowledge – of private lives originally written for intimates. Such knowledge makes us feel a similar, unexpected intimacy, an attachment to the speaker that makes us feel almost as if we were being addressed personally. This feeling of intimacy is not only caused by our initiation into what is normally kept secret inside families but is also the result of the sheer volume of the detail of the rhythms of daily life that is communicated in these letters. People come alive for us in their concern with details, the state of the weather and the crops, the cost of dress fabric and writing paper, the news and gossip of the neighbourhood. Through such details we begin to live inside the lives of the correspondents and to care for the men they wrote to, to live in their relational world.

The most powerful attraction of these private letters lies in this relational nature. As readers not addressed by the correspondence, we inhabit an imaginary space between the correspondents. In the case of these letters, we are almost accidental readers of words never meant for us, and yet we become part of a relationship, living between the writer who desired to reach the loved one and the loved one who never received the letter. The letters are undelivered to the intended addressee but, in a strange way, have been delivered – to us. And in accepting the delivery, we enter the lives of people in the past in a way that is qualitatively different from the narratives of both fiction and history. All life writing accomplishes this difference to one degree or another – this special sense of authenticity, of closeness to the narrative voice – that happens when actual persons attempt to represent themselves in writing. However, letters do it in a particularly compelling way that other formats do not. A personal letter is always reaching out to a particular reader, a particular person. When accidents of history make such writing public, the effect can be to give readers a vivid sense of being personally addressed, personally called into the lives of others. As editors we have felt this intensity often while working on these letters and we hope that sharing them with readers can bring this closeness to actual people in a time far away from our own, to help us realize their different world, and to understand the common humanity we share with them.

Appendix A: Ships

Beaver

The 187-ton paddlewheel steamer *Beaver* was built by Green, Wigrams & Green at their Blackwall Yards in 1834-5 for the Hudson's Bay Company's Pacific Northwest coast fur trade (HBCA, PAM, A.6/23 p. 238). She measured 30.7 by 6 metres (100.75 by 20 feet), with a speed of nine and three-quarter miles per hour. She sailed out to the coast, schooner or brigantine rigged, under the command of David Home, leaving 29 August 1835 and arriving on the coast 19 March 1836 and at Fort Vancouver 10 April 1836 (log published in Wright 1961, 15-17). On arrival at the coast she was fitted with her boilers and carried on the coasting trade under the successive commands of William Henry McNeill (1837-42), William Brotchie (1842-3), Alexander Duncan (1843-4), Charles Humphreys (1844-5), Charles Dodd (1845-51), Charles E. Stuart (1851-2), Charles Dodd (1852-6), John Swanson (1856-8), J.L. Sinclair (1859), and Herbert Lewis (1859-60) (HBCA, PAM, C.1/207-10; E.109). In 1851 she was seized by US forces (HBCA, PAM, A.8/7). In 1853 she was relegated to transporting general freight and passengers between outposts, and after use between Victoria and the Fraser River during the gold rush, she was laid up in Victoria Harbour 1860-2. After being used by the British government to survey the coast 1863-70 (HBCA, PAM, C.7/15) she was again laid up in Victoria Harbour and sold in 1874 for $15,700. The ship's logs cover 1847-70 (HBCA, PAM, C.1/207-10; E.109). See also Lamb 1938a, 1958, and McCann 1980.

Cadboro

The 71-ton schooner *Cadboro* (*Cadborough*) was built in Rye, England, in 1826 and was purchased by the Hudson's Bay Company for the Pacific Northwest coast fur trade for £800 (HBCA, PAM, A.1/55 fo. 55; A.7/1 fo. 68d; A.5/8 fo. 73). She measured 17 by 5 metres (56 by 17 feet), with a crew of thirty-five (HBCA, PAM, A.7/1 fo. 68d). She travelled out to the coast under the command of James P. Swan, leaving 25 September 1826 and arriving on 24 April 1827 (HBCA, PAM, C.1/217). On arrival at the coast she carried on the coasting trade under the successive commands of Aemilius Simpson (1827-31), William Ryan (1834), Alexander Duncan (1835), William Heath (1836), William Brotchie (1837), James Allan Scarborough (1839-46), James Sangster (1849-52), and Charles E. Stuart (1853-4) (HBCA, PAM, C.1/218-22). In 1846-7 she was chartered by Captain Howison of the *Shark* for £500 to convey the crew to California after it was wrecked (HBCA, PAM, B.223/b/35 fo. 65). In 1850 she was seized by US forces at Nisqually (Tacoma, Washington) (HBCA, PAM, A.11/72 fo. 250). In 1857 she was laid up in harbour to be dismantled and was sold to Captain Edward Howard; she was wrecked in 1860 while carrying lumber from Puget Sound (HBCA, PAM, B.226/b/13 fo. 102-3). The ship's logs cover 1826-50 (HBCA, PAM, C.1/217-22). The Archives holds a map on which her route into the Columbia River in 1847 is laid out (HBCA, PAM, G.1/285).

Columbia

The 400-ton barque *Columbia* was built by Messrs Green Wigram & Green and launched in 1835 (HBCA, PAM, A.1/59 fo. 65d-6; A.7/1 fo. 68d). She left the Downs 29 August 1835 as escort to the *Beaver* with Captain William Darby in command, and reached the coast 22 March 1836 (HBCA, PAM, A.1/62 fo. 11; A.5/13 p. 97; B.223/b/28 fo. 25d). On the coast she travelled to the Sandwich Islands (Hawai'i) in June, then returned to London under the command of Captain Robert Royal, leaving on 30 November 1836 and arriving 12 May 1837. Her second trip, under the command of Captain Charles Humphreys, took her out from London 18 November 1837 to 24 May 1838 and back 11 November 1838 to 21 May 1839, with trips to the north while on the coast. The third voyage departed London on 18 September 1839 under Humphreys's command, arriving at the Columbia on 15 March 1840. After a stay during which she visited California twice, she returned to London leaving 24 December 1841 and arriving there 7 July 1842. Her fourth voyage to the coast departed London on 10 September 1842 again under Humphreys, arriving 6 May 1843. She left the coast on 5 December 1844 under the command of Captain Alexander Duncan and arrived in London on 22 May 1845. Her fifth voyage to the coast departed London on 4 October 1845 under the command of Captain Alexander Duncan, arriving at Fort Victoria in spring 1846 and returning 10 November 1847, arriving in London on 22 May 1848. Her sixth and final voyage under the command of Captain James Cooper left London on 12 September 1848, arriving on the coast 16 March 1849, with the return voyage departing 1 November 1849 and arriving in London 17 April 1850, when the Company decided to sell her (HBCA, PAM, A.1/66 p. 183). The ship's logs cover 1835-50 (HBCA, PAM, C.1/243-54, 1064; E.316).

Cowlitz

The 400-ton barque *Cowlitz* was built by Messrs Green Wigram & Green and launched in 1840 (HBCA, PAM, A.1/61 fo. 114; A.5/13 pp. 81, 86, 87; A.6/25 fo. 104d, 110d; A.7/1 fo. 68d). She left the Downs on 24 August 1840 with Captain William Brotchie in command and entered the Columbia River 5 February 1841, reaching Fort Vancouver on 6 March 1841 (HBCA, PAM, A.1/62 fo. 11; A.5/13 p. 97; B.223/b/28 fo. 25d). On the coast she delivered goods to the Russian American Company, and delivered Sir George Simpson from Fort George (now Astoria, Oregon) to Stikine, 3 December 1841-27 April 1842 (HBCA, PAM, C.1/257). She returned to London under the command of Captain William Henry McNeill, leaving on 16 November 1842 and arriving 9 May 1843. Her second trip took her from London on 23 September 1843, arriving at Victoria on 24 March 1844. After a stay on the coast of more than a year under the command of Charles Humphreys, she returned to London on 18 December 1845 with Humphreys as a passenger and Captain William Heath at the helm, arriving 27 June 1846. The third voyage departed London on 8 October 1846 under the command of Captain J.A. Weynton, arriving in Victoria 21 March 1847 and Fort Vancouver three days later. After an extended stay during which she visited the Sandwich Islands (Hawai'i) and New Archangel (Sitka, Alaska), she returned to London, leaving 7 December 1848 and arriving there 19 May 1849. Her fourth and final voyage to the coast departed London on 4 August 1849, arriving 12 March 1850 after a delay when the crew deserted in Honolulu. This time she carried some emigrant labourers recruited by Mr Henry Berens, a member of the HBC London Committee. She left the coast on 10 July 1850 and arrived in London on 21 April 1851 after a call at St. Helena (HBCA, PAM, A.6/29 fo. 74), and was sold for £3,250 soon after (HBCA, PAM, A.1/67 fo. 112). The ship's logs cover 1840-50 (HBCA, PAM, C.1/257-66).

Dryad

The 203-ton brig *Dryad* (*Drade*) was built in Fishborn, Isle of Wight, in 1825 and was chartered by the Hudson's Bay Company for the Pacific Northwest coast fur trade (HBCA, PAM, A.1/55 fo. 6-6d, 10d). She arrived on the coast on 1 June 1826 under the command of James Davidson, who died on 19 December at Valparaiso, Chile, on the return voyage (HBCA, PAM, Rich 1960:612). A. Dunn, the chief mate, sailed her home (HBCA, PAM, A.1/56 fo. 8). In 1829 she was purchased from Cotfield & Shepard by the Hudson's Bay Company (HBCA, PAM, A.1/56 fo. 105d). She left London in January 1830 under the command of Captain John Minors, who was described as drunken and incompetent, arriving on the coast on 10 August 1830 with eight apprentices from the Royal Hospital, Greenwich (Rich 1960, 627; HBCA, PAM, A.6/22 fo. 53-4). The captain was forced to resign in 1831 and Aemilius Simpson, who took over, died at Nass in September 1831 (Rich 1960, 627 and 630). Captain Alexander Duncan was in command in 1832 (HBCA, PAM, C.1/281) and Charles Kipling in 1834-6. She left the coast on 20 October 1835 and arrived in London on 10 April 1836 (HBCA, PAM, C.4/1; C.1/281-2; A.6/24 fo. 35d). In June she was sold to Thomas Gillespy Jr., an agent for Peter Ainsley, for £1,450 (HBCA, PAM, A.1/60 fo. 21; A.7/1 fo. 68d; A.6/24 fo. 59d). The ship's logs cover 1831-6 (HBCA, PAM, C.1/218, 281-2). The Archives hold maps on which her routes in 1830 and 1835-6 are laid out (HBCA, PAM, G.3/887, 888, 891, 892).

Eagle

The 194-ton brigantine *Eagle* was built at Lynn, Norfolk, in 1824 and was bought by the Hudson's Bay Company for the Pacific Northwest coast fur trade in 1827 (HBCA, PAM, A.1/55 fo. 6-6d, 10d). On her first voyage she left London on 16 September 1827 and arrived on the coast on 19 May 1828 under the command of Captain John Costello Grave, with her return voyage taking from 20 August 1828 to 10 February 1829 (HBCA, PAM, C.4/1). On the second voyage, she left London 1 November 1829 and arrived on the coast on 2 June 1830, with her return voyage taking from 29 October 1830 to 17 April 1831 (HBCA, PAM, C.4/1). The third voyage took her from 24 September 1831 to 19 May 1832 and, after a trip to the Sandwich Islands (Hawai'i) in June, she returned to London, leaving the coast on 6 November 1832 and arriving 30 May 1833 (HBCA, PAM, C.4/1). Her fourth voyage was her last to the coast, under the command of William Darby, leaving London on 8 December 1833 and arriving on 20 September 1834, with the return to London taking from 25 November 1834 to 6 June 1835 (HBCA, PAM, C.4/1). On her last trip in 1836 she sailed to Hudson Bay and was stranded on the rocks off Button Island, wintering in the Hayes River (HBCA, PAM, A.6/24 fo. 41d). She returned to London under the command of Charles Humphreys and was sold to G. & H.A. Castle for £1,140, not being worth the expense of a thorough repair (HBCA, PAM, C.7/1 fo. 68d; C.7/44). The ship's logs cover 1827-37 (HBCA, PAM, C.1/283-8).

Ganymede

The 213-ton barque *Ganymede* (*Ganemede*) was built at Chepstow in 1827 and was chartered from Richard Drew by the Hudson's Bay Company for the Pacific Northwest coast fur trade in 1828 (HBCA, PAM, A.1/55 fo. 6-6d, 10d). On her first voyage under Captain Leonard John Hayne, she left London with the *William & Ann* on 16 September 1828, but parted from her in a heavy gale on 24 September (HBCA, PAM, A.6/22 fo. 13d, 35d). She arrived back in London on 31 May 1830, after a detour that took her to Van Dieman's Land (present-day Tasmania) (HBCA, PAM, A.1/57 fo. 25d; A.6/22 fo. 69). Although she had been described as large and dull, the Company bought her for £2,700 (HBCA, PAM, A.7/1 fo. 68d). On 16 November 1830 she left London under the command of Captain Charles Kipling, arriving on 17 July 1831 at Fort Vancouver. By 7 November she was on her way home with William Ryan as master via the Sandwich Islands (Hawai'i), where seven of the crew were placed in confinement after "they conducted themselves in a very turbulent manner in Wohoa [Oahu]" (HBCA, PAM, A.6/22 fo. 128, 133-3d). After her arrival in London on 15 May 1832 she was refitted for a return voyage under Robert Royal, leaving 15 September 1832, arriving at Fort Vancouver 1 May 1833, leaving the coast 19 September 1833 and back in London 23 February 1834 (HBCA, PAM, A.1/58 fo. 100-100d; C.4/1). After travelling to Moose Factory with supplies for the Southern Department from 6 June to 10 November, she set out on the final trip to the coast on 10 December 1834 under the command of William Eales (HBCA, PAM, A.6/23 fo. 98; B.38/b/2 fo. 20, 22; D.4/127 p. 140; C.4/1). She spent from 27 July 1835 to 19 October 1836 on the coast, then returned to London by 30 March 1837 (HBCA, PAM, A.6/24 fo. 138d; C.4/1). On 5 June 1837 she was sold to W. Mulley (HBCA, PAM, A.1/60 fo. 76; A.6/24 fo. 97). The ship's logs cover 1832-7 (HBCA, PAM, C.1/333-8).

Harpooner

The 213-ton brigantine or barque *Harpooner* was chartered in 1848 to carry labourers for the settlement on Vancouver Island. She left in mid-December 1848 and arrived in Victoria on 31 May 1849, where she discharged the emigrants, including the oversman John Muir, his family, and seven other Scottish miners with their families, eight working men recruited by Captain Walter Colquhoun Grant, James Yates the shipwright, and several carpenters and bakers. She also delivered the cargo of goods to replace those lost on the *Vancouver*. The men stayed three months in Victoria before proceeding to the mines at Fort Rupert in August, while the ship proceeded to Fort Vancouver and the Sandwich Islands (Hawai'i) (Bowsfield 1979; Sale 1979, 28 and 153). The ship's logs have not been preserved in the Hudson's Bay Company Archives because she was a chartered vessel.

Isabella

The 195-ton brig (also listed as a snow) *Isabella* measured 27 by 8 by 5 metres (90 by 26 by 16 feet) and sailed with a crew of three officers and twelve men. She was built in 1825 at Shoreham, Sussex, for Messrs Gilmour & Richardson and worked in the British maritime trade until 1829. On 10 October 1829 the Hudson's Bay Company purchased her for £2,900 to replace the *William & Ann,* which had wrecked (HBCA, PAM, A.1/56 fo. 188). She left Blackwall for the Columbia via the Sandwich Islands (Hawai'i) on 30 October 1829 under the command of William Ryan, arriving on 2 May 1830, when she also wrecked on the Columbia bar but with no loss of life (HBCA, PAM, C.1/355). On 4 June the crew arrived at Fort Vancouver (HBCA, PAM, C.1/355; B.223/b/6 fo. 13-14; B.223/d/31). The ship's logs cover 1829-30 (HBCA, PAM, C.1/355).

Lama

The 145-ton brigantine *Lama* (*Llama*) was built in Boston about 1826 and cruised on the Northwest coast between 1829 and 1831 (HBCA, PAM, B.223/b/8 fo. 23d-4d). The Company bought her in Oahu for US$5,000 from Captain McNeill (HBCA, PAM, B.223/b/8 fo. 9-10, 22d, 23d-4d). In September 1832 she left Oahu under the command of William Henry McNeill. In May 1834 she rescued some Japanese after their ship was wrecked at Cape Flattery. Although she was judged too small for the trade, she could not be sent to

Britain since she was registered in the United States. She was sent to San Francisco with corn and lumber under the command of William Brotchie, who attempted to sell her (HBCA, PAM, B.223/b/15 fo. 59d-60). Plans were made to sell her to Captain John Bancroft for US$5,500 on her return from California, and she was delivered to Bancroft in Honolulu, who made an arrangement with the Company that he would pay in sea otter skins for goods it supplied (HBCA, PAM, B.223/a/22 fo. 33d; B.223/b/17 fo. 13, 15, 38-8d). The ship's logs have not been preserved in the Hudson's Bay Company Archives.

Mary Dare

The 149-ton brigantine *Mary Dare* was purchased in London by the Hudson's Bay Company in the summer of 1846 (HBCA, PAM, A.1/64; A.7/1 fo. 68d). She had been built at Bridport, Dorset, in 1842 (HBCA, PAM, A.7/1 fo. 68d). She left London under the command of James Cooper on 3 November 1846 and arrived at Fort Victoria on 14 April 1847 (HBCA, PAM, C.4/1; C.1/504). She spent the following years under the commands of James Allen Scarborough and William Mouat mainly employed in the conveyance of supplies between Forts Vancouver and Victoria and Honolulu in the Sandwich Islands (Hawai'i). On 14 December 1853 she left the coast for London, arriving 27 May 1854. In July she was purchased by William Sadler of Wivenhoe near Colchester, Essex (HBCA, PAM, A.1/69). The ship's logs cover 1850-4 (HBCA, PAM, C.1/459-62) and the log for 1849-50 has been preserved at the Oregon Historical Society. The Archives holds maps on which her route in 1846-7 is laid out (HBCA, PAM, G.3/888 copy 1 and 893).

HMS *Modeste*

This 568-ton sloop was commissioned to the British naval fleet in the Pacific in 1843, and in 1844 under the command of Captain Thomas Baillie visited and reported on the British settlements on the northwest coast (Knuth 1960, 408). After visiting Fort Victoria and Fort Simpson, Nass, in the summer of 1844, she lay off Fort Vancouver until May 1847, when word arrived that the Oregon Territory had become part of the United States (Knuth 1960, 410-14).

Nereide

The 253-ton brig *Nereide* (*Nereid*) was built at Kidderpore in 1821 and the Hudson's Bay Company bought her in 1833 for the Pacific Northwest coast fur trade for £3,650 (HBCA, PAM, A.1/58 fo. 37; A.6/23 fo. 17d; A.7/1 fo. 68d). On her first voyage under Captain J.M. Langtry, she left London on 6 May 1833, but a leak was discovered and she had to put in to Spithead, Plymouth, and again at Lisbon for repairs (HBCA, PAM, A.6/22 fo. 28; A.6/23 fo. 48; B.223/b/10 fo. 22d). She sailed from Lisbon on 28 July and arrived on the coast on 14 April 1834 (HBCA, PAM, B.223/b/10 fo. 13). She left the coast on 20 June 1834 and arrived back in London on 27 May 1835, after calling in at Valparaiso, Chile, and Copiapo (HBCA, PAM, A.6/23 fo. 26d, 138, 138d; C.4/1). On 13 February 1836 she left London under the command of Robert Royal, arriving on 26 August 1836 at Fort Vancouver. She travelled along the coast to Fort Stikine, Fort Langley, Fort Nisqually, California, and over to the Sandwich Islands (Hawai'i) under the command of Captains Robert Royal and David Home, experiencing a strike of the crew in May 1837. By 18 November 1839 she was on her way home with William Brotchie as master and arrived in London 19 April 1840 (HBCA, PAM, C.4/1). After her arrival in London she was sold to Joseph Somes, Ratcliffe, London (HBCA, PAM, A.1/62; A.10/13). The ship's logs cover 1833-4, 1839-40 (HBCA, PAM, C.1/609-10).

Norman Morison

The 529-ton vessel *Norman Morison* was purchased in London in November 1848 to replace the *Vancouver* (HBCA, PAM, A.1/65 p. 214; A.6/28 fo. 27d; A.5/16 pp. 64-5; A.6/27 fo. 172d). She had originally been built in Burma teak for the East India Company (*Victoria Colonist*, 17 June 1853, from HBCA, PAM, SF "Ships, *Norman Morison*"). She left Gravesend under the command of Captain David Durham Wishart on 20 October 1849 for the trip to the west coast with 250 tons of goods for the Russian American Company, 15 tons for the Hudson's Bay Company, and sixty-five passengers, sixty of whom were "of the labouring class" and "between decks" and four of whom were women "permitted to accompany their husbands." The men had been hired for five years at £17 a year (HBCA, PAM, A.6/28 fo. 67). She arrived in Victoria on 24 March 1850 after a five-month trip, a month shorter than the norm (HBCA, PAM, A.11/72 fo. 201-6d). On 23 September 1850 she left the coast for London, arriving 20 February 1851. Her second trip out commenced on 28 May 1851, and she remained on the coast from 30 October 1851 until her departure for London on 21 January 1852, arriving 12 June 1852. Her third trip out took place on 20 August 1852. She arrived in Esquimalt on 16 January 1853 and returned 19 March 1853 with furs and gold dust, arriving on 31 July 1853. She was then sold for £6,700 and replaced by the *Princess Royal* (Bowsfield 1979; HBCA, PAM, B.226/z/1 fo. 1-32; Nesbitt 1949, 91 n. 3; Mouat 1939). The ship's logs cover 1850-4 (HBCA, PAM, C.1/459-62).

Princess Royal

The 583-ton vessel *Princess Royal* was built in 1853 for the Hudson's Bay Company by Money, Wigrams & Sons to replace the *Norman Morison* (HBCA, PAM, A.5/18 fo. 160; A.10/32; A.6/31 p. 5; B.226/b/12). She left on 6 June 1854 under the command of Captain David D. Wishart carrying the miners under George Robinson who were sent out from Staffordshire, arriving at Esquimalt on 23 November 1854 (HBCA, PAM, A.6/31 pp. 32, 52; C.1/975; A.10/35 fo. 307; Nicholls 1991-4). The miners left for Colviletown (Nanaimo) in the *Beaver* and the *Recovery* on 26 November 1854 (HBCA, PAM, B.226/b/11). After sailing back to England, departing 17 January 1855 and arriving 25 May 1855, she made a second trip out under the same commander leaving July 1855 and arriving back in London in June 1856 (HBCA, PAM, C1/976). Her third voyage left 20 August 1856 and returned to England on 5 July 1857 (HBCA, PAM, C.4/1). These trips continued with few breaks until in 1885 she was sent to Moose Factory and broke her keel on a sandbar near Moose Island during a snowstorm (HBCA, PAM, A.11/47 fo. 314-15; B.134/c/155 fo. 128). The ship's logs cover 1854-71 (HBCA, PAM, C.1/975-99). The Archives hold maps on which her routes in 1857-60 are laid out (HBCA, PAM, G.1/174-76).

Recovery

The 154-ton brigantine *Recovery* was purchased by the Hudson's Bay Company agent in Honolulu for £520 (US$2,500) in January 1852. She had originally been built in Dorchester County, Maryland, in 1845 and sailed under the name *Orbit* (HBCA, PAM, A.11/63 fo. 31; D.7/1 fo. 250-50d). In March 1852 she was sent to the Queen Charlotte Islands with a party of five officers and forty-two men under Chief Trader John F. Kennedy to hunt for gold (HBCA, PAM, A.11/73 fo. 332d). Between 1854 and 1857 she was used for trading voyages to Hawai'i with lumber and shingles (Lamb 1938b; Spoehr 1988). In July 1858 she was fitted up as a guard ship to be stationed in the Fraser River to control the issuing of gold licences to the miners by the government (HBCA, PAM, B.226/b/15 fo. 69d, 84;

B.226/b/16 fo. 86d). By 1859 the ship had been sold to the government, and the same year she was sold to Lennard & Green of Portland, Oregon, to operate in the Sandwich Islands (Hawai'i) and China trade (HBCA, PAM, B.226/b/18 fo. 15-15d). From 1852 to 1858 her master was William Mitchell (HBCA, PAM, B.239/k/3 pp. 39, 60, 84). The ship's logs have not been preserved in the Hudson's Bay Company Archives.

Sumatra

The barque *Sumatra* was chartered from Messrs McCalmont & Co. on 21 December 1836 and left London under the command of Captain Alexander Duncan on 3 February 1837, arriving on the coast on 4 September 1837 (HBCA, PAM, A.6/24 fo. 62, 71). On 21 November 1837 she headed back to London, arriving on 10 April 1838 (HBCA, PAM, C.4/1). The ship's log covers 1837-8 (HBCA, PAM, C.1/1061). The Archives holds maps on which her route in 1837-8 is laid out (HBCA, PAM, G.3/887-8, 892, 896).

Tory

The barque *Tory* was chartered in October 1850 from F.W. Green to carry labourers for the settlement on Vancouver Island. It left under the command of Captain Edward Duncan and arrived in Victoria in May 1851. Labourers were recruited in Orkney by Edward Clouston, the Hudson's Bay Company's agent and in Essex by Captain Richard Wilson Pelly, a member of the HBC Committee. There were seventy-seven labourers aboard as well as cabin passengers Richard Golledge, William McDonald, and John Wark, apprentice clerks; Andrew Hunter and John Henry Johnson, engineers; George Johnstone, surgeon and clerk; William Mitchell, master mariner; William Henry Newton, agricultural assistant; Edward Edwards Langford and family, Thomas Bayly and family, and Thomas Dean and family, bailiffs. By 15 May thirty men were transferred to Edward Edwards Langford for the Puget's Sound Agricultural Company's farm near Esquimalt and six more would go with Thomas Dean to Nisqually (Tacoma, Washington), with sixteen on the Hudson's Bay Company's Uplands farm at Cadboro Bay with Thomas Bayly. The others were to be distributed as required (Bowsfield 1979; HBCA, PAM, B.226/z/1 fo. 1-32; Nesbitt 1949, 91 n. 3). The ship's logs have not been preserved in the Hudson's Bay Company Archives.

Una

The 135-ton brigantine *Una* was purchased in London from William Mitcheson for £950 by the Hudson's Bay Company on 5 December 1849 (HBCA, PAM, A.10/27; A.1/66 p. 127). She left under the command of Charles E. Stuart on 6 January 1850 (HBCA, PAM, C.4/1; A.10/28 fo. 194). After arriving on the coast William Mitchell took command. On 25 December 1851, she was driven on the shore of Neah Bay in a gale during the night. The American sloop *Susan Sturges* delivered officers and crew, along with a cargo of furs and gold from the Queen Charlotte Islands to Fort Victoria. Aboriginal people set fire to the ship and it was burnt to the water's edge (HBCA, PAM, A.11/73; D.7/1 fo. 250). The ship's logs have not been preserved in the Hudson's Bay Company Archives.

Vancouver (I, II, III)

(I) The schooner *Vancouver,* of less than 100 tons, was built at Fort Vancouver in 1826 with unseasoned timbers that warped, so by 1829 she had not yet been launched (HBCA, PAM, D.4/93 fo. 61d; *The Beaver,* December 1926, p. 7; D.4/93 fo. 61d; D.4/121 fo. 23). In 1830 and 1831 she made trips along coast (HBCA, PAM, B.223/z/4 fo. 171a-b; C.7/177 fo. 8d, 10, 13-13d, 17-17d, 23-25d). On 3 March 1834 she wrecked on Point Rose, Queen Charlotte Islands, and the crew was forced to flee, leaving wreck and cargo in possession of the Natives (HBCA, PAM, D.4/102, fo. 28; B.223/c/1, fo. 30). Her masters included William Ryan (1830-1 and 1833), Charles Kipling (1831-2), and Alexander Duncan (1834). The ship's logs cover 1831-2 (HBCA, PAM, C.1/1062).

(II) The 400-ton barque *Vancouver* was built by Messrs Green Wigram & Green and launched in 1838 (HBCA, PAM, A.6/25 fo. 13). She left London on 6 November 1838 with Alexander Duncan in command, and reached the coast 3 May 1839 (HBCA, PAM, B.223/b/23 fo. 1). On the coast she travelled twice to the Sandwich Islands and to Sitka (in present-day Alaska), then returned to London, leaving on 29 November 1840 and arriving 3 June 1841. Her second trip out under Alexander Duncan took from 9 September 1841 to 3 April 1842. She returned to London under William Brotchie, 29 November 1843 to 10 June 1844. The third voyage, under Andrew Cook Mott, left London on 4 September 1844, arriving at Fort Victoria on 18 February 1845 and returning to London 12 December 1846 to 12 July 1847. On her fourth visit, she wrecked at the mouth of the Columbia in May 1848 (HBCA, PAM, A.11/70 fo. 280-94). The ship's logs cover 1841-7 (HBCA, PAM, C.1/1063-5). Henry J. Warre depicted the ship in his drawing entitled "Cape Disappointment" (HBCA, PAM, P-63).

(III) The 192-ton brigantine *Vancouver* reached the coast, under the command of James Murray Reid, in December 1852 (HBCA, PAM, A.11/73 fo. 658). On 3 August 1853, she wrecked off Cape Rose, Queen Charlotte Islands, with the Fort Simpson outfit valued at £3,200 (HBCA, PAM, D.4/46 pp. 260-1). The ship's logs have not been preserved in the Hudson's Bay Company Archives.

William & Ann

The 161-ton brig *William & Ann* was built in 1818 at Bermuda (HBCA, PAM, A.6/20 fo. 161; A.7/1 fo. 68d). The Hudson's Bay Company purchased her, with her stores, for £1,500 on 19 May 1824 (HBCA, PAM, A.5/7 pp. 276-7). She left Gravesend with a crew of three officers and fourteen men and the botanist David Douglas on 27 July 1824 (HBCA, PAM, C.1/1066). She sailed via Rio de Janeiro and Juan Fernandez Island, under the command of Captain Henry Hanwell Jr., arriving on 8 April 1825 (HBCA, PAM, C.4/1; C.1/1066). Between 2 June and 5 September she travelled north along the coast, exploring the territory that Britain anticipated being granted in negotiations with Russia (HBCA, PAM, B.223/a/1; C.1/1066). On 25 October 1825 she crossed the Columbia bar on the return journey to London, arriving on 13 April 1826 (HBCA, PAM, C.4/1; C.1/1068; A.6/21 fo. 88d). A second trip to the coast under Hanwell took from 25 September 1826 to 29 January 1827, with the return lasting from 23 August 1827 to 8 February 1828. She sailed from Plymouth in company with the *Ganymede* on her third voyage, but continued alone from the Bay of Biscay (HBCA, PAM, A.6/22 fo. 13d, 35d). She wrecked on arrival at the bar of the Columbia River and all hands were lost, probably drowned (HBCA, PAM, B.223/b/5 fo. 8-9). The ship's logs cover 1824-8 (HBCA, PAM, C.1/1066-1070). Her story was told in Payette 1962, 672-3.

Appendix B: Posts

Fort Colvile

Fort Colvile (Colville, Washington) named for Andrew Colvile, a member of the Hudson's Bay Company's London Committee, was established on the south side of the Columbia River, 1.2 kilometres (three-quarters of a mile) above the portage around Kettle Falls (HBCA, PAM D.4/7 fo. 206-6d; D.3/1 fo. 99d-100). By 7 April 1826 Spokane House was abandoned and the employees and stores were moved to Fort Colvile (Elliott 1914, 276-83). In 1828 Governor George Simpson described the post:

> This establishment which is uppermost in the Columbia River, and situated about 300 miles below the Mountain Portage, was previous to Outfit 1825 so much connected, and its affairs so much blended with those of the Snake Country Expedition, that it is now scarcely possible to separate them so as to give, a comparative statement of the result of each up to that period: but since 1825, they have been kept distinct ... The removal of this Establishment from Spokane to the Banks of the Columbia, has not only been advantageous to its own immediate business, but to all the other Posts on the communication, as by attention to Agriculture here, for the situation of the place together with the Soil and climate are favourable, it supplies all the Grain required for the interior, rendering it unnecessary to furnish any Provisions at the coast except for consumption on the Voyage; whereas formerly, there were about 30 men employed in the transport of Provisions alone, for the use of the interior (HBCA, PAM, D.4/93 fo. 16-75, para. 38).

Francis Heron was chief trader in charge from 1829 to 1831, kept the post journal (HBCA, PAM, B.45/a/1) and wrote the reports (HBCA, PAM, B.45/e/2-3) that cover the period when John Mongle (Jean Monde) (entry 76) was employed there. Archibald McDonald was chief factor from 1842-4 and Francis Ermatinger was chief trader from 1844-6 when Alexander Morison (entry 85) was there (HBCA, PAM, B.239/k/2 pp. 258, 280, 332, 361). During the time Peter Irvine (entry 89) served, there were three men in charge: Alexander Caulfield Anderson, chief trader (1852-3); A.E. Pelly, chief trader (1853-4); and Angus McDonald, clerk (1854-6) (HBCA, PAM, B.239/k/3 pp. 14, 36, 59, 83).

Fort George

Fort George (Prince George, British Columbia) was established in 1807 by Simon Fraser of the North West Company at the junction of the Nechako and Fraser rivers to build craft to explore Fraser River to the Pacific, but was abandoned in 1808 (Morice 1904, 71; HBCA, PAM, B.188/e/1). In 1820 the same Company established it for the fur trade, and it was turned over to the Hudson's Bay Company in November 1821 at the merger of the two companies (HBCA, PAM, B.188/b/1 fo. 26-6d). By 1823 a store was erected at a new site at the 'point of the forks' but the post was abandoned in spring 1824 (HBCA, PAM,

B.119/e/1; B.188/b/2 fo. 30d). The post was re-established in 1829-30, and it was near here that William Johnston (entry 81) drowned on 7 July 1835 (HBCA, PAM, B.239/g/5; D.4/95 fo. 11d). George Linton, clerk (entry 82) was in charge of this post from 1831 to his death in November 1835 (HBCA, PAM, B.239/k/1 p. 217; B.239/k/2 pp. 17, 44, 74, 97).

Fort George

Fort George (Astoria, Oregon) was established in 1811 by the Pacific Fur Company at the mouth of the Columbia River and named Astoria in honour of John Jacob Astor. In October 1813 it was purchased by the North West Company and renamed Fort George. In 1821 it became a Hudson's Bay Company post and headquarters of the Columbia Department on the union of the Hudson's Bay Company and the North West Company. In 1825 the headquarters moved to Fort Vancouver and Fort George was abandoned except as a "minor outlook station" (Merk 1931, 323). By 1839 it was described as consisting of a small house for Mr. Birnie, two or three sheds for the Canadians, and a pine stick with a red ensign (Belcher 1843). By 1847 a new establishment was built at Cape Disappointment with one employee in charge of both. In 1850 United States officers under Major Hathaway took possession of the post (HBCA, PAM, Fort George [OR] Post History). The post managers included Pisk Kipling, in charge from 1833 to 1835; John Dunn, postmaster, from 1835 to 1838, during the time that George Prattent (entry 20) spent six months there in 1836; James Birnic, clerk, from 1839 to 1846, who kept the only journal and report preserved in the HBCA (B.76/a/1 and B.76/e/1); Alexander Lattie, mate, from 1846 to 1847; Charles Forrest, clerk, from 1847 to 1848; William H. McNeill, chief trader, from 1848 to 1849; William Craigie, labourer, from 1849 to 1850; and Edward Spencer, interpreter, who was appointed but did not serve from 1850 to 1851.

Fort Nisqually

Fort Nisqually (Tacoma, Washington) was established in 1833 by John McLoughlin at the southern end of Puget Sound as a farming centre and shipping depot. On 23 December 1840 the farming operations were transferred to the Puget's Sound Agricultural Company, while the fur trade remained in the Company's hands. In 1846 with the settlement of the Oregon boundary it was in United States territory. In January 1858 all the Hudson's Bay Company's stock was transferred to the Puget's Sound Agricultural Company and the effects of the fort were disposed of by public auction and were bought by Edward Huggins (HBCA, PAM, SF "Nisqually"). During the time that Joseph Thomas Heath (brother to William Heath, entry 29) (1844-9) and Edward Hoare (1850) (entry 98) were at Nisqually (also Tacoma, Washington), William Fraser Tolmie, clerk/surgeon and later chief trader, was in charge of the farm.

Fort Rupert

Fort Rupert (near Port Hardy, British Columbia) was established in 1849 by the Hudson's Bay Company on Beaver Harbour at the northeast end of Vancouver Island and was named after the first Governor of the Hudson's Bay Company, Prince Rupert. Until 1852 it served as the headquarters for the Company's commercial coal mining operations. Once the centre of these operations moved to Nanaimo, the post focused on trading furs and salmon until Robert Hunt bought the post in 1883 (Johnson 1972, 12 and 14). The men sent to Fort Rupert between 1849 and 1854 included: miners William Smith (entry 51); John Willoughby (entry 97); William Ritch (entry 106); and Richard Whiffen (entry 101). A number of the sailors deserted or died there in 1850, including Charles Lobb (entry 65) and George and James Wishart (entry 66). During this time the post managers included William Henry McNeill, chief trader (1849-50); George Blenkinsop, clerk (1850-2); John Work (1852-3); and George Blenkinsop (1853-5) (HBCA, PAM, A.11/72 fo. 87-7d; B.239/k/2 fo. 243d; B.239/k/3 pp. 15, 39, 60, 84).

Fort Vancouver
Fort Vancouver (Vancouver, Washington) was officially opened by the Hudson's Bay Company on 19 March 1825, having been removed from the Astoria site used from 1821 (HBCA, PAM, D.4). It was named in honour of George Vancouver in order to reinforce the British claim to the coast. It originally occupied the north bank of the Columbia River and in 1829 was moved to the plain in front of the former site (HBCA, PAM, B.223/z/4 fo. 193-204). On 27 September 1844 a devastating fire raged at the post (HBCA, PAM, B.223/b/31 fo. 218). Until 1849 it was the headquarters of the Columbia Department, but that year the headquarters on the coast was transferred to Fort Victoria. The post was abandoned in 1860. Chief Factor John McLoughlin was in charge of the district from 1825 to 1846, with Chief Trader James Douglas serving from 1846 to 1849. Once the headquarters transferred to Fort Victoria, Chief Factor Peter Skene Ogden was in charge from 1849 to 1851 and Chief Factor John Ballenden from 1851 to 1853. In 1853 it became the headquarters of the newly formed Oregon Department and James A. Grahame, first clerk and later chief trader, was in charge from 1853 to 1860. The men posted at Fort Vancouver included Murdoch McLeod, labourer and middleman (1834-47) (entry 85); James Dickson, blacksmith (1836-43) (entry 83); Angus McDonald, labourer (1842-3) (entry 86); William Swanston, slooper (1843) (entry 84); Allen MacIsaac, labourer (1851-3) (entry 87); and Hugh Mouat (1852-4) (entry 88). It was the main destination of the sailors until 1849, when Fort Victoria took pre-eminence.

Fort Victoria
Fort Victoria (Victoria, British Columbia) was established in 1843 by James Douglas and John McLoughlin near the southeast corner of Vancouver Island and named in honour of Queen Victoria. It was intended to function as a depot for the Pacific trade (HBCA, PAM, D.5/8 fo. 143-4d). In 1849 the Hudson's Bay Company headquarters was transferred here from Fort Vancouver and from 1849 to 1859 Fort Victoria also functioned as the headquarters of the colony. In 1864 the old fort was demolished and the land advertised for sale. The men posted at Fort Victoria included Angus McDonald, labourer (1843-5) (entry 86). The emigrant labourers working in the area included James Rose (1848-50) (entry 93); George Miller (March to July 1850) (entry 100); Richard Ribbins (entry 95); John Shadrach Blundell (entry 96); Benjamin Wickham (entry 102); George Horne (entry 103); Henry Horne (entry 104); William Ross (March to September 1850) (entry 105); Philip Cole (entry 108); and Peter Brown (1851-2) (entry 109). The post managers during this time were Charles Ross, chief trader (1844-5); Dugald Mactavish, clerk and chief trader (1845-7); George Holland (1847-8); and Roderick Finlayson, clerk (1848-9). Chief Factor James Douglas took charge of the Columbia Department from 1849 to 1853, with Roderick Finlayson, now chief trader, continuing with responsibility for the post operations until 1855.

Nanaimo
In 1852 J.D. Pemberton made a geological survey of the coal beds discovered earlier by Joseph William McKay (entry 90) at Nanaimo (in present-day British Columbia), and in

1853 a bastion was built to protect the miners, with the main floor used as an office and store (HBCA, PAM, A.11/73 fo. 585-7). In March 1854 George Robinson of Eardington Colliery, Bridgnorth, was engaged as manager of the Company's coal works on Vancouver Island and he hired colliers at Brierley Hill to be sent out on the *Princess Royal* (HBCA, PAM, A.5/18 fo. 282; A.10/35 fo. 305d, 309, 340). Terms were agreed for the Company to purchase the land in 1854-5, and in 1862 the Company sold the coal mines to the Vancouver Coal Mining and Land Company (HBCA, PAM, A.1/70 pp. 6, 8-9, 64; A.6/31 fo. 184; A.11/75 fo. 228d, 450, 453-4; A.11/79 fo. 21-38; F.33/1 pp. 1-7, 24, 191-7). Joseph William McKay (entry 90) was in charge of the Nanaimo coalfields from 1852 to 1854.

Nisqually
See Fort Nisqually.

San Francisco
In 1824 the Company began trading in the area of present-day San Francisco, California, in order to stock the Company's farms with sheep, cattle, and horses but trading was abandoned in 1832 (HBCA, PAM, A.92/17/117 fo. 127). In 1841 an agency was established but after the agent, William Glen Rae, committed suicide on 19 January 1845, the business was wound up by Dugald Mactavish (HBCA, PAM, A.11/64 fo. 9-12). In 1846 Mellus and Howard purchased the Company's building (Blake 1949, 254).

Sandwich Islands (Oahu, Hawai'i)
The Company used Honolulu, Oahu, as a station to repair their vessels and tranship mail and cargo even before 1833, when George Simpson suggested that an agency be established (HBCA, PAM, A.1/58). George Pelly was appointed agent and travelled on the *Eagle,* arriving in 1834. By 1837 the Company considered trade was disappointing, but in 1842 the Company was seeking wharf and waterside premises (HBCA, PAM, A.11/61; D.4/60). The Company ships regularly stopped on their way between England and the Columbia River, and a trade in lumber and salmon was pursued. In 1837 Francis Hardy (entry 19) and Thomas Lorkin (entry 22) both deserted in Honolulu, and in April 1847 Jonathan Buck (entry 47) was freed from his agreement. In 1850 the *Cowlitz* had a difficult time with her crew and John Bracebridge (entry 58) was discharged for foul language on 21 January, while William Dean (entry 59), George Mouat (entry 61), and George Micklefield (entry 62) all deserted on 31 January. Jeremiah McCarthy (entry 60) was one of the few who did not desert but he was discharged in Hawai'i on 16 October 1850. The agency began winding up business in 1859 and by 1861 the business was brought to a close (Thrum 1912; HBCA, PAM, B.226/b/20 pp. 164, 209).

Thompson's River
David Stuart of the Pacific Fur Company founded the Thompson's River post (now Kamloops, British Columbia) on the south shore of the South Thompson River in 1812 as a post for the Shuswap trade (Coues). In October 1813 all posts in the Columbia and Thompson River Districts were sold to the North West Company and in 1821 they became Hudson's Bay Company posts on the union of the latter two companies. The fur trade reached its zenith at this post in 1823 and by 1827 the trade was declining at the post, now referred to as Kamloops (a word meaning "the meeting place of waters") (HBCA, PAM, B.97/e/1). In 1842 under the direction of John Tod (entry 92), a new fort was constructed on the west side of the North Thompson River (MacKay 1937). It was here that William Swanston (entry 84) was based as slooper from 1842 to 1843.

$\mathcal{N}otes$

Introduction

For a general introduction to the history of the Hudson's Bay Company no work has yet surpassed E.E. Rich's masterful volume (Rich 1959), although some might prefer the less academic approach of Peter C. Newman (1987). A useful introduction to Canadian postal history and letter writing is found in Jane E. Harrison's work (1997).

Biographical sheets, ships' histories, and post histories – which are constantly being revised and expanded – are available from the Hudson's Bay Company Archives, Provincial Archives of Manitoba, 200 Vaughan Street, Winnipeg, Manitoba, R3C 1T5, Canada.

The following acronyms, representing collections described more fully in the references, appear in source citations in these notes:

BCA	British Columbia Archives
CduP	Centre du patrimoine
FHC	Family History Center
HSA	Hawai'i State Archives
HMCS	Hawaiian Mission Children's Society Collections
HBCA, PAM	Hudson's Bay Company Archives, Provincial Archives of Manitoba
MGS	Manitoba Genealogical Society
OHS	Oregon Historical Society
OA	Orkney Archives
PANS	Public Archives of Nova Scotia

Men on the Ships

For information on the men who served on the Company's ships, we rely heavily on Dick Wilson's work (1997) based on his thesis, and on the various Hudson's Bay Record Society volumes dedicated to the activities on the West Coast of North America (Rich 1941; Rich 1943; 1944; Ormsby 1979). For a discussion of the difficulties between the HBC and mariners on the west coast, please see Burley 1997, 204-7. For the statistical analyses of seamen, please see Wilson 1997, especially 38-45.

The dates for leaving London are complicated by which place is used as the European point of departure: Gravesend; the Downs, where ships often had a long wait for favourable winds; or some other point. Similarly, the dates for arriving on the west coast depend on whether the date of arrival at the bar of the Columbia River or the arrival at Fort Vancouver is used – or, for the later period, arrival at the harbour of Esquimalt or Fort Victoria. The dates given here correspond to the dates provided for departure from Gravesend and arrival at the coast in the Book of Ship's Movements (HBCA, PAM,

C.4/1) rather than date provided in the various ships' logs. Sometimes the time spent by the crew on the ship is different from the actual sailing dates: the men usually entered the ship before it departed and stayed on it after its arrival, both in London and on the coast. Apprentices and ship's officers were on board longer than the seamen were.

- 1830 brief quotations on apprentices "lads intended to go out" (HBCA, PAM, A.1/56, p. 216); "they be treated with kindness" (HBCA, PAM, A.6/22 fo. 53d-54).

1 WILLIAM WILSON
Wilson (Willson) entered the Company's ship as a seaman on 11 September 1826 and on 16 September he signed with his mark for three years at £30 per year, giving Kirkwall, Orkney, as his parish of origin (HBCA, PAM, A.32/59 fo. 135). He was given the designation "b" after his name to distinguish him from other men by the same name employed by the Company. He travelled on the *Cadboro,* leaving Gravesend on 25 September 1826 and arriving at the Columbia Department 24 April 1827 (HBCA, PAM, B.223/d/12 fo. 4; C.3/13 fo. 66; C.4/1; C.7/21). After two and a half years on the coast, he returned on the *Eagle,* leaving on 29 October 1830 and arriving in London 17 April 1831 (HBCA, PAM, C.3/13 fo. 87; C.4/1).
- 17 June 1830 letter (HBCA, PAM, E.31/2/1 fo. 343-4d)
- 22 June 1830 letter (HBCA, PAM, E.31/2/1 fo. 345-6d).

2a JAMES CURTIS
Entering the Company's ship as a boatswain on 28 December 1829, Curtis on 9 January 1830 signed with his mark a three-year contract for £34 4s. per year (HBCA, PAM, A.32/24 fo. 530). He travelled out on the *Dryad,* accompanied by his son William, leaving Gravesend in January 1830 and arriving at the Columbia Department on 10 August 1830 (HBCA, PAM, A.67/29 fo. 286B; C.3/13 fo. 97; C.4/1). After serving with the *Vancouver* on the coast, he returned on the *Ganymede,* leaving on 7 November 1831 and arriving in London 15 May 1832 (HBCA, PAM, C.3/13 fo. 101; C.4/1). In 1832 he sailed to New South Wales with Aly & Price on the *Windsor* (HBCA, PAM, E.31/2/1 fo. 81-2d). He and his wife, Mary (Litchfield?), had at least three children: Mary, Hugh (bapt. 1811), and William (bapt. 1813) (FHC).

2b WILLIAM CURTIS
Curtis (b. c. 1811) entered the Company's ship as a seaman on 28 December 1829 and on 9 January 1830 signed a three-year contract for £30 per year (HBCA, PAM, A.32/24 fo. 531). He travelled out on the *Dryad,* accompanying his father James, leaving Gravesend in January 1830 and arriving at the Columbia Department on 10 August 1830 (HBCA, PAM, A.67/29 fo. 286B; C.3/13 fo. 97; C.4/1). He served with the *Ganymede* and the *Cadboro* on the coast (HBCA, PAM, B.223/d/28, 29, 37, 47; B.239/g/11-12; C.7/177 fo. 14d, 18d). While on the *Cadboro,* he was involved in a riot in which he got drunk and used insolent language, and was put in irons, along with Robert Nicholls and Peter Calder (Rich 1941, 316; HBCA, PAM, B.223/b/8 fo. 18-20). He returned on the *Eagle,* leaving on 6 November 1832 and arriving in London 30 May 1833 (HBCA, PAM, C.3/14 fo. 3; C.4/1).

2c HENRY BEE
Entering the Company's ship as a cook on 28 December 1829, Bee on 9 January 1830 signed a three-year contract for £30 per year (HBCA, PAM, A.32/21 fo. 263). He travelled

on the *Dryad,* leaving Gravesend in January 1830 and arriving at the Columbia Department on 10 August 1830 (HBCA, PAM, A.67/29 fo. 265d-6; C.3/13 fo. 97; C.4/1). After serving with the *Dryad* on the coast, he deserted, possibly at Monterey, in 1831 (HBCA, PAM, B.223/d/28; B.223/z/4 fo. 170a).

Accounts of Burke and Hare can be found in the *Harmsworth Enclycopaedia* (n.d., 422) and the fourteenth edition of the *Encyclopaedia Britannica,* among others.
- 28 January 1832 letter (HBCA, PAM, E.31/2/1 fo. 79-80d)
- 27 August 1832 letter (HBCA, PAM, E.31/2/1 fo. 81-2d)
- October(?) 1832 quotation "sent in irons" (HBCA, PAM, B.223/b/8 fo. 18-20).

3 ROBERT NICHOLLS
Entering the Company's ship as a seaman on 8 November 1830, Nicholls on 20 November signed a three-year contract for £30 per year giving his parish of origin as Falmouth, Rol, Cornwall (HBCA, PAM, A.32/48 fo. 43). He left London on the *Ganymede* on 16 November 1830 and arrived at the Columbia Department in July 1831 (HBCA, PAM, C.3/13 fo. 100; C.4/1; C.7/59). He served with the *Ganymede, Vancouver,* and *Cadboro* on the coast (HBCA, PAM, B.239/g/11-12; C.7/177 fo. 14d, 18d). While on the *Cadboro,* he was involved in a riot in which he got drunk and used insolent language, and was put in irons, along with William Curtis and Peter Calder (Rich 1941, 316; HBCA, PAM, B.223/b/8 fo. 18-20). He was sent home as a passenger on the *Eagle,* leaving the coast on 6 November 1832 and arriving in London on 30 May 1833 (HBCA, PAM, C.3/14 fo. 3; C.4/1).
- 13 May 1832 letter (HBCA, PAM, C.7/59 fo. 1-2d).

4 JOSEPH BINNINGTON
Binnington entered the Company ship on 6 October and on 20 November 1830 signed a three-year contact as a seaman at £30 per year giving Hull, Yorkshire, as his parish of origin (HBCA, PAM, A.32/21 fo. 381). He travelled on the *Ganymede,* leaving Gravesend on 16 November 1830 and arriving at the Columbia Department on 17 July 1831 (HBCA, PAM, C.3/13 fo. 99; C.4/1; C.7/59). After serving with the *Ganymede* and *Cadboro* on the coast, he went home as a seaman on the *Eagle,* leaving the coast on 6 November 1832 and arriving in London on 30 May 1833 (HBCA, PAM, B.223/d/37, 47; B.239/g/11-12; C.3/14 fo. 3; C.4/1; C.7/177 fo. 14d). For a discussion of malaria at Fort Vancouver, please see Gibson 1997, 145-7.
- 12 September 1832 letter (HBCA, PAM, C.7/21 fo. 5-6d)
- 20 February 1833 letter (HBCA, PAM, E.31/2/1 fo. 12-13d).

5 JAMES BLACKIE
Blackie (Blackey, Blakey) joined as a seaman in London and travelled on the *Prince of Wales* to Hudson Bay between 12 May and 7 November 1828 (HBCA, PAM, C.3/13 fo. 71). He entered the *Dryad* on 28 December 1829 and signed a three-year contract at £30 per year on 9 January 1830, giving no parish of origin (HBCA, PAM, A.32/21 fo. 448). He travelled as a seaman, leaving Gravesend in January 1830 and arriving at the Columbia Department on 10 August 1830 (HBCA, PAM, C.3/13 fo. 97; C.4/1). He was promoted to boatswain on the *Dryad,* then served in that capacity with the *Ganymede* on the coast and on the return voyage to London, departing on 19 September 1833 and arriving in London 23 February 1834 (HBCA, PAM, B.223/d/28-9, 37, 47, 54; B.239/g/11-13; C.3/14 fo. 6, 14; C.4/1; C.7/177 fo. 12d, 19d, 26, 27A). In 1835 and 1838-58 he was boatswain on

the yearly trips between Moose Factory and London: on the *Prince of Wales* until 1841, on the *Prince Albert* 1842-53, and on the *Prince Arthur* 1854-8 (HBCA, PAM, C.3/14 fo. 24, 61, 71, 78, 90, 107, 114; C.3/15 fo. 6, 17, 23, 31, 40, 48, 56, 72, 87, 98, 107, 121B; C.3/16 fo. 1, 8, 17).
- 2 October 1832 letter (HBCA, PAM, E.31/2/1 fo. 14-15d).

6   ARCHIBALD CAMPBELL
Campbell signed a three-year contract as a seaman for £30 per year on 30 September 1829, giving his parish of origin as Renfrew, Scotland (HBCA, PAM, A.32/23 fo. 91). He travelled on the *Isabella,* which left Gravesend on 1 November 1829 and wrecked at the Columbia bar on 2 May 1830 (HBCA, PAM, C.3/13 fo. 89; C.4/1). He was promoted to steward after his efforts to save the ship and salvage the cargo, serving on the *Cadboro* and *Dryad* on the coast, before returning in the same capacity with the *Eagle,* departing on 6 November 1832 and arriving in London 30 May 1833 (HBCA, PAM, B.223/b/6 fo. 13-14; B.223/d/28, 37; B.239/g/11-12; C.3/14 fo. 3; C.4/1; C.7/177 fo. 9d, 12d, 19d).
- 27 January 1833 letter (HBCA, PAM, E.31/2/1 fo. 53-4d)
- 11 October 1830 letter extract (HBCA, PAM, B.223/b/6 fo. 13-18d; Rich 1941, 83).

7   JOHN FLINN
Flinn (Flynn) entered the *Isabella* on 28 September and on 31 October 1829 he signed a three-year contract as a seaman at £30 per year, giving his parish of origin as Waterford, Ireland (HBCA, PAM, A.32/28 fo. 329). He travelled out on the *Isabella,* leaving Gravesend on 1 November 1829 and wrecking at the Columbia bar on 2 May 1830 (HBCA, PAM, C.3/13 fo. 89; C.4/1). He served on the *Vancouver, Cadboro,* and *Dryad* on the coast before returning on the *Eagle,* departing on 6 November 1832 and arriving in London 30 May 1833 (HBCA, PAM, B.223/d/28, 29, 37, 47; B.223/g/2; B.239/g/11-12; C.3/14 fo. 3; C.4/1; C.7/177 fo. 9d, 10, 19d).
- 29 January 1833 letter (HBCA, PAM, E.31/2/1 fo. 105-6)
- May [1833] letter (HBCA, PAM, E.31/2/1 fo. 107-8d).

8   SAMUEL PARSONS
Entering the ship on 6 October, Parsons on 20 November 1830 signed a three-year contract for £30 per year as a seaman, giving his parish of origin as Liverpool, Lancashire (HBCA, PAM, A.32/49 fo. 86; C.3/13 fo. 99). He travelled on the *Ganymede,* which left Gravesend on 16 November 1830 and arrived at the Columbia Department on 17 July 1831 (HBCA, PAM, C.3/13 fo. 99; C.4/1). He served on the *Vancouver* and *Dryad* on the coast before returning on the *Ganymede,* departing on 19 September 1833 and arriving in London 23 February 1834 (HBCA, PAM, B.223/d/105; B.239/g/11-13; C.3/14 fo. 6; C.4/1; C.7/177 fo. 17d, 22Bd, 27A).
- 31 May 1833 letter (HBCA, PAM, E.31/2/1 fo. 239-40d).

9   CHARLES FRASER
Fraser (Frazer), entering as a ship's boy on 1 October 1829 at a pay rate of £15 per year, travelled out on the *Eagle,* leaving Gravesend on 1 November 1829 and arriving at the Columbia Department on 2 June 1830 (HBCA, PAM, C.3/13 fo. 88; C.4/1). He served on the coast on the *Eagle, Dryad, Cadboro,* and once again on the *Dryad,* before returning on the *Ganymede,* departing on 19 September 1833 and arriving in London 23 February 1834 (HBCA, PAM, B.239/g/11-13; C.3/13 fo. 89; C.4/1; C.7/177 fo. 12d, 19d, 27A).
- 1 June 1833 letter (HBCA, PAM, E.31/2/1 fo. 109-11).

10 ROBERT ALLAN
Allan (Allen) (1800-45) signed with his mark a three-year contract at £30 per year on 31 October 1829, giving his parish of origin as Greenwich, Kent (HBCA, PAM, A.32/20 fo. 151). He was given the designation "a" after his name to distinguish him from other men with the same name in the Company's service. He entered the *Isabella* as a seaman on 1 November 1829, leaving London the same day and arriving at the Columbia bar on 2 May 1830, where the ship was wrecked (HBCA, PAM, B.223/b/6 fo. 134; C.3/13 fo. 89). He served on the coast on the *Cadboro* and *Dryad* before returning on the *Ganymede,* departing on 19 September 1833 and arriving in London 23 February 1834 (HBCA, PAM, B.223/d/28, 37; B.239/g/11-13; C.1/337; C.3/13, 14 fo. 7, 14; C.4/1; C.7/177 fo. 9d, 12d, 19d, 27A). He sailed to Hudson Bay on the *Ganymede* in the summer of 1834. On 13 December 1834 (one day after the ship left the Downs), he once more signed with his mark, this time for a five-year contract at £24 per year, again giving his parish of origin as Greenwich, Kent (HBCA, PAM, A.32/20 fo. 152; C.4/1). He returned to the Columbia, leaving London 10 December 1834 and arriving on the coast on 27 July 1835 (HBCA, PAM, C.3/14 fo. 14; C.4/1). He served on the *Cadboro* and *Nereide* before settling at Chinook in Oregon Territory (HBCA, PAM, B.223/d/77, 88, 100, 121, 141, 145, 152, 157; B.239/g/15-24; C.3/14 fo. 39; C.7/177 fo. 42d, 58, 65, 67d, 68d, 70, 81, 85d). He died at Fort Vancouver on 7 March 1845 and Captain James Allan Scarborough was the executor of his will, with Alexander Caulfield Anderson a trustee. In his will his parish of origin was given as Portsmouth, Hampshire (HBCA, PAM, A.10/19 fo. 166; A.10/21 fo. 41-41d; B.239/g/27, 29). His parents were probably John and Mary Allan of Portsea and, if so, his sister Mary was baptized 8 December 1798, while he was born 2 March 1800 (FHC). He married Charlotte Scarborough, according to C.D. Denney, but James Scarborough also came out in 1829 and could not have had a daughter old enough to be married by 1840 (HBCA, PAM, SF "Allen, Robert"). Allan's daughter Mary Anne was born about 1840, and was baptized at Fort Dunvegan (in present-day Alberta) on 10 August 1846 (HBCA, PAM, A.10/19 fo. 166). Though both her parents died when she was young, she remembered having some brothers and sisters who were living in Oregon in 1859 (HBCA, PAM, E.69/2 fo. 50d). She married William Lucas Hardisty (1824-81) in the summer of 1857 (HBCA, PAM, E.69/1 fo. 68). Their children included Richard (1862-85); Isabella (b. 1864); Frank Allan (b. 1866); Mary Louisa; Thomas Alexander; David Alexander; and William Lucas. In Winnipeg in June 1883 she married Edwin Stewart Thomas (1850-1932), son of Harriet Stewart Thomas (1819-1910) (MGS, Stonewall Anglican Register). She died 16 January 1930 and was buried in All Saints, Victoria Cemetery near Stonewall, Manitoba (MGS, Stonewall Anglican Register). We have been in touch with a number of people concerning Mary Allen, including Robin McLay and Professor Donald Smith. For information on marriages in the fur trade, see Brown 1980, Hussey 1991, and Van Kirk 1980.
• 4 June 1833 letter (HBCA, PAM, C.7/21 fo. 7-8d).
• 1857 letter extract (HBCA, PAM, D.5/45 fo. 263d-4d).

11a JAMES WILSON
Wilson (b. 1804) signed a five-year contract at £24 per year in Orkney on 24 January 1828, giving his parish of origin as Stromness, Orkney (HBCA, PAM, A.32/59 fo. 105). He was given the designation "a" in the Company's accounts to distinguish him from other men of the same name. He travelled as a sailor to York Factory and crossed the continent with

the brigade to the Columbia, serving on the coast on the *Dryad* and the *Ganymede* (HBCA, PAM, B.223/d/47 fo. 17d; B.223/d/54 p. 16; B.239/g/8-13; C.7/177 fo. 223d). He returned on the *Ganymede,* departing on 19 September 1833 and arriving in London 23 February 1834 (HBCA, PAM, C.3/14 fo. 7; C.4/1; C.7/177 fo. 27A). His parents, Robert Wilson and Janet McKinnie (or McKemie), married on 20 December 1798 in Stromness and their children included Robert (bapt. 12 November 1799, d. 29 March 1864, see next entry), Janet (bapt. April 1801), John (bapt. 8 August 1802), and William (bapt. 16 January 1806) (FHC).

11b ROBERT WILSON

In Orkney, Wilson (1799-1864) signed a five-year contract as a boatbuilder at £30 per year on 7 June 1820, giving his parish of origin as Stromness, Orkney (HBCA, PAM, A.32/59 fo. 117). He was given the designation "a" in the Company's accounts to distinguish him from other men of the same name. He travelled as a boatbuilder to York Factory and served at Norway House, then in the Saskatchewan and Swan River districts (HBCA, PAM, A.16/39; B.239/g/1-11; B.239/u/1 #2211). He returned to Norway House as boatbuilder and postmaster in 1832, and became postmaster at Severn in 1834 and at York Factory in 1839 (Macleod 1947; HBCA, PAM, A.10/11 fo. 148-9; B.239/g/12-28). In 1849 he was promoted to clerk at York Factory, and in 1854 he was sent as clerk in charge at Oxford House (Macleod 1947; HBCA, PAM, B.239/g/29-44; B.239/k/3). He died on 29 March 1864 (HBCA, PAM, A.44/4 fo. 60; B.239/c/15, 31 March 1864; B.239/g/44). For family details, see entry 11a. He married Jane Flett on 4 September 1851 at York Factory, and they had a son, Robert Cummins Wilson (1852-1913), who also worked for the Company (Macleod 1947; PAM, St. John's Marriages; HBCA, PAM, A.44/4 fo. 62).
- 21 June 1833 letter (HBCA, PAM, E.31/2/1 fo. 339-40d)
- 7 July 1833 letter (HBCA, PAM, E.31/2/1 fo. 341-2)
- 5 September 1840 letter (HBCA, PAM, A.10/11 fo. 148-9).

12 WALTER PREDITH

Predith signed a three-year contract at £34 4s. per year as a steward on 4 May 1833, giving his parish of origin as Stepney, Middlesex (HBCA, PAM, C.3/14 fo. 16). He travelled on the *Nereide,* leaving Gravesend on 6 May 1833 and arriving at the Columbia Department on 14 April 1834 (HBCA, PAM, C.1/609; C.4/1). He served on the *Nereide* until arriving at Valparaiso, Chile, where he deserted on 25 March 1835 (HBCA, PAM, C.1/609; C.3/14 fo. 16).
- 2 October 1833 letter (HBCA, PAM, E.31/2/1 fo. 247-8d)
- 4 December 1833 letter (HBCA, PAM, E.31/2/1 fo. 249-50d).

13 HENRY WILLIAM HARMSWORTH

Harmsworth (1816-1906) was a pupil at the Royal Hospital School in Greenwich, Kent, and entered the Company's ship as an apprentice on 19 October 1830 (Glegg 1984; HBCA, PAM, C.3/13 fo. 100). He travelled on the *Ganymede,* leaving Gravesend on 16 November 1830 and arriving at the Columbia River on 17 July 1831 (HBCA, PAM, C.3/13 fo. 100; C.4/1). He served on the *Nereide, Cadboro,* and *Lama* on the coast before returning on the *Nereide,* departing on 20 June 1834 and arriving in London 27 May 1835 after a delay in Valparaiso and Copiapo under the command of Captain J.M. Langtry (HBCA, PAM, B.239/g/11-13; C.3/14 fo. 18; C.4/1; C.7/177 fo. 14d, 18d, 22A, 33). He sailed to Ungava and returned on the *Esquimaux* in the 1835 season, then returned to the Columbia Department on the *Nereide,* departing Gravesend on 13 February 1836 and arriving on the coast on 26 August 1836 (HBCA, PAM, A.67/27 fo. 396; B.223/z/4 fo. 180; C.1/325a; C.3/14 fo. 20, 48; C.4/1). He served on the coast on board the *Nereide* before returning to London on the *Sumatra,* departing on 21 November 1837 and arriving on 10 April 1838 (HBCA, PAM, B.239/g/16-17; C.3/14 fo. 67; C.4/1; C.7/98, 177 fo. 53, 137). After he was released from the Hudson's Bay Company he went to work on other ships, including *Mayflower, William Broderick,* and *Waverley* (Glegg 1984, 61). He died in England on 22 July 1906 (Glegg 1984). His parents were Henry Harmsworth (1785-1833) and Elizabeth Ann Burney (1786-1870), and his siblings were John Henry (b. 1813), Elizabeth Studd (1824-1903) and Mary Ann (b. 1828) (Glegg 1984). In 1856 he married Ann Brooke (1827-1917), and their children were Harry (1857-1939), Frank Brooke (1861-1947), Herbert William (1865-1943), Annie Elizabeth (1866-7), Annie Grace (1867-73), Pattie (1868-1921) and Josephine (1872-1961) (Glegg 1984). For general information on the family and for details on Henry Harmsworth's life after HBC service, please see Glegg 1984.

- quotations on apprentices "when in Harbour" (HBCA, PAM, B.223/b/9 fo. 11d-13d) and "I am certain he would not" (HBCA, PAM, B.223/b/9 fo. 13d-14)
- For the Company's replies to his father's, please see HBCA, PAM, A.5/9 fo. 170 and A.5/10 fo. 24.
- 12 January 1835 letter (HBCA, PAM, E.31/2/1 fo. 122-3d)
- 4 February 1835 letter (HBCA, PAM, E.31/2/1 fo. 124-5d)
- [1836] letter (HBCA, PAM, E.31/2/1 fo. 126-7d)
- 26 November [1836] letter (HBCA, PAM, E.31/2/1 fo. 128-9d)
- September 1837 letter (HBCA, PAM, E.31/2/1 fo. 130-1d)
- 12 November 1837 letter (HBCA, PAM, E.31/2/1 fo. 132-3d).

14 ALEXANDER DUNCAN

Duncan entered the Company's service as a seaman at £30 per year on 19 July 1824 (HBCA, PAM, C.3/13 fo. 50). He travelled on the *William & Ann,* leaving Gravesend on 27 July, arriving at the Columbia River on 8 April 1825 and returning as boatswain, with an additional £12 per year, on a voyage that took from 25 October 1825 to 13 April 1826 (HBCA, PAM, C.1/1066-68; C.3/13 fo. 50; C.4/1). He signed a three-year contract at £52 10s. per year as mate of the schooner and clerk on 4 September 1826, giving his parish of origin as Carronshore, Larbor (Larbert), Stirlingshire (HBCA, PAM, A.32/26 fo. 189). After a second trip out on the *William & Ann* from 25 September 1826 to 29 January 1827, he was offered, and declined, the position as second-in-command of the *Cadboro,* preferring instead to return to London as mate on the *William & Ann,* travelling between 23 August 1827 and 8 February 1828 (Rich 1941, 42, 42n; HBCA, PAM, C.1/1070; C.4/1). For the next two seasons he made the Hudson Bay trip as second mate on the *Prince of Wales* (Rich 1941, 90 and 97; HBCA, PAM, A.1/56 fo. 79d, 105d). On 29 December 1829 he once more entered the ship, signing another three-year contract at £75 12s. per year on 9 January 1830 (HBCA, PAM, A.32/26 fo. 190). He returned to the Columbia River on the *Dryad* as first mate, leaving Gravesend in January 1830 and arriving on the coast on 10 August 1830. He served on the coast as master and mate on the *Dryad, Ganymede, Vancouver* (until it wrecked on 3 March 1834) and *Cadboro* (Rich 1941, 101-2; HBCA, PAM, SF "Columbia" and "Duncan, Alexander"; HBCA, PAM, A.1/56 fo. 105d; B.223/b/7 fo. 12d; B.239/g/12-14; C.1/281; C.4/1). On 20 October 1835 he left the coast as a passenger on full pay on the *Dryad,* arriving in London on 10 April 1836 (Rich 1941, 140; HBCA,

PAM, A.10/3 fo. 10, 75, 187; B.239/g/15; C.4/1). On 30 November 1836 he signed a five-year contract for £126 per year as master of any vessel, giving his parish of origin as Kincardine, Stirling (HBCA, PAM, A.32/26 fo. 191). He now sailed to the Columbia River as master of the *Sumatra,* travelling out between 3 February and 4 September 1837 and returning between 21 November 1837 and 10 April 1838 (HBCA, PAM, A.6/24 fo. 61d, 154d; A.10/4 fo. 67, 213; A.10/5 fo. 44, 261; A.10/6 fo. 276; B.239/g/17; C.4/1). In November 1838 he returned once more, this time in command of the *Vancouver,* signing a five-year contract at £126 per year on 5 November 1838 (HBCA, PAM, A.10/7 fo. 312; A.32/26 fo. 192). After arriving on 3 May 1839 he travelled twice to the Sandwich Islands (Hawai'i) and to Sitka (in present-day Alaska) before returning to London between 29 November 1840 and 3 June 1841 (Rich 1943, 30; HBCA, PAM, A.6/24 fo. 154d; A.10/6 fo. 276; A.10/11 fo. 399; A.10/12 fo. 561, 588-90, 598, 601-6; A.10/13 fo. 1, 77; B.239/g/17-22; C.4/1). He left London once more on 9 September 1840 and arrived on 3 April 1841, serving on the *Vancouver* and *Beaver* before returning to London on the *Columbia* between 5 December 1844 and 22 May 1845 (Rich 1943, 47 and 52; HBCA, PAM, A.10/13 fo. 172; A.10/14 fo. 6; B.239/g/23-4; C.1/248-9; C.4/1). His final trip out to the coast, on the *Columbia,* kept him away from London between 4 October 1845 and 22 May 1848, when he retired from the Company's service (HBCA, PAM, A.5/15 fo. 18; A.10/20 fo. 205-6; A.10/24 fo. 435, 475; A.10/25 fo. 18; B.223/z/4 fo. 215d; B.239/g/27; C.1/250-3; C.4/1; C.7/32 fo. 65-74). By 1849 he had moved, with his family, to a farm in the United States (variously given as New York or Oakland County, Michigan) (HBCA, PAM, B.223/z/4 fo. 215d; C.7/32 fo. 65-74). His father was Alexander Duncan (HBCA, PAM, A.5/9 fo. 103d), and his siblings were John, Peter, and Andrew. On 15 March 1829 he married Ann Simpson in Larbert, Stirling, and their children were Ann (b. 15 May 1837); Margaret (b. 20 March 1839); and John Alexander (b. 28 April 1846) (FHC).

- 3 February 1835 letter (HBCA, PAM, E.31/2/1 fo. 93-4d)
- 1 June 1836 brief quotation (HBCA, PAM, A.10/3 fo. 75); for Alexander Duncan's letters to the Company on 1 June 1836, 8 July 1836, and 31 January 1837, please see HBCA, PAM, A.10/3 fo. 75, A.10/3 fo. 187, and A.10/4 fo. 67.
- 21 May 1837 letter (HBCA, PAM, E.31/2/1 fo. 95-6d)
- 5 November 1837 letter (HBCA, PAM, E.31/2/1 fo. 97-8d)
- 25 April 1838 brief quotation (HBCA, PAM, A.10/6 fo. 276)
- 11 May 1840 letter (HBCA, PAM, E.31/2/1 fo. 99-100d)
- 28 January 1841 letter (HBCA, PAM, E.31/2/1 fo. 101-2d); for Ann's 11 December 1840 letter to William Smith, please see HBCA, PAM, A.10/11 fo. 399; for some of the many letters describing the conflict between Alexander Duncan and James McLoughlin, please see HBCA, PAM, A.10/12 fo. 561-61d, 588-90, 598-98d, 601-6; A.10/13 fo. 1a; for Ann's letter dated 9 May 1841 to William Smith, please see HBCA, PAM, A.10/12 fo. 378.
- 1841 brief quotation (HBCA, PAM, A.10/12 fo. 588)
- 10 March 1841 letter (HBCA, PAM, E.31/2/1 fo. 103-4d)
- 9 September 1845 letter (HBCA, PAM, A.10/20 fo. 205-6)
- 7 June 1848 brief quotation (HBCA, PAM, A.10/24 fo. 435); for his 13 June 1848 letter and the Company secretary's notes, please see HBCA, PAM, A.10/24 fo. 475.

15 JAMES JOHNSTON
Johnston (Johnstone) (b. 1795) entered the Company's ship *Isabella* on 28 September 1829 and signed a three-year contract at £30 per year on 28 October 1829, giving his parish of

origin as Stromness, Orkney (HBCA, PAM, A.32/35 fo. 136; C.3/13 fo. 89). In the Company's records he was distinguished from other men of the same name by the designation "D" after his name. He travelled out as a seaman, leaving Gravesend on 1 November 1829 and wrecking at the Columbia bar on 2 May 1830 (HBCA, PAM, C.3/13 fo. 89; C.4/1). He served on the *Vancouver, Dryad,* and *Cadboro* on the coast before being promoted to boatswain on the *Dryad* and then second mate on the *Ganymede* (HBCA, PAM, B.239/g/11-14; C.7/177 fo. 8d, 10d, 12d, 22Bd, 31, 45). He returned on the *Ganymede,* departing on 19 October 1836 and arriving in London on 30 March 1837 (HBCA, PAM, B.239/g/15-16; C.3/14 fo. 39; C.4/1). His parents were probably Peter Johnston and Elspeth Sutherland of Walls & Flotta, Orkney, and his siblings William (b. 1787) and Peter (bapt. 29 March 1801) (FHC).

• 27 June 1835 letter (HBCA, PAM, E.31/2/1 fo. 172-3d)
• 17 April 1847 letter extract (HBCA, PAM, A.10/23 fo. 235)
• "only one person of the name" (HBCA, PAM, A.10/23 fo. 235d).

16a JOSEPH SPENCE
Spence (b. 1803) signed a five-year contract at £21 per year as a sailor on 14 January 1828, giving his parish of origin as Beaboran, Harray in Orkney (HBCA, PAM, A.32/54 fo. 314). He went out to York Factory, crossing the continent to serve in the Columbia Department (HBCA, PAM, B.239/g/8). He served as a sailor at Fort Vancouver 1829-33, then as a carpenter on the *Vancouver, Lama, Cadboro,* and *Columbia* before deserting in Oahu in August 1836 (HBCA, PAM, B.239/g/9-19). His parents were Jacob Spence and Jacobina Spence (d. 1814) of Tufta, Harray. His stepmother, Mary Flett, was a widow with three children: William (a seaman); John (in a mill in Russland); and Margaret (who married Thomas Johnston). Information on the family was supplied by Janice Sinclair of Harray.

16b JOHN SPENCE
Spence (c. 1798-1865) signed a five-year contract at £30 per year on 6 June 1820, giving his parish of origin as Stromness, Orkney (HBCA, PAM, A.32/54 fo. 294). He went out as a boatbuilder to York Factory, then to Cumberland House until 1825, when he crossed the continent to Forts Vancouver and Simpson in the Columbia Department (HBCA, PAM, B.239/g/1-12; B.223/d/19, 28, 39, 27, 105a). He retired to Orkney across the continent, after wintering at Churchill and York Factory (HBCA, PAM, A.5/10 p. 280; B.239/g/13-14). From 1835 to 1838 he served as carpenter on the *Prince Rupert* on her annual voyage into Hudson Bay from Stromness and return (HBCA, PAM, C.3/14 fo. 26d, 35d, 54, 58). On 24 October 1838 he signed a five-year contract at £50 8s. as carpenter with the *Vancouver* and made the long trip out to the Columbia Department once more, this time by sea (HBCA, PAM, A.32/54 fo. 300; C.7/164 fo. 12; C.3/14 fo. 76; C.4/1). He served as boatbuilder or carpenter on the *Cadboro* and at Fort Vancouver until he travelled home on the *Vancouver,* leaving the coast on 29 November 1843, arriving at London 3 June 1844, and proceeding to Stromness in July (HBCA, PAM, A.10/11 fo. 77; A.10/22 fo. 79; B.239/g/19-23; C.3/15 fo. 4; C.4/1). On 4 September 1844 he left Gravesend once again on the *Vancouver* and arrived at Fort Victoria on 18 Februrary 1845 to serve on the *Vancouver* and *Beaver* until he retired in 1861 (HBCA, PAM, C.3/15 fo. 21; A.10/22 fo. 79; B.239/g/25-32; B.226/d/3 fo. 521; B.226/g/1-12). From 1820 to 1835 he was designated "John Spence C" to distinguish him from others by the same name on the Company's Northern Department account books. After 1853, he was shown as "John Spence A" in

the Western Department, since he was the only one by that name on these books. He began buying property in 1854 and at the time of his death he owned part of lot 1772, subdivisions 1, 5, 6 (BCA, C/AA/30.7/2; AA/30.1/1; HBCA, PAM, B.226/z/1 fo. 39). He died on 29 September 1865 and was buried in the naval corner of the Quadra Cemetery on 2 October 1865 (BCA, C/AA/30.1/1; *Victoria Colonist,* 30 September 1865, 3). His uncle was John Spence (HBCA, PAM, A.5/10 p. 317). His sister Betsy Clouston was married to Thomas Clouston, a grocer, Plain Stones, Stromness, Orkney, and had two daughters, Janet or Janette (1827-90), who married John Rae, a bookseller in Stromness, and Christina or Christian (b. 1830), who married Robert Eunson (information on the family was supplied by Janice Sinclair of Harray; HBCA, PAM, A.10/11 fo. 77; A.10/13 fo. 198; A.10/15 fo. 425; A.10/22 fo. 79, 175; A.10/23 fo. 703; A.10/35 fo. 85). On 17 February 1863 John married Maria Robinson, sister of George Robinson, who came out to Nanaimo with her brother, who was foreman in the Company's coal mine (HBCA, PAM, E.196/1 pp. 120-6). In his will, dated 26 September 1865, he left bequests to his relatives in Orkney as well as to the United Presbyterian Church in Stromness and the Pandora Street Society of Wesleyan Methodists in Victoria (a copy from BCA is on HBCA, PAM, SF "Spence, John C").

- 17 September 1835 letter (HBCA, PAM, E.31/2/1 fo. 285-6d)
- 18 June 1843 letter (HBCA, PAM, E.31/2/1 fo. 280-2d)
- 29 September 1843 letter (HBCA, PAM, E.31/2/1 fo. 283-4d).

17 THOMAS FRANCIS
Entering the Company's ship on 1 September 1830, Francis signed a three-year contract as a cook at £34 4s. on 24 September 1831, giving his parish of origin as the Isle of Fyal (HBCA, PAM, A.32/29 fo. 179). He travelled out on the *Eagle,* leaving Gravesend the day he signed on, and arriving at the Columbia River on 19 May 1832 (HBCA, PAM, C.3/14 fo. 2; C.4/1). He served on the *Ganymede* on the coast before returning on the *Eagle,* departing on 6 November 1832 and arriving in London 30 May 1833 (HBCA, PAM, B.223/d/63; C.3/14 fo. 19; C.4/1). He entered the ship on 2 December 1833 and signed a five-year contract at £28 4s. on 7 December 1833, giving his parish of origin as Poplar, Middlesex (London) (HBCA, PAM, A.32/29 fo. 180). On this trip he left on the *Eagle* on 8 December 1833 and arrived on the coast on 20 September 1834 (HBCA, PAM, C.3/14 fo. 18d-19; C.4/1). After serving as cook on the *Eagle* until 10 November 1834, he filled the same position at Fort Vancouver, then returned on the *Columbia,* taking up a position as seaman on 4 February 1837 after the ship left Hawai'i and arriving in London on 12 May 1837 (HBCA, PAM, B.239/g/15-16; C.3/14 fo. 44; C.4/1). On his return he petitioned the Company for compensation because he was allowed no spirits (HBCA, PAM, A.10/5 fo. 505).
- 14 January 1836 letter (HBCA, PAM, C.7/42 fo. 1-2d)
- 1835 letter extract (HBCA, PAM, A.1/59 fo. 69d-70)
- 1837 petition extract (HBCA, PAM, A.10/5 fo. 505).

18 WILLIAM POUCHER
Poucher signed a five-year contract at £24 per year in June 1833, giving his parish of origin as St. George, Middlesex (HBCA, PAM, A.32/49 fo. 398). He travelled as a steward to Captain Darby on the *Eagle,* leaving on 8 December 1833 and arriving at the Columbia River on 20 September 1834 (HBCA, PAM, C.3/14 fo. 19; C.4/1). He served on the *Lama* and *Ganymede* on the coast before returning on the *Ganymede* as a seaman, departing on 19 October 1836 and arriving in London 30 March 1837 (HBCA, PAM, B.239/g/14-16;

C.3/14 fo. 39; C.4/1; C.7/177 fo. 47). After suffering an accident on the way home and spending time in the hospital, he was working as a gardener at Shorter's, Sydenham Common in Kent by November 1837 (HBCA, PAM, A.10/5 fo. 331-31d).

* 10 February 1836 letter (HBCA, PAM, E.31/2/1 fo. 241-2d)
* 28 February 1836 two letters (HBCA, PAM, E.31/2/1 fo. 243-4d)
* 13 November 1837 letter (HBCA, PAM, A.10/5 fo. 331); for mentions in the log of Poucher's injury, please see HBCA, PAM, C.1/337.

19 FRANCIS JOSEPH HARDY

Hardy (b. c. 1812) signed a five-year contract at £24 per year on 24 August 1835 giving his parish of origin as Limehouse, Middlesex, after having served on the *Dunkin [Duncan?] Gibbs* with Thomas Wheeler (HBCA, PAM, A.32/32 fo. 71; C.7/32 fo. 18). He travelled as a seaman on the *Columbia,* leaving Gravesend 29 August 1835 and arriving at the Columbia River on 22 March 1836 (HBCA, PAM, C.1/243; C.4/1). He served on the *Cadboro* and *Lama* on the coast before deserting at Oahu, Hawai'i, in August 1837 (HBCA, PAM, B.223/d/100; B.223/g/4; B.239/g/16-17; C.7/177 fo. 78).

* 22 September 1836 letter (HBCA, PAM, E.31/2/1 fo. 118-19d)
* 18 May 1838 letter (HBCA, PAM, E.31/2/1 fo. 120-1d)
* February 1836 quotation "returned on board drunk" (HBCA, PAM, C.1/243); for Henry Hardy's letters dated 18 May 1838 and 10 July 1839 and for note of the Company's reply 12 July 1839, please see HBCA, PAM, A.10/6 fo. 336 and A.10/9 fo. 17.

20 GEORGE PRATTENT

Prattent signed a three-year contract at £50 8s. per year on 4 May 1833, giving his parish of origin as Devonport, Devon (HBCA, PAM, A.32/49 fo. 408). He travelled out as second mate on the *Nereide,* leaving on 6 May 1833 and arriving at the Columbia River on 14 April 1834, and made the return trip via Valparaiso and Copiapo, arriving back in London on 27 May 1835 (HBCA, PAM, C.1/609; C.4/1). He set out once more, signing a five-year contract at £34 4s. per month on 29 August 1835, leaving as second mate on the *Columbia,* but being promoted to chief mate when Peter Corney died on 31 August (HBCA, PAM, A.5/11 p. 44, 64; A.32/49 fo. 409; C.1/243; C.7/32 fo. 18). In Hawai'i, when he was accused of drunkenness by Captain Darby, Prattent charged Darby with trading furs privately and he was exchanged with the mate of the *Beaver* until he arrived on the coast on 19 March 1836 (Rich 1941, 160; Lamb 1938, 171; HBCA, PAM, A.10/3 fo. 13; C.4/1). In May 1836 after a Court of Inquiry, he was dismissed for intoxication, sent to Fort George (formerly Astoria), and returned home as a passenger on the *Columbia,* leaving the coast on 30 November 1836 and arriving on 12 May 1837 (HBCA, PAM, A.1/60 fo. 55d; A.6/24 fo. 117; A.10/4 fo. 387-9; B.223/b/12 fo. 12-14d, p. 50; B.239/g/16; C.4/1). The Governor and Committee in London were displeased with both Prattent and Darby, and both were dismissed (HBCA, PAM, A.6/24 fo. 117; A.10/4 fo. 330, 387-9, 398, 421-2, 507). In October 1837 Prattent wrote concerning a dispute between himself and Captain Darby over a watch (HBCA, PAM, A.10/5 fo. 257-9). On 18 August 1835 he married Anne Coull at St. Paul, Middlesex (HBCA, PAM, A.10/4 fo. 141-3). Assistance in the analysis of Anne's medical condition was provided by Marion McKay and Professor Ian Carr of Winnipeg, who have both conducted research in medical history.

* 1835(?) witness and charge statements (HBCA, PAM, B.223/b/12 fo. 12-14d)
* October 1836 petition quotation "take into consideration" (HBCA, PAM, B.223/b/12 fo. 50)

- 27 February 1837 letter (HBCA, PAM, E.31/2/1 fo. 245-6d)
- identification of medical condition "severe Bilious Remittant Fever" (HBCA, PAM, A.10/4 fo. 143); for Anne's letter dated 28 February 1837 and the secretary's notes, please see HBCA, PAM, A.10/4 fo. 141-3.
- 14 May 1837 petition extract (HBCA, PAM, A.10/4 fo. 387-9); for letters dated 15 May and 28 October 1837, please see HBCA, PAM, A.10/4 fo. 398, 421-2, A.10/5 fo. 257-8.

21 CHARLES BAKER

Baker (b. c. 1804) signed a five-year contract at £24 per year on 2 December 1833, giving his parish of origin as Plymouth, Newdevonport, Devon (HBCA, PAM, A.32/21 fo. 56). He travelled out as a seaman on the *Eagle,* leaving Gravesend on 8 December and arriving at the Columbia River on 20 September 1834 (HBCA, PAM, C.3/14 fo. 19; C.4/1). He served on the *Lama* on the coast before returning on the *Columbia* as a seaman, departing on 30 November 1836 and arriving in London on 12 May 1837 (HBCA, PAM, B.223/d/61, 63, 77, 88; B.239/g/14-16; C.3/14 fo. 43; C.4/1; C.7/177 fo. 38, 46d). His parents were Charles Baker and Elizabeth Waycot, who married 11 December 1800 and his siblings were John (bapt. 15 November 1801) and William (bapt. 21 January 1807). He married Mary Ireland on 20 March 1827 in Ashburton, and their children included John (bapt. 7 March 1830) and Elizabeth (bapt. 4 February 1835) (FHC). For a general discussion of women "in service," please see Stanley 1984.

- 4 March 1837 letter (HBCA, PAM, E.31/2/1 fo. 4-5d).

22 THOMAS LORKIN

Lorkin (Larkin, Lorkins) (b. c. 1804) signed a five-year contract at £24 per year on 25 August 1835, the day after he entered the Company's ship, giving no parish of origin (his contract was made out to William Lorkin, but signed Thomas) (HBCA, PAM, A.32/39 fo. 28). Before entering the Company's service, he had worked on the *Pearl* (HBCA, PAM, C.7/32 fo. 18). He travelled out as a seaman on the *Columbia,* leaving Gravesend on 29 August 1835 and arriving at the Columbia River on 22 March 1836 (HBCA, PAM, C.1/243; C.3/14 fo. 46; C.4/1). He served on the *Lama* on the coast before deserting at Oahu, Hawai'i, on 31 July 1837 (HBCA, PAM, B.239/g/16-17). We have been in touch with Jo Spencer of Kent, England, and Eric Larkin of Newfoundland about their possible connection with Thomas Lorkin.

- 2 July 1837, "Dear cousin, I received a letter" (HBCA, PAM, E.31/2/1 fo. 183-5)
- [2 July 1837] three letters (HBCA, PAM, E.31/2/1 fo. 181-2d, 185).

23 DAVID NEIL

Neil (Neill) (b. c. 1812) entered the Company's ship on 24 August 1835 and signed a five-year contract at £24 per year on 29 August 1835, giving no parish of origin. His contract was made out to William Neil, but signed David (HBCA, PAM, A.32/48 fo. 19). Before entering the Company's service, he had worked on the *Guiana* (HBCA, PAM, C.7/32 fo. 18). He travelled out as a seaman on the *Columbia,* leaving Gravesend on 29 August 1835, and arriving at the Columbia River on 22 March 1836 (HBCA, PAM, C.1/243; C.3/14 fo. 46; C.4/1). He served on the *Lama* and *Cadboro* on the coast before deserting with Henry Napuko at San Francisco on a trip to Monterey on 1 October 1837 (HBCA, PAM, B.239/g/16-17; C.7/177 fo. 59).

- 21 July 1837 two letters (HBCA, PAM, E.31/2/1 fo. 217-18d).

24   CHARLES HUMPHREYS
Humphreys (Humphrey, Humphries) (b. c. 1810) family lived in Stromness, Orkney, and
he entered the Company's service as a seaman at £37 16s. in May 1833 (HBCA, PAM,
C.3/14 fo. 9). His first voyage on the *Prince of Wales* was ill fated: he was forced to winter
at Charlton Island. In 1834 he returned as first mate at twice his former rate when the captain and first mate perished, and served in this position on the 1835 journey (Rich 1943,
391). In 1836 he was appointed master of the *Eagle,* but once more he wintered in the Bay
after encountering bad ice conditions (HBCA, PAM, A.10/3; A.10/5 fo. 178; C.1/285-8;
C.3/14 fo. 49; C.4/1). He was examined in "Navigation and Nautical Astronomy" and was
found "perfectly conversant with these subjects," so was appointed master of the barque
Columbia bound for the Columbia River after signing a three-year contract at £126 per
year (HBCA, PAM, A.32/33 fo. 180; A.6/24 fo. 118-18d; A.10/5 fo. 410, 432). He served in
this capacity from 1837 to 1844, completing two round trips from 18 November 1837 to
21 May 1839 and 18 September 1839 to 7 July 1842 (HBCA, PAM, A.10/5 fo. 410, 432;
A.10/6 fo. 305; A.10/15 fo. 38, 40; A.67/27 fo. 471; B.239/g/20-1; B.239/k/2 pp. 229, 281;
C.1/245-7; C.3/14 fo. 64, 84, 101; C.4/1; D.4/110 fo. 73). He set out from London on 10
September 1842 on his third trip out on the *Columbia,* arriving on 6 May 1843 (HBCA,
PAM, A.10/22 fo. 56; C.3/15 fo. 2; C.4/1). On the coast he served until November on the
Columbia and then on the *Beaver,* but in September he was replaced by Charles Dodd
when it was feared that Humphreys's mind was deranged (HBCA, PAM, A.10/22 fo. 130;
B.223/b/33 fo. 89-92d; B.239/k/2 pp. 333, 362; C.1/248). He was sent back home as a pas-
senger on the *Cowlitz,* arriving in London on 27 June 1846, in spite of an attempt to com-
mit suicide by taking laudanum (HBCA, PAM, A.10/21 fo. 79; A.10/22 fo. 31, 56, 132;
C.1/262; C.3/15 fo. 27). After his return he was seeking a job with the Oriental Navigation Company and his mother unsuccessfully petitioned to have him reinstated with the
Company (HBCA, PAM, A.1/64 p. 209; A.10/22 fo. 368, 444). His parents were George
Humphreys (b. 1766, died before 1837, a schoolteacher) and Margaret Allan (b. 1773, running a hospital for scurvy-ridden sailors in 1836, and a midwife in 1851) (HBCA, PAM,
A.1/64 p. 209; A.10/3; A.10/22 fo. 368). His siblings were: William (b. 1792); Margaret (b.
1793); Robert (b. 1795, died before 1802); George (b. 1796); Alex (b. 1797); Jean (b. 1799,
mantilla maker in 1821 Census); John (b. 1800, married Elizabeth Wylie, 25 December
1856); Robert Stewart (b. 1802, cabinet maker in 1851); James (b. 1806, a doctor in Halifax, Mexico during the Spanish-American War, and Boston); Mary (1808-37, married
Robert Dunn, 1 May 1832); Thomas (b. 1812, to Halifax with a drug store, returning in
1855 to Orkney and establishing the Humphrey Bequest to educate poor children); Ann
(b. 1815) (FHC; PANS F109 H13; HBCA, PAM, A.10/3 fo. 509; A.10/14 fo. 35; A.10/22 fo.
444; C.7/32 fo. 30-3, 37-8d; E.31/2/1 fo. 164-5d). His mother wrote frequent letters to the
Company (HBCA, PAM, A.10/3 fo. 509; A.10/13 fo. 462; A.10/14 fo. 378, 537). He
appears to have married in 1842 (HBCA, PAM, A.10/15 fo. 189, 194, 310; B.223/b/33 fo.
92d). Information on the Humphreys also came from Jim Troup, Bruce Watson, and Janice Sinclair, based on research in the Orkney Library and elsewhere in Orkney.
• 13 November 1837 letter (HBCA, PAM, C.7/32 fo. 30-1d); for the letter dated 15
  December 1836, please see HBCA, PAM, A.5/11 pp. 300-1.
• 29 December 1837 letter (HBCA, PAM, C. 7/32 fo. 32-3d)
• [after 29 December 1837] letter (HBCA, PAM, C.7/32 fo. 33-33d)
• 28 May 1838 letter (HBCA, PAM, C.7/32 fo. 37-8d)
• 1 September 1838 letter (HBCA, PAM, E.31/2/1 fo. 164-5d)
• 1840 quotation "I have done myself the satisfaction" (HBCA, PAM, A.10/15 fo. 40)

- brief quotation "[i]f i am ill tempered" (HBCA, PAM, A.10/15 fo. 38)
- August 1846 letter extract (HBCA, PAM, A.10/22 fo. 130)
- brief quotation "complain[ed] to Mr. Work" (HBCA, PAM, A.10/22 fo. 56)
- brief quotation "poor son is my Sole dependance" (HBCA, PAM, A.10/14 fo. 537)
- 1841 or 1842 letter extract (HBCA, PAM, A.10/22 fo. 444).

25 WILLIAM RIDLER
Ridler (Redlur) (d. 1838) entered the Company's ship on 10 February 1836 and signed a five-year contract at £25 4s. per year on 13 February 1836, giving his parish of origin as Gravesend, Kent (HBCA, PAM, A.32/50 fo. 233). He travelled out as a seaman and gunner on the *Nereide*, leaving London the same day he signed on, and arriving at the Columbia River on 26 August 1836 (HBCA, PAM, A.10/7 fo. 297; C.3/14 fo. 48; C.4/1). He served on the *Nereide* and *Columbia* on the coast, and was promoted to boatswain in 1837 (HBCA, PAM, B.239/g/16-17; C.7/177 fo. 53, 57, 61d). However, when he refused to make a whip to punish the mutineers on the *Nereide*, he was demoted to foretopman (Rich 1941, 193). On 26 January 1838 he drowned in the Columbia River, along with Captain David Home and Quinton Hooten (HBCA, PAM, B.239/g/17). For a discussion of the *Nereide* mutiny please see Burley 1997, 238-9.
- "At this urgent moment" (HBCA, PAM, B.223/b/20 fo. 68-83d; Rich 1941, 274-5)
- "On the 14th I went on board" (HBCA, PAM, B.223/b/18 fo. 3d-5; Rich 1941, 192-3)
- 20 May 1838 (HBCA, PAM, E.31/2/1 fo. 253-4d)
- "a widow" and "consequently in great distress" (HBCA, PAM, A.10/7 fo. 297-9d)
- "look in" (HBCA, PAM, A.5/12 fo. 227-9).

26 QUINTON HOOTEN
Quinton (Quintin) Hooten (Hooton) (1812-38) entered the Company's ship on 10 February 1836 and signed a five-year contract at £24 per year on 13 February 1836, giving his parish of origin as Shadwell, Middlesex (HBCA, PAM, A.32/33 fo. 86; C.3/14 fo. 48). He travelled out as a seaman on the *Nereide*, leaving Gravesend the same day he signed on, and arriving at the Columbia River on 26 August 1836 (HBCA, PAM, C.3/14 fo. 48; C.4/1; C.7/98). He served on the *Nereide* and *Columbia* on the coast (HBCA, PAM, B.239/g/16-17; C.7/177 fo. 53, 57). In June 1837 he was put on prisoners' rations of bread and water for the part he played in the mutiny (HBCA, PAM, B.223.b/18 fo. 3-5; B.223/b/20 fo. 72d-3). On 26 January 1838 he drowned in the Columbia River, along with Captain David Home and William Ridler (HBCA, PAM, B.223/b/20 fo. 74d-5; B.239/g/17).
- 27 November 1838 letter (HBCA, PAM, E.31/2/1 fo. 149-50d)
- January 1838 extract (Rich 1941, 276-7; HBCA, PAM, B.223/b/20 fo. 68-83d); for his mother's letter dated 27 May 1839 and the Company's response, please see HBCA, PAM, A.5/12 p. 285; A.10/8 fo. 287.

27 JOHN WILMOT
Wilmot (Wilmore, Willmore, Wilbner) entered the Company ship on 10 February 1836 and signed with his mark a five-year contract at £24 per year on 13 February 1836, giving his parish of origin as London, Middlesex (HBCA, PAM, A.32/59 fo. 92; C.3/14 fo. 48). He travelled out as a seaman on the *Nereide*, leaving Gravesend the same day he signed on and arriving at the Columbia River on 26 August 1836 (HBCA, PAM, C.3/14 fo. 48; C.4/1). He served on the *Nereide* on the coast, was one of the striking sailors punished

for mutiny, and left on the *Columbia* on 11 November 1838, arriving in London on 21 May 1839 (HBCA, PAM, B.223/b/18 fo. 3d-5; B.223/b/20 fo. 72d-3; B.239/g/16-18; C.3/14 fo. 64; C.4/1; C.7/98; C.7/177 fo. 53, 57, 65, 66d). On 17 September 1839 he signed another five-year contract at £24 per year (HBCA, PAM, A.32/59 fo. 93). He made two more return voyages on the *Columbia*, the first departing 18 September 1839 and returning 7 July 1842, and the second departing 10 September 1842 and returning 22 May 1845, with more than a year on the coast both times (HBCA, PAM, B.239/g/22-4; C.3/14 fo. 84, 101; C.3/15 fo. 2, 13; C.4/1).

• 21 May 1838 letter (HBCA, PAM, E.31/2/1 fo. 337-8d).

28 JOHN COON
Coon (Coun, Coone) (b. c. 1791) signed with his mark a three-year contract at £30 per year on 15 September 1832, giving his parish of origin as Limehouse, Middlesex (HBCA, PAM, A.32/24 fo. 184). He travelled out as a seaman on the *Ganymede,* leaving Gravesend the same day he signed, and arriving at the Columbia River on 1 May 1833 (HBCA, PAM, C.3/14 fo. 5; C.4/1). He served on the *Ganymede* and *Lama* on the coast and left on the *Eagle* on 25 November 1834, arriving in London 6 June 1835 (HBCA, PAM, B.223/d/54, 161; B.239/g/13-14; C.3/14 fo. 21; C.4/1; C.7/177 fo. 32d). He signed with his mark a five-year contract at £24 per year on 29 August 1835, and another as boatswain on 18 November 1837 at £30 per year, and made two more return voyages to the coast on the *Columbia,* the first departing 29 August 1835 and returning 12 May 1837, and the second departing 18 November 1837 and returning 21 May 1839 (HBCA, PAM, A.32/24 fo. 185-6; B.223/d/88; B.239/g/16; C.1/243; C.3/14 fo. 42, 65; C.4/1). William Green collected his wages for him (HBCA, PAM, A.10/8 fo. 118).

• 22 April 1838 letter (HBCA, PAM, C.7/32 fo. 34-6d); for the letter dated 31 August 1839, please see HBCA, PAM, A.10/9 fo. 118.

29 WILLIAM HEATH
William Heath (b. 15 May 1810) signed a three-year contract at £50 8s. per year on 15 September 1832, giving his parish of origin as Marlow, Buckinghamshire (HBCA, PAM, A.32/32 fo. 172). He left the same day and travelled out as second mate on the *Ganymede* under the command of Captain Royal, and arrived on the coast on 1 May 1833 (HBCA, PAM, C.3/14 fo. 5; C.4/1). After serving on the coast as mate on the *Ganymede, Vancouver, Cadboro,* and a second time on the *Ganymede,* he returned on the *Columbia,* leaving the coast on 30 November 1836 and arriving in London on 12 May 1837 (Rich 1941, 345-6; HBCA, PAM, A.10/2 fo. 478; A.10/3 fo. 24a; B.239/g/14-16; C.1/220; C.3/14 fo. 42; C.4/1; C.7/32 fo. 18; C.7/177 fo. 40d, 45, 47, 49d). He refused duty in Oahu, Hawai'i, and was replaced by Charles Chitty, but petitioned the London Committee on his return (HBCA, PAM, A.10/4 fo. 474-474d; A.11/61 fo. 22b). On hearing that the *Columbia* was set to sail, he offered his services and re-entered the ship on 1 November 1837, signing a five-year contract at £70 12s. per year as first mate with Captain Humphreys on 18 November 1837 (HBCA, PAM, A.5/12 p. 70; A.10/5 fo. 157; A.32/32 fo. 173; C.3/14 fo. 64). He left Gravesend the day he signed and arrived at the coast on 24 May 1838, returning between 11 November 1838 and 21 May 1839 (HBCA, PAM, C.3/14 fo. 64, 66d; C.4/1). He entered the ship on 11 September 1839 and signed another five-year contract at £75 12s. per year as first officer on 17 September 1839 (HBCA, PAM, A.32/32 fo. 174; C.3/14 fo. 84). He left on the *Columbia* the next day and arrived on the coast on 15 March 1840 (HBCA, PAM, C.1/245-7; C.3/14 fo. 84; C.4/1). He served on the *Columbia* until 31

October and, after an incident in which Captain Humphreys accused him of refusing duty, he served as first mate of the *Cadboro* and *Beaver*, returning to London on the *Cowlitz* on a trip that took from 16 November 1842 to 9 May 1843 (Rich 1943, 69-80; HBCA, PAM, A.10/11 fo. 233; A.10/16 fo. 434; B.239/g/20; B.239/k/2 p. 281; C.1/259; C.4/1). His final trip took him out on the *Cowlitz* between 23 September 1843 and 24 March 1844, the arrival at Fort Victoria (HBCA, PAM, B.239/k/2 p. 333; C.1/259; C.3/15 fo. 11; C.4/1). After travelling on the coast, he returned as master of the *Cowlitz*, leaving the coast on 18 December 1845 and arriving in London on 27 June 1846, when he was dismissed for intoxication (HBCA, PAM, A.1/64, 8 July 1846; A.6/27 fo. 80d; A.10/21 fo. 488; A.10/23 fo. 633; B.239/g/24-6; B.239/k/2 p. 362; C.1/260-2; C.4/1). He wrote to Sir John Henry Pelly asking for passage to join his brother Joseph on the coast but was told his request "cannot be complied with" (HBCA, PAM, A.5/15 p. 262; A.10/23 fo. 633-4). When he asked that the Company certify his abilities as a navigator and seaman, he received no reply (HBCA, PAM, A.10/25 fo. 120). He took up farming at Mill End Farm, but did not appear in the 1869 Directory (Information from Mrs. Sisam, Marlow, Buckinghamshire).

His grandfather was George (1745-1822), second son of Benjamin Heath and Rose Marie Michelet, his wife. George married Mary Keen and was Headmaster at Eton 1791-1801 (Beinecke Library, Yale University). His parents were Joseph Heath (eldest son of George, d. 1 April 1837) and his wife, who wrote and taught music at Henley in 1838 (HBCA, PAM, E.31/2/1 fo. 139-44d). His siblings were: Joseph Thomas (Joe) (b. 22 September 1804) – who left England and leased a farm at Nisqually (Tacoma, Washington) in 1844, and died 7 March 1849 in Steilacoom, Lewis County, Oregon (Beinecke Library, Yale University; HBCA, PAM, A.10/28 fo. 129; A.10/30 fo. 240); Thomas (Tom) Mason (b. 10 September 1805, applied to take over Joseph's farm and in 1851 asked for a farm on Vancouver Island, but both requests were refused and he went to New Zealand and became head of Wellington Public Library); John (Jack) (b. 25 December 1806, married Helena with children Jane and Agnes Mary in 1851); Emma (b. 1 March 1808); Ellen (b. 29 March 1809, married John Earwaker); Fanny (b. 9 November 1811, married Dr. George Faithorn in 1839, he died in 1871 and she in 1872, their daughter Fanny died on 24 February 1929 and the local newspaper carried a tribute by the Vicar of Chesham); Jane (Jenney) (b. 24 May 1813, married a Mr. Smith) (Dickey 1989, index). Mary, Harry, Harriet, Anne, and Charles (tutor to the Czar of Russia who died 6 December 1900) may have been half siblings (Yale University, Joseph T. Heath Papers). The County Record Office holds a lease dated 18 December 1818 between the Rev. Charles Hughes and Joseph Heath for the properties of Grove Farm (133 hectares [328 acres]), Friars Farm (41 hectares [102 acres]), Mill End Farm (41 hectares [102 acres] with two cottages), Park Lane Farm (10.5 hectares [26 acres]), and sundry other parcels of land, for a rent of £500 per year for fourteen years. On 16 June 1837, after the death of Joseph Heath Senior, several of the farms were sold by auction (McDonald 1979).

Laura Arksey provided a link to family sources in England and at the Beinecke Library at Yale, discovered during her work on Joseph Thomas Heath. William Torrens, Local Studies Librarian, Buckinghamshire, provided much of the local and family information from the County Record Office. Mrs. P.J. Sisam of Marlow, Buckinghamshire, also provided information and the name of a possible descendant, Garry Heath. Since there were many Heaths in the area, he may be descended from another line. See also Buss 2002. Of the legendary character "Old Parr," it was said that "in 1588 he was constrained to do penance in a white sheet in the neighbouring church of Alberbury for having begotten a bastard child" (*Harmsworth Encyclopaedia* n.d., 364-5).

- 24 May 1838 letter (HBCA, PAM, E.31/2/1 fo. 137-8d)
- 17 October 1838 letter (HBCA, PAM, E.31/2/1 fo. 139-40d)
- 15 October 1838, two letters (HBCA, PAM, E.31/2/1 fo. 141-2d and 142-2d
- 17 February 1839 letter (HBCA, PAM, E.31/2/1 fo. 143-4d)
- October 1840 letter extract (HBCA, PAM, A.10/11 fo. 233)
- 1845 quotation "you well know Sir" (HBCA, PAM, D.5/13 fo. 176-9)
- 1846 quotation "being weak in her water ways" (HBCA, PAM, A.10/21 fo. 488)
- 14 August 1847 quotation "other vicious habits" (HBCA, PAM, A.10/23 fo. 633-4); for William's and Thomas's letter of 14 August 1847 and William's of 14 August 1848, please see HBCA, PAM, A.10/23 fo. 633-4, A.10/25 fo. 120; for Thomas Heath's letter to the Company on 26 August 1851, please see HBCA, PAM, A.10/28 fo. 129-9d.

30   GEORGE GORDON
Entering the Company's ship on 24 August, Gordon (Gaddarn) signed a five-year contract at £24 per year on 29 August 1835, giving his parish of origin as Milford, Stainton, Pembroke, Wales (HBCA, PAM, A.32/31 fo. 110; C.3/14 fo. 47). He travelled out as a seaman on the new Company ship, the *Beaver,* leaving Gravesend the same day he signed on and arriving at the Columbia River on 19 March 1836 (HBCA, PAM, C.3/14 fo. 47; C.4/1). He served on the coast until he joined the mutineers on the *Beaver* and was sent to Fort Vancouver on the *Cowlitz* and home on the *Columbia,* arriving in London on 21 May 1839 (HBCA, PAM, A.10/8 fo. 298, 309; B.223/b/21 fo. 92-4; B.223/d/88, 100; B.223/g/3-4; B.239/g/16-18; C.3/14 fo. 66; C.4/1; C.7/177 fo. 50d). On 28 May 1839 he, James Starling, and William Willson lodged an appeal with Frederick Clarkson of Doctors Commons concerning the Company's withholding of six months' pay (HBCA, PAM, A.10/8 fo. 298, 309). For a discussion of corporal punishment and of the mutiny on the *Beaver,* please see Burley 1997, 174-9, 239-43. George Gaddarn, William Gaddarn's descendant through another son, Charles, provided information. Charles and James Gaddarn served their time as shipwrights and became quite famous ship builders. They owned a yard at Neyland and built several clippers for the China tea trade. James died in 1890 at sixty-eight, Charles a few years later.
- 19 August 1838 letter (HBCA, PAM, E.31/2/1, fo. 112-13d)
- 1838 quotations "lost patience," "yielded," and "prisoners at large" (HBCA, PAM, B.223/b/21 fo. 92-4)
- 25 June 1851 quotation re William McNeill (HBCA, PAM, B.226/b/3)
- 22 October 1838 letter (HBCA, PAM, E.31/2/1 fo. 114-15d)
- 31 May 1839 quotations "wished that," "constantly advised," and "from his threats" (HBCA, PAM, A. 10/8 fo. 309).

31   GEORGE WILLIAM BARTON
Barton (bapt. 1816) signed on as a Greenwich apprentice in London and travelled as a ship's boy on the *Ganymede,* leaving on 16 November 1830 and arriving at the Columbia Department on 17 July 1831 (HBCA, PAM, B.223/d/47; C.3/13 fo. 100; C.4/1; C.7/59). After serving with the *Vancouver* and *Dryad* on the coast, he returned on the *Dryad,* leaving the coast on 20 October 1835 and arriving in London on 10 April 1836 (HBCA, PAM, B.223/d/59, 61; B.239/g/12-15; C.1/177). In 1836 he was appointed second mate of the *Eagle* but he wintered in Hudson Bay after encountering bad ice conditions (HBCA, PAM, A.5/11 p. 222; A.10/3, A.10/5 fo. 178, 291; C.1/285-8; C.3/14 fo. 49; C.7/44 fo. 4, 9). On 18 November 1837 and on 17 September 1839, he signed five-year contracts at £50 8s. as second mate, giving Blackwall, Middlesex, as his parish of origin (HBCA, PAM,

A.32/21 fo. 138-9). He made two round trips, travelling out on the *Columbia* between 18 November 1837 and 24 May 1838, and returning 11 November 1838, arriving in London 21 May 1839, and again 18 September 1839 to 15 March 1840 and back to London 24 December 1841 to 7 July 1842 (HBCA, PAM, A.10/15 fo. 76, 148-148d, 150, 167; B.223/d/141, 168; B.223/g/6; B.239/g/20-1; C.1/245; C.3/14 fo. 65; C.4/1). His parents were Samuel and Olive Barton, who married at St. Dunstan, Stepney, London, and his siblings were: Samuel Robert (bapt. 8 November 1812), who applied unsuccessfully to the Company as a second mate in 1837 and was in the Caribbean in 1838; Richard, who was in Quebec in 1838; and Harriet Jane (bapt. 2 July 1820) (FHC; HBCA, PAM, A.5/12 p. 140; A.10/6 fo. 233). He married Maria Ridley in the summer of 1839, and they had a child by 1842 (HBCA, PAM, A.10/15 fo. 148-8d). For accounts of Chief Factor McLoughlin whipping a man and for the cost of rations for Aboriginal wives, please see Hussey 1991, 276 and 290.

- 6 November 1837 extract from memorial of Robert Stewart (HBCA, PAM, A.10/5 fo. 291)
- [23 August 1838] letter (HBCA, PAM, E.31/2/1 fo. 6-7d)
- 10 October 1838 letter (HBCA, PAM, E.31/2/1 fo. 8-9d)
- 31 October 1838 letter (HBCA, PAM, E.31/2/1 fo. 10-11d)
- 21 July 1842 quotations "Chest and bedding," "what capacity," and "Captn Humphrey's" (HBCA, PAM, A.10/15 fo. 76)
- 24 August 1842 quotations "refer to Captn Humphrey," "Being out of employment" (HBCA, PAM, A.10/15 fo. 148-8d); for the letter with the Company's offer of £10, please see HBCA, PAM, A.10/15 fo. 167.

32 JAMES DOWDEN BUCK
Buck (b. c. 1815) signed articles as a Greenwich apprentice at £8 per year for two years, £10 per year for two years, £12 per year for two years, and the last year at £15, and travelled on the *Ganymede* leaving London on 16 November 1830 and arriving at the Columbia Department on 31 July 1831 (HBCA, PAM, A.6/22 fo. 78d; C.3/13 fo. 100; D.4/97 fo. 20d). He served beyond his indentures with the *Cadboro, Vancouver, Lama,* and *Nereide* on the coast and the *Sumatra* in Oahu, August 1837, before he returned on the *Columbia,* leaving the coast on 11 November 1838 and arriving in London on 21 May 1839 (HBCA, PAM, A.5/12 p. 291; A.10/7 fo. 395-5d; A.10/8 fo. 292, 295, 323-6; B.223/b/9 fo. 13d-14; B.223/d/37, 47, 54, 71, 88, 100, 168; B.239/g/11-18; C.1/1061 fo. 91; C.3/14 fo. 65; C.4/1; C.7/177 fo. 64, 66d). His parents were Richard and Elizabeth Buck of Hope Quay, Weymouth, Dorset, and his siblings were Richard and possibly Ann (HBCA, PAM, A.10/6 fo. 31). There were several exchanges of correspondence between his parents and the Company (HBCA, PAM, A.5/10 p. 329; A.5/12 p. 124, 211; A.10/6 fo. 31; A.10/7 fo. 248).

- 4 January 1830 quotations "for the due fulfillment" (HBCA, PAM, A.1/56 fo. 109d-10) and "a proper supply of good warm clothing" (HBCA, PAM, A.6/22 fo. 53d-4)
- 28 October 1838 letter (HBCA, PAM, E.31/2/1 fo. 29-31)
- 9 February 1838 letter (HBCA, PAM, A.10/7 fo. 395-5d)
- 22 October 1838 quotation "being detained" (HBCA, PAM, A.10/7 fo. 248); for the Company's reply, please see HBCA, PAM, A.5/12 p. 211.
- 28 May 1839 quotation "[I] had the misfortune" (HBCA, PAM, A.10/8 fo. 292); for the letters and responses concerning Buck's compensation, please see HBCA, PAM, A.5/12 p. 291; A.10/8 fo. 323-6.

33 WILLIAM GREEN
Signing a two-year contract at £30 per year with Chief Factor John McLoughlin at Fort Vancouver on 30 March 1834, Green worked on the coast as a seaman on the *Dryad,* leaving

for London on 20 October 1835 and arriving on 10 April 1836 (HBCA, PAM, A.32/31 fo. 246; B.223/d/168; B.239/g/14-15; C.3/14 fo. 30; C.4/1; C.7/177 fo. 31, 39, 43d). He signed a five-year contract at £24 per year on 18 November 1837 and left as a seaman on the *Columbia* the same day, arriving on the coast on 24 May 1838, then returning 11 November 1838 to arrive in London on 21 May 1839 (HBCA, PAM, A.32/31 fo. 247; C.1/245 fo. 2; C.3/14 fo. 65; C.4/1; C.7/177 fo. 64, 66d). On 31 August 1839 he collected the balance of wages for John Coon, the ship keeper, on the authority of a letter signed by George W. Barton (HBCA, PAM, A.10/9 fo. 118). On his next trip he signed a five-year contract on 17 September 1839 as steward at £24 per year, giving his parish of origin as Northampton, and left on the *Columbia* the next day, arriving on the coast on 15 March 1840 (HBCA, PAM, A.10/13 fo. 513; A.10/22 fo. 93; A.32/31 fo. 248; C.4/1). He served on the coast on the *Columbia, Cowlitz, Vancouver,* and *Beaver* before returning to London on the *Cowlitz,* travelling from 18 December 1845 to 27 June 1846 (HBCA, PAM, A.10/13 fo. 513; B.239/g/20-9; C.3/15 fo. 19; C.4/1). Captain Charles Humpheys wrote two letters on his behalf, one dated 3 December 1841 at the Columbia River and another on 29 July 1846, in support of his receiving a bonus promised by Captain Drew (HBCA, PAM, A.10/13 fo. 513; A.10/22 fo. 93-4).
• 3 November 1838 letter (HBCA, PAM, E.31/2/1 fo. 116-17d).

34 WILLIAM MARTINDELL
Martindell (Martindale, Martingale) (1824-58) was sent to sign his indentures as an apprentice on 28 May 1838, starting at £8 per year, and set off on the *Prince of Wales* on her annual trip to Hudson Bay, returning in October 1838 (HBCA, PAM, A.10/6 fo. 374; C.3/14 fo. 62d-3). He made two trips out to the Columbia Department as an apprentice on the *Vancouver.* The first left Gravesend on 6 November 1838, arriving on the coast on 3 May 1839, then returning, after trips to the Sandwich Islands (Hawai'i) and Sitka (in present-day Alaska), departing the coast on 29 November 1840 and arriving in London on 3 June 1841 (HBCA, PAM, B.239/g/18-21; C.3/14 fo. 77, 88; C.4/1; C.7/177 fo. 6d-7). The second left on 9 September 1841, arriving on the coast on 3 April 1842, then departing the coast on 29 November 1843 and arriving in London on 10 June 1844 (HBCA, PAM, B.239/g/23; C.3/14 fo. 88; C.3/15 fo. 4; C.4/1). He made another voyage out on the *Columbia,* leaving on 4 October 1845 and arriving at Fort Victoria in the spring of 1846 sick and in need of medical attention (HBCA, PAM, C.1/253; C.3/7 fo. 15; C.3/15 fo. 29; C.4/1). Once on the coast, he travelled to Sitka on the *Columbia,* then transferred to the *Cadboro,* where he was among those who, on 20 February 1847, refused to work if William Mouat, the mate, stayed on board (HBCA, PAM, B.239/g/26-7; C.1/222 fo. 32d). He transferred to the *Mary Dare* as seaman and cook on 29 October 1847, and on 17 July 1850 he deserted from the ship (HBCA, PAM, B.223/d/195; B.226/d/3 fo. 609; B.239/g/28-32; C.1/222 fo. 90). In 1850 he was a labourer at Nisqually (Tacoma, Washington) and appeared in the Lewis County Census, Schedule 1 #146. In 1851 he settled on a claim of 130 hectares (320 acres) in Pacific County, where he was shot and killed by Joseph Duprey on 2 July 1858. The reference to these events in the US 1850 Census and *Weekly Oregonian,* 10 July 1858, were supplied by Bruce Watson. For the fate of Joseph Duprey, please see the same source. For J.H. Pelly's letter dated 28 May 1838, please see HBCA, PAM, A.10/6 fo. 374.
• 31 May 1840 letter (HBCA, PAM, E.31/2/1 fo. 202-4)
• For the ship's log recording the 1847 Mouat incident, please see HBCA, PAM, C.1/222 fo. 32d; for the fate of W.A. Mouat, please see Dickey 1989, entry for 27 February 1850.

35 JAMES SANGSTER

Sangster (c. 1812-58) served as a ship's boy at £15 per year for two return trips on the *Eagle*, from Gravesend to the Columbia River, 16 September 1827 to 19 May 1828, and returning 20 August 1828 to 6 October 1829, and again London to Columbia, 1 November 1829 to 2 June 1830, and returning 29 October 1830 to 17 April 1831 (HBCA, PAM, C.3/13 fo. 74, 88; C.4/1). He entered the ship on 1 September and, on 24 September 1831, he signed a three-year contract at £30 per year, giving Port Glasgow, Renfrewshire, as his parish of origin, and travelled as a seaman out on the *Eagle*, leaving London the same day and arriving at the Columbia Department on 19 May 1832 (HBCA, PAM, A.32/52 fo. 198; C.3/14 fo. 3). He served on the *Vancouver* as a seaman and later second mate, then as first mate on the *Cadboro, Lama,* and on the *Beaver* as first mate and then master (HBCA, PAM, B.239/g/12-21; B.239/k/2 p. 96, 139; C.7/177 fo. 25, 40d, 42d, 82). As first mate of the *Vancouver*, he travelled to London 29 November 1840 to 3 June 1841 and returned 9 September 1841 to 3 April 1842 (HBCA, PAM, A.5/13 pp. 227, 262; A.10/13 fo. 223; C.4/1). Just before he left, he wrote to the London Committee asking to be permitted to return in order to prove himself capable of promotion, which he observed was faster in Europe than at the Columbia River (HBCA, PAM, A.10/13 fo. 223). Once back on the coast he served as master of the *Beaver*, second mate of the *Cowlitz*, the clerk in charge of pilotage at Fort Vancouver, and finally master of the *Cadboro* and the *Una* (HBCA, PAM, B.239/g/23-30). On 6 July 1851 he retired at Victoria, British Columbia, to become a pilot, harbourmaster, collector of customs, and Victoria's first postmaster (Smith 1975, 125; HBCA, PAM, A.11/74 fo. 238; B.226/z/1 fo. 38). In 1855 he held more than eight hectares (twenty acres) near Colwood Farm, and in July 1858 he retired in consequence of failing health; on 18 October 1858, however, he committed suicide and died in Esquimalt (*Victoria Gazette*, 19 October, 20 October, 25 December 1858; 26 February, 7 March 1861; Smith 1975, 126; HBCA, PAM, B.226/z/1 fo. 38). John Royn (wine and spirit merchant and Mrs. Sangster's guarantor) exchanged later letters with the Hudson's Bay Company (HBCA, PAM, A.5/15 p. 523; A.5/18 p. 11; A.5/19 p. 238, 226; A.10/23 fo. 592; A.10/33 fo. 310; A.10/34 fo. 462, 478; A.10/38 fo. 147-7a). Danda Humphreys of Victoria, British Columbia, used the undelivered letter in one of her columns in the *Victoria Times-Colonist*.

- June 1840 letter (HBCA, PAM, E.31/2/1 fo. 271-2d)
- 1840-1 quotation "promotion was more rapid" (HBCA, PAM, A.10/13 fo. 223)
- 1842 and 1845 quotations "a confirmed drunkard" (HBCA, PAM, D.4/III fo. 42-67d) and "pulls hard on the bottle" (HBCA, PAM, D.5/13 fo. 176-9)
- 1855 quotation "as to writing her" (HBCA, PAM, A. 10/38 fo. 147a).

36 JAMES ADAMS

Adams (d. 1841) entered the Company's ship on 20 August and signed a five-year contract at £24 per year on 24 August 1840, giving London, Middlesex, as his parish of origin (HBCA, PAM, A.32/1 fo. 11; C.3/14 fo. 100). He left London the same day on the *Cowlitz*, arriving on the coast on 5 February 1841 (HBCA, PAM, C.3/14 fo. 100; C.4/1). On 1 April 1841, he drowned at Fort Vancouver (HBCA, PAM, C.1/257 fo. 94d).

- 10 November 1841 letter (HBCA, PAM, E.31/2/1 fo. 1-3)
- 1 April 1841 quotation "with the assistance" (HBCA, PAM, C.1/257).

37 JAMES SIMPSON

Simpson signed a five-year contract at £50 8s. per year on 5 November 1838 (HBCA, PAM, A.32/53 fo. 86). He travelled as a ship's carpenter on the *Vancouver*, leaving

London on 6 November 1838, arriving at the Columbia River on 3 May 1839 (HBCA, PAM, C.3/14 fo. 76; C.4/1). He travelled along the coast to Sitka (in present-day Alaska) and to the Sandwich Islands (Hawai'i) on the *Vancouver, Cadboro,* and *Beaver,* then returned to London on the *Cowlitz,* leaving 16 November 1842 and arriving in London on 9 May 1843 (HBCA, PAM, B.239/g/19-21; C.4/1; C.7/177 fo. 81, 85d). Another trip out to the coast kept him away from London on the *Columbia* between 12 September 1848 and 17 April 1850 (HBCA, PAM, C.3/7 fo. 34, 51; C.3/15 fo. 52, 54; C.4/1). In 1850 he made the trip to York Factory in Hudson Bay on the *Prince Rupert* from 3 June to 7 October but seems to have then left the service of the Company (HBCA, PAM, C.3/15 fo. 61). One sister, Ann, was married to Alexander Duncan (entry 14).

- February 1839 quotation "I have no other thing" (HBCA, PAM, A.10/8 fo. 183)
- 22 August 1842 letter (HBCA, PAM, E.31/2/1 fo. 273-4d)
- 18 March 1843 letter (HBCA, PAM, E.31/2/1 fo. 275-6d)
- 26 June 1849 letter (HBCA, PAM, C.7/32 fo. 65-6d)
- 16 July 1849 letter (HBCA, PAM, C.7/32 fo. 67-8)
- 12 October 1849 letter (HBCA, PAM, C.7/32 fo. 69-71)
- 17 December 1849 letter (HBCA, PAM, C.7/32 fo. 72-4d)

38 EDWIN ROBERTS
Roberts signed a five-year contract on 24 August 1840 at £24 per year, giving Liverpool, Lancashire, as his parish of origin (HBCA, PAM, A.32/51 fo. 22). He left London the same day on the *Cowlitz,* arriving on the coast on 5 February 1841 and returning between 16 November 1842 and 9 May 1843 (HBCA, PAM, B.239/g/21-2; C.3/14 fo. 100, 110; C.4/1). He entered the *Cowlitz* once more on 11 July 1843 and left London on 23 September, arriving at Fort Victoria on 24 March 1844 (HBCA, PAM, C.3/15 fo. 10d-11; C.4/1). While on the coast he served as seaman on the *Cowlitz* and *Beaver,* and as boatswain and second mate at £50 8s. on the *Columbia* (HBCA, B.239/g/24-7). He left the coast on the same ship on 10 November 1847 and arrived home on 22 May 1848 (HBCA, PAM, C.3/7 fo. 34; C.3/15 fo. 37d-8; C.4/1). He returned as second mate on the *Columbia,* entering the ship on 1 August 1848, leaving London on 12 September 1848 and arriving on the coast on 16 March 1849 (HBCA, PAM, C.3/15 fo. 51d-2; C.4/1). He deserted in May 1849 – along with James Brooks, steward; John Phillips, cook; and seamen William Baker, John Thompson, William Murray, Abraham Dyke, Abraham Holland, Peter Petrelius, and Alex Brands – and joined an American party travelling to the gold fields (Bowsfield 1979, 15n; HBCA, PAM, A.11/70 fo. 368-9; B.226/d/3 fo. 805; B.239/g/26 fo. 28, 91; C.3/15 fo. 51d-2).

- 25 October 1842 letter (HBCA, PAM, E.31/2/1 fo. 255-6d)
- 8 October 1847 quotations "towing down," "swept the vessel," and "making water" (HBCA, PAM, A.11/72 fo. 22).

39 JOHN CRELLY
Crelly (Creely) was a seaman on another ship when he joined the Company's ship *Cowlitz* in 1842 at £24 per year and travelled to London between 16 November 1842 and 9 May 1843 (HBCA, PAM, B.239/g/22-3; C.3/14 fo. 110; C.4/1; E.31/2/1 fo. 77-8d).

- 10 May [1843] letter (HBCA, PAM, E.31/2/1 fo. 77-8d).

40 ARNOLD OR JOHN NICHOLS
Although Martha Nichols addressed her letter to her son Arnold Nichols, there is only one man with the surname Nichols on a Company ship at that time, a John Nichols. He

signed a five-year contract at £24 per year on 17 September 1839, giving no parish of origin (HBCA, PAM, A.32/48 fo. 44). He sailed as a seaman on the *Columbia* the next day (HBCA, PAM, C.3/14 fo. 84; C.4/1). He arrived on the coast on 15 March 1840 and returned on the *Cowlitz*, leaving the coast on 16 November 1842 and arriving in London on 9 May 1843 (HBCA, PAM, B.239/g/21-3; C.3/14 fo. 111; C.4/1).

- 11 May 1843 letter (HBCA, PAM, E.31/2/1 fo. 219-20d).

41 ISAAC R. CHRISTOPHER

Joining the *Vancouver* on 30 August 1841 as a seaman at £24 per year, Christopher sailed on 9 September for the coast, arriving 3 April 1842 (HBCA, PAM, C.3/14 fo. 112d-13; C.3/15 fo. 4; C.4/1). He served on the *Vancouver* and *Cadboro* on the coast, then returned home on the *Vancouver*, leaving the coast on 29 November 1843 and arriving in London on 10 June 1844 (HBCA, PAM, B.239/g/23-4; C.3/15 fo. 4; C.4/1). The undelivered letter mentions his siblings Fanny, Martha, Caleb, and Evan. These may be the children of Frances and James Christopher, Frances being baptized 7 March 1819, with the others all baptized in Wales on 5 January 1834: Martha (b. 10 January 1825), Caleb (b. 25 February 1827), Diana (b. 15 January 1832), and Joshua (FHC). The letters were postmarked Pembroke, Wales, though addressed from Jerusalem (Dorset or Lincolnshire?).

- 13 May 1843 letter (HBCA, PAM, E.31/2/1 fo. 68-9d).
- 12 May 1843 letter (IIBCA, PAM, E.31/2/1 fo. 65-7).

42 THOMAS STOREY

Storey signed a five-year contract at £24 per year on 5 November 1838, giving his parish of origin as London, Middlesex (HBCA, PAM, A.32/55 fo. 158). He sailed as a seaman on the *Vancouver* the next day and arrived on the coast on 3 May 1839 (HBCA, PAM, C.3/14 fo. 76; C.4/1). After sailing on the coast, including trips to the Sandwich Islands (Hawai'i) and Sitka (in present-day Alaska), he left the coast on 29 November 1840 and arrived in London on 3 June 1841 (HBCA, PAM, B.239/g/19-21; C.3/14 fo. 88; C.4/1; C.7/177 fo. 71, 73, 76d). He joined the *Vancouver* again on 1 September 1841 and sailed on 9 September for the coast, arriving 3 April 1842 (HBCA, PAM, C.3/14 fo. 113; C.4/1). He returned on the *Vancouver*, leaving the coast on 29 November 1843 and arriving in London on 10 June 1844 (HBCA, PAM, B.239/g/23-4; C.3/15 fo. 4; C.4/1). In 1849 a Thomas Storey was on the crew list for the *Norman Morison* with the notation "did not embark" (HBCA, PAM, C.3/7 fo. 41d).

- 26 May 1843 letter (HBCA, PAM, E.31/2/1 fo. 287-90d).

43 JOHN OXLEY

Joining the *Vancouver* on 26 August 1841 as second mate at £50 8s. per year, Oxley sailed on 9 September for the coast, arriving 3 April 1842 (HBCA, PAM, C.3/14 fo. 111d; C.4/1). He returned on the *Vancouver*, leaving the coast on 29 November 1843 but left the ship at Honolulu in January 1844, after being judged incapable of acting as first mate once Alexander Lattie was dismissed (Rich 1943, 142; HBCA, PAM, A.10/18 fo. 468; A.11/70 fo. 47; B.223/b/30 fo. 52-67 para. 56; B.239/g/22-4; C.3/15 fo. 4; C.4/1; C.7/164 fo. 18). By June 1845 he was back in London and approved the arrangements that had been made to pay his account to his aunt to go into his mother's estate (HBCA, PAM, A.10/18 fo. 465-8).

- 28 May 1843 letter (HBCA, PAM, E.31/2/1 fo. 224-6)
- 19 August 1843 letter (HBCA, PAM, E.31/2/1 fo. 227-9)
- 2 March 1844 letter (HBCA, PAM, C.7/164 fo. 17-18d)

- 1844 Company notations re Oxley's whereabouts on March letter, and quotation re discharge on "having no inclination" (HBCA, PAM, A.11/70 fo. 47); for a petition dated 28 June 1844 and certified by Oxley on 23 June 1845, and a statement of wages due dated 29 December 1843, please see HBCA, PAM, A.11/18 fo. 465-8.

44 FREDERICK W. REA

Rea (Rae) joined the *Columbia* on 5 September 1842 as an ordinary seaman at £18 per year and sailed on 10 September for the coast, arriving 6 May 1843 (HBCA, PAM, C.3/15 fo. 2d-3; C.4/1). He transferred to the *Vancouver* on 9 June 1843 and left the coast on 29 November 1843, was promoted to boatswain at £27 per year on 20 December 1843, and arrived in London on 10 June 1844 (HBCA, PAM, C.1/248 fo. 128; C.3/15 fo. 5; C.4/1).
- 12 August 1843 letter (HBCA, PAM, E.31/2/1 fo. 251-2d).

45 WILLIAM CARRACK

Carrack (d. 1844) joined the *Cowlitz* on 11 July 1843 as second mate at £50 8s. per year, and sailed on 23 September for the coast. On 4 February he drowned, and the ship arrived at Fort Victoria without him on 24 March 1844 (HBCA, PAM, C.1/259; C.3/15 fo. 10d-11; C.4/1). The Company paid £54 (seven and a half months pay plus £60 6s. from the sale of his effects at Fort Vancouver, minus advances) to the Merchant Seaman's Office on 13 June 1845 (HBCA, PAM, C.3/15 fo. 11).
- 13 November 1843 letter (HBCA, PAM, E.31/2/1 folio 55-6d)
- 16 November 1843 letter (HBCA, PAM, E.31/2/1 folio 57-8d)
- 7 March 1844 letter (HBCA, PAM, E.31/2/1 folio 59-60d)
- 29 August 1844 letter (HBCA, PAM, E.31/2/1 folio 61-2d)
- 1 September 1844 letter (HBCA, PAM, E.31/2/1 folio 63-4d)
- 18 February 1844 report extract and quotations on drowning (HBCA, PAM, C.1/359)
- For his mother's petition dated 15 April 1845, please see HBCA, PAM, A.10/19 fo. 180; 1845 quotation from Company response "as you have no claim on the Company" (HBCA, PAM, A.5/15 p. 15) and quotation from her reply "humane generosity" (HBCA, PAM, A.10/19 fo. 220); for the calculation of the sums due, please see HBCA, PAM, C.3/15 fo. 11.

46 DANIEL HOPKIRK

Joining the *Vancouver* on 30 August 1841 as seaman at £24 per year, Hopkirk sailed on 9 September for the coast, arriving 3 April 1842 (HBCA, PAM, C.3/14 fo. 112d-13; C.4/1). He returned on the *Vancouver,* leaving the coast on 29 November 1843 and arriving in London on 10 June 1844 (HBCA, PAM, B.223/d/152; B.239/g/22-3; C.3/15 fo. 4). We have been in contact with John Hopkirk, who thinks that James is from the Sunderland Hopkirk family, which maintains a Web site at <www.hopkirk.org/hopkirk>.
- 14 February [1844] letter (HBCA, PAM, E.31/2/1 fo. 151-2d).

47 JONATHAN BUCK

Buck (d. 1850?) signed articles on 22 August 1842, joined the *Columbia* the same day as second mate at £50 8s. per year, and sailed on 10 September for the coast, arriving 6 May 1843 (HBCA, PAM, C.1/248; C.3/15 fo. 1d-2). After serving on the coast, he returned on the same ship, leaving on 5 December 1844, arriving in London on 22 May 1845 (HBCA, PAM, B.223/d/32, 156; B.223/g/8; B.239/g/23-4; B.239/k/2 p. 333; C.3/15 fo. 12d-13).

He continued on the ship's crew during his stay, signed articles as second mate on 23 September 1845, and left London on the *Columbia* on 4 October 1845, arriving at Fort Victoria in the spring of 1846 (HBCA, PAM, B.223/d/169; C.1/253; C.3/15 fo. 28d-9). He joined the *Beaver* steamer as first mate from 1 June to 31 October, before rejoining the *Columbia* at his former rank (HBCA, PAM, B.223/d/169 fo. 33; B.226/d/3 p. 23; C.1/253 fo. 128d). In late April 1847 he left the ship and was described variously as "free at Woahoo [Oahu]" or "free at S[andwich]. Islands [Hawai'i]" (HBCA, PAM, B.239/g/27; C.1/253; C.7/32 fo. 59-60). He returned to the coast as a settler at Willamette, Oregon, and was listed as a single lumberman in Clatsop County in the 1850 Census but, in a family record, he was noted as having died at the gold diggings in California that year (US Census 1850, Schedule 1 #90, quoted by Watson n.d.; ffolliott 1975, 22; HBCA, PAM, B.239/g/29-30).

His great-grandfather and grandfather were both named Jonathan Buck, silversmiths: the first married Faith c. 1726, and died in 1762; the second married Elizabeth Sidney in 1751 and died in 1786. His father Frederick was a well-known miniaturist, who died on 7 September 1840 (*Cork Constitution,* 8 September 1840, reference provided thanks to Alicia St. Leger). He married Eliza Reily on 9 February 1796 and had at least two children: Elizabeth (b. c. 1797), living in Cork, then Inishannon; and Samuel, living in the country at Curra. Faith may also have been a child from that marriage. Elizabeth married Robert Olden in 1814 and had at least seventeen children: Frederick (b. 1815); Sarah (b. 1816); Elizabeth or Liz or Lizzy (b. 1817); Robert (b. 1818, d. before 1822); Andrew (a.k.a Ducky[?]) (b. 1819, m. Mary Roberts); Maria or Mary (b. 1820); Robert or Bob (b. 1822); Thomas (1823-1900); Ann (b. 1824); George (1825-47?); Emily Montague (b. 1827); Sidney (b. 1829, to China in 1848); Adelaide Constance (b. 1832, m. Longfield Davis); Francis (b. 1833); Louisa (b. 1834); Caroline (b. 1837); Richard (a.k.a. Ducky[?]) (b. 1838). Samuel had at least ten children including: Sam or Sammy; Fred or Freddy; John; Ruth, who settled in America; Emily (living in 1885); Elizabeth (m. Mr. Gulder and had issue); Charlotte (m. Mr. Standish and had issue); Henrietta (b. 1828); Harriet (m. Mr. Gash and had issue); Sarah (m. Mr. Ludgate); and possibly Dorothy, or Doty or Doaty. Four daughters, excluding Harriet, were unmarried in 1866. Samuel Buck died 7 June 1874 with effects under £500.

Frederick married his second wife, Harriet Mahoney, widow of William Craig, in October 1816. She lived until 16 January 1870 and her probate records initially indicated effects of less than £800, then £1,000, and, by October 1871, under £1,500. The children from this second marriage included Frederick or Fred (a.k.a Fuz or Buz) (d. 17 September 1894 with effects totalling £322 6s. 7d.); Adam, who was still living in 1866; Jonathan or Jonty (d. c. 1850 with effects totalling £464); John or Johnny, who was still living in 1866; Alfred or Alfy (b. 1829), who married Fanny Buck (c. 1848) and had a daughter Anne or Annie, who was still living in 1866; Sidney, who was still living in 1901; and Harriet, who married Robert Vincent and was still living in 1866, with a son Edward Percival. A son, William, who seems to have been from her first marriage, to William Craig, had most likely died by 1866. A daughter, Ellen, was also from that marriage. Ellen married Samuel Buck and died 15 October 1884. Because of the number of Bucks marrying Bucks, there may be some incorrect assumptions about relations.

A great deal of assistance has been provided by Alicia St. Leger of Cork, Ireland, who heard about the letters from her relatives the Oldens through a newspaper article published by Campbell Thomas in 1998. She unearthed the two articles on Frederick Buck, miniaturist, by Rosemary ffolliott (1975; 1984) and conducted research in the National

Archives in Dublin, Ireland, where some of the grants of probate survived the 1922 fires. She also checked a number of directories for Ireland, including Griffith's Valuation for 1852, a survey of all land and buildings in the country.
- 6 September 1844 letter (HBCA, PAM, E.31/2/1 fo. 32-5, 42)
- 3 December 1844 letter (HBCA, PAM, E.31/2/1 fo. 36-7d, 42)
- 6 December 1844 two letters (HBCA, PAM, E.31/2/1 fo. 38-40d, 42)
- 22 January [1848] letter (HBCA, PAM, C.7/32 fo. 39-41d)
- 8 February 1848 letter (HBCA, PAM, C.7/32 fo. 42-5d)
- 21 February 1848 letter (HBCA, PAM, C.7/32 fo. 46-8d)
- 23 February 1848 letter from Emily Olden (HBCA, PAM, C.7/32 fo. 49-51d)
- 23 Feburary 1848 letter from Liz Olden (HBCA, PAM, E.31/2/1 fo. 43-5)
- 26 February 1848 letters (HBCA, PAM, C.7/32 fo. 52-4d)
- 1 March 1848 letter from John Buck (HBCA, PAM, C.7/32 fo. 55-7d)
- 1 March [1848] letter from Faith (HBCA, PAM, E.31/2/1 fo. 49-50d)
- 1 March 1848 letter from mother Harriet Buck (HBCA, PAM, E.31/2/1 fo. 46-8)
- 2 March 1848 letter from Alfred Buck (HBCA, PAM, C.7/32 fo. 58, 61)
- [4 March 1848] letter (HBCA, PAM, C.7/32 fo. 59-60).

48 JOHN HARRIER
Harrier joined the *Cowlitz* in September 1843 as steward at £30 per year and sailed on 23 September for the coast, arriving at Fort Victoria on 24 March 1844 (HBCA, PAM, C.3/15 fo. 10d-11; C.4/1). Harrier returned on the *Cowlitz,* leaving the coast on 18 December 1845, and arriving in London on 27 June 1846 (HBCA, PAM, B.223/d/214 fo. 116; B.226/z/2 fo. 1b; B.239/g/24; C.3/15 fo. 19; C.4/1).
- 5 June 1845 letter (HBCA, PAM, E.31/2/1 fo. 134-6d)
- 1844 quotations "broke the after storeroom out" (HBCA, PAM, C.1/259 fo. 119d) and "if he goes to work" (HBCA, PAM, C.1/22 fo. 82d).

49 ABRAHAM NORGATE
Abraham (Abram) Norgate (Norget) joined the *Vancouver* on 30 August 1841 as seaman at £24 per year and sailed on 9 September for the coast, arriving 3 April 1842 (HBCA, PAM, C.3/14 fo. 111d-12; C.4/1). He served on the coast on the *Vancouver, Columbia,* and *Cadboro,* hurting his finger when he was sent to kill a bullock for meat on 6 July 1845 and going ashore without permission on 3 September 1845 (HBCA, PAM, B.239/d/162 fo. 17; B.239/g/22-5; C.1/221 fo. 107d, 116). He returned home on the *Cowlitz,* leaving the coast on 18 December 1845 and arriving in London on 27 June 1846 (HBCA, PAM, C.3/15 fo. 20; C.4/1).
- 7 June 1845 letter (HBCA, PAM, E.31/2/1 fo. 221-3).

50 JAMES JOHNSON
Johnson (Johnston, Johnstone) (d. 1845) joined the *Vancouver* as an apprentice at £8 per year, and sailed on 4 September 1844 for the coast, arriving at Fort Victoria on 18 February 1845 (HBCA, PAM, C.3/15 fo.229; C.4/1). On 2 April 1845 he drowned at Fort Vancouver (HBCA, PAM, E.31/2/1 fo. 176). When James's balance of 19s. 8d. was paid out to his mother, she was at Marsh Street, Walthamstow, Essex (HBCA, PAM, C.3/15 fo. 22).
- 22 and 23 June 1845 letter (HBCA, PAM, E.31/2/1 fo. 174-6).

51 WILLIAM SMITH
Smith joined the *Mary Dare* on 28 October 1846 as a seaman at £24 per year, and sailed on 3 November 1846 for the coast, arriving at Fort Victoria on 23 May 1847 (HBCA,

PAM, C.3/15 fo. 36d-7; C.4/1). He was given the letter "A" after his name to distinguish him from the other men with the same name working at the same time. On 10 November 1847 he left the coast on the *Columbia* and arrived in London on 22 May 1848, receiving his pay on 25 May (HBCA, PAM, C.3/15 fo. 37d-8; C.4/1). The two William Smiths serving on the *Columbia* are listed in HBCA, PAM, C.3/15 fo. 38d-9.

- 4 April 1847 letter (HBCA, PAM, C.7/92 fo. 1-3).

52   JOHN WATKIN

Watkin (Watkins) joined the *Columbia* on 29 September 1845 as a seaman at £24 per year, and sailed on 4 October 1845 for the coast, arriving at Fort Victoria in the spring of 1846 (HBCA, PAM, C.3/15 fo. 29d-30; C.4/1). After a year and a half plying the coast, on 10 November 1847 he left the coast on the *Columbia* and arrived in London on 22 May 1848 (HBCA, PAM, B.226/d/3 fo. 619; B.239/g/26-7; C.3/15 fo. 39; C.4/1).

- 6 September 1847 letter (HBCA, PAM, E.31/2/1 fo. 311-13).

53   CHARLES WALLIS

Wallis was engaged as an apprentice for six years, 30 November 1842 to 30 November 1848, with no advance from the Company. He accompanied another apprentice, James Franklin, on the *Diamond* with Captain Fowler, who was to pay him until his discharge at the rate of £8, £10, and £12 per year for two years each (Rich 1943, 303; HBCA, PAM, A.6/21 fo. 34-9d, para. 21). He joined the *Columbia* on the coast and travelled back to London between 5 December 1844 and 22 May 1845 (HBCA, PAM, B.239/g/23-4; C.3/15 fo. 14; C.4/1). He returned to the coast on the same ship, leaving on 4 October 1845, and arriving at Fort Victoria in the spring of 1846 (HBCA, PAM, C.3/15 fo. 30; C.4/1). After a year plying the coast, on 10 November 1847, he left the coast on the *Columbia* and arrived in London on 22 May 1848 (HBCA, PAM, B.226/d/3 fo. 619; B.239/g/26-7; C.3/15 fo. 39).

- 19 September 1847 letter (HBCA, PAM, E.31/2/1 fo. 297-8d, 307)
- 17 September 1847 letter from Susannah (HBCA, PAM, E.31/2/1 fo. 302-3d)
- 17 September 1847 two letters (HBCA, PAM, E.31/2/1 fo. 299-300, 306)
- 19 September 1847 letter and drawing from Edward (HBCA, PAM, E.31/2/1 fo. 301-1d).
- [19 September 1847] letter from Louisa (HBCA, PAM, E.31/2/1 fo. 304-5).

54   WILLIAM MURRAY

Entering the *Columbia* on 6 September 1848, Murray travelled out as a seaman at £24 per year, leaving on 12 September and arriving on the coast on 16 March 1849 (HBCA, PAM, C.3/15 fo. 51d-2; C.4/1). In 1849 he deserted to California (HBCA, PAM, A.11/70 fo. 368-9; B.226/d/2 fo. 29; B.226/d/3 fo. 762; C.3/7 fo. 34).

- 23 April 1849 letter (HBCA, PAM, C.7/32 fo. 63A-4)
- 26 February 1850 quotation "by letting me know" (HBCA, PAM, A.10/28 fo. 294)
- 4 April 1850 letter (HBCA, PAM, C.7/32 fo. 75-7).

55   WILLIAM BLAIR

Blair (bapt. 1829) joined the *Columbia* on 29 September 1845 as a seaman at £24 per year, and sailed on 4 October 1845 for the coast, arriving at Fort Victoria in the spring of 1846 (HBCA, PAM, C.3/15 fo. 28d-9; C.4/1). In 1847 he left the *Columbia* and entered the

Mary Dare, serving with her until he deserted on 20 August 1849 (HBCA, PAM, B.226/d/169, 176, 184; B.239/g/26-32; C.7/92 fo. 4-6). His mother, Janet Clement or Clairmont, was probably Janet Crammond who married Francis Blair, and whose son William was baptized in Angus, 7 May 1829 (FHC).

- March 1847 quotation "there has, as yet" (HBCA, PAM, A.10/23 fo. 159)
- 25 June 1849 letter (HBCA, PAM, C.7/92 fo. 4-6d)
- Douglas quotation "we live in hourly apprehension" (HBCA, PAM, A.11/72 fo. 87-96d, para. 37).

56 THOMAS PEREGRINE LEWIS

Lewis (bapt. 1830) joined the *Columbia* on 2 October 1845 as an apprentice and sailed on 4 October for the coast, arriving at Fort Victoria in the spring of 1846 (HBCA, PAM, C.3/15 fo. 29d-30; C.4/1). He served on the coast on the *Columbia,* leaving the coast on 10 November 1847, arriving in London on 22 May 1848 and leaving the ship on 1 June (HBCA, PAM, B.239/g/26-7; C.3/15 fo. 38d-9; C.4/1). His father wrote to Archibald Barclay, the Company secretary, informing him that Thomas had left to rejoin the ship a few days late and asking for a position for a second son (HBCA, PAM, A.10/25 fo. 147). Thomas returned to the coast on the same ship, leaving on 12 September 1848 and arriving at Fort Victoria on 16 March 1849, then returning to London between 1 November 1849 and 17 April 1850 and leaving the ship on 1 May (HBCA, PAM, B.226/d/3 fo. 782; B.239/g/28; C.3/15 fo. 52d-3; C.4/1). He asked to be released from his indentures but made another voyage with the Company, this time to Hudson Bay on the *Prince Rupert* in 1850, to complete his apprenticeship (HBCA, PAM, A.5/16 p. 267; A.10/28 fo. 578). In 1851 his father applied to the Company on Thomas's behalf but was told that there was no position available (HBCA, PAM, A.5/17 p. 146; A.10/30 fo. 445). Thomas's parents, Emma Evans and Thomas James Lewis, were married on 22 September 1829, and their children were: Thomas Peregrine (bapt. 30 August 1830); Harry (Henry, bapt. 29 March 1832); Emma Elizabeth (bapt. 27 July 1835 in Hudderston, Pembroke, Wales, d. 21 March 1849); Georgina Mary (bapt. 26 August 1836) (FHC). The undelivered letter was written from Milford, Wales.

- For the letter acknowledging Thomas junior's arrival, please see HBCA, PAM, A.10/24 fo. 399.
- Quotations "the first direct opportunity," "the favor and privilege" (HBCA, PAM, A.10/25 fo. 147)
- 14 July 1849 letter (HBCA, PAM, E.31/2/1 fo. 186-7, 191)
- 18 July 1849 letter (HBCA, PAM, E.31/2/1 fo. 188-91)
- For Thomas P. Lewis's 1850 letter, please see HBCA, PAM, A.10/28 fo. 578-8d.
- Quotation "provided he has a chance for promotion" (HBCA, PAM, A.10/30 fo. 445-5d).

57 GEORGE HILDRED

Hildred joined the *Albion* on 20 March 1849 as a carpenter at wages of £60 per year and sailed from 1849-50 from London to Sydney, Australia, and then to the west coast (HBCA, PAM, A.67/30 fo. 77-8). Although his wife thought he was on the *Fifeshire,* she addressed the letter to the Company, but he had deserted from the *Albion* on 22 April 1850 with sixteen others on the way to San Francisco (HBCA, PAM, A.67/30 fo. 77-8).

- 1 March 1850 letter (HBCA, PAM, E.31/2/1 fo. 145-6d).

58   JOHN BRACEBRIDGE
     Joining the *Cowlitz* on 1 August 1849 as a seaman at £24 per year, Bracebridge sailed on
     4 August 1849 for the west coast (HBCA, PAM, C.1/265; C.3/7 fo. 40d-1; C.4/1). For a
     description of the grog shops in Honolulu at mid-nineteenth century, please see Greer
     1970 and 1994.
     • 31 October 1849 letter (HBCA, PAM, C.7/38 fo. 9-10d)
     • 30 November 1849 letter (HBCA, PAM, E.31/2/1 fo. 21-3)
     • 6 December 1849 letter (HBCA, PAM, E.31/2/1 fo. 24-5d)
     • 1851 quotation "using threatening and abusive language to the Captain" (HBCA,
       PAM, C.1/253).

59   WILLIAM DEAN
     Dean (b. 1832) joined the *Cowlitz* as an apprentice at £8 per year and sailed on 8 Octo-
     ber 1846 for the coast, arriving at Fort Victoria on 21 March 1847 (HBCA, PAM, C.3/7
     fo. 21d-2; C.4/1). He returned on the same ship, leaving the coast on 7 December 1848
     and arriving in London on 19 May 1849 (HBCA, PAM, B.223/d/176 fo. 25; B.223/d/184
     fo. 27; C.3/15 fo. 46d-7; C.4/1). He left again on 4 August 1849, arriving at Fort Victoria
     on 12 March 1850 (HBCA, PAM, C.3/7 fo. 40d; C.4/1). In less than a month he had
     deserted with several of the crew (HBCA, PAM, A.11/72 fo. 218-18d; B.239/g/27-9; C.3/7
     fo. 41). Barbara Petraglia of Arizona and James Lane of Massachusetts have been in touch
     with us to check whether he was an ancestor but no connection has yet been confirmed.
     • 30 December [1849] letter, (HBCA, PAM, C.7/38 fo. 7A-8d)
     • 15 July 1836 quotation "The Captain of the Nereide" (HMCS, Levi Chamberlain
       diary)
     • 2 February 1850 extract and three quotations "Point out to the Marshal," "unless the
       unruly seamen," and "the want of irons" (HSA, FO & EX 403-11-159) and "came to
       ask the Captain pardon" (HBCA, PAM, C.1/265 fo. 83)
     • 3 April 1850 extract (HBCA, PAM, A.11/72 fo. 218-18d; Bowsfield 1979, 76-8).

60   JEREMIAH MCCARTHY
     McCarthy (bapt. 1818) entered the *Vancouver* on 26 August 1844 as a seaman at £24 per
     year and left on 4 September, arriving at Fort Victoria on 18 February 1845 (HBCA, PAM,
     C.3/15 fo. 20d-1; C.4/1; C.7/164 fo. 19d-20). He served on the *Vancouver* along the coast
     until the end of October, when he joined the crew of the *Cowlitz,* and travelled back,
     leaving the coast on 18 December 1845 and arriving in London on 27 June 1846 (HBCA,
     PAM, B.226/z/2 fo. 1b; C.3/15 fo. 27; C.4/1). In 1848 he travelled on the *Prince Rupert* to
     and from Hudson Bay (HBCA, PAM, C.3/15 fo. 42d-3). He joined the *Cowlitz* as a
     boatswain at £30 per year and sailed on 4 August 1849 for the coast, arriving on 12 March
     1850. He left for London on 10 July 1850 and received his discharge on 16 October 1850
     at Oahu, Hawai'i (HBCA, PAM, C.1/265 fo. 131d; C.3/15 fo. 74; C.4/1). He had been bap-
     tized on 7 June 1818. His parents, Hannah Fourhane (or Houron) and Florence
     McCarthy, were living in London in 1850; his siblings included Mary (bapt. 15 January
     1811), Margaret (bapt. 17 March 1813), Charley (bapt. 3 September 1815), Felix, Patrick,
     Owen, Florence, and John (FHC).
     • 1 March 1850 letter (HBCA, PAM, E.31/2/1 fo. 192-4)
     • 25 July 1850 letter (HBCA, PAM, E.31/2/1 fo. 195-6)

61 GEORGE MOUAT

Mouat (Moad) joined the *Cowlitz* as a seaman at £24 per year and sailed on 4 August 1849 for the coast. While on a stop at Hawai'i on 31 January 1850, he deserted (HBCA, PAM, C.1/265 fo. 82d; C.3/7 fo. 41; A.4/1). For comparison of British and American pay, please see HBCA, PAM, A.11/72 fo. 87-96d, para. 37.

• 14 August 1850 letter (HBCA, PAM, E.31/2/1 fo. 214-16).

62 GEORGE MICKLEFIELD

George Micklefield (bapt. 1816) joined the *Cowlitz* as a seaman at £24 per year and sailed on 4 August 1849 for the coast, arriving at Fort Victoria on 12 March 1850 (HBCA, PAM, C.3/7 fo. 40d-41; C.4/1). He served on the coast until he deserted while on a stop at Hawai'i on 31 January 1850, with the intention of making his way to the gold fields of California. The Company paid US$100 for his board and expenses in prison from 2 February to 13 May 1850 (HSA, FO & EX 403-11-159, 21-2 May 1850; HBCA, PAM, A.11/72 fo. 218-18d; B.239/g/29; C.1/265 fo. 82d; C.3/7 fo. 40-1d). He had been baptized on 5 July 1816 at St. Mary Whitechapel, Stepney, and his parents were Mary Ann Rose and Richard Micklefield. His siblings included Mary Ann (also bapt. 5 July 1816), Sarah Elizabeth (bapt. 13 May 1818), John (bapt. 8 October 1820), Matilda (bapt. 3 March 1822, d. 24 October 1850), Harriet (bapt. 22 June 1823), Elizabeth (bapt. 30 September 1832), and William (FHC).

• 1 December 1850 letter (HBCA, PAM, E.31/2/1 fo. 205-7).

63 JOHN THOMPSON

Thompson (Thomson) joined the *Norman Morison* on 13 October 1849 as a seaman at £24 per year and sailed for the coast on 20 October 1849, arriving at Fort Victoria on 24 March 1850 and returning on the same ship between 23 September 1850 and 20 February 1851 (HBCA, PAM, C.1/613; C.3/15 fo. 62d-3, 65d-6; C.4/1). On his arrival in London, he signed a petition with others, notifying the Company that Chief Factor James Douglas at Vancouver Island had authorized a £25 gratuity for good conduct (HBCA, PAM, A.10/30 fo. 144-5). He was not on the next return voyage of the same ship in 1851-2. A man by the same name made another round trip on the same vessel, leaving on 20 August 1852, arriving on the coast on 16 January 1853, then returning between 19 March 1853 and 31 July 1853 (HBCA, PAM, A.11/74 fo. 87; C.3/15 fo. 89d; C.4/1). He also signed a petition on his return to London complaining that a gratuity that had been promised had not been paid (HBCA, PAM, A.10/30 fo. 144). In 1854 a miner with that name came out on the *Princess Royal*. However, since these men signed with their mark and the name is a common one, it is not certain that these were the same man (HBCA, PAM, A.10/34 fo. 13; C.1/615 fo. 87-7d).

• 5 July 1850 letter (HBCA, PAM, C.7/99 fo. 3-4).
• 14 May 1850 quotation "was willing to look over" (HBCA, PAM, C.1/613 pp. 83-3d).

64 FRANCIS MANNOCK

Between 1839 and 1844, Mannock (d. 1855) travelled as an apprentice on the *Prince Rupert* and *Prince Albert* on their annual voyages into Hudson Bay (HBCA, PAM, A.5/14 p. 327; A.10/8 fo. 232; C.3/14 fo. 69d, 82d, 96d, 104d). He joined the *Norman Morison* as a seaman at £24 per year on 13 October 1849 and sailed for the coast on 20 October 1849, arriving at Fort Victoria on 24 March 1850 (HBCA, PAM, C.3/15 fo. 64d-65; C.4/1). On the coast he transferred to the *Cowlitz* on 20 April 1850 and travelled to Oahu, Hawai'i, from

10 July to 28 September 1850, when he received a discharge (HBCA, PAM, B.226/d/3 fo. 788; C.1/265 fo. 130; C.1/613; C.3/15 fo. 75-6d; C.4/1). On 24 December 1852 he had made his way back to London and signed articles at the Sailor's Home in Poplar, entering the *Otter* as seaman at £30 per year; he left London on 28 December 1852 and arrived at Fort Victoria on 5 August 1853 (HBCA, PAM, C.1/625; C.3/15 fo. 100d; C.4/1). He participated in the coastal trade on the *Otter* until he died at Esquimalt on 23 July 1855, the same day the ship took Governor James Douglas to Victoria (HBCA, PAM, C.1/625). He was buried in Victoria on 3 August 1855 (BCA, Burials, Christ Church supplied by Bruce Watson). His parents were John, master of the *Prince Rupert* until his death on 1 October 1833, and M. Mannock (HBCA, PAM, A.10/8 fo. 232). His siblings included Jessy, Edward, and William, who was an apprentice seaman on the *Ganymede* from 1835 to 1837 (HBCA, PAM, A.10/6 fo. 235-7; A.32/44 fo. 126; B.223/g/3; C.3/14 fo. 39d; C.7/177 fo. 45, 47).

- 31 July 1850 letter (HBCA, PAM, C.7/99 fo. 9-10d)
- 14 May 1850 quotations "refused to take their grog" and "in consequence of bad weather" (HBCA, PAM, C.1/613).

65 CHARLES LOBB

Lobb (d. 1850) joined the *Norman Morison* on 13 October as a seaman at £24 per year and sailed for the coast on 20 October 1849, arriving at Fort Victoria on 24 March 1850 (HBCA, PAM, C.1/613; C.3/15 fo. 64d-5; C.4/1). He deserted from the ship on 11 May 1850 and went to Fort Rupert on the *England,* which was picking up coal there before proceeding to California. He was killed on 7 July 1850 near Fort Rupert (Smith 1975, 308-14; HBCA, PAM, A.10/30 fo. 336; A.10/33 fo. 325; A.11/72 fo. 326-8d). Once his body was recovered, he was buried at the fort on 16 July 1850 (information from Bruce Watson; HBCA, PAM, A.11/72 fo. 326-8d).

His mother, Judith, wrote to the Company inquiring about how to contact her son (HBCA, PAM, A.10/28 fo. 210) and the Company responded (HBCA, PAM, A.5/16 p. 222).

- 7 July 1850 letter (HBCA, PAM, C.7/99 fo. 6-8)
- 1851 extract "A canoe of Newittians" (HBCA, PAM, A.11/73 fo. 8)
- For the May 1851 letter to Robert Pyke, please see HBCA, PAM, A.10/30 fo. 336-6b.
- 21 November [18]52 letter (HBCA, PAM, A.10/33 fo. 325-5d).

66a GEORGE WISHART

Wishart (d. 1850) joined the *Norman Morison* as a seaman at £18 per year and sailed for the coast on 20 October 1849, arriving at Fort Victoria on 24 March 1850 (HBCA, PAM, C.1/613; C.3/15 fo. 64d-5; C.4/1). He deserted from the ship on 11 May 1850 and went to Fort Rupert on the *England,* which was picking up coal there before proceeding to California (HBCA, PAM, A.10/30 fo. 336; A.10/33 fo. 325; A.11/72 fo. 326-8d). For sources on his death and burial, see note for Charles Lobb (entry 65).

66b JAMES WISHART

Joining the *Norman Morison* as a seaman at £24 per year, Wishart sailed for the coast on 20 October 1849, arriving at Fort Victoria on 24 March 1850 (HBCA, PAM, C.1/613; C.3/7 fo. 41d; C.4/1). On the way out he refused to go to prayers, but when the sailors returned to standing orders and the captain ordered grog he was among those who refused to take it. The next day, when given the opportunity, he was the only one who accepted the grog (HBCA, PAM, C.1/613 fo. 64). He deserted from the ship on 11 May 1850 and went to Fort Rupert on the *England,* which was picking up coal there before

proceeding to California (HBCA, PAM, A.10/30 fo. 336; A.10/33 fo. 325; A.11/72 fo. 326-8d).
He sailed away on the *England* bound for California (HBCA, PAM, A.11/72 fo. 326-8d).

His parents, signing simply "J," were possibly James and Ann who married on 24
February 1829 in Orphir, and whose son James was baptized on 14 February 1830 in
Stromness. A James Wishart, who may have been the same man, married Eliza Flett in
British Columbia on 22 September 1853, and their children included Barbara (b. 1855),
Joseph (b. 1857), George (b. 1859), Peter (b. 1861), Margaret (b. 1863), David (b. 1865),
Mary (b. 1868) (BCA, 1870 Census). These Census data are from Bruce Watson.

- 2 September 1850 letter (HBCA, PAM, E.31/2/1 fo. 347-8d)
- 12 and 13 July 1850 extract "½ past 12" (HBCA, PAM, A.11/73 fo. 5-6)
- 1851 Blanshard quotation "the three men" (HBCA, PAM, A.11/73 fo. 7); magistrate's
  quoted response "mere fabrication" and report extract "A great many men having
  deserted" (HBCA, PAM, A.11/73 fo. 8-8d); for an account of the July 1851 campaign,
  please see HBCA, PAM, A.11/73 fo. 150-2.
- September 1851 quotation "a party of Neweetis" (HBCA, PAM, A.11/73 fo. 171-2)
- For the letter to Robert Pyke, please see HBCA, PAM, A.10/30 fo. 336-6b.

67 SAMUEL PEPPER

Pepper joined the *Norman Morison* on 13 October as a seaman at £24 per year and sailed
for the coast on 20 October 1849, arriving at Fort Victoria on 24 March 1850 (HBCA,
PAM, C.1/613; C.3/15 fo. 64d-5; C.4/1). He served on the coast in that ship until 20 April
1850, when he transferred to the *Beaver* (HBCA, PAM, C.3/7 fo. 41). On 19 June 1850, he
deserted from the ship at Fort Victoria, along with three others (HBCA, PAM, B.226/d/3
fo. 817; B.223/d/195; B.239/g/32; C.1/208).

- [2 October 1850] letter (HBCA, PAM, C.7/99 fo. 1-2d).

68 THOMAS WALSH

Joining the *Norman Morison* on 22 May 1851 as a seaman on a five-year contract at £24
per year, Walsh sailed for the coast on 28 May 1851; he arrived at Fort Victoria on 30 October 1851 and served on the *Una* until she was wrecked in December 1851 (HBCA, PAM,
B.226/d/214 fo. 868; C.1/614; C.3/15 fo. 81d-2; C.4/1). After the loss of the *Una*, he joined
the *Recovery* and served until January, 1852, when he deserted at the Queen Charlotte
Islands (HBCA, PAM, B.226/l/1 fo. 22; B.239/g/31-2).

- 21 June 1852 letter (HBCA, PAM, E.31/2/1 fo. 308-10)
- 1851 quotation "Dr. Kennedy thinks" (HBCA, PAM, A.11/73 fo. 258-9d).

69 ALFRED A. MOSS

Moss joined the *Norman Morison* as an able seaman at £24 per year and sailed for the
coast on 20 August 1852, arriving at Fort Victoria on 16 January 1853 (HBCA, PAM,
C.1/615; C.3/15 fo. 90d; C.4/1). He served on the coast in that ship then returned, leaving the coast on 19 March 1853 and arriving in London on 31 July 1853 (HBCA, PAM,
C.3/15 fo. 90d). John Betts of Yarmouth inquired after him (HBCA, PAM, A.10/33 fo.
388). Roxanne Moss Puddicombe of Newfoundland was in touch trying to trace a connection with Alfred, which to date has not been established.

- 7 October 1852 letter (HBCA, PAM, C.7/99 fo. 45-6d)
- August 1853 petition extract "As regards our refusing duty on the 9th March" (HBCA,
  PAM, A.10/34 fo. 13) and 23 May 1853 report extract by chief factor "The crew of the
  'Norman Morison'" (HBCA, PAM, A.11/74 fo. 87-7d).

70 GEORGE NAUNTON
Joining the *Norman Morison* as an apprentice seaman at £8 per year, Naunton sailed for the coast on 20 October 1849; he arrived at Fort Victoria on 24 March 1850 and returned on the same ship between 23 September 1850 and 20 February 1851 (HBCA, PAM, C.1/613; C.3/7 fo. 43d; C.4/1). He made a second voyage on the same ship, leaving London on 28 May 1851 and arriving at Fort Victoria on 30 October 1851, then returning between 21 January 1852 and 12 June 1852 (HBCA, PAM, C.3/15 fo. 81d-2; C.4/1). He rejoined the *Norman Morison* and sailed for the coast on 20 August 1852, arriving at Fort Victoria on 16 January 1853 (HBCA, PAM, C.1/614; C.3/7 fo. 49d; C.4/1). He served on the coast in that ship then returned, leaving the coast on 19 March 1853 and arriving in London on 31 July 1853 (HBCA, PAM, C.1/615; C.3/7 fo. 67d; C.4/1). His final voyage as apprentice was on the *Princess Royal* (C.3/15).
• 1 December 1852 letter (HBCA, PAM, C.7/99 fo. 47-9d).

71 THOMAS HOLMAN
Before Holman began his service with the Company, he served as second mate on the barque *Wanderer* from London to China and return and on the brig *Earl Stanhope* to Green Island (Greenland?) and return, and as chief officer on the barque *Earl Durham* to New York and Quebec and return (HBCA, PAM, A.10/27 fo. 531-3). He joined the *Una* as first mate on 31 December 1849 at £63 per year and sailed for the coast on 4 January 1850, arriving at Fort Victoria and serving on the same ship until she was wrecked in December 1851 (HBCA, PAM, A.1/66 p. 139; A.11/73 fo. 135-7d, 184-4d; C.3/15 fo. 78d-9; C.4/1). He returned home as a passenger on the *Norman Morison* (HBCA, PAM, A.11/73 fo. 218-19d; C.1/614 fo. 2). His mother wrote to the Company in 1852 to ask how to send a parcel to her son (HBCA, PAM, A.5/17 p. 263; A.10/31 fo. 288).
• 25 December 1850 letter (HBCA, PAM, C.7/163 fo. 1-3d)
• 5 April 1851 letter (HBCA, PAM, C.7/163 fo. 4-6d)
• 4 October 1851 letter (HBCA, PAM, C.7/163 fo. 7-9d)
• 14 November 1851 letter (HBCA, PAM, C.7/163 fo. 10-12d)
• 20 November 1851 extract "we commenced blasting" (HBCA, PAM, B.226/c/1 fo. 166-8); for an account of the incident involving the *Una,* please see HBCA, PAM, A.10/31 fo. 439.
• 5 May 1852 letter (HBCA, PAM, C.7/163 fo. 13-15d).

72 THOMAS MORROW
Morrow joined the *Una* as an apprentice on 25 October 1849 at £8 per year and sailed for the coast on 4 January 1850, arriving at Fort Victoria; he served on the same ship until she was wrecked in December 1851 (HBCA, PAM, A.1/66 p. 139; A.11/73 fo. 135-7d, 184-4d; B.223/d/195 fo. 24; C.3/15 fo. 78d; C.4/1). After the loss of the *Una,* he joined the *Recovery* and served until 1 November 1852, when he deserted with three others (HBCA, PAM, B.226/l/1 fo. 22; B.239/g/31-2). For the working conditions at the Queen Charlotte Islands gold mine, please see HBCA, PAM, A.11/73 fo. 462-2d.
• 19 October 1852 two letters (HBCA, PAM, C.7/163 fo. 18-21).

73 JAMES M. PHILLIPS
Joining the *Norman Morison* as a landsman at £12 per year, Phillips sailed for the coast on 20 August 1852, arriving at Fort Victoria on 16 January 1853 (HBCA, PAM, C.1/615; C.3/15 fo. 91d; C.4/1). He served on the coast in that ship then returned, leaving the coast on 19

March 1853 and arriving in London on 31 July 1853 (HBCA, PAM, C.3/15 fo. 91d; C.4/1).
- 23 December 1852 letter (HBCA, PAM, C.7/99 fo. 50-2).

74   ROBERT WILSON
Wilson joined the *Princess Royal* on 2 June 1854 as a seaman at £48 per year and sailed for the coast on 6 June 1854, arriving at Fort Victoria on 23 November 1854 (HBCA, PAM, C.3/15 fo. 109d-10; C.4/1). He served at Fort Victoria in that ship, then returned, leaving the coast on 17 January 1855 and arriving in London on 25 May 1855 (HBCA, PAM, C.3/15 fo. 109d-10; C.4/1).
- 23 November(?) 1854 quotation "death, misery and dissatisfaction" (HBCA, PAM, C.1/975)
- 5 June 1854 letter (HBCA, PAM, C.7/154 fo. 35A-6).

Voyageurs
We relied heavily on Carolyn Podruchny's recent thesis for the background on the *voyageurs* and their origins (Podruchny 1999) and on Allan Greer's work for the social context of the fur trade in New France and the significance of the *pays d'en haut* (Greer 1997, 77-9, 82, 101-4, 119).

75   JOSEPH GRENIER
Joseph Grenier (Pierre, Joseph dit Massa, Grinier) (1797-1830) came out from Maskinongé with the North West Company in 1815 as a *milieu* and in 1818 was promoted to a *devant* in the Columbia Department. (HBCA, PAM, F.4/32 fo. 429; F.5/3 fo. 29). In 1821 he continued to deal with the Hudson's Bay Company as a freeman (HBCA, PAM, B.239/g/1-3). By 1824 he was a regular member of Peter Skene Ogden's Snake Country expeditions, acting in the capacity of *milieu* until his death by drowning in the Columbia River on 3 July 1830 (HBCA, PAM, B.202/a/2, 6; B.223/d/10, 19, 28; B.239/g/4-11). His grandparents were Antoinette Marchand (b. 3 June 1743) and Amable Sicard, who married at Trois-Rivières on 25 June 1764, and Laurent Grenier and Geneviève Hamel, who married at Ste-Croix on 6 October 1769. His parents were Joseph Grenier and Marie Sicard of Ruisseau des Chênes, who married at Maskinongé on 9 February 1795. (CduP, Maskinongé, Ste-Croix, and Trois-Rivières Parish Registers). He married Thérèse Spokan (a.k.a. Okanagan, Quilquil, or Sihan) and had a daughter Marie-Anne (1829-50), who married Gédéon Senegal on 27 February 1843. After Joseph's death, Thérèse married Joseph Corneiller (Corneille, Cournoyer, or Cournoillé) on 11 July 1839. At the time of their marriage they recognized their own children Victoire, aged eight, and Joseph, six months, as well as the children of Thérèse by two previous husbands, now deceased: Marie Anne Grenier aged nine years, Martial Lavallée aged twenty-one years, and Pierre Lavallée aged eighteen years (Munnick 1972, 50 M-63; Munnick 1979a, A-40, 68 B-97, 68 M-15; Munnick 1982, 22 S-8).
- April 1831 letter (HBCA, PAM, E.31/2/2 fo. 9-10d)
- 20 April 1831 letter (HBCA, PAM, E.31/2/2 fo. 7-8d)
- July 1830 Hargrave extract (HBCA, PAM, B.223/b/6 fo. 13-18d)
- 5 February 1832 letter (HBCA, PAM, B.134/c/13 fo. 106-7).

76   JOHN MONGLE
John Mongle (Jean Mongall, Mongls, Jean Monde) (1801-30) came out from Maskinongé with the North West Company in 1816 as a *milieu,* making purchases at Nipigon in 1817

and at Lake Winnipeg in 1819, after which he returned to Lower Canada (HBCA, PAM, F.4/32 fo. 749). In 1821 he signed on with the North West Company for three years as a *milieu* before that Company united with the Hudson's Bay Company (HBCA, PAM, F.4/40 fo. 125). In 1829 he signed on for the more senior position of *boute* and worked at Fort Colvile until his death by drowning in the Columbia River on 25 October 1830 (HBCA, PAM, B.45/a/1 fo. 22; B.239/g/9-10). His parents were Marie-Judith Panneton and Johan or Jean Andres Mongel, a Hessian soldier with the Hanau Chasseurs who had fled to Lower Canada after the American Revolution. His first wife, Marie Carret (or Comette), appears to have died, after which he married Marie St-Germain at L'Assomption on 9 January 1827 (CduP, Maskinongé and L'Assomption Parish Registers, Drouin Index). Their children's marriages are recorded (CduP, L'Assomption and Joliette Parish Registers).

- 20 April 1830 letter (HBCA, PAM, E.31/2/2 fo. 24-5d)
- 12 April 1830 letter (HBCA, PAM, B.134/c/13 fo. 32)
- 13 January 1832 letter (HBCA, PAM, B.134/c/13 fo. 30)
- October 1830 quotations "not over too well manned" and "Four of our men" (HBCA, PAM, B.45/a/1).

77 OLIVIER ST. PIERRE

St. Pierre (1806-30) came out from Trois-Rivières with the Hudson's Bay Company as a *milieu* in the Columbia Department in 1830 (HBCA, PAM, B.223/d/28 fo. 4; B.239/g/10). He drowned in the Columbia River on 25 October 1830 (HBCA, PAM, B.45/a/1 fo. 22; B.239/g/10). His parents were Joseph St. Pierre and Marie-Anne Blondin, who married in Trois-Rivières in 1792. His siblings were Joseph (b. 1792), Claude (b. 1793, m. 1814 Marguerite Duguay dit Duplacy), Marie Marguerite (b. 1794), Pierre (b. 1795, d. 1797), Angélique (b. 1797, d. at 4 months), Josephe (b. 1798), Joseph (b. 1799) (CduP, Trois-Rivières Parish Registers). He married Nelly (Eléonore) Duplessis, daughter of Charles Duplessis and Josephte Lewis, in 1827 (CduP, Trois-Rivières Parish Registers). Another daughter was Heriette (perhaps Harriette or Henriette).

- 28 March 1831 two letters (HBCA, PAM, E.31/2/2 fo. 30-1d)
- April 1830 quotations "could not be taken" and "a minor under the care of his Tutor" (HBCA, PAM, B.134/c/7 fo. 183-4) and May quotation from magistrate "be kept in gaol" (HBCA, PAM, B.134/c/7 fo. 316, 362-3)
- 28 March 1831 letter extract (HBCA, PAM, E.31/2/2 fo. 31)
- October 1830 McLoughlin report extract (HBCA, PAM, B.223/b/6 fo. 25).

78 FÉLIX LEBRUN

Lebrun (1807-30) came out from Maskinongé with the Hudson's Bay Company as a *milieu* in the Columbia Department in 1830 (HBCA, PAM, B.223/d/28 fo. 4; B.239/g/10). He drowned in the Columbia River on 25 October 1830 (HBCA, PAM, B.45/a/1 fo. 22; B.239/g/10). His grandparents were Charles Lebrun from Port-Royale and Marie-Josephte Lord, who came to Maskinongé from Acadia via Massachusetts and New Hampshire. His parents were Louis Lebrun (b. 1767) and Marie Etiennette Belair, who married in Maskinongé in 1794. His siblings were Louis (b. 1797, m. Genevieve Duteau in St-Cuthbert in 1828, whose young son died 22 July 1830), Amable (b. 1798 in Rivière du Loup, m. Elisabeth Landry in 1829 and Louise Juneau in 1841), Julie (m. Louis Paquin in Maskinongé in 1820), and David (b. 1809) (CduP, Rivière du Loup, St-Cuthbert, and Maskinongé Parish Registers). Davide Sigard's correct name was Sicard de Carifel.

- 19 April 1831 letter (HBCA, PAM, E.31/2/2 fo. 11-12d)
- 20 April 1831 letter (HBCA, PAM, E.31/2/2 fo. 13-14d).

79 HERCULE LEBRUN
    Hercule (Louis-Hercule) Lebrun (1810-c. 1857) came out from Maskinongé with the
    Hudson's Bay Company as a *milieu* in the Columbia Department in 1830 (HBCA, PAM,
    B.223/d/28 fo. 4; B.239/g/10). He returned to Canada in 1833 (HBCA, PAM, B.239/g/12).
    In 1845 he reappeared in the Pacific Northwest and took land near the centre of the
    French Prairie in 1849, becoming a citizen in 1852 (Munnick 1979b, A-58 and 11 M-7). He
    appears to have died between 1856 and 1858. His grandparents were Charles Lebrun from
    Port-Royale and Marie-Josephte Lord and his parents were Charles Lebrun (bapt. 1767)
    and Marie Anne Lemire (daughter of Gabriel Lemyre Gonneville and Angélique Deserre),
    whom Charles married in Maskinongé in 1799 after his first wife, Madeleine Lesieur, died.
    Hercule's siblings were Charles Edouard (b. 1806, m. 1838 in Chateauguay), Adolphe,
    Maxime, Agathe, Félix (m. 1831 Marie-Anne Masson), and Moise. His nephew, Olivier
    Fizette, was the son of Josephte Lemire and Louis Fiset. Anastasie and Catherine, men-
    tioned in the undelivered letters, were the daughters of Joseph Lebrun and Euphro-
    sine Grenier. Louis Paquin was married to his cousin Julie Lebrun, sister to Félix (CduP,
    Chateauguay and Maskinongé Parish Registers). On 18 September 1848 he married
    Marie-Anne (later referred to as Louise) Ouvrie (Ouvré), the daughter of the late Jean
    Baptiste Ouvré and a Cowlitz woman. They had five daughters: Flavie (b. 30 September
    1850, buried 18 January 1851); Marie Louise Philomène (b. 3 November 1851, buried 23
    February 1858); Marie Mélanie (b. 3 February 1854); Esther (b. 7 October 1855, buried 7
    March 1858); and Virginie (b. 27 April 1857, buried 2 January 1858). After Hercule's death,
    Louise married Adolphe L'Oiseau on 10 May 1858 and brought only four-year-old
    Mélanie to the new marriage (Munnick 1979b, A-58, 11 M-7, 29 B-22, 33 S-3, 43 B-26, 60
    B-4, 75 B-23, 85 B-10, 90 S-1, 92 S-5 and S-7, 94 M-4).
- 12 March 1831 letter (HBCA, PAM, E.31/2/2 fo. 15-16d)
- April 18, 1831 letter (HBCA, PAM, E.31/2/2 fo. 17-18d).

80 JOHN McKAY
    McKay (McKee, McKy, McKisse) (b. 1812) came out from York (St-Cuthbert) with the
    Hudson's Bay Company as a *milieu* (middleman) in the Columbia Department in 1832
    (HBCA, PAM, B.239/g/12-14). He was the second man of that name to be employed on
    the coast, so he was called John McKay "b" on the Company's books to distinguish him
    from others. He returned to Canada in 1835 (HBCA, PAM, B.239/g/14). He may have
    been the man recorded as son of Jean and Magdaleine McKay, who married Angélique
    Chapdelaine dit LaRivière on 12 January 1841 and whose son Henry married Philomène
    Roberge on 2 February 1863 (CduP, St-Cuthbert Parish Registers).
- 12 April 1833 letter (HBCA, PAM, E.31/2/2 fo. 19-20d).

Men at the Posts
For information on the men who served in the Company's posts, we relied heavily on the
various Hudson's Bay Record Society volumes dedicated to the activities on the West
Coast of North America (Rich 1941; 1943; 1944; Ormsby 1979) and on Richard Mackie's
more recent work (1997).

81 WILLIAM JOHNSTON
Johnston (c. 1811-35) signed on at Kirkwall and came out to York Factory as a labourer in 1833 (HBCA, PAM, A.32/35 fo. 179; B.239/g/13). Because there were other men with the same name, the Company gave him the letter "c" after his name to distinguish him in their books. He travelled out as a middleman to the Columbia Department on the brigade that crossed the continent (HBCA, PAM, B.239/g/14). On 7 July 1835 his life was cut short when he drowned in the Fraser River near Fort George (present-day Prince George, British Columbia) (HBCA, PAM, B.239/g/15). Two Orkney Hugh Johnstons with sons named William appear in the International Genealogical Index (FHC), one married to Margaret Spence and one to Katharine Harvey, but neither seem to correspond to this family.
- 15 June 1834 letter (HBCA, PAM, E.31/2/1 fo. 177-8d)
- 16 June 1835 letter (HBCA, PAM, E.31/2/1 fo. 179-80d)
- December 1839 quotation "You will do a poor man" (HBCA, PAM, A.10/9 fo. 385); for the reply that there were two men by that name, please see HBCA, PAM, A.5/13 p. 14; September 1840 quotation "verbal reports from" (HBCA, PAM, A.10/10 fo. 183); for the Company secretary's request for a certificate, please see HBCA, PAM, A.5/13 p. 108; B.239/g/16.

82 GEORGE LINTON
Linton (1800-35) signed a six-year contract with the North West Company on 1 October 1818 and came to the Athabasca District as an apprentice clerk in 1819 (HBCA, PAM, F.4/32 fo. 1036). In 1821, when the North West Company and the Hudson's Bay Company united, he continued as a clerk with the Hudson's Bay Company (HBCA, PAM, A.32/1 p. 68; B.135/k/1 p. 56). In 1824 he was transferred to Fort Pelly in the Swan River District (in present-day Saskatchewan) and in 1826 he went to the Saskatchewan District, serving in Fort Edmonton and Fort Assiniboine and in Lesser Slave Lake (HBCA, PAM, B.239/k/1 pp. 86, 121, 170, 209, 244, 264, 285). In 1831 he transferred to New Caledonia and was placed in charge at Fort George (present-day Prince George, British Columbia) (HBCA, PAM, B.239/k/1 p. 317; B.239/k/2 pp. 17, 44, 74, 97). On 8 November 1835 he died on the Fraser River between Fort George and Fort Alexandria (HBCA, PAM, D.4/22 pp. 32-3, 64). At the time he was assumed to have drowned but years later another story was told of his death (see his story and HBCA, PAM, B.5/a/4 fo. 10-10d). Some references to him (see Cole 2001) mistakenly call him Robert. His wife and family perished with him on the Fraser River in 1835. By 1836 his heirs appear to have been his widowed mother, Elizabeth Linton of Woolwich, and his sister H.A. (Mrs. Arthur) Douglas of Darmellington, Scotland (HBCA, PAM, A.10/3 fo. 557; A.10/4 fo. 180; A.10/5 fo. 1-2, 162).
- 1832 quotation from Simpson "An Englishman (Londoner)" (HBCA, PAM, A.34/2 Clerk No. 46)
- 2 March 1834 letter (HBCA, PAM, E.31/2/4 fo. 16-17d)
- December 1836 quotation "Eighty years of age" (HBCA, PAM, A.10/3 fo. 557); for the March 1837 letter from Mrs. Linton to Company Secretary Smith, please see HBCA, PAM, A.10/4 fo. 180; for her July 1837 letter, see HBCA, PAM, A.10/5 fo. 1, and for Smith's responses "further measures are taken" and "some property," see HBCA, PAM, A.10/5 fo. 2.
- "That poor Gentleman" (Cole 2001, 113)

- March 1838 extract "I have a conversation with Toule whates Widow" (HBCA, PAM, B.5/a/4 fo. 10-10d).

83 JAMES DICKSON
Dickson (Dixon) (1787-1861) was hired from Feolquoy Farm, Harray, Orkney, as a black-smith in 1825 (HBCA, PAM, A.32/26 fo. 30; B.59/a/110 fo. 9; B.186/e/10 fo. 12d-13 and information from Bruce Watson and Janice Sinclair). He served 1825-9 at Eastmain and 1829-34 at Moose Factory before returning to Orkney from London to Leith in the *Duke of Buccleugh,* then by smack to Orkney (HBCA, PAM, A.5/10 p. 256; B.135/g/7-18; B.186/e/9, 11, 13, 14; C.1/826; C.4/1 fo. 20). On 3 April 1835 he signed on as blacksmith in the Columbia Department and served at Fort Vancouver until 31 October 1843, when he joined the crew as a seaman on the *Vancouver.* The ship left the coast on 29 November 1843 and arrived in London on 10 June 1844 (HBCA, PAM, C.4/1). His parents were Robert Dickson and Christian Firth, who married in 1786. His siblings were: Margaret (b. 1793), who married William Corrigal of Vola, Harray; Christian (b. 1796), who mar-ried Thomas Isbister and cared for James Dickson's son James; William (b. 1798), who married Christian Clouston; Helen (Nelly) (b. 1805), who married James Robertson of Doehouse, Sandwick; and Robert (b. 1807), who married Cecelia Firth and appeared in the 1851 Census for Sandwick. James first married Jean Flett and had a son, James, who lived with his aunt Christian Isbister after his mother died and his father left for the Columbia Department.

   According to family information supplied by Janice Sinclair, Dickson married Mary Johnstone in 1843, although he does not appear to have come home in 1843. Janice Sinclair put us in touch with E.S. Adamson (née Wilson), G. Barclay, John K. Bews, V. Copland, Jemima D. Flett, Alfred J.R. Merriman, William C. Merriman, Robertina S. Paterson, E. Sabiston, D. Wilson, J.C. Wilson, and William J. Wilson, descendants of the Dickson family in Orkney. For other articles discussing the "Great Disruption," please see *New Encyclopaedia Britannica* 1961, 4: 963, MacWhirter 1956, 30-3, and Good-fellow 1903, 110-30.
- 6 June 1843 letter (HBCA, PAM, E.31/2/1 fo. 83-4d)
- 12 June 1843 letter (HBCA, PAM, E.31/2/1 fo. 85-6d)
- 16 June 1843 letter (HBCA, PAM, E.31/2/1 fo. 87-7d)
- 19 June 1843 letter (HBCA, PAM, E.31/2/1 fo. 88-9d).

84 WILLIAM SWANSTON
Swanston (Swanson) (1819-43) began work as an apprentice sailor at Moose Factory in 1835, becoming a sailor there in 1840 (HBCA, PAM, B.135/g/19-24). To distinguish him from his father, another William, he was given the designation "B" after his name in the Company books. In 1841 he went out to the Columbia Department as a sailor, serving as a slooper at Thompson River (now Kamloops) and Fort Vancouver until his death by drowning at the Dalles of the Columbia River in July 1843 (HBCA, PAM, B.239/g/21-3). He was the son of William Swanston and Anne (Nancy) Brown (daughter of Joseph Brown, who had died a widower in 1818) and was born in Rupert's Land, as were his sib-lings Elizabeth (b. 1816), Anne (b. 1818), Joseph (b. 1821), Charlotte (b. 1824), John (b. 1827), Sarah (b. 1828), and James (b. 1832). Janice Sinclair of Harray, Orkney, provided information on the Swanston family and gave help on the interpretation of some of the Orkney vocabulary in the letters and the other people mentioned in them. Other infor-mation on the family can be found in Bailey 1992.

His brother Joseph began work with the Company in 1835 as an apprentice cooper and carpenter on Hudson Bay and Lake Superior before going to the Company's agency in California in 1841 (HBCA, PAM, B.135/g/19-23; B.239/g/81). After serving as a middleman and a slooper, he was discharged in California in 1845-6 (HBCA, PAM, B.239/g/82-5).

Brother John chose the seafaring life and served as an apprentice sailor on the *Cadborough, Vancouver, Columbia,* and *Cowlitz* from 1842 to 1848 (HBCA, PAM, A.11/72 fo. 201d; B.223/g/7-8; B.239/g/82-7). In just one year he went from seaman to second mate on the *Cowlitz,* serving one year before becoming second mate on the *Beaver* from 1850 to 1852 (HBCA, PAM, B.239/g/88-9; B.239/k/3 p. 14, 40; C.1/208; C.1/266). He served as first mate on *Mary Dare,* 1852-4, then as master of the *Beaver,* 1856-8, the *Labouchere,* 1859-66, and the *Enterprise* from 1866 until his death on 21 October 1872 (HBCA, PAM, B.226/b/6 p. 40; B.226/b/20 fo. 306; B.226/b/27 fo. 37, 136, 304; B.226/b/34 fo. 42, 152, 346; B.226/b/40 fo. 84; B.226/b/45 fo. 344; B.226/g/4, 5; B.239/k/3 p. 60; C.1/461; C.1/625).

Andrew Linklater's parish of origin was given as Brick, Harray, when Linklater (c. 1807-60) signed on with the Company on 14 April 1828 (HBCA, PAM, A.32/38 fo. 190). He served in the Moose District as a middleman and sailor on the *Union* sloop (HBCA, PAM, A.16/21; B.135/g/10-22). While he worked the small craft at Company posts, he was more closely integrated into the life of the post than the seamen working the seagoing ships. On 16 October 1839 he sailed home on the *Prince of Wales* with his wife and family (HBCA, PAM, A.16/22). He was whaling in Davis Straits in 1844 (HBCA, PAM, E.31/2/1 fo. 291-1d). In the early morning of 21 November 1860 he drowned in Houseby Loch in Birsay, Orkney, on his way home to Ooter Dykes, Knarston, Harray, from a farm sale in Stromness. (Information was sent by Janice Sinclair and Stuart Linklater, based on newspaper reports in the *Orcadian* and *The Orkney Herald.*) His father, Andrew, was born in 1775. He married Elizabeth (Betsy) Swanston, sister of William, in 1834 and had children named Kitty (Katherine), Ann (b. 1837), Elizabeth (b. 1840), William (b. 1842), Mary (b. 1845), Margaret (b. 1848), John (b. 1850), Andrew (b. 1854), and James (b. 1857). Information on the family was supplied by Janice Sinclair and Stuart Linklater. We have been in touch with J. Shand and Stuart Linklater, descendants of the Linklater family.
- 3 January 1844 letter (HBCA, PAM, E.31/2/1 fo. 291-2d)
- 12 August 1843 quotation from McLoughlin (HBCA, PAM, A.11/70) and 15 November 1843 extract "I am pained" (HBCA, PAM, B.223/b/30 fo. 52-67 para. 25).

85a ALEXANDER MORISON

Morison (Morrison) (c. 1819-97) signed on with the Company on 15 June 1840, giving his parish of origin as Skegursta, Isle of Lewis (HBCA, PAM, A.32/46 fo. 234). He sailed from Stornoway on the *Prince Rupert* on 23 June, arriving at York Factory on 9 August (HBCA, PAM, B.239/g/20; C.4/1 fo. 20d). He crossed the continent with the brigade and served as a middleman in the Columbia Department for a year before becoming a labourer at Fort Colvile from 1842 to 1846 (HBCA, PAM, B.239/g/21-5). He left the coast by the spring express (a rapid brigade trip) and sailed for home from York Factory on the *Prince Rupert* in the fall of 1846 (HBCA, PAM, B.239/g/25-6; C.1/250, 259-62). Sometime between 1851 and 1861, Alexander moved to Croft Number 6, Branahuie. He died in 1897. His parents, John Morison and Mary MacDonald, were born about 1778 and in the 1851 Census they occupied Croft Number 20, Branahuie, Isle of Lewis. His brother John (b. 1809) married Ann (Anne) McLeod (MacLeod) (1812-53) of Uig and, in the 1851 Census, they were living in Melbost with their five children. Brother Donald (b. 1817) and his wife, Marion, were living in Branahuie with their four children in 1851. On 28

December 1846, Alexander married Ann McLeod of Knock, a village about three kilometres (two miles) from Branahuie, and by 1851 they had a son, John (Norman). A
daughter, Catherine, was born in 1853. Ann died the next year and Alexander subsequently married Isabella Montgomery, with whom he had three daughters, including
Isabella and Ann. Family information came from Bill Lawson, Isle of Harris, a genealogist, and William Macleod of Branahuie, Isle of Lewis, a great-grandson of Alexander. We
have been in touch with Bellann Macleod, a great-grandchild of Alexander Morison.

85b MURDOCH MCLEOD
His parish of origin was given as Shader Aird, Isle of Lewis, when Murdoch (Murdock,
Murdo) McLeod (Macleod) (c. 1808-c. 1855) signed on as a labourer with the Company
on 19 June 1832 (HBCA, PAM, A.32/43 fo. 158). He sailed from Stornoway on the *Prince
Rupert* on 23 June, arriving at York Factory on 24 August, and was given the designation
"a" after his name to distinguish him from other men of the same name (HBCA, PAM,
B.239/g/12; C.1/923 fo. 1d). He went inland to Saskatchewan and then crossed the continent with the brigade and served as a labourer and middleman at Fort Vancouver in the
Columbia Department from 1834 to 1847 (HBCA, PAM, B.239/g/12-28). He sailed for
home on the *Columbia* in November 1847, arriving in London on 22 May 1848 (HBCA,
PAM, C.1/251-2, 263-4). He died between 1851 and 1855. In the undelivered letter, his
mother was still alive, and his sister Ann (Anne) was married to John Morison of Melbost. Murdoch married Kirsty (Christian, Chirsty) McLeod (MacLeod) of Melbost in
December 1849 and settled in Shulishader. After Murdoch's death, Kirsty married
Alexander Munro and had two daughters (family information from Bill Lawson, Isle of
Harris, and William Macleod of Branahuie, Isle of Lewis). For the 12 December 1846 letter from Leitch, please see HBCA, PAM, A.10/22 fo. 523.
• 8-9 June 1845 two letters (HBCA, PAM, E.31/2/1 fo. 212-13d).

86 ANGUS MCDONALD
His parish of origin was given as Markethill, Stornoway, Isle of Lewis, when McDonald
(b. c. 1824) signed on as a labourer with the Company on 17 June 1841 (HBCA, PAM,
B.239/u/1 #1257). He was given the designation "e" after his name to distinguish him
from other men of the same name. Sailing from Stornoway on the *Prince Rupert* for York
Factory (HBCA, PAM, B.239/u/1 #1257; C.1/923 fo. 1d), he crossed the continent with
the brigade and served as a labourer at Fort Vancouver (1842-3), Fort Victoria (1843-5),
and Nisqually (1845-6) in the Columbia Department (HBCA, PAM, B.239/g/21-5). He
crossed back east with the express brigade and went home on the *Prince Rupert* in 1846
(HBCA, PAM, B.239/g/25-6). His father, Murdo, born c. 1801 and his mother, Margaret
(possibly McLeod of Gress and married in 1821), who was born about 1791, were living
with their seventeen-year-old son Angus in Old Markethill in the 1841 Census. Murdo
did not appear in the 1851 Census, so presumably he had died; Angus, aged twenty-eight,
was living with his wife Margaret of Uig. Family information came from Bill Lawson, Isle
of Harris.
• 16 February 1846 letter (HBCA, PAM, E.31/2/1 fo. 353-4).

87 ALLAN MACISAAC
His parish of origin was given as South Uist, Outer Hebrides, when MacIsaac (McIsaac)
signed on as a labourer with the Company on 14 June 1849 (HBCA, PAM, B.239/u/1
#1395). He sailed from Stornoway on the *Prince Rupert* for York Factory and crossed the

continent with the brigade (HBCA, PAM, B.239/g/29-30). He served as a labourer at one of the inland posts in the Columbia Department from 1850 to 1851, then was listed as a "discharged" labourer from the Vancouver depot from 1851 to 1853 (HBCA, PAM, B.239/g/31-2). His balances appeared on the Oregon Department account books from 1853 to 1856 (HBCA, PAM, B.223/g/9-11). In the 1851 Census, his sweetheart Mary Mac-Donald (aged twenty-four) lived at Widow's Row, Sandwick, on the eastern outskirts of Stornoway with her widowed mother Mary (forty-five) and siblings Peggy (twenty-five), Donald (nineteen), Janet (fifteen), and Lexy (nine). The census also records neighbours Murdina Campbel and Neil MacKay, mentioned in the letter. Family and census information came from Bill Lawson, Isle of Harris. The story of the drowning on the steamer comes from a reference in the *Victoria Colonist,* 29 May 1862, 3, BCA.

• 1 October 1851 letter (HBCA, PAM, E.31/2/1 fo. 197-8d).

88 Hugh Mouat

His parish of origin was given as Instar, Rousay, Orkney, when Mouat (Mowat) signed on as a labourer with the Company on 10 December 1850 (HBCA, PAM, B.239/u/1 #2282). He sailed from Stomness for York Factory and crossed the continent with the brigade (HBCA, PAM, B.239/g/31). He served as a labourer at Fort Vancouver in the Columbia and later the Oregon Department from 1852 to 1854, then was listed as a steward at the Vancouver depot from 1854 to 1860 (HBCA, PAM, B.223/g/9-16; B.239/g/32). Hugh, the youngest of five children of Rousay farmers, John and Catherine, was born 4 December 1828 and baptized 7 February 1829 (OA, OPR 24/2); this information was made available thanks to Bruce Watson.

• 31 December 1851 letter (HBCA, PAM, E.31/2/1 fo. 355-7)
• 1 January 1852 letter (HBCA, PAM, E.31/2/1 fo. 358-9).

89 Peter Irvine

His parish of origin was given as South Yell, Shetland, when Irvine signed on as a labourer with the Company on 7 March 1850 (HBCA, PAM, B.239/u/1 #1019). The letter "A" after his name was used by the Company to distinguish him from several men with the same name. He sailed to York Factory and crossed the continent with the brigade (HBCA, PAM, B.223/d/214 fo. 846; B.239/g/30-1). He served as a labourer at Fort Colvile in the Columbia Department from 1852 to 1856, when he was listed "left" (HBCA, PAM, B.223/g/11-12). His balances appeared on the Oregon Department account books from 1856 to 1860 (HBCA, PAM, B.223/g/13-15). If he was the Peter Irvine baptized on 27 September 1828 into the Delting family headed by John Irvine and his wife Christina Mouat, his siblings may have been Margaret, (bapt. 26 May 1820), Andrew (bapt. 1 November 1821), and John (bapt. 29 August 1826) (FHC). His account of £17 9s. was written off in 1860 (HBCA, PAM, B.223/g/11-15).

• 1 February 1852 letter (HBCA, PAM, E.31/2/1 fo. 169-71)
• 22 June 1852 letter (HBCA, PAM, E.31/2/1 fo. 166-8).

90 Joseph William McKay

McKay (Mackay) (1829-1900) was a fur trader, explorer, businessman, politician, justice of the peace, Indian agent, and office holder. He joined the Hudson's Bay Company in 1844 and by 1853, when this letter was written, he had been in charge of their Nanaimo coalfields for a year, during which he had opened a coal mine, a sawmill, a saltern, and a school. (For detailed biography, please see Mackie 1990.) He was born at Rupert's House

(Waskaganish, Quebec), son of William McKay and Mary Bunn. Both were of Aboriginal and European ancestry. In 1860 he married Helen Holmes in Victoria, British Columbia, and they had four daughters and two sons. He died there on 21 December 1900 (Mackie 1990). For Catherine McKay's accounts, please see Annuitants and Servants Accounts, HBCA, PAM, B.135/g/26-48.
- 13 July 1853 letter (HBCA, PAM, E.31/2/1 fo. 199-201)
- May 1842 quotation "having kept his bed" (HBCA, PAM, B.186/b/45 fo. 2d).

91a EDWIN KITTSON
In 1857 Edwin Kittson (Kitson) (b. 1840) was at the Blue Coat School in Greenwich. After he left the school his name appears on the Company Sundries list at Langley for 1858-9, receiving £20 in wages, but spending more than £66. His debt continued on the books for one more year but he was no longer being paid (HBCA, PAM, B.226/g/6-7). He was the son of William Kittson and Hélène McDonald, born at Fort Nisqually.
     William Kittson (1792-1841) was a militia officer and fur trader. Born in Lower Canada, he died on Christmas Day in 1841 at Fort Vancouver. (For detailed biography, please see Holmgren 1988.) He had an Aboriginal wife, a Walla Walla woman named Marie, by whom he had two sons, Jules and Peter (Pierre) Charles. He later married Hélène, daughter of Finan McDonald, and they had four children: Jesse (c. 1832-7); Caroline (1834-7); Eloisa Jemima (1836-1927), who married William Sinclair III; and Edwin (b. 1840). Hélène married Richard Grant in 1845 (Holmgren 1988; Roxanne Woodruff, <www.geocities.com/Heartland/Oaks/2189/Kittson.htm>; Dickey 1989).

91b JAMES DOUGLAS
James Douglas (1803-77) was a Hudson's Bay Company officer who had initially worked for the North West Company and later became governor of Vancouver Island and of the Crown colony of British Columbia. (For a detailed biography, please see Ormsby 1972.) He was born at Demerara, British Guiana, son of John Douglas and a Creole woman. He married Amelia Connolly – daughter of William Connolly and his Cree wife – and seven of their thirteen children died young (Van Kirk 1980; Ormsby 1972). For other versions of the Chief Kwah restitution story, please see Frieda Esau Klippenstein 1996, 124-40.
- 14 January 1857 letter from James Douglas (HBCA, PAM, E.31/2/1 fo. 90-2).

92 JOHN TOD
Tod (1794-1882) came to North America in 1811 and rose to chief trader in the Hudson's Bay Company, retiring in October 1858. Our account of Tod's life relies heavily on Wolfenden 1982. For a more extensive biography, please see Belyk 1995. An Aboriginal wife who bore him at least one daughter when he was at McLeod's Lake between 1824 and 1834 may have been Mackoodzie, a Sickannie (Sekani) woman, who was listed in the Outstanding Balances for 1834-5 as "formerly with John Tod" (HBCA, PAM, B.239/g/14 fo. 84). For reference to the Wilson-Tod affair, please see HBCA, PAM, D.4/102 fo. 6. On arrival in England in 1837 Tod placed Emmeline under the protection of her great-aunt, Miss M. Greenshields, and Eliza with her mother (HBCA, PAM, A.36/12 fo. 151-61). Eliza entered the Lunatic House at Guy's Hospital in 1844 and died, aged forty-nine, on 12 May 1857 (HBCA, PAM, Search File "John Tod").
- 24 February 1838 extract from Waugh letter (HBCA, PAM, A.10/6 fo. 117-17d) and accompanying doctor's report (HBCA, PAM, A.10/6 fo. 118)

- 1842 quotation from Tod "two aged parents" (HBCA, PAM, D.5/7 fo. 27-8)
- 1842 quotation from Simpson "charitable" (HBCA, PAM, D.6/62 fo. 64); 1846 response by Tod "your benevolent arrangement" (HBCA, PAM, D.5/16 fo. 466-8)
- [26 May 1857] letter and funeral invoice (HBCA, PAM, E.31/2/1 fo. 293-6).

Emigrant Labourers
For a general discussion of emigration sponsored by the Hudson's Bay Company, please see Richard Mackie 1992-3 and Margaret A. Ormsby 1979, xi-xciv. A discussion of the challenges of a homo-social culture can be found in Perry 2000. For a discussion of crime and traditional Aboriginal methods of dealing with it, please see Reid 1999, 75-84. Accounts of the miners and their complaints can be found in Ralston 1983, 44, Leynard 1982, Nicholls 1991-4, and Burley 1997, 207-13. The agricultural projects of the Puget's Sound Agricultural Company are outlined in Gibson 1985, with the example of operations at Nisqually (Tacoma, Washington) described in Dickey 1989 and McDonald 1979. See also Beattie 2002.

93   JAMES ROSE
Rose came out in 1848 on the *Harpooner* (Sale 1979, 153) and was bound for Sooke River as a blacksmith and engineer, according to the address on the undelivered letter. A note indicates that in the spring of 1850 he went to Oregon City. In the 1851 Census for Nairn, Scotland, his mother Margaret (b. c. 1793 in Inverness) was shown as the head of the family living with her milliner daughter, Betsy (twenty-five), Betsy's carpenter husband, George Gauld, and their son, Alexander (b. 26 March 1850) at 27 High Street Nairn, Scotland. Brother Alexander (Sandy) was living in Nairn with Mr. Dalles (1851 Census, thanks to Barbara A. MacLeod, Balintor Cawdor, Nairn in 1997). Their brother Tom is mentioned in the undelivered letters.
- 19 September 1849 letter (HBCA, PAM, E.31/2/1 fo. 257-9d)
- 9 April 1850 from sister and husband (HBCA, PAM, E.31/2/1 fo. 262-4)
- 9 April 1850 from brother (HBCA, PAM, E.31/2/1 fo. 260-1d).

94   JOHN SMITH
Smith came out in 1848 on the *Harpooner* and was one of the Scottish miners (a collier labourer) bound for Fort Rupert (Sale 1979, 153; Bowsfield 1979, lviiin). He came out at the age of twenty-five with a wife, Marion, and a child (HBCA, PAM, A.10/25 fo. 401; B.239/g/29). He was sent to work at Fort Rupert but not long after his arrival he deserted along with Peter Leach, John Willoughby, and Richard Whitton on 18 June 1850, and went aboard the *England* bound for California (Bowsfield 1979, 102-3, 111-12; HBCA, PAM, A.11/72 fo. 87-96d, 289; B.226/d/3, 195; B.239/g/32).
- 1848(?) extract by Landale "I trust" (HBCA, PAM, A.10/25 fo. 401-1d)
- 2 December 1848 quotation from Company Secretary Smith (HBCA, PAM, A.10/25 fo. 517-17d)
- quotation from captain "*roughly spoken* to" (HBCA, PAM, A.11/72 fo. 87-96d)
- 23 October 1850 letter (HBCA, PAM, E.31/2/1 fo. 277-9).

95a   EDWARD PARROT
Parrot came out from Kent in August 1849 on the *Cowlitz* as a farm labourer (HBCA, PAM, B.226/d/3 fo. 464; C.7/38 fo. 6). On 27 January 1850 he drowned at Kapena Falls and Pool in Nu'uana Valley, Sandwich Islands (Hawai'i) and was buried in the public

cemetery (Bowsfield 1979, 78; HBCA, PAM, A.10/28 fo. 248; A.11/62 fo. 448; A.11/72 fo. 201-6d; A.11/72 fo. 387).

95b RICHARD RIBBINS
Ribbins (Ribbens) came out from Ruxley, Kent, in August 1849 on the *Cowlitz* (HBCA, PAM, B.239/g/89; C.7/38 fo. 6). From his arrival in March 1850 he was a labourer in Victoria (HBCA, PAM, B.239/g/30-1). He left in September 1850, signing on as a seaman to work his passage back to England on the *Norman Morison* and arriving in London in February 1851 (HBCA, PAM, B.226/d/3 fo. 11d, 487; B.239/g/31-2). His family consisted of his parents John and Margaret and siblings James (bapt. 1825), Jeremiah (bapt. 1827), Joseph (bapt. 1830), John (bapt. 1832), Oliver (bapt. 1835), Elizabeth (bapt. 1836), Solomon (bapt. 1839), Mary Anne (bapt. 1842), and George (bapt. 1847) (FHC).
• 2 April 1850 three letters (HBCA, PAM, E.31/2/1 fo. 230-1, 232-3, 234-8)
• 27 January 1850 quotation "unfortunately drowned" (HBCA, PAM, A.11/72 fo. 201-6d).

96 JOHN SHADRACH BLUNDELL
Blundell (b. c. 1816) came out at about thirty-three years of age from St. Paul's Cray, Kent, in August 1849 on the *Cowlitz* (HBCA, PAM, B.239/g/89; C.7/38 fo. 6). From his arrival in March 1850, he was a farm labourer in Victoria and Nanaimo (Sale 1979, 28; HBCA, PAM, B.239/g/30-1). He left in September 1850, signing on as a seaman to work his passage back to England on the *Norman Morison,* and arriving in London in February 1851 (HBCA, PAM, B.226/b/3 fo. 11d; B.226/d/3 fo. 68; B.239/g/32; C.1/613 fo. 110d; C.3/15 fo. 68). His family consisted of his parents Jane and Thomas and younger siblings Thomas (bapt. 1819), William (bapt. 1824), Elizabeth (bapt. 1826), Charlotte (bapt. 1828), and Henry (bapt. 1830) (FHC). He married Ann of St. Mary's Cray and had four girls: Mary Ann (bapt. 1855), Sarah Jane (bapt. 1857), Virginia (bapt. 1862), and Emma (bapt. 1864) (FHC). We have been in contact with possible descendants Lynette Royan (from Bundaberg, Queensland, Australia) and Mary Skinner.
• 3 April 1850 from sweetheart (HBCA, PAM, E.31/2/1, fo. 16-17, 20).
• 3 April 1850 from mother (HBCA, PAM, E.31/2/1 fo. 18-20).

97 JOHN WILLOUGHBY
Willoughby came out from near Orpington, Kent, as an emigrant labourer on the first voyage of the *Norman Morison,* which departed from London on 20 October 1849. On 18 June 1850 he deserted from Fort Rupert with Peter Leach, John Smith, Richard Whiffen, and the Muirs (HBCA, PAM, A.11/72 fo. 289; B.239/g/32). His father T. (or J.) Willoughby and mother R. mentioned siblings James, Thomas, Joseph, Alexander, and Ruth in the undelivered letter. Contact has been made with possible descendant Graham Willoughby of Winnipeg, Manitoba, and his sister in New Zealand.
• 2 April 1850 letter (HBCA, PAM, E.31/2/1 fo. 327-30)
• [1 October 1850] letter (HBCA, PAM, E.31/2/1 fo. 331-3)
• [29 October 1850] letter (HBCA, PAM, E.31/2/1 fo. 334-6).

98 EDWARD HOARE
Hoare (Hoar, Hore) came out from St. Mary's Cray, Kent, as an emigrant labourer on the first voyage of the *Norman Morison,* leaving on 20 October 1849 and arriving on the coast on 24 March 1850 (Bowsfield 1979, 79; Mouat 1939, 213). He worked on the Puget's

Sound Agricultural Company farm at Nisqually (Tacoma, Washington) until he deserted in October. By April 1851 he was still in the vicinity (Dickey 1989).
- 3 April [1850] letter (HBCA, PAM, E.31/2/1 fo. 147-8)
- 15 October 1850 "The Englishman Hore," 6 February 1851 "The Englishman Edwards off duty," 27 February 1851 "driven high and dry off Whitby Island" (Dickey 1989)
- 8 July 1851 letter (HBCA, PAM, E.31/2/1 fo. 350-2).

99 WILLIAM BURGESS

Burgess came out from St. Mary's Cray, Kent, as a twenty-one-year-old emigrant labourer on the first voyage of the *Norman Morison,* leaving London on 20 October 1849 (Bowsfield 1979, 79; Mouat 1939, 213). He took ill on 30 October and died on 17 November 1849, being buried at sea (Mouat 1939, 208; HBCA, PAM, A.11/70 fo. 491; B.226/b/8 fo. 17; C.1/613).
- 3 April 1850 letter (HBCA, PAM, E.31/2/1 fo. 51-2d)
- November 1850 quotation "committed the body" (HBCA, PAM, C.1/613, fo. 14).

100 GEORGE MILLER

Miller (Millar) came out from Dartford, Kent, as an emigrant labourer for Captain W.C. Grant on the first voyage of the *Norman Morison,* leaving on 20 October 1849 and arriving on the coast on 24 March 1850 (Bowsfield 1979, 79; Mouat 1939, 213). Not long after his arrival he deserted along with an apprentice clerk, Samuel Robertson, on 17 July 1850 (HBCA, PAM, A.11/72 fo. 274-5d, 289; B.226/d/3, 195; B.239/g/89; D.5/29 fo. 58d). His mother may have been Mary, who had a son George in 1822 in Tenterton, Kent (FHC). Information on the Royal Gunpowder Magazines in Purfleet came from Jonathan Catton.
- 28 and 29 May 1850 two letters (HBCA, PAM, E.31/2/1 fo. 208-9d, 210, 211)
- 16 July 1850 two James Douglas quotations "Mr. Samuel Robertson" and "day labourer" (HBCA, PAM, A.11/72, fo. 274-5; D.5/29 fo. 58d).

101 RICHARD WHIFFEN

Whiffen (Whiffin) came out from Farnborough near Bromley, Kent, as an emigrant labourer on the first voyage of the *Norman Morison,* leaving on 20 October 1849 and arriving on the coast on 24 March 1850 (Mouat 1939, 213; HBCA, PAM, A.11/72 fo. 290-3d). He was sent to work at Fort Rupert but not long after his arrival he deserted along with Peter Leach, John Willoughby, and John Smith, on 18 June 1850, and went aboard the *England* bound for California (Bowsfield 1979, 102-3, 111-12; HBCA, PAM, A.11/72 fo. 289; B.226/d/3, 195; B.239/g/32). He apparently drowned at California (note on HBCA, PAM, E.31/2/1 fo. 316). We have been in contact with possible descendant Carolyn Whiffen Murray, Tewkesbury, Maine.
- 1 August 1850, "My Dear Couson, I am very thankful to hear" (HBCA, PAM, E.31/2/1 fo. 314-16)
- 1 August 1850, "My Dear Brother, We was all so very glad" (HBCA, PAM, E.31/2/1 fo. 317-19).

102 BENJAMIN WICKHAM

Wickham came out from Orpington, Kent, in October 1849 on the first voyage of the *Norman Morison,* leaving London on 20 October 1849 (Bowsfield 1979, 79; Mouat 1939, 213). He was hired as a farm labourer by Henry Berens, a member of the HBC London

Committee (HBCA, PAM, B.239/g/89; A.19/39 fo. 72). From his arrival in March 1850 he was a labourer in Victoria (HBCA, PAM, B.239/g/29). He left in September 1850, signing on as a seaman to work his passage back to England on the *Norman Morison* and arriving in London in February 1851 (HBCA, PAM, B.226/b/3 fo. 11d; B.226/d/3 fo. 68; B.239/g/32; C.1/613 fo. 110d; C.3/15 fo. 68).
• 5 September 1850 letter (HBCA, PAM, E.31/2/1 fo. 320-2).

103   GEORGE HORNE
Horne (Horn) came out from Wick or Orkney as an emigrant labourer on the first voyage of the *Norman Morison,* leaving on 20 October 1849 and arriving on the coast on 24 March 1850 (Bowsfield 1979, 79; Mouat 1939, 213; HBCA, PAM, B.226/d/3; B.239/g/89). He left in September 1850, signing on as a seaman to work his passage back to England on the *Norman Morison* and arriving in London in February 1851 (HBCA, PAM, B.226/b/3 fo. 11d; B.226/d/3 fo. 68; B.239/g/32; C.1/613 fo. 110d; C.3/15 fo. 68).
• 9 July 1850 letter to George (HBCA, PAM, E.31/2/1 fo. 153-6).
• 4 October 1850 letter to George (HBCA, PAM, E.31/2/1 fo. 157-9).

104   HENRY HORNE
Horne (Horn) came out from Wick or Orkney as an emigrant labourer on the first voyage of the *Norman Morison,* leaving on 20 October 1849 and arriving on the coast on 24 March 1850 (Bowsfield 1979, 79; Mouat 1939, 213; HBCA, PAM, B.226/d/3; B.239/g/89). He left in September 1850, signing on as a seaman to work his passage back to England on the *Norman Morison,* and arriving in London in February 1851 (HBCA, PAM, B.226/b/3 fo. 11d; B.226/d/3 fo. 68; B.239/g/32; C.1/613 fo. 110d; C.3/15 fo. 68). His siblings included George, who accompanied him on the trip out and back, and Anne, Elizabeth, George, and Catherine, who are mentioned in the undelivered letters. On 17 February 1852 he married Anne Watters in Kirkwall (based on information supplied by Alison Fraser, Orkney Library, Kirkwall).
• 9 July 1850 letter to Henry (HBCA, PAM, F.31/2/1 fo. 160-1d)
• 12 October 1850 letter to Henry (HBCA, PAM, E.31/2/1 fo. 162-3d)
• quotation from Ross letter "was to be appointed" (HBCA, PAM, E.31/2/1 fo. 268-70).

105   WILLIAM ROSS
Ross came out from Kirkwall, Orkney, as an eighteen-year-old emigrant labourer on the first voyage of the *Norman Morison,* leaving on 20 October 1849 and arriving on the coast on 24 March 1850 (Bowsfield 1979, 79; Mouat 1939, 213; HBCA, PAM, B.226/d/3; B.239/g/89). He worked as an overseer of drains (HBCA, PAM, B.239/g/89; E.31/2/1 fo. 265-70). He left in September 1850, signing on as a seaman to work his passage back to England on the *Norman Morison* and arriving in London in February 1851 (HBCA, PAM, B.226/b/3 fo. 11d; B.226/d/3 fo. 68; B.239/g/32; C.1/613 fo. 110d; C.3/15 fo. 68). His parents were William Ross and Isabella Finlayson, and his siblings included Jean, Alexander, David, Catherine Graham (bapt. 1834), and Isabella Elrick (bapt. 1837) (FHC and HBCA, PAM, E.31/2/1 fo. 265-70).
• 11 July 1850 letter (HBCA, PAM, E.31/2/1 fo. 265-7)
• 12 September 1850 letter (HBCA, PAM, E.31/2/1 fo. 268-70)
• 15 May 1850 Douglas quotation "A quantity of Rum" (HBCA, PAM, A.11/72 fo. 240-3d).

106 WILLIAM RITCH

Ritch was hired in Stromness by Company agent Edward Clouston on 1 September 1850, left for London on 15 October 1850 by the *Queen,* then came out in steerage cabin 6 on the *Tory* (HBCA, PAM, A.10/29 fo. 311; B.226/z/1 fo. 1-2, 30-1). He worked at Fort Rupert after his arrival in 1851, and went to Nanaimo in 1853, but disappeared from Company books in 1854 (HBCA, PAM, B.239/g/30-2; B.226/d/214 fo. 804; B.226/l/1 fo. 23). In the 1881 Census he was living with Anne Ritch and died in hospital at Nanaimo on 30 March 1888 (*Nanaimo Free Press,* 31 March 1888); this information is available thanks to Bruce Watson. Help in interpreting the letter was provided by James R. Harvey, who was researching the headstones of Swordies in the Kirkwall cemetery in 1996. For the occupants of the *Tory,* please see the list in HBCA, PAM, B.226/z/1 fo. 30d. For references to William Ritch's work at Fort Rupert please see HBCA, PAM, B.185/a/1.
- 30 October 1850 letter (HBCA, PAM, E.31/2/4 fo. 23-4).

107 THOMAS CRAIGIE

Craigie was hired in Stromness by Company agent Edward Clouston on 1 September 1850 and came out in steerage cabin 2 on the *Tory* at the age of twenty (HBCA, PAM, B.226/z/1 fo. 1-2, 18d, 30-1). He worked as a farm labourer at Victoria after his arrival in 1851 and went to Esquimalt farm for the Puget's Sound Agricultural Company in 1852-4 (HBCA, PAM, B.226/d/3 fo. 726; B.239/g/30-2; E.15/22a fo. 16d). He married Mary Ann Porter at St. Paul's Anglican Church in Esquimalt on 13 October 1870 and died on 18 June 1882 (BCA 1882-09-002444, reel B13077, supplied by Bruce Watson).
- September 1850 quotations "to step forward" and "seized by a Sheriff" (HBCA, PAM, A.10/29 fo. 311)
- For the occupants of the *Tory,* please see the list in HBCA, PAM, B.226/z/1 fo. 30d.
- 4 November 1850 letter (HBCA, PAM, E.31/2/1 fo. 74-6).

108 PHILIP COLE

Cole was hired in 1850 by Captain Richard Wilson Pelly and came out from Aveley, Essex, in steerage cabin 11 on the *Tory* at the age of twenty-three with his older single brother Thomas and two others (HBCA, PAM, A.5/17 p. 15; A.10/29 fo. 281; B.226/z/1 fo. 1-2, 15d, 26, 30-1). He worked as a farm labourer at Victoria after his arrival in 1851 but disappears from the books in 1852 (HBCA, PAM, B.239/g/30-2). A William Cole had drowned on 26 January 1838 (see Ridler and Hooten stories, entries 25 and 26) and, when his father James made the claim for his pay on 5 June 1839, he enclosed a baptismal certificate showing that William, son of James and Sarah Cole, was born 16 June 1816 and baptized in Stepney on 21 July 1816 (HBCA, PAM, A.10/8 fo. 333-3A and 336). This may have been Philip's older brother, with a second child named William after his death. A Philip Ford Cole (b. 1825) married Jane Sarah Morris in 1854 in Stepney and this may be the same person (FHC). Jonathan Catton, Heritage and Museum Officer, Thurrock Council, has tried to identify this family for us and has supplied details on those who furnished letters of reference.
- 1850 two quoted application references (HBCA, PAM, A.5/17 p. 15; A.10/29 fo. 281)
- For the occupants of the *Tory,* please see the list in HBCA, PAM, B.226/z/1 fo. 30d.
- 1 and 3 December 1851 two letters (HBCA, PAM, E.31/2/1 fo. 70-1d, 72-3).

109   PETER BROWN
      Brown came out from Harray, Orkney, as a twenty-year-old emigrant labourer on the sec-
      ond voyage of the *Norman Morison,* leaving on 28 May 1851 and arriving on the coast on
      30 October 1851 (HBCA, PAM, C.1/614 fo. 1d-2). He worked as shepherd at Lake Hill
      Farm until he was found shot in the chest on 5 November 1852 (Pethick 1968, 107-9). His
      parents were James Brown and Jane Marwick, married 9 January 1827. Their other chil-
      dren were Margaret (b. 1826), James (bapt. 1829), William (bapt. 1834), Jean (bapt. 1837),
      and Betty (b. 1840) (FHC).

      • 19 [June?] 1852 two letters (HBCA, PAM, E.31/2/1 fo. 26, 26d, 27-7d, 28)
      • 5 November 1852 and 4 January 1853 two extracts from Douglas reports to Company
        Secretary Barclay (HBCA, PAM, A.11/73 fo. 636-7, received 29 January 1853; A.11/73
        fo. 38-41).

References

Archival Sources

Beinecke Library, Yale University
Joseph T. Heath Papers.

British Columbia Archives, Victoria
C/AA/30.1/1. Vancouver Island Colonial Secretary. Record of marriage licences, 1859-61.
C/AA/30.7/2. Vancouver Island Lands and Works Dept. Land sales, 1860-5.
Electronic Index to Biographical References.
MS-0520 and 1500. Burials, Christ Church.
PDP. Prints, Drawings and Paintings.
Reel B13077, 1882-09-002444. St. Paul's Registers.

Centre du patrimoine, Winnipeg
Drouin Index.
Parish Registers (Chateauguay, Joliette, L'Assomption, Maskinongé, Rivière du Loup, Ste-Croix, St-Cuthbert, Trois-Rivières).
Voyageur Contracts Database.

Family History Center, Winnipeg
International Genealogical Index.

Hawai'i State Archives, Honolulu
Foreign Office and Executive (FO & EX) Series 402 (402-3-54, 402-7-184, 190, 402-9-205, 207) and Series 403 (403-11-159).
Public Safety (PS) Series 310, vol. 1.

Hawaiian Mission Children's Society Collections, Honolulu
Levi Chamberlain Journal, vols. 20-5.

Hudson's Bay Company Archives, Provincial Archives of Manitoba, Winnipeg
A.1. London Minute Books.
A.5. London Correspondence Books Outward – General Series.
A.6. London Correspondence Books Outward – HBC Official.
A.7. London Locked Private Letterbooks.
A.8. London Correspondence with His Majesty's Government.
A.10. London Inward Correspondence – General.
A.11. London Inward Correspondence from HBC Posts.
A.16. Officers' and Servants' Ledgers and Account Books.

A.32. Servants' Contracts.

A.34. Servants' Characters and Staff Records.

A.36. Officers' and Servants' Wills.

A.44. Register Book of Wills and Administrations.

A.67. Miscellaneous Papers.

B.5. Fort Alexandria Records.

B.38. Fort Chimo Records.

B.45. Fort Colvile Records.

B.59. Eastmain Records.

B.76. Fort George (Columbia) Records.

B.134. Montreal Records.

B.135. Moose Factory Records.

B.185. Fort Rupert Records.

B.186. Rupert House Records.

B.202. Snake Country Records.

B.223. Fort Vancouver Records.

B.226. Fort Victoria Records.

B.239. York Factory Records.

C.1. Ships' Logs.

C.2. Seamen's Wages Books.

C.3. Portledge Books.

C.4. Book of Ships' Movements.

C.7. Ships' Miscellaneous Paper.

D.3. George Simpson Journals.

D.4. George Simpson Correspondence Books.

D.5. George Simpson Inward Correspondence.

E.31. HBC Employees: Undelivered and Unallocated Letters.

E.69. Joseph Wordsworth Hardisty fonds.

E.109. Copy of *Beaver* Logs in Public Record Office.

E.196. George Robinson fonds.

E.316. Copy of *Columbia* Log from Columbia River Maritime Museum.

E.353. Dale Forster Collection: Fur Trade Letters.

F.4. North West Company Account Books.

F.5. North West Company Servants' Contracts.

F.15. Puget's Sound Agricultural Company Accounts.

G.1. Manuscript Maps.

G.3. Published Maps.

P. Documentary Art.

SF. Search Files.

Manitoba Genealogical Society, Winnipeg
Cemetery Listings.

Oregon Historical Society, Portland
Log of *Mary Dare* 1849-50.

Orkney Archives, Kirkwall
Births in Old Parish Registers, Microfilm OPR 24/2.

Public Archives of Nova Scotia, Halifax
F109 H13 *Halifax and Its Businesses 1876: Drug Businesses and Druggists.*

Other Sources

Arksey, Laura. 2000. Prodigal Son at Nisqually. Paper delivered at Spokane Corral of Westerners, Spokane, WA, February.

Bailey, Lloyd. 1992. Captain John Swanson and the HBC in Frontier BC, 1842-1872. Monograph. HBCA Library.

Barman, Jean, with Bruce M. Watson. 1999. Fort Colvile's Fur Trade Families and the Dynamics of Race in the Pacific Northwest. *Pacific Northwest Quarterly* 32, 4 (Summer): 140-53.

Bartholomew, J.G. 1914. *The Survey Gazetteer of the British Isles: Topographical, Statistical and Commercial Compiled from the 1911 Census and the Latest Official Returns.* Edinburgh: J.G. Bartholomew.

Beattie, Judith Hudson. 1993. Letters from Home: Undelivered Letters to Seamen on the West Coast, 1832-1867. Paper presented at the Columbia Department Fur Trade Conference, University of Victoria, Victoria, 1-3 October.

– . 1995a. The Hudson's Bay Company Link to the International Seafaring Community, 1830-1860. Paper presented at the Seventh North American Fur Trade Conference, Halifax, 24-7 May.

– . 1995b. Alfy's Marriage: A Story in Nine Chapters with Preface and Introduction. Paper presented at the Provincial Archives of Manitoba Open House, Winnipeg, 16 November.

– . 1996. Letters to the Backside of the World: Undelivered Letters to Hudson's Bay Company Seamen on the West Coast, 1830-1850. Paper presented at the annual meeting of the Manitoba Historical Society, Winnipeg, 8 June.

– . 2000a. The Undelivered Letters. Paper presented at the Centre for Rupert's Land Studies colloquium, Vancouver, Washington, 24-8 May.

– . 2000b. The Lost Art of Letter-Writing. Paper presented to the Antique Arts group, Winnipeg, 20 November.

– . 2001a. Glimpses of Manitoba's Past through Three Undelivered Letters. *Manitoba History* 41 (Spring/Summer): 26-30.

– . 2001b. The Undelivered Letters. Paper presented to the Fort Garry Historical Society, Winnipeg, 27 October.

– . 2002. Recruiting English Emigrant Labourers for the Hudson's Bay Company, 1849-1850: The Kent Experience As Seen through Some Undelivered Letters. In *Selected Papers of Rupert's Land Colloquium 2002,* comp. David G. Malaher, 81-9. Winnipeg: Centre for Rupert's Land Studies, 2002.

– . 2003. Half a Year and Half a World Away: The Voyage of the Hudson's Bay Company's Brig *Dryad,* 1830-1836. *Mains'l Haul* 31, 1 (January).

Belcher, Edward. 1843. *Narrative of a Voyage Round the World, Performed in Her Majesty's Ship Sulphur ...* London: Henry Colburn.

Belyk, Robert C. 1995. *John Tod: Rebel in the Ranks.* Victoria: Horsdal and Schubart.

Blake, Anson S. 1949. The Hudson's Bay Company in San Francisco. *California Historical Society Quarterly* 28 (2): 97-112; 28 (3): 243-58.

Bowsfield, Hartwell, ed. 1979. *Fort Victoria Letters 1846-51.* Vol. 31. Winnipeg: Hudson's Bay Record Society.

Brown, Jennifer S.H. 1980. *Strangers in Blood: Fur Trade Families in Indian Country.* Vancouver: UBC Press.

Burley, Edith I. 1997. *Servants of the Honourable Company: Work, Discipline, and Conflict in the Hudson's Bay Company, 1770-1879.* Toronto: Oxford University Press.

Buss, Helen M. 1989. The Dear Domestic Circle: Frameworks for the Literary Study of Women's Personal Narratives in Archival Collections. *Studies in Canadian Literature* 14 (1): 1-17.

–. 2000. Constructing Female Subjects in the Archive: A Reading of Three Versions of One Woman's Subjectivity. *Working in Women's Archive: Researching Women's Private Literature and Archival Documents,* ed. Helen M. Buss and Marlene Kadar, 23-5. Waterloo, ON: Wilfrid Laurier University Press.

–. 2002a. Mothers in "Undelivered Letters." In *Selected Papers of Rupert's Land Colloquium 2002,* comp. David G. Malaher, 107-13. Winnipeg: Centre for Rupert's Land Studies, 2002.

–. 2002b. The "Undelivered Letters" and Jane Austen's England. Paper presented to the Centre for Rupert's Land Studies colloquium, Oxford, 10 April.

Cole, Jean Murray. 1979. *Exile in the Wilderness: The Biography of Chief Factor Archibald McDonald, 1790-1853.* Don Mills, ON: Burns and McEachern.

–, ed. 2001. *This Blessed Wilderness: Archibald McDonald's Letters from the Columbia, 1822-44.* Vancouver: UBC Press.

Coues, Elliott. 1897. *New Light on the Early History of the Greater North-West: The Manuscript Journals of Alexander Henry ... and of David Thompson, 1799-1814.* New York: Francis P. Harper.

Davies, K.G., ed. 1961. *Peter Skene Ogden's Snake Country Journals, 1826-27.* Vol. 23. London: Hudson's Bay Record Society.

Devine, T.M. 1999. *The Scottish Nation: 1700-2000.* London: Penguin.

Dickey, George, ed. 1989. *The Journal of Occurrences at Fort Nisqually Commencing May 30, 1833 Ending September 27, 1859.* Nisqually, WA: Fort Nisqually Association.

Elliott, T.C. 1994. Journal of John Work. *Washington Historical Quarterly* 5: 83-115, 258-87.

Encyclopaedia Britannica. 1929. 14th ed. London: The Encyclopaedia Britannica Company.

Farnham, Thomas J. 1844. *Travels in the Californias.* New York.

Fisher, Robin. 1992. *Contact and Conflict: Indian-European Relations in British Columbia, 1774-1890.* 2nd ed. Vancouver: UBC Press.

ffolliott, Rosemary. 1975. The Swift Rise and Slow Decline of Frederick Buck. *The Irish Ancestor* 7 (1): 15-24.

– . 1984. The Unmistakable Hand of Frederick Buck. *Irish Arts Review* 1 (2): 46-50.

Fuchs, Denise. 2000. Native Sons of Rupert's Land 1760 to the 1860s. Ph.D. diss., University of Manitoba.

Gibson, James R. 1985. *Farming the Frontier: The Agricultural Opening of the Oregon Country, 1786-1846.* Vancouver: UBC Press.

– . 1997. *The Lifeline of the Oregon Country: The Fraser-Columbia Brigade System, 1811-1847.* Vancouver: UBC Press.

Glegg, Eleanor. 1984. *A Harmsworth Saga of the Nineteenth Century.* Privately published.

Goodfellow, The Rev. Alexander. 1903. *Birsay Church History including Harray with sketches of the Ministers and people from the earliest times, a list of Orkney tokens, appendix and index.* Kirkwall, Orkney: W.R. Mackintosh.

Greer, Allan. 1997. *The People of New France.* Toronto: University of Toronto Press.

Greer, Richard A. 1970. Honolulu in 1847. *Hawaiian Journal of History* 4: 59-88.

– . 1994. Grog Shops and Hotels: Bending the Elbow in Old Honolulu. *Hawaiian Journal of History* 28: 35-67.

Harmsworth Encyclopaedia. n.d. London: The Amalgamated Press and Thomas Nelson and Sons.

Harris, Cole. 1997-8. Social Power and Cultural Change in Pre-Colonial British Columbia. *Native Peoples and Colonials,* ed. Cole Harris and Jean Barman. Special double issue of *BC Studies* 115-16 (Autumn/Winter): 45-82.

Harrison, Jane E. 1997. *Until Next Year: Letter Writing and the Mails in the Canadas, 1640-1830.* Hull, QC: Canadian Museum of Civilization.

Haynes, Bessie Doak. 1966. Gold on the Queen Charlotte Island. *The Beaver,* outfit 297 (Winter): 4-11.

Hill, Bridgit. 1996. *Servants: English Domestics in the Eighteenth Century.* Oxford: The Clarendon Press.

Holmgren, Eric. 1988. William Kittson. In *Dictionary of Canadian Biography,* 7: 473. Toronto: University of Toronto Press.

Humphreys, Danda. 1999. *On the Street Where You Live: Pioneer Pathways of Early Victoria.* Surrey, BC: Heritage House.

Hussey, John A. 1991. The Women of Fort Vancouver. *Oregon Historical Quarterly* 82 (Fall): 265-308.

Johnson, P.M. 1972. Fort Rupert. *The Beaver,* outfit 302 (Spring): 4-13.

Klippenstein, Frieda Esau. 1994. Domestic Servants and Fur Trade Households. In *Papers of the 1994 Rupert's Land Colloquium,* ed. Ian MacLaren, Michael Payne, and Heather Rollason, 255-70. Winnipeg: Centre for Rupert's Land Studies.

– . 1996. The Challenge of James Douglas and Carrier Chief Kwah. In *Reading beyond Words: Contexts for Native History,* ed. Jennifer S.H. Brown and Elizabeth Vibert, 124-40. Peterborough, ON: Broadview Press.

Kluckner, Michael. 1986. *The Way It Was.* North Vancouver, BC: Whitecap Books.

Knuth, Priscilla. 1960. HMS *Modeste* on the Pacific Coast 1843-47: Logs and Letters. *Oregon Historical Quarterly* 61, 4 (December): 415-34.

Kuykendall, Ralph S. 1938. *The Hawaiian Kingdom 1778-1854: Formation and Transformation.* Honolulu: The University of Hawaii.

Lamb, W. Kaye. 1938a. The Advent of the "Beaver." *British Columbia Historical Quarterly* 2 (3): 163-84.

– . 1938b. Early Lumbering on Vancouver's Island. *British Columbia Historical Quarterly* 2 (1): 51-2.

–, ed. 1943. The Diary of Robert Melrose. *British Columbia Historical Quarterly* 7 (2): 119-34, 199-218, 283-95.

– . 1958. S.S. *Beaver. The Beaver,* outfit 289 (Winter): 10-17.

– . 1985. John McLoughlin. In *Dictionary of Canadian Biography,* 8: 575-81. Toronto: University of Toronto Press.

Lawson, Bill. 1997. Returning Home – Lewismen with the HBC. In *Papers of the 1994 Rupert's Land Colloquium,* ed. Ian MacLaren, Michael Payne, and Heather Rollason, 271-8. Winnipeg: Centre for Rupert's Land Studies.

Leynard, Arthur. 1982. *The Coal Mines of Nanaimo.* Nanaimo, BC: Nanaimo Historical Society.

Loo, Tina. 1994. *Making Law, Order and Authority in British Columbia, 1821-1871.* Toronto: University of Toronto Press.

McCann, Leonard G. 1980. *The Honourable Company's Beaver.* Vancouver: Vancouver Maritime Museum.

McDonald, Lucille, ed. 1979. *Memoirs of Nisqually by Joseph Heath*. Fairfield, WA: Ye Galleon Press.

[MacKay, Douglas]. 1937. Kamloops 1812-1937. *The Beaver,* outfit 268, no. 1 (June): 36-8.

Mackie, Richard Somerset. 1990. Joseph William McKay. In *Dictionary of Canadian Biography,* 12: 641-3. Toronto: University of Toronto Press.

– . 1992-3. The Colonization of Vancouver Island, 1849-1858. *BC Studies* 96 (Winter): 3-40.

– . 1997. *Trading beyond the Mountains: The British Fur Trade on the Pacific, 1793-1843.* Vancouver: UBC Press.

Macleod, Margaret Arnett, ed. 1947. *The Letters of Letitia Hargrave.* Vol. 28. Toronto: The Champlain Society.

MacWhirter, Archibald. 1956. Separations and Unions in the Church of Scotland. *Orkney Miscellany* 3: n.p.

Merk, Frederick, ed. 1931. *Fur Trade and Empire: George Simpson's Journal. Remarks Connected with the Fur Trade in the Course of a Voyage from York Factory to Fort George and back to York Factory 1824-25, together with Accompanying Documents.* Cambridge, MA: Harvard University Press.

Morice, Adrien Gabriel. 1904. *The History of the Northern Interior of British Columbia.* Toronto: William Briggs.

Morris, Derek. 1990. Stepney and Trinity House. *East London Record* no. 13: 33-8.

Morrison, Dorothy Nafus. 1999. *Outpost: John McLoughlin and the Far Northwest.* Portland, OR: Oregon Historical Society Press.

Mouat, A.N. 1939. Notes on the "Norman Morison." *British Columbia Historical Quarterly* 3 (3): 203-14.

Munnick, Harriet Duncan. 1972. *Catholic Church Records of the Pacific Northwest: Vancouver.* Vol. 1. Portland, OR: Binford and Mort.

– . 1979a. *Catholic Church Records of the Pacific Northwest: St. Paul, Oregon 1839-1847.* Vol. 1. Portland, OR: Binford and Mort.

– . 1979b. *Catholic Church Records of the Pacific Northwest: St. Paul, Oregon 1847-1864.* Vol. 2. Portland, OR: Binford and Mort.

– . 1982. *Catholic Church Records of the Pacific Northwest: St. Louis 1845-1868.* Vol. 1. Portland, OR: Binford and Mort.

Nesbitt, James K., ed. 1949. The Diary of Martha Cheney Ella, 1853-1856. *British Columbia Historical Quarterly* 13 (2): 91-112; 13 (3-4): 257-70.

New Encyclopaedia Britannica. n.d. 15th ed. London: Encyclopaedia Britannica.

Newman, Peter C. 1987. *Caesars of the Wilderness.* Markham, ON: Viking.

Nicholls, Peggy. 1991-4. *From the Black Country to Nanaimo.* Nanaimo, BC: Nanaimo Historical Society.

Norcross, E. Blanche, ed. 1979. *Nanaimo Retrospective: The First Century.* Nanaimo, BC: Nanaimo Historical Society.

– . 1983. *The Company on the Coast.* Nanaimo, BC: Nanaimo Historical Society.

[Ogden, Peter Skene]. 1853. *Traits of American-Indian Life and Character by a Fur Trader.* London: Smith, Elder.

Ormsby, Margaret A. 1972. Sir James Douglas. In *Dictionary of Canadian Biography,* 10: 238-49. Toronto: University of Toronto Press.

– . 1979. Introduction. In *Fort Victoria Letters 1846-1851,* ed. Hartwell Bowsfield. Winnipeg: Hudson's Bay Record Society.

Payne, Michael. 1989. *The Most Respectable Place in the Territory: Everyday Life in Hudson's Bay Company Service, York Factory, 1788 to 1870*. Studies in Archaeology, Architecture and History. Ottawa: National Historic Parks and Sites.

Payette, B.C., compiler. 1962. *The Oregon Country under the Union Jack*. Montreal: Payette Radio.

Perry, Adele. 2000. *On the Edge of Empire: Gender, Race and the Making of British Columbia, 1849-1871*. Toronto: University of Toronto Press.

Peterson, Jaqueline, and Jennifer S.H. Brown. 1985. Introduction. *The New Peoples: Being and Becoming Métis in North America*, ed. J.S.H. Brown and J. Peterson, 3-18. Winnipeg: University of Manitoba Press.

Pethick, Derek. 1968. *Victoria: The Fort*. Vancouver: Mitchell Press.

Podruchny, Carolyn. 1999. "Sons of the Wilderness": Work, Culture, and Identity among Voyageurs in the Montreal Fur Trade, 1780-1821. Ph.D. diss., University of Toronto.

Ralston, H. Keith. 1983. Miners and Managers: The Organization of Coal Production on Vancouver Island by the Hudson's Bay Company, 1848-1862. In *The Company on the Coast*, ed. E. Blanche Norcross, 42-55. Nanaimo, BC: Nanaimo Historical Society.

Reksten, Terry. 1986. *"More English Than the English": A Very Social History of Victoria*. Victoria, BC: Orca Books.

Reid, John Phillip. 1999. *Patterns of Vengeance: Crosscultural Homicide in the North American Fur Trade*. [Pasadena, CA]: Ninth Judicial Circuit Historical Society.

Rich, E.E. 1959. *History of the Hudson's Bay Company, 1763-1870*. Vol. 22. London: Hudson's Bay Record Society.

–, ed. 1941. *The Letters of John McLoughlin from Fort Vancouver to the Governor and Committee*. First series, *1825-38*. Vol. 4. London: Champlain Society for the Hudson's Bay Record Society.

–, ed. 1943. *The Letters of John McLoughlin from Fort Vancouver to the Governor and Committee*. Second series, *1839-43*. Vol. 6. London: Champlain Society for the Hudson's Bay Record Society.

–, ed. 1944. *The Letters of John McLoughlin from Fort Vancouver to the Governor and Committee*. Third series, *1844-46*. Vol. 7. London: Champlain Society for the Hudson's Bay Record Society.

–, ed. 1950. *Peter Skene Ogden's Snake Country Journals, 1824-25 and 1825-26*. Vol. 13. London: Hudson's Bay Record Society.

Sale, T.D. 1979. Two Arrivals (Princess Royal and Harpooner). In *Nanaimo Retrospective, The First Century*, ed. E. Blanche Norcross, 28-30, 153. Nanaimo, BC: Nanaimo Historical Society.

Saw, Reginald. 1940. Sir John H. Pelly, Bart., Governor, Hudson's Bay Company, 1822-1852. *British Columbia Historical Quarterly* 13 (1): 23-32.

Sexton, Sean. 1994. *Ireland in Old Photographs*. Boston: Bullfinch Press, Little-Brown.

Shoemaker, Robert B. 1998. *Gender in English Society 1650-1850: The Emergence of Separate Spheres?* London and New York: Longman.

Smith, Dorothy Blakey, ed. 1975. *The Reminiscences of Doctor John Sebastian Helmcken*. Vancouver: UBC Press.

Somerville-Large, Peter. 1995. *The Irish Country House: A Social History*. London: Sinclair-Stevenson.

Spoehr, Alexander. 1988. A 19th Century Chapter in Hawaii's Maritime History: Hudson's Bay Company Merchant Shipping 1829-1859. *Hawaiian Journal of History* 22: 70-100.

Stanley, Liz. 1984. Introduction. *The Diaries of Hannah Cullwick, Victorian Maidservant,* ed. Liz Stanley, 1-28. London: Virago.

Strickland, W.G. 1913. *A Dictionary of Irish Artists.* Dublin: n.p.

Thrum, Thomas G. 1912. History of Hudson's Bay Company's Agency in Honolulu. In *Hawaiian Annual for 1912,* 43-59. N.p.

Tinch, David M.N. 1988. *Shoal and Sheaf: Orkney's Pictorial Heritage.* Kirkwall: The Orkney Library.

Tolmie, William Fraser. 1963. *The Journals of William Fraser Tolmie.* Vancouver, BC: Mitchell Press.

Van Kirk, Sylvia. 1980. *"Many Tender Ties": Women in Fur-Trade Society, 1670-1870.* Winnipeg: Watson and Dwyer.

– . 1997-8. Tracing the Fortunes of Five Founding Families of Victoria. In *Native Peoples and Colonials,* ed. Cole Harris and Jean Barman. Special double issue of *BC Studies* 115-16 (Autumn/Winter): 148-79.

Walls, Hugh. 1896. A Little Sanday Church History. *Orkney View* 65 (April/May): unpaginated.

Watson, Bruce. n.d. Biographical dictionary of men in the fur trade. Author's private collection.

Williams, Glyndwr, ed. 1971. *Peter Skene Ogden's Snake Country Journals, 1827-28 and 1828-29.* Vol. 28. London: Hudson's Bay Record Society.

Wilson, Dick. 1997. Below Decks: Seamen and Landsmen Aboard Hudson's Bay Company Vessels in the Pacific Northwest 1821-1850. In *Papers of the 1994 Rupert's Land Colloquium,* ed. Ian MacLaren, Michael Payne, and Heather Rollason, 26-50. Winnipeg: Centre for Rupert's Land Studies.

Wolfenden, Madge. 1982. John Tod. *Dictionary of Canadian Biography,* 11: 881-3. Toronto: University of Toronto Press.

Wright, E.W. 1961. *Marine History of the Pacific Northwest.* New York: Antiquarian Press.

Credits

Following p. 114

Hudson's Bay Company Archives, Provincial Archives of Manitoba, P-220 (N5403), watercolour by Thomas Colman Dibdin, 1854

Hudson's Bay Company Archives, Provincial Archives of Manitoba, P-63 (N5275), lithograph by Henry James Warre, [1848]

Hudson's Bay Company Archives, Provincial Archives of Manitoba, P-60 (N5273), lithograph by Henry James Warre, [1848]

Hudson's Bay Company Archives, Provincial Archives of Manitoba, G.2/24 (N4179), drawn by R[ichard] Covington, 1846

Hudson's Bay Company Archives, Provincial Archives of Manitoba, P-55 (N5267), lithograph by Henry James Warre, [1848]

Hudson's Bay Company Archives, Provincial Archives of Manitoba, P-164 (N5350), engraving from *The Illustrated London News*, 26 August 1848

Hudson's Bay Company Archives, Provincial Archives of Manitoba, P-349 (N5566), engraving from *The Illustrated London News*, 10 February 1849

British Columbia Archives, PDP 02819, Ezra Meeker, date unknown

Hudson's Bay Company Archives, Provincial Archives of Manitoba, P-111 (N5296), [Captain Edwin Porcher], 1866

Hudson's Bay Company Archives, Provincial Archives of Manitoba, E.36/4 fo. 6 (N9287), Alexander Grant Dallas, 1858-60. Published with permission of Dr. O.V. Briscoe and donated by him without restrictions, November 2002.

British Columbia Archives, PDP 00468, 1854

Hudson's Bay Company Archives, Provincial Archives of Manitoba, E.31/2/1 fo. 349

Hudson's Bay Company Archives, Provincial Archives of Manitoba, E.31/2/1 fo. 14

Hudson's Bay Company Archives, Provincial Archives of Manitoba, A.67/27 fo. 396

Hudson's Bay Company Archives, Provincial Archives of Manitoba, E.31/2/1 fo. 285. Shingle with York Factory brand courtesy Judith Hudson Beattie

Hudson's Bay Company Archives, Provincial Archives of Manitoba, E.31/2/1 fo. 245

Hudson's Bay Company Archives, Provincial Archives of Manitoba, A.10/8 fo. 286-7

Hudson's Bay Company Archives, Provincial Archives of Manitoba, E.31/2/1 fo. 140. Snuff box courtesy Judith Hudson Beattie

Hudson's Bay Company Archives, Provincial Archives of Manitoba, C.7/32 fo. 65-70. Ointment bottle courtesy Judith Hudson Beattie

Hudson's Bay Company Archives, Provincial Archives of Manitoba, E.31/2/1 fo. 301

Hudson's Bay Company Archives, Provincial Archives of Manitoba, E.31/2/1 fo. 301d

Selection from Hudson's Bay Company Archives, Provincial Archives of Manitoba, C.7/32 fo. 39-57d; E.31/2/1 fo. 32-45. Inkwell and pen courtesy Manitoba Museum

Following p. 306

Hudson's Bay Company Archives, Provincial Archives of Manitoba, E.31/2/1 fo. 134-6d (artifact no. 541-1)

Hudson's Bay Company Archives, Provincial Archives of Manitoba, C.7/163 fo. 14

Hudson's Bay Company Archives, Provincial Archives of Manitoba, E.31/2/1 fo.7-9

Hudson's Bay Company Archives, Provincial Archives of Manitoba, B.134/c/13 fo. 32. Inkwell/jar courtesy HBC Gallery, Manitoba Museum

Hudson's Bay Company Archives, Provincial Archives of Manitoba, E.31/2/1 fo. 197d-8 (artifact no. 541-3)

Hudson's Bay Company Archives, Provincial Archives of Manitoba, E.31/2/1 fo. 293-6

British Columbia Archives, PDP 00117, artist and date unknown

British Columbia Archives, PDP 03242, artist and date unknown

British Columbia Archives, PDP A-01483, artist and date unknown

Hudson's Bay Company Archives, Provincial Archives of Manitoba, E.31/2/1 fo. 279

Hudson's Bay Company Archives, Provincial Archives of Manitoba, E.31/2/1 fo. 16-20

Hudson's Bay Company Archives, Provincial Archives of Manitoba, E.31/2/1 fo. 327d-30 (artifact no. 541-2)

Hudson's Bay Company Archives, Provincial Archives of Manitoba, E.31/2/1 fo. 147-8 (artifact no. 607)

Hudson's Bay Company Archives, Provincial Archives of Manitoba, E.31/2/1 fo. 160

Hudson's Bay Company Archives, Provincial Archives of Manitoba, E.31/2/1 fo. 161d

Hudson's Bay Company Archives, Provincial Archives of Manitoba, E.31/2/1 fo. 26-8

Index

E = Entry, I = Illustration